TEXAS TECH UNIVERSITY
Department of Economics
Principles of Microeconomics (ECO 2301)
Course Syllabus

Dear Student: **This is a general syllabus for all sections of this course—Principles of Microeconomics (ECO 2301). You will receive a copy from your instructor that is specifically designed for your course and section number on, or before, the first day of class. The Department of Economics welcomes you to this course. We hope that you will benefit from it and find it useful and relevant to your daily life.**

Reading Material:

- Case, Fair, Oster, "*Principles of Microeconomics*", Texas Tech University customized edition. Pearson Publishers.
- Class notes.

Course Description

This course emphasis is on theories of the firm, value and price determination, and functional distribution, with the application of these theories to the problem of particular firms, industries and markets.

Course Purpose

The Uniform Undergraduate Degree Requirements apply to all Texas Tech undergraduates regardless of their major in college. There are 5 components to these requirements. This course fulfills a Core Social and Behavioral Sciences—Individual or Group Behavior requirement. Students graduating from Texas Tech University should be able to demonstrate the ability to access critically claims about social issues, human behavior and diversity in human behavior. This course is also a required course for all lower-division undergraduate students in the Rawls College of Business.

Learning Outcomes

Upon completion of this course, students should be able to:

- Identify and critique alternative explanations for claims about social issues and human behavior, i.e., why do consumers and producers behave the way they do?
- Learn how to "think like an economist"
- Understand the economic problem of scarcity and choice and their impact on consumer and firms
- Understand the concepts of demand, supply, and market equilibrium

- Demonstrate knowledge on how to apply demand and supply analysis on real world examples
- Distinguish between various market structures—from perfectly competitive markets to imperfectly competitive markets to monopoly
- Predict firms' behavior and strategy under each market structure

Methods of Assessing the Expected Learning Outcomes

The expected learning outcomes for the course will be assessed through exams, in-class application activities, graded and non-graded quizzes, class discussion and participation, and homework.

Description of How Grades are Determined

Exams

There will be 3 midterm exams and a cumulative Final Exam. Each exam will include several multiple choice questions. Each midterm exam will consist of 30 to 40 multiple choice questions. The Final Exam will include 50 multiple choice questions. Exam dates will be announced in the syllabus you will receive from your instructor at the beginning of the semester.

Of the 3 midterm exams, your lowest grade weighs 15% of our final grade, and your remaining 2 grades weigh 20% each. Thus, the 3 midterm exams weigh 55% of your total final grade.

The Final Exam is cumulative, and will weigh 30% of your total final grade.

Class Activities/Quizzes/Homework

These will weigh 15% of your final grade. Details will be discussed with you in class.

Grading Scale

A = 90% - 100%
B = 80% - 89%
C = 70% - 79%
D = 60% - 69%
F = 0% = 59%

Exams =   85% (3 midterms and a Final Exam)
Class Activities =   15%

Extra Credit Policy

There is no extra credit policy offered in this course.

Important Dates to Remember

There will be specific dates to remember on the syllabus that you will receive from your instructor on the first day of class.

Examination Calendar

The dates of the 3 midterm exams, the makeup exam, and the departmental final exam will be listed on the syllabus which you will receive from your instructor on the first day of class.

Read Carefully:

- If you miss one of the first three exams because of an emergency, the makeup exam's grade will replace it. The makeup exam's grade will not replace (i) the final exam's grade, or (ii) your lowest midterm grade.
- Under no circumstances will a student be allowed to do any additional work to improve his/her grade.

Notes

1. Students are expected to assist in maintaining a classroom environment which is conducive to learning. In order to assure that all students have an opportunity to gain from time spent in class, unless otherwise approved by the instructor, **students are prohibited from using cellular phones or beepers, eating or drinking in class, making offensive remarks, using laptops for nonrelated class activities, reading newspapers, sleeping or engaging in any other form of distraction.** Inappropriate behavior in the classroom shall result in, minimally, a request to leave class.

2. Attendance is REQUIRED and will be MONITORED throughout the semester. Incidences of excessive absence will be dealt with in a manner consistent with University policy and procedures.

3. American with Disability ACT. Any student who, because of a disabling condition, may require some special arrangements in order to meet course requirements should contact the instructor as soon as possible to make necessary accommodations. Students should present appropriate verification for Disabled Students Services, Dean of Students Office.

3. Student Absence for Observation of Religious Holy Days. A student who is absent from classes for the observation of a religious holy day shall be allowed to take an examination or complete an assignment scheduled for that day within a reasonable time after the absence if, not later than the fifteenth day after the first day of the semester, the student had notified the instructor of each scheduled class that the student would be absent for a

religious holy day.

4. Students are expected to have their ID's with them in class. The instructor reserves the right to ask a student to show his/her ID, especially during exams.

5. Any instance of cheating will result in an (F) for the course. The instructor reserves the right to pursue the matter further.

6. You will be given a grade of a zero for any test you miss until you replace it with the makeup exam's grade, granted that you have demonstrated valid justification for missing a scheduled exam.

Economics is concerned with the problems of scarcity and choice in society.   Economics majors learn how to use analytical reasoning and logic to understand and to predict the economic behavior of producers and consumers within the limitations imposed by market competition and government regulation.   The insightful understanding of the economic process and the development of problem-solving skills qualify economics majors for many careers in academics, business and governmental service.   Because the economic mode of reasoning may be applied to a wide range of issues, the economics major is considered to be an excellent preparation for law school, as well as for an MBA or for further study in economics.

The Department of Economics at Texas Tech University offers three distinct undergraduate degree programs through the College of Arts and Sciences to accommodate a variety of interests and career objectives.   Students can pursue a Bachelor of Arts (B.A.) a Bachelor of Science (B.S.), or a Bachelor of Science in International Economics (B.S.I.E.) Additionally, the Rawls College of Business offers a Bachelor of Business Administration (B.B.A) with an economics major.

The Bachelor of Arts degree allows students to pursue a broad liberal arts education while specializing in economics to achieve an understanding of the complex relationships among consumers, producers, and government in an economic system.   Those who select this option may choose a minor to combine with their economic training to create a unique and individualized course of study.

The Bachelor of Science program is more highly structured and technically oriented.   It is intended for students who want to combine a liberal arts education with rigorous and extensive training in theoretical and mathematical economics.   This degree requires a minor in mathematics and is recommended for students considering graduate study in economics.

The Bachelor of Science in International Economics provides understanding of international economics and commercial relationships in a global economy through concentrations of coursework in international politics and international business combined with specialized training in economics.

The Bachelor of Business Administration program introduces students to many facets of business while building a strong foundation in economics.

The Department of Economics houses the Zeta chapter of Omicron Delta Epsilon, an international honor society in Economics that recognizes scholastic attainment and honors outstanding achievements in economics.   This society offers a great way to learn more about economics and to network with faculty as well as other economics students.   All of the department's teaching faculty are involved in undergraduate education, so students benefit from their accessibility to them and from the variety of course offerings in the curriculum.   The list that follows includes descriptions of courses you may want to consider in order to expand your knowledge of economics.

Economics (ECO) Courses

2000 Level Courses

2301. Principles of Economics I (3:3:0). Emphasis on theories of the firm, value and price determination, and functional distribution, with the application of these theories to the problems of particular firms, industries, and markets. Fulfills Core Social and Behavioral Sciences B Individual or Group Behavior requirement.

2302. Principles of Economics II (3:3:0). An introduction to modern economic society and theories of production and exchange. Emphasis upon monetary and fiscal policy and macroeconomics. Fulfills Core Social and Behavioral Sciences B Individual or Group Behavior requirement.

2305. Principles of Economics (3:3:0). An abridged course for students not majoring in economics or business. Covers the most significant portions of ECO 2301 and 2302, with emphasis upon monetary and fiscal policy. Credit will not be given for both ECO 2305 and 2302. Fulfills Core Social and Behavioral Sciences B Individual or Group Behavior requirement.

3000 Level Courses

3305. Game Theory (3:3:0). Analysis of strategic interaction. Strategies of rational choice will be derived and analyzed in economics and other environments.

3311. Intermediate Macroeconomics (3:3:0). Prerequisite: ECO 2302. Analysis of the determinants of aggregate demand and supply with special emphasis on macroeconomic problems such as unemployment and inflation and on techniques used to forecast macroeconomic variables.

3312. Intermediate Economic Theory (3:3:0). Prerequisite: ECO 2301. Intermediate price theory and introduction to welfare theory. Includes theory of demand, theory of the firm, and welfare theory.

3320. Managerial Economics (3:3:0). Prerequisite: ECO 2301. The application of economic theory to problems of business enterprise.

3323. Principles of Money, Banking, and Credit (3:3:0). Prerequisite: ECO 2301 and 2302. A basic course which deals with the commercial banking system, the Federal Reserve System, and other matters associated with money, prices, and credit control.

3324. Taxation and Public Expenditure (3:3:0). Explores the justification for and effects of the entrance of government into the U.S. marketplace.

3325. Special Topics in Applied Economics (3:3:0). Prerequisites: ECO 2301 and 2302 or consent of instructor. Analysis of selected economic issues, theories, and policies in microeconomics or macroeconomics. May be repeated once for credit when topics vary.

3326. Industrial Organization, Antitrust, and Regulation (3:3:0). Prerequisite: ECO 2301. Combines the latest theories with empirical evidence about the organization of firms and industries. Particular attention is paid to antitrust and regulation issues.

3333. International Economics (3:3:0). Prerequisite: ECO 2301 and 2302 or consent of instructor. Principles of international trade, balance of payments, trade policies, and agreements.

3336. Environmental Economics (3:3:0). Prerequisite: ECO 2301 and 2302 or consent of instructor. Applies economic models to current local and global environmental issues with an emphasis on evaluating policies.

4000 Level Courses

4300. Economic Research (3). Prerequisite: ECO 3311 and 3312. Consent of instructor and the director of undergraduate studies or the department chairperson. Directed undergraduate student research in selected areas under the supervision of selected departmental faculty. (Writing Intensive)

4305. Introduction to Econometrics (3:3:0). Prerequisite: ECO 2301, 2302, 3311, and MATH 2345 or equivalent, or consent of instructor. Application of linear regression analysis including simple statistics, probability, distributions, hypothesis testing, and linear regression. (Writing Intensive)

4314. Development of Economic Doctrines (3:3:0). Prerequisite: ECO 2301 and 2302. The basis, nature, and effects of economic doctrines from ancient times through the 19th century. (Writing Intensive)

4322. The Economics of Labor Markets (3:3:0). Prerequisite: ECO 3312 or ECO 3320. Labor as a factor of production, labor market participation and hours worked, compensating wage differentials, human capital investment, income inequality, migration, and discrimination. (Writing Intensive)

4323. Monetary Theory (3:3:0). Prerequisite: ECO 3311. Analysis of money supply, money demand, interest rates, income and price level determination, and transmission mechanisms. Emphases include monetary policies in an open economy context. (Writing Intensive)

4331. Economics of Multinational Enterprise (3:3:0). Prerequisite: ECO 2301 or consent of instructor. Examination of the economics of international enterprise and associations with the major dimensions of the international economy and international political economy. (Writing Intensive)

4332. International Finance (3:3:0). Prerequisite: ECO 3323 or 3333 or consent of instructor. Analysis of international monetary system theory, policy, and institutions. Includes attention to foreign exchange markets and roles of international banking and international managerial finance. (Writing Intensive)

Students learn best when they attend lectures and keep up with their reading and assignments… but learning shouldn't end when class is over.

MyEconLab *Picks Up Where Lectures and Office Hours Leave Off*

Instructors choose MyEconLab:

"MyEconLab offers them a way to practice every week. They receive immediate feedback and a feeling of personal attention. As a result, my teaching has become more targeted and efficient."

—Kelly Blanchard, Purdue University

"Students tell me that offering them MyEconLab is almost like offering them individual tutors."

—Jefferson Edwards, Cypress Fairbanks College

"Chapter quizzes offset student procrastination by ensuring they keep on task. If a student is having a problem, MyEconLab indicates exactly what they need to study."

—Diana Fortier, Waubonsee Community College

Students choose MyEconLab:

In a recent study, 87 percent of students who used MyEconLab regularly felt it improved their grade.

"It was very useful because it had EVERYTHING, from practice exams to exercises to reading. Very helpful."

—student, Northern Illinois University

"It was very helpful to get instant feedback. Sometimes I would get lost reading the book, and these individual problems would help me focus and see if I understood the concepts."

—student, Temple University

"I would recommend taking the quizzes on MyEconLab because they give you a true account of whether or not you understand the material."

—student, Montana Tech

myeconlab

Get Ahead of the Curve

MICROECONOMIC STRUCTURE

The organization of the microeconomics chapters continues to reflect the authors' belief that the best way to understand how market economies operate—and the best way to understand basic economic theory—is to work through a simple model of a perfectly competitive market system first, including discussions of output markets (goods and services) and input markets (land, labor, and capital), and the connections between them. Only then do the authors turn to noncompetitive market structures such as monopoly and oligopoly. When students have worked through a simple model of a perfectly competitive market system, they begin to understand how the pieces of the economy "fit together." Learning perfect competition first also enables students to see the power of the market system. It is impossible to discuss the efficiency of markets as well as the problems that arise from markets until students have seen how a simple perfectly competitive market produces and distributes goods and services. The accompanying visual gives you an overview of the structure.

CHAPTERS 6–8 provide an overview of firm and household decision making in simple perfectly competitive markets.

CHAPTERS 9–11 show how firms and households interact in output markets (goods and services) and input markets (labor, land, and capital) to determine prices, wages, and profits.

CHAPTER 12 is a pivotal chapter that links simple perfectly competitive markets with a discussion of market imperfections and the role of government.

CHAPTERS 13–19 cover the three noncompetitive market structures (monopoly, oligopoly, and monopolistic competition), externalities, public goods, uncertainty and asymmetric information, and income distribution as well as taxation and government finance.

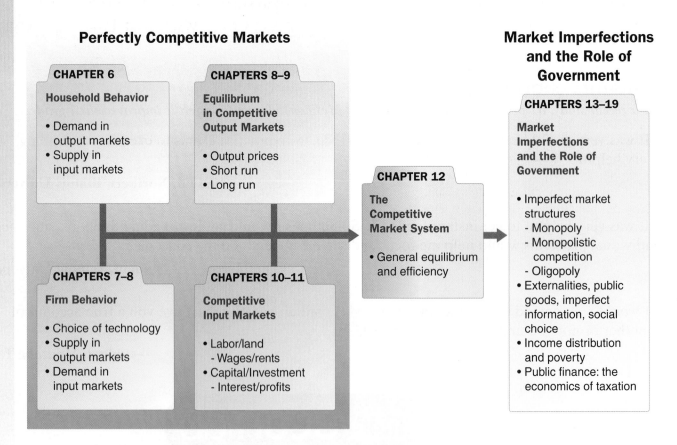

▲ Understanding the Microeconomy and the Role of Government

ECONOMICS IN PRACTICE FEATURE

To help pique students' interest in the economic world, the authors include the chapter feature entitled *Economics in Practice*. This feature either (1) describes a personal observation or a research idea and provides an analysis using the concepts of the chapter or (2) presents a newspaper excerpt that relates to the concepts of the chapter.

The Pearson Series in Economics

Abel/Bernanke/Croushore
Macroeconomics*

Bade/Parkin
Foundations of Economics*

Berck/Helfand
The Economics of the Environment

Bierman/Fernandez
Game Theory with Economic Applications

Blanchard
Macroeconomics*

Blau/Ferber/Winkler
The Economics of Women, Men and Work

**Boardman/Greenberg/Vining/
Weimer**
Cost-Benefit Analysis

Boyer
Principles of Transportation Economics

Branson
Macroeconomic Theory and Policy

Brock/Adams
The Structure of American Industry

Bruce
Public Finance and the American Economy

Carlton/Perloff
Modern Industrial Organization

Case/Fair/Oster
Principles of Economics*

Caves/Frankel/Jones
World Trade and Payments: An Introduction

Chapman
*Environmental Economics: Theory,
Application, and Policy*

Cooter/Ulen
Law & Economics

Downs
An Economic Theory of Democracy

Ehrenberg/Smith
Modern Labor Economics

Ekelund/Ressler/Tollison
Economics*

Farnham
Economics for Managers

Folland/Goodman/Stano
The Economics of Health and Health Care

Fort
Sports Economics

Froyen
Macroeconomics

Fusfeld
The Age of the Economist

Gerber
International Economics*

Gordon
Macroeconomics*

Greene
Econometric Analysis

Gregory
Essentials of Economics

Gregory/Stuart
*Russian and Soviet Economic Performance
and Structure*

Hartwick/Olewiler
The Economics of Natural Resource Use

Heilbroner/Milberg
The Making of the Economic Society

Heyne/Boettke/Prychitko
The Economic Way of Thinking

Hoffman/Averett
*Women and the Economy: Family, Work,
and Pay*

Holt
Markets, Games and Strategic Behavior

Hubbard/O'Brien
Economics*

Money, Banking, and the Financial System*

Hughes/Cain
American Economic History

Husted/Melvin
International Economics

Jehle/Reny
Advanced Microeconomic Theory

Johnson-Lans
A Health Economics Primer

Keat/Young
Managerial Economics

Klein
Mathematical Methods for Economics

Krugman/Obstfeld/Melitz
International Economics: Theory & Policy*

Laidler
The Demand for Money

Leeds/von Allmen
The Economics of Sports

Leeds/von Allmen/Schiming
Economics*

Lipsey/Ragan/Storer
Economics*

Lynn
*Economic Development: Theory and Practice
for a Divided World*

Miller
Economics Today*

Understanding Modern Economics

Miller/Benjamin
The Economics of Macro Issues

Miller/Benjamin/North
The Economics of Public Issues

Mills/Hamilton
Urban Economics

Mishkin
*The Economics of Money, Banking, and
Financial Markets**

*The Economics of Money, Banking, and
Financial Markets, Business School Edition**

Macroeconomics: Policy and Practice*

Murray
Econometrics: A Modern Introduction

Nafziger
The Economics of Developing Countries

O'Sullivan/Sheffrin/Perez
*Economics: Principles, Applications
and Tools**

Parkin
Economics*

Perloff
Microeconomics*

*Microeconomics: Theory and Applications
with Calculus**

Perman/Common/McGilvray/Ma
*Natural Resources and Environmental
Economics*

Phelps
Health Economics

Pindyck/Rubinfeld
Microeconomics*

**Riddell/Shackelford/Stamos/
Schneider**
*Economics: A Tool for Critically
Understanding Society*

Ritter/Silber/Udell
*Principles of Money, Banking & Financial
Markets**

Roberts
*The Choice: A Fable of Free Trade and
Protection*

Rohlf
Introduction to Economic Reasoning

Ruffin/Gregory
Principles of Economics

Sargent
Rational Expectations and Inflation

Sawyer/Sprinkle
International Economics

Scherer
*Industry Structure, Strategy, and Public
Policy*

Schiller
*The Economics of Poverty and
Discrimination*

Sherman
Market Regulation

Silberberg
Principles of Microeconomics

Stock/Watson
Introduction to Econometrics

Introduction to Econometrics, Brief Edition

Studenmund
Using Econometrics: A Practical Guide

Tietenberg/Lewis
*Environmental and Natural Resource
Economics*

Environmental Economics and Policy

Todaro/Smith
Economic Development

Waldman
Microeconomics

Waldman/Jensen
*Industrial Organization: Theory and
Practice*

Weil
Economic Growth

Williamson
Macroeconomics

PEARSON ALWAYS LEARNING

Karl E. Case • Ray C. Fair • Sharon M. Oster

Principles of Microeconomics

A Custom Edition for Texas Tech University

Taken from:
Principles of Microeconomics, Tenth Edition
by Karl E. Case, Ray C. Fair, and Sharon M. Oster

Pearson Learning Solutions, 501 Boylston Street, Suite 900, Boston, MA 02116
A Pearson Education Company
www.pearsoned.com

Printed in the United States of America

1 2 3 4 5 6 7 8 9 10 V011 16 15 14 13 12 11

000200010270783016

RH

ISBN 10: 1-256-32158-3
ISBN 13: 978-1-256-32158-3

About the Authors

Karl E. Case is Professor of Economics Emeritus at Wellesley College where he has taught for 34 years and served several tours of duty as Department Chair. He is a Senior Fellow at the Joint Center for Housing Studies at Harvard University and a founding partner in the real estate research firm of Fiserv Case Shiller Weiss, which produces the S&P Case-Shiller Index of home prices. He serves as a member of the Index Advisory Committee of Standard and Poor's, and along with Ray Fair he serves on the Academic Advisory Board of the Federal Reserve Bank of Boston.

Before coming to Wellesley, he served as Head Tutor in Economics (director of undergraduate studies) at Harvard, where he won the Allyn Young Teaching Prize. He was Associate Editor of the *Journal of Economic Perspectives* and the *Journal of Economic Education,* and he was a member of the AEA's Committee on Economic Education.

Professor Case received his B.A. from Miami University in 1968; spent three years on active duty in the Army, and received his Ph.D. in Economics from Harvard University in 1976.

Professor Case's research has been in the areas of real estate, housing, and public finance. He is author or coauthor of five books, including *Principles of Economics, Economics and Tax Policy,* and *Property Taxation: The Need for Reform,* and he has published numerous articles in professional journals.

For the last 25 years, his research has focused on real estate markets and prices. He has authored numerous professional articles, many of which attempt to isolate the causes and consequences of boom and bust cycles and their relationship to regional and national economic performance.

Ray C. Fair is Professor of Economics at Yale University. He is a member of the Cowles Foundation at Yale and a Fellow of the Econometric Society. He received a B.A. in Economics from Fresno State College in 1964 and a Ph.D. in Economics from MIT in 1968. He taught at Princeton University from 1968 to 1974 and has been at Yale since 1974.

Professor Fair's research has primarily been in the areas of macroeconomics and econometrics, with particular emphasis on macroeconometric model building. He also has done work in the areas of finance, voting behavior, and aging in sports. His publications include *Specification, Estimation, and Analysis of Macroeconometric Models* (Harvard Press, 1984); *Testing Macroeconometric Models* (Harvard Press, 1994); and *Estimating How the Macroeconomy Works* (Harvard Press, 2004).

Professor Fair has taught introductory and intermediate macroeconomics at Yale. He has also taught graduate courses in macroeconomic theory and macroeconometrics.

Professor Fair's U.S. and multicountry models are available for use on the Internet free of charge. The address is http://fairmodel.econ.yale.edu. Many teachers have found that having students work with the U.S. model on the Internet is a useful complement to an introductory macroeconomics course.

Sharon M. Oster is the Dean of the Yale School of Management, where she is also the Frederic Wolfe Professor of Economics and Management. Professor Oster joined Case and Fair as a coauthor in the ninth edition of this book. Professor Oster has a B.A. in Economics from Hofstra University and a Ph.D. in Economics from Harvard University.

Professor Oster's research is in the area of industrial organization. She has worked on problems of diffusion of innovation in a number of different industries, on the effect of regulations on business, and on competitive strategy. She has published a number of articles in these areas and is the author of several books, including *Modern Competitive Analysis* and *The Strategic Management of Nonprofits.*

Prior to joining the School of Management at Yale, Professor Oster taught for a number of years in Yale's Department of Economics. In the department, Professor Oster taught introductory and intermediate microeconomics to undergraduates as well as several graduate courses in industrial organization. Since 1982, Professor Oster has taught primarily in the Management School, where she teaches the core microeconomics class for MBA students and a course in the area of competitive strategy. Professor Oster also consults widely for businesses and nonprofit organizations and has served on the boards of several publicly traded companies and nonprofit organizations.

Brief Contents

Contents

4 Demand and Supply Applications 79

5 Elasticity 97

Preface

Our goal in the 10th edition, as it was in the first edition, is to instill in students a fascination with both the functioning of the economy and the power and breadth of economics. The first line of every edition of our book has been "The study of economics should begin with a sense of wonder." We hope that readers come away from our book with a basic understanding of how market economies function, an appreciation for the things they do well, and a sense of the things they do poorly. We also hope that readers begin to learn the art and science of economic thinking and begin to look at some policy and even personal decisions in a different way.

What's New in This Edition?

- In microeconomics, there has been a good deal of exciting new work in the areas of economic development, behavioral economics, and experimental economics. This edition has added material in various places throughout the microeconomics chapters that describe this work. A particular highlight is Chapter 21, which carefully lays out the methodological approach used by researchers doing randomized experiments in the economic development area and describes some of the results of that work.

- This edition has augmented the current research focus of many of the *Economics in Practice* boxes. Historically, the boxes have focused principally on newspaper excerpts related to the subject of the chapter. Beginning last edition and pushed through more strongly this edition, we have added boxes that we hope will demonstrate more clearly the ideas that lie at the heart of economic thinking. Thus, two thirds of the boxes in the chapters relate an economic principle either to a personal observation (why does Denzel Washington get paid what he does?) or to a recent piece of economic research (new work by Emmanuel Saez on the fact that much of modern wealth comes from wages rather than interest, Carola Frydman's work on executive compensation, and Rachel Croson's work on gender and trust). When possible, we focus on work by younger scholars and on more recent research. It is our hope that new students will be inspired by the wide breadth and exciting nature of the research currently going on in economics as they read these boxes.

- Many graphs and tables have been heavily revised and updated to include the most recent data available from 2008 to as recent as the fall of 2010. The inclusion of up-to-date studies and data is essential to promoting a better understanding of recent microeconomic developments.

- A number of the chapters have been reworked to improve their readability. Chapters 9, 12, and 18 have been most affected.
- We have added many new problems in the end-of-chapter materials, aiming for more text-specific questions.

Economics is a social science. Its value is measured in part in terms of its ability to help us understand the world around us and to grapple with some of the social issues of the times: How do markets work, and why are they so powerful? Why do firms earn profits, and how are wages determined? Does it matter to consumers if there are many firms in an industry or only one? In 2006, the top 20 percent of the households in the United States earned 48 percent of all income generated. Why do we see this income inequality, and why has it been growing? There is enormous poverty in many parts of the world. Are there ways to intervene, either at the country level or the individual level? In almost any marketplace in the United States we see goods that were produced in countries from all over the world. U.S. goods also travel to far corners of the world to be sold to consumers in Europe, Asia, and Latin America. Why do we see the pattern we do? Across the globe, people are increasingly worried about global warming. What tools can an economist bring to the table in helping to solve this complex problem? These questions are microeconomic questions. To answer them, we need to learn how households and firms make decisions and how those decisions are interconnected. As we begin to see the way in which market outcomes—like prices, profits, industry growth, and the like—emerge from the interplay of decisions made by a legion of households and firms, acting largely in their own interests, we hope that the reader's sense of wonder will grow.

The Foundation

The themes of *Principles of Microeconomics*, 10th edition, are the same themes of the first nine editions. The purposes of this book are to introduce the discipline of economics and to provide a basic understanding of how economies function. This requires a blend of economic theory, institutional material, and real-world applications. We have maintained a balance between these ingredients in every chapter. The hallmark features of our book are its:

1. Three-tiered explanations of key concepts (*stories-graphs-equations*)
2. Intuitive and accessible structure
3. International coverage

Three-Tiered Explanations: Stories-Graphs-Equations

Professors who teach principles of economics are faced with a classroom of students with different abilities, backgrounds, and learning styles. For some students, analytical material is difficult no matter how it is presented; for others, graphs and equations seem to come naturally. The problem facing instructors and textbook authors is how to convey the core principles of the discipline to as many students as possible without selling the better students short. Our approach to this problem is to present most core concepts in the following three ways:

First, we present each concept in the context of a simple intuitive *story* or example in words often followed by a table. Second, we use a *graph* in most cases to illustrate the story or example. And finally, in many cases where appropriate, we use an *equation* to present the concept with a mathematical formula.

Microeconomic Structure

The organization of the microeconomic chapters continues to reflect our belief that the best way to understand how market economies operate—and the best way to understand basic economic theory—is to work through the perfectly competitive model first, including discussions of output markets (goods and services) and input markets (land, labor, and capital), and the connections between them before turning to noncompetitive market structures such as monopoly and oligopoly. When students understand how a simple, perfectly competitive system works, they can start thinking about how the pieces of the economy "fit together." We think this is a better approach to teaching economics than some of the more traditional approaches, which encourage students to think of economics as a series of disconnected alternative market models.

Learning perfect competition first also enables students to see the power of the market system. It is impossible for students to discuss the efficiency of markets as well as the problems that arise from markets until they have seen how a simple, perfectly competitive market system produces and distributes goods and services. This is our purpose in Chapter 6 through 11.

Chapter 12, "General Equilibrium and the Efficiency of Perfect Competition," is a pivotal chapter that links simple, perfectly competitive markets with a discussion of market imperfections and the role of government. Chapter 13 through 15 cover three noncompetitive market structures—monopoly, monopolistic competition, and oligopoly. Chapter 16 covers externalities, public goods, and social choice. Chapter 17, which is new to this edition, covers uncertainty and asymmetric information. Chapters 18 and 19 cover income distribution as well as taxation and government finance. The visual below (Figure II.2 from page 118), gives you an overview of our structure.

International Coverage

As in previous editions, we continue to integrate international examples and applications throughout the text. This probably goes without saying: The days in which an introductory economics text could be written with a closed economy in mind have long since gone.

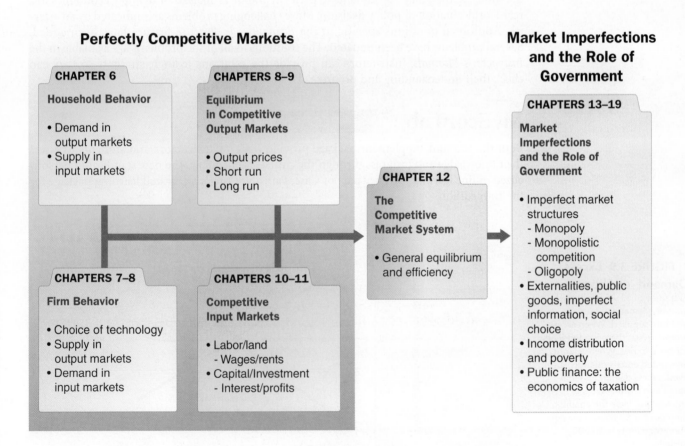

▲ FIGURE II.2 **Understanding the Microeconomy and the Role of Government**

Tools for Learning

As authors and teachers, we understand the challenges of the principles of economics course. Our pedagogical features are designed to illustrate and reinforce key economic concepts through real-world examples and applications.

Economics in Practice

As described earlier, the *Economics in Practice* feature presents a real-world personal observation, current research work, or a news article that supports the key concept of the chapter and helps students think critically about how economics is a part of their daily lives. The end-of-chapter problem sets include a question specific to each *Economics in Practice* feature. Students can visit www.myeconlab.com for additional updated news articles and related exercises.

Graphs

Reading and interpreting graphs is a key part of understanding economic concepts. The Chapter 1 Appendix, "How to Read and Understand Graphs," shows readers how to interpret the 200-plus graphs featured in this book. We use red curves to illustrate the behavior of firms and blue curves to show the behavior of households. We use a different shade of red and blue to signify a shift in a curve.

Problems and Solutions

Each chapter and appendix ends with a problem set that asks students to think about and apply what they've learned in the chapter. These problems are not simple memorization questions. Rather, they ask students to perform graphical analysis or to apply economics to a real-world situation or policy decision. More challenging problems are indicated by an asterisk. Additional questions specific to the *Economics in Practice* feature have been added. Several problems have been updated. The solutions to all of the problems are available in the *Instructor's Manuals*. Instructors can provide the solutions to their students so they can check their understanding and progress.

MyEconLab myeconlab

Both the text and supplement package provide ways for instructors and students to assess their knowledge and progress through the course. MyEconLab, the new standard in personalized online learning, is a key part of Case, Fair, and Oster's integrated learning package for the 10th edition.

▶ **FIGURE 3.9 Excess Demand, or Shortage**
At a price of $1.75 per bushel, quantity demanded exceeds quantity supplied. When excess *demand* exists, there is a tendency for price to rise. When quantity demanded equals quantity supplied, excess demand is eliminated and the market is in equilibrium. Here the equilibrium price is $2.50 and the equilibrium quantity is 35,000 bushels.

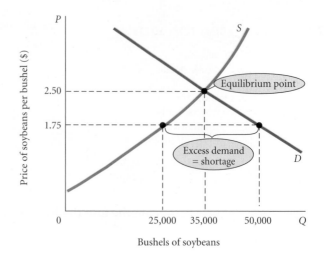

For the Instructor

MyEconLab is an online course management, testing, and tutorial resource. Instructors can choose how much or how little time to spend setting up and using MyEconLab. Each chapter contains two Sample Tests, Study Plan Exercises, and Tutorial Resources. Student use of these materials requires no initial setup by their instructor. The online Gradebook records each student's performance and time spent on the Tests and Study Plan and generates reports by student or by chapter. Instructors can assign tests, quizzes, and homework in MyEconLab using four resources:

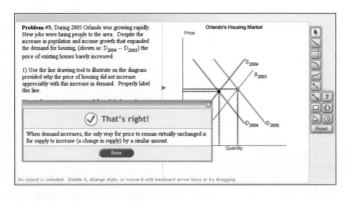

- Preloaded Sample Tests
- Problems similar to the end-of-chapter problems
- Test Item File questions
- Self-authored questions using Econ Exercise Builder

Exercises use multiple-choice, graph drawing, and free-response items, many of which are generated algorithmically so that each time a student works them, a different variation is presented. MyEconLab grades every problem, even those with graphs. When working homework exercises, students receive immediate feedback with links to additional learning tools.

Customization and Communication   MyEconLab in CourseCompass™ provides additional optional customization and communication tools. Instructors who teach distance learning courses or very large lecture sections find the CourseCompass format useful because they can upload course documents and assignments, customize the order of chapters, and use communication features such as Digital Drop Box and Discussion Board.

Experiments in MyEconLab

Experiments are a fun and engaging way to promote active learning and mastery of important economic concepts. Pearson's experiments program is flexible and easy for instructors and students to use.

- Single-player experiments allow your students to play an experiment against virtual players from anywhere at anytime with an Internet connection.
- Multiplayer experiments allow you to assign and manage a real-time experiment with your class. In both cases, pre- and post-questions for each experiment are available for assignment in MyEconLab.

For the Student

MyEconLab puts students in control of their learning through a collection of tests, practice, and study tools tied to the online interactive version of the textbook, as well as other media resources. Within MyEconLab's structured environment, students practice what they learn, test their understanding, and pursue a personalized Study Plan generated from their performance on Sample Tests and tests set by their instructors. At the core of MyEconLab are the following features:

- Sample Tests, two per chapter
- Personal Study Plan
- Tutorial Instruction
- Graphing Tool

Sample Tests   Two Sample Tests for each chapter are preloaded in MyEconLab, enabling students to practice what they have learned, test their understanding, and identify areas in which they need further work. Students can study on their own, or they can complete assignments created by their instructor.

Personal Study Plan
Based on a student's performance on tests, MyEconLab generates a personal Study Plan that shows where the student needs further study. The Study Plan consists of a series of additional practice exercises with detailed feedback and guided solutions that are keyed to other tutorial resources.

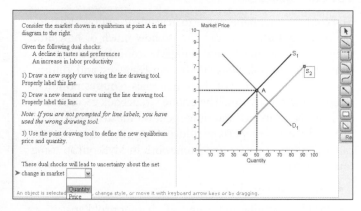

Tutorial Instruction
Launched from many of the exercises in the Study Plan, MyEconLab provides tutorial instruction in the form of step-by-step solutions and other media-based explanations.

Graphing Tool A graphing tool is integrated into the Tests and Study Plan exercises to enable students to make and manipulate graphs. This feature helps students understand how concepts, numbers, and graphs connect.

Additional MyEconLab Tools MyEconLab includes the following additional features:

1. **Economics in the News**—This feature provides weekly updates during the school year of news items with links to sources for further reading and discussion questions.

2. **eText**—While students are working in the Study Plan or completing homework assignments, one of the tutorial resources available is a direct link to the relevant page of the text so that students can review the appropriate material to help them complete the exercise.

3. **Glossary**—This searchable version of the textbook glossary provides additional examples and links to related terms.

4. **Glossary Flashcards**—Every key term is available as a flashcard, allowing students to quiz themselves on vocabulary from one or more chapters at a time.

5. **Research Navigator (CourseCompass™ version only)**—This feature offers extensive help on the research process and provides four exclusive databases of credible and reliable source material, including the *New York Times*, the *Financial Times*, and peer-reviewed journals.

MyEconLab content has been created through the efforts of:

Charles Baum, Middle Tennessee State University; Sarah Ghosh, University of Scranton; Russell Kellogg, University of Colorado–Denver; Bert G. Wheeler, Cedarville University; and Noel Lotz and Douglas A. Ruby, Pearson Education.

Resources for the Instructor

The following supplements are designed to make teaching and testing flexible and easy.

Instructor's Manuals

Prepared by Tony Lima of California State University, East Bay (Hayward, California), the *Instructor's Manual* is designed to provide the utmost teaching support for instructors. It includes the following content:

- Detailed *Chapter Outlines* include key terminology, teaching notes, and lecture suggestions.

- *Topics for Class Discussion* provide topics and real-world situations that help ensure that economic concepts resonate with students.

- Unique *Economics in Practice* features that are not in the main text provide extra real-world examples to present and discuss in class.

- *Teaching Tips* provide tips for alternative ways to cover the material and brief reminders on additional help to provide students. These tips include suggestions for exercises and experiments to complete in class.

- *Extended Applications* include exercises, activities, and experiments to help make economics relevant to students.
- *Excel Workbooks*, available for many chapters, make it easy to customize numerical examples and produce graphs.
- *Solutions* are provided for all problems in the book.

Three Test Item Files

We have tailored the Test Item Files to help instructors easily and efficiently assess student understanding of economic concepts and analyses. Test questions are annotated with the following information:

- **Difficulty:** 1 for straight recall, 2 for some analysis, 3 for complex analysis
- **Type:** Multiple-choice, true/false, short-answer, essay
- **Topic:** The term or concept the question supports
- **Skill:** Fact, definition, analytical, conceptual
- **AACSB:** See description in the next section.

The Test Item Files include questions with tables that students must analyze to solve for numerical answers. The Test Item Files also contain questions based on the graphs that appear in the book. The questions ask students to interpret the information presented in the graph. Many questions require students to sketch a graph on their own and interpret curve movements.

Microeconomics Test Item File 1, by Randy Methenitis of Richland College: Test Item File 1 (TIF1) includes over 2,700 questions. All questions are machine gradable and are either multiple-choice or true/false. This Test Item File is for use with the 10th edition of *Principles of Microeconomics* in the first year of publication. TIF1 is available in a computerized format using TestGen EQ test-generating software and is included in MyEconLab.

Microeconomics Test Item File 2, by Randy Methenitis of Richland College: This additional Test Item File contains another 2,700 machine-gradable questions based on the TIF1 but regenerated to provide instructors with fresh questions when using the book the second year. This Test Item File is available in a computerized format using TestGen EQ test-generating software.

Microeconomics Test Item File 3, by Richard Gosselin of Houston Community College: This third Test Item File includes 1,000 conceptual problems, essay questions, and short-answer questions. Application-type problems ask students to draw graphs and analyze tables. The Word files are available on the Instructor's Resource Center (www.pearsonhighered.com/educator).

The Test Item Files were checked for accuracy by the following professors:

Leon J. Battista, Bronx Community College; Margaret Brooks, Bridgewater State College; Mike Cohick, Collin County Community College; Dennis Debrecht, Carroll College; Amrik Dua, California State Polytechnic University, Pomona; Mitchell Dudley, The College of William & Mary; Ann Eike, University of Kentucky; Connel Fullencamp, Duke University; Craig Gallet, California State University, Sacramento; Michael Goode, Central Piedmont Community College; Steve Hamilton, California State Polytechnic University; James R. Irwin, Central Michigan University; Aaron Jackson, Bentley College; Rus Janis, University of Massachusetts, Amherst; Jonatan Jelen, The City College of New York; Kathy A. Kelly, University of Texas, Arlington; Kate Krause, University of New Mexico; Gary F. Langer, Roosevelt University; Leonard Lardaro, University of Rhode Island; Ross LaRoe, Denison University; Melissa Lind, University of Texas, Arlington; Solina Lindahl, California State Polytechnic University; Pete Mavrokordatos, Tarrant County College; Roberto Mazzoleni, Hofstra University; Kimberly Mencken, Baylor University; Ida Mirzaie, Ohio State University; Shahruz Mohtadi, Suffolk University; Mary Pranzo, California State University, Fresno; Ed Price, Oklahoma State University; Robert Shoffner, Central Piedmont Community College; James Swofford, University of South Alabama; Helen Tauchen, University of North Carolina, Chapel Hill; Eric Taylor, Central Piedmont Community College; Henry Terrell, University of Maryland; John Tommasi, Bentley College; Mukti Upadhyay, Eastern Illinois University; Robert Whaples, Wake Forest University; and Timothy Wunder, University of Texas, Arlington.

The Association to Advance Collegiate Schools of Business (AACSB) The authors of the Test Item File have connected select Test Item File questions to the general knowledge and skill guidelines found in the AACSB assurance of learning standards.

What Is the AACSB? AACSB is a not-for-profit corporation of educational institutions, corporations, and other organizations devoted to the promotion and improvement of higher education in business administration and accounting. A collegiate institution offering degrees in business administration or accounting may volunteer for AACSB accreditation review. The AACSB makes initial accreditation decisions and conducts periodic reviews to promote continuous quality improvement in management education. Pearson Education is a proud member of the AACSB and is pleased to provide advice to help you apply AACSB assurance of learning standards.

What Are AACSB Assurance of Learning Standards? One of the criteria for AACSB accreditation is quality of the curricula. Although no specific courses are required, the AACSB expects a curriculum to include learning experiences in areas such as the following:

- Communication
- Ethical Reasoning
- Analytic Skills
- Use of Information Technology
- Multicultural and Diversity
- Reflective Thinking

Questions that test skills relevant to these guidelines are appropriately tagged. For example, a question testing the moral questions associated with externalities would receive the Ethical Reasoning tag.

How Can Instructors Use the AACSB Tags? Tagged questions help you measure whether students are grasping the course content that aligns with the AACSB guidelines noted. In addition, the tagged questions may help instructors identify potential applications of these skills. This in turn may suggest enrichment activities or other educational experiences to help students achieve these skills.

TestGen

The computerized TestGen package allows instructors to customize, save, and generate classroom tests. The test program permits instructors to edit, add, or delete questions from the Test Item Files; create new graphics; analyze test results; and organize a database of tests and student results. This software allows for extensive flexibility and ease of use. It provides many options for organizing and displaying tests, along with search and sort features. The software and the Test Item Files can be downloaded from the Instructor's Resource Center (**www.pearsonhighered.com/educator**).

PowerPoint® Lecture Presentations

Three sets of PowerPoint® slides, prepared by Fernando Quijano of Dickinson State University and his assistant Shelly Tefft, are available:

- A comprehensive set of PowerPoint® slides that can be used by instructors for class presentations or by students for lecture preview or review. The presentation includes all the figures, photos, tables, key terms, and equations in the textbook. Two versions are available—the first is in step-by-step mode so that you can build graphs as you would on a blackboard, and the second is in automated mode, using a single click per slide.

- A comprehensive set of PowerPoint® slides with Classroom Response Systems (CRS) questions built in so that instructors can incorporate CRS "clickers" into their classroom lectures. For more information on Pearson's partnership with CRS, see the description below. Instructors may download these PowerPoint presentations from the Instructor's Resource Center (**www.pearsonhighered.com/educator**).

- Student versions of the PowerPoint presentations are available as .pdf files from the book's MyEconLab course. This version allows students to print the slides and bring them to class for note taking.

Instructor's Resource CD-ROM

The Instructor's Resource CD-ROM contains all the faculty and student resources that support this text. Instructors have the ability to access and edit the following three supplements:

- *Instructor's Manuals*
- Test Item Files
- PowerPoint® presentations

By clicking on a chapter or searching for a key word, faculty can access an interactive library of resources. Faculty can pick and choose from the various supplements and export them to their hard drives.

Classroom Response Systems

Classroom Response Systems (CRS) is an exciting new wireless polling technology that makes large and small classrooms even more interactive because it enables instructors to pose questions to their students, record results, and display the results instantly. Students can answer questions easily by using compact remote-control transmitters. Pearson has partnerships with leading providers of classroom response systems and can show you everything you need to know about setting up and using a CRS system. We provide the classroom hardware, text-specific PowerPoint® slides, software, and support; and we show you how your students can benefit. Learn more at www.pearsonhighered.com/crs.

Blackboard® and WebCT® Course Content

Pearson offers fully customizable course content for the Blackboard® and WebCT® Course Management Systems.

Resources for the Student

The following supplements are designed to help students understand and retain the key concepts of each chapter.

MyEconLab

MyEconLab allows students to practice what they learn, test their understanding, and pursue a personalized Study Plan generated from their performance on Sample Tests and tests set by their instructors. Here are MyEconLab's key features. (See page xx of this preface for more details on MyEconLab.)

- Sample Tests, two per chapter
- Personal Study Plan
- Tutorial Instruction
- Graphing Tool

Study Guide

The Study Guide, prepared by Thomas M. Beveridge of Durham Technical Community College, provides students with additional applications and exercises.

Each chapter of the Study Guide contains the following elements:

- **Point-by-Point Chapter Objectives** A list of learning goals for the chapter. Each objective is followed up with a summary of the material, learning tips for each concept, and practice questions with solutions.

- *Economics in Practice* **Questions** A question that requires students to apply concepts of the chapter to the *Economics in Practice* feature. The answer accompanies the question.

- **Practice Tests**   Approximately 20 multiple-choice questions and answers and application questions that require students to use graphic or numerical analysis to solve economic problems.
- **Solutions**   Worked-out solutions to all questions in the Study Guide.
- **Comprehensive Part Exams**   Multiple-choice and application questions to test students' overall comprehension. Solutions to all questions are also provided.

CourseSmart

CourseSmart is an exciting new *choice* for students looking to save money. As an alternative to purchasing the print textbook, students can purchase an electronic version of the same content and save up to 50 percent off the suggested list price of the print text. With a CourseSmart eTextbook, students can search the text, make notes online, print out reading assignments that incorporate lecture notes, and bookmark important passages for later review. For more information or to purchase access to the CourseSmart eTextbook, visit **www.coursesmart.com**.

Student Subscriptions

Staying on top of current economic issues is critical to understanding and applying microeconomic theory in and out of class. Keep students engaged by packaging, at a discount, a semester-long subscription to the *Financial Times* or Economist.com with each student text. Contact your local Pearson Prentice Hall representative for more information about benefits of these subscriptions and how to order them for your students.

Acknowledgments

We are grateful to the many people who helped us prepare the 10th edition. We thank David Alexander, our editor, and Lindsey Sloan and Melissa Pellerano, our project managers, for their help and enthusiasm.

Lori DeShazo, Executive Marketing Manager, carefully crafted the marketing message. Nancy Freihofer, production editor, and Nancy Fenton, our production managing editor, ensured that the production process of the book went smoothly. In addition, we also want to thank Marisa Taylor of GEX Publishing Services, who kept us on schedule, and Diahanne Dowridge, who researched the many photographs that appear in the book.

We want to give special thanks to Patsy Balin, Murielle Dawdy, and Tracy Waldman for their research assistance.

We also owe a debt of gratitude to those who reviewed and checked the 10th edition for accuracy. They provided us with valuable insight as we prepared this edition and its supplement package.

Reviewers of the Current Edition

Mohsen Bahmani, University of Wisconsin—Milwaukee

Klaus Becker, Texas Tech University

Jeff Bookwalter, University of Montana

Suparna Chakraborty, City University of New York—Baruch

Scott Cunningham, Baylor University

Elisabeth Curtis, Dartmouth

Erwin Ehrhardt, University of Cincinnati

Barbara Fischer, Cardinal Stritch University

Bill Galose, Drake University

Brett Katzman, Kennesaw State University

Heather Kohls, Marquette University

Daniel Lawson, Drew University

Ming Lo, St. Cloud State University

Nathan Perry, University of Utah

Joe Petry, University of Illinois-Urbana-Champaign

Chris Phillips, Somerset Community College

Jeff Phillips, Morrisville Community College

David Spigelman, University of Miami

John Watkins, Westminster

Janice Weaver, Drake University

Reviewers of Previous Editions

The following individuals were of immense help in reviewing all or part of previous editions of this book and the teaching/learning package in various stages of development:

Cynthia Abadie, Southwest Tennessee Community College

Shawn Abbott, College of the Siskiyous

Fatma Abdel-Raouf, Goldey-Beacom College

Lew Abernathy, University of North Texas

Rebecca Abraham, Nova Southeastern University

Basil Adams, Notre Dame de Namur University

Jack Adams, University of Maryland

Douglas K. Adie, Ohio University

Douglas Agbetsiafa, Indiana University, South Bend

Sheri Aggarwal, University of Virginia

Carlos Aguilar, El Paso Community College

Ehsan Ahmed, James Madison University

Ferhat Akbas, Texas A&M University

Sam Alapati, Rutgers University

Terence Alexander, Iowa State University

John W. Allen, Texas A&M University

Polly Allen, University of Connecticut

Stuart Allen, University of North Carolina at Greensboro

Hassan Aly, Ohio State University

Alex Anas, University at Buffalo, The State University of New York

David Anderson, Centre College

Joan Anderssen, Arapahoe Community College

Jim Angresano, Hampton-Sydney College

Kenneth S. Arakelian, University of Rhode Island

Harvey Arnold, Indian River Community College

Nick Apergis, Fordham University

Bevin Ashenmiller, Occidental College

Richard Ashley, Virginia Technical University

Birjees Ashraf, Houston Community College Southwest

Kidane Asmeron, Pennsylvania State University

Musa Ayar, University of Texas, Austin

James Aylesworth, Lakeland Community College

Moshen Bahmani, University of Wisconsin-Milwaukee

Asatar Bair, City College of San Francisco

Diana Bajrami, College of Alameda

Mohammad Bajwa, Northampton Community College

Rita Balaban, University of North Carolina, Chapel Hill

A. Paul Ballantyne, University of Colorado, Colorado Springs

Richard J. Ballman, Jr., Augustana College

King Banaian, St. Cloud State University

Nick Barcia, Baruch College

Henry Barker, Tiffin University

Robin Bartlett, Denison University

Laurie Bates, Bryant University

Kari Battaglia, University of North Texas

Leon Battista, Bronx Community College

Amanda Bayer, Swarthmore College

Klaus Becker, Texas Tech University

Richard Beil, Auburn University

Clive Belfield, Queens College

Willie J. Belton, Jr., Georgia Institute of Technology

Daniel K. Benjamin, Clemson University

Charles A. Bennett, Gannon University

Emil Berendt, Siena Heights University

Daniel Berkowitz, University of Pittsburgh

Kurt Beron, University of Texas, Dallas

Derek Berry, Calhoun Community College

Tibor Besedes, Georgia Institute of Technology

Thomas Beveridge, Durham Technical Community College

Anoop Bhargava, Finger Lakes CC

Eugenie Bietry, Pace University

Kelly Blanchard, Purdue University

Mark Bock, Loyola College in Maryland

Howard Bodenhorn, Lafayette College

Bruce Bolnick, Northeastern University

Frank Bonello, University of Notre Dame

Jeffrey Bookwalter, University of Montana

Antonio Bos, Tusculum College

Maristella Botticini, Boston University

G. E. Breger, University of South Carolina

Dennis Brennan, William Rainey Harper Junior College

Anne E. Bresnock, California State Polytechnic University, Pomona, and the University of California, Los Angeles

Barry Brown, Murray State University

Bruce Brown, California State Polytechnic University, Pomona

Jennifer Brown, Eastern Connecticut State University

David Brownstone, University of California, Irvine

Don Brunner, Spokane Falls Community College

Jeff Bruns, Bacone College

David Bunting, Eastern Washington University

Barbara Burnell, College of Wooster

Alison Butler, Willamette University

Charles Callahan, III, State University of New York at Brockport

Fred Campano, Fordham University

Douglas Campbell, University of Memphis

Beth Cantrell, Central Baptist College

Kevin Carlson, University of Massachusetts, Boston

Leonard Carlson, Emory University

Arthur Schiller Casimir, Western New England College

Lindsay Caulkins, John Carroll University

Atreya Chakraborty, Boston College

Suparna Chakraborty, Baruch College of the City University of New York

Winston W. Chang, University at Buffalo, The State University of New York

Janie Chermak, University of New Mexico

David Ching, University of Hawaii – Honolulu

Harold Christensen, Centenary College

Daniel Christiansen, Albion College

Susan Christoffersen, Philadelphia University

Samuel Kim-Liang Chuah, Walla Walla College

Dmitriy Chulkov, Indiana University, Kokomo

David Colander, Middlebury College

Daniel Condon, University of Illinois at Chicago; Moraine Valley Community College

Karen Conway, University of New Hampshire

Cesar Corredor, Texas A&M University

David Cowen, University of Texas, Austin

Tyler Cowen, George Mason University

Amy Cramer, Pima Community College, West Campus

Peggy Crane, Southwestern College

Barbara Craig, Oberlin College

Jerry Crawford, Arkansas State University

James Cunningham, Chapman University

James D'Angelo, University of Cincinnati

David Dahl, University of St. Thomas

Sheryll Dahlke, Lees-McRae College

Joseph Dahms, Hood College

Sonia Dalmia, Grand Valley State University

Rosa Lea Danielson, College of DuPage

David Danning, University of Massachusetts, Boston

Minh Quang Dao, Eastern Illinois University

Amlan Datta, Cisco Junior College

David Davenport, McLennan Community College

Stephen Davis, Southwest Minnesota State University

Dale DeBoer, Colorado University, Colorado Springs

Dennis Debrecht, Carroll College

Juan J. DelaCruz, Fashion Institute of Technology and Lehman College

Greg Delemeester, Marietta College

Yanan Di, State University of New York, Stony Brook

Amy Diduch, Mary Baldwin College

Timothy Diette, Washington and Lee University

Vernon J. Dixon, Haverford College

Alan Dobrowolksi, Manchester Community College

Eric Dodge, Hanover College

Carol Dole, Jacksonville University

Michael Donihue, Colby College

Shahpour Dowlatshahi, Fayetteville Technical Community College

Joanne M. Doyle, James Madison University

Robert Driskill, Ohio State University

James Dulgeroff, San Bernardino Valley College

Kevin Duncan, Colorado State University

Yvonne Durham, Western Washington University

Debra Sabatini Dwyer, State University of New York, Stony Brook

Gary Dymski, University of Southern California

David Eaton, Murray State University

Jay Egger, Towson State University

Ann Eike, University of Kentucky

Eugene Elander, Plymouth State University

Ronald D. Elkins, Central Washington University

Tisha Emerson, Baylor University

Michael Enz, Western New England College

Erwin Erhardt III, University of Cincinnati

William Even, Miami University

Dr. Ali Faegh, Houston Community College, Northwest

Noel J. J. Farley, Bryn Mawr College

Mosin Farminesh, Temple University

Dan Feaster, Miami University of Ohio

Susan Feiner, Virginia Commonwealth University

Getachew Felleke, Albright College

Lois Fenske, South Puget Sound Community College

William Field, DePauw University

Deborah Figart, Richard Stockton College

Mary Flannery, Santa Clara University

Bill Foeller, State University of New York, Fredonia

Fred Foldvary, Santa Clara University

Roger Nils Folsom, San Jose State University

Mathew Forstater, University of Missouri-Kansas City

Kevin Foster, The City College of New York

Richard Fowles, University of Utah

Sean Fraley, College of Mount Saint Joseph

Johanna Francis, Fordham University

Roger Frantz, San Diego State University

Mark Frascatore, Clarkson University

Amanda Freeman, Kansas State University

Morris Frommer, Owens Community College

Brandon Fuller, University of Montana

David Fuller, University of Iowa

Mark Funk, University of Arkansas, Little Rock

Alejandro Gallegos, Winona State University

Craig Gallet, California State University, Sacramento

N. Galloro, Chabot College

Bill Ganley, Buffalo State College

Martin A. Garrett, Jr., College of William and Mary

Tom Gausman, Northern Illinois University

Shirley J. Gedeon, University of Vermont

Jeff Gerlach, Sungkyunkwan Graduate School of Business

Lisa Giddings, University of Wisconsin, La Crosse

Gary Gigliotti, Rutgers University

Lynn Gillette, Spalding University

Donna Ginther, University of Kansas

James N. Giordano, Villanova University

Amy Glass, Texas A&M University

Sarah L. Glavin, Boston College

Roy Gobin, Loyola University, Chicago

Bill Godair, Landmark College

Bill Goffe, University of Mississippi

Devra Golbe, Hunter College

Roger Goldberg, Ohio Northern University

Joshua Goodman, New York University

Ophelia Goma, DePauw University

John Gonzales, University of San Francisco

David Gordon, Illinois Valley College

Richard Gosselin, Houston Community College

Eugene Gotwalt, Sweet Briar College

John W. Graham, Rutgers University

Douglas Greenley, Morehead State University

Thomas A. Gresik, University of Notre Dame

Lisa M. Grobar, California State University, Long Beach

Wayne A. Grove, Le Moyne College

Daryl Gruver, Mount Vernon Nazarene University

Osman Gulseven, North Carolina State University

Mike Gumpper, Millersville University

Benjamin Gutierrez, Indiana University, Bloomington

A. R. Gutowsky, California State University, Sacramento

Anthony Gyapong, Penn State University, Abington

David R. Hakes, University of Missouri, St. Louis

Bradley Hansen, University of Mary Washington

Stephen Happel, Arizona State University

Mehdi Haririan, Bloomsburg University of Pennsylvania

David Harris, Benedictine College

David Harris, San Diego State University

James Hartley, Mount Holyoke College

Bruce Hartman, California Maritime Academy of California State University

Mitchell Harwitz, University at Buffalo, The State University of New York

Dewey Heinsma, Mt. San Jacinto College

Sara Helms, University of Alabama, Birmingham

Brian Hill, Salisbury University

David Hoaas, Centenary College

Arleen Hoag, Owens Community College

Carol Hogan, University of Michigan, Dearborn

Harry Holzer, Michigan State University

Ward Hooker, Orangeburg-Calhoun Technical College

Bobbie Horn, University of Tulsa

John Horowitz, Ball State University

Daniel Horton, Cleveland State University

Ying Huang, Manhattan College

Janet Hunt, University of Georgia

E. Bruce Hutchinson, University of Tennessee, Chattanooga

Creed Hyatt, Lehigh Carbon Community College

Ana Ichim, Louisiana State University

Aaron Iffland, Rocky Mountain College

Fred Inaba, Washington State University

Richard Inman, Boston College

Aaron Jackson, Bentley College

Brian Jacobsen, Wisconsin Lutheran College

Russell A. Janis, University of Massachusetts, Amherst

Jonatan Jelen, The City College of New York

Eric Jensen, The College of William & Mary

Aaron Johnson, Missouri State University

Donn Johnson, Quinnipiac University

Paul Johnson, University of Alaska Anchorage

Shirley Johnson, Vassar College

Farhoud Kafi, Babson College

R. Kallen, Roosevelt University

Arthur E. Kartman, San Diego State University

Hirshel Kasper, Oberlin College

Brett Katzman, Kennesaw State University

Bruce Kaufman, Georgia State University

Dennis Kaufman, University of Wisconsin, Parkside

Pavel Kapinos, Carleton College

Russell Kashian, University of Wisconsin, Whitewater

Amoz Kats, Virginia Technical University

David Kaun, University of California, Santa Cruz

Brett Katzman, Kennesaw State University

Fred Keast, Portland State University

Stephanie Kelton, University of Missouri, Kansas City

Deborah Kelly, Palomar College

Erasmus Kersting, Texas A&M University

Randall Kesselring, Arkansas State University

Alan Kessler, Providence College

Dominique Khactu, The University of North Dakota

Gary Kikuchi, University of Hawaii, Manoa

Hwagyun Kim, State University of New York, Buffalo

Keon-Ho Kim, University of Utah

Kil-Joong Kim, Austin Peay State University

Sang W. Kim, Hood College

Phillip King, San Francisco State University

Barbara Kneeshaw, Wayne County Community College

Inderjit Kohli, Santa Clara University

Heather Kohls, Marquette University

Janet Koscianski, Shippensburg University

Vani Kotcherlakota, University of Nebraska, Kearney

Barry Kotlove, Edmonds Community College

Kate Krause, University of New Mexico

David Kraybill, University of Georgia

David Kroeker, Tabor College

Stephan Kroll, California State University, Sacramento

Joseph Kubec, Park University

Jacob Kurien, Helzberg School of Management

Rosung Kwak, University of Texas at Austin

Sally Kwak, University of Hawaii-Manoa

Steven Kyle, Cornell University

Anil K. Lal, Pittsburg State University

Melissa Lam, Wellesley College

David Lang, California State University, Sacramento

Gary Langer, Roosevelt University

Anthony Laramie, Merrimack College

Leonard Lardaro, University of Rhode Island

Ross LaRoe, Denison University

Michael Lawlor, Wake Forest University

Pareena Lawrence, University of Minnesota, Morris

Daniel Lawson, Drew University

Mary Rose Leacy, Wagner College

Margaret D. Ledyard, University of Texas, Austin

Jim Lee, Fort Hays State University

Judy Lee, Leeward Community College

Sang H. Lee, Southeastern Louisiana University

Don Leet, California State University, Fresno

Robert J. Lemke, Lake Forest College

Gary Lemon, DePauw University

Alan Leonard, Wilson Technical Community College

Mary Lesser, Iona College

Ding Li, Northern State University

Zhe Li, Stony Brook University

Larry Lichtenstein, Canisius College

Benjamin Liebman, Saint Joseph's University

Jesse Liebman, Kennesaw State University

George Lieu, Tuskegee University

Stephen E. Lile, Western Kentucky University

Jane Lillydahl, University of Colorado at Boulder

Tony Lima, California State University, East Bay, Hayward, CA

Melissa Lind, University of Texas, Arlington

Al Link, University of North Carolina Greensboro

Charles R. Link, University of Delaware

Robert Litro, U.S. Air Force Academy

Samuel Liu, West Valley College

Jeffrey Livingston, Bentley College

Ming Chien Lo, St. Cloud State University

Burl F. Long, University of Florida

Alina Luca, Drexel University

Adrienne Lucas, Wellesley College

Nancy Lutz, Virginia Technical University, Virginia Tech

Kristina Lybecker, Colorado College

Gerald Lynch, Purdue University

Karla Lynch, University of North Texas

Ann E. Lyon, University of Alaska Anchorage

Bruce Madariaga, Montgomery College

Michael Magura, University of Toledo

Marvin S. Margolis, Millersville University of Pennsylvania

Tim Mason, Eastern Illinois University

Don Mathews, Coastal Georgia Community College

Don Maxwell, Central State University

Nan Maxwell, California State University at Hayward

Roberto Mazzoleni, Hofstra University

Cynthia S. McCarty, Jacksonville State University

J. Harold McClure, Jr., Villanova University

Patrick McEwan, Wellesley College

Rick McIntyre, University of Rhode Island

James J. McLain, University of New Orleans

Dawn McLaren, Mesa Community College

B. Starr McMullen, Oregon State University

K. Mehtaboin, College of St. Rose

Randy Methenitis, Richland College

Martin Melkonian, Hofstra University

Alice Melkumian, Western Illinois University

William Mertens, University of Colorado, Boulder

Randy Methenitis, Richland College

Art Meyer, Lincoln Land Community College

Carrie Meyer, George Mason University

Meghan Millea, Mississippi State University

Jenny Minier, University of Miami

Ida Mirzaie, The Ohio State University

David Mitchell, Missouri State University

Bijan Moeinian, Osceola Campus

Robert Mohr, University of New Hampshire

Shahruz Mohtadi, Suffolk University

Amyaz Moledina, College of Wooster

Gary Mongiovi, St. John's University

Terry D. Monson, Michigan Technological University

Barbara A. Moore, University of Central Florida

Joe L. Moore, Arkansas Technical University

Myra Moore, University of Georgia

Robert Moore, Occidental College

Norma C. Morgan, Curry College

W. Douglas Morgan, University of California, Santa Barbara

David Murphy, Boston College

John Murphy, North Shore Community College, Massachusetts

Ellen Mutari, Richard Stockton College of New Jersey

Steven C. Myers, University of Akron

Veena Nayak, University at Buffalo, The State University of New York

Ron Necoechea, Robert Wesleyan College

Doug Nelson, Spokane Community College

Randy Nelson, Colby College

David Nickerson, University of British Columbia

Sung No, Southern University and A&M College

Rachel Nugent, Pacific Lutheran University

Akorlie A. Nyatepe-Coo, University of Wisconsin LaCrosse

Norman P. Obst, Michigan State University

William C. O'Connor, Western Montana College

Constantin Ogloblin, Georgia Southern University

David O'Hara, Metropolitan State University

Albert Okunade, University of Memphis

Ronald Olive, University of Massachusetts, Lowell

Martha L. Olney, University of California, Berkeley

Kent Olson, Oklahoma State University

Jaime Ortiz, Florida Atlantic University

Theresa Osborne, Hunter College

Donald J. Oswald, California State University, Bakersfield

Mete Ozcan, Brooklyn College

Alexandre Padilla, Metropolitan State College of Denver

Aaron Pankratz, Fresno City College

Niki Papadopoulou, University of Cyprus

Walter Park, American University

Carl Parker, Fort Hays State University

Spiro Patton, Rasmussen College

Andrew Pearlman, Bard College

Richard Peck, University of Illinois at Chicago

Don Peppard, Connecticut College

Elizabeth Perry, Randolph College

Nathan Perry, University of Utah

Joseph A. Petry, University of Illinois

Mary Ann Pevas, Winona State University

Chris Phillips, Somerset Community College

Frankie Pircher, University of Missouri, Kansas City

Tony Pizelo, Spokane Community College

Dennis Placone, Clemson University

Mike Pogodzinski, San Jose State University

Linnea Polgreen, University of Iowa

Elizabeth Porter, University of North Florida

Bob Potter, University of Central Florida

Ed Price, Oklahoma State University

Abe Qastin, Lakeland College

Kevin Quinn, St. Norbert College

Ramkishen S. Rajan, George Mason University

James Rakowski, University of Notre Dame

Amy Ramirez-Gay, Eastern Michigan University

Paul Rappoport, Temple University

Artatrana Ratha, St. Cloud State University

Michael Rendich, Westchester Community College

Lynn Rittenoure, University of Tulsa

Brian Roberson, Miami University

Michael Robinson, Mount Holyoke College

Juliette Roddy, University of Michigan, Dearborn

Michael Rolleigh, University of Minnesota

Belinda Roman, Palo Alto College

S. Scanlon Romer, Delta College

Brian Rosario, University of California, Davis

Paul Roscelli, Canada College

David C. Rose, University of Missouri-St. Louis

Greg Rose, Sacramento City College

Richard Rosenberg, Pennsylvania State University

Robert Rosenman, Washington State University

Robert Rosenthal, Stonehill College

Howard Ross, Baruch College

Paul Rothstein, Washington University

Charles Roussel, Louisiana State University

Jeff Rubin, Rutgers University

Mark Rush, University of Florida

Dereka Rushbrook, Ripon College

Jerard Russo, University of Hawaii

Luz A. Saavedra, University of St. Thomas

William Samuelson, Boston University School of Management

Allen Sanderson, University of Chicago

David Saner, Springfield College – Benedictine University

Ahmad Saranjam, Bridgewater State College

David L. Schaffer, Haverford College

Eric Schansberg, Indiana University – Southeast

Robert Schenk, Saint Joseph's College

Ramon Schreffler, Houston Community College System (retired)

Adina Schwartz, Lakeland College

Jerry Schwartz, Broward Community College

Amy Scott, DeSales University

Gary Sellers, University of Akron

Atindra Sen, Miami University

Chad Settle, University of Tulsa

Jean Shackleford, Bucknell University

Ronald Shadbegian, University of Massachusetts, Dartmouth

Linda Shaffer, California State University, Fresno

Dennis Shannon, Southwestern Illinois College

Stephen L. Shapiro, University of North Florida

Paul Shea, University of Oregon

Geoff Shepherd, University of Massachusetts Amherst

Bih-Hay Sheu, University of Texas at Austin

David Shideler, Murray State University

Alden Shiers, California Polytechnic State University

Gerald Shilling, Eastfield College

Dongsoo Shin, Santa Clara University

Elias Shukralla, St. Louis Community College, Meramec

Anne Shugars, Harford Community College

Richard Sicotte, University of Vermont

William Simeone, Providence College

Scott Simkins, North Carolina Agricultural and Technical State University

Larry Singell, University of Oregon

Priyanka Singh, University of Texas, Dallas

Sue Skeath, Wellesley College

Edward Skelton, Southern Methodist University

Ken Slaysman, York College

John Smith, New York University

Paula Smith, Central State University, Oklahoma

Donald Snyder, Utah State University

Marcia Snyder, College of Charleston

David Sobiechowski, Wayne State University

John Solow, University of Iowa

Angela Sparkman, Itawamba Community College

Martin Spechler, Indiana University

Arun Srinivasa, Indiana University, Southeast

David J. St. Clair, California State University at Hayward

Sarah Stafford, College of William & Mary

Richard Stahl, Louisiana State University

Rebecca Stein, University of Pennsylvania

Mary Stevenson, University of Massachusetts, Boston

Susan Stojanovic, Washington University, St. Louis

Courtenay Stone, Ball State University

Ernst W. Stromsdorfer, Washington State University

Edward Stuart, Northeastern Illinois University

Chris Stufflebean, Southwestern Oklahoma State University

Chuck Stull, Kalamazoo College

Della Sue, Marist College

Abdulhamid Sukar, Cameron University

Christopher Surfield, Saginaw Valley State University

Rodney B. Swanson, University of California, Los Angeles

James Swofford, University of Alabama

Bernica Tackett, Pulaski Technical College

Michael Taussig, Rutgers University

Samia Tavares, Rochester Institute of Technology

Timothy Taylor, Stanford University

William Taylor, New Mexico Highlands University

Sister Beth Anne Tercek, SND, Notre Dame College of Ohio

Henry Terrell, University of Maryland

Jennifer Thacher, University of New Mexico

Donna Thompson, Brookdale Community College

Robert Tokle, Idaho State University

David Tolman, Boise State University

Susanne Toney, Hampton University

Karen M. Travis, Pacific Lutheran University

Jack Trierweler, Northern State University

Brian M. Trinque, University of Texas at Austin

HuiKuan Tseng, University of North Carolina at Charlotte

Boone Turchi, University of North Carolina, Chapel Hill

Kristin Van Gaasbeck, California State University, Sacramento

Amy Vander Laan, Hastings College

Ann Velenchik, Wellesley College

Lawrence Waldman, University of New Mexico

Chris Waller, Indiana University, Bloomington

William Walsh, University of St. Thomas

Chunbei Wang, University of St. Thomas

Bruce Webb, Gordon College

Ross Weiner, The City College of New York

Elaine Wendt, Milwaukee Area Technical College

Walter Wessels, North Carolina State University

Christopher Westley, Jacksonville State University

Joan Whalen-Ayyappan, DeVry Institute of Technology

Robert Whaples, Wake Forest University

Leonard A. White, University of Arkansas

Alex Wilson, Rhode Island College

Wayne Winegarden, Marymount University

Jennifer Wissink, Cornell University

Arthur Woolf, University of Vermont

Paula Worthington, Northwestern University

Bill Yang, Georgia Southern University

Ben Young, University of Missouri, Kansas City

Darrel Young, University of Texas

Michael Youngblood, Rock Valley College

Jay Zagorsky, Boston University

Alexander Zampieron, Bentley College

Sourushe Zandvakili, University of Cincinnati

Walter J. Zeiler, University of Michigan

Abera Zeyege, Ball State University

James Ziliak, Indiana University, Bloomington

Jason Zimmerman, South Dakota State University

We welcome comments about the 10th edition. Please write to us care of David Alexander, Executive Editor, Pearson Economics, 75 Arlington Suite 300, Boston, MA 02116.

Karl E. Case

Ray C. Fair

Sharon M. Oster

Save a Tree!

Many of the components of the teaching and learning package are available online. Online supplements conserve paper and allow you to select and print only the material you plan to use. For more information, please contact your Pearson Prentice Hall sales representative.

The Scope and Method of Economics

1

The study of economics should begin with a sense of wonder. Pause for a moment and consider a typical day in your life. It might start with a bagel made in a local bakery with flour produced in Minnesota from wheat grown in Kansas and bacon from pigs raised in Ohio packaged in plastic made in New Jersey. You spill coffee from Colombia on your shirt made in Texas from textiles shipped from South Carolina.

After class you drive with a friend on an interstate highway that is part of a system that took 20 years and billions of dollars to build. You stop for gasoline refined in Louisiana from Saudi Arabian crude oil brought to the United States on a supertanker that took 3 years to build at a shipyard in Maine.

Later you log onto the Web with a laptop assembled in Indonesia from parts made in China and Skype with your brother in Mexico City, and you call a buddy on your iPhone with parts from a dozen countries. You use or consume tens of thousands of things, both tangible and intangible, every day: buildings, music, staples, paper, toothpaste, tweezers, pizza, soap, digital watches, fire protection, banks, electricity, eggs, insurance, football fields, buses, rugs, subways, health services, sidewalks, and so forth. Somebody made all these things. Somebody organized men and women and materials to produce and distribute them. Thousands of decisions went into their completion. Somehow they got to you.

In the United States, over 139 million people—almost half the total population—work at hundreds of thousands of different jobs producing over $14 trillion worth of goods and services every year. Some cannot find work; some choose not to work. Some are rich; others are poor.

The United States imports over $200 billion worth of automobiles and parts and about $300 billion worth of petroleum and petroleum products each year; it exports around $62 billion worth of agricultural products, including food. Every month the United States buys around $25 billion worth of goods and services from China, while China buys about $5 billion worth from the United States. High-rise office buildings go up in central cities. Condominiums and homes are built in the suburbs. In other places, homes are abandoned and boarded up.

Some countries are wealthy. Others are impoverished. Some are growing. Some are not. Some businesses are doing well. Others are going bankrupt. As the 10th edition of our text goes to press, the world is beginning to recover from a period during which many people felt the pain of a major economic downturn. In the United States at the beginning of 2010 more than 15 million people who wanted to work could not find a job. Millions around the world found themselves with falling incomes and wealth.

At any moment in time, every society faces constraints imposed by nature and by previous generations. Some societies are handsomely endowed by nature with fertile land, water, sunshine,

1

and natural resources. Others have deserts and few mineral resources. Some societies receive much from previous generations—art, music, technical knowledge, beautiful buildings, and productive factories. Others are left with overgrazed, eroded land, cities leveled by war, or polluted natural environments. *All* societies face limits.

economics The study of how individuals and societies choose to use the scarce resources that nature and previous generations have provided.

> **Economics** is the study of how individuals and societies choose to use the scarce resources that nature and previous generations have provided. The key word in this definition is *choose*. Economics is a behavioral, or social, science. In large measure, it is the study of how people make choices. The choices that people make, when added up, translate into societal choices.

The purpose of this chapter and the next is to elaborate on this definition and to introduce the subject matter of economics. What is produced? How is it produced? Who gets it? Why? Is the result good or bad? Can it be improved?

Why Study Economics?

There are four main reasons to study economics: to learn a way of thinking, to understand society, to understand global affairs, and to be an informed citizen.

To Learn a Way of Thinking

Probably the most important reason for studying economics is to learn a way of thinking. Economics has three fundamental concepts that, once absorbed, can change the way you look at everyday choices: opportunity cost, marginalism, and the working of efficient markets.

Opportunity Cost What happens in an economy is the outcome of thousands of individual decisions. People must decide how to divide their incomes among all the goods and services available in the marketplace. They must decide whether to work, whether to go to school, and how much to save. Businesses must decide what to produce, how much to produce, how much to charge, and where to locate. It is not surprising that economic analysis focuses on the process of decision making.

Nearly all decisions involve trade-offs. A key concept that recurs in analyzing the decision-making process is the notion of *opportunity cost*. The full "cost" of making a specific choice includes what we give up by not making the alternative choice. The best alternative that we forgo, or give up, when we make a choice or a decision is called the **opportunity cost** of that decision.

opportunity cost The best alternative that we forgo, or give up, when we make a choice or a decision.

When asked how much a movie costs, most people cite the ticket price. For an economist, this is only part of the answer: to see a movie takes not only a ticket but also time. The opportunity cost of going to a movie is the value of the other things you could have done with the same money and time. If you decide to take time off from work, the opportunity cost of your leisure is the pay that you would have earned had you worked. Part of the cost of a college education is the income you could have earned by working full-time instead of going to school. If a firm purchases a new piece of equipment for $3,000, it does so because it expects that equipment to generate more profit. There is an opportunity cost, however, because that $3,000 could have been deposited in an interest-earning account. To a society, the opportunity cost of using resources to launch astronauts on a space shuttle is the value of the private/civilian or other government goods that could have been produced with the same resources.

scarce Limited.

Opportunity costs arise because resources are scarce. **Scarce** simply means limited. Consider one of our most important resources—time. There are only 24 hours in a day, and we must live our lives under this constraint. A farmer in rural Brazil must decide whether it is better to continue to farm or to go to the city and look for a job. A hockey player at the

University of Vermont must decide whether to play on the varsity team or spend more time studying.

Marginalism   A second key concept used in analyzing choices is the notion of **marginalism**. In weighing the costs and benefits of a decision, it is important to weigh only the costs and benefits that arise from the decision. Suppose, for example, that you live in New Orleans and that you are weighing the costs and benefits of visiting your mother in Iowa. If business required that you travel to Kansas City, the cost of visiting Mom would be only the additional, or *marginal*, time and money cost of getting to Iowa from Kansas City.

> **marginalism** The process of analyzing the additional or incremental costs or benefits arising from a choice or decision.

Consider the video game business. It has been estimated that to create and produce a complex multiplayer role-playing game like World of Warcraft (WOW) costs as much as $500 million. Once the game has been developed, however, the cost of selling and delivering it to another player is close to zero. The original investment (by Activision) made to create WOW is considered a **sunk cost**. Once the game has been developed, Activision cannot avoid these costs because they have already been incurred. Activision's business decisions about pricing and distributing WOW depend not on the sunk costs of production, but on the incremental or *marginal* costs of production. For Activision, those costs are close to zero.

> **sunk costs** Costs that cannot be avoided because they have already been incurred.

There are numerous examples in which the concept of marginal cost is useful. For an airplane that is about to take off with empty seats, the marginal cost of an extra passenger is essentially zero; the total cost of the trip is roughly unchanged by the addition of an extra passenger. Thus, setting aside a few seats to be sold at big discounts through www.priceline.com or other Web sites can be profitable even if the fare for those seats is far below the average cost per seat of making the trip. As long as the airline succeeds in filling seats that would otherwise have been empty, doing so is profitable.

Efficient Markets—No Free Lunch   Suppose you are ready to check out of a busy grocery store on the day before a storm and seven checkout registers are open with several people in each line. Which line should you choose? Usually, the waiting time is approximately the same no matter which register you choose (assuming you have more than 12 items). If one line is much shorter than the others, people will quickly move into it until the lines are equalized again.

As you will see later, the term *profit* in economics has a very precise meaning. Economists, however, often loosely refer to "good deals" or risk-free ventures as *profit opportunities*. Using the term loosely, a profit opportunity exists at the checkout lines when one line is shorter than the others. In general, such profit opportunities are rare. At any time, many people are searching for them; as a consequence, few exist. Markets like this, where any profit opportunities are eliminated almost instantaneously, are said to be **efficient markets**. (We discuss *markets*, the institutions through which buyers and sellers interact and engage in exchange, in detail in Chapter 2.)

> **efficient market** A market in which profit opportunities are eliminated almost instantaneously.

The common way of expressing the efficient markets concept is "there's no such thing as a free lunch." How should you react when a stockbroker calls with a hot tip on the stock market? With skepticism. Thousands of individuals each day are looking for hot tips in the market. If a particular tip about a stock is valid, there will be an immediate rush to buy the stock, which will quickly drive up its price. This view that very few profit opportunities exist can, of course, be carried too far. There is a story about two people walking along, one an economist and one not. The non-economist sees a $20 bill on the sidewalk and says, "There's a $20 bill on the sidewalk." The economist replies, "That is not possible. If there were, somebody would already have picked it up."

There are clearly times when profit opportunities exist. Someone has to be first to get the news, and some people have quicker insights than others. Nevertheless, news travels fast, and there are thousands of people with quick insights. The general view that large profit opportunities are rare is close to the mark.

The study of economics teaches us a way of thinking and helps us make decisions.

To Understand Society

Another reason for studying economics is to understand society better. Past and present economic decisions have an enormous influence on the character of life in a society. The current state of the physical environment, the level of material well-being, and the nature and number of jobs are all products of the economic system.

To get a sense of the ways in which economic decisions have shaped our environment, imagine looking out a top-floor window of an office tower in any large city. The workday is about to begin. All around you are other tall glass and steel buildings full of workers. In the distance, you see the smoke of factories. Looking down, you see thousands of commuters pouring off trains and buses and cars backed up on freeway exit ramps. You see trucks carrying goods from one place to another. You also see the face of urban poverty: Just beyond the freeway is a large public housing project and, beyond that, burned-out and boarded-up buildings.

What you see before you is the product of millions of economic decisions made over hundreds of years. People at some point decided to spend time and money building those buildings and factories. Somebody cleared the land, laid the tracks, built the roads, and produced the cars and buses.

Economic decisions not only have shaped the physical environment but also have determined the character of society. At no time has the impact of economic change on a society been more evident than in England during the late eighteenth and early nineteenth centuries, a period that we now call the **Industrial Revolution**. Increases in the productivity of agriculture, new manufacturing technologies, and development of more efficient forms of transportation led to a massive movement of the British population from the countryside to the city. At the beginning of the eighteenth century, approximately 2 out of 3 people in Great Britain worked in agriculture. By 1812, only 1 in 3 remained in agriculture; by 1900, the figure was fewer than 1 in 10. People jammed into overcrowded cities and worked long hours in factories. England had changed completely in two centuries—a period that in the run of history was nothing more than the blink of an eye.

It is not surprising that the discipline of economics began to take shape during this period. Social critics and philosophers looked around and knew that their philosophies must expand to accommodate the changes. Adam Smith's *Wealth of Nations* appeared in 1776. It was followed by the writings of David Ricardo, Karl Marx, Thomas Malthus, and others. Each tried to make sense out of what was happening. Who was building the factories? Why? What determined the level of wages paid to workers or the price of food? What would happen in the future, and what *should* happen? The people who asked these questions were the first economists.

Similar changes continue to affect the character of life in more recent times. In fact, many argue that the late 1990s marked the beginning of a new Industrial Revolution. As we turned the corner into the new millennium, the "e" revolution was clearly having an impact on virtually every aspect of our lives: the way we buy and sell products, the way we get news, the way we plan vacations, the way we communicate with each other, the way we teach and take classes, and on and on. These changes have had and will clearly continue to have profound impacts on societies across the globe, from Beijing to Calcutta to New York.

These changes have been driven by economics. Although the government was involved in the early years of the World Wide Web, private firms that exist to make a profit (such as Facebook, YouTube, Yahoo!, Microsoft, Google, Monster.com, Amazon.com, and E-Trade) created almost all the new innovations and products. How does one make sense of all this? What will the effects of these innovations be on the number of jobs, the character of those jobs, the family incomes, the structure of our cities, and the political process both in the United States and in other countries?

During the last days of August 2005, Hurricane Katrina slammed into the coasts of Louisiana and Mississippi, causing widespread devastation, killing thousands, and leaving hundreds of thousands homeless. The economic impact of this catastrophic storm was huge. Thinking about various markets involved helps frame the problem.

For example, the labor market was massively affected. By some estimates, over 400,000 jobs were lost as the storm hit. Hotels, restaurants, small businesses, and oil refineries, to name just a

---

Industrial Revolution The period in England during the late eighteenth and early nineteenth centuries in which new manufacturing technologies and improved transportation gave rise to the modern factory system and a massive movement of the population from the countryside to the cities.

few, were destroyed. All the people who worked in those establishments instantaneously lost their jobs and their incomes. The cleanup and rebuilding process took time to organize, and it eventually created a great deal of employment.

The storm created a major disruption in world oil markets. Loss of refinery capacity sent gasoline prices up immediately, nearly 40 percent to over $4 per gallon in some locations. The price per gallon of crude oil rose to over $70 per barrel. Local governments found their tax bases destroyed, with no resources to pay teachers and local officials. Hundreds of hospitals were destroyed, and colleges and universities were forced to close their doors, causing tens of thousands of students to change their plans.

While the horror of the storm hit all kinds of people, the worst hit were the very poor, who could not get out of the way because they had no cars or other means of escape. The storm raised fundamental issues of fairness, which we will be discussing for years to come.

The study of economics is an essential part of the study of society.

To Understand Global Affairs

A third reason for studying economics is to understand global affairs. News headlines are filled with economic stories. The environmental disaster associated with BP's oil spill has the potential to affect the future price of oil if deep sea drilling is banned, the price of fish, the extent of tourism, and tourist-related employment in the Gulf and numerous other markets. The discovery in 2010 of major new diamond deposits in Zimbabwe has implications for the future stability of Mugabe's government, with implications for developments in the rest of the region. China's new position as a major trading partner of both the United States and Europe clearly has implications for political interactions among these nations. Greece's economic struggles in 2010 over its large debt is affecting the enthusiasm of the rest of Europe's citizens for the European Union.

In a relatively open, market-oriented world, it is impossible to understand political affairs without a grounding in economics. While there is much debate about whether or not economic considerations dominate international relations, it is clear that they play a role as political leaders seek the economic well-being of their citizenry.

An understanding of economics is essential to an understanding of global affairs.

To Be an Informed Citizen

A knowledge of economics is essential to being an informed citizen. In 2009, most of the world suffered from a major recession, with diminished economic growth and high unemployment. Millions of people around the world lost their jobs. Governments from China to the United Kingdom to the United States all struggled to figure out policies to help their economies recover. Understanding what happens in a recession and what the government can and cannot do to help in a recovery is an essential part of being an informed citizen.

Economics is also essential in understanding a range of other everyday government decisions at the local and federal levels. Why do governments pay for public schools and roads, but not cell phones? In 2010, the federal government under President Obama moved toward universal health care for U.S. citizens. How do you understand the debate of whether this is or is not a good idea? In some states, scalping tickets to a ball game is illegal. Is this a good policy or not? Some governments control the prices that firms can charge for some goods, especially essentials like milk and bread. Is this a good idea? Every day, across the globe, people engage in political decision making around questions like these, questions that depend on an understanding of economics.

To be an informed citizen requires a basic understanding of economics.

iPod and the World

It is impossible to understand the workings of an economy without first understanding the ways in which economies are connected across borders. The United States was importing goods and services at a rate of over $2 trillion per year in 2007 and was exporting at a rate of over $1.5 trillion per year.

For literally hundreds of years, the virtues of free trade have been the subject of heated debate. Opponents have argued that buying foreign-produced goods costs Americans jobs and hurts American producers. Proponents argue that there are gains from trade—that all countries can gain from specializing in the production of the goods and services they produce best.

In the modern world, it is not always easy to track where products are made. A sticker that says "Made in China" can often be misleading. Recent studies of two iconic U.S. products, the iPod and the Barbie doll, make this complexity clear.

The Barbie doll is one of Mattel's best and longest selling products. The Barbie was designed in the United States. It is made of plastic fashioned in Taiwan, which came originally from the Mideast in the form of petroleum. Barbie's hair comes from Japan, while the cloth for her clothes mostly comes from China. Most of the assembly of the Barbie also is done in China, using, as we see, pieces from across the globe. A doll that sells for $10 in the United States carries an export value when leaving Hong Kong of $2, of which only 35 cents is for Chinese labor, with most of the rest covering transportation and raw materials. Because the Barbie comes to the United States from assembly in China and transport from Hong Kong, some would count it as being produced in China. Yet, for this Barbie, $8 of its retail value of $10 is captured by the United States![1]

The iPod is similar. A recent study by three economists, Greg Linden, Kenneth Kraemer, and Jason Dedrick, found that once one

includes Apple's payment for its intellectual property, distribution costs, and production costs for some components, almost 80% of the retail price of the iPod is captured by the United States.[2] Moreover, for some of the other parts of the iPod, it is not easy to tell exactly where they are produced. The hard drive, a relatively expensive component, was produced in Japan by Toshiba, but some of the components of that hard drive were actually produced elsewhere in Asia. Indeed, for the iPod, which is composed of many small parts, it is almost impossible to accurately tell exactly where each piece was produced without pulling it apart.

So, next time you see a label saying "Made in China" keep in mind that from an economics point of view one often has to dig a little deeper to see what is really going on.

[1] For a discussion of the Barbie see Robert Feenstra, "Integration of Trade and Disintegration of Production in the Global Economy," *Journal of Economic Perspectives*, Fall 1998, 31–50.
[2] Greg Linden, Kenneth Kraemer, and Jason Dedrick, "Who Profits from Innovation in Global Value Chains?" *Industrial and Corporate Change*, 2010: 19(1), 81–116.

The Scope of Economics

Most students taking economics for the first time are surprised by the breadth of what they study. Some think that economics will teach them about the stock market or what to do with their money. Others think that economics deals exclusively with problems such as inflation and unemployment. In fact, it deals with all those subjects, but they are pieces of a much larger puzzle.

Economics has deep roots in and close ties to social philosophy. An issue of great importance to philosophers, for example, is distributional justice. Why are some people rich and others poor? And whatever the answer, is this fair? A number of nineteenth-century social philosophers wrestled with these questions, and out of their musings, economics as a separate discipline was born.

The easiest way to get a feel for the breadth and depth of what you will be studying is to explore briefly the way economics is organized. First of all, there are two major divisions of economics: microeconomics and macroeconomics.

Microeconomics and Macroeconomics

microeconomics The branch of economics that examines the functioning of individual industries and the behavior of individual decision-making units—that is, firms and households.

Microeconomics deals with the functioning of individual industries and the behavior of individual economic decision-making units: firms and households. Firms' choices about what to produce and how much to charge and households' choices about what and how much to buy help to explain why the economy produces the goods and services it does.

Another big question addressed by microeconomics is who gets the goods and services that are produced. Wealthy households get more than poor households, and the forces that determine this distribution of output are the province of microeconomics. Why does poverty exist? Who is poor? Why do some jobs pay more than others?

Think again about what you consume in a day, and then think back to that view over a big city. Somebody decided to build those factories. Somebody decided to construct the roads, build the housing, produce the cars, and smoke the bacon. Why? What is going on in all those buildings? It is easy to see that understanding individual microdecisions is very important to any understanding of society.

Macroeconomics looks at the economy as a whole. Instead of trying to understand what determines the output of a single firm or industry or what the consumption patterns are of a single household or group of households, macroeconomics examines the factors that determine national output, or national product. Microeconomics is concerned with *household* income; macroeconomics deals with *national* income.

Whereas microeconomics focuses on individual product prices and relative prices, macroeconomics looks at the overall price level and how quickly (or slowly) it is rising (or falling). Microeconomics questions how many people will be hired (or fired) this year in a particular industry or in a certain geographic area and focuses on the factors that determine how much labor a firm or an industry will hire. Macroeconomics deals with *aggregate* employment and unemployment: how many jobs exist in the economy as a whole and how many people who are willing to work are not able to find work.

To summarize:

> Microeconomics looks at the individual unit—the household, the firm, the industry. It sees and examines the "trees." Macroeconomics looks at the whole, the aggregate. It sees and analyzes the "forest."

macroeconomics The branch of economics that examines the economic behavior of aggregates—income, employment, output, and so on—on a national scale.

Table 1.1 summarizes these divisions of economics and some of the subjects with which they are concerned.

TABLE 1.1   Examples of Microeconomic and Macroeconomic Concerns

Division of Economics	Production	Prices	Income	Employment
Microeconomics	*Production/output in individual industries and businesses* How much steel How much office space How many cars	*Prices of individual goods and services* Price of medical care Price of gasoline Food prices Apartment rents	*Distribution of income and wealth* Wages in the auto industry Minimum wage Executive salaries Poverty	*Employment by individual businesses and industries* Jobs in the steel industry Number of employees in a firm Number of accountants
Macroeconomics	*National production/output* Total industrial output Gross domestic product Growth of output	*Aggregate price level* Consumer prices Producer prices Rate of inflation	*National income* Total wages and salaries Total corporate profits	*Employment and unemployment in the economy* Total number of jobs Unemployment rate

The Diverse Fields of Economics

Individual economists focus their research and study in many diverse areas. Many of these specialized fields are reflected in the advanced courses offered at most colleges and universities. Some are concerned with economic history or the history of economic thought. Others focus on international economics or growth in less developed countries. Still others study the economics of cities (urban economics) or the relationship between economics and law. These fields are summarized in Table 1.2.

TABLE 1.2 The Fields of Economics

Behavioral economics	uses psychological theories relating to emotions and social context to help understand economic decision making and policy. Much of the work in behavioral economics focuses on the biases that individuals have that affect the decisions they make.
Comparative economic systems	examines the ways alternative economic systems function. What are the advantages and disadvantages of different systems?
Econometrics	applies statistical techniques and data to economic problems in an effort to test hypotheses and theories. Most schools require economics majors to take at least one course in statistics or econometrics.
Economic development	focuses on the problems of low-income countries. What can be done to promote development in these nations? Important concerns of development for economists include population growth and control, provision for basic needs, and strategies for international trade.
Economic history	traces the development of the modern economy. What economic and political events and scientific advances caused the Industrial Revolution? What explains the tremendous growth and progress of post–World War II Japan? What caused the Great Depression of the 1930s?
Environmental economics	studies the potential failure of the market system to account fully for the impacts of production and consumption on the environment and on natural resource depletion. Have alternative public policies and new economic institutions been effective in correcting these potential failures?
Finance	examines the ways in which households and firms actually pay for, or finance, their purchases. It involves the study of capital markets (including the stock and bond markets), futures and options, capital budgeting, and asset valuation.
Health economics	analyzes the health care system and its players: government, insurers, health care providers, and patients. It provides insight into the demand for medical care, health insurance markets, cost-controlling insurance plans (HMOs, PPOs, IPAs), government health care programs (Medicare and Medicaid), variations in medical practice, medical malpractice, competition versus regulation, and national health care reform.
The history of economic thought,	which is grounded in philosophy, studies the development of economic ideas and theories over time, from Adam Smith in the eighteenth century to the works of economists such as Thomas Malthus, Karl Marx, and John Maynard Keynes. Because economic theory is constantly developing and changing, studying the history of ideas helps give meaning to modern theory and puts it in perspective.
Industrial organization	looks carefully at the structure and performance of industries and firms within an economy. How do businesses compete? Who gains and who loses?
International economics	studies trade flows among countries and international financial institutions. What are the advantages and disadvantages for a country that allows its citizens to buy and sell freely in world markets? Why is the dollar strong or weak?
Labor economics	deals with the factors that determine wage rates, employment, and unemployment. How do people decide whether to work, how much to work, and at what kind of job? How have the roles of unions and management changed in recent years?
Law and economics	analyzes the economic function of legal rules and institutions. How does the law change the behavior of individuals and businesses? Do different liability rules make accidents and injuries more or less likely? What are the economic costs of crime?
Public economics	examines the role of government in the economy. What are the economic functions of government, and what should they be? How should the government finance the services that it provides? What kinds of government programs should confront the problems of poverty, unemployment, and pollution? What problems does government involvement create?
Urban and regional economics	studies the spatial arrangement of economic activity. Why do we have cities? Why are manufacturing firms locating farther and farther from the center of urban areas?

ECONOMICS IN PRACTICE

Trust and Gender

As you study economics, you will see that economists study quite a large range of topics. In the experimental area, this seems to be especially true. An interesting recent example is a paper on gender and trust by Nancy Buchan, Rachel Croson, and Sara Solnick.[1]

While many transactions happen in anonymous markets in which buyers and sellers don't know one another, there are many other occasions in which markets operate more effectively if individuals develop some trust in one another. Trust in the goodwill of your employer or of the staff of your local day care can make a big difference in the ways in which you transact business. What can economists say about who is or is not trustworthy?

To answer this question, Buchan et al. used a game economists call the Investment Game to explore the behavior of people when they are not being observed. In this game, there are two players, a responder and a sender, and the game begins with each person receiving $10 from the experimenter. The sender and responder are not known to each other and are put in separate rooms. Sender begins and is told he or she can send any or all of the $10 to the responder. Whatever is sent will be tripled by the experimenter. The responder then can send any or all of the money back.

Clearly the sender–responder pair stand to gain the most if the sender sends all $10 and has it tripled by the experimenter. In this way the pair could turn a starting sum of $20 ($10 each) to $40 (the tripled $10 plus the responder's original $10). As you will see in Chapter 14, economists who work on game theory expect no money to be sent in either direction: Because the sender doesn't trust the responder to share, he or she sends nothing in the first place.

What do Buchan et al. find? In experiments run at the University of Wisconsin and the University of Miami, the experimenters found that almost all subjects sent some money. Perhaps more interestingly, men sent significantly more than women did, but women returned significantly more than men. As the researchers conclude, "We find that men trust more than women, and women are more trustworthy than men."

[1] Nancy Buchan, Rachel Croson, and Sara Solnick. "Trust and Gender: An Examination of Behavior, Biases, and Beliefs in the Investment Game." *Journal of Economic Behavior and Organization*, 2008: 68(3), 466–476.

Economists also differ in the emphasis they place on theory. Some economists specialize in developing new theories, whereas other economists spend their time testing the theories of others. Some economists hope to expand the frontiers of knowledge, whereas other economists are more interested in applying what is already known to the formulation of public policies.

As you begin your study of economics, look through your school's course catalog and talk to the faculty about their interests. You will discover that economics encompasses a broad range of inquiry and is linked to many other disciplines.

The Method of Economics

Economics asks and attempts to answer two kinds of questions: positive and normative. **Positive economics** attempts to understand behavior and the operation of economic systems *without making judgments* about whether the outcomes are good or bad. It strives to describe what exists and how it works. What determines the wage rate for unskilled workers? What would happen if we abolished the corporate income tax? The answers to such questions are the subject of positive economics.

In contrast, **normative economics** looks at the outcomes of economic behavior and asks whether they are good or bad and whether they can be made better. Normative economics involves judgments and prescriptions for courses of action. Should the government subsidize or regulate the cost of higher education? Should medical benefits to the elderly under Medicare be available only to those with incomes below some threshold? Should the

positive economics An approach to economics that seeks to understand behavior and the operation of systems without making judgments. It describes what exists and how it works.

normative economics An approach to economics that analyzes outcomes of economic behavior, evaluates them as good or bad, and may prescribe courses of action. Also called *policy economics*.

United States allow importers to sell foreign-produced goods that compete with U.S.-made products? Should we reduce or eliminate inheritance taxes? Normative economics is often called *policy economics*.

Of course, most normative questions involve positive questions. To know whether the government *should* take a particular action, we must know first if it *can* and second what the consequences are likely to be. (For example, if we lower import fees, will there be more competition and lower prices?)

Some claim that positive, value-free economic analysis is impossible. They argue that analysts come to problems with biases that cannot help but influence their work. Furthermore, even in choosing what questions to ask or what problems to analyze, economists are influenced by political, ideological, and moral views.

Although this argument has some merit, it is nevertheless important to distinguish between analyses that attempt to be positive and those that are intentionally and explicitly normative. Economists who ask explicitly normative questions should be required to specify their grounds for judging one outcome superior to another.

Descriptive Economics and Economic Theory

descriptive economics The compilation of data that describe phenomena and facts.

Positive economics is often divided into descriptive economics and economic theory. **Descriptive economics** is simply the compilation of data that describe phenomena and facts. Examples of such data appear in the *Statistical Abstract of the United States*, a large volume of data published by the Department of Commerce every year that describes many features of the U.S. economy. Massive volumes of data can now be found on the World Wide Web. As an example, look at www.bls.gov (Bureau of Labor Statistics).

Where do these data come from? The Census Bureau collects an enormous amount of raw data every year, as do the Bureau of Labor Statistics, the Bureau of Economic Analysis, and nongovernment agencies such as the University of Michigan Survey Research Center. One important study now published annually is the *Survey of Consumer Expenditure*, which asks individuals to keep careful records of all their expenditures over a long period of time. Another is the *National Longitudinal Survey of Labor Force Behavior*, conducted over many years by the Center for Human Resource Development at the Ohio State University.

economic theory A statement or set of related statements about cause and effect, action and reaction.

Economic theory attempts to generalize about data and interpret them. An **economic theory** is a statement or set of related statements about cause and effect, action and reaction. One of the first theories you will encounter in this text is the *law of demand*, which was most clearly stated by Alfred Marshall in 1890: When the price of a product rises, people tend to buy less of it; when the price of a product falls, people tend to buy more.

Theories do not always arise out of formal numerical data. All of us have been observing people's behavior and their responses to economic stimuli for most of our lives. We may have observed our parents' reaction to a sudden increase—or decrease—in income or to the loss of a job or the acquisition of a new one. We all have seen people standing in line waiting for a bargain. Of course, our own actions and reactions are another important source of data.

Theories and Models

model A formal statement of a theory, usually a mathematical statement of a presumed relationship between two or more variables.

In many disciplines, including physics, chemistry, meteorology, political science, and economics, theorists build formal models of behavior. A **model** is a formal statement of a theory. It is usually a mathematical statement of a presumed relationship between two or more variables.

A **variable** is a measure that can change from time to time or from observation to observation. Income is a variable—it has different values for different people and different values for the same person at different times. The rental price of a movie on a DVD is a variable; it has different values at different stores and at different times. There are countless other examples.

variable A measure that can change from time to time or from observation to observation.

Because all models simplify reality by stripping part of it away, they are abstractions. Critics of economics often point to abstraction as a weakness. Most economists, however, see abstraction as a real strength.

The easiest way to see how abstraction can be helpful is to think of a map. A map is a representation of reality that is simplified and abstract. A city or state appears on a piece of paper as a series of lines and colors. The amount of reality that the mapmaker can strip away before the map loses something essential depends on what the map will be used for. If you want to drive from St. Louis to Phoenix, you need to know only the major interstate highways and roads. You lose absolutely nothing and gain clarity by cutting out the local streets and roads. However, if you need to get around Phoenix, you may need to see every street and alley.

Most maps are two-dimensional representations of a three-dimensional world; they show where roads and highways go but do not show hills and valleys along the way. Trail maps for hikers, however, have "contour lines" that represent changes in elevation. When you are in a car, changes in elevation matter very little; they would make a map needlessly complex and more difficult to read. However, if you are on foot carrying a 50-pound pack, a knowledge of elevation is crucial.

Like maps, economic models are abstractions that strip away detail to expose only those aspects of behavior that are important to the question being asked. The principle that irrelevant detail should be cut away is called the principle of **Ockham's razor** after the fourteenth-century philosopher William of Ockham.

Ockham's razor The principle that irrelevant detail should be cut away.

Be careful—although abstraction is a powerful tool for exposing and analyzing specific aspects of behavior, it is possible to oversimplify. Economic models often strip away a good deal of social and political reality to get at underlying concepts. When an economic theory is used to help formulate actual government or institutional policy, political and social reality must often be reintroduced if the policy is to have a chance of working.

The key here is that the appropriate amount of simplification and abstraction depends on the use to which the model will be put. To return to the map example: You do not want to walk around San Francisco with a map made for drivers—there are too many very steep hills.

All Else Equal: *Ceteris Paribus*

It is usually true that whatever you want to explain with a model depends on more than one factor. Suppose, for example, that you want to explain the total number of miles driven by automobile owners in the United States. The number of miles driven will change from year to year or month to month; it is a variable. The issue, if we want to understand and explain changes that occur, is what factors cause those changes.

Obviously, many things might affect total miles driven. First, more or fewer people may be driving. This number, in turn, can be affected by changes in the driving age, by population growth, or by changes in state laws. Other factors might include the price of gasoline, the household's income, the number and age of children in the household, the distance from home to work, the location of shopping facilities, and the availability and quality of public transport. When any of these variables change, the members of the household may drive more or less. If changes in any of these variables affect large numbers of households across the country, the total number of miles driven will change.

Very often we need to isolate or separate these effects. For example, suppose we want to know the impact on driving of a higher tax on gasoline. This change would raise the price of gasoline at the pump but would not (at least in the short run) affect income, workplace location, number of children, and so on.

To isolate the impact of one single factor, we use the device of *ceteris paribus*, or **all else equal**. We ask, "What is the impact of a change in gasoline price on driving behavior, *ceteris paribus*, or assuming that nothing else changes?" If gasoline prices rise by 10 percent, how much less driving will there be, assuming no simultaneous change in anything else—that is, assuming that income, number of children, population, laws, and so on, all remain constant? Using the device of *ceteris paribus* is one part of the process of abstraction. In formulating economic theory, the concept helps us simplify reality to focus on the relationships that interest us.

ceteris paribus, *or* **all else equal** A device used to analyze the relationship between two variables while the values of other variables are held unchanged.

Expressing Models in Words, Graphs, and Equations

Consider the following statements: Lower airline ticket prices cause people to fly more frequently. Higher interest rates slow the rate of home sales. When firms produce more output, employment increases. Higher gasoline prices cause people to drive less and to buy more fuel-efficient cars.

Each of those statements expresses a relationship between two variables that can be quantified. In each case, there is a stimulus and a response, a cause and an effect. Quantitative relationships can be expressed in a variety of ways. Sometimes words are sufficient to express the essence of a theory, but often it is necessary to be more specific about the nature of a relationship or about the size of a response. The most common method of expressing the quantitative relationship between two variables is *graphing* that relationship on a two-dimensional plane. In fact, we will use graphic analysis extensively in Chapter 2 and beyond. Because it is essential that you be familiar with the basics of graphing, the appendix to this chapter presents a careful review of graphing techniques.

Quantitative relationships between variables can also be presented through *equations*. For example, suppose we discovered that over time, U.S. households collectively spend, or consume, 90 percent of their income and save 10 percent of their income. We could then write:

$$C = .90\,Y \text{ and } S = .10Y$$

where C is consumption spending, Y is income, and S is saving. Writing explicit algebraic expressions like these helps us understand the nature of the underlying process of decision making. Understanding this process is what economics is all about.

Cautions and Pitfalls   In formulating theories and models, it is especially important to avoid two pitfalls: the *post hoc* fallacy and the fallacy of composition.

post hoc, ergo propter hoc
Literally, "after this (in time), therefore because of this." A common error made in thinking about causation: If Event A happens before Event B, it is not necessarily true that A caused B.

The* Post Hoc *Fallacy   Theories often make statements or sets of statements about cause and effect. It can be quite tempting to look at two events that happen in sequence and assume that the first caused the second to happen. This is not always the case. This common error is called the ***post hoc, ergo propter hoc*** (or "after this, therefore because of this") fallacy.

There are thousands of examples. The Colorado Rockies have won seven games in a row. Last night you went to the game and they lost. You must have jinxed them. They lost *because* you went to the game.

Stock market analysts indulge in what is perhaps the most striking example of the *post hoc* fallacy in action. Every day the stock market goes up or down, and every day some analyst on some national news program singles out one or two of the day's events as *the* cause of some change in the market: "Today the Dow Jones industrial average rose 5 points on heavy trading; analysts say that the increase was due to progress in talks between Israel and Syria." Research has shown that daily changes in stock market averages are very largely random. Although major news events clearly have a direct influence on certain stock prices, most daily changes cannot be linked directly to specific news stories.

Very closely related to the *post hoc* fallacy is the often erroneous link between correlation and causation. Two variables are said to be *correlated* if one variable changes when the other variable changes. However, correlation does not imply causation. Cities that have high crime rates also have many automobiles, so there is a very high degree of correlation between number of cars and crime rates. Can we argue, then, that cars *cause* crime? No. The reason for the correlation may have nothing to do with cause and effect. Big cities have many people, many people have many cars; therefore, big cities have many cars. Big cities also have high crime rates for many reasons—crowding, poverty, anonymity, unequal distribution of wealth, and readily available drugs, to mention only a few. However, the presence of cars is probably not one of them.

This caution must also be viewed in reverse. Sometimes events that seem entirely unconnected actually *are* connected. In 1978, Governor Michael Dukakis of Massachusetts ran for reelection. Still quite popular, Dukakis was nevertheless defeated in the Democratic primary that year by a razor-thin margin. The weekend before, the Boston Red Sox, in the thick of the division championship race, had been badly beaten by the New York Yankees in four straight games. Some very respectable political analysts believe that hundreds of thousands of Boston sports fans vented their anger on the incumbent governor the following Tuesday.

The Fallacy of Composition   To conclude that what is true for a part is necessarily true for the whole is to fall into the **fallacy of composition**. Suppose that a large group of cattle ranchers graze their cattle on the same range. To an individual rancher, more cattle and more grazing mean a higher income. However, because its capacity is limited, the land can support only so many cattle. If every cattle rancher increased the number of cattle sent out to graze, the land would become overgrazed and barren; as a result, everyone's income would fall. In short, theories that seem to work well when applied to individuals or households often break down when they are applied to the whole.

fallacy of composition   The erroneous belief that what is true for a part is necessarily true for the whole.

Testing Theories and Models: Empirical Economics   In science, a theory is rejected when it fails to explain what is observed or when another theory better explains what is observed. The collection and use of data to test economic theories is called **empirical economics**.

Numerous large data sets are available to facilitate economic research. For example, economists studying the labor market can now test behavioral theories against the actual working experiences of thousands of randomly selected people who have been surveyed continuously since the 1960s. Macroeconomists continuously monitoring and studying the behavior of the national economy at the National Bureau of Economic Research (NBER) pass thousands of items of data, collected by both government agencies and private companies, over the Internet.

empirical economics   The collection and use of data to test economic theories.

In the natural sciences, controlled experiments, typically done in the lab, are a standard way of testing theories. In recent years, economics has seen an increase in the use of experiments, both in the field and in the lab, as a tool to test its theories. One economist, John List of Chicago, tested the effect of changing the way an auction was run on bid prices for rare baseball cards with the help of the sports memorabilia dealers in trade show. (The experiment used a standard Cal Ripkin Jr. card.) Another economist, Keith Chen of Yale, has used experiments with monkeys to investigate the deeper biological roots of human decision making. The *Economics in Practice* on p. 9 describes another experiment on trust and gender.

Economic Policy

Economic theory helps us understand how the world works, but the formulation of *economic policy* requires a second step. We must have objectives. What do we want to change? Why? What is good and what is bad about the way the system is operating? Can we make it better?

Such questions force us to be specific about the grounds for judging one outcome superior to another. What does it mean to be better? Four criteria are frequently applied in judging economic outcomes:

1. Efficiency
2. Equity
3. Growth
4. Stability

Efficiency   In physics, "efficiency" refers to the ratio of useful energy delivered by a system to the energy supplied to it. An efficient automobile engine, for example, is one that uses a small amount of fuel per mile for a given level of power.

In economics, **efficiency** means *allocative efficiency*. An efficient economy is one that produces what people want at the least possible cost. If the system allocates resources to the production of goods and services that nobody wants, it is inefficient. If all members of a particular society were vegetarians and somehow half of all that society's resources were used to produce meat, the result would be inefficient. It is inefficient when steel beams lie in the rain and rust because somebody fouled up a shipping schedule. If a firm could produce its product using 25 percent less labor and energy without sacrificing quality, it too is inefficient.

efficiency   In economics, allocative efficiency. An efficient economy is one that produces what people want at the least possible cost.

The clearest example of an efficient change is a voluntary exchange. If you and I each want something that the other has and we agree to exchange, we are both better off and no one loses. When a company reorganizes its production or adopts a new technology that enables it to produce more of its product with fewer resources, without sacrificing quality, it has made an efficient change. At least potentially, the resources saved could be used to produce more of something.

Inefficiencies can arise in numerous ways. Sometimes they are caused by government regulations or tax laws that distort otherwise sound economic decisions. Suppose that land in Ohio is best suited for corn production and that land in Kansas is best suited for wheat production. A law that requires Kansas to produce only corn and Ohio to produce only wheat would be inefficient. If firms that cause environmental damage are not held accountable for their actions, the incentive to minimize those damages is lost and the result is inefficient.

equity   Fairness.

Equity   While efficiency has a fairly precise definition that can be applied with some degree of rigor, **equity** (fairness) lies in the eye of the beholder. To many, fairness implies a more equal distribution of income and wealth. Fairness may imply alleviating poverty, but the extent to which the poor should receive cash benefits from the government is the subject of enormous disagreement. For thousands of years, philosophers have wrestled with the principles of justice that should guide social decisions. They will probably wrestle with such questions for thousands of years to come.

Despite the impossibility of defining equity or fairness universally, public policy makers judge the fairness of economic outcomes all the time. Rent control laws were passed because some legislators thought that landlords treated low-income tenants unfairly. Certainly, most social welfare programs are created in the name of equity.

economic growth   An increase in the total output of an economy.

Growth   As the result of technological change, the building of machinery, and the acquisition of knowledge, societies learn to produce new goods and services and to produce old ones better. In the early days of the U.S. economy, it took nearly half the population to produce the required food supply. Today less than 2.0 percent of the country's population works in agriculture.

When we devise new and better ways of producing the goods and services we use now and when we develop new goods and services, the total amount of production in the economy increases. **Economic growth** is an increase in the total output of an economy. If output grows faster than the population, output per capita rises and standards of living increase. Presumably, when an economy grows, it produces more of what people want. Rural and agrarian societies become modern industrial societies as a result of economic growth and rising per capita output.

Some policies discourage economic growth, and others encourage it. Tax laws, for example, can be designed to encourage the development and application of new production techniques. Research and development in some societies are subsidized by the government. Building roads, highways, bridges, and transport systems in developing countries may speed up the process of economic growth. If businesses and wealthy people invest their wealth outside their country rather than in their country's industries, growth in their home country may be slowed.

stability   A condition in which national output is growing steadily, with low inflation and full employment of resources.

Stability   Economic **stability** refers to the condition in which national output is growing steadily, with low inflation and full employment of resources. During the 1950s and 1960s, the U.S. economy experienced a long period of relatively steady growth, stable prices, and low unemployment. Between 1951 and 1969, consumer prices never rose more than 5 percent in a single year, and in only 2 years did the number of unemployed exceed 6 percent of the labor force. From the end of the Gulf War in 1991 to the beginning of 2001, the U.S. economy enjoyed price stability and strong economic growth with rising employment. It was the longest expansion in American history.

The decades of the 1970s and 1980s, however, were not as stable. The United States experienced two periods of rapid price inflation (over 10 percent) and two periods of severe unemployment. In 1982, for example, 12 million people (10.8 percent of the workforce) were looking for work. The beginning of the 1990s was another period of instability, with a recession occurring in 1990–1991. In 2008–2009 much of the world, including the United States, experienced a large contraction in output and rise in unemployment. This was clearly an unstable period.

The causes of instability and the ways in which governments have attempted to stabilize the economy are the subject matter of macroeconomics.

An Invitation

This chapter has prepared you for your study of economics. The first part of the chapter invited you into an exciting discipline that deals with important issues and questions. You cannot begin to understand how a society functions without knowing something about its economic history and its economic system.

The second part of the chapter introduced the method of reasoning that economics requires and some of the tools that economics uses. We believe that learning to think in this very powerful way will help you better understand the world.

As you proceed, it is important that you keep track of what you have learned in earlier chapters. This book has a plan; it proceeds step-by-step, each section building on the last. It would be a good idea to read each chapter's table of contents at the start of each chapter and scan each chapter before you read it to make sure you understand where it fits in the big picture.

———————————— SUMMARY ————————————

1. *Economics* is the study of how individuals and societies choose to use the scarce resources that nature and previous generations have provided.

WHY STUDY ECONOMICS? *p. 2*

2. There are many reasons to study economics, including (a) to learn a way of thinking, (b) to understand society, (c) to understand global affairs, and (d) to be an informed citizen.

3. The best alternative that we forgo when we make a choice or a decision is the *opportunity cost* of that decision.

THE SCOPE OF ECONOMICS *p. 6*

4. *Microeconomics* deals with the functioning of individual markets and industries and with the behavior of individual decision-making units: business firms and households.

5. *Macroeconomics* looks at the economy as a whole. It deals with the economic behavior of aggregates—national output, national income, the overall price level, and the general rate of inflation.

6. Economics is a broad and diverse discipline with many special fields of inquiry. These include economic history, international economics, and urban economics.

THE METHOD OF ECONOMICS *p. 9*

7. Economics asks and attempts to answer two kinds of questions: positive and normative. *Positive economics* attempts to understand behavior and the operation of economies

without making judgments about whether the outcomes are good or bad. *Normative economics* looks at the results of economic behavior and asks whether they are good or bad and whether they can be improved.

8. Positive economics is often divided into two parts. *Descriptive economics* involves the compilation of data that accurately describe economic facts and events. *Economic theory* attempts to generalize and explain what is observed. It involves statements of cause and effect—of action and reaction.

9. An economic *model* is a formal statement of an economic theory. Models simplify and abstract from reality.

10. It is often useful to isolate the effects of one variable on another while holding "all else constant." This is the device of *ceteris paribus*.

11. Models and theories can be expressed in many ways. The most common ways are in words, in graphs, and in equations.

12. Because one event happens before another, the second event does not necessarily happen as a result of the first. To assume that "after" implies "because" is to commit the fallacy of *post hoc, ergo propter hoc*. The erroneous belief that what is true for a part is necessarily true for the whole is the *fallacy of composition*.

13. *Empirical economics* involves the collection and use of data to test economic theories. In principle, the best model is the one that yields the most accurate predictions.

14. To make policy, one must be careful to specify criteria for making judgments. Four specific criteria are used most often in economics: *efficiency, equity, growth,* and *stability*.

———— REVIEW TERMS AND CONCEPTS ————

ceteris paribus, or all else equal, *p. 11*

descriptive economics, *p. 10*

economic growth, *p. 14*

economic theory, *p. 10*

economics, *p. 2*

efficiency, *p. 13*

efficient market, *p. 3*

empirical economics, *p. 13*

equity, *p. 14*

fallacy of composition, *p. 13*

Industrial Revolution, *p. 4*

macroeconomics, *p. 7*

marginalism, *p. 3*

microeconomics, *p. 6*

model, *p. 10*

normative economics, *p. 9*

Ockham's razor, *p. 11*

opportunity cost, *p. 2*

positive economics, *p. 9*

post hoc, ergo propter hoc, p. 12

scarce, *p. 2*

stability, *p. 14*

sunk costs, *p. 3*

variable, *p. 10*

———— PROBLEMS ————

All problems are available on www.myeconlab.com

1. One of the scarce resources that constrain our behavior is time. Each of us has only 24 hours in a day. How do you go about allocating your time in a given day among competing alternatives? How do you go about weighing the alternatives? Once you choose a most important use of time, why do you not spend all your time on it? Use the notion of opportunity cost in your answer.

2. In the summer of 2007, the housing market and the mortgage market were both in decline. Housing prices in most U.S. cities began to decline in mid-2006. With prices falling and the inventory of unsold houses rising, the production of new homes fell to around 1.5 million in 2007 from 2.3 million in 2005. With new construction falling dramatically, it was expected that construction *employment* would fall and that this would have the potential of slowing the national economy and increasing the general unemployment rate. Go to www.bls.gov and check out the recent data on total employment and construction employment. Have they gone up or down from their levels in August 2007? What has happened to the unemployment rate? Go to www.fhfa.gov and look at the housing price index. Have home prices risen or fallen since August 2007? Finally, look at the latest GDP release at www.bea.gov. Look at residential and nonresidential investment (Table 1.1.5) during the last 2 years. Do you see a pattern? Does it explain the employment numbers? Explain your answer.

3. Which of the following statements are examples of positive economic analysis? Which are examples of normative analysis?
   a. The inheritance tax should be repealed because it is unfair.
   b. Allowing Chile to join NAFTA would cause wine prices in the United States to drop.
   c. The first priorities of the new regime in the Democratic Republic of Congo (DRC, formerly Zaire) should be to rebuild schools and highways and to provide basic health care.

4. Sarita signed up with Netflix for a fixed fee of $16.99 per month. For this fee, she can receive up to 3 DVDs at a time in the mail and exchange each DVD as often as she likes. She also receives unlimited instant access to movies being streamed from Netflix to her computer or TV. During the average month in 2010, Sarita received and watched 6 movies sent to her through the mail and she watched an additional 13 movies which were streamed to her computer. What is the average cost of a movie to Sarita? What is the marginal cost of an additional movie?

5. A question facing many U.S. states is whether to allow casino gambling. States with casino gambling have seen a substantial increase in tax revenue flowing to state government. This revenue can be used to finance schools, repair roads, maintain social programs, or reduce other taxes.
   a. Recall that efficiency means producing what people want at the least cost. Can you make an efficiency argument in favor of allowing casinos to operate?
   b. What nonmonetary costs might be associated with gambling? Would these costs have an impact on the efficiency argument you presented in part **a**?
   c. Using the concept of equity, argue for or against the legalization of casino gambling.

6. For each of the following situations, identify the full cost (opportunity cost) involved:
   a. A worker earning an hourly wage of $8.50 decides to cut back to part-time to attend Houston Community College.
   b. Sue decides to drive to Los Angeles from San Francisco to visit her son, who attends UCLA.
   c. Tom decides to go to a wild fraternity party and stays out all night before his physics exam.
   d. Annie spends $200 on a new dress.
   e. The Confab Company spends $1 million to build a new branch plant that will probably be in operation for at least 10 years.
   f. Alex's father owns a small grocery store in town. Alex works 40 hours a week in the store but receives no compensation.

7. [**Related to the** *Economics in Practice* **on p. 6**] Log onto www.census.gov. Click on "Foreign Trade," then on "Statistics," and finally on "State Export Data." There you will find a list of the products produced in your state and exported to countries around the world. In looking over that list, are you surprised by anything? Do you know of any firms that produce these items? Search the Web to find a company that does. Do some research and write a paragraph about your company: what it produces, how many people it employs, and whatever else you can learn about the firm. You might even call the company to obtain the information.

8. Explain the pitfalls in the following statements.
   a. Whenever Jeremy decides to wash his car, the next day it usually rain. Since Jeremy's town is suffering from a severe drought, he decided to wash his car and, just as he expected, the next day the thunderstorms rolled in. Obviously it rained because Jeremy washed his car.

b. The principal of Hamilton High School found that requiring those students who were failing algebra to attend an after-school tutoring program resulted in a 30 percent average increase in their algebra grades. Based on this success, the principal decided to hire more tutors and require that all students must attend after-school tutoring, so everyone's algebra grades would improve.

c. People who drive hybrid automobiles recycle their trash more than people who do not drive hybrids. Therefore, recycling trash causes people to drive hybrid automobiles.

9. Explain whether each of the following is an example of a macroeconomic concern or a microeconomic concern.

a. Ford Motor Company is contemplating increasing the production of full-size SUVs based on projected future consumer demand.

b. Congress is debating the option of implementing a value-added tax as a means to cut the federal deficit.

c. The Federal Reserve announces it is increasing the discount rate in an attempt to slow the rate of inflation.

d. The Bureau of Labor Statistics projects a 22.5 percent increase in the number or workers in the healthcare industry from 2008 to 2018.

10. On the *Forbes* 2010 list of the World's Billionaires, Mexico's Carlos Slim Helu ranks at the top with a net worth of U.S. $53.5 billion. Does this "richest man in the world" face scarcity, or does scarcity only affect those with more limited incomes and lower net worth?

Source: "The World's Billionaires," *Forbes*, March 10, 2010.

CHAPTER 1 APPENDIX

How to Read and Understand Graphs

Economics is the most quantitative of the social sciences. If you flip through the pages of this or any other economics text, you will see countless tables and graphs. These serve a number of purposes. First, they illustrate important economic relationships. Second, they make difficult problems easier to understand and analyze. Finally, they can show patterns and regularities that may not be discernible in simple lists of numbers.

A **graph** is a two-dimensional representation of a set of numbers, or data. There are many ways that numbers can be illustrated by a graph.

Time Series Graphs

It is often useful to see how a single measure or variable changes over time. One way to present this information is to plot the values of the variable on a graph, with each value corresponding to a different time period. A graph of this kind is called a **time series graph.** On a time series graph, time is measured along the horizontal scale and the variable being graphed is measured along the vertical scale. Figure 1A.1 is a time series graph that presents the total disposable personal

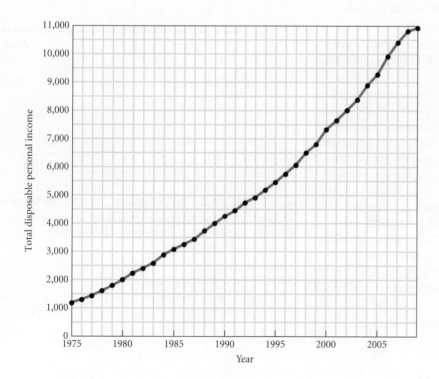

◀ **FIGURE 1A.1 Total Disposable Personal Income in the United States: 1975–2009 (in billions of dollars)**

Source: See Table 1A.1.

income in the U.S. economy for each year between 1975 and 2009.[1] This graph is based on the data found in Table 1A.1. By displaying these data graphically, we can see that (1) total disposable personal income has increased steadily since 1975 and (2) during certain periods, income has increased at a faster rate than during other periods.

TABLE 1A.1	Total Disposable Personal Income in the United States, 1975–2009 (in billions of dollars)		
Year	Total Disposable Personal Income	Year	Total Disposable Personal Income
1975	1,187.3	1993	4,921.6
1976	1,302.3	1994	5,184.3
1977	1,435.0	1995	5,457.0
1978	1,607.3	1996	5,759.6
1979	1,790.8	1997	6,074.6
1980	2,002.7	1998	6,498.9
1981	2,237.1	1999	6,803.3
1982	2,412.7	2000	7,327.2
1983	2,599.8	2001	7,648.5
1984	2,891.5	2002	8,009.7
1985	3,079.3	2003	8,377.8
1986	3,258.8	2004	8,889.4
1987	3,435.3	2005	9,277.3
1988	3,726.3	2006	9,915.7
1989	3,991.4	2007	10,403.1
1990	4,254.0	2008	10,806.4
1991	4,444.9	2009	10,923.6
1992	4,736.7		

Source: U.S. Department of Commerce, Bureau of Economic Analysis.

Graphing Two Variables on a Cartesian Coordinate System

More important than simple graphs of one variable are graphs that contain information on two variables at the same time. The most common method of graphing two variables is the **Cartesian coordinate system**. This system is constructed by drawing two perpendicular lines: a horizontal line, or **X-axis**, and a vertical line, or **Y-axis**. The axes contain measurement scales that intersect at 0 (zero). This point is called the **origin**. On the vertical scale, positive numbers lie above the horizontal axis (that is, above the origin) and negative numbers lie below it. On the horizontal scale, positive numbers lie to the right of the vertical axis (to the right of the origin) and negative numbers lie to the left of it. The point at which the graph intersects the *Y*-axis is called the **Y-intercept**. The point at which the graph intersects the *X*-axis is called the **X-intercept**.

When two variables are plotted on a single graph, each point represents a pair of numbers. The first number is measured on the *X*-axis, and the second number is measured on the *Y*-axis. For example, the following points (X, Y) are plotted on the set of axes

drawn in Figure 1A.2: (4, 2), (2, −1), (−3, 4), (−3, −2). Most, but not all, of the graphs in this book are plots of two variables where both values are positive numbers [such as (4, 2) in Figure 1A.2]. On these graphs, only the upper-right quadrant of the coordinate system (that is, the quadrant in which all *X* and *Y* values are positive) will be drawn.

Plotting Income and Consumption Data For Households

Table 1A.2 presents data collected by the Bureau of Labor Statistics (BLS). In a recent survey, 5,000 households were asked to keep track of all their expenditures. This table shows average income and average spending for those households,

TABLE 1A.2	Consumption Expenditures and Income, 2008	
	Average Income Before Taxes	Average Consumption Expenditures
Bottom fifth	$ 10,263	$22,304
2nd fifth	27,442	31,751
3rd fifth	47,196	42,659
4th fifth	74,090	58,632
Top fifth	158,652	97,003

Source: Consumer Expenditures in 2008, U.S. Bureau of Labor Statistics.

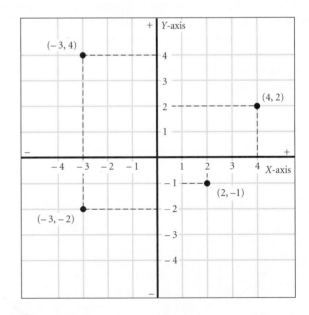

▲ **FIGURE 1A.2 A Cartesian Coordinate System**

A Cartesian coordinate system is constructed by drawing two perpendicular lines: a vertical axis (the *Y*-axis) and a horizontal axis (the *X*-axis). Each axis is a measuring scale.

---

[1] The measure of income presented in Table 1A.1 and in Figure 1A.1 is disposable personal income in billions of dollars. It is the total personal income received by all households in the United States minus the taxes that they pay.

ranked by income. For example, the average income for the top fifth (20 percent) of the households was $158,652. The average spending for the top 20 percent was $97,003.

Figure 1A.3 presents the numbers from Table 1A.2 graphically using the Cartesian coordinate system. Along the horizontal scale, the X-axis, we measure average income. Along the vertical scale, the Y-axis, we measure average consumption spending. Each of the five pairs of numbers from the table is represented by a point on the graph. Because all numbers are positive numbers, we need to show only the upper right quadrant of the coordinate system.

To help you read this graph, we have drawn a dotted line connecting all the points where consumption and income would be equal. *This 45° line does not represent any data.* Instead, it represents the line along which all variables on the X-axis correspond exactly to the variables on the Y-axis, for example, (10,000, 10,000), (20,000, 20,000), and (37,000, 37,000). The heavy blue line traces the data; the purpose of the dotted line is to help you read the graph.

There are several things to look for when reading a graph. The first thing you should notice is whether the line slopes upward or downward as you move from left to right. The blue line in Figure 1A.3 slopes upward, indicating that there seems to be a **positive relationship** between income and spending: The higher a household's income, the more a household tends to consume. If we had graphed the percentage of each group receiving welfare payments along the Y-axis, the line would presumably slope downward, indicating that welfare payments are lower at higher income levels. The income level/welfare payment relationship is thus a **negative relationship**.

Slope

The **slope** of a line or curve is a measure that indicates whether the relationship between the variables is positive or negative and how much of a response there is in Y (the variable on the vertical axis) when X (the variable on the horizontal axis) changes. The slope of a line between two points is the change in the quantity measured on the Y-axis divided by the change in the quantity measured on the X-axis. We will normally use Δ (the Greek letter *delta*) to refer to a change in a variable. In Figure 1A.4, the slope of the line between points A and B is ΔY divided by ΔX. Sometimes it is easy to remember slope as "the rise over the run," indicating the vertical change over the horizontal change.

To be precise, ΔX between two points on a graph is simply X_2 minus X_1, where X_2 is the X value for the second point and X_1 is the X value for the first point. Similarly, ΔY is defined as Y_2 minus Y_1, where Y_2 is the Y value for the second point and Y_1 is the Y value for the first point. Slope is equal to

$$\frac{\Delta Y}{\Delta X} = \frac{Y_2 - Y_1}{X_2 - X_1}$$

As we move from A to B in Figure 1A.4(a), both X and Y increase; the slope is thus a positive number. However, as we move from A to B in Figure 1A.4(b), X increases [$(X_2 - X_1)$ is a positive number], but Y decreases [$(Y_2 - Y_1)$ is a negative number]. The slope in Figure 1A.4(b) is thus a negative number because a negative number divided by a positive number results in a negative quotient.

To calculate the numerical value of the slope between points A and B in Figure 1A.3, we need to calculate ΔY and ΔX. Because consumption is measured on the Y-axis, ΔY is 9,447 [$(Y_2 - Y_1) = (31,751 - 22,304)$]. Because income is measured along the X-axis, ΔX is 17,179 [$(X_2 - X_1) = (27,442 - 10,263)$]. The slope between A and B is $\Delta Y/\Delta X$ = 9,447/17,179 = + 0.55.

▶ **FIGURE 1A.3**
Household Consumption and Income

A graph is a simple two-dimensional geometric representation of data. This graph displays the data from Table 1A.2. Along the horizontal scale (X-axis), we measure household income. Along the vertical scale (Y-axis), we measure household consumption.
Note: At point A, consumption equals $22,304 and income equals $10,263. At point B, consumption equals $31,751 and income equals $27,442.

Source: See Table 1A.2.

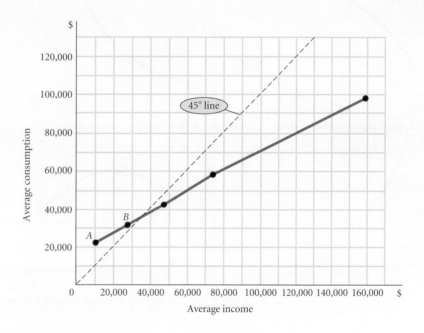

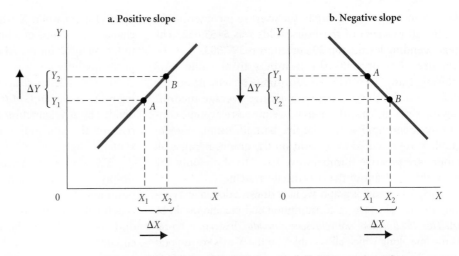

▲ **FIGURE 1A.4 A Curve with (a) Positive Slope and (b) Negative Slope**
A *positive* slope indicates that increases in *X* are associated with increases in *Y* and that decreases in *X* are associated with decreases in *Y*. A *negative* slope indicates the opposite—when *X* increases, *Y* decreases; and when *X* decreases, *Y* increases.

Another interesting thing to note about the data graphed in Figure 1A.3 is that all the points lie roughly along a straight line. (If you look very closely, however, you can see that the slope declines as you move from left to right; the line becomes slightly less steep.) A straight line has a constant slope. That is, if you pick any two points along it and calculate the slope, you will always get the same number. A horizontal line has a zero slope (ΔY is zero); a vertical line has an "infinite" slope because ΔY is too big to be measured.

Unlike the slope of a straight line, the slope of a *curve* is continually changing. Consider, for example, the curves in Figure 1A.5. Figure 1A.5(a) shows a curve with a positive slope that decreases as you move from left to right. The easiest way to think about the concept of increasing or decreasing

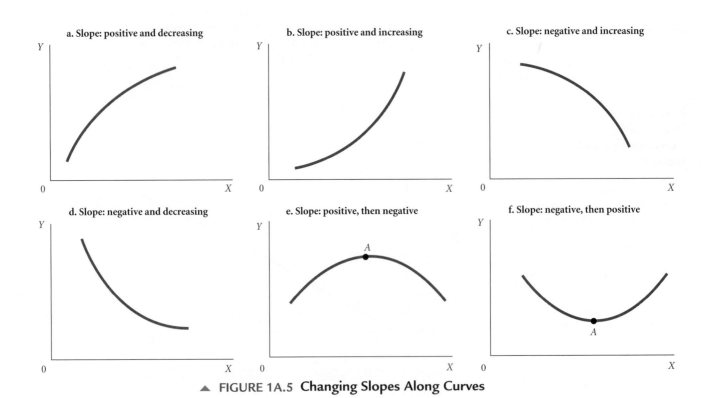

▲ **FIGURE 1A.5 Changing Slopes Along Curves**

slope is to imagine what it is like walking up a hill from left to right. If the hill is steep, as it is in the first part of Figure 1A.5(a), you are moving more in the Y direction for each step you take in the X direction. If the hill is less steep, as it is further along in Figure 1A.5(a), you are moving less in the Y direction for every step you take in the X direction. Thus, when the hill is steep, slope ($\Delta Y/\Delta X$) is a larger number than it is when the hill is flatter. The curve in Figure 1A.5(b) has a positive slope, but its slope *increases* as you move from left to right.

The same analogy holds for curves that have a negative slope. Figure 1A.5(c) shows a curve with a negative slope that increases (in absolute value) as you move from left to right. This time think about skiing down a hill. At first, the descent in Figure 1A.5(c) is gradual (low slope), but as you proceed down the hill (to the right), you descend more quickly (high slope). Figure 1A.5(d) shows a curve with a negative slope that *decreases* (in absolute value) as you move from left to right.

In Figure 1A.5(e), the slope goes from positive to negative as X increases. In Figure 1A.5(f), the slope goes from negative to positive. At point A in both, the slope is zero. [Remember, slope is defined as $\Delta Y/\Delta X$. At point A, Y is not changing ($\Delta Y = 0$). Therefore, the slope at point A is zero.]

Some Precautions

When you read a graph, it is important to think carefully about what the points in the space defined by the axes represent. Table 1A.3 and Figure 1A.6 present a graph of consumption and income that is very different from the one

TABLE 1A.3	Aggregate National Income and Consumption for the United States, 1930–2009 (in billions of dollars)	
	Aggregate National Income	Aggregate Consumption
1930	82.9	70.1
1940	90.9	71.3
1950	263.9	192.2
1960	473.9	331.8
1970	929.5	648.3
1980	2,433.0	1,755.8
1990	5,059.8	3,835.5
2000	8,938.9	6,830.4
2005	11,273.8	8,819.0
2006	12,031.2	9,322.7
2007	12,448.2	9,826.4
2008	12,635.2	10,129.9
2009	12,280.0	10,089.1

Source: U.S. Department of Commerce, Bureau of Economic Analysis.

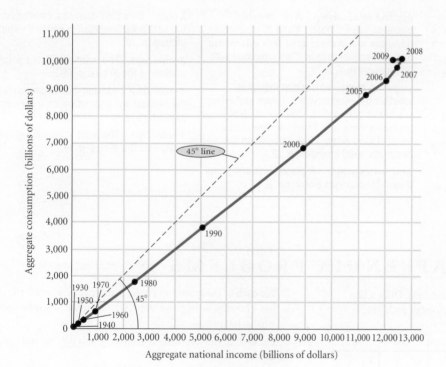

▲ **FIGURE 1A.6 National Income and Consumption**

It is important to think carefully about what is represented by points in the space defined by the axes of a graph. In this graph, we have graphed income with consumption, as in Figure 1A.3, but here each observation point is national income and aggregate consumption in *different years*, measured in billions of dollars.

Source: See Table 1A.3.

in Table 1A.2 and Figure 1A.3. First, each point in Figure 1A.6 represents a different year; in Figure 1A.3, each point represented a different group of households at the *same* point in time (2008). Second, the points in Figure 1A.6 represent *aggregate* consumption and income for the whole nation measured in *billions* of dollars; in Figure 1A.3, the points represented average *household* income and consumption measured in dollars.

It is interesting to compare these two graphs. All points on the aggregate consumption curve in Figure 1A.6 lie below the 45° line, which means that aggregate consumption is always less than aggregate income. However, the graph of average household income and consumption in Figure 1A.3 crosses the 45° line, implying that for some households, consumption is larger than income.

APPENDIX SUMMARY

1. A *graph* is a two-dimensional representation of a set of numbers, or data. A *time series graph* illustrates how a single variable changes over time.

2. The most common method of graphing two variables on one graph is the *Cartesian coordinate system*, which includes an X (horizontal)-*axis* and a Y (vertical)-*axis*. The points at which the two axes intersect is called the *origin*. The point at which a graph intersects the Y-axis is called the *Y-intercept*. The point at which a graph intersects the X-axis is called the *X-intercept*.

3. The *slope* of a line or curve indicates whether the relationship between the two variables graphed on a Cartesian coordinate system is positive or negative and how much of a response there is in Y (the variable on the vertical axis) when X (the variable on the horizontal axis) changes. The slope of a line between two points is the change in the quantity measured on the Y-axis divided by the change in the quantity measured on the X-axis.

APPENDIX REVIEW TERMS AND CONCEPTS

Cartesian coordinate system A common method of graphing two variables that makes use of two perpendicular lines against which the variables are plotted. *p. 18*

graph A two-dimensional representation of a set of numbers or data. *p. 17*

negative relationship A relationship between two variables, X and Y, in which a decrease in X is associated with an increase in Y and an increase in X is associated with a decrease in Y. *p. 19*

origin On a Cartesian coordinate system, the point at which the horizontal and vertical axes intersect. *p. 18*

positive relationship A relationship between two variables, X and Y, in which a decrease in X is associated with a decrease in Y, and an increase in X is associated with an increase in Y. *p. 19*

slope A measurement that indicates whether the relationship between variables is positive or negative and how much of a response there is in Y (the variable on the vertical axis) when X (the variable on the horizontal axis) changes. *p. 19*

time series graph A graph illustrating how a variable changes over time. *p. 17*

X-axis On a Cartesian coordinate system, the horizontal line against which a variable is plotted. *p. 18*

X-intercept The point at which a graph intersects the X-axis. *p. 18*

Y-axis On a Cartesian coordinate system, the vertical line against which a variable is plotted. *p. 18*

Y-intercept The point at which a graph intersects the Y-axis. *p. 18*

APPENDIX PROBLEMS

1. Graph each of the following sets of numbers. Draw a line through the points and calculate the slope of each line.

1		2		3		4		5		6	
X	Y	X	Y	X	Y	X	Y	X	Y	X	Y
1	5	1	25	0	0	0	40	0	0	0.1	100
2	10	2	20	10	10	10	30	10	10	0.2	75
3	15	3	15	20	20	20	20	20	20	0.3	50
4	20	4	10	30	30	30	10	30	10	0.4	25
5	25	5	5	40	40	40	0	40	0	0.5	0

2. For each of the graphs in Figure 1, determine whether the curve has a positive or negative slope. Give an intuitive explanation for what is happening with the slope of each curve.

3. For each of the following equations, graph the line and calculate its slope.
   a. $P = 10 - 2q_D$ (Put q_D on the X-axis.)
   b. $P = 100 - 4q_D$ (Put q_D on the X-axis.)
   c. $P = 50 + 6q_S$ (Put q_S on the X-axis.)
   d. $I = 10,000 - 500r$ (Put I on the X-axis.)

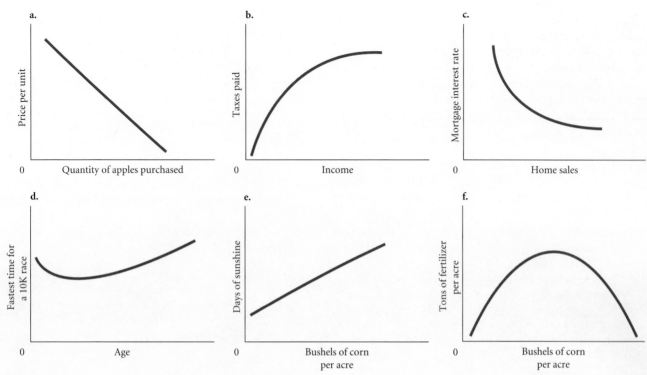

▲ FIGURE 1

4. The following table shows the relationship between the price of a dozen roses and the number of roses sold by Fiona's Flowers.
   a. Is the relationship between the price of roses and the number of roses sold by Fiona's Flowers a positive relationship or a negative relationship? Explain.
   b. Plot the data from the table on a graph, draw a line through the points, and calculate the slope of the line.

PRICE PER DOZEN	QUANTITY OF ROSES (DOZENS)	MONTH
$20	30	January
50	90	February
25	40	March
30	50	April
40	70	May

5. Calculate the slope of the demand curve at point A and at point B in the following figure.

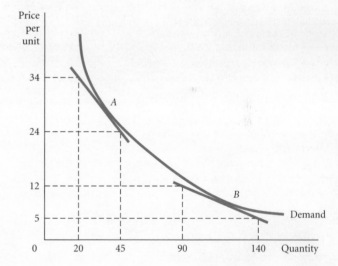

The Economic Problem: Scarcity and Choice

2

Chapter 1 began with a very broad definition of economics. Every society, no matter how small or large, no matter how simple or complex, has a system or process that works to transform the resources that nature and previous generations provide into useful form. Economics is the study of that process and its outcomes.

Figure 2.1 illustrates three basic questions that must be answered to understand the functioning of the economic system:

- What gets produced?
- How is it produced?
- Who gets what is produced?

This chapter explores these questions in detail. In a sense, this entire chapter *is* the definition of economics. It lays out the central problems addressed by the discipline and presents a framework that will guide you through the rest of the book. The starting point is the presumption that *human wants are unlimited but resources are not.* Limited or scarce resources force individuals and societies to choose among competing uses of resources—alternative combinations of produced goods and services—and among alternative final distributions of what is produced among households.

These questions are *positive* or *descriptive*. That is, they ask how the system functions without passing judgment about whether the result is good or bad. They must be answered first before we ask more normative questions such as these:

- Is the outcome good or bad?
- Can it be improved?

The term *resources* is very broad. The sketch on the left side of Figure 2.1 shows several categories of resources. Some resources are the products of nature: land, wildlife, fertile soil, minerals, timber, energy, and even the rain and wind. In addition, the resources available to an economy include things such as buildings and equipment that have been produced in the past but are now being used to produce other things. And perhaps the most important resource of a society is its human workforce with people's talents, skills, and knowledge.

Things that are produced and then used in the production of other goods and services are called capital resources, or simply **capital**. Buildings, equipment, desks, chairs, software, roads, bridges, and highways are a part of the nation's stock of capital.

The basic resources available to a society are often referred to as **factors of production**, or simply **factors**. The three key factors of production are land, labor, and capital. The process that transforms scarce resources into useful goods and services is called **production**. In many societies, most of the production of goods and services is done by private firms.

capital Things that are produced and then used in the production of other goods and services.

factors of production (or factors) The inputs into the process of production. Another term for resources.

production The process that transforms scarce resources into useful goods and services.

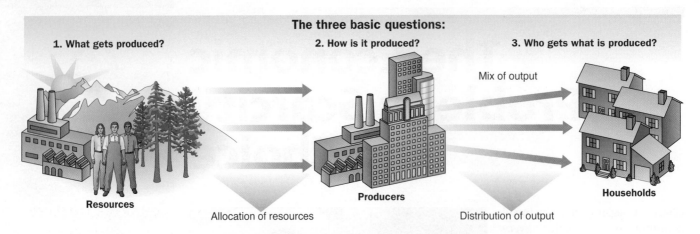

▲ FIGURE 2.1 **The Three Basic Questions**
Every society has some system or process that transforms its scarce resources into useful goods and services. In doing so, it must decide what gets produced, how it is produced, and to whom it is distributed. The primary resources that must be allocated are land, labor, and capital.

Private airlines in the United States use land (runways), labor (pilots and mechanics), and capital (airplanes) to produce transportation services. But in all societies, some production is done by the public sector, or government. Examples of government-produced or government-provided goods and services include national defense, public education, police protection, and fire protection.

Resources or factors of production are the **inputs** into the process of production; goods and services of value to households are the **outputs** of the process of production.

inputs *or* resources
Anything provided by nature or previous generations that can be used directly or indirectly to satisfy human wants.

outputs Goods and services of value to households.

Scarcity, Choice, and Opportunity Cost

In the second half of this chapter we discuss the global economic landscape. Before you can understand the different types of economic systems, it is important to master the basic economic concepts of scarcity, choice, and opportunity cost.

Scarcity and Choice in a One-Person Economy

The simplest economy is one in which a single person lives alone on an island. Consider Bill, the survivor of a plane crash, who finds himself cast ashore in such a place. Here individual and society are one; there is no distinction between social and private. *Nonetheless, nearly all the same basic decisions that characterize complex economies must also be made in a simple economy.* That is, although Bill will get whatever he produces, he still must decide how to allocate the island's resources, what to produce, and how and when to produce it.

First, Bill must decide *what* he wants to produce. Notice that the word *needs* does not appear here. Needs are absolute requirements; but beyond just enough water, basic nutrition, and shelter to survive, needs are very difficult to define. What is an "absolute necessity" for one person may not be for another person. In any case, Bill must put his wants in some order of priority and make some choices.

Next, he must look at the *possibilities*. What can he do to satisfy his wants given the limits of the island? In every society, no matter how simple or complex, people are constrained in what they can do. In this society of one, Bill is constrained by time, his physical condition, his knowledge, his skills, and the resources and climate of the island.

Given that resources are limited, Bill must decide *how* to best use them to satisfy his hierarchy of wants. Food would probably come close to the top of his list. Should he spend his time gathering fruits and berries? Should he hunt for game? Should he clear a field and plant seeds?

The answers to those questions depend on the character of the island, its climate, its flora and fauna (*are* there any fruits and berries?), the extent of his skills and knowledge (does he know anything about farming?), and his preferences (he may be a vegetarian).

Opportunity Cost The concepts of *constrained choice* and *scarcity* are central to the discipline of economics. They can be applied when discussing the behavior of individuals such as Bill and when analyzing the behavior of large groups of people in complex societies.

Given the scarcity of time and resources, if Bill decides to hunt, he will have less time to gather fruits and berries. He faces a trade-off between meat and fruit. There is a trade-off between food and shelter too. If Bill likes to be comfortable, he may work on building a nice place to live, but that may require giving up the food he might have produced. As we noted in Chapter 1, the best alternative that we give up, or forgo, when we make a choice is the **opportunity cost** of that choice.

Bill may occasionally decide to rest, to lie on the beach, and to enjoy the sun. In one sense, that benefit is free—he does not have to buy a ticket to lie on the beach. In reality, however, relaxing does have an opportunity cost. The true cost of that leisure is the value of the other things Bill could have produced, but did not, during the time he spent on the beach.

During 2010, more than a dozen cities, including Minneapolis, Los Angeles, and Houston, were actively considering public funding for new football, soccer, and basketball arenas. An important part of that debate was the opportunity cost of the taxpayers' dollars: What else could tax dollars be spent on, and how much value would the alternatives bring to the local taxpayers? Perhaps without the new arena, taxes could be lower. Here the opportunity cost would include the value taxpayers receive from goods and services they would consume with the earnings that are no longer taxed. Most discussions of public expenditures at all levels of government include active considerations of opportunity costs.

In making everyday decisions, it is often helpful to think about opportunity costs. Should you go to the dorm party or not? First, it costs $4 to attend. When you pay money for anything, you give up the other things you could have bought with that money. Second, it costs 2 or 3 hours. Time is a valuable commodity for a college student. You have exams next week, and you need to study. You could go to a movie instead of the party. You could go to another party. You could sleep. Just as Bill must weigh the value of sunning on the beach against more food or better housing, so you must weigh the value of the fun you may have at the party against everything else you might otherwise do with the time and money.

opportunity cost The best alternative that we give up, or forgo, when we make a choice or decision.

Scarcity and Choice in an Economy of Two or More

Now suppose that another survivor of the crash, Colleen, appears on the island. Now that Bill is not alone, things are more complex and some new decisions must be made. Bill's and Colleen's preferences about what things to produce are likely to be different. They will probably not have the same knowledge or skills. Perhaps Colleen is very good at tracking animals and Bill has a knack for building things. How should they split the work that needs to be done? Once things are produced, the two castaways must decide how to divide them. How should their products be distributed?

The mechanism for answering these fundamental questions is clear when Bill is alone on the island. The "central plan" is his; he simply decides what he wants and what to do about it. The minute someone else appears, however, a number of decision-making arrangements immediately become possible. One or the other may take charge, in which case that person will decide for both of them. The two may agree to cooperate, with each having an equal say, and come up with a joint plan; or they may agree to split the planning as well as the production duties. Finally, they may go off to live alone at opposite ends of the island. Even if they live apart, however, they may take advantage of each other's presence by specializing and trading.

Modern industrial societies must answer the same questions that Colleen and Bill must answer, but the mechanics of larger economies are more complex. Instead of two people living together, the United States has over 300 million people. Still, decisions must be made about what to produce, how to produce it, and who gets it.

ECONOMICS IN PRACTICE

Frozen Foods and Opportunity Costs

In 2007, $27 billion of frozen foods were sold in U.S. grocery stores, one quarter of it in the form of frozen dinners and entrees. In the mid-1950s, sales of frozen foods amounted to only $1 billion, a tiny fraction of the overall grocery store sales. One industry observer attributes this growth to the fact that frozen food tastes much better than it did in the past. Can you think of anything else that might be occurring?

The growth of the frozen dinner entrée market in the last 50 years is a good example of the role of opportunity costs in our lives. One of the most significant social changes in the U.S. economy in this period has been the increased participation of women in the labor force. In 1950, only 24 percent of married women worked; by 2000, that fraction had risen to 61 percent. Producing a meal takes two basic ingredients: food and time. When both husbands and wives work, the opportunity cost of time for housework—including making meals—goes up. This tells us that making a home-cooked meal became more expensive in the last 50 years. A natural result is to shift people toward labor-saving ways to make meals. Frozen foods are an obvious solution to the problem of increased opportunity costs.

Another, somewhat more subtle, opportunity cost story is at work encouraging the consumption of frozen foods. In 1960, the first microwave oven was introduced. The spread of this device into America's kitchens was rapid. The microwave turned out to be a quick way to defrost and cook those frozen entrées. So this technology lowered the opportunity cost of making frozen dinners, reinforcing the

advantage these meals had over home-cooked meals. Microwaves made cooking with frozen foods cheaper once opportunity cost was considered while home-cooked meals were becoming more expensive.

The entrepreneurs among you also might recognize that the rise we described in the opportunity cost of the home-cooked meal *contributed* in part to the spread of the microwave, creating a reinforcing cycle. In fact, many entrepreneurs find that the simple tools of economics—like the idea of opportunity costs—help them anticipate what products will be profitable for them to produce in the future. The growth of the two-worker family has stimulated many entrepreneurs to search for labor-saving solutions to family tasks.

The public policy students among you might be interested to know that some researchers attribute part of the growth in obesity in the United States to the lower opportunity costs of making meals associated with the growth of the markets for frozen foods and the microwave. (See David M.Cutler, Edward L. Glaeser, and Jesse M. Shapiro, "Why Have Americans Become More Obese?" *Journal of Economic Perspectives*, Summer 2003, 93–118.)

Specialization, Exchange, and Comparative Advantage   The idea that members of society benefit by specializing in what they do best has a long history and is one of the most important and powerful ideas in all of economics. David Ricardo, a major nineteenth-century British economist, formalized the point precisely. According to Ricardo's **theory of comparative advantage**, specialization and free trade will benefit all trading parties, even when some are "absolutely" more efficient producers than others. Ricardo's basic point applies just as much to Colleen and Bill as it does to different nations.

theory of comparative advantage   Ricardo's theory that specialization and free trade will benefit all trading parties, even those that may be "absolutely" more efficient producers.

To keep things simple, suppose that Colleen and Bill have only two tasks to accomplish each week: gathering food to eat and cutting logs to burn. If Colleen could cut more logs than Bill in 1 day and Bill could gather more nuts and berries than Colleen could, specialization would clearly lead to more total production. Both would benefit if Colleen only cuts logs and Bill only gathers nuts and berries, as long as they can trade.

Suppose that Bill is slow and somewhat clumsy in his nut gathering and that Colleen is better at cutting logs *and* gathering food. At first, it might seem that since Colleen is better at everything, she should do everything. But that cannot be right. Colleen's time is limited after all, and even though Bill is clumsy and not very clever, he must be able to contribute something.

One of Ricardo's lasting contributions to economics has been his analysis of exactly this situation. His analysis, which is illustrated in Figure 2.2, shows both how Colleen and Bill should divide the work of the island and how much they will gain from specializing and exchanging even if, as in this example, one party is absolutely better at everything than the other party.

absolute advantage   A producer has an absolute advantage over another in the production of a good or service if he or she can produce that product using fewer resources.

Suppose Colleen can cut 10 logs per day and Bill can cut only 4. Also suppose Colleen can gather 10 bushels of food per day and Bill can gather only 8. A producer has an **absolute advantage** over another in the production of a good or service if he or she can produce the good or service using fewer resources, including time. Since Colleen can cut more logs per day than Bill, we say that she has an absolute advantage in the production of logs. Similarly, Colleen has an absolute advantage over Bill in the production of food.

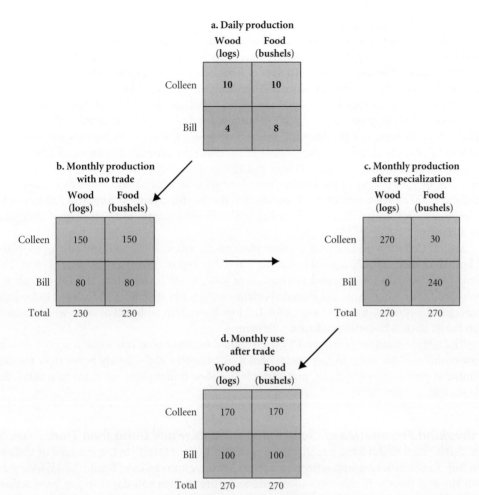

a. Daily production

	Wood (logs)	Food (bushels)
Colleen	10	10
Bill	4	8

b. Monthly production with no trade

	Wood (logs)	Food (bushels)
Colleen	150	150
Bill	80	80
Total	230	230

c. Monthly production after specialization

	Wood (logs)	Food (bushels)
Colleen	270	30
Bill	0	240
Total	270	270

d. Monthly use after trade

	Wood (logs)	Food (bushels)
Colleen	170	170
Bill	100	100
Total	270	270

◀ **FIGURE 2.2**

Comparative Advantage and the Gains from Trade

In this figure, (a) shows the number of logs and bushels of food that Colleen and Bill can produce for every day spent at the task and (b) shows how much output they could produce in a month, assuming they wanted an equal number of logs and bushels. Colleen would split her time 50/50, devoting 15 days to each task and achieving total output of 150 logs and 150 bushels of food. Bill would spend 20 days cutting wood and 10 days gathering food. As shown in (c) and (d), by specializing and trading, both Colleen and Bill will be better off. Going from (c) to (d), Colleen trades 100 logs to Bill in exchange for 140 bushels of food.

Thinking just about productivity and the output of food and logs, you might conclude that it would benefit Colleen to move to the other side of the island and be by herself. Since she is more productive in cutting logs and gathering food, would she not be better off on her own? How could she benefit by hanging out with Bill and sharing what they produce?

To answer that question we must remember that Colleen's time is limited: This limit creates opportunity cost. A producer has a **comparative advantage** over another in the production of a good or service if he or she can produce the good or service at a lower opportunity cost. First, think about Bill. He can produce 8 bushels of food per day, or he can cut 4 logs. To get 8 additional bushels of food, he must give up cutting 4 logs. Thus, *for Bill, the opportunity cost of 8 bushels of food is 4 logs*. Think next about Colleen. She can produce 10 bushels of food per day, or she can cut 10 logs. She thus gives up 1 log for each additional bushel; so *for Colleen, the opportunity cost of 8 bushels of food is 8 logs*. Bill has a comparative advantage over Colleen in the production of food because he gives up only 4 logs for an additional 8 bushels, whereas Colleen gives up 8 logs.

Think now about what Colleen must give up in terms of food to get 10 logs. To produce 10 logs she must work a whole day. If she spends a day cutting 10 logs, she gives up a day of gathering 10 bushels of food. Thus, *for Colleen, the opportunity cost of 10 logs is 10 bushels of food*. What must Bill give up to get 10 logs? To produce 4 logs, he must work 1 day. For each day he cuts logs, he gives up 8 bushels of food. He thus gives up 2 bushels of food for each log; so *for Bill, the opportunity cost of 10 logs is 20 bushels of food*. Colleen has a comparative advantage over Bill in the production of logs since she gives up only 10 bushels of food for an additional 10 logs, whereas Bill gives up 20 bushels.

Ricardo argues that two parties can benefit from specialization and trade even if one party has an absolute advantage in the production of both goods. Suppose Colleen and Bill both want

comparative advantage A producer has a comparative advantage over another in the production of a good or service if he or she can produce that product at a lower *opportunity cost*.

equal numbers of logs and bushels of food. If Colleen goes off on her own, in a 30-day month she can produce 150 logs and 150 bushels, devoting 15 days to each task. For Bill to produce equal numbers of logs and bushels on his own requires that he spend 10 days on food and 20 days on logs. This yields 80 bushels of food (10 days × 8 bushels per day) and 80 logs (20 days × 4 logs per day). Between the two, they produce 230 logs and 230 bushels of food.

Let's see if specialization and trade can work. If Bill spends all his time on food, he produces 240 bushels in a month (30 days × 8 bushels per day). If Colleen spends 3 days on food and 27 days on logs, she produces 30 bushels of food (3 days × 10 bushels per day) and 270 logs (27 days × 10 logs per day). Between the two, they produce 270 logs and 270 bushels of food, which is more than the 230 logs and 230 bushels they produced when not specializing. Thus, by specializing in the production of the good in which they enjoyed a comparative advantage, there are more of both goods. We see in this example how the fundamental concept of opportunity cost covered earlier in this chapter relates to the theory of comparative advantage.

Even if Colleen were to live at another place on the island, she could specialize, producing 30 bushels of food and 270 logs, then trading 100 of her logs to Bill for 140 bushels of food. This would leave her with 170 logs and 170 bushels of food, which is more than the 150 of each she could produce on her own. Bill would specialize completely in food, producing 240 bushels. Trading 140 bushels of food to Colleen for 100 logs leaves him with 100 of each, which is more than the 80 of each he could produce on his own.

The simple example of Bill and Colleen should begin to give you some insight into why most economists see value in free trade. Even if one country is absolutely better than another country at producing everything, our example has shown that there are gains to specializing and trading.

A Graphical Presentation of Comparative Advantage and Gains from Trade Graphs can also be used to show the benefits from specialization and trade in the example of Colleen and Bill. To construct a graph reflecting Colleen's production choices (Figure 2.3 [a]), we start with the end points. If she were to devote an entire month (30 days) to log production, she could cut 300 logs—10 logs per day × 30 days. Similarly, if she were to devote an entire month to food gathering, she could produce 300 bushels. If she chose to split her time evenly (15 days to logs and 15 days to food), she would have 150 bushels and 150 logs. Her production possibilities are illustrated by the straight line between A and B and illustrate the trade-off that she faces between logs and food: By reducing her time spent in food gathering, Colleen is able to devote more time to logs; and for every 10 bushels of food that she gives up, she gets 10 logs.

In Figure 2.3(b), we construct a graph of Bill's production possibilities. Recall that Bill can produce 8 bushels of food per day, but he can cut only 4 logs. Again, starting with the end points, if Bill devoted all his time to food production, he could produce 240 bushels— 8 bushels of food per day × 30 days. Similarly, if he were to devote the entire 30 days to log cutting, he could cut 120 logs—4 logs per day × 30 days. By splitting his time, with 20 days spent on log cutting and 10 days spent gathering food, Bill could produce 80 logs and 80 bushels of food. His production possibilities are illustrated by the straight line between D and E. By shifting his resources and time from logs to food, he gets 2 bushels for every log.

Figures 2.3(a) and 2.3(b) illustrate the maximum amounts of food and logs that Bill and Colleen can produce acting independently with no specialization or trade, which is 230 logs and 230 bushels. Now let us have each specialize in producing the good in which he or she has a comparative advantage. Back in Figure 2.2 on p. 29, we showed that if Bill devoted all his time to food production, producing 240 bushels (30 days × 8 bushels per day), and Colleen devoted the vast majority of her time to cutting logs (27 days) and just a few days to gathering food (3 days), their combined total would be 270 logs and 270 bushels of food. Colleen would produce 270 logs and 30 bushels of food to go with Bill's 240 bushels of food.

Finally, we arrange a trade, and the result is shown in Figures 2.4(a) and 2.4(b). Bill trades 140 bushels of food to Colleen for 100 logs, and he ends up with 100 logs and 100 bushels of food, 20 more of each than he would have had before the specialization and trade.

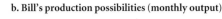

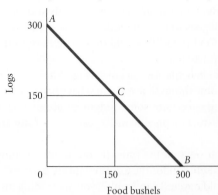

▲ **FIGURE 2.3 Production Possibilities with No Trade**

The figure in (a) shows all of the combinations of logs and bushels of food that Colleen can produce by herself. If she spends all 30 days each month on logs, she produces 300 logs and no food (point *A*). If she spends all 30 days on food, she produces 300 bushels of food and no logs (point *B*). If she spends 15 days on logs and 15 days on food, she produces 150 of each (point *C*).

The figure in (b) shows all of the combinations of logs and bushels of food that Bill can produce by himself. If he spends all 30 days each month on logs, he produces 120 logs and no food (point *D*). If he spends all 30 days on food, he produces 240 bushels of food and no logs (point *E*). If he spends 20 days on logs and 10 days on food, he produces 80 of each (point *F*).

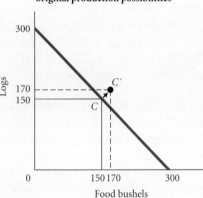

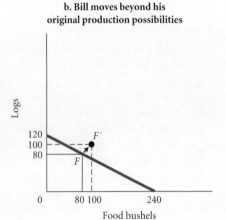

▲ **FIGURE 2.4 Colleen and Bill Gain from Trade**

By specializing and engaging in trade, Colleen and Bill can move beyond their own production possibilities. If Bill spends all his time producing food, he will produce 240 bushels of food and no logs. If he can trade 140 of his bushels of food to Colleen for 100 logs, he will end up with 100 logs and 100 bushels of food. The figure in (b) shows that he can move from point *F* to point *F′*.

If Colleen spends 27 days cutting logs and 3 days producing food, she will produce 270 logs and 30 bushels of food. If she can trade 100 of her logs to Bill for 140 bushels of food, she will end up with 170 logs and 170 bushels of food. The figure in (a) shows that she can move from point *C* to point *C′*.

Colleen ends up with 170 logs and 170 bushels, again 20 more of each than she would have had before the specialization and trade. Both are better off. Both move beyond their individual production possibilities.

Weighing Present and Expected Future Costs and Benefits   Very often we find ourselves weighing benefits available today against benefits available tomorrow. Here, too, the notion of opportunity cost is helpful.

While alone on the island, Bill had to choose between cultivating a field and just gathering wild nuts and berries. Gathering nuts and berries provides food now; gathering seeds and clearing a field for planting will yield food tomorrow if all goes well. Using today's time to farm may well be worth the effort if doing so will yield more food than Bill would otherwise have in the future. By planting, Bill is trading present value for future value.

The simplest example of trading present for future benefits is the act of saving. When you put income aside today for use in the future, you give up some things that you could have had today in exchange for something tomorrow. Because nothing is certain, some judgment about future events and expected values must be made. What will your income be in 10 years? How long are you likely to live?

We trade off present and future benefits in small ways all the time. If you decide to study instead of going to the dorm party, you are trading present fun for the expected future benefits of higher grades. If you decide to go outside on a very cold day and run 5 miles, you are trading discomfort in the present for being in better shape later.

Capital Goods and Consumer Goods   A society trades present for expected future benefits when it devotes a portion of its resources to research and development or to investment in capital. As we said earlier in this chapter, *capital* in its broadest definition is anything that has already been produced that will be used to produce other valuable goods or services over time.

Building capital means trading present benefits for future ones. Bill and Colleen might trade gathering berries or lying in the sun for cutting logs to build a nicer house in the future. In a modern society, resources used to produce capital goods could have been used to produce **consumer goods**—that is, goods for present consumption. Heavy industrial machinery does not directly satisfy the wants of anyone, but producing it requires resources that could instead have gone into producing things that do satisfy wants directly—for example, food, clothing, toys, or golf clubs.

consumer goods Goods produced for present consumption.

Capital is everywhere. A road is capital. Once a road is built, we can drive on it or transport goods and services over it for many years to come. A house is also capital. Before a new manufacturing firm can start up, it must put some capital in place. The buildings, equipment, and inventories that it uses comprise its capital. As it contributes to the production process, this capital yields valuable services over time.

In Chapter 1, we talked about the enormous amount of capital—buildings, factories, housing, cars, trucks, telephone lines, and so on—that you might see from a window high in a skyscraper. Much of that capital was put in place by previous generations, yet it continues to provide valuable services today; it is part of this generation's endowment of resources. To build every building, every road, every factory, every house, and every car or truck, society must forgo using resources to produce consumer goods today. To get an education, you pay tuition and put off joining the workforce for a while.

Capital does not need to be tangible. When you spend time and resources developing skills or getting an education, you are investing in human capital—your own human capital. This capital will continue to exist and yield benefits to you for years to come. A computer program produced by a software company and available online may cost nothing to distribute, but its true intangible value comes from the ideas embodied in the program itself. It too is capital.

investment The process of using resources to produce new capital.

The process of using resources to produce new capital is called **investment**. (In everyday language, the term *investment* often refers to the act of buying a share of stock or a bond, as in "I invested in some Treasury bonds." In economics, however, investment *always* refers to the creation of capital: the purchase or putting in place of buildings, equipment, roads, houses, and the like.) A wise investment in capital is one that yields future benefits that are more valuable than the present cost. When you spend money for a house, for example, presumably you value its future benefits. That is, you expect to gain more from living in it than you would from the things you could buy today with the same money. Capital can also be intangible. Consider education that builds skills or knowledge in workers. Clearly education can yield decades of future "benefits" including higher wages. Because resources are scarce, the opportunity cost of every investment in capital is forgone present consumption.

The Production Possibility Frontier

A simple graphic device called the **production possibility frontier (ppf)** illustrates the principles of constrained choice, opportunity cost, and scarcity. The ppf is a graph that shows all the combinations of goods and services that can be produced if all of a society's resources are used efficiently. Figure 2.5 shows a ppf for a hypothetical economy.

On the Y-axis, we measure the quantity of capital goods produced. On the X-axis, we measure the quantity of consumer goods. All points below and to the left of the curve (the shaded area) represent combinations of capital and consumer goods that are possible for the society given the resources available and existing technology. Points above and to the right of the curve, such as point G, represent combinations that cannot be reached. If an economy were to end up at point A on the graph, it would be producing no consumer goods at all; all resources would be used for the production of capital. If an economy were to end up at point B, it would be devoting all its resources to the production of consumer goods and none of its resources to the formation of capital.

While all economies produce some of each kind of good, different economies emphasize different things. About 17.1 percent of gross output in the United States in 2005 was new capital. In Japan, capital historically accounted for a much higher percent of gross output, while in the Congo, the figure was 7 percent. Japan is closer to point A on its ppf, the Congo is closer to B, and the United States is somewhere in between.

Points that are actually on the ppf are points of both full resource employment and production efficiency. (Recall from Chapter 1 that an efficient economy is one that produces the things that people want at the least cost. *Production efficiency* is a state in which a given mix of outputs is produced at the least cost.) Resources are not going unused, and there is no waste. Points that lie within the shaded area but that are not on the frontier represent either unemployment of resources or production inefficiency. An economy producing at point D in Figure 2.5 can produce more capital goods and more consumer goods, for example, by moving to point E. This is possible because resources are not fully employed at point D or are not being used efficiently.

production possibility frontier (ppf) A graph that shows all the combinations of goods and services that can be produced if all of society's resources are used efficiently.

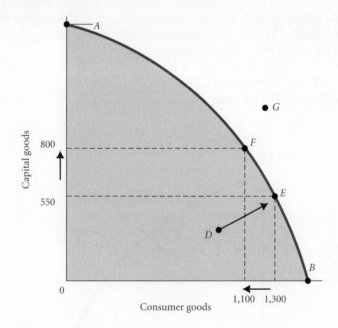

▲ **FIGURE 2.5 Production Possibility Frontier**

The ppf illustrates a number of economic concepts. One of the most important is *opportunity cost*. The opportunity cost of producing more capital goods is fewer consumer goods. Moving from *E* to *F*, the number of capital goods increases from 550 to 800, but the number of consumer goods decreases from 1,300 to 1,100.

Unemployment   During the Great Depression of the 1930s, the U.S. economy experienced prolonged unemployment. Millions of workers found themselves without jobs. In 1933, 25 percent of the civilian labor force was unemployed. This figure stayed above 14 percent until 1940. More recently, between the end of 2007 and 2010, the United States lost over 8 million payroll jobs and unemployment rose to over 15 million.

In addition to the hardship that falls on the unemployed, unemployment of labor means unemployment of capital. During economic downturns or recessions, industrial plants run at less than their total capacity. When there is unemployment of labor and capital, we are not producing all that we can.

Periods of unemployment correspond to points inside the ppf, points such as *D* in Figure 2.5. Moving onto the frontier from a point such as *D* means achieving full employment of resources.

Inefficiency   Although an economy may be operating with full employment of its land, labor, and capital resources, it may still be operating inside its ppf (at a point such as *D* in Figure 2.5). It could be using those resources *inefficiently*.

Waste and mismanagement are the results of a firm operating below its potential. If you are the owner of a bakery and you forget to order flour, your workers and ovens stand idle while you figure out what to do.

Sometimes inefficiency results from mismanagement of the economy instead of mismanagement of individual private firms. Suppose, for example, that the land and climate in Ohio are best suited for corn production and that the land and climate in Kansas are best suited for wheat production. If Congress passes a law forcing Ohio farmers to plant 50 percent of their acreage with wheat and Kansas farmers to plant 50 percent with corn, neither corn nor wheat production will be up to potential. The economy will be at a point such as *A* in Figure 2.6—inside the ppf. Allowing each state to specialize in producing the crop that it produces best increases the production of both crops and moves the economy to a point such as *B* in Figure 2.6.

The Efficient Mix of Output   To be efficient, an economy must produce what people want. This means that in addition to operating *on* the ppf, the economy must be operating at the *right point* on the ppf. This is referred to as *output efficiency*, in contrast to production efficiency. Suppose that an economy devotes 100 percent of its resources to beef production and that the beef industry runs efficiently using the most modern techniques. Also suppose that everyone in the society is a vegetarian. The result is a total waste of resources (assuming that the society cannot trade its beef for vegetables produced in another country).

Points *B* and *C* in Figure 2.6 are points of production efficiency and full employment. Whether *B* is more or less efficient than *C*, however, depends on the preferences of members of society and is not shown in the ppf graph.

▶ **FIGURE 2.6**
Inefficiency from Misallocation of Land in Farming
Society can end up inside its ppf at a point such as *A* by using its resources inefficiently. If, for example, Ohio's climate and soil were best suited for corn production and those of Kansas were best suited for wheat production, a law forcing Kansas farmers to produce corn and Ohio farmers to produce wheat would result in less of both. In such a case, society might be at point *A* instead of point *B*.

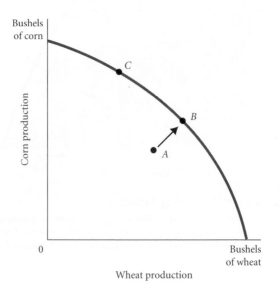

Negative Slope and Opportunity Cost   As we have seen, points that lie on the ppf represent points of full resource employment and production efficiency. Society can choose only one point on the curve. Because a society's choices are constrained by available resources and existing technology, when those resources are fully and efficiently employed, it can produce more capital goods only by reducing production of consumer goods. The opportunity cost of the additional capital is the forgone production of consumer goods.

The fact that scarcity exists is illustrated by the negative slope of the ppf. (If you need a review of slope, see the Appendix to Chapter 1.) In moving from point *E* to point *F* in Figure 2.5, capital production *increases* by 800 − 550 = 250 units (a positive change), but that increase in capital can be achieved only by shifting resources out of the production of consumer goods. Thus, in moving from point *E* to point *F* in Figure 2.5, consumer goods production *decreases* by 1,300 − 1,100 = 200 units (a negative change). The slope of the curve, the ratio of the change in capital goods to the change in consumer goods, is negative.

The value of the slope of a society's ppf is called the **marginal rate of transformation (MRT)**. In Figure 2.5, the MRT between points *E* and *F* is simply the ratio of the change in capital goods (a positive number) to the change in consumer goods (a negative number).

marginal rate of transformation (MRT)   The slope of the production possibility frontier (ppf).

The Law of Increasing Opportunity Cost   The negative slope of the ppf indicates the trade-off that a society faces between two goods. We can learn something further about the shape of the frontier and the terms of this trade-off. Let's look at the trade-off between corn and wheat production in Ohio and Kansas. In a recent year, Ohio and Kansas together produced 510 million bushels of corn and 380 million bushels of wheat. Table 2.1 presents these two numbers, plus some hypothetical combinations of corn and wheat production that might exist for Ohio and Kansas together. Figure 2.7 graphs the data from Table 2.1.

TABLE 2.1	Production Possibility Schedule for Total Corn and Wheat Production in Ohio and Kansas	
Point on ppf	Total Corn Production (Millions of Bushels per Year)	Total Wheat Production (Millions of Bushels per Year)
A	700	100
B	650	200
C	510	380
D	400	500
E	300	550

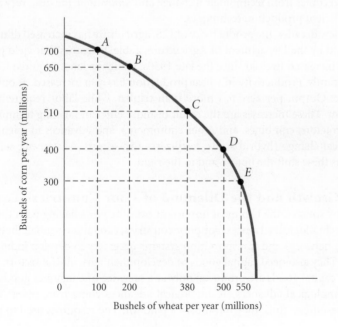

◀ **FIGURE 2.7 Corn and Wheat Production in Ohio and Kansas**

The ppf illustrates that the opportunity cost of corn production increases as we shift resources from wheat production to corn production. Moving from point *E* to *D*, we get an additional 100 million bushels of corn at a cost of 50 million bushels of wheat. Moving from point *B* to *A*, we get only 50 million bushels of corn at a cost of 100 million bushels of wheat. The *cost per bushel* of corn—measured in lost wheat—has increased.

Suppose that society's demand for corn dramatically increases. If this happens, farmers would probably shift some of their acreage from wheat production to corn production. Such a shift is represented by a move from point C (where corn = 510 and wheat = 380) up and to the left along the ppf toward points A and B in Figure 2.7. As this happens, it becomes more difficult to produce additional corn. The best land for corn production was presumably already in corn, and the best land for wheat production was already in wheat. As we try to produce more corn, the land is less well suited to that crop. As we take more land out of wheat production, we are taking increasingly better wheat-producing land. In other words, the opportunity cost of more corn, measured in terms of wheat, increases.

Moving from point E to D, Table 2.1 shows that we can get 100 million bushels of corn $(400 - 300)$ by sacrificing only 50 million bushels of wheat $(550 - 500)$—that is, we get 2 bushels of corn for every bushel of wheat. However, when we are already stretching the ability of the land to produce corn, it becomes harder to produce more and the opportunity cost increases. Moving from point B to A, we can get only 50 million bushels of corn $(700 - 650)$ by sacrificing 100 million bushels of wheat $(200 - 100)$. For every bushel of wheat, we now get only half a bushel of corn. However, if the demand for *wheat* were to increase substantially and we were to move down and to the right along the ppf, it would become increasingly difficult to produce wheat and the opportunity cost of wheat, in terms of corn, would increase. This is the *law of increasing opportunity cost.*

If you think about the example we discussed earlier of Colleen and Bill producing logs and food on an island, you will recognize that the production possibilities described were highly simplified. In that example, we drew a downward slope, *straight line ppf*; to make the problem easier, we assumed constant opportunity costs. In a real economy, ppf's would be expected to look like Figure 2.5.

Although it exists only as an abstraction, the ppf illustrates a number of very important concepts that we will use throughout the rest of this book: scarcity, unemployment, inefficiency, opportunity cost, the law of increasing opportunity cost, economic growth, and the gains from trade.

It is important to remember that the ppf represents choices available within the constraints imposed by the current state of agricultural technology. In the long run, technology may improve, and when that happens, we have *growth*.

economic growth An increase in the total output of an economy. It occurs when a society acquires new resources or when it learns to produce more using existing resources.

Economic Growth   **Economic growth** is characterized by an increase in the total output of an economy. It occurs when a society acquires new resources or learns to produce more with existing resources. New resources may mean a larger labor force or an increased capital stock. The production and use of new machinery and equipment (capital) increase workers' productivity. (Give a man a shovel, and he can dig a bigger hole; give him a steam shovel, and wow!) Improved productivity also comes from technological change and *innovation*, the discovery and application of new, more efficient production techniques.

In the past few decades, the productivity of U.S. agriculture has increased dramatically. Based on data compiled by the Department of Agriculture, Table 2.2 shows that yield per acre in corn production has increased fivefold since the late 1930s, while the labor required to produce it has dropped significantly. Productivity in wheat production has also increased, at only a slightly less remarkable rate: Output per acre has more than tripled, while labor requirements are down nearly 90 percent. These increases are the result of more efficient farming techniques, more and better capital (tractors, combines, and other equipment), and advances in scientific knowledge and technological change (hybrid seeds, fertilizers, and so on). As you can see in Figure 2.8, increases such as these shift the ppf up and to the right.

Sources of Growth and the Dilemma of Poor Countries   Economic growth arises from many sources, the two most important over the years having been the accumulation of capital and technological advances. For poor countries, capital is essential; they must build the communication networks and transportation systems necessary to develop industries that function efficiently. They also need capital goods to develop their agricultural sectors.

Recall that capital goods are produced only at a sacrifice of consumer goods. The same can be said for technological advances. Technological advances come from research and development that use resources; thus, they too must be paid for. The resources used to produce capital

TABLE 2.2 Increasing Productivity in Corn and Wheat Production in the United States, 1935–2009

	Corn		Wheat	
	Yield per Acre (Bushels)	Labor Hours per 100 Bushels	Yield per Acre (Bushels)	Labor Hours per 100 Bushels
1935–1939	26.1	108	13.2	67
1945–1949	36.1	53	16.9	34
1955–1959	48.7	20	22.3	17
1965–1969	78.5	7	27.5	11
1975–1979	95.3	4	31.3	9
1981–1985	107.2	3	36.9	7
1985–1990	112.8	NAᵃ	38.0	NAᵃ
1990–1995	120.6	NAᵃ	38.1	NAᵃ
1998	134.4	NAᵃ	43.2	NAᵃ
2001	138.2	NAᵃ	43.5	NAᵃ
2006	145.6	NAᵃ	42.3	NAᵃ
2007	152.8	NAᵃ	40.6	NAᵃ
2008	153.9	NAᵃ	44.9	NAᵃ
2009	164.9	NAᵃ	44.3	NAᵃ

ᵃData not available.

Source: U.S. Department of Agriculture, Economic Research Service, Agricultural Statistics, Crop Summary.

goods—to build a road, a tractor, or a manufacturing plant—*and* to develop new technologies could have been used to produce consumer goods.

When a large part of a country's population is very poor, taking resources out of the production of consumer goods (such as food and clothing) is very difficult. In addition, in some countries, people wealthy enough to invest in domestic industries choose instead to invest abroad because of political turmoil at home. As a result, it often falls to the governments of poor countries to generate revenues for capital production and research out of tax collections.

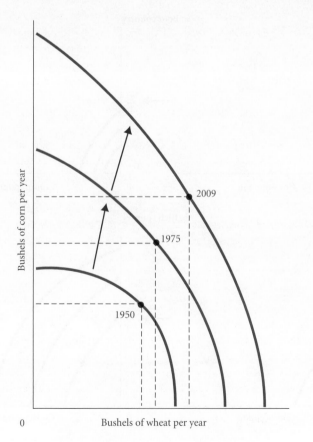

◀ **FIGURE 2.8 Economic Growth Shifts the PPF Up and to the Right**
Productivity increases have enhanced the ability of the United States to produce both corn and wheat. As Table 2.2 shows, productivity increases were more dramatic for corn than for wheat. Thus, the shifts in the ppf were not parallel.

Note: The ppf also shifts if the amount of land or labor in corn and wheat production changes. Although we emphasize productivity increases here, the actual shifts between years were due in part to land and labor changes.

All these factors have contributed to the growing gap between some poor and rich nations. Figure 2.9 shows the result using ppf's. On the left, the rich country devotes a larger portion of its production to capital while the poor country produces mostly consumer goods. On the right, you see the results: The ppf of the rich country shifts up and out farther and faster.

The importance of capital goods and technological developments to the position of workers in less developed countries is well illustrated by Robert Jensen's study of South India's industry. Conventional telephones require huge investments in wires and towers and, as a result, many less developed areas are without landlines. Mobile phones, on the other hand, require a less expensive investment; thus, in many areas, people upgraded from no phones directly to cell phones. Jensen found that in small fishing villages, the advent of cell phones allowed fishermen to determine on any given day where to take their catch to sell, resulting in a large decrease in fish wasted and an increase in fishing profits. The ability of newer communication technology to aid development is one of the exciting features of our times. (See Robert Jensen, "The Digital Provide: Information Technology, Market Performance, and Welfare in the South Indian Fisheries Sector," *Quarterly Journal of Economics*, August 2007, 879–924.)

The Economic Problem

Recall the three basic questions facing all economic systems: (1) What gets produced? (2) How is it produced? and (3) Who gets it?

When Bill was alone on the island, the mechanism for answering those questions was simple: He thought about his own wants and preferences, looked at the constraints imposed by the resources of the island and his own skills and time, and made his decisions. As Bill set about his work, he allocated available resources quite simply, more or less by dividing up his available time. Distribution of the output was irrelevant. Because Bill was the society, he got it all.

▶ FIGURE 2.9 **Capital Goods and Growth in Poor and Rich Countries**

Rich countries find it easier than poor countries to devote resources to the production of capital, and the more resources that flow into capital production, the faster the rate of economic growth. Thus, the gap between poor and rich countries has grown over time.

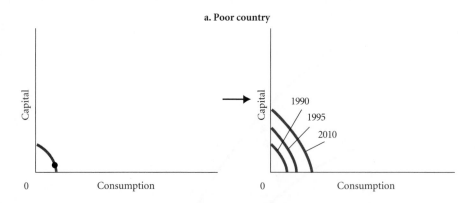

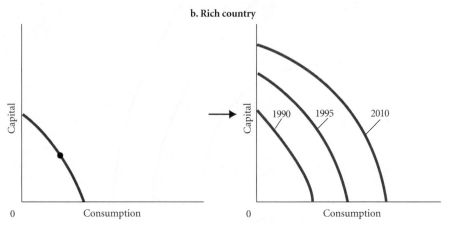

ECONOMICS IN PRACTICE

Trade-Offs among the Rich and Poor

In all societies, for all people, resources are limited relative to people's demands. There are, however, quite large differences in the kinds of trade-offs individuals face in rich versus poor countries.

In 1990, the World Bank defined the extremely poor people of the world as those earning less than $1 a day. Among development economists and policy makers, this figure continues to be used as a rough rule of thumb. In a recent survey, Esther Duflo and Abhijit Banerjee, two MIT economists, surveyed individuals living at this level in 13 countries across the world.[1] What did they learn about the consumption trade-offs faced by these individuals versus consumers in the United States?

It should not surprise you to learn that for the extremely poor, food is a much larger component of the budget. On average over the 13 countries, between 56 percent and 78 percent of consumption was spent on food. In the United States just under 10 percent of the average budget goes to food. Even for the poorest consumers, however, biological need is not all determining. The Banerjee and Duflo study finds that in Udaipur, India, almost 10 percent of the typical food budget goes to sugar and processed foods rather than more nutritionally valuable grains. So even at these very low levels of income, some choice remains. Perhaps more interestingly, almost 10 percent of the budget of those surveyed goes to weddings, funerals, and other festivals. In societies with very few entertainment

outlets, Banerjee and Duflo suggest we may see more demand for festivals, indicating that even in extremely poor societies, household choice plays a role.

[1] Abhijit Banerjee and Esther Duflo, "The Economic Lives of the Poor," *Journal of Economic Perspective*, Winter 2007, 21(1), 141–167.

Introducing even one more person into the economy—in this case, Colleen—changed all that. With Colleen on the island, resource allocation involves deciding not only how each person spends his or her time but also who does what; now there are two sets of wants and preferences. If Bill and Colleen go off on their own and form two separate self-sufficient economies, there will be lost potential. Two people can do more things together than each person can do alone. They may use their comparative advantages in different skills to specialize. Cooperation and coordination may give rise to gains that would otherwise not be possible.

When a society consists of millions of people, the problem of coordination and cooperation becomes enormous, but so does the potential for gain. In large, complex economies, specialization can go wild, with people working in jobs as different in their detail as an impressionist painting is from a blank page. The range of products available in a modern industrial society is beyond anything that could have been imagined a hundred years ago, and so is the range of jobs.

The amount of coordination and cooperation in a modern industrial society is almost impossible to imagine. Yet something seems to drive economic systems, if sometimes clumsily and inefficiently, toward producing the goods and services that people want. Given scarce resources, how do large, complex societies go about answering the three basic economic questions? This is the economic problem, which is what this text is about.

Economic Systems and the Role of Government

Thus far we have described the questions that the economic system must answer. Now we turn to the mechanics of the system. Here the basic debate concerns the role of government.

On the one hand, many favor leaving the economy alone and keeping the government at bay while others believe that there are many circumstances in which the government may be able to improve the functioning of the market.

In November 2008, President Barack Obama was elected during a period of turmoil in the world economy. In the United States during the month of the election over 700,000 jobs were lost. A year later the unemployment rate was over 10 percent, and even into 2010, more than 15 million were unemployed. At the same time, the banking system nearly collapsed when massive home mortgage defaults led to bankruptcy filings by giants Bear Sterns and Lehmann Brothers. The Federal Reserve System and the Treasury in response took action to save some big banks and big auto companies with the Troubled Asset Relief Program (TARP). While some called it a "bail out," much of the federal expenditure on these troubled institutions was paid back with interest.

In addition, during his first year, President Obama pushed hard for major reform of the health care system, for much stronger government regulation of the financial markets, and for a system designed to more effectively regulate energy consumption and protect the environment.

All of a sudden, the debate is all about the nature of the system. What should the government be doing, and which decisions should be left to the free, private markets? Is it true that the government should save companies or banks in trouble on the grounds that they are "too big to fail"?

Command Economies

During the long struggle between the United States and the Soviet Union it was an all or nothing proposition. The Soviet Union had a planned economy run by the government. In a pure **command economy**, the basic economic questions are answered by a central government. Through a combination of government ownership of state enterprises and central planning, the government, either directly or indirectly, sets output targets, incomes, and prices.

While the extremes of central planning have been rejected, so too has the idea that "markets solve all problems." The real debate is not about whether we have government at all, it is about the extent and the character of a limited government role in the economy. One of the major themes of this book is that government involvement, in theory, may improve the efficiency and fairness of the allocation of a nation's resources. At the same time, a poorly functioning government can destroy incentives, lead to corruption, and result in the waste of a society's resources.

command economy An economy in which a central government either directly or indirectly sets output targets, incomes, and prices.

Laissez-Faire Economies: The Free Market

At the opposite end of the spectrum from the command economy is the **laissez-faire economy**. The term *laissez-faire*, which translated literally from French means "allow [them] to do," implies a complete lack of government involvement in the economy. In this type of economy, individuals and firms pursue their own self-interest without any central direction or regulation; the sum total of millions of individual decisions ultimately determines all basic economic outcomes. The central institution through which a laissez-faire system answers the basic questions is the **market**, a term that is used in economics to mean an institution through which buyers and sellers interact and engage in exchange.

The interactions between buyers and sellers in any market range from simple to complex. Early explorers of the North American Midwest who wanted to exchange with Native Americans did so simply by bringing their goods to a central place and trading them. Today the Internet is revolutionizing exchange. A jewelry maker in upstate Maine can exhibit wares through digital photographs on the Web. Buyers can enter orders or make bids and pay by credit card. Companies such as eBay facilitate the worldwide interaction of tens of thousands of buyers and sellers sitting at their computers.

In short:

laissez-faire economy Literally from the French: "allow [them] to do." An economy in which individual people and firms pursue their own self-interest without any central direction or regulation.

market The institution through which buyers and sellers interact and engage in exchange.

Some markets are simple and others are complex, but they all involve buyers and sellers engaging in exchange. The behavior of buyers and sellers in a laissez-faire economy determines what gets produced, how it is produced, and who gets it.

The following chapters explore market systems in great depth. A quick preview is worthwhile here, however.

Consumer Sovereignty   In a free, unregulated market, goods and services are produced and sold only if the supplier can make a profit. In simple terms, making a *profit* means selling goods or services for more than it costs to produce them. You cannot make a profit unless someone wants the product that you are selling. This logic leads to the notion of **consumer sovereignty**: The mix of output found in any free market system is dictated ultimately by the tastes and preferences of consumers who "vote" by buying or not buying. Businesses rise and fall in response to consumer demands. No central directive or plan is necessary.

consumer sovereignty   The idea that consumers ultimately dictate what will be produced (or not produced) by choosing what to purchase (and what not to purchase).

Individual Production Decisions: Free Enterprise   Under a free market system, individual producers must also determine how to organize and coordinate the actual production of their products or services. The owner of a small shoe repair shop must alone buy the needed equipment and tools, hang signs, and set prices. In a big corporation, so many people are involved in planning the production process that in many ways, corporate planning resembles the planning in a command economy. In a free market economy, producers may be small or large. One person who hand-paints eggshells may start to sell them as a business; a person good with computers may start a business designing Web sites. On a larger scale, a group of furniture designers may put together a large portfolio of sketches, raise several million dollars, and start a bigger business. At the extreme are huge corporations such as Microsoft, Mitsubishi, and Intel, each of which sells tens of billions of dollars' worth of products every year. Whether the firms are large or small, however, production decisions in a market economy are made by separate private organizations acting in what they perceive to be their own interests.

Often the market system is called a free enterprise system. **Free enterprise** means the freedom of individuals to start private businesses in search of profits. Because new businesses require capital investment before they can begin operation, starting a new business involves risk. A well-run business that produces a product for which demand exists is likely to succeed; a poorly run business or one that produces a product for which little demand exists now or in the future is likely to fail. It is through free enterprise that new products and new production techniques find their way into use.

free enterprise   The freedom of individuals to start and operate private businesses in search of profits.

Proponents of free market systems argue that free enterprise leads to more efficient production and better response to diverse and changing consumer preferences. If a producer produces inefficiently, competitors will come along, fight for the business, and eventually take it away. Thus, in a free market economy, competition forces producers to use efficient techniques of production. It is competition, then, that ultimately dictates how output is produced.

Distribution of Output   In a free market system, the distribution of output—who gets what—is also determined in a decentralized way. The amount that any one household gets depends on its income and wealth. *Income* is the amount that a household earns each year. It comes in a number of forms: wages, salaries, interest, and the like. *Wealth* is the amount that households have accumulated out of past income through saving or inheritance.

To the extent that income comes from working for a wage, it is at least in part determined by individual choice. You will work for the wages available in the market only if these wages (and the products and services they can buy) are sufficient to compensate you for what you give up by working. Your leisure certainly has a value also. You may discover that you can increase your income by getting more education or training. You *cannot* increase your income, however, if you acquire a skill that no one wants.

Price Theory   The basic coordinating mechanism in a free market system is price. A price is the amount that a product sells for per unit, and it reflects what society is willing to pay. Prices of inputs—labor, land, and capital—determine how much it costs to produce a product. Prices of various kinds of labor, or *wage rates*, determine the rewards for working in different jobs and professions. Many of the independent decisions made in a market economy involve the weighing of prices and costs, so it is not surprising that much of economic theory focuses on the factors that influence and determine prices. This is why microeconomic theory is often simply called *price theory*.

In sum:

> In a free market system, the basic economic questions are answered without the help of a central government plan or directives. This is what the "free" in free market means—the system is left to operate on its own with no outside interference. Individuals pursuing their own self-interest will go into business and produce the products and services that people want. Other individuals will decide whether to acquire skills; whether to work; and whether to buy, sell, invest, or save the income that they earn. The basic coordinating mechanism is price.

Mixed Systems, Markets, and Governments

The differences between command economies and laissez-faire economies in their pure forms are enormous. In fact, these pure forms do not exist in the world; all real systems are in some sense "mixed." That is, individual enterprise exists and independent choice is exercised even in economies in which the government plays a major role.

Conversely, no market economies exist without government involvement and government regulation. The United States has basically a free market economy, but government purchases accounted for just over 20 percent of the country's total production in 2010. Governments in the United States (local, state, and federal) directly employ about 14 percent of all workers (15 percent including active duty military). They also redistribute income by means of taxation and social welfare expenditures, and they regulate many economic activities.

One of the major themes in this book, and indeed in economics, is the tension between the advantages of free, unregulated markets and the desire for government involvement. Advocates of free markets argue that such markets work best when left to themselves. They produce only what people want; without buyers, sellers go out of business. Competition forces firms to adopt efficient production techniques. Wage differentials lead people to acquire needed skills. Competition also leads to innovation in both production techniques and products. The result is quality and variety, but market systems have problems too. Even staunch defenders of the free enterprise system recognize that market systems are not perfect. First, they do not always produce what people want at the lowest cost—there are inefficiencies. Second, rewards (income) may be unfairly distributed and some groups may be left out. Third, periods of unemployment and inflation recur with some regularity.

Many people point to these problems as reasons for government involvement. Indeed, for some problems, government involvement may be the only solution. However, government decisions are made by people who presumably, like the rest of us, act in their own self-interest. While governments may be called on to improve the functioning of the economy, there is no guarantee that they will do so. Just as markets may fail to produce an allocation of resources that is perfectly efficient and fair, governments may fail to improve matters. We return to this debate many times throughout this text.

Looking Ahead

This chapter described the economic problem in broad terms. We outlined the questions that all economic systems must answer. We also discussed very broadly the two kinds of economic systems. In the next chapter, we analyze the way market systems work.

SUMMARY

1. Every society has some system or process for transforming into useful form what nature and previous generations have provided. Economics is the study of that process and its outcomes.

2. *Producers* are those who take resources and transform them into usable products, or *outputs*. Private firms, households, and governments all produce something.

SCARCITY, CHOICE, AND OPPORTUNITY COST *p. 26*

3. All societies must answer *three basic questions*: What gets produced? How is it produced? Who gets what is produced? These three questions make up the *economic problem*.

4. One person alone on an island must make the same basic decisions that complex societies make. When a society consists of more than one person, questions of distribution, cooperation, and specialization arise.

5. Because resources are scarce relative to human wants in all societies, using resources to produce one good or service implies *not* using them to produce something else. This concept of *opportunity cost* is central to an understanding of economics.

6. Using resources to produce *capital* that will in turn produce benefits in the future implies *not* using those resources to produce consumer goods in the present.

7. Even if one individual or nation is absolutely more efficient at producing goods than another, all parties will gain if they specialize in producing goods in which they have a *comparative advantage*.

8. A *production possibility frontier* (ppf) is a graph that shows all the combinations of goods and services that can be produced if all of society's resources are used efficiently. The ppf illustrates a number of important economic concepts: scarcity, unemployment, inefficiency, increasing opportunity cost, and economic growth.

9. *Economic growth* occurs when society produces more, either by acquiring more resources or by learning to produce more with existing resources. Improved productivity may come from additional capital or from the discovery and application of new, more efficient techniques of production.

ECONOMIC SYSTEMS AND THE ROLE OF GOVERNMENT *p. 39*

10. In some modern societies, government plays a big role in answering the three basic questions. In pure *command economies*, a central authority directly or indirectly sets output targets, incomes, and prices.

11. A *laissez-faire economy* is one in which individuals independently pursue their own self-interest, without any central direction or regulation, and ultimately determine all basic economic outcomes.

12. A *market* is an institution through which buyers and sellers interact and engage in exchange. Some markets involve simple face-to-face exchange; others involve a complex series of transactions, often over great distances or through electronic means.

13. There are no purely planned economies and no pure laissez-faire economies; all economies are mixed. Individual enterprise, independent choice, and relatively free markets exist in centrally planned economies; there is significant government involvement in market economies such as that of the United States.

14. One of the great debates in economics revolves around the tension between the advantages of free, unregulated markets and the desire for government involvement in the economy. Free markets produce what people want, and competition forces firms to adopt efficient production techniques. The need for government intervention arises because free markets are characterized by inefficiencies and an unequal distribution of income, and experience regular periods of inflation and unemployment.

REVIEW TERMS AND CONCEPTS

absolute advantage, *p. 28*

capital, *p. 25*

command economy, *p. 40*

comparative advantage, *p. 29*

consumer goods, *p. 32*

consumer sovereignty, *p. 41*

economic growth, *p. 36*

factors of production (*or* factors), *p. 25*

free enterprise, *p. 41*

inputs *or* resources, *p. 26*

investment, *p. 32*

laissez-faire economy, *p. 40*

marginal rate of transformation (MRT), *p. 35*

market, *p. 40*

opportunity cost, *p. 27*

outputs, *p. 26*

production, *p. 25*

production possibility frontier (ppf), *p. 33*

theory of comparative advantage, *p. 28*

PROBLEMS

All problems are available on www.myeconlab.com

1. For each of the following, describe some of the potential opportunity costs:
   a. Studying for your economics test
   b. Spending 2 hours playing computer games
   c. Buying a new car instead of keeping the old one
   d. A local community voting to raise property taxes to increase school expenditures and to reduce class size
   e. A number of countries working together to build a space station
   f. Going to graduate school

2. "As long as all resources are fully employed and every firm in the economy is producing its output using the best available technology, the result will be efficient." Do you agree or disagree with this statement? Explain your answer.

3. You are an intern to the editor of a small-town newspaper in Mallsburg, Pennsylvania. Your boss, the editor, asks you to write the first draft of an editorial for this week's paper. Your assignment is to describe the costs and the benefits of building a new bridge across the railroad tracks in the center of town. Currently, most people who live in this town must drive 2 miles through thickly congested traffic to the existing bridge to get to the main shopping and employment center. The bridge will cost the citizens of Mallsburg $25 million, which will be paid for with a tax on their incomes over the next 20 years. What are the opportunity costs of building this bridge? What are the benefits that citizens will likely receive if the bridge is built? What other factors might you consider in writing this editorial?

4. Kristen and Anna live in the beach town of Santa Monica. They own a small business in which they make wristbands and pot holders and sell them to people on the beach. As shown in the table on the following page, Kristen can make 15 wristbands per hour but only 3 pot holders. Anna is a bit slower and can make only 12 wristbands or 2 pot holders in an hour.

	OUTPUT PER HOUR	
	WRISTBANDS	POT HOLDERS
Kristen	15	3
Anna	12	2

   a. For Kristen and for Anna, what is the opportunity cost of a pot holder? Who has a comparative advantage in the production of pot holders? Explain your answer.
   b. Who has a comparative advantage in the production of wristbands? Explain your answer.
   c. Assume that Kristen works 20 hours per week in the business. Assuming Kristen is in business on her own, graph the possible combinations of pot holders and wristbands that she could produce in a week. Do the same for Anna.
   d. If Kristen devoted half of her time (10 out of 20 hours) to wristbands and half of her time to pot holders, how many of each would she produce in a week? If Anna did the same, how many of each would she produce? How many wristbands and pot holders would be produced in total?
   e. Suppose that Anna spent all 20 hours of her time on wristbands and Kristen spent 17 hours on pot holders and 3 hours on wristbands. How many of each item would be produced?
   f. Suppose that Kristen and Anna can sell all their wristbands for $1 each and all their pot holders for $5.50 each. If each of them worked 20 hours per week, how should they split their time between wristbands and pot holders? What is their maximum joint revenue?

5. Briefly describe the trade-offs involved in each of the following decisions. Specifically, list some of the opportunity costs associated with each decision, paying particular attention to the trade-offs between present and future consumption.
   a. After a stressful senior year in high school, Sherice decides to take the summer off instead of working before going to college.
   b. Frank is overweight and decides to work out every day and to go on a diet.
   c. Mei is diligent about taking her car in for routine maintenance even though it takes 2 hours of her time and costs $100 four times each year.
   d. Jim is in a hurry. He runs a red light on the way to work.

*6. The countries of Figistan and Blah are small island countries in the South Pacific. Both produce fruit and timber. Each island has a labor force of 1,200. The following table gives production per month for each worker in each country.

	BASKETS OF FRUIT	BOARD FEET OF TIMBER
Figistan workers	10	5
Blah workers	30	10

Productivity of one worker for one month

   a. Which country has an absolute advantage in the production of fruit? Which country has an absolute advantage in the production of timber?
   b. Which country has a comparative advantage in the production of fruit? of timber?
   c. Sketch the ppf's for both countries.
   d. Assuming no trading between the two, if both countries wanted to have equal numbers of feet of timber and baskets of fruit, how would they allocate workers to the two sectors?
   e. Show that specialization and trade can move both countries beyond their ppf's.

7. Suppose that a simple society has an economy with only one resource, labor. Labor can be used to produce only two commodities—*X*, a necessity good (food), and *Y*, a luxury good (music and merriment). Suppose that the labor force consists of 100 workers. One laborer can produce either 5 units of necessity per month (by hunting and gathering) or 10 units of luxury per month (by writing songs, playing the guitar, dancing, and so on).

    a. On a graph, draw the economy's ppf. Where does the ppf intersect the *Y*-axis? Where does it intersect the *X*-axis? What meaning do those points have?

    b. Suppose the economy produced at a point *inside* the ppf. Give at least two reasons why this could occur. What could be done to move the economy to a point *on* the ppf?

    c. Suppose you succeeded in lifting your economy to a point on its ppf. What point would you choose? How might your small society decide the point at which it wanted to be?

    d. Once you have chosen a point on the ppf, you still need to decide how your society's production will be divided. If you were a dictator, how would you decide? What would happen if you left product distribution to the free market?

*8. Match each diagram in Figure 1 with its description here. Assume that the economy is producing or attempting to produce at point *A* and that most members of society like meat and not fish. Some descriptions apply to more than one diagram, and some diagrams have more than one description.

    a. Inefficient production of meat and fish

    b. Productive efficiency

    c. An inefficient mix of output

    d. Technological advances in the production of meat and fish

    e. The law of increasing opportunity cost

    f. An impossible combination of meat and fish

9. A nation with fixed quantities of resources is able to produce any of the following combinations of bread and ovens:

LOAVES OF BREAD (MILLIONS)	OVENS (THOUSANDS)
75	0
60	12
45	22
30	30
15	36
0	40

These figures assume that a certain number of previously produced ovens are available in the current period for baking bread.

    a. Using the data in the table, graph the ppf (with ovens on the vertical axis).

    b. Does the principle of "increasing opportunity cost" hold in this nation? Explain briefly. (*Hint:* What happens to the opportunity cost of bread—measured in number of ovens—as bread production increases?)

    c. If this country chooses to produce both ovens and bread, what will happen to the ppf over time? Why?

*Note: Problems marked with an asterisk are more challenging.

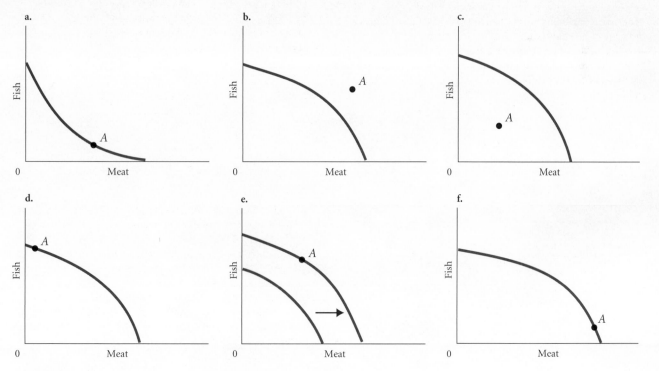

▲ FIGURE 1

Now suppose that a new technology is discovered that allows twice as many loaves of bread to be baked in each existing oven.

d. Illustrate (on your original graph) the effect of this new technology on the ppf.

e. Suppose that before the new technology is introduced, the nation produces 22 ovens. After the new technology is introduced, the nation produces 30 ovens. What is the effect of the new technology on the production of bread? (Give the number of loaves before and after the change.)

10. [Related to the *Economics in Practice* on p. 28] An analysis of a large-scale survey of consumer food purchases by Mark Aguiar and Erik Hurst indicates that retired people spend less for the same market basket of food than working people do. Use the concept of opportunity cost to explain this fact.

*11. Dr. Falk is a dentist who performs two basic procedures: filling cavities and whitening teeth. Falk charges $50 per cavity filled, a process that takes him 15 minutes per tooth and requires no help or materials. For tooth whitening, a process requiring 30 minutes, Falk charges $150 net of materials. Again, no help is required. Is anything puzzling about Falk's pricing pattern? Explain your answer.

12. In 2010, the Texas Lottery Commission began selling $5 Dallas Cowboys scratch-off game tickets. Prizes for winning tickets included cash, team merchandise, and Cowboys' season tickets for the 2010 season at their new $1.15 billion stadium. Suppose you received one of these Cowboys' scratch-off games as a birthday present and you won free season tickets for the 2010 season. Would there be a cost to you to attend the Cowboys' games during the 2010 season?

13. Describe a command economy and a laissez-faire economy. Do any economic systems in the world reflect the purest forms of command or laissez-faire economies? Explain.

14. The nation of Rougarou is able to produce turnips and potatoes in combinations represented by the data in the following table. Each number represents thousands of bushels.

	A	B	C	D	E
Turnips	100	90	70	40	0
Potatoes	0	10	20	30	40

Plot this data on a production possibilities graph and explain why the data shows that Rougarou experiences increasing opportunity costs.

15. Explain how each of the following situations would affect a nation's production possibilities curve.

a. A technological innovation allows the nation to more efficiently convert solar energy into electricity.

b. A prolonged recession increases the number of unemployed workers in the nation.

c. A category 5 hurricane destroys over 40 percent of the nation's productive capacity.

d. The quality of education in the nation's colleges and universities improves greatly.

e. The nation passes a law requiring all employers to give their employees 16 weeks of paid vacation each year. Prior to this law, employers were not legally required to give employees any paid vacation time.

Demand, Supply, and Market Equilibrium

3

Chapters 1 and 2 introduced the discipline, methodology, and subject matter of economics. We now begin the task of analyzing how a market economy actually works. This chapter and the next present an overview of the way individual markets work. They introduce some of the concepts needed to understand both microeconomics and macroeconomics.

As we proceed to define terms and make assumptions, it is important to keep in mind what we are doing. In Chapter 1 we explained what economic theory attempts to do. Theories are abstract representations of reality, like a map that represents a city. We believe that the models presented here will help you understand the workings of the economy just as a map helps you find your way around a city. Just as a map presents one view of the world, so too does any given theory of the economy. Alternatives exist to the theory that we present. We believe, however, that the basic model presented here, while sometimes abstract, is useful in gaining an understanding of how the economy works.

In the simple island society discussed in Chapter 2, Bill and Colleen solved the economic problem directly. They allocated their time and used the island's resources to satisfy their wants. Bill might be a farmer, Colleen a hunter and carpenter. He might be a civil engineer, she a doctor. Exchange occurred, but complex markets were not necessary.

In societies of many people, however, production must satisfy wide-ranging tastes and preferences. Producers therefore specialize. Farmers produce more food than they can eat so that they can sell it to buy manufactured goods. Physicians are paid for specialized services, as are attorneys, construction workers, and editors. When there is specialization, there must be exchange, and *markets* are the institutions through which exchange takes place.

This chapter begins to explore the basic forces at work in market systems. The purpose of our discussion is to explain how the individual decisions of households and firms together, without any central planning or direction, answer the three basic questions: What gets produced? How is it produced? Who gets what is produced? We begin with some definitions.

Firms and Households: The Basic Decision-Making Units

Throughout this book, we discuss and analyze the behavior of two fundamental decision-making units: *firms*—the primary producing units in an economy—and *households*—the consuming units in an economy. Both are made up of people performing different functions and playing different roles. In essence, what we are developing is a theory of human behavior.

47

firm An organization that transforms resources (inputs) into products (outputs). Firms are the primary producing units in a market economy.

A **firm** exists when a person or a group of people decides to produce a product or products by transforming *inputs*—that is, resources in the broadest sense—into *outputs*, the products that are sold in the market. Some firms produce goods; others produce services. Some are large, many are small, and some are in between. All firms exist to transform resources into goods and services that people want. The Colorado Symphony Orchestra takes labor, land, a building, musically talented people, instruments, and other inputs and combines them to produce concerts. The production process can be extremely complicated. For example, the first flautist in the orchestra uses training, talent, previous performance experience, score, instrument, conductor's interpretation, and personal feelings about the music to produce just one contribution to an overall performance.

Most firms exist to make a profit for their owners, but some do not. Columbia University, for example, fits the description of a firm: It takes inputs in the form of labor, land, skills, books, and buildings and produces a service that we call education. Although the university sells that service for a price, it does not exist to make a profit; instead, it exists to provide education of the highest quality possible.

Still, most firms exist to make a profit. They engage in production because they can sell their product for more than it costs to produce it. The analysis of a firm's behavior that follows rests on the assumption that *firms make decisions in order to maximize profits.* Sometimes firms suffer losses instead of earning profits. In recent years this has occurred frequently. When firms suffer losses, we will assume that they act to minimize those losses.

entrepreneur A person who organizes, manages, and assumes the risks of a firm, taking a new idea or a new product and turning it into a successful business.

An **entrepreneur** is someone who organizes, manages, and assumes the risks of a firm. When a new firm is created, someone must organize the new firm, arrange financing, hire employees, and take risks. That person is an entrepreneur. Sometimes existing firms introduce new products, and sometimes new firms develop or improve on an old idea, but at the root of it all is entrepreneurship, which some see as the core of the free enterprise system.

households The consuming units in an economy.

The consuming units in an economy are **households**. A household may consist of any number of people: a single person living alone, a married couple with four children, or 15 unrelated people sharing a house. Household decisions are presumably based on individual tastes and preferences. The household buys what it wants and can afford. In a large, heterogeneous, and open society such as the United States, wildly different tastes find expression in the marketplace. A six-block walk in any direction on any street in Manhattan or a drive from the Chicago Loop south into rural Illinois should be enough to convince anyone that it is difficult to generalize about what people do and do not like.

Even though households have wide-ranging preferences, they also have some things in common. All—even the very rich—have ultimately limited incomes, and all must pay in some way for the goods and services they consume. Although households may have some control over their incomes—they can work more hours or fewer hours—they are also constrained by the availability of jobs, current wages, their own abilities, and their accumulated and inherited wealth (or lack thereof).

Input Markets and Output Markets: The Circular Flow

Households and firms interact in two basic kinds of markets: product (or output) markets and input (or factor) markets. Goods and services that are intended for use by households are exchanged in **product *or* output markets**. In output markets, firms *supply* and households *demand*.

product *or* output markets The markets in which goods and services are exchanged.

input *or* factor markets The markets in which the resources used to produce goods and services are exchanged.

To produce goods and services, firms must buy resources in **input *or* factor markets**. Firms buy inputs from households, which supply these inputs. When a firm decides how much to produce (supply) in output markets, it must simultaneously decide how much of each input it needs to produce the desired level of output. To produce automobiles, Ford Motor Company must use many inputs, including tires, steel, complicated machinery, and many different kinds of labor.

Figure 3.1 shows the *circular flow* of economic activity through a simple market economy. Note that the flow reflects the direction in which goods and services flow through input and output markets. For example, real goods and services flow from firms to households through output—or product—markets. Labor services flow from households to firms through input markets. Payment (most often in money form) for goods and services flows in the opposite direction.

In input markets, households *supply* resources. Most households earn their incomes by working—they supply their labor in the **labor market** to firms that demand labor and pay workers for their time and skills. Households may also loan their accumulated or inherited savings to firms for interest or exchange those savings for claims to future profits, as when a household buys shares of stock in a corporation. In the **capital market**, households supply the funds that firms use to buy capital goods. Households may also supply land or other real property in exchange for rent in the **land market**.

Inputs into the production process are also called **factors of production**. Land, labor, and capital are the three key factors of production. Throughout this text, we use the terms *input* and *factor of production* interchangeably. Thus, input markets and factor markets mean the same thing.

Early economics texts included entrepreneurship as a type of input, just like land, labor, and capital. Treating entrepreneurship as a separate factor of production has fallen out of favor, however, partially because it is unmeasurable. Most economists today implicitly assume that

labor market The input/factor market in which households supply work for wages to firms that demand labor.

capital market The input/factor market in which households supply their savings, for interest or for claims to future profits, to firms that demand funds to buy capital goods.

land market The input/factor market in which households supply land or other real property in exchange for rent.

factors of production The inputs into the production process. Land, labor, and capital are the three key factors of production.

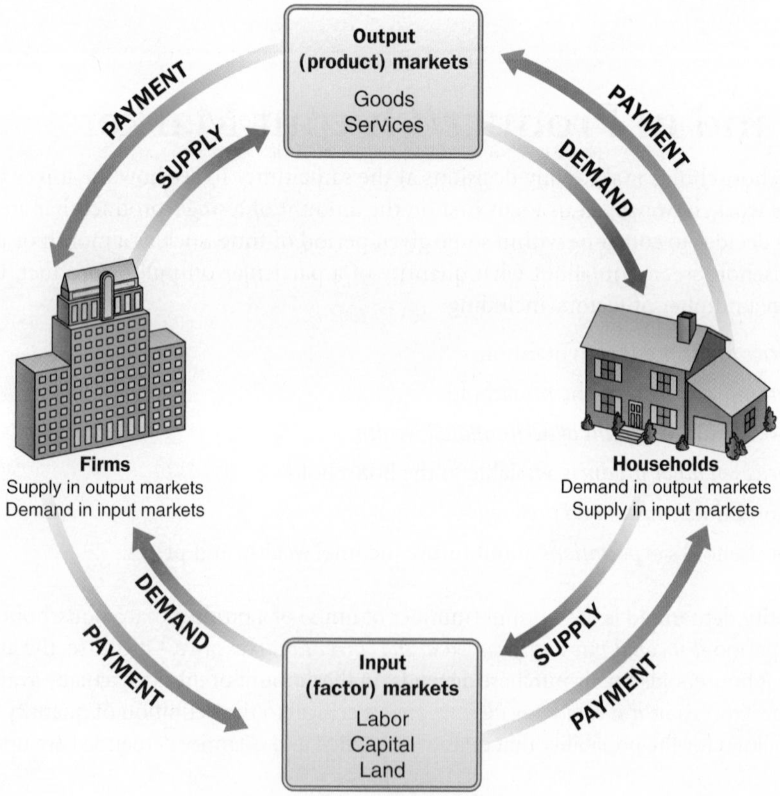

▲ **FIGURE 3.1 The Circular Flow of Economic Activity**

Diagrams like this one show the circular flow of economic activity, hence the name *circular flow diagram*. Here goods and services flow clockwise: Labor services supplied by households flow to firms, and goods and services produced by firms flow to households. Payment (usually money) flows in the opposite (counterclockwise) direction: Payment for goods and services flows from households to firms, and payment for labor services flows from firms to households.

Note: Color Guide—In Figure 3.1 households are depicted in *blue* and firms are depicted in *red*. From now on all diagrams relating to the behavior of households will be blue or shades of blue and all diagrams relating to the behavior of firms will be red or shades of red.

entrepreneurship is in plentiful supply. That is, if profit opportunities exist, it is likely that entrepreneurs will crop up to take advantage of them. This assumption has turned out to be a good predictor of actual economic behavior and performance.

The supply of inputs and their prices ultimately determine household income. Thus, the amount of income a household earns depends on the decisions it makes concerning what types of inputs it chooses to supply. Whether to stay in school, how much and what kind of training to get, whether to start a business, how many hours to work, whether to work at all, and how to invest savings are all household decisions that affect income.

As you can see:

> Input and output markets are connected through the behavior of both firms and households. Firms determine the quantities and character of outputs produced and the types and quantities of inputs demanded. Households determine the types and quantities of products demanded and the quantities and types of inputs supplied.[1]

The following analysis of demand and supply will lead up to a theory of how market prices are determined. Prices are determined by the interaction between demanders and suppliers. To understand this interaction, we first need to know how product prices influence the behavior of demanders and suppliers *separately*. Therefore, we discuss output markets by focusing first on demanders, then on suppliers, and finally on their interaction.

Demand in Product/Output Markets

In real life, households make many decisions at the same time. To see how the forces of demand and supply work, however, let us focus first on the amount of a *single* product that an *individual* household decides to consume within some given period of time, such as a month or a year.

A household's decision about what quantity of a particular output, or product, to demand depends on a number of factors, including:

- The *price of the product* in question.
- The *income available* to the household.
- The household's *amount of accumulated wealth*.
- The *prices of other products* available to the household.
- The household's *tastes and preferences*.
- The household's *expectations* about future income, wealth, and prices.

quantity demanded The amount (number of units) of a product that a household would buy in a given period if it could buy all it wanted at the current market price.

Quantity demanded is the amount (number of units) of a product that a household would buy in a given period *if it could buy all it wanted at the current market price*. Of course, the amount of a product that households finally purchase depends on the amount of product actually available in the market. The expression *if it could buy all it wanted* is critical to the definition of quantity demanded because it allows for the possibility that quantity supplied and quantity demanded are unequal.

---

[1] Our description of markets begins with the behavior of firms and households. Modern orthodox economic theory essentially combines two distinct but closely related theories of behavior. The "theory of household behavior," or "consumer behavior," has its roots in the works of nineteenth-century utilitarians such as Jeremy Bentham, William Jevons, Carl Menger, Leon Walras, Vilfredo Parcto, and F. Y. Edgeworth. The "theory of the firm" developed out of the earlier classical political economy of Adam Smith, David Ricardo, and Thomas Malthus. In 1890, Alfred Marshall published the first of many editions of his *Principles of Economics*. That volume pulled together the main themes of both the classical economists and the utilitarians into what is now called *neoclassical economics*. While there have been many changes over the years, the basic structure of the model that we build can be found in Marshall's work.

Changes in Quantity Demanded versus Changes in Demand

The most important relationship in individual markets is that between market price and quantity demanded. For this reason, we need to begin our discussion by analyzing the likely response of households to changes in price using the device of *ceteris paribus*, or "all else equal." That is, we will attempt to derive a relationship between the quantity demanded of a good per time period and the price of that good, holding income, wealth, other prices, tastes, and expectations constant.

It is very important to distinguish between price changes, which affect the quantity of a good demanded, and changes in other factors (such as income), which change the entire relationship between price and quantity. For example, if a family begins earning a higher income, it might buy more of a good at every possible price. To be sure that we distinguish between changes in price and other changes that affect demand, throughout the rest of the text, we will be very precise about terminology. Specifically:

> Changes in the price of a product affect the *quantity demanded* per period. Changes in any other factor, such as income or preferences, affect *demand*. Thus, we say that an increase in the price of Coca-Cola is likely to cause a decrease in the *quantity of Coca-Cola demanded*. However, we say that an increase in income is likely to cause an increase in the *demand* for most goods.

Price and Quantity Demanded: The Law of Demand

A **demand schedule** shows how much of a product a person or household is willing to purchase per time period (each week or each month) at different prices. Clearly that decision is based on numerous interacting factors. Consider Alex who just graduated from college with an entry-level job at a local bank. During her senior year, Alex got a car loan and bought a used Mini Cooper. The Mini gets 25 miles per gallon of gasoline. Alex lives with several friends in a house 10 miles from her workplace and enjoys visiting her parents 50 miles away.

demand schedule A table showing how much of a given product a household would be willing to buy at different prices.

How often Alex will decide to drive herself to work and parties, visit her family, or even go joy riding depends on many things, including her income and whether she likes to drive. But the price of gasoline also plays an important role, and it is this relationship between price and quantity demanded that we focus on in the law of demand. With a gasoline price of $3.00 a gallon, Alex might decide to drive herself to work every day, visit her parents once a week, and drive another 50 miles a week for other activities. This driving pattern would add up to 250 miles a week, which would use 10 gallons of gasoline in her Mini. The demand schedule in Table 3.1 thus shows that at a price of $3.00 per gallon, Alex is willing to buy 10 gallons of gasoline. We can see that this demand schedule reflects a lot of information about Alex including where she lives and works and what she likes to do in her spare time.

Now suppose an international crisis in the Middle East causes the price of gasoline at the pump to rise to $5.00 per gallon. How does this affect Alex's demand for gasoline, assuming that everything else remains the same? Driving is now more expensive, and we would not be surprised if Alex decided to take the bus some mornings or share a ride with friends. She might visit her parents less frequently as well. On the demand schedule given in Table 3.1, Alex cuts her desired consumption of gasoline by half to 5 gallons when the price goes to $5.00. If, instead, the price of gasoline fell substantially, Alex might well spend more time driving, and that is in fact the pattern we see in the table. This same information presented graphically is called a **demand curve**. Alex's demand curve is presented in Figure 3.2. You will note in Figure 3.2 that *quantity* (q) is measured along the horizontal axis and *price* (P) is measured along the vertical axis. This is the convention we follow throughout this book.

demand curve A graph illustrating how much of a given product a household would be willing to buy at different prices.

TABLE 3.1	Alex's Demand Schedule for Gasoline	
Price (per Gallon)	Quantity Demanded (Gallons per Week)
$8.00	0
7.00	2
6.00	3
5.00	5
4.00	7
3.00	10
2.00	14
1.00	20
0.00	26

Demand Curves Slope Downward   The data in Table 3.1 show that at lower prices, Alex buys more gasoline; at higher prices, she buys less. Thus, there is a *negative, or inverse, relationship between quantity demanded and price*. When price rises, quantity demanded falls, and when price falls, quantity demanded rises. Thus, demand curves always slope downward. This negative relationship between price and quantity demanded is often referred to as the **law of demand**, a term first used by economist Alfred Marshall in his 1890 textbook.

law of demand The negative relationship between price and quantity demanded: As price rises, quantity demanded decreases; as price falls, quantity demanded increases.

Some people are put off by the abstraction of demand curves. Of course, we do not actually draw our own demand curves for products. When we want to make a purchase, we usually face only a single price and how much we would buy at other prices is irrelevant. However, demand curves help analysts understand the kind of behavior that households are *likely* to exhibit if they are actually faced with a higher or lower price. We know, for example, that if the price of a good rises enough, the quantity demanded must ultimately drop to zero. The demand curve is thus a tool that helps us explain economic behavior and predict reactions to possible price changes.

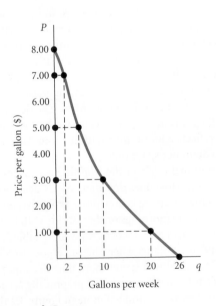

▲ **FIGURE 3.2 Alex's Demand Curve**

The relationship between price (*P*) and quantity demanded (*q*) presented graphically is called a demand curve. Demand curves have a negative slope, indicating that lower prices cause quantity demanded to increase. Note that Alex's demand curve is blue; demand in product markets is determined by household choice.

Marshall's definition of a social "law" captures the idea:

The term "law" means nothing more than a general proposition or statement of tendencies, more or less certain, more or less definite . . . a *social law* is a statement of social tendencies; that is, that a certain course of action may be expected from the members of a social group under certain conditions.[2]

It seems reasonable to expect that consumers will demand more of a product at a lower price and less of it at a higher price. Households must divide their incomes over a wide range of goods and services. At $3.00 per gallon and 25 miles to a gallon, driving the 20 miles round trip to work costs Alex $2.40. At $5.00 per gallon, the trip now costs $4.00. With the higher prices, Alex may have to give up her morning latte if she drives, and that may turn out to be too big a sacrifice for her. As the price of gasoline rises, the opportunity cost of driving in terms of other types of consumption also rises and that is why Alex ends up driving less as the price of gasoline rises. Goods compete with one another for our spending.

Economists use the concept of *utility* to explain the slope of the demand curve. Presumably, we consume goods and services because they give us utility or satisfaction. As we consume more of a product within a given period of time, it is likely that each additional unit consumed will yield successively less satisfaction. The utility you gain from a second ice cream cone is likely to be less than the utility you gained from the first, the third is worth even less, and so on. This *law of diminishing marginal utility* is an important concept in economics. If each successive unit of a good is worth less to you, you are not going to be willing to pay as much for it. Thus, it is reasonable to expect a downward slope in the demand curve for that good.

Thinking about the ways that people are affected by price changes also helps us see what is behind the law of demand. Consider this example: Luis lives and works in Mexico City. His elderly mother lives in Santiago, Chile. Last year the airlines servicing South America got into a price war, and the price of flying between Mexico City and Santiago dropped from 20,000 pesos to 10,000 pesos. How might Luis's behavior change?

First, he is better off. Last year he flew home to Chile three times at a total cost of 60,000 pesos. This year he can fly to Chile the same number of times, buy exactly the same combination of other goods and services that he bought last year, and have 30,000 pesos left over. Because he is better off—his income can buy more—he may fly home more frequently. Second, the opportunity cost of flying home has changed. Before the price war, Luis had to sacrifice 20,000 pesos worth of other goods and services each time he flew to Chile. After the price war, he must sacrifice only 10,000 pesos worth of other goods and services for each trip. The trade-off has changed. Both of these effects are likely to lead to a higher quantity demanded in response to the lower price.

In sum:

It is reasonable to expect quantity demanded to fall when price rises, *ceteris paribus*, and to expect quantity demanded to rise when price falls, *ceteris paribus*. Demand curves have a negative slope.

Other Properties of Demand Curves Two additional things are notable about Alex's demand curve. First, it intersects the *Y*, or price, axis. This means that there is a price above which she buys no gasoline. In this case, Alex simply stops driving when the price reaches $8 per gallon. As long as households have limited incomes and wealth, all demand curves will intersect the price axis. For any commodity, there is always a price above which a household will not or cannot pay. Even if the good or service is very important, all households are ultimately constrained, or limited, by income and wealth.

[2] Alfred Marshall, *Principles of Economics*, 8th ed. (New York: Macmillan, 1948), p. 33. (The first edition was published in 1890.)

Second, Alex's demand curve intersects the *X*, or quantity, axis. Even at a zero price, there is a limit to how much she will drive. If gasoline were free, she would use 26 gallons, but not more. That demand curves intersect the quantity axis is a matter of common sense. Demand in a given period of time is limited, if only by time, even at a zero price.

To summarize what we know about the shape of demand curves:

1. They have a negative slope. An increase in price is likely to lead to a decrease in quantity demanded, and a decrease in price is likely to lead to an increase in quantity demanded.
2. They intersect the quantity (*X*-) axis, a result of time limitations and diminishing marginal utility.
3. They intersect the price (*Y*-) axis, a result of limited income and wealth.

That is all we can say; it is not possible to generalize further. The actual shape of an individual household demand curve—whether it is steep or flat, whether it is bowed in or bowed out—depends on the unique tastes and preferences of the household and other factors. Some households may be very sensitive to price changes; other households may respond little to a change in price. In some cases, plentiful substitutes are available; in other cases, they are not. Thus, to fully understand the shape and position of demand curves, we must turn to the other determinants of household demand.

Other Determinants of Household Demand

Of the many factors likely to influence a household's demand for a specific product, we have considered only the price of the product. Other determining factors include household income and wealth, the prices of other goods and services, tastes and preferences, and expectations.

Income and Wealth   Before we proceed, we need to define two terms that are often confused, *income* and *wealth*. A household's **income** is the sum of all the wages, salaries, profits, interest payments, rents, and other forms of earnings received by the household *in a given period of time*. Income is thus a *flow* measure: We must specify a time period for it—income *per month* or *per year*. You can spend or consume more or less than your income in any given period. If you consume less than your income, you save. To consume more than your income in a period, you must either borrow or draw on savings accumulated from previous periods.

income   The sum of all a household's wages, salaries, profits, interest payments, rents, and other forms of earnings in a given period of time. It is a flow measure.

Wealth is the total value of what a household owns minus what it owes. Another word for wealth is **net worth**—the amount a household would have left if it sold all of its possessions and paid all of its debts. Wealth is a *stock* measure: It is measured at a given point in time. If, in a given period, you spend less than your income, you save; the amount that you save is added to your wealth. Saving is the flow that affects the stock of wealth. When you spend more than your income, you *dissave*—you reduce your wealth.

wealth *or* **net worth**   The total value of what a household owns minus what it owes. It is a stock measure.

Households with higher incomes and higher accumulated savings or inherited wealth can afford to buy more goods and services. In general, we would expect higher demand at higher levels of income/wealth and lower demand at lower levels of income/wealth. Goods for which demand goes up when income is higher and for which demand goes down when income is lower are called **normal goods**. Movie tickets, restaurant meals, telephone calls, and shirts are all normal goods.

normal goods   Goods for which demand goes up when income is higher and for which demand goes down when income is lower.

However, generalization in economics can be hazardous. Sometimes demand for a good falls when household income rises. Consider, for example, the various qualities of meat available. When a household's income rises, it is likely to buy higher-quality meats—its demand for filet mignon is likely to rise—but its demand for lower-quality meats—chuck steak, for example—is likely to fall. Transportation is another example. At higher incomes, people can afford to fly. People who can afford to fly are less likely to take the bus long distances. Thus, higher income may *reduce* the number of times someone takes a bus. Goods for which demand tends to fall when income rises are called **inferior goods**.

inferior goods   Goods for which demand tends to fall when income rises.

Prices of Other Goods and Services   No consumer decides in isolation on the amount of any one commodity to buy. Instead, each decision is part of a larger set of decisions that are made simultaneously. Households must apportion their incomes over many different goods and services. As a result, the price of any one good can and does affect the demand for other goods. This is most obviously the case when goods are substitutes for one another. For Alex the bus is an alternative that she uses when gasoline gets expensive.

ECONOMICS IN PRACTICE

Kindle in the College Market?

Most of you are likely quite aware of the high price of text-books. For some students, high prices lead to sharing texts or using library copies. Jeff Bezos, who runs Amazon, the producer of the Kindle, thinks the high prices of printed text books provides an opportunity for his company to increase the demand for the Kindle.

People buy Kindles so that they can read books on them. Books are thus a complement to the Kindle. The cheaper the electronic books you can buy are, the higher your demand for the Kindle device. As the article here suggests, Amazon is working with several universities and textbook publishers to make textbooks available—for a much lower price—on the Kindle. As the last line of the article tells us, this move is clearly intended to build demand for the Kindle itself. The president of Amazon is well aware of the role of complements in his business.

Amazon to Launch Kindle for Textbooks

The Wall Street Journal

Beginning this fall, some students at Case Western Reserve University in Cleveland will be given large-screen Kindles with textbooks for chemistry, computer science, and a freshman seminar already installed, said Lev Gonick, the school's chief information officer. The university plans to compare the experiences of students who get the Kindles and those who use traditional textbooks, he said.

Amazon has worked out a deal with several textbook publishers to make their materials available for the device. Five other universities are involved in the Kindle project, according to people briefed on the matter. They are Pace, Princeton, Reed, Darden School at the University of Virginia, and Arizona State. The moves are the latest by Amazon to promote the Kindle, which is the company's first consumer-electronics device.

Source: The Wall Street Journal, excerpted from "Amazon to Launch Kindle for Textbooks" by Geoffrey A. Fowler and Ben Worthen. Copyright 2009 by *Dow Jones & Company, Inc.* Reproduced with permission of *Dow Jones & Company, Inc.* via Copyright Clearance Center.

When an *increase* in the price of one good causes demand for another good to *increase* (a positive relationship), we say that the goods are **substitutes**. A *fall* in the price of a good causes a *decline* in demand for its substitutes. Substitutes are goods that can serve as replacements for one another.

substitutes Goods that can serve as replacements for one another; when the price of one increases, demand for the other increases.

To be substitutes, two products do not need to be identical. Identical products are called **perfect substitutes**. Japanese cars are not identical to American cars. Nonetheless, all have four wheels, are capable of carrying people, and run on gasoline. Thus, significant changes in the price of one country's cars can be expected to influence demand for the other country's cars. Restaurant meals are substitutes for meals eaten at home, and flying from New York to Washington, D.C., is a substitute for taking the train.

perfect substitutes Identical products.

Often two products "go together"—that is, they complement each other. Bacon and eggs are **complementary goods**, as are cars and gasoline, and cameras and film. When two goods are **complements**, a *decrease* in the price of one results in an *increase* in demand for the other and vice versa. The makers of Guitar Hero and Rock Band, two popular and competitive video games, understand that there is a strong connection between how many songs can be played on their operating platforms and how strong the demand is for their games. For iPods and Kindles as well, the availability of content at low prices stimulates demand for the devices. The *Economics in Practice* above talks about the complementarity between the Kindle and e-books.

complements, complementary goods Goods that "go together"; a decrease in the price of one results in an increase in demand for the other and vice versa.

Tastes and Preferences Income, wealth, and prices of goods available are the three factors that determine the combinations of goods and services that a household is *able* to buy. You know that you cannot afford to rent an apartment at $1,200 per month if your monthly income is only $400, but within these constraints, you are more or less free to choose what to buy. Your final choice depends on your individual tastes and preferences.

Changes in preferences can and do manifest themselves in market behavior. Thirty years ago the major big-city marathons drew only a few hundred runners. Now tens of thousands enter and run. The demand for running shoes, running suits, stopwatches, and other running items has greatly increased. For many years, people drank soda for refreshment. Today convenience stores are filled with a dizzying array of iced teas, fruit juices, natural beverages, and mineral waters.

Within the constraints of prices and incomes, preference shapes the demand curve, but it is difficult to generalize about tastes and preferences. First, they are volatile: Five years ago more people smoked cigarettes and fewer people had computers. Second, tastes are idiosyncratic: Some people like to text, whereas others still prefer to use e-mail; some people prefer dogs, whereas others are crazy about cats. Some eat fried cockroaches. The diversity of individual demands is almost infinite.

One of the interesting questions in economics is why, in some markets, diverse consumer tastes give rise to a variety of styles, while in other markets, despite a seeming diversity in tastes, we find only one or two varieties. All sidewalks in the United States are a similar gray color, yet houses are painted a rainbow of colors. Yet it is not obvious on the face of it that people would not prefer as much variety in their sidewalks as in their houses. To answer this type of question, we need to move beyond the demand curve. We will revisit this question in a later chapter.

Expectations What you decide to buy today certainly depends on today's prices and your current income and wealth. You also have expectations about what your position will be in the future. You may have expectations about future changes in prices too, and these may affect your decisions today.

There are many examples of the ways expectations affect demand. When people buy a house or a car, they often must borrow part of the purchase price and repay it over a number of years. In deciding what kind of house or car to buy, they presumably must think about their income today, as well as what their income is likely to be in the future.

As another example, consider a student in the final year of medical school living on a scholarship of $12,000. Compare that student with another person earning $6 an hour at a full-time job, with no expectation of a significant change in income in the future. The two have virtually identical incomes because there are about 2,000 working hours in a year (40 hours per week × 50 work weeks per year). But even if they have the same tastes, the medical student is likely to demand different goods and services, simply because of the expectation of a major increase in income later on.

Increasingly, economic theory has come to recognize the importance of expectations. We will devote a good deal of time to discussing how expectations affect more than just demand. For the time being, however, it is important to understand that demand depends on more than just *current* incomes, prices, and tastes.

Shift of Demand versus Movement Along a Demand Curve

Recall that a demand curve shows the relationship between quantity demanded and the price of a good. Demand curves are derived while holding income, tastes, and other prices constant. If income, tastes, or other prices change, we would have to derive an entirely new relationship between price and quantity.

Let us return once again to Alex. (See Table 3.1 and Figure 3.2 on p. 52.) Suppose that when we derived the demand curve in Figure 3.1 Alex was receiving a salary of $500 per week after taxes. If Alex faces a price of $3.00 per gallon and chooses to drive 250 miles per week, her total weekly expenditure works out to be $3.00 per gallon times 10 gallons of $30 per week. That amounts to 6.0 percent of her income.

Suppose now she were to receive a raise to $700 per week after taxes. Then if she continued to buy only 10 gallons of gasoline a week it would absorb a smaller percentage of her income. The higher income may well raise the amount of gasoline being used by Alex *regardless* of what she was using before. Notice in Figure 3.3 that the entire curve has shifted to the right—at $3.00 a gallon the curve shows an increase in the quantity demanded from 10 to 15 gallons. At $5.00, the quantity demanded by Alex increases from 5 gallons to 10 gallons.

The fact that demand *increased* when income increased implies that gasoline is a *normal good* to Alex.

TABLE 3.2   Shift of Alex's Demand Schedule Due to an Increase in Income

	Schedule D_0	Schedule D_1
Price (per Gallon)	Quantity Demanded (Gallons per Week at an Income of $500 per Week)	Quantity Demanded (Gallons per Week at an Income of $700 per Week)
$8.00	0	3
7.00	2	5
6.00	3	7
5.00	5	10
4.00	7	12
3.00	10	15
2.00	14	19
1.00	20	24
0.00	26	30

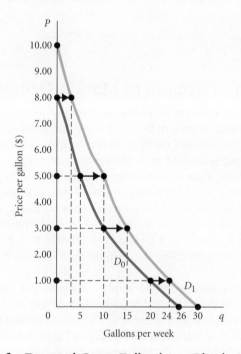

▲ **FIGURE 3.3 Shift of a Demand Curve Following a Rise in Income**
When the price of a good changes, we move *along* the demand curve for that good. When any other factor that influences demand changes (income, tastes, and so on), the relationship between price and quantity is different; there is a *shift* of the demand curve, in this case from D_0 to D_1. Gasoline is a normal good.

shift of a demand curve
The change that takes place in a demand curve corresponding to a new relationship between quantity demanded of a good and price of that good. The shift is brought about by a change in the original conditions.

movement along a demand curve The change in quantity demanded brought about by a change in price.

The conditions that were in place at the time we drew the original demand curve have now changed. In other words, a factor that affects Alex's demand for gasoline (in this case, her income) has changed, and there is now a new relationship between price and quantity demanded. Such a change is referred to as a **shift of a demand curve**.

It is very important to distinguish between a change in quantity demanded—that is, some movement *along* a demand curve—and a shift of demand. Demand schedules and demand curves show the relationship between the price of a good or service and the quantity demanded per period, *ceteris paribus*. If price changes, quantity demanded will change—this is a **movement along a demand curve**. When any of the *other* factors that influence demand change, however, a new relationship between price and quantity demanded is established—this is a *shift of a demand curve*. The result, then, is a *new* demand curve. Changes in income, preferences, or prices of other goods cause a demand curve to shift:

Change in price of a good or service leads to
└──➤ Change in *quantity demanded* (**movement along a demand curve**).

Change in income, preferences, or prices of other goods or services leads to
└──➤ Change in *demand* (**shift of a demand curve**).

Figure 3.4 on the next page illustrates the differences between movement along a demand curve and shifting demand curves. In Figure 3.4(a), an increase in household income causes demand for hamburger (an inferior good) to decline, or shift to the left from D_0 to D_1. (Because quantity is measured on the horizontal axis, a decrease means a *shift to the left*.) In contrast, demand for steak (a normal good) increases, or *shifts to the right*, when income rises.

In Figure 3.4(b), an increase in the price of hamburger from $1.49 to $3.09 a pound causes a household to buy less hamburger each month. In other words, the higher price causes the *quantity demanded* to decline from 10 pounds to 5 pounds per month. This change represents a movement *along* the demand curve for hamburger. In place of hamburger, the household buys more chicken. The household's demand for chicken (a substitute for hamburger) rises—the demand curve shifts to the right. At the same time, the demand for ketchup (a good that complements hamburger) declines—its demand curve shifts to the left.

From Household Demand to Market Demand

market demand The sum of all the quantities of a good or service demanded per period by all the households buying in the market for that good or service.

Market demand is simply the sum of all the quantities of a good or service demanded per period by all the households buying in the market for that good or service. Figure 3.5 shows the derivation of a market demand curve from three individual demand curves. (Although this market demand curve is derived from the behavior of only three people, most markets have thousands, or even millions of demanders.) As the table in Figure 3.5 shows, when the price of a pound of coffee is $3.50, both household A and household C would purchase 4 pounds per month, while household B would buy none. At that price, presumably, B drinks tea. Market demand at $3.50 would thus be a total of 4 + 4, or 8 pounds. At a price of $1.50 per pound, however, A would purchase 8 pounds per month; B, 3 pounds; and C, 9 pounds. Thus, at $1.50 per pound, market demand would be 8 + 3 + 9, or 20 pounds of coffee per month.

The total quantity demanded in the marketplace at a given price is simply the sum of all the quantities demanded by all the individual households shopping in the market *at that price*. A market demand curve shows the total amount of a product that would be sold at each price if households could buy all they wanted at that price. As Figure 3.5 shows, the market demand curve is the sum of all the individual demand curves—that is, the sum of all the individual quantities demanded at each price. Thus, the market demand curve takes its shape and position from the shapes, positions, and number of individual demand curves. If more people decide to shop in

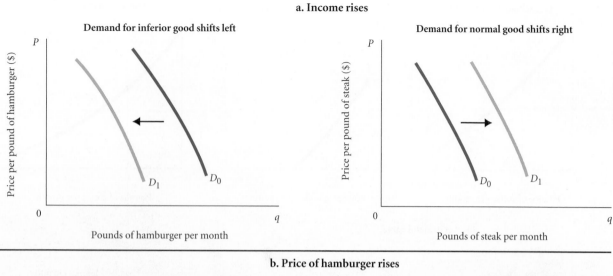

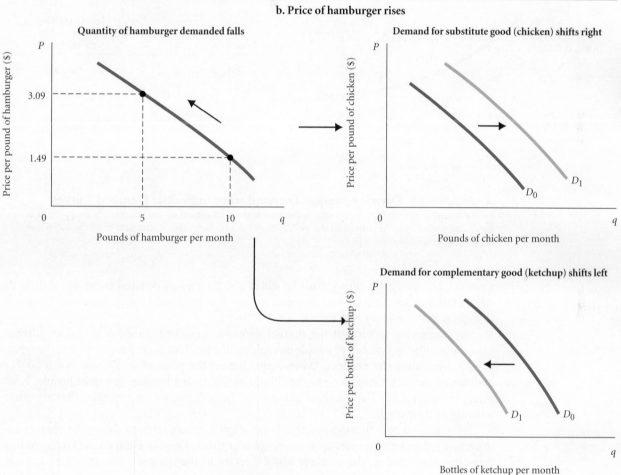

▲ **FIGURE 3.4 Shifts versus Movement Along a Demand Curve**
a. When income increases, the demand for inferior goods *shifts to the left* and the demand for normal goods *shifts to the right*. **b.** If the price of hamburger rises, the quantity of hamburger demanded declines—this is a movement along the demand curve. The same price rise for hamburger would shift the demand for chicken (a substitute for hamburger) to the right and the demand for ketchup (a complement to hamburger) to the left.

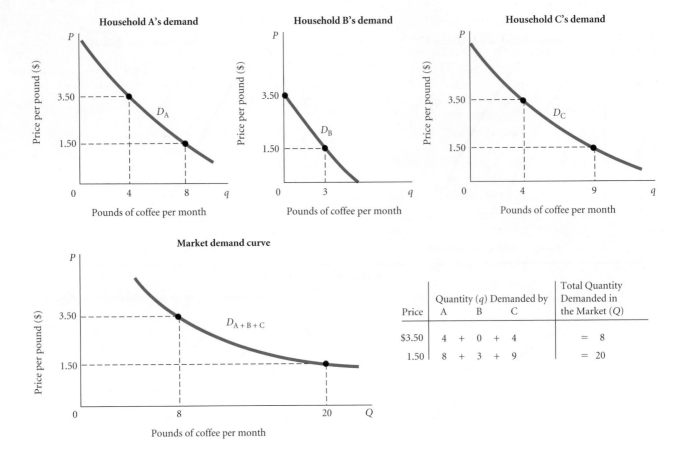

▲ **FIGURE 3.5 Deriving Market Demand from Individual Demand Curves**
Total demand in the marketplace is simply the sum of the demands of all the households shopping in a particular market. It is the sum of all the individual demand curves—that is, the sum of all the individual quantities demanded at each price.

a market, more demand curves must be added and the market demand curve will shift to the right. Market demand curves may also shift as a result of preference changes, income changes, or changes in the number of demanders.

An interesting fact about the market demand curve in Figure 3.5 is that at different prices, not only the number of people demanding the product may change but also the *type* of people demanding the product. When Apple halved the price of its iPhone in fall 2007, it announced that it wanted to make the iPhone available to a broader group of people. When prices fall, people like those in household B in Figure 3.5 move into markets that are otherwise out of their reach.

As a general rule throughout this book, capital letters refer to the entire market and lowercase letters refer to individual households or firms. Thus, in Figure 3.5, Q refers to total quantity demanded in the market, while q refers to the quantity demanded by individual households.

Supply in Product/Output Markets

We turn now to explore the other half of markets, the firms that supply the goods and services consumers want to purchase. What determines their willingness to produce and distribute the goods and services that people want? How do we understand the supply part of the market?

Firms build factories, hire workers, and buy raw materials because they believe they can sell the products they make for more than it costs to produce them. In other words, firms supply goods and services because they believe it will be profitable to do so. Supply decisions thus depend on profit potential. Because **profit** is the difference between revenues and costs, supply is likely to react to changes in revenues and changes in production costs. The amount of revenue that a firm earns depends on what the price of its product in the market is and on how much it sells. Costs of production depend on many factors, the most important of which are (1) the kinds of inputs needed to produce the product, (2) the amount of each input required, and (3) the prices of inputs.

profit The difference between revenues and costs.

In later chapters, we will focus on how firms decide *how* to produce their goods and services and explore the cost side of the picture more formally. For now, we will begin our examination of firm behavior by focusing on the output supply decision and the relationship between quantity supplied and output price, *ceteris paribus*.

Price and Quantity Supplied: The Law of Supply

Quantity supplied is the amount of a particular product that firms would be willing and able to offer for sale at a particular price during a given time period. A **supply schedule** shows how much of a product firms will sell at alternative prices.

quantity supplied The amount of a particular product that a firm would be willing and able to offer for sale at a particular price during a given time period.

Let us look at an agricultural market as an example. Table 3.3 itemizes the quantities of soybeans that an individual representative farmer such as Clarence Brown might sell at various prices. If the market paid $1.50 or less for a bushel for soybeans, Brown would not supply any soybeans: When Farmer Brown looks at the costs of growing soybeans, including the opportunity cost of his time and land, $1.50 per bushel will not compensate him for those costs. At $1.75 per bushel, however, at least some soybean production takes place on Brown's farm, and a price increase from $1.75 to $2.25 per bushel causes the quantity supplied by Brown to increase from 10,000 to 20,000 bushels per year. The higher price may justify shifting land from wheat to soybean production or putting previously fallow land into soybeans, or it may lead to more intensive farming of land already in soybeans, using expensive fertilizer or equipment that was not cost-justified at the lower price.

supply schedule A table showing how much of a product firms will sell at alternative prices.

TABLE 3.3	Clarence Brown's Supply Schedule for Soybeans
Price (per Bushel)	Quantity Supplied (Bushels per Year)
$1.50	0
1.75	10,000
2.25	20,000
3.00	30,000
4.00	45,000
5.00	45,000

Generalizing from Farmer Brown's experience, we can reasonably expect an increase in market price, *ceteris paribus*, to lead to an increase in quantity supplied for Brown and farmers like him. In other words, there is a positive relationship between the quantity of a good supplied and price. This statement sums up the **law of supply**: An increase in market price will lead to an increase in quantity supplied, and a decrease in market price will lead to a decrease in quantity supplied.

law of supply The positive relationship between price and quantity of a good supplied: An increase in market price will lead to an increase in quantity supplied, and a decrease in market price will lead to a decrease in quantity supplied.

supply curve A graph illustrating how much of a product a firm will sell at different prices.

The information in a supply schedule may be presented graphically in a **supply curve**. Supply curves slope upward. The upward, or positive, slope of Brown's curve in Figure 3.6 reflects this positive relationship between price and quantity supplied.

Note in Brown's supply schedule, however, that when price rises from $4 to $5, quantity supplied no longer increases. Often an individual firm's ability to respond to an increase in price is constrained by its existing scale of operations, or capacity, in the short run. For example, Brown's ability to produce more soybeans depends on the size of his farm, the fertility of his soil, and the types of equipment he has. The fact that output stays constant at 45,000 bushels per year suggests that he is running up against the limits imposed by the size of his farm, the quality of his soil, and his existing technology.

In the longer run, however, Brown may acquire more land or technology may change, allowing for more soybean production. The terms *short run* and *long run* have very precise meanings in economics; we will discuss them in detail later. Here it is important only to understand that time plays a critical role in supply decisions. When prices change, firms' immediate response may be different from what they are able to do after a month or a year. Short-run and long-run supply curves are often different.

Other Determinants of Supply

Of the factors we have listed that are likely to affect the quantity of output supplied by a given firm, we have thus far discussed only the price of output. Other factors that affect supply include the cost of producing the product and the prices of related products.

The Cost of Production For a firm to make a profit, its revenue must exceed its costs. As an individual producer, like Farmer Brown, thinks about how much to supply at a particular price, the producer will be looking at his or her costs. Brown's supply decision is likely to change in response to changes in the cost of production. Cost of production depends on a

▶ **FIGURE 3.6 Clarence Brown's Individual Supply Curve**
A producer will supply more when the price of output is higher. The slope of a supply curve is positive. Note that the supply curve is red: Supply is determined by choices made by firms.

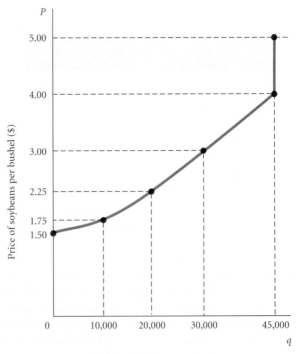

Bushels of soybeans produced per year

number of factors, including the available technologies and the prices and quantities of the inputs needed by the firm (labor, land, capital, energy, and so on).

Technological change can have an enormous impact on the cost of production over time. Consider agriculture. The introduction of fertilizers, the development of complex farm machinery, and the use of bioengineering to increase the yield of individual crops have all powerfully affected the cost of producing agricultural products. Farm productivity in the United States has been increasing dramatically for decades. Yield per acre of corn production has increased fivefold since the late 1930s, and the amount of labor required to produce 100 bushels of corn has fallen from 108 hours in the late 1930s to 20 hours in the late 1950s to less than 2 hours today. (See Table 2.2 on p. 37.)

When a technological advance lowers the cost of production, output is likely to increase. When yield per acre increases, individual farmers can and do produce more. The output of the Ford Motor Company increased substantially after the introduction of assembly-line techniques. The production of electronic calculators, and later personal computers, boomed with the development of inexpensive techniques to produce microprocessors.

Cost of production is also directly affected by the price of the factors of production. In the spring of 2008, the world price of oil rose to more than $100 per barrel from below $20 in 2002. As a result, cab drivers faced higher gasoline prices, airlines faced higher fuel costs, and manufacturing firms faced higher heating bills. The result: Cab drivers probably spent less time driving around looking for customers, airlines cut a few low-profit routes, and some manufacturing plants stopped running extra shifts. The moral of this story: Increases in input prices raise costs of production and are likely to reduce supply. The reverse occurred in 2009–2010 when oil prices fell back to $75 per barrel.

The Prices of Related Products   Firms often react to changes in the prices of related products. For example, if land can be used for either corn or soybean production, an increase in soybean prices may cause individual farmers to shift acreage out of corn production into soybeans. Thus, an increase in soybean prices actually affects the amount of corn supplied.

Similarly, if beef prices rise, producers may respond by raising more cattle. However, leather comes from cowhide. Thus, an increase in beef prices may actually increase the supply of leather.

To summarize:

> Assuming that its objective is to maximize profits, a firm's decision about what quantity of output, or product, to supply depends on:
>
> 1. The price of the good or service.
> 2. The cost of producing the product, which in turn depends on:
>   - the price of required inputs (labor, capital, and land), and
>   - the technologies that can be used to produce the product.
> 3. The prices of related products.

Shift of Supply versus Movement Along a Supply Curve

A supply curve shows the relationship between the quantity of a good or service supplied by a firm and the price that good or service brings in the market. Higher prices are likely to lead to an increase in quantity supplied, *ceteris paribus*. Remember: The supply curve is derived holding everything constant except price. When the price of a product changes *ceteris paribus*, a change in the quantity supplied follows—that is, a **movement along a supply curve** takes place. As you have seen, supply decisions are also influenced by factors other than price. New relationships between price and quantity supplied come about when factors other than price change, and the

movement along a supply curve The change in quantity supplied brought about by a change in price.

shift of a supply curve
The change that takes place in a supply curve corresponding to a new relationship between quantity supplied of a good and the price of that good. The shift is brought about by a change in the original conditions.

result is a **shift of a supply curve**. When factors other than price cause supply curves to shift, we say that there has been a *change in supply*.

Recall that the cost of production depends on the price of inputs and the technologies of production available. Now suppose that a major breakthrough in the production of soybeans has occurred: Genetic engineering has produced a superstrain of disease- and pest-resistant seed. Such a technological change would enable individual farmers to supply more soybeans at *any* market price. Table 3.4 and Figure 3.7 describe this change. At $3 a bushel, farmers would have produced 30,000 bushels from the old seed (schedule S_0 in Table 3.4); with the lower cost of production and higher yield resulting from the new seed, they produce 40,000 bushels (schedule S_1 in Table 3.4). At $1.75 per bushel, they would have produced 10,000 bushels from the old seed; but with the lower costs and higher yields, output rises to 23,000 bushels.

Increases in input prices may also cause supply curves to shift. If Farmer Brown faces higher fuel costs, for example, his supply curve will shift to the left—that is, he will produce less at any

TABLE 3.4 Shift of Supply Schedule for Soybeans Following Development of a New Disease-Resistant Seed Strain

	Schedule S_0	Schedule S_1
Price (per Bushel)	Quantity Supplied (Bushels per Year Using Old Seed)	Quantity Supplied (Bushels per Year Using New Seed)
$1.50	0	5,000
1.75	10,000	23,000
2.25	20,000	33,000
3.00	30,000	40,000
4.00	45,000	54,000
5.00	45,000	54,000

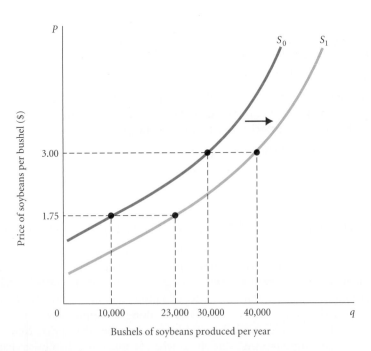

▲ **FIGURE 3.7 Shift of the Supply Curve for Soybeans Following Development of a New Seed Strain**

When the price of a product changes, we move *along* the supply curve for that product; the quantity supplied rises or falls. When any other factor affecting supply changes, the supply curve *shifts*.

given market price. If Brown's soybean supply curve shifted far enough to the left, it would intersect the price axis at a higher point, meaning that it would take a higher market price to induce Brown to produce any soybeans at all.

As with demand, it is very important to distinguish between *movements along* supply curves (changes in quantity supplied) and *shifts in* supply curves (changes in supply):

Change in price of a good or service leads to
└──→ Change in *quantity supplied* (**movement along a supply curve**).

Change in costs, input prices, technology, or prices of related goods and services leads to
└──→ Change in *supply* (**shift of a supply curve**).

From Individual Supply to Market Supply

Market supply is determined in the same fashion as market demand. It is simply the sum of all that is supplied each period by all producers of a single product. Figure 3.8 derives a market supply curve from the supply curves of three individual firms. (In a market with more firms, total market supply would be the sum of the amounts produced by each of the firms in that market.) As the table in Figure 3.8 shows, at a price of $3, farm A supplies 30,000 bushels of soybeans,

market supply The sum of all that is supplied each period by all producers of a single product.

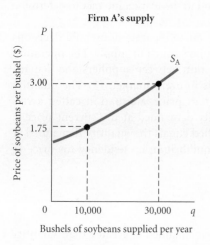

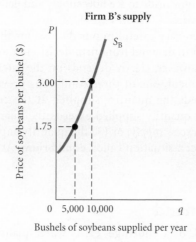

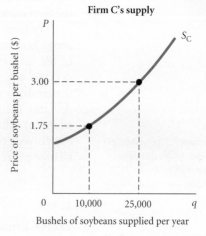

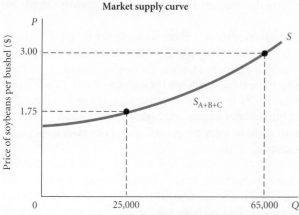

Price	Quantity (q) Supplied by			Total Quantity Supplied in the Market (Q)
	A	B	C	
$3.00	30,000 +	10,000 +	25,000	= 65,000
1.75	10,000 +	5,000 +	10,000	= 25,000

▲ **FIGURE 3.8 Deriving Market Supply from Individual Firm Supply Curves**
Total supply in the marketplace is the sum of all the amounts supplied by all the firms selling in the market. It is the sum of all the individual quantities supplied at each price.

farm B supplies 10,000 bushels, and farm C supplies 25,000 bushels. At this price, the total amount supplied in the market is 30,000 + 10,000 + 25,000, or 65,000 bushels. At a price of $1.75, however, the total amount supplied is only 25,000 bushels (10,000 + 5,000 + 10,000). Thus, the market supply curve is the simple addition of the individual supply curves of all the firms in a particular market—that is, the sum of all the individual quantities supplied at each price.

The position and shape of the market supply curve depends on the positions and shapes of the individual firms' supply curves from which it is derived. The market supply curve also depends on the number of firms that produce in that market. If firms that produce for a particular market are earning high profits, other firms may be tempted to go into that line of business. When the technology to produce computers for home use became available, literally hundreds of new firms got into the act. The popularity and profitability of professional football has, three times, led to the formation of new leagues. When new firms enter an industry, the supply curve shifts to the right. When firms go out of business, or "exit" the market, the supply curve shifts to the left.

Market Equilibrium

So far, we have identified a number of factors that influence the amount that households demand and the amount that firms supply in product (output) markets. The discussion has emphasized the role of market price as a determinant of both quantity demanded and quantity supplied. We are now ready to see how supply and demand in the market interact to determine the final market price.

We have been very careful in our discussions thus far to separate household decisions about how much to demand from firm decisions about how much to supply. The operation of the market, however, clearly depends on the interaction between suppliers and demanders. At any moment, one of three conditions prevails in every market: (1) The quantity demanded exceeds the quantity supplied at the current price, a situation called *excess demand*; (2) the quantity supplied exceeds the quantity demanded at the current price, a situation called *excess supply*; or (3) the quantity supplied equals the quantity demanded at the current price, a situation called **equilibrium**. At equilibrium, no tendency for price to change exists.

Excess Demand

Excess demand, or a **shortage**, exists when quantity demanded is greater than quantity supplied at the current price. Figure 3.9, which plots both a supply curve and a demand curve on the same graph, illustrates such a situation. As you can see, market demand at $1.75 per bushel (50,000 bushels) exceeds the amount that farmers are currently supplying (25,000 bushels).

When excess demand occurs in an unregulated market, there is a tendency for price to rise as demanders compete against each other for the limited supply. The adjustment mechanisms may differ, but the outcome is always the same. For example, consider the mechanism of an auction. In an auction, items are sold directly to the highest bidder. When the auctioneer starts the bidding at a low price, many people bid for the item. At first, there is a shortage: Quantity demanded exceeds quantity supplied. As would-be buyers offer higher and higher prices, bidders drop out until the one who offers the most ends up with the item being auctioned. Price rises until quantity demanded and quantity supplied are equal.

At a price of $1.75 (see Figure 3.9 again), farmers produce soybeans at a rate of 25,000 bushels per year, but at that price, the demand is for 50,000 bushels. Most farm products are sold to local dealers who in turn sell large quantities in major market centers, where bidding would push prices up if quantity demanded exceeded quantity supplied. As price rises above $1.75, two things happen: (1) The quantity demanded falls as buyers drop out of the market and perhaps choose a

equilibrium The condition that exists when quantity supplied and quantity demanded are equal. At equilibrium, there is no tendency for price to change.

excess demand *or* **shortage** The condition that exists when quantity demanded exceeds quantity supplied at the current price.

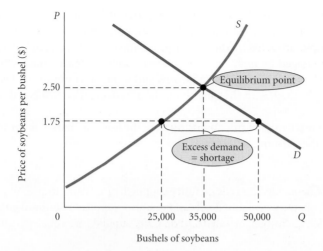

▲ **FIGURE 3.9 Excess Demand, or Shortage**

At a price of $1.75 per bushel, quantity demanded exceeds quantity supplied. When excess *demand* exists, there is a tendency for price to rise. When quantity demanded equals quantity supplied, excess demand is eliminated and the market is in equilibrium. Here the equilibrium price is $2.50 and the equilibrium quantity is 35,000 bushels.

substitute, and (2) the quantity supplied increases as farmers find themselves receiving a higher price for their product and shift additional acres into soybean production.[3]

This process continues until the shortage is eliminated. In Figure 3.9, this occurs at $2.50, where quantity demanded has fallen from 50,000 to 35,000 bushels per year and quantity supplied has increased from 25,000 to 35,000 bushels per year. When quantity demanded and quantity supplied are equal and there is no further bidding, the process has achieved an equilibrium, a situation in which *there is no natural tendency for further adjustment.* Graphically, the point of equilibrium is the point at which the supply curve and the demand curve intersect.

Increasingly, items are auctioned over the Internet. Companies such as eBay connect buyers and sellers of everything from automobiles to wine and from computers to airline tickets. Auctions are occurring simultaneously with participants located across the globe. The principles through which prices are determined in these auctions are the same: When excess demand exists, prices rise.

While the principles are the same, the process through which excess demand leads to higher prices is different in different markets. Consider the market for houses in the hypothetical town of Boomville with a population of 25,000 people, most of whom live in single-family homes. Normally, about 75 homes are sold in the Boomville market each year. However, last year a major business opened a plant in town, creating 1,500 new jobs that pay good wages. This attracted new residents to the area, and real estate agents now have more buyers than there are properties for sale. Quantity demanded now exceeds quantity supplied. In other words, there is a shortage.

Properties are sold very quickly, and housing prices begin to rise. Boomville sellers soon learn that there are more buyers than usual, and they begin to hold out for higher offers. As

---

[3] Once farmers have produced in any given season, they cannot change their minds and produce more, of course. When we derived Clarence Brown's supply schedule in Table 3.3, we imagined him reacting to prices that existed at the time he decided how much land to plant in soybeans. In Figure 3.9, the upward slope shows that higher prices justify shifting land from other crops. Final price may not be determined until final production figures are in. For our purposes here, however, we have ignored this timing problem. The best way to think about it is that demand and supply are *flows*, or *rates*, of production—that is, we are talking about the number of bushels produced *per production period*. Adjustments in the rate of production may take place over a number of production periods.

prices for Boomville houses rise, quantity demanded eventually drops off and quantity supplied increases: (1) Encouraged by the high prices, builders begin constructing new houses, and (2) some people, attracted by the higher prices their homes will fetch, put their houses on the market. Discouraged by higher prices, however, some potential buyers (demanders) may begin to look for housing in neighboring towns and settle on commuting. Eventually, equilibrium will be reestablished, with the quantity of houses demanded just equal to the quantity of houses supplied.

Although the mechanics of price adjustment in the housing market differ from the mechanics of an auction, the outcome is the same:

> When quantity demanded exceeds quantity supplied, price tends to rise. When the price in a market rises, quantity demanded falls and quantity supplied rises until an equilibrium is reached at which quantity demanded and quantity supplied are equal.

This process is called *price rationing*. When a shortage exists, some people will be satisfied and some will not. When the market operates without interference, price increases will distribute what is available to those who are willing and able to pay the most. As long as there is a way for buyers and sellers to interact, those who are willing to pay more will make that fact known somehow. (We discuss the nature of the price system as a rationing device in detail in Chapter 4.)

Excess Supply

excess supply *or* **surplus**
The condition that exists when quantity supplied exceeds quantity demanded at the current price.

Excess supply, or a **surplus**, exists when the quantity supplied exceeds the quantity demanded at the current price. As with a shortage, the mechanics of price adjustment in the face of a surplus can differ from market to market. For example, if automobile dealers find themselves with unsold cars in the fall when the new models are coming in, you can expect to see price cuts. Sometimes dealers offer discounts to encourage buyers; sometimes buyers themselves simply offer less than the price initially asked. In any event, products do no one any good sitting in dealers' lots or on warehouse shelves. The auction metaphor introduced earlier can also be applied here: If the initial asking price is too high, no one bids and the auctioneer tries a lower price. It is almost always true that certain items do not sell as well as anticipated during the Christmas holidays. After Christmas, most stores have big sales during which they lower the prices of overstocked items. Quantities supplied exceeded quantities demanded at the current prices, so stores cut prices.

Figure 3.10 illustrates another excess supply/surplus situation. At a price of $3 per bushel, suppose farmers are supplying soybeans at a rate of 40,000 bushels per year, but buyers are demanding only 20,000. With 20,000 (40,000 minus 20,000) bushels of soybeans going unsold, the market price falls. As price falls from $3.00 to $2.50, quantity supplied decreases from 40,000 bushels per year to 35,000. The lower price causes quantity demanded to rise from 20,000 to 35,000. At $2.50, quantity demanded and quantity supplied are equal. For the data shown here, $2.50 and 35,000 bushels are the equilibrium price and quantity, respectively.

Although oil prices rose to record levels in 2008, back in 2001, crude oil production worldwide exceeded the quantity demanded and prices fell significantly as competing producer countries tried to maintain their share of world markets. Although the mechanism by which price is adjusted is different for automobiles, housing, soybeans, and crude oil, the outcome is the same:

> When quantity supplied exceeds quantity demanded at the current price, the price tends to fall. When price falls, quantity supplied is likely to decrease and quantity demanded is likely to increase until an equilibrium price is reached where quantity supplied and quantity demanded are equal.

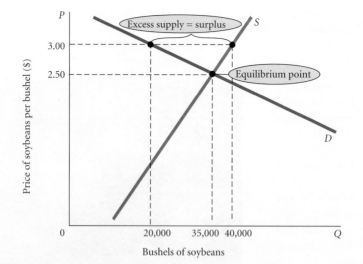

◀ FIGURE 3.10 **Excess Supply, or Surplus**
At a price of $3.00, quantity supplied exceeds quantity demanded by 20,000 bushels. This excess supply will cause the price to fall.

Changes in Equilibrium

When supply and demand curves shift, the equilibrium price and quantity change. The following example will help to illustrate this point.

South America is a major producer of coffee beans. A cold snap there can reduce the coffee harvest enough to affect the world price of coffee beans. In the mid-1990s, a major freeze hit Brazil and Colombia and drove up the price of coffee on world markets to a record $2.40 per pound. Severe hurricanes in the Caribbean caused a similar shift of supply in 2005.

Figure 3.11 illustrates how the freeze pushed up coffee prices. Initially, the market was in equilibrium at a price of $1.20. At that price, the quantity demanded was equal to quantity supplied (13.2 billion pounds). At a price of $1.20 and a quantity of 13.2 billion pounds, the demand curve (labeled D) intersected the initial supply curve (labeled S_0). (Remember that equilibrium exists when quantity demanded equals quantity supplied—the point at which the supply and demand curves intersect.)

The freeze caused a decrease in the supply of coffee beans. That is, the freeze caused the supply curve to shift to the left. In Figure 3.11, the new supply curve (the supply curve that shows the relationship between price and quantity supplied after the freeze) is labeled S_1.

At the initial equilibrium price, $1.20, there is now a shortage of coffee. If the price were to remain at $1.20, quantity demanded would not change; it would remain at 13.2 billion pounds.

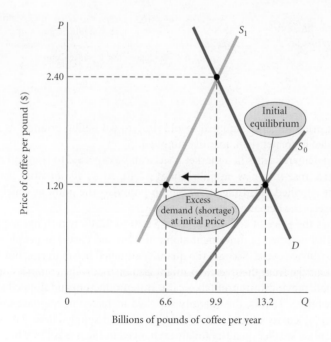

◀ FIGURE 3.11 **The Coffee Market: A Shift of Supply and Subsequent Price Adjustment**
Before the freeze, the coffee market was in equilibrium at a price of $1.20 per pound. At that price, quantity demanded equaled quantity supplied. The freeze shifted the supply curve to the left (from S_0 to S_1), increasing the equilibrium price to $2.40.

High Prices for Tomatoes

The winter of 2010 was a very cold one for Florida, where much of the U.S. fresh fruit and vegetable supply is produced. The article below describes the effect on the price of fresh tomatoes resulting from the freeze. With fewer tomatoes around (the supply curve shifted left due to the freeze), the price of tomatoes increased fivefold. What the reporter calls a shortage, we economists simply note as a shift in the supply curve!

Note the interesting comment by Mr. Brown, the executive vice president of the Florida Tomato Growers Exchange, when people complained to him about the high price of tomatoes. "Doesn't matter," he opined, "because there isn't anything to sell." It is precisely *because* there is less to sell that the price has in fact risen!

Tomatoes Get Sliced From Menus

The Wall Street Journal

A shortage of tomatoes from weather-battered Florida is forcing restaurants and supermarkets to ration supplies amid soaring prices for America's most popular fresh vegetable.

Fast-food restaurant chains such as Wendy's have stopped automatically including tomatoes in sandwiches; now customers have to know to ask.

Even then, consumers might not get what they usually do. At Lloyd's, a white-table cloth restaurant across the street from the Chicago Mercantile Exchange, signs went up this week warning that only plum tomatoes are available.

"People love having tomatoes in their salad and in sandwiches, but we want people to know ahead of time that the quality just isn't what they are used to," said Sam Berngard, president of Taste America Restaurant Group LLC, which operates Lloyd's and two Chicago seafood restaurants.

Subway is continuing to offer tomatoes on its sandwiches, but the chain is using different varieties to ensure that it has enough on hand.

Fresh tomatoes are in short supply because of the unusual spell of freezing temperatures that hugged Florida in January. The cold temperatures that dented citrus production also destroyed roughly 70% of the tomato crop in Florida, which is the largest source of U.S.-grown fresh tomatoes this time of year.

Reggie Brown, executive vice president of Florida Tomato Growers Exchange, a Maitland, Florida, trade group, said Tuesday that a 25-pound box of tomatoes is trading for $30, compared with $6.45 a year ago.

Some restaurants have been told they would have to spend up to $45 for a box of tomatoes in recent days. "Doesn't matter though, because there isn't anything to sell," said Mr. Brown, who calculates the state's shipments are running at about 30% of normal.

Source: The Wall Street Journal, excerpted from "Tomatoes Get Sliced from Menus" by Scott Kilman and Julie Jargon. Copyright 2010 by *Dow Jones & Company, Inc.* Reproduced with permission of *Dow Jones & Company, Inc.* via Copyright Clearance Center.

However, at that price, quantity supplied would drop to 6.6 billion pounds. At a price of $1.20, quantity demanded is greater than quantity supplied.

When excess demand exists in a market, price can be expected to rise, and rise it did. As the figure shows, price rose to a new equilibrium at $2.40. At $2.40, quantity demanded is again equal to quantity supplied, this time at 9.9 billion pounds—the point at which the new supply curve (S_1) intersects the demand curve.

Notice that as the price of coffee rose from $1.20 to $2.40, two things happened. First, the quantity demanded declined (a movement along the demand curve) as people shifted to substitutes such as tea and hot cocoa. Second, the quantity supplied began to rise, but within the limits imposed by the damage from the freeze. (It might also be that some countries or areas with high costs of production, previously unprofitable, came into production and shipped to the world market at the higher price.) That is, the quantity supplied increased in response to the higher price *along* the new supply curve, which lies to the left of the old supply curve. The final result was a higher price ($2.40), a smaller quantity finally exchanged in the market (9.9 billion pounds), and coffee bought only by those willing to pay $2.40 per pound.

Since many market prices are driven by the interaction of millions of buyers and sellers, it is often difficult to predict how they will change. A series of events in the mid-1990s led to the leftward shift in supply, thus driving up the price of coffee, but the opposite occurred more recently. Today coffee beans are exported by over 50 countries, with Brazil being the largest producer with about 30 percent of the market. Large increases in production have kept prices low. In July 2007, the average price per pound was $1.06.

Figure 3.12 summarizes the possible supply and demand shifts that have been discussed and the resulting changes in equilibrium price and quantity. Study the graphs carefully to ensure that you understand them.

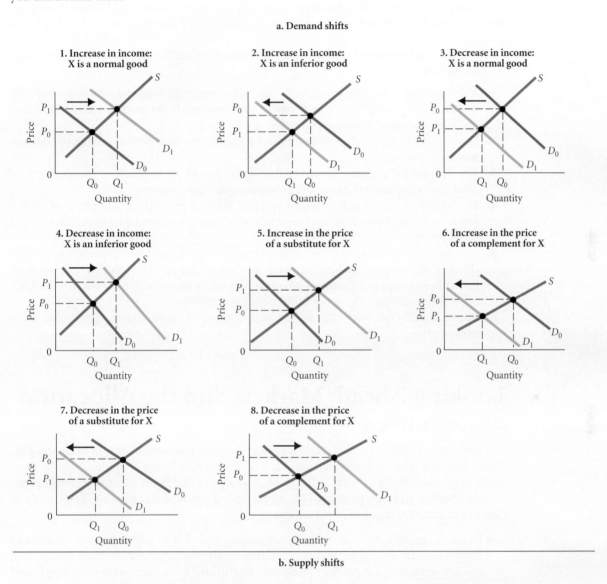

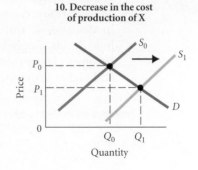

▲ FIGURE 3.12 Examples of Supply and Demand Shifts for Product X

Demand and Supply in Product Markets: A Review

As you continue your study of economics, you will discover that it is a discipline full of controversy and debate. There is, however, little disagreement about the basic way that the forces of supply and demand operate in free markets. If you hear that a freeze in Florida has destroyed a good portion of the citrus crop, you can bet that the price of oranges will rise. If you read that the weather in the Midwest has been good and a record corn crop is expected, you can bet that corn prices will fall. When fishermen in Massachusetts go on strike and stop bringing in the daily catch, you can bet that the price of local fish will go up.

Here are some important points to remember about the mechanics of supply and demand in product markets:

1. A demand curve shows how much of a product a household would buy if it could buy all it wanted at the given price. A supply curve shows how much of a product a firm would supply if it could sell all it wanted at the given price.
2. Quantity demanded and quantity supplied are always per time period—that is, per day, per month, or per year.
3. The demand for a good is determined by price, household income and wealth, prices of other goods and services, tastes and preferences, and expectations.
4. The supply of a good is determined by price, costs of production, and prices of related products. Costs of production are determined by available technologies of production and input prices.
5. Be careful to distinguish between movements along supply and demand curves and shifts of these curves. When the price of a good changes, the quantity of that good demanded or supplied changes—that is, a movement occurs along the curve. When any other factor changes, the curve shifts, or changes position.
6. Market equilibrium exists only when quantity supplied equals quantity demanded at the current price.

Looking Ahead: Markets and the Allocation of Resources

You can already begin to see how markets answer the basic economic questions of what is produced, how it is produced, and who gets what is produced. A firm will produce what is profitable to produce. If the firm can sell a product at a price that is sufficient to ensure a profit after production costs are paid, it will in all likelihood produce that product. Resources will flow in the direction of profit opportunities.

■ Demand curves reflect what people are willing and able to pay for products; demand curves are influenced by incomes, wealth, preferences, prices of other goods, and expectations. Because product prices are determined by the interaction of supply and demand, prices reflect what people are willing to pay. If people's preferences or incomes change, resources will be allocated differently. Consider, for example, an increase in demand—a shift in the market demand curve. Beginning at an equilibrium, households simply begin buying more. At the equilibrium price, quantity demanded becomes greater than quantity supplied. When there is excess demand, prices will rise, and higher prices mean higher profits for firms in the industry. Higher profits, in turn,

ECONOMICS IN PRACTICE

Why Do the Prices of Newspapers Rise?

In 2006, the average price for a daily edition of a Baltimore newspaper was $0.50. In 2007, the average price had risen to $0.75. Three different analysts have three different explanations for the higher equilibrium price.

Analyst 1: The higher price for Baltimore newspapers is good news because it means the population is better informed about public issues. These data clearly show that the citizens of Baltimore have a new, increased regard for newspapers.

Analyst 2: The higher price for Baltimore newspapers is bad news for the citizens of Baltimore. The higher cost of paper, ink, and distribution reflected in these higher prices will further diminish the population's awareness of public issues.

Analyst 3: The higher price for Baltimore newspapers is an unfortunate result of newspapers trying to make money as many consumers have turned to the Internet to access news coverage for free.

As economists, we are faced with two tasks in looking at these explanations: Do they make sense based on what we know about economic principles? And if they do make sense, can we figure out which explanation applies to the case of rising newspaper prices in Baltmore?

What is Analyst 1 saying? Her observation about consumers' new increased regard for newspapers tells us something about the demand curve. Analyst 1 seems to be arguing that tastes have changed in favor of newspapers, which would mean a shift in the demand curve to the right. With upward-sloping supply, such a shift would produce a price increase. So Analyst 1's story is plausible.

Analyst 2 refers to an increased cost of newsprint. This would cause production costs of newspapers to rise, shifting the supply curve to the left. A downward-sloping demand curve also results in increased prices. So Analyst 2 also has a plausible story.

Since Analyst 1 and Analyst 2 have plausible stories based on economic principles, we can look at evidence to see who is in fact right. If you go back to the graphs in Figure 3.12 on p. 71, you will find a clue. When demand shifts to the right (as in Analyst 1's story) the price rises, but so does the quantity as shown in Figure (a). When supply shifts to the left (as in Analyst 2's story) the price rises, but the quantity falls as shown in Figure (b). So we would look at what happened to newspaper circulation during this period to see whether the price increase is from the demand side or the supply side. In fact, in most markets, including Baltimore, quantities of newspapers bought have been falling, so Analyst 2 is most likely correct.

But be careful. Both analysts may be correct. If demand shifts to the right and supply shifts to the left by a greater amount, the price will rise and the quantity sold will fall.

What about Analyst 3? Analyst 3 clearly never had an economics course! Free Internet access to news is a substitute for print media. A decrease in the price of this substitute should shift the demand for newspapers to the left. The result should be a lower price, not a price increase. The fact that the newspaper publishers are "trying to make money" faced with this new competition does not change the laws of supply and demand.

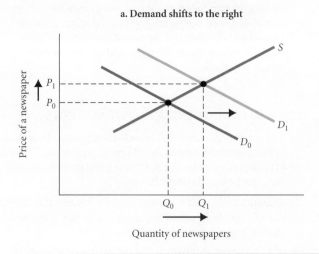

a. Demand shifts to the right

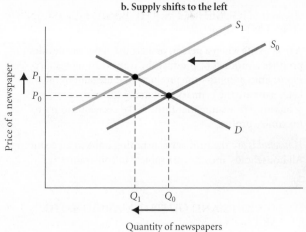

b. Supply shifts to the left

provide existing firms with an incentive to expand and new firms with an incentive to enter the industry. Thus, the decisions of independent private firms responding to prices and profit opportunities determine *what* will be produced. No central direction is necessary.

Adam Smith saw this self-regulating feature of markets more than 200 years ago:

> Every individual . . . by pursuing his own interest . . . promotes that of society. He is led . . . by an invisible hand to promote an end which was no part of his intention.[4]

The term Smith coined, the *invisible hand*, has passed into common parlance and is still used by economists to refer to the self-regulation of markets.

■ Firms in business to make a profit have a good reason to choose the best available technology— lower costs mean higher profits. Thus, individual firms determine *how* to produce their products, again with no central direction.

■ So far, we have barely touched on the question of distribution—*who* gets what is produced? You can see part of the answer in the simple supply and demand diagrams. When a good is in short supply, price rises. As they do, those who are willing and able to continue buying do so; others stop buying.

The next chapter begins with a more detailed discussion of these topics. How, exactly, is the final allocation of resources (the mix of output and the distribution of output) determined in a market system?

—————— SUMMARY ——————

1. In societies with many people, production must satisfy wide-ranging tastes and preferences, and producers must therefore specialize.

FIRMS AND HOUSEHOLDS: THE BASIC DECISION-MAKING UNITS *p. 47*

2. A *firm* exists when a person or a group of people decides to produce a product or products by transforming resources, or *inputs*, into *outputs*—the products that are sold in the market. Firms are the primary producing units in a market economy. We assume that firms make decisions to try to maximize profits.

3. *Households* are the primary consuming units in an economy. All households' incomes are subject to constraints.

INPUT MARKETS AND OUTPUT MARKETS: THE CIRCULAR FLOW *p. 48*

4. Households and firms interact in two basic kinds of markets: *product* or *output markets* and *input* or *factor markets*. Goods and services intended for use by households are exchanged in output markets. In output markets, competing firms supply and competing households demand. In input markets, competing firms demand and competing households supply.

5. Ultimately, firms choose the quantities and character of outputs produced, the types and quantities of inputs demanded, and the technologies used in production. Households choose the types and quantities of products demanded and the types and quantities of inputs supplied.

DEMAND IN PRODUCT/OUTPUT MARKETS *p. 50*

6. The quantity demanded of an individual product by an individual household depends on (1) price, (2) income, (3) wealth, (4) prices of other products, (5) tastes and preferences, and (6) expectations about the future.

7. *Quantity demanded* is the amount of a product that an individual household would buy in a given period if it could buy all that it wanted at the current price.

8. A *demand schedule* shows the quantities of a product that a household would buy at different prices. The same information can be presented graphically in a *demand curve*.

---

[4] Adam Smith, *The Wealth of Nations*, Modern Library Edition (New York: Random House, 1937), p. 456 (1st ed., 1776).

9. The *law of demand* states that there is a negative relationship between price and quantity demanded: As price rises, quantity demanded decreases and vice versa. Demand curves slope downward.

10. All demand curves eventually intersect the price axis because there is always a price above which a household cannot or will not pay. Also, all demand curves eventually intersect the quantity axis because demand for most goods is limited, if only by time, even at a zero price.

11. When an increase in income causes demand for a good to rise, that good is a *normal good*. When an increase in income causes demand for a good to fall, that good is an *inferior good*.

12. If a rise in the price of good X causes demand for good Y to increase, the goods are *substitutes*. If a rise in the price of X causes demand for Y to fall, the goods are *complements*.

13. *Market demand* is simply the sum of all the quantities of a good or service demanded per period by all the households buying in the market for that good or service. It is the sum of all the individual quantities demanded at each price.

SUPPLY IN PRODUCT/OUTPUT MARKETS *p. 60*

14. *Quantity supplied* by a firm depends on (1) the price of the good or service; (2) the cost of producing the product, which includes the prices of required inputs and the technologies that can be used to produce the product; and (3) the prices of related products.

15. *Market supply* is the sum of all that is supplied in each period by all producers of a single product. It is the sum of all the individual quantities supplied at each price.

16. It is very important to distinguish between *movements* along demand and supply curves and *shifts* of demand and supply curves. The demand curve shows the relationship between price and quantity demanded. The supply curve shows the relationship between price and quantity supplied. A change in price is a movement along the curve. Changes in tastes, income, wealth, expectations, or prices of other goods and services cause demand curves to shift; changes in costs, input prices, technology, or prices of related goods and services cause supply curves to shift.

MARKET EQUILIBRIUM *p. 66*

17. When quantity demanded exceeds quantity supplied at the current price, *excess demand* (or a *shortage*) exists and the price tends to rise. When prices in a market rise, quantity demanded falls and quantity supplied rises until an equilibrium is reached at which quantity supplied and quantity demanded are equal. At *equilibrium*, there is no further tendency for price to change.

18. When quantity supplied exceeds quantity demanded at the current price, *excess supply* (or a *surplus*) exists and the price tends to fall. When price falls, quantity supplied decreases and quantity demanded increases until an equilibrium price is reached where quantity supplied and quantity demanded are equal.

———————— R E V I E W   T E R M S   A N D   C O N C E P T S ————————

capital market, *p. 49*

complements, complementary goods, *p. 55*

demand curve, *p. 51*

demand schedule, *p. 51*

entrepreneur, *p. 48*

equilibrium, *p. 66*

excess demand *or* shortage, *p. 66*

excess supply *or* surplus, *p. 68*

factors of production, *p. 49*

firm, *p. 48*

households, *p. 48*

income, *p. 54*

inferior goods, *p. 54*

input *or* factor markets, *p. 48*

labor market, *p. 49*

land market, *p. 49*

law of demand, *p. 52*

law of supply, *p. 61*

market demand, *p. 58*

market supply, *p. 65*

movement along a demand curve, *p. 58*

movement along a supply curve, *p. 63*

normal goods, *p. 54*

perfect substitutes, *p. 55*

product *or* output markets, *p. 48*

profit, *p. 61*

quantity demanded, *p. 50*

quantity supplied, *p. 61*

shift of a demand curve, *p. 58*

shift of a supply curve, *p. 64*

substitutes, *p. 55*

supply curve, *p. 62*

supply schedule, *p. 61*

wealth *or* net worth, *p. 54*

PROBLEMS

All problems are available on www.myeconlab.com

1. Illustrate the following with supply and demand curves:
   a. With increased access to wireless technology and lighter weight, the demand for laptop computers has increased substantially. Laptops have also become easier and cheaper to produce as new technology has come online. Despite the shift of demand, prices have fallen.
   b. Cranberry production in Massachusetts totaled 2.37 million barrels in 2008, a 56 percent increase from the 1.52 million barrels produced in 2007. Demand increased by even more than supply, pushing 2008 prices to $56.70 per barrel from $49.80 in 2007.
   c. During the high-tech boom in the late 1990s, San Jose office space was in very high demand and rents were very high. With the national recession that began in March 2001, however, the market for office space in San Jose (Silicon Valley) was hit very hard, with rents per square foot falling. In 2005, the employment numbers from San Jose were rising slowly and rents began to rise again. Assume for simplicity that no new office space was built during the period.
   d. Before economic reforms were implemented in the countries of Eastern Europe, regulation held the price of bread substantially below equilibrium. When reforms were implemented, prices were deregulated and the price of bread rose dramatically. As a result, the quantity of bread demanded fell and the quantity of bread supplied rose sharply.
   e. The steel industry has been lobbying for high taxes on imported steel. Russia, Brazil, and Japan have been producing and selling steel on world markets at $610 per metric ton, well below what equilibrium would be in the United States with no imports. If no imported steel was permitted into the country, the equilibrium price would be $970 per metric ton. Show supply and demand curves for the United States, assuming no imports; then show what the graph would look like if U.S. buyers could purchase all the steel that they wanted from world markets at $610 per metric ton; show the quantity of imported steel.

2. On Sunday, August 19, the Detroit Tigers and the New York Yankees played baseball at Yankee Stadium. Both teams were in pursuit of league championships. Tickets to the game were sold out, and many more fans would have attended if additional tickets had been available. On that same day, the Cleveland Indians and the Tampa Bay Rays played each other and sold tickets to only 22,500 people in Tampa.

   The Rays stadium, Tropicana Field, holds 43,772. Yankee Stadium holds 57,478. Assume for simplicity that tickets to all regular-season games are priced at $40.
   a. Draw supply and demand curves for the tickets to each of the two games. (*Hint:* Supply is fixed. It does not change with price.) Draw one graph for each game.
   b. Is there a pricing policy that would have filled the ballpark for the Tampa game? If the Rays adopted such a strategy, would it bring in more or less revenue?
   c. The price system was not allowed to work to ration the New York tickets when they were initially sold to the public. How do you know? How do you suppose the tickets were rationed?

3. During the last 10 years, Orlando, Florida, grew rapidly, with new jobs luring young people into the area. Despite increases in population and income growth that expanded demand for housing, the price of existing houses barely increased. Why? Illustrate your answer with supply and demand curves.

4. Do you agree or disagree with each of the following statements? Briefly explain your answers and illustrate each with supply and demand curves.
   a. The price of a good rises, causing the demand for another good to fall. Therefore, the two goods are substitutes.
   b. A shift in supply causes the price of a good to fall. The shift must have been an increase in supply.
   c. During 2009, incomes fell sharply for many Americans. This change would likely lead to a decrease in the prices of both normal and inferior goods.
   d. Two normal goods cannot be substitutes for each other.
   e. If demand increases and supply increases at the same time, price will clearly rise.
   f. The price of good A falls. This causes an increase in the price of good B. Therefore, goods A and B are complements.

5. The U.S. government administers two programs that affect the market for cigarettes. Media campaigns and labeling requirements are aimed at making the public aware of the health dangers of cigarettes. At the same time, the Department of Agriculture maintains price supports for tobacco. Under this program, the supported price is above the market equilibrium price and the government limits the amount of land that can be devoted to tobacco production. Are these two programs at odds with the goal of reducing cigarette consumption? As part of your answer, illustrate graphically the effects of both policies on the market for cigarettes.

6. During the period 2006 through 2010, housing production in the United States fell from a rate of over 2.27 million housing starts per year to a rate of under 500,000, a decrease of over 80 percent. At the same time, the number of new households slowed to a trickle. Students without a job moved in with their parents, fewer immigrants came to the United States, and more of those already here went home. If there are fewer households, it is a decline in demand. If fewer new units are built, it is a decline in supply.
   a. Draw a standard supply and demand diagram which shows the demand for new housing units that are purchased each month, and the supply of new units built and put on the market each month. Assume that the quantity supplied and quantity demanded are equal at 45,000 units and at a price of $200,000.
   b. On the same diagram show a decline in demand. What would happen if this market behaved like most markets?
   c. Now suppose that prices did not change immediately. Sellers decided not to adjust price even though demand is below supply. What would happen to the number of homes for sale (the inventory of unsold new homes) if prices stayed the same following the drop in demand?

d. Now supposed that the supply of new homes put on the market dropped, but price still stayed the same at $200,000. Can you tell a story that brings the market back to equilibrium without a drop in price?

e. Go to www.census.gov/newhomesales. Look at the current press release, which contains data for the most recent month and the past year. What trends can you observe?

7. The following sets of statements contain common errors. Identify and explain each error:

a. Demand increases, causing prices to rise. Higher prices cause demand to fall. Therefore, prices fall back to their original levels.

b. The supply of meat in Russia increases, causing meat prices to fall. Lower prices always mean that Russian households spend more on meat.

8. For each of the following statements, draw a diagram that illustrates the likely effect on the market for eggs. Indicate in each case the impact on equilibrium price and equilibrium quantity.

a. A surgeon general warns that high-cholesterol foods cause heart attacks.

b. The price of bacon, a complementary product, decreases.

c. An increase in the price of chicken feed occurs.

d. Caesar salads become trendy at dinner parties. (The dressing is made with raw eggs.)

e. A technological innovation reduces egg breakage during packing.

*9. Suppose the demand and supply curves for eggs in the United States are given by the following equations:

$$Q_d = 100 - 20P$$
$$Q_s = 10 + 40P$$

where Q_d = millions of dozens of eggs Americans would like to buy each year; Q_s = millions of dozens of eggs U.S. farms would like to sell each year; and P = price per dozen of eggs.

a. Fill in the following table:

PRICE (PER DOZEN)	QUANTITY DEMANDED (Q_d)	QUANTITY SUPPLIED (Q_s)
$ .50	___	___
$1.00	___	___
$1.50	___	___
$2.00	___	___
$2.50	___	___

b. Use the information in the table to find the equilibrium price and quantity.

c. Graph the demand and supply curves and identify the equilibrium price and quantity.

10. Housing policy analysts debate the best way to increase the number of housing units available to low-income households. One strategy—the demand-side strategy—is to provide people with housing vouchers, paid for by the government, that can be used to rent housing supplied by the private market. Another—a supply-side strategy—is to have the government subsidize housing suppliers or to build public housing.

a. Illustrate supply- and demand-side strategies using supply and demand curves. Which results in higher rents?

b. Critics of housing vouchers (the demand-side strategy) argue that because the supply of housing to low-income households is limited and does not respond to higher rents, demand vouchers will serve only to drive up rents and make landlords better off. Illustrate their point with supply and demand curves.

*11. Suppose the market demand for pizza is given by $Q_d = 300 - 20P$ and the market supply for pizza is given by $Q_s = 20P - 100$, where P = price (per pizza).

a. Graph the supply and demand schedules for pizza using $5 through $15 as the value of P.

b. In equilibrium, how many pizzas would be sold and at what price?

c. What would happen if suppliers set the price of pizza at $15? Explain the market adjustment process.

d. Suppose the price of hamburgers, a substitute for pizza, doubles. This leads to a doubling of the demand for pizza. (At each price, consumers demand twice as much pizza as before.) Write the equation for the new market demand for pizza.

e. Find the new equilibrium price and quantity of pizza.

12. [Related to the *Economics in Practice* on p. 70] In the winter, which is the peak season for coats, the price of coats is typically higher than it is in the summer. In the case of strawberries, however, the reverse is true: The price of strawberries is lower in the peak season than it is in the winter season. How do we explain this seeming contradiction?

13. [Related to the *Economics in Practice* on p. 73] Analyst 1 suggested that the demand curve for newspapers in Baltimore might have shifted to the right because people were becoming more literate. Think of two other plausible stories that would result in this demand curve shifting to the right.

14. Explain whether each of the following statements describes a change in demand or a change in quantity demanded, and specify whether each change represents an increase or a decrease.

a. Baby Steps Footwear experiences a 40 percent increase in sales of baby shoes during a 3-day, half-price sale.

b. Tabitha gets a promotion and 15 percent increase in her salary and decides to reward herself by purchasing a new 3-D television.

c. When the price of peaches unexpectedly rises, many consumers choose to purchase plums instead.

d. Due to potential problems with its breaking system, Asteriod Motors has experienced a decline in sales of its Galactica automobile.

e. Antonio, an accountant working for the city of Santa Cristina, decides to forego his annual vacation to Hawaii when word leaks out that the city may be cutting all employees' salaries by 10 percent at the end of the year.

15. For each of the five statements (a–e) in the previous question, draw a demand graph representing the appropriate change in quantity demanded or change in demand.

16. Until 2008, General Motors held the title of the world's largest automobile manufacturer for 78 years. The recession of 2007–2009 and its accompanying financial crisis saw GM declare bankruptcy, receive over $50 billion in government bailout funds, and experience a significant decrease in demand

* Note: Problems marked with an asterisk are more challenging.

for its products. One area where GM saw huge declines in demand was its highly profitable large truck and SUV sector. In response to the fall in demand, GM drastically reduced the production of large trucks and SUVs, including discontinuing its Hummer brand. Explain what determinants of household demand contributed to the decision by GM to significantly reduce production of its large trucks and SUVs.

17. The market for manicures is made up of five firms, and the data in the following table represents each firm's quantity supplied at various prices. Fill in the column for the quantity supplied in the market, and draw a supply graph showing the market data.

Quantity supplied by:

PRICE	FIRM A	FIRM B	FIRM C	FIRM D	FIRM E	MARKET
$10	3	2	0	2	4	
20	4	4	2	3	5	
30	5	6	3	4	7	
40	6	8	5	5	8	

18. The following table represents the market for disposable digital cameras. Plot this data on a supply and demand graph and identify the equilibrium price and quantity. Explain what would happen if the market price is set at $30, and show this on the graph. Explain what would happen if the market price is set at $15, and show this on the graph.

PRICE	QUANTITY DEMANDED	QUANTITY SUPPLIED
$ 5.00	15	0
10.00	13	3
15.00	11	6
20.00	9	9
25.00	7	12
30.00	5	15
35.00	3	18

Demand and Supply Applications

4

Every society has a system of institutions that determines what is produced, how it is produced, and who gets what is produced. In some societies, these decisions are made centrally, through planning agencies or by government directive. However, in every society, many decisions are made in a *decentralized* way, through the operation of markets.

Markets exist in all societies, and Chapter 3 provided a bare-bones description of how markets operate. In this chapter, we continue our examination of demand, supply, and the price system.

The Price System: Rationing and Allocating Resources

The market system, also called the *price system*, performs two important and closely related functions. First, it provides an automatic mechanism for distributing scarce goods and services. That is, it serves as a **price rationing** device for allocating goods and services to consumers when the quantity demanded exceeds the quantity supplied. Second, the price system ultimately determines both the allocation of resources among producers and the final mix of outputs.

Price Rationing

Consider the simple process by which the price system eliminates a shortage. Figure 4.1 shows hypothetical supply and demand curves for wheat. Wheat is produced around the world, with large supplies coming from Russia and from the United States. Wheat is sold in a world market and used to produce a range of food products, from cereals and breads to processed foods, which line the kitchens of the average consumer. Wheat is thus demanded by large food companies as they produce breads, cereals, and cake for households.

As Figure 4.1 shows, the equilibrium price of wheat was $160 per millions of metric tons in the spring of 2010. At this price, farmers from around the world were expected to bring 61.7 million metric tons to market. Supply and demand were equal. Market equilibrium existed at a price of $160 per millions of metric tons because at that price, quantity demanded was equal to quantity supplied. (Remember that equilibrium occurs at the point where the supply and demand curves intersect. In Figure 4.1, this occurs at point C.)

In the summer of 2010, Russia experienced its warmest summer on record. Fires swept through Russia, destroying a substantial portion of the Russia wheat crop. With almost a third of the world wheat normally produced in Russia, the effect of this environmental disaster on world

price rationing The process by which the market system allocates goods and services to consumers when quantity demanded exceeds quantity supplied.

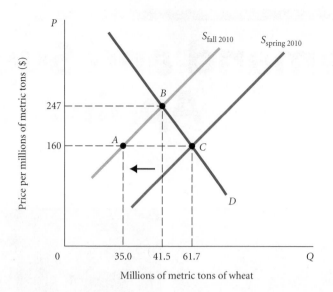

▲ **FIGURE 4.1 The Market for Wheat**

Fires in Russia in the summer of 2010 caused a shift in the world's supply of wheat to the left, causing the price to increase from $160 per millions of metric tons to $247. The equilibrium moved from C to B.

wheat supply was substantial. In the figure, the supply curve for wheat, which had been drawn in expectation of harvesting all the wheat planted in Russia along with the rest of the world, now shifted to the left, from $S_{\text{spring 2010}}$ to $S_{\text{fall 2010}}$. This shift in the supply curve created a situation of excess demand at the old price of $160. At that price, the quantity demanded is 61.7 million metric tons but the burning of much of the Russia supply left the world with only 35 millions of metric tons expected to be supplied. Quantity demanded exceeded quantity supplied at the original price by 26.7 million metric tons.

The reduced supply caused the price of wheat to rise sharply. As the price rises, the available supply is "rationed." Those who are willing and able to pay the most get it. You can see the market's rationing function clearly in Figure 4.1. As the price rises from $160, the quantity demanded declines along the demand curve, moving from point C (61.7 million tons) toward point B (41.5 million tons). The higher prices mean that prices for products like Pepperidge Farm bread and Shredded Wheat cereal, which use wheat as an essential ingredient, also rise. People bake fewer cakes, and begin to eat more rye bread and switch from Shredded Wheat to Corn Flakes in response to the price changes.

As prices rise, wheat farmers also change their behavior, though supply responsiveness is limited in the short term. Farmers outside of Russia, seeing the price rise, harvest their crops more carefully, getting more precious grains from each stalk. Perhaps some wheat is taken out of storage and brought to market. Quantity supplied increases from 35 million metric tons (point A) to 41.5 million tons (point B). The price increase has encouraged farmers who can to make up for part of the Russia wheat loss.

A new equilibrium is established at a price of $247 per millions of metric tons, with 41.5 million tons transacted. The market has determined who gets the wheat: *The lower total supply is rationed to those who are willing and able to pay the higher price.*

This idea of "willingness to pay" is central to the distribution of available supply, and willingness depends on both desire (preferences) and income/wealth. Willingness to pay does not necessarily mean that only the very rich will continue to buy wheat when the price increases. For anyone to continue to buy wheat at a higher price, his or her enjoyment comes at a higher cost in terms of other goods and services.

In sum:

> The adjustment of price is the rationing mechanism in free markets. Price rationing means that whenever there is a need to ration a good—that is, when a shortage exists—in a free market, the price of the good will rise until quantity supplied equals quantity demanded—that is, until the market clears.

ECONOMICS IN PRACTICE

Prices and Total Expenditure: A Lesson From the Lobster Industry in 2008–2009

It is very important to distinguish between the *price* of a product and *total expenditure* from that product. A recent report on the lobster market in New England shows how it can be confusing. See if you can figure out what happened to the price and quantity of lobsters trapped in Maine between 2008 and 2009.

The following short passage was taken from an Associated Press article dated March 1, 2010.

Lobster Prices Plummet As Maine Fisherman Catch Way Too Many

Business Insider

PORTLAND, Maine (AP)—Officials say Maine lobstermen had a record harvest in 2009, but the value of the catch continued to plunge amid the sour global economy.

The Department of Marine Resources announced Monday that lobstermen caught 75.6 million pounds last year, up 8 percent from 2008. But the value of the catch fell $23 million, to $221.7 million.

Source: Used with permission of The Associated Press. Copyright © 2010. All rights reserved.

Total revenue or expenditure in a market is simply the number of units sold multiplied by the price. The author of this article seems surprised that the total revenue in the lobster business (or *value* as he calls it) has fallen despite an increase in the catch. But of course, when supply curves shift right, as has happened here, prices typically fall, unless something has simultaneously happened to shift the demand curve. With an increase in volume and a decrease in price, total revenue could go up or down. In 2009, in the lobster market, revenue apparently fell.

Incidentally, the data given in the article allows you to find prices for 2008 and 2009 as well as quantities. (The price in 2008 was $3.50 and in 2009, $2.93.) Make sure you see how these numbers are derived.

There is some price that will clear any market you can think of. Consider the market for a famous painting such as Jackson Pollock's *No. 5, 1948*, illustrated in Figure 4.2. At a low price, there would be an enormous excess demand for such an important painting. The price would be bid up until there was only one remaining demander. Presumably, that price would be very high. In fact, the Pollock painting sold for a record $140 million in 2006. If the product is in strictly scarce supply, as a single painting is, its price is said to be *demand-determined*. That is,

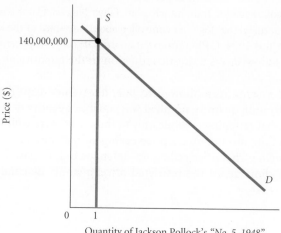

Quantity of Jackson Pollock's *"No. 5, 1948"*

◀ **FIGURE 4.2 Market for a Rare Painting**

There is some price that will clear any market, even if supply is strictly limited. In an auction for a unique painting, the price (bid) will rise to eliminate excess demand until there is only one bidder willing to purchase the single available painting. Some estimate that the *Mona Lisa* would sell for $600 million if auctioned.

its price is determined solely and exclusively by the amount that the highest bidder or highest bidders are willing to pay.

One might interpret the statement that "there is some price that will clear any market" to mean "everything has its price," but that is not exactly what it means. Suppose you own a small silver bracelet that has been in your family for generations. It is quite possible that you would not sell it for *any* amount of money. Does this mean that the market is not working, or that quantity supplied and quantity demanded are not equal? Not at all. It simply means that *you* are the highest bidder. By turning down all bids, you must be willing to forgo what anybody offers for it.

Constraints on the Market and Alternative Rationing Mechanisms

On occasion, both governments and private firms decide to use some mechanism other than the market system to ration an item for which there is excess demand at the current price. Policies designed to stop price rationing are commonly justified in a number of ways.

The rationale most often used is fairness. It is not "fair" to let landlords charge high rents, not fair for oil companies to run up the price of gasoline, not fair for insurance companies to charge enormous premiums, and so on. After all, the argument goes, we have no choice but to pay— housing and insurance are necessary, and one needs gasoline to get to work. Although it is not precisely true that price rationing allocates goods and services solely on the basis of income and wealth, income and wealth do constrain our wants. Why should all the gasoline or all the tickets to the World Series go just to the rich?

Various schemes to keep price from rising to equilibrium are based on several perceptions of injustice, among them (1) that price-gouging is bad, (2) that income is unfairly distributed, and (3) that some items are necessities and everyone should be able to buy them at a "reasonable" price. Regardless of the rationale, the following examples will make two things clear:

1. Attempts to bypass price rationing in the market and to use alternative rationing devices are more difficult and more costly than they would seem at first glance.
2. Very often such attempts distribute costs and benefits among households in unintended ways.

Oil, Gasoline, and OPEC   One of the most important prices in the world is the price of crude oil. Millions of barrels of oil are traded every day. It is a major input into virtually every product produced. It heats our homes, and it is used to produce the gasoline that runs our cars. Its production has led to massive environmental disasters as well as wars. Its price has fluctuated wildly, leading to major macroeconomic problems. But oil is like other commodities in that its price is determined by the basic forces of supply and demand. Oil provides a good example of how markets work and how markets sometimes fail.

The Organization of the Petroleum Exporting Countries (OPEC) is an organization of twelve countries (Algeria, Angola, Ecuador, Iran, Iraq, Kuwait, Libya, Nigeria, Qatar, Saudi Arabia, the United Arab Emirates, and Venezuela) that together controlled about one-third of the known supply of oil in the year 2010. In 1973 and 1974, OPEC imposed an embargo on shipments of crude oil to the United States. What followed was a drastic reduction in the quantity of gasoline available at local gas pumps.

Had the market system been allowed to operate, refined gasoline prices would have increased dramatically until quantity supplied was equal to quantity demanded. However, the government decided that rationing gasoline only to those who were willing and able to pay the most was unfair, and Congress imposed a **price ceiling**, or maximum price, of $0.57 per gallon of leaded regular gasoline. That price ceiling was intended to keep gasoline "affordable," but it also perpetuated the shortage. At the restricted price, quantity demanded remained greater

price ceiling   A maximum price that sellers may charge for a good, usually set by government.

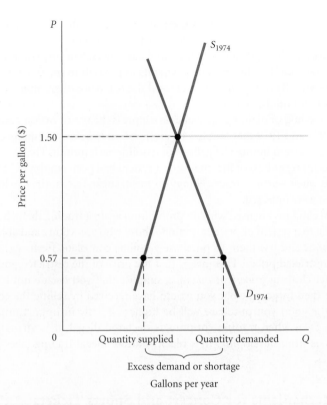

▲ **FIGURE 4.3 Excess Demand (Shortage) Created by a Price Ceiling**
In 1974, a ceiling price of $0.57 cents per gallon of leaded regular gasoline was imposed. If the price had been set by the interaction of supply and demand instead, it would have increased to approximately $1.50 per gallon. At $0.57 per gallon, the quantity demanded exceeded the quantity supplied. Because the price system was not allowed to function, an alternative rationing system had to be found to distribute the available supply of gasoline.

than quantity supplied, and the available gasoline had to be divided up somehow among all potential demanders.

You can see the effects of the price ceiling by looking carefully at Figure 4.3. If the price had been set by the interaction of supply and demand, it would have increased to approximately $1.50 per gallon. Instead, Congress made it illegal to sell gasoline for more than $0.57 per gallon. At that price, quantity demanded exceeded quantity supplied and a shortage existed. Because the price system was not allowed to function, an alternative rationing system had to be found to distribute the available supply of gasoline.

Several devices were tried. The most common of all nonprice rationing systems is **queuing**, a term that means waiting in line. During 1974, very long lines formed daily at gas stations, starting as early as 5 A.M. Under this system, gasoline went to those people who were willing to pay the most, but the sacrifice was measured in hours and aggravation instead of dollars.[1]

queuing Waiting in line as a means of distributing goods and services: a nonprice rationing mechanism.

---

[1] You can also show formally that the result is inefficient—that there is a resulting net loss of total value to society. First, there is the cost of waiting in line. Time has a value. With price rationing, no one has to wait in line and the value of that time is saved. Second, there may be additional lost value if the gasoline ends up in the hands of someone who places a lower value on it than someone else who gets no gas. Suppose, for example, that the market price of gasoline if unconstrained would rise to $2 but that the government has it fixed at $1. There will be long lines to get gas. Imagine that to motorist A, 10 gallons of gas is worth $35 but that she fails to get gas because her time is too valuable to wait in line. To motorist B, 10 gallons is worth only $15, but his time is worth much less, so he gets the gas. In the end, A could pay B for the gas and both would be better off. If A pays B $30 for the gas, A is $5 better off and B is $15 better off. In addition, A does not have to wait in line. Thus, the allocation that results from nonprice rationing involves a net loss of value. Such losses are called *deadweight losses*. See p. 92 of this chapter.

favored customers Those who receive special treatment from dealers during situations of excess demand.

ration coupons Tickets or coupons that entitle individuals to purchase a certain amount of a given product per month.

black market A market in which illegal trading takes place at market-determined prices.

A second nonprice rationing device used during the gasoline crisis was that of **favored customers**. Many gas station owners decided not to sell gasoline to the general public, but to reserve their scarce supplies for friends and favored customers. Not surprisingly, many customers tried to become "favored" by offering side payments to gas station owners. Owners also charged high prices for service. By doing so, they increased the real price of gasoline but hid it in service overcharges to get around the ceiling.

Yet another method of dividing up available supply is the use of **ration coupons**. It was suggested in both 1974 and 1979 that families be given ration tickets or coupons that would entitle them to purchase a certain number of gallons of gasoline each month. That way, everyone would get the same amount regardless of income. Such a system had been employed in the United States during the 1940s when wartime price ceilings on meat, sugar, butter, tires, nylon stockings, and many other items were imposed.

When ration coupons are used with no prohibition against trading them, however, the result is almost identical to a system of price rationing. Those who are willing and able to pay the most buy up the coupons and use them to purchase gasoline, chocolate, fresh eggs, or anything else that is sold at a restricted price.[2] This means that the price of the restricted good will effectively rise to the market-clearing price. For instance, suppose that you decide not to sell your ration coupon. You are then forgoing what you would have received by selling the coupon. Thus, the "real" price of the good you purchase will be higher (if only in opportunity cost) than the restricted price. Even when trading coupons is declared illegal, it is virtually impossible to stop black markets from developing. In a **black market**, illegal trading takes place at market-determined prices.

Rationing Mechanisms for Concert and Sports Tickets Tickets for sporting events such as the World Series, the Super Bowl, and the World Cup command huge prices in the open market. In many cases, the prices are substantially above the original issue price. One of the hottest basketball tickets ever was one to the Boston Celtics and Los Angeles Lakers' NBA final series in 2010 that LA won in seven games. The online price for a courtside seat to one of the games in Los Angeles was $19,000. On September 16, 2007, Justin Timberlake performed at the Staples Center in Los Angeles. The day before the concert, you could buy a front row ticket for $16,000 on the StubHub Web site.

You might ask why a profit-maximizing enterprise would not charge the highest price it could? The answer depends on the event. If the Chicago Cubs got into the World Series, the people of Chicago would buy all the tickets available for thousands of dollars each. But if the Cubs actually *charged* $2,000 a ticket, the hard-working fans would be furious: "Greedy Cubs Gouge Fans" the headlines would scream. Ordinary loyal fans earning reasonable salaries would not be able to afford those prices. Next season, perhaps some of those irate fans would change loyalties, supporting the White Sox over the Cubs. In part to keep from alienating loyal fans, prices for championship games are held down. But not every concert promoter or sports team behaves this way. In 2000, Barbra Streisand gave a concert in Sydney, Australia. Tickets were issued with a *face value* of $1,530, a record for a concert that still stands today.

Let's consider a concert at the Staples Center, which has 20,000 seats. The supply of tickets is thus fixed at 20,000. Of course, there are good seats and bad seats, but to keep things simple, let's assume that all seats are the same and that the promoters charge $50 per ticket for all tickets. This is illustrated in Figure 4.4. Supply is represented by a vertical line at

---

[2] Of course, if you are assigned a number of tickets and you sell them, you are better off than you would be with price rationing. Ration coupons thus serve as a way of redistributing income.

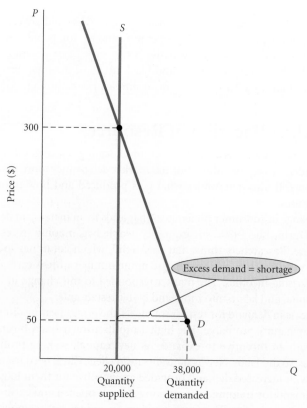

▲ **FIGURE 4.4 Supply of and Demand for a Concert at the Staples Center**

At the face-value price of $50, there is excess demand for seats to the concert. At $50 the quantity demanded is greater than the quantity supplied, which is fixed at 20,000 seats. The diagram shows that the quantity demanded would equal the quantity supplied at a price of $300 per ticket.

20,000. Changing the price does not change the supply of seats. In the figure the quantity demanded at the price of $50 is 38,000, so at this price there is excess demand of 18,000.

Who would get to buy the $50 tickets? As in the case of gasoline, a variety of rationing mechanisms might be used. The most common is queuing, waiting in line. The tickets would go on sale at a particular time, and people would show up and wait. Now ticket sellers have virtual waiting rooms online. Tickets for the World Series go on sale at a particular time in September, and the people who log on to team Web sites at the right moment get into an electronic queue and can buy tickets. Often tickets are sold out in a matter of minutes.

There are also, of course, favored customers. Those who get tickets without queuing are local politicians, sponsors, and friends of the artist or friends of the players.

But "once the dust settles," the power of technology and the concept of *opportunity cost* take over. Even if you get the ticket for the (relatively) low price of $50, that is not the true cost. The true cost is what you give up to sit in the seat. If people on eBay, StubHub, or Ticketmaster are willing to pay $300 for your ticket, that's what you must pay, or sacrifice, to go to the concert. Many people—even strong fans—will choose to sell that ticket. Once again, it is difficult to stop the market from rationing the tickets to those people who are willing and able to pay the most.

No matter how good the intentions of private organizations and governments, it is very difficult to prevent the price system from operating and to stop people's willingness to pay from asserting itself. Every time an alternative is tried, the price system seems to sneak in the back door. With favored customers and black markets, the final distribution may be even more unfair than what would result from simple price rationing.

Prices and the Allocation of Resources

Thinking of the market system as a mechanism for allocating scarce goods and services among competing demanders is very revealing, but the market determines more than just the distribution of final outputs. It also determines what gets produced and how resources are allocated among competing uses.

Consider a change in consumer preferences that leads to an increase in demand for a specific good or service. During the 1980s, for example, people began going to restaurants more frequently than before. Researchers think that this trend, which continues today, is partially the result of social changes (such as a dramatic rise in the number of two-earner families) and partially the result of rising incomes. The market responded to this change in demand by shifting resources, both capital and labor, into more and better restaurants.

With the increase in demand for restaurant meals, the price of eating out rose and the restaurant business became more profitable. The higher profits attracted new businesses and provided old restaurants with an incentive to expand. As new capital, seeking profits, flowed into the restaurant business, so did labor. New restaurants need chefs. Chefs need training, and the higher wages that came with increased demand provided an incentive for them to get it. In response to the increase in demand for training, new cooking schools opened and existing schools began to offer courses in the culinary arts. This story could go on and on, but the point is clear:

Price changes resulting from shifts of demand in output markets cause profits to rise or fall. Profits attract capital; losses lead to disinvestment. Higher wages attract labor and encourage workers to acquire skills. At the core of the system, supply, demand, and prices in input and output markets determine the allocation of resources and the ultimate combinations of goods and services produced.

Price Floor

As we have seen, price ceilings, often imposed because price rationing is viewed as unfair, result in alternative rationing mechanisms that are inefficient and may be equally unfair. Some of the same arguments can be made for price floors. A **price floor** is a minimum price below which exchange is not permitted. If a price floor is set above the equilibrium price, the result will be excess supply; quantity supplied will be greater than quantity demanded.

price floor A minimum price below which exchange is not permitted.

minimum wage A price floor set for the price of labor.

The most common example of a price floor is the **minimum wage**, which is a floor set for the price of labor. Employers (who demand labor) are not permitted under federal law to pay a wage less than $7.25 per hour (in 2010) to workers (who supply labor). Critics argue that since the minimum wage is above equilibrium, the result will be wasteful unemployment. At the wage of $7.25, the quantity of labor demanded is less than the quantity of labor supplied. Whenever a price floor is set above equilibrium, there will be an excess supply.

Supply and Demand Analysis: An Oil Import Fee

The basic logic of supply and demand is a powerful tool of analysis. As an extended example of the power of this logic, we will consider a proposal to impose a tax on imported oil. The idea of taxing imported oil is hotly debated, and the tools we have learned thus far will show us the effects of such a tax.

The Price Mechanism at Work for Shakespeare

Every summer, New York City puts on free performances of Shakespeare in the Park. Tickets are distributed on a first-come-first-serve basis at the Delacorte Theatre in the park beginning at 1 P.M. on the day of the show. People usually begin lining up at 6 A.M. when the park opens; by 10 A.M. the line has typically reached a length sufficient to give away all available tickets.

When you examine the people standing in line for these tickets, most of them seem to be fairly young. Many carry book bags identifying them as students in one of New York's many colleges. Of course, all college students may be fervent Shakespeare fans, but can you think of another reason for the composition of the line? Further, when you attend one of the plays and look around, the audience appears much older and much sleeker than the people who were standing in line. What is going on?

While the tickets are "free" in terms of financial costs, their true price includes the value of the time spent standing in line. Thus, the tickets are cheaper for people (for example, students) whose time value is lower than they are for high-wage earners, like an investment banker from Goldman Sachs. The true cost of a ticket is $0 plus the opportunity cost of the time spent in line. If the average person spends 4 hours in line, as is done in the Central Park case, for someone with a high wage, the true cost of the ticket might be very high. For example, a lawyer who earns $300 an hour would be giving up $1,200 to wait in line. It should not surprise you to see more people waiting in line for whom the tickets are inexpensive.

What about the people who are at the performance? Think about our discussion of the power of entrepreneurs. In this case, the students who stand in line as consumers of the tickets also can play a

role as producers. In fact, the students can produce tickets relatively cheaply by waiting in line. They can then turn around and sell those tickets to the high-wage Shakespeare lovers. These days eBay is a great source of tickets to free events, sold by individuals with low opportunity costs of their time who queued up. Craigslist even provides listings for people who are willing to wait in line for you.

Of course, now and again we do encounter a busy businessperson in one of the Central Park lines. Recently, one of the authors encountered one and asked him why he was waiting in line rather than using eBay, and he replied that it reminded him of when he was young, waiting in line for rock concerts.

Consider the facts. Between 1985 and 1989, the United States increased its dependence on oil imports dramatically. In 1989, total U.S. demand for crude oil was 13.6 million barrels per day. Of that amount, only 7.7 million barrels per day (57 percent) were supplied by U.S. producers, with the remaining 5.9 million barrels per day (43 percent) imported. The price of oil on world markets that year averaged about $18. This heavy dependence on foreign oil left the United States vulnerable to the price shock that followed the Iraqi invasion of Kuwait in August 1990. In the months following the invasion, the price of crude oil on world markets shot up to $40 per barrel.

Even before the invasion, many economists and some politicians had recommended a stiff oil import fee (or tax) that would, it was argued, reduce the U.S. dependence on foreign oil by (1) reducing overall consumption and (2) providing an incentive for increased domestic production. An added bonus would be improved air quality from the reduction in driving.

Supply and demand analysis makes the arguments of the import fee proponents easier to understand. Figure 4.5(a) shows the U.S. market for oil. The world price of oil is assumed to be $18, and the United States is assumed to be able to buy *all the oil that it wants* at this price. This means that domestic producers cannot charge any more than $18 per barrel. The curve labeled *Supply*$_{US}$ shows the amount that domestic suppliers will produce at each price level. At a price of $18, domestic production is 7.7 million barrels. U.S. producers will produce at point *A* on the supply curve. The total quantity of oil demanded in the United States in 1989 was 13.6 million barrels per day. At a price of $18, the quantity demanded in the United States is point *B* on the demand curve.

▶ FIGURE 4.5 **The U.S. Market for Crude Oil, 1989**

At a world price of $18, domestic production is 7.7 million barrels per day and the total quantity of oil demanded in the United States is 13.6 million barrels per day. The difference is total imports (5.9 million barrels per day).

If the government levies a 33 1/3 percent tax on imports, the price of a barrel of oil rises to $24. The quantity demanded falls to 12.2 million barrels per day. At the same time, the quantity supplied by domestic producers increases to 9.0 million barrels per day and the quantity imported falls to 3.2 million barrels per day.

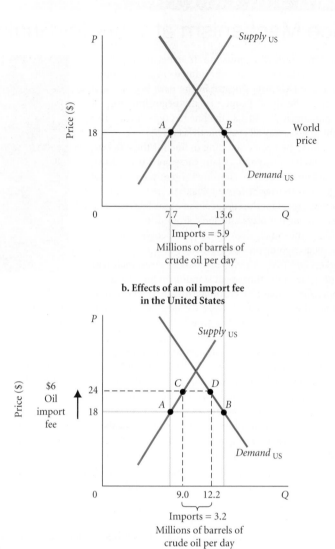

The difference between the total quantity demanded (13.6 million barrels per day) and domestic production (7.7 million barrels per day) is total imports (5.9 million barrels per day).

Now suppose that the government levies a tax of 33 1/3 percent on imported oil. Because the import price is $18, a tax of $6 (or .3333 × $18) per barrel means that importers of oil in the United States will pay a total of $24 per barrel ($18 + $6). This new, higher price means that U.S. producers can also charge up to $24 for a barrel of crude. Note, however, that the tax is paid only on imported oil. Thus, the entire $24 paid for domestic crude goes to domestic producers.

Figure 4.5(b) shows the result of the tax. First, because of a higher price, the quantity demanded drops to 12.2 million barrels per day. This is a movement *along* the demand curve from point *B* to point *D*. At the same time, the quantity supplied by domestic producers increased to 9.0 million barrels per day. This is a movement *along* the supply curve from point *A* to point *C*.

With an increase in domestic quantity supplied and a decrease in domestic quantity demanded, imports decrease to 3.2 million barrels per day (12.2 − 9.0).[3]

The tax also generates revenues for the federal government. The total tax revenue collected is equal to the tax per barrel ($6) times the number of imported barrels. When the quantity imported is 3.2 million barrels per day, total revenue is $6 × 3.2 million, or $19.2 million *per day* (about $7 billion per year).

What does all of this mean? In the final analysis, an oil import fee would (1) increase domestic production and (2) reduce overall consumption. To the extent that one believes that Americans are consuming too much oil, the reduced consumption may be a good thing.

Supply and Demand and Market Efficiency

Clearly, supply and demand curves help explain the way that markets and market prices work to allocate scarce resources. Recall that when we try to understand "how the system works," we are doing "positive economics."

Supply and demand curves can also be used to illustrate the idea of market efficiency, an important aspect of "normative economics." To understand the ideas, you first must understand the concepts of consumer and producer surplus.

Consumer Surplus

The argument, made several times already, that the market forces us to reveal a great deal about our personal preferences is an extremely important one, and it bears repeating at least once more here. If you are free to choose within the constraints imposed by prices and your income and you decide to buy, for example, a hamburger for $2.50, you have "revealed" that a hamburger is worth at least $2.50 to you.

A simple market demand curve such as the one in Figure 4.6(a) illustrates this point quite clearly. At the current market price of $2.50, consumers will purchase 7 million hamburgers per month. There is only one price in the market, and the demand curve tells us how many hamburgers households would buy if they could purchase all they wanted at the posted price of $2.50. Anyone who values a hamburger at $2.50 or more will buy it. Anyone who does not value a hamburger that highly will not buy it.

Some people, however, value hamburgers at more than $2.50. As Figure 4.6(a) shows, even if the price were $5.00, consumers would still buy 1 million hamburgers. If these people were able to buy the good at a price of $2.50, they would earn a **consumer surplus**. Consumer surplus is the difference between the maximum amount a person is willing to pay for a good and its current market price. The consumer surplus earned by the people willing to pay $5.00 for a hamburger is approximately equal to the shaded area between point *A* and the price, $2.50.

The second million hamburgers in Figure 4.6(a) are valued at more than the market price as well, although the consumer surplus gained is slightly less. Point *B* on the market demand curve shows the maximum amount that consumers would be willing to pay for the second million hamburgers. The consumer surplus earned by these people is equal to the shaded area between *B* and the price, $2.50. Similarly, for the third million hamburgers, maximum willingness to pay is given by point *C*; consumer surplus is a bit lower than it is at points *A* and *B*, but it is still significant.

The total value of the consumer surplus suggested by the data in Figure 4.6(a) is roughly equal to the area of the shaded triangle in Figure 4.6(b). To understand why this is so, think about offering hamburgers to consumers at successively lower prices. If the good were actually sold for $2.50, those near point *A* on the demand curve would get a large surplus; those at point *B* would get a smaller surplus. Those at point *E* would get no surplus.

consumer surplus The difference between the maximum amount a person is willing to pay for a good and its current market price.

---

[3] These figures were not chosen randomly. It is interesting to note that in 1985, the world price of crude oil averaged about $24 a barrel. Domestic production was 9.0 million barrels per day and domestic consumption was 12.2 million barrels per day, with imports of only 3.2 million. The drop in the world price between 1985 and 1989 increased imports to 5.9 million, an 84 percent increase.

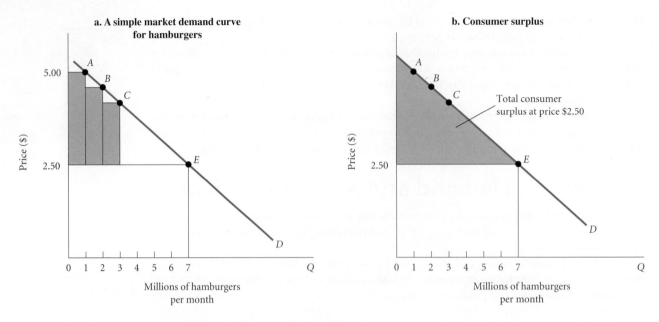

a. A simple market demand curve for hamburgers

b. Consumer surplus

▲ **FIGURE 4.6 Market Demand and Consumer Surplus**
As illustrated in Figure 4.6(a), some consumers (see point *A*) are willing to pay as much as $5.00 each for hamburgers. Since the market price is just $2.50, they receive a consumer surplus of $2.50 for each hamburger that they consume. Others (see point *B*) are willing to pay something less than $5.00 and receive a slightly smaller surplus. Since the market price of hamburgers is just $2.50, the area of the shaded triangle in Figure 4.6(b) is equal to total consumer surplus.

Producer Surplus

Similarly, the supply curve in a market shows the amount that firms willingly produce and supply to the market at various prices. Presumably it is because the price is sufficient to cover the costs or the opportunity costs of production and give producers enough profit to keep them in business. When speaking of cost of production, we include everything that a producer must give up in order to produce a good.

A simple market supply curve like the one in Figure 4.7(a) illustrates this point quite clearly. At the current market price of $2.50, producers will produce and sell 7 million hamburgers. There is only one price in the market, and the supply curve tells us the quantity supplied at each price.

Notice, however, that if the price were just $0.75 (75 cents), although production would be much lower—most producers would be out of business at that price—a few producers would actually be supplying burgers. In fact, producers would supply about 1 million burgers to the market. These firms must have lower costs: They are more efficient or they have access to raw beef at a lower price or perhaps they can hire low-wage labor.

producer surplus The difference between the current market price and the full cost of production for the firm.

If these efficient, low-cost producers are able to charge $2.50 for each hamburger, they are earning what is called a **producer surplus**. Producer surplus is the difference between the current market price and the full cost of production for the firm. The first million hamburgers would generate a producer surplus of $2.50 minus $0.75, or $1.75 per hamburger: a total of $1.75 million. The second million hamburgers would also generate a producer surplus because the price of $2.50 exceeds the producers' total cost of producing these hamburgers, which is above $0.75 but much less than $2.50.

The total value of the producer surplus received by producers of hamburgers at a price of $2.50 per burger is roughly equal to the shaded triangle in Figure 4.7(b). Those producers just able to make a profit producing burgers will be near point *E* on the supply curve and will earn very little in the way of surplus.

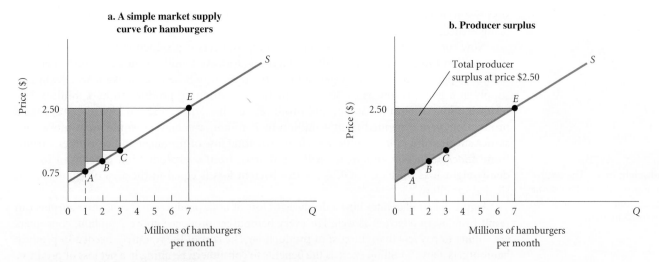

▲ FIGURE 4.7 Market Supply and Producer Surplus

As illustrated in Figure 4.7(a), some producers are willing to produce hamburgers for a price of $0.75 each. Since they are paid $2.50, they earn a producer surplus equal to $1.75. Other producers are willing to supply hamburgers at a price of $1.00; they receive a producer surplus equal to $1.50. Since the market price of hamburgers is $2.50, the area of the shaded triangle in Figure 4.7(b) is equal to total producer surplus.

Competitive Markets Maximize the Sum of Producer and Consumer Surplus

In the preceding example, the quantity of hamburgers supplied and the quantity of hamburgers demanded are equal at $2.50. Figure 4.8 shows the total net benefits to consumers and producers resulting from the production of 7 million hamburgers. Consumers receive benefits in excess of the price they pay and equal to the blue shaded area between the demand curve and the price line at $2.50; the area is equal to the amount of consumer surplus being earned. Producers receive compensation in excess of costs and equal to the red shaded area between the

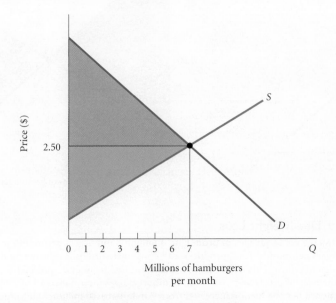

▲ FIGURE 4.8 Total Producer and Consumer Surplus

Total producer and consumer surplus is greatest where supply and demand curves intersect at equilibrium.

supply curve and the price line at $2.50; the area is equal to the amount of producer surplus being earned.

Now consider the result to consumers and producers if production were to be reduced to 4 million burgers. Look carefully at Figure 4.9(a). At 4 million burgers, consumers are willing to pay $3.75 for hamburgers and there are firms whose costs make it worthwhile to supply at a price as low as $1.50, yet something is stopping production at 4 million. The result is a loss of both consumer and producer surplus. You can see in Figure 4.9(a) that if production were expanded from 4 million to 7 million, the market would yield more consumer surplus and more producer surplus. The total loss of producer and consumer surplus from *underproduction* and, as we will see shortly, from overproduction is referred to as a **deadweight loss**. In Figure 4.9(a) the deadweight loss is equal to the area of triangle *ABC* shaded in yellow.

deadweight loss The total loss of producer and consumer surplus from underproduction or overproduction.

Figure 4.9(b) illustrates how a deadweight loss of both producer and consumer surplus can result from *overproduction* as well. For every hamburger produced above 7 million, consumers are willing to pay less than the cost of production. The cost of the resources needed to produce hamburgers above 7 million exceeds the benefits to consumers, resulting in a net loss of producer and consumer surplus equal to the yellow shaded area *ABC*.

Potential Causes of Deadweight Loss From Under- and Overproduction

Most of the next few chapters will discuss perfectly competitive markets in which prices are determined by the free interaction of supply and demand. As you will see, when supply and demand interact freely, competitive markets produce what people want at the least cost, that

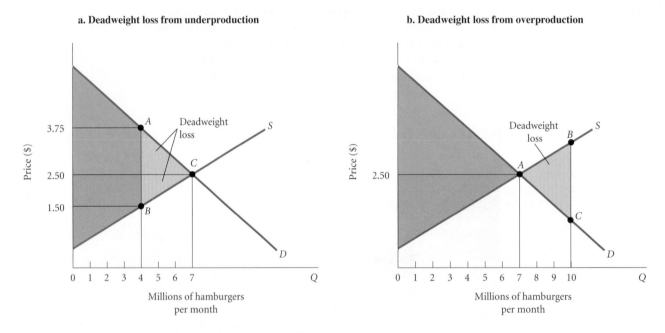

a. Deadweight loss from underproduction

b. Deadweight loss from overproduction

▲ **FIGURE 4.9 Deadweight Loss**

Figure 4.9(a) shows the consequences of producing 4 million hamburgers per month instead of 7 million hamburgers per month. Total producer and consumer surplus is reduced by the area of triangle *ABC* shaded in yellow. This is called the deadweight loss from underproduction. Figure 4.9(b) shows the consequences of producing 10 million hamburgers per month instead of 7 million hamburgers per month. As production increases from 7 million to 10 million hamburgers, the full cost of production rises above consumers' willingness to pay, resulting in a deadweight loss equal to the area of triangle *ABC*.

is, they are efficient. Beginning in Chapter 13, however, we will begin to relax assumptions and will discover a number of naturally occurring sources of market failure. Monopoly power gives firms the incentive to underproduce and overprice, taxes and subsidies may distort consumer choices, external costs such as pollution and congestion may lead to over- or underproduction of some goods, and artificial price floors and price ceilings may have the same effects.

Looking Ahead

We have now examined the basic forces of supply and demand and discussed the market/price system. These fundamental concepts will serve as building blocks for what comes next. Whether you are studying microeconomics or macroeconomics, you will be studying the functions of markets and the behavior of market participants in more detail in the following chapters.

Because the concepts presented in the first four chapters are so important to your understanding of what is to come, this might be a good time for you to review this material.

--- S U M M A R Y ---

THE PRICE SYSTEM: RATIONING AND ALLOCATING RESOURCES *p. 79*

1. In a market economy, the market system (or price system) serves two functions. It determines the allocation of resources among producers and the final mix of outputs. It also distributes goods and services on the basis of willingness and ability to pay. In this sense, it serves as a *price rationing* device.

2. Governments as well as private firms sometimes decide not to use the market system to ration an item for which there is excess demand. Examples of nonprice rationing systems include *queuing*, *favored customers*, and *ration coupons*. The most common rationale for such policies is "fairness."

3. Attempts to bypass the market and use alternative nonprice rationing devices are more difficult and costly than it would seem at first glance. Schemes that open up opportunities for favored customers, black markets, and side payments often end up less "fair" than the free market.

SUPPLY AND DEMAND ANALYSIS: AN OIL IMPORT FEE *p. 86*

4. The basic logic of supply and demand is a powerful tool for analysis. For example, supply and demand analysis shows that an oil import tax will reduce quantity of oil demanded, increase domestic production, and generate revenues for the government.

SUPPLY AND DEMAND AND MARKET EFFICIENCY *p. 89*

5. Supply and demand curves can also be used to illustrate the idea of market efficiency, an important aspect of normative economics.

6. *Consumer surplus* is the difference between the maximum amount a person is willing to pay for a good and the current market price.

7. *Producer surplus* is the difference between the current market price and the full cost of production for the firm.

8. At free market equilibrium with competitive markets, the sum of consumer surplus and producer surplus is maximized.

9. The total loss of producer and consumer surplus from underproduction or overproduction is referred to as a *deadweight loss*.

REVIEW TERMS AND CONCEPTS
---

black market, *p. 84*

consumer surplus, *p. 89*

deadweight loss, *p. 92*

favored customers, *p. 84*

minimum wage, *p. 86*

price ceiling, *p. 82*

price floor, *p. 86*

price rationing, *p. 79*

producer surplus, *p. 90*

queuing, *p. 83*

ration coupons, *p. 84*

PROBLEMS

All problems are available on www.myeconlab.com

1. Illustrate the following with supply and demand curves:
   a. In the summer of 2010, Spanish artist Pablo Picasso's *Portrait d'Angel Fernández de Soto* was sold in London for $51.6 million.
   b. In 2010, hogs in the United States were selling for 81 cents per pound, up from 58 cents per pound a year before. This was due primarily to the fact that supply had decreased during the period.
   c. Early in 2009, a survey of greenhouses indicated that the demand for houseplants was rising sharply. At the same time, large numbers of low-cost producers started growing plants for sale. The overall result was a drop in the average price of houseplants and an increase in the number of plants sold.

2. Every demand curve must eventually hit the quantity axis because with limited incomes, there is always a price so high that there is no demand for the good. Do you agree or disagree? Why?

3. When excess demand exists for tickets to a major sporting event or a concert, profit opportunities exist for scalpers. Explain briefly using supply and demand curves to illustrate. Some argue that scalpers work to the advantage of everyone and are "efficient." Do you agree or disagree? Explain briefly.

4. In an effort to "support" the price of some agricultural goods, the Department of Agriculture pays farmers a subsidy in cash for every acre that they leave *unplanted*. The Agriculture Department argues that the subsidy increases the "cost" of planting and that it will reduce supply and increase the price of competitively produced agricultural goods. Critics argue that because the subsidy is a payment to farmers, it will reduce costs and lead to lower prices. Which argument is correct? Explain.

5. The rent for apartments in New York City has been rising sharply. Demand for apartments in New York City has been rising sharply as well. This is hard to explain because the law of demand says that higher prices should lead to lower demand. Do you agree or disagree? Explain your answer.

6. Illustrate the following with supply and/or demand curves:
   a. The federal government "supports" the price of wheat by paying farmers not to plant wheat on some of their land.

   b. An increase in the price of chicken has an impact on the price of hamburger.
   c. Incomes rise, shifting the demand for gasoline. Crude oil prices rise, shifting the supply of gasoline. At the new equilibrium, the quantity of gasoline sold is less than it was before. (Crude oil is used to produce gasoline.)

7. Illustrate the following with supply and/or demand curves:
   a. A situation of excess labor supply (unemployment) caused by a "minimum wage" law.
   b. The effect of a sharp increase in heating oil prices on the demand for insulation material.

8. Suppose that the world price of oil is $70 per barrel and that the United States can buy all the oil it wants at this price. Suppose also that the demand and supply schedules for oil in the United States are as follows:

PRICE ($ PER BARREL)	U.S. QUANTITY DEMANDED	U.S. QUANTITY SUPPLIED
68	16	4
70	15	6
72	14	8
74	13	10
76	12	12

   a. On graph paper, draw the supply and demand curves for the United States.
   b. With free trade in oil, what price will Americans pay for their oil? What quantity will Americans buy? How much of this will be supplied by American producers? How much will be imported? Illustrate total imports on your graph of the U.S. oil market.
   c. Suppose the United States imposes a tax of $4 per barrel on imported oil. What quantity would Americans buy? How much of this would be supplied by American producers? How much would be imported? How much tax would the government collect?
   d. Briefly summarize the impact of an oil import tax by explaining who is helped and who is hurt among the following groups: domestic oil consumers, domestic oil producers, foreign oil producers, and the U.S. government.

9. Use the data in the preceding problem to answer the follow-ing questions. Now suppose that the United States allows no oil imports.
   a. What are the equilibrium price and quantity for oil in the United States?
   b. If the United States imposed a price ceiling of $74 per bar-rel on the oil market and prohibited imports, would there be an excess supply or an excess demand for oil? If so, how much?
   c. Under the price ceiling, quantity supplied and quantity demanded differ. Which of the two will determine how much oil is purchased? Briefly explain why.

10. Use the following diagram to calculate total consumer sur-plus at a price of $8 and production of 6 million meals per day. For the same equilibrium, calculate total producer surplus. Assuming price remained at $8 but production was cut to 3 million meals per day, calculate producer surplus and consumer surplus. Calculate the deadweight loss from underproduction.

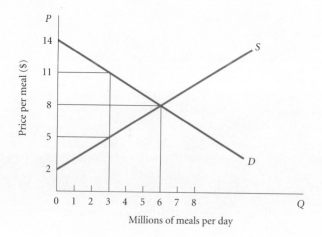

Millions of meals per day

11. In early 2008, many predicted that in a relatively short period of time, unleaded regular gasoline at the pump would be selling for over $4. Do some research on the price of gasoline. Have those dire predictions materialized? What is the price of unleaded regular today in your city or town? If it is below $4 per gallon, what are the reasons? Similarly, if it is higher than $4, what has happened to drive up the price? Illustrate with supply and demand curves.

12. [Related to the *Economics in Practice* on *p. 87*] Many cruise lines offer 5-day trips. A disproportionate number of these trips leave port on Thursday and return late Monday. Why might this be true?

13. [Related to the *Economics in Practice* on *p. 87*] Lines for free tickets to see Shakespeare in Central Park are often long. A local politician has suggested that it would be a great service if the park provided music to entertain those who are waiting in line. What do you think of this suggestion?

14. Suppose the market demand for burritos is given by $Q_d = 40 - 5P$ and the market supply for burritos is given by $Q_s = 10P - 20$, where P = price (per burrito).
    a. Graph the supply and demand schedules for burritos.
    b. What is the equilibrium price and equilibrium quantity?
    c. Calculate consumer surplus and producer surplus, and iden-tify these on the graph.

15. On April 20, 2010, an oil-drilling platform owned by British Petroleum exploded in the Gulf of Mexico, causing oil to leak into the gulf at estimates of 1.5 to 2.5 million gallons per day for well over two months. Due to the oil spill, the government closed over 25 percent of federal waters, which has devastated the commercial fishing industry in the area. Explain how the reduction in supply from the reduced fishing waters will either increase or decrease consumer surplus and producer surplus, and show these changes graphically.

16. The following graph represents the market for DVDs.

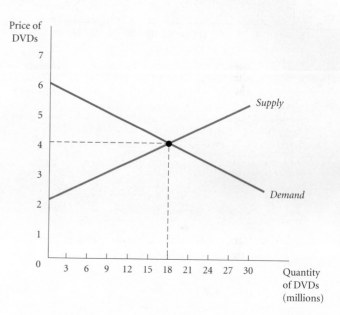

    a. Find the values of consumer surplus and producer surplus when the market is in equilibrium, and identify these areas on the graph.
    b. If underproduction occurs in this market, and only 9 million DVDs are produced, what happens to the amounts of consumer surplus and producer surplus? What is the value of the deadweight loss? Identify these areas on the graph.
    c. If overproduction occurs in this market, and 27 million DVDs are produced, what happens to the amounts of con-sumer surplus and producer surplus? Is there a deadweight loss with overproduction? If so, what is its value? Identify these areas on the graph.

17. The following graph represents the market for wheat. The equilibrium price is $20 per bushel and the equilibrium quantity is 14 million bushels.

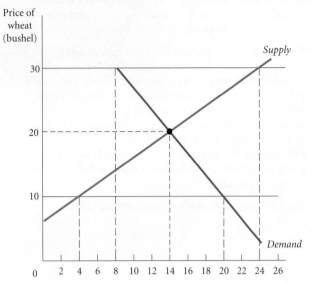

Price of wheat (bushel)

Quantity of wheat (millions of bushels)

a. Explain what will happen if the government establishes a price ceiling of $10 per bushel of wheat in this market? What if the price ceiling was set at $30?

b. Explain what will happen if the government establishes a price floor of $30 per bushel of wheat in this market. What if the price floor was set at $10?

18. **[Related to the *Economics in Practice* on *p. 81*]** Go back to the *Economics in Practice* on page 81. Using the numbers in the newspaper article, find the total revenue, total catch, and market prices for lobsters in the years 2008 and 2009.

Elasticity 5

In economics, simple logic often tells us how a change in one variable, such as the price of a good or an interest rate, is likely to affect behavior. It is a safe bet, for example, that when Barnes & Noble and Amazon.com both lowered the price of their e-Readers in the summer of 2010, sales increased. When many universities lowered the price of football tickets to students (many to a price of zero), the schools did so in an attempt to increase the number of student fans in their stadiums. If the government helps to raise the price of cigarettes by increasing cigarette taxes, it is likely that tobacco sales will suffer.

The work we did in earlier chapters tells us the direction of the changes we would expect to see from price changes in markets. But in each of the preceding examples and in most other situations, knowing the direction of a change is not enough. What we really need to know to help us make the right decisions is how big the reactions are. How many more fans would come to a football game if the price were lowered? Is the added team spirit worth the lost ticket revenue? Would the university get more fans by charging students but giving them free hot dogs at the game? For profit-making firms, knowing the quantity that would be sold at a lowered price is key. If sales increases following a price cut are large enough, revenues may rise. To answer these questions, we must know more than just direction; we must know something about market responsiveness.

Understanding the responsiveness of consumers and producers in markets to price changes is key to answering a wide range of economic problems. Should McDonald's lower the price of its Big Mac? For McDonald's, the answer depends on whether that price cut increases or decreases its profits. The answer to that, in turn, depends on how its customers are likely to respond to the price cut. How many more Big Macs will be sold, and will the new sales come at the expense of the sandwiches sold at Subway or be a substitution of McDonald's Chicken McNuggets for Big Macs? How many potential new smokers will be deterred from smoking by higher cigarette prices the government has induced? Questions such as these lie at the core of economics. To answer these questions, we need to measure the magnitude of market responses.

The importance of actual measurement cannot be overstated. Much of the research being done in economics today involves the collection and analysis of quantitative data that measure behavior. The ability to analyze large amounts of data increased enormously with the advent of modern computers.

Economists commonly measure responsiveness using the concept of **elasticity**. Elasticity is a general concept that can be used to quantify the response in one variable when another variable

elasticity A general concept used to quantify the response in one variable when another variable changes.

changes. If some variable *A* changes in response to changes in another variable *B*, the elasticity of *A* with respect to *B* is equal to the percentage change in *A* divided by the percentage change in *B*:

$$\text{elasticity of } A \text{ with respect to } B = \frac{\%\Delta A}{\%\Delta B}$$

In the examples discussed previously, we often consider responsiveness or elasticity by looking at prices: How does demand for a product respond when its price changes? This is known as the price elasticity of demand. How does supply respond when prices change? This is the price elasticity of supply. As in the McDonald's example, sometimes it is important to know how the price of one good—for example, the Big Mac—affects the demand for another good—Chicken McNuggets. This is called the cross-price elasticity of demand.

But the concept of elasticity goes well beyond responsiveness to price changes. As we will see, we can look at elasticities as a way to understand responses to changes in income and almost any other major determinant of supply and demand in a market. We begin with a discussion of price elasticity of demand.

Price Elasticity of Demand

You have already seen the law of demand at work. Recall that *ceteris paribus*, when prices rise, quantity demanded can be expected to decline. When prices fall, quantity demanded can be expected to rise. The normal negative relationship between price and quantity demanded is reflected in the downward slope of demand curves.

Slope and Elasticity

The slope of a demand curve may in a rough way reveal the responsiveness of the quantity demanded to price changes, but slope can be quite misleading. In fact, it is not a good formal measure of responsiveness.

Consider the two identical demand curves in Figure 5.1. The only difference between the two is that quantity demanded is measured in pounds in the graph on the left and in ounces in the graph on the right. When we calculate the numerical value of each slope, however, we get very different

▶ **FIGURE 5.1 Slope Is Not a Useful Measure of Responsiveness**

Changing the unit of measure from pounds to ounces changes the numerical value of the demand slope dramatically, but the behavior of buyers in the two diagrams is identical.

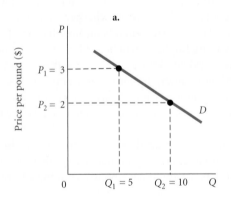

a.

Slope: $\dfrac{\Delta Y}{\Delta X} = \dfrac{P_2 - P_1}{Q_2 - Q_1}$

$= \dfrac{2 - 3}{10 - 5} = -\dfrac{1}{5}$

Pounds of steak per month

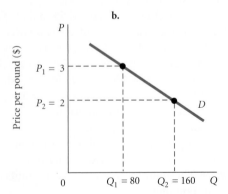

b.

Slope: $\dfrac{\Delta Y}{\Delta X} = \dfrac{P_2 - P_1}{Q_2 - Q_1}$

$= \dfrac{2 - 3}{160 - 80} = -\dfrac{1}{80}$

Ounces of steak per month

answers. The curve on the left has a slope of −1/5, and the curve on the right has a slope of −1/80; yet the two curves represent the *exact same behavior*. If we had changed dollars to cents on the Y-axis, the two slopes would be −20 and −1.25, respectively. (Review the Appendix to Chapter 1 if you do not understand how these numbers are calculated.)

The problem is that the numerical value of slope depends on the units used to measure the variables on the axes. To correct this problem, we must convert the changes in price and quantity to *percentages*. By looking at by how much the *percent* quantity demanded changes for a given *percent* price change, we have a measure of responsiveness that does not change with the unit of measurement. The price increase in Figure 5.1 leads to a decline of 5 pounds, or 80 ounces, in the quantity of steak demanded—a decline of 50 percent from the initial 10 pounds, or 160 ounces, whether we measure the steak in pounds or ounces.

We define **price elasticity of demand** simply as the ratio of the percentage of change in quantity demanded to the percentage change in price.

$$\text{price elasticity of demand} = \frac{\% \text{ change in quantity demanded}}{\% \text{ change in price}}$$

Percentage changes should always carry the sign (plus or minus) of the change. Positive changes, or increases, take a (+). Negative changes, or decreases, take a (−). The law of demand implies that price elasticity of demand is nearly always a negative number: Price increases (+) will lead to decreases in quantity demanded (−), and vice versa. Thus, the numerator and denominator should have opposite signs, resulting in a negative ratio.

Types of Elasticity

The elasticity of demand can vary between 0 and minus infinity. An elasticity of 0 indicates that the quantity demanded does not respond *at all* to a price change. A demand curve with an elasticity of 0 is called **perfectly inelastic** and is illustrated in Figure 5.2(a). A demand curve in which even the smallest price increase reduces quantity demanded to zero is known as a **perfectly elastic** demand curve and is illustrated in Figure 5.2(b). A good way to remember the difference between the two perfect elasticities is

> Perfectly **E**lastic
> and Perfectly **I**nelastic

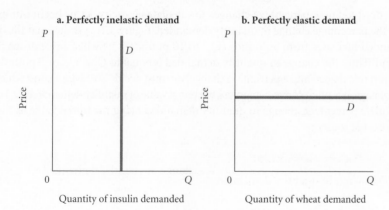

a. Perfectly inelastic demand

b. Perfectly elastic demand

Quantity of insulin demanded

Quantity of wheat demanded

▲ **FIGURE 5.2 Perfectly Inelastic and Perfectly Elastic Demand Curves**
Figure 5.2(a) shows a perfectly inelastic demand curve for insulin. Price elasticity of demand is zero. Quantity demanded is fixed; it does not change at all when price changes. Figure 5.2(b) shows a perfectly elastic demand curve facing a wheat farmer. A tiny price increase drives the quantity demanded to zero. In essence, perfectly elastic demand implies that individual producers can sell all they want at the going market price but cannot charge a higher price.

price elasticity of demand The ratio of the percentage of change in quantity demanded to the percentage of change in price; measures the responsiveness of quantity demanded to changes in price.

perfectly inelastic demand Demand in which quantity demanded does not respond at all to a change in price.

perfectly elastic demand Demand in which quantity drops to zero at the slightest increase in price.

What type of good might have a perfectly elastic demand curve? Suppose there are two identical vendors selling Good Humor bars on a beach. If one vendor increased his price, all the buyers would flock to the second vendor. In this case, a small price increase costs the first vendor all his business; the demand he faces is perfectly elastic. Products with perfectly inelastic demand are harder to find, but some life-saving medical products like insulin may be close, in that very high price increases may elicit no response in terms of quantity demanded.

Of course, a lot of products have elasticities between the two extremes. When an elasticity is over −1.0 in absolute value,[1] we refer to the demand as **elastic**. In this case, the percentage change in quantity is larger in absolute value than the percentage change in price. Here consumers are responding a lot to a price change. When an elasticity is less than 1 in absolute value, it is referred to as **inelastic**. In these markets, consumers respond much less to price changes. The demand for oil is inelastic, for example, because even with a price increase, it is hard to substitute oil for other products. The demand for a Nestlé Crunch bar is much more elastic, in part because there are so many more substitutes.

A special case is one in which the elasticity of demand is minus one. Here, we say demand has **unitary elasticity**. In this case, the percentage change in price is exactly equal to the percentage change in quantity demanded, in absolute value terms. As you will see when we look at the relationship between revenue and elasticities later in this chapter, unitary elastic demand curves have some very interesting properties.

A warning: You must be very careful about signs. Because it is generally understood that demand elasticities are negative (demand curves have a negative slope), they are often reported and discussed without the negative sign. For example, a technical paper might report that the demand for housing "appears to be inelastic with respect to price, or less than 1 (.6)." What the writer means is that the estimated elasticity is −.6, which is between zero and −1. Its absolute value is less than 1.

elastic demand A demand relationship in which the percentage change in quantity demanded is larger than the percentage change in price in absolute value (a demand elasticity with an absolute value greater than 1).

inelastic demand Demand that responds somewhat, but not a great deal, to changes in price. Inelastic demand always has a numerical value between zero and −1.

unitary elasticity A demand relationship in which the percentage change in quantity of a product demanded is the same as the percentage change in price in absolute value (a demand elasticity of −1).

Calculating Elasticities

Elasticities must be calculated cautiously. Return for a moment to the demand curves in Figure 5.1 on p. 98. The fact that these two identical demand curves have dramatically different slopes should be enough to convince you that slope is a poor measure of responsiveness. As we will see shortly, a given straight line, which has the same slope all along it, will show different elasticities at various points.

The concept of elasticity circumvents the measurement problem posed by the graphs in Figure 5.1 by converting the changes in price and quantity to percentage changes. Recall that elasticity of demand is the *percentage* change in quantity demanded divided by the *percentage* change in price.

Calculating Percentage Changes

Because we need to know percentage changes to calculate elasticity, let us begin our example by calculating the percentage change in quantity demanded. Figure 5.1(a) shows that the quantity of steak demanded increases from 5 pounds (Q_1) to 10 pounds (Q_2) when price drops from \$3 to \$2 per pound. Thus, the change in quantity demanded is equal to $Q_2 - Q_1$, or 5 pounds.

To convert this change into a percentage change, we must decide on a *base* against which to calculate the percentage. It is often convenient to use the initial value of quantity demanded (Q_1) as the base.

To calculate percentage change in quantity demanded using the initial value as the base, the following formula is used:

$$\% \text{ change in quantity demanded} = \frac{\text{change in quantity demanded}}{Q_1} \times 100\%$$

$$= \frac{Q_2 - Q_1}{Q_1} \times 100\%$$

---

[1] *Absolute value* or *absolute size* means ignoring the sign. The absolute value of −4 is 4.

In Figure 5.1, $Q_2 = 10$ and $Q_1 = 5$. Thus,

$$\text{\% change in quantity demanded} = \frac{10 - 5}{5} \times 100\% = \frac{5}{5} \times 100\% = 100\%$$

Expressing this equation verbally, we can say that an increase in quantity demanded from 5 pounds to 10 pounds is a 100 percent increase from 5 pounds. Note that you arrive at exactly the same result if you use the diagram in Figure 5.1(b), in which quantity demanded is measured in ounces. An increase from Q_1 (80 ounces) to Q_2 (160 ounces) is a 100 percent increase.

We can calculate the percentage change in price in a similar way. Once again, let us use the initial value of P—that is, P_1—as the base for calculating the percentage. By using P_1 as the base, the formula for calculating the percentage of change in P is

$$\begin{aligned}\text{\% change in price} &= \frac{\text{change in price}}{P_1} \times 100\% \\ &= \frac{P_2 - P_1}{P_1} \times 100\%\end{aligned}$$

In Figure 5.1(a), P_2 equals 2 and P_1 equals 3. Thus, the change in P, or ΔP, is a negative number: $P_2 - P_1 = 2 - 3 = -1$. This is true because the change is a decrease in price. Plugging the values of P_1 and P_2 into the preceding equation, we get

$$\text{\% change in price} = \frac{2 - 3}{3} \times 100\% = \frac{-1}{3} \times 100\% = -33.3\%$$

In other words, decreasing the price from \$3 to \$2 is a 33.3 percent decline.

Elasticity Is a Ratio of Percentages

Once the changes in quantity demanded and price have been converted to percentages, calculating elasticity is a matter of simple division. Recall the formal definition of elasticity:

$$\text{price elasticity of demand} = \frac{\text{\% change in quantity demanded}}{\text{\% change in price}}$$

If demand is elastic, the ratio of percentage change in quantity demanded to percentage change in price will have an absolute value greater than 1. If demand is inelastic, the ratio will have an absolute value between 0 and 1. If the two percentages are equal, so that a given percentage change in price causes an equal percentage change in quantity demanded, elasticity is equal to −1; this is unitary elasticity.

Substituting the preceding percentages, we see that a 33.3 percent decrease in price leads to a 100 percent increase in quantity demanded; thus,

$$\text{price elasticity of demand} = \frac{+100\%}{-33.3\%} = -3.0$$

According to these calculations, the demand for steak is elastic when we look at the range between \$2 and \$3.

The Midpoint Formula

Although simple, the use of the initial values of P and Q as the bases for calculating percentage changes can be misleading. Let us return to the example of demand for steak in Figure 5.1(a), where we have a change in quantity demanded of 5 pounds. Using the initial value Q_1 as the base, we calculated that this change represents a 100 percent increase over the base. Now suppose that the price of steak rises to \$3 again, causing the quantity demanded to drop back to 5 pounds. How much of a percentage decrease in quantity demanded is this? We now have $Q_1 = 10$ and $Q_2 = 5$. With the same formula we used earlier, we get

$$\text{\% change in quantity demanded} = \frac{\text{change in quantity demanded}}{Q_1} \times 100\%$$

$$= \frac{Q_2 - Q_1}{Q_1} \times 100\%$$

$$= \frac{5 - 10}{10} \times 100\% = -50\%$$

Thus, an increase from 5 pounds to 10 pounds is a 100 percent increase (because the initial value used for the base is 5), but a decrease from 10 pounds to 5 pounds is only a 50 percent decrease (because the initial value used for the base is 10). This does not make much sense because in both cases, we are calculating elasticity on the same interval on the demand curve. Changing the "direction" of the calculation should not change the elasticity.

To describe percentage changes more accurately, a simple convention has been adopted. Instead of using the initial values of Q and P as the bases for calculating percentages, we use the *midpoints* of these variables as the bases. That is, we use the value halfway between P_1 and P_2 for the base in calculating the percentage change in price and the value halfway between Q_1 and Q_2 as the base for calculating percentage change in quantity demanded.

Thus, the **midpoint formula** for calculating the percentage change in quantity demanded becomes

midpoint formula A more precise way of calculating percentages using the value halfway between P_1 and P_2 for the base in calculating the percentage change in price and the value halfway between Q_1 and Q_2 as the base for calculating the percentage change in quantity demanded.

$$\text{\% change in quantity demanded} = \frac{\text{change in quantity demanded}}{(Q_1 + Q_2)/2} \times 100\%$$

$$= \frac{Q_2 - Q_1}{(Q_1 + Q_2)/2} \times 100\%$$

Substituting the numbers from the original Figure 5.1(a), we get

$$\text{\% change in quantity demanded} = \frac{10 - 5}{(5 + 10)/2} \times 100\% = \frac{5}{7.5} \times 100\% = 66.7\%$$

Using the point halfway between P_1 and P_2 as the base for calculating the percentage change in price, we get

$$\text{\% change in price} = \frac{\text{change in price}}{(P_1 + P_2)/2} \times 100\%$$

$$= \frac{P_2 - P_1}{(P_1 + P_2)/2} \times 100\%$$

Substituting the numbers from the original Figure 5.1(a) yields

$$\text{\% change in price} = \frac{2 - 3}{(3 + 2)/2} \times 100\% = \frac{-1}{2.5} \times 100\% = -40.0\%$$

We can thus say that a change from a quantity of 5 to a quantity of 10 is a +66.7 percent change using the midpoint formula and that a change in price from \$3 to \$2 is a −40 percent change using the midpoint formula.

Using these percentages to calculate elasticity yields

$$\text{price elasticity of demand} = \frac{\text{\% change in quantity demanded}}{\text{\% change in price}} = \frac{66.7\%}{-40.0\%} = -1.67$$

Using the midpoint formula in this case gives a lower demand elasticity, but the demand remains elastic because the percentage change in quantity demanded is still greater than the percentage change in price in absolute size.

The calculations based on the midpoint approach are summarized in Table 5.1.

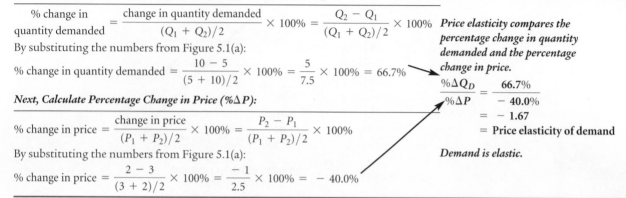

TABLE 5.1 Calculating Price Elasticity with the Midpoint Formula

First, Calculate Percentage Change in Quantity Demanded (%ΔQ_D):

$$\frac{\% \text{ change in}}{\text{quantity demanded}} = \frac{\text{change in quantity demanded}}{(Q_1 + Q_2)/2} \times 100\% = \frac{Q_2 - Q_1}{(Q_1 + Q_2)/2} \times 100\%$$

By substituting the numbers from Figure 5.1(a):

$$\% \text{ change in quantity demanded} = \frac{10 - 5}{(5 + 10)/2} \times 100\% = \frac{5}{7.5} \times 100\% = 66.7\%$$

Price elasticity compares the percentage change in quantity demanded and the percentage change in price.

$$\frac{\%\Delta Q_D}{\%\Delta P} = \frac{66.7\%}{-40.0\%}$$
$$= -1.67$$
$$= \textbf{Price elasticity of demand}$$

Next, Calculate Percentage Change in Price (%ΔP):

$$\% \text{ change in price} = \frac{\text{change in price}}{(P_1 + P_2)/2} \times 100\% = \frac{P_2 - P_1}{(P_1 + P_2)/2} \times 100\%$$

By substituting the numbers from Figure 5.1(a):

$$\% \text{ change in price} = \frac{2 - 3}{(3 + 2)/2} \times 100\% = \frac{-1}{2.5} \times 100\% = -40.0\%$$

Demand is elastic.

Elasticity Changes Along a Straight-Line Demand Curve

An interesting and important point is that elasticity changes from point to point along a demand curve even when the slope of that demand curve does not change—that is, even along a straight-line demand curve. Indeed, the differences in elasticity along a demand curve can be quite large.

Before we go through the calculations to show how elasticity changes along a demand curve, it is useful to think *why* elasticity might change as we vary price. Consider again McDonald's decision to reduce the price of a Big Mac. Suppose McDonald's found that at the current price of $3, a small price cut would generate a large number of new customers who wanted burgers. Demand, in short, was relatively elastic. What happens as McDonald's continues to cut its price? As the price moves from $2.50 to $2.00, for example, new customers lured in by the price cuts are likely to decrease; in some sense, McDonald's will be running out of customers who are interested in its burgers at any price. It should come as no surprise that as we move down a typical straight-line demand curve, price elasticity falls. Demand becomes less elastic as price is reduced. This lesson has important implications for price-setting strategies of firms.

Consider the demand schedule shown in Table 5.2 and the demand curve in Figure 5.3. Herb works about 22 days per month in a downtown San Francisco office tower. On the top floor

TABLE 5.2 Demand Schedule for Office Dining Room Lunches

Price (per Lunch)	Quantity Demanded (Lunches per Month)
$11	0
10	2
9	4
8	6
7	8
6	10
5	12
4	14
3	16
2	18
1	20
0	22

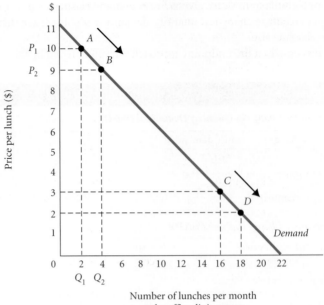

of the building is a nice dining room. If lunch in the dining room were $10, Herb would eat there only twice a month. If the price of lunch fell to $9, he would eat there 4 times a month. (Herb would bring his lunch to work on other days.) If lunch were only a dollar, he would eat there 20 times a month.

Let us calculate price elasticity of demand between points A and B on the demand curve in Figure 5.3. Moving from A to B, the price of a lunch drops from $10 to $9 (a decrease of $1) and the number of dining room lunches that Herb eats per month increases from two to four (an increase of two). We will use the midpoint approach.

First, we calculate the percentage change in quantity demanded:

$$\% \text{ change in quantity demanded} = \frac{Q_2 - Q_1}{(Q_1 + Q_2)/2} \times 100\%$$

Substituting the numbers from Figure 5.3, we get

$$\% \text{ change in quantity demanded} = \frac{4 - 2}{(2 + 4)/2} \times 100\% = \frac{2}{3} \times 100\% = 66.7\%$$

Next, we calculate the percentage change in price:

$$\% \text{ change in price} = \frac{P_2 - P_1}{(P_1 + P_2)/2} \times 100\%$$

Substituting the numbers from Figure 5.3, we get

$$\% \text{ change in price} = \frac{9 - 10}{(10 + 9)/2} \times 100\% = \frac{-1}{9.5} \times 100\% = -10.5\%$$

Finally, we calculate elasticity by dividing

$$\text{elasticity of demand} = \frac{\% \text{ change in quantity demanded}}{\% \text{ change in price}}$$

$$= \frac{66.7\%}{-10.5\%} = -6.4$$

The percentage change in quantity demanded is 6.4 times larger than the percentage change in price. In other words, Herb's demand between points A and B is quite responsive; his demand between points A and B is elastic.

Now consider a different movement along the *same* demand curve in Figure 5.3. Moving from point *C* to point *D*, the graph indicates that at a price of $3, Herb eats in the office dining room 16 times per month. If the price drops to $2, he will eat there 18 times per month. These changes expressed in numerical terms are exactly the same as the price and quantity changes between points *A* and *B* in the figure—price falls $1, and quantity demanded increases by two meals. Expressed in *percentage* terms, however, these changes are very different.

By using the midpoints as the base, the $1 price decline is only a 10.5 percent reduction when price is around $9.50, between points *A* and *B*. The same $1 price decline is a 40 percent reduction when price is around $2.50, between points *C* and *D*. The two-meal increase in quantity demanded is a 66.7 percent increase when Herb averages only 3 meals per month, but it is only an 11.76 percent increase when he averages 17 meals per month. The elasticity of demand between points *C* and *D* is thus 11.76 percent divided by −40 percent, or −0.294. (Work these numbers out for yourself by using the midpoint formula.)

The percentage changes between *A* and *B* are very different from those between *C* and *D*, and so are the elasticities. Herb's demand is quite elastic (−6.4) between points *A* and *B*; a 10.5 percent reduction in price caused a 66.7 percent increase in quantity demanded. However, his demand is inelastic (−0.294) between points *C* and *D*; a 40 percent decrease in price caused only an 11.76 percent increase in quantity demanded.

Again, it is useful to keep in mind the underlying economics as well as the mathematics. At high prices, there is a great deal of potential demand for the dining room to capture. Hence, quantity is likely to respond well to price cuts. At low prices, everyone who is likely to come to the dining room already has.

Elasticity and Total Revenue

As we saw in Chapter 4, the oil-producing countries have had some success keeping oil prices high by controlling supply. To some extent, reducing supply and driving up prices has increased the total oil revenues to the producing countries. We would not, however, expect this strategy to work for everyone. If the organization of banana-exporting countries (OBEC) had done the same thing, the strategy would not have worked.

Why? Suppose OBEC decides to cut production by 30 percent to drive up the world price of bananas. At first, when the quantity of bananas supplied declines, the quantity demanded is greater than the quantity supplied and the world price rises. The issue for OBEC, however, is *how much* the world price will rise. That is, how much will people be willing to pay to continue consuming bananas? Unless the percentage *increase* in price is greater than the percentage *decrease* in output, the OBEC countries will lose revenues.

A little research shows us that the prospects are not good for OBEC. There are many reasonable substitutes for bananas. As the price of bananas rises, people simply eat fewer bananas as they switch to eating more pineapples or oranges. Many people are simply not willing to pay a higher price for bananas. The quantity of bananas demanded declines 30 percent—to the new quantity supplied—after only a modest price rise, and OBEC fails in its mission; its revenues decrease instead of increase.

We have seen that oil-producing countries often can increase their revenues by restricting supply and pushing up the market price of crude oil. We also argued that a similar strategy by banana-producing countries would probably fail. Why? The quantity of oil demanded is not as responsive to a change in price as is the quantity of bananas demanded. In other words, the demand for oil is more inelastic than is the demand for bananas. One of the very useful features of elasticity is that knowing the value of price elasticity allows us to quickly see what happens to a firm's revenue as it raises and cuts its prices. When demand is inelastic, raising prices will raise revenues; when (as in the banana case) demand is elastic, price increases reduce revenues.

We can now use the more formal definition of elasticity to make more precise our argument of why oil producers would succeed and banana producers would fail as they raise prices. In any market, $P \times Q$ is total revenue (*TR*) received by producers:

$$TR = P \times Q$$
total revenue = price × quantity

The oil producers' total revenue is the price per barrel of oil (P) times the number of barrels its participant countries sell (Q). To banana producers, total revenue is the price per bunch times the number of bunches sold.

When price increases in a market, quantity demanded declines. As we have seen, when price (P) declines, quantity demanded (Q_D) increases. This is true in all markets. The two factors, P and Q_D, move in opposite directions:

> effects of price changes
> on quantity demanded:
>
> $$P \uparrow \rightarrow Q_D \downarrow$$
> and
> $$P \downarrow \rightarrow Q_D \uparrow$$

Because total revenue is the product of P and Q, whether TR rises or falls in response to a price increase depends on which is bigger: the percentage increase in price or the percentage decrease in quantity demanded. If the percentage decrease in quantity demanded is smaller than the percentage increase in price, total revenue will rise. This occurs when demand is *inelastic*. In this case, the percentage price rise simply outweighs the percentage quantity decline and $P \times Q = (TR)$ rises:

> effect of price increase on
> a product with inelastic demand:
>
> $$\uparrow P \times Q_D \downarrow = TR \uparrow$$

If, however, the percentage decline in quantity demanded following a price increase is larger than the percentage increase in price, total revenue will fall. This occurs when demand is *elastic*. The percentage price increase is outweighed by the percentage quantity decline:

> effect of price increase on
> a product with elastic demand:
>
> $$\uparrow P \times Q_D \downarrow = TR \downarrow$$

The opposite is true for a price cut. When demand is elastic, a cut in price increases total revenues:

> effect of price cut on a product
> with elastic demand:
>
> $$\downarrow P \times Q_D \uparrow = TR \uparrow$$

When demand is inelastic, a cut in price reduces total revenues:

> effect of price cut on a product
> with inelastic demand:
>
> $$\downarrow P \times Q_D \uparrow = TR \downarrow$$

Review the logic of these equations to make sure you thoroughly understand the reasoning. Having a responsive (or elastic) market is good when we are lowering price because it means that we are dramatically increasing our units sold. But that same responsiveness is unattractive as we contemplate raising prices because now it means that we are losing customers. And, of course, the reverse logic works in the inelastic market. Note that if there is unitary elasticity, total revenue is unchanged if the price changes.

With this knowledge, we can now see why reducing supply by the oil-producing countries was so effective. The demand for oil is inelastic. Restricting the quantity of oil available led to a huge increase in the price of oil—the percentage increase was larger in absolute value than the percentage decrease in the quantity of oil demanded. Hence, oil producers' total revenues went up. In contrast, a banana cartel would not be effective because the demand for bananas is elastic. A small increase in the price of bananas results in a large decrease in the quantity of bananas demanded and thus causes total revenues to fall.

The Determinants of Demand Elasticity

Elasticity of demand is a way of measuring the responsiveness of consumers' demand to changes in price. As a measure of behavior, it can be applied to individual households or to market demand as a whole. You love peaches, and you would hate to give them up. Your demand for peaches is therefore inelastic. However, not everyone is crazy about peaches; in fact, the market demand for peaches is relatively elastic. Because no two people have exactly the same preferences, reactions to price changes will be different for different people, which makes generalizations risky. Nonetheless, a few principles do seem to hold.

Availability of Substitutes

Perhaps the most obvious factor affecting demand elasticity is the availability of substitutes. Consider a number of farm stands lined up along a country road. If every stand sells fresh corn of roughly the same quality, Mom's Green Thumb will find it very difficult to charge a price much higher than the competition charges because a nearly perfect substitute is available just down the road. The demand for Mom's corn is thus likely to be very elastic: An increase in price will lead to a rapid decline in the quantity demanded of Mom's corn.

In the oil versus banana example, the demand for oil is inelastic in large measure due to the lack of substitutes. When the price of crude oil went up in the early 1970s, 130 million motor vehicles, getting an average of 12 miles per gallon and consuming over 100 billion gallons of gasoline each year, were on the road in the United States. Millions of homes were heated with oil, and industry ran on equipment that used petroleum products. When the oil-producing countries (OPEC) cut production, the price of oil rose sharply. Quantity demanded fell somewhat, but price increased over 400 percent. What makes the cases of OPEC and OBEC different is the *magnitude* of the response in the quantity demanded to a change of price.

The Importance of Being Unimportant

When an item represents a relatively small part of our total budget, we tend to pay little attention to its price. For example, if you pick up a pack of mints once in a while, you might not notice an increase in price from 25 cents to 35 cents. Yet this is a 40 percent increase in price (33.3 percent using the midpoint formula). In cases such as these, we are not likely to respond very much to changes in price and demand is likely to be inelastic.

Who Are the Elastic Smokers?

In the United States, taxes are imposed on cigarettes at the state level. As a result, there are large differences among states. As of July 1, 2010, three states had cigarette taxes in excess of $3.00 per pack: Rhode Island, Connecticut, and Washington. Seven more had rates between $2.00 and $3.00 (including the District of Columbia). Missouri had the lowest rate among the 50 states at $0.17 a pack. The following article describes a proposal to raise taxes by $1.00 per pack in the state of Washington.

We would expect an increase in the tax on cigarettes to increase their price to consumers. An interesting question from the point of view of health and tax revenue is how much a price increase lowers demand. One of the commentators in the article claims that increasing cigarette prices by 10 percent reduces youth smokers by 6–7 percent; this is an implied demand elasticity of –0.6 (6%/10%). How do you think this compares to what we would expect from adult smokers? Many people would argue that because more young people are new smokers and because they have less money than adults, their demand for cigarettes would be more elastic. On the other hand, if peer pressure favors smoking, this could lower demand elasticity for youths.

One problem that states face as they increase their cigarette taxes is that people will seek cigarette substitutes from cheaper areas. In Washington, the state pressured Indian tribes to raise the tribal tax rate on cigarettes to the overall state level. By making these substitutes to state-taxed cigarettes more expensive, the loss of customers in response to the state tax increase would be less.

Bill Aims to Raise Tax on Cigarettes

Seattle Times

OLYMPIA—If lawmakers pass a House bill raising the state cigarette tax to $2.50 a pack, Washington would be the second most expensive place in the country to buy cigarettes.

The proposed tax would raise the current $1.425 a pack by more than a dollar. The additional revenue would generate an estimated $300 million in two years for the state's health-care fund, according to bill sponsors. Proponents also say the substantial tax would deter people from smoking, saving nearly $1 billion in future health-care costs.

Eric Lindblom, manager for policy research at Campaign for Tobacco-Free Kids, said "raising cigarette prices is one of the quickest, most effective ways to reduce youth smoking."

Every time a state increases cigarette taxes by 10 percent, there is a 6 to 7 percent decrease in youth smokers, he said.

Source: Copyright 2005, Seattle Times Company. Used with permission.

The Time Dimension

When the oil-producing nations first cut output and succeeded in pushing up the price of crude oil, few substitutes were immediately available. Demand was relatively inelastic, and prices rose substantially. During the last 30 years, however, there has been some adjustment to higher oil prices. Automobiles manufactured today get on average more miles per gallon, and some drivers have cut down on their driving. Millions of home owners have insulated their homes, most people have turned down their thermostats, and some people have explored alternative energy sources.

Oil prices again rose dramatically during the weeks following Hurricane Katrina in 2005 because of the disruption to oil refineries and oil rigs. Once again, the response of demand to the resulting higher gasoline prices took place slowly over time. This time many former SUV drivers switched to hybrids.

All of this illustrates a very important point: The elasticity of demand in the short run may be very different from the elasticity of demand in the long run. In the longer run, demand is likely to become more elastic, or responsive, simply because households make adjustments over time and producers develop substitute goods.

ECONOMICS IN PRACTICE

Elasticities at a Delicatessen in the Short Run and Long Run

Frank runs a corner delicatessen and decides one Monday morning to raise the prices of his sandwiches by 10 percent. Because Frank knows a little economics, he expects that this price increase will cause him to lose some business, since demand curves slope down, but he decides to try it anyway. At the end of the day, Frank discovers that his revenue has, in fact, gone up in the sandwich department. Feeling pleased with himself, Frank hires someone to create signs showing the new prices for the sandwich department. At the end of the month, however, he discovers that sandwich revenue is way down. What is going on?

The first thing to notice about this situation is that it poses a puzzle about what happens to revenue following a price increase. Seeing a linkage between price increases (or cuts) and revenue immediately leads an economist to think about *elasticity*. We remember from earlier in the chapter that *when demand is elastic,* (that is, an *absolute value* greater than 1), *price increases reduce revenue* because a small price increase will bring a large quantity decrease, thus depressing revenue. Conversely, when demand is inelastic (that is, an absolute value less than 1), price increases do little to curb demand and revenues rise. In this case, Monday's price increase brings increases in revenue; therefore, this pattern tells us that the demand from Frank's customers appears to be inelastic. In the longer term, however, demand appears to be more elastic (revenue is down after a month). Another way to pose this puzzle is to ask why the monthly demand curve might have a different elasticity than the daily demand.

To answer that question, you need to think about what determines elasticity. The most fundamental determinant of demand elasticity is the availability of substitutes. In this case, the product we are looking at is sandwiches. At first, you might think that the substitutes for Monday's sandwich would be the same as the substitutes for the sandwiches for the rest of the month. But this is not correct. Once you are in Frank's store, planning to buy a sandwich, your demand tends to be relatively inelastic because your ability to substitute by going elsewhere or choosing a different lunch item is relatively limited. You have already come to the part of town where Frank's Delicatessen is located, and you may already have chosen chips and a beverage to go along with your sandwich. Once you know that Frank's sandwiches are expensive, you can make different plans, and this broadening of your substitute choices increases your elasticity. In general, longer-term demand curves tend to be more elastic than shorter-term curves because customers have more choices.

The graph below shows the expected relationship between long-run and short-run demand for Frank's sandwiches. Notice if you raise prices above the current level, the expected quantity change read off the short-run curve is less than that from the long-run curve.

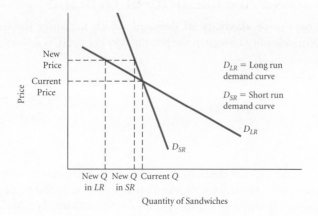

Other Important Elasticities

So far, we have been discussing price elasticity of demand, which measures the responsiveness of quantity demanded to changes in price. However, as we noted earlier, elasticity is a general concept. If B causes a change in A and we can measure the change in both, we can calculate the elasticity of A with respect to B. Let us look briefly at three other important types of elasticity.

Income Elasticity of Demand

Income elasticity of demand, which measures the responsiveness of demand to changes in income, is defined as

$$\text{income elasticity of demand} = \frac{\% \text{ change in quantity demanded}}{\% \text{ change in income}}$$

Measuring income elasticity is important for many reasons. Government policy makers spend a great deal of time and money weighing the relative merits of different policies. During the 1970s, for example, the Department of Housing and Urban Development (HUD) conducted a huge experiment in four cities to estimate the income elasticity of housing demand. In this "housing allowance demand experiment," low-income families received housing vouchers over an extended period of time and researchers watched their housing consumption for several years. Most estimates, including the ones from the HUD study, put the income elasticity of housing demand between 0.5 and 0.8. That is, a 10 percent increase in income can be expected to raise the quantity of housing demanded by a household by 5 percent to 8 percent.

Income elasticities can be positive or negative. During periods of rising income, people increase their spending on some goods (positive income elasticity) but reduce their spending on other goods (negative income elasticity). The income elasticity of demand for jewelry is positive, while the income elasticity of demand for low-quality beef is negative. As incomes rise in many low-income countries, the birth rate falls, implying a negative income elasticity of demand for children. Also, as incomes rise in most countries, the demand for education and health care rises, a positive income elasticity.

Cross-Price Elasticity of Demand

Cross-price elasticity of demand, which measures the response of quantity of one good demanded to a change in the price of another good, is defined as

$$\text{cross-price elasticity of demand} = \frac{\% \text{ change in quantity of } Y \text{ demanded}}{\% \text{ change in price of } X}$$

Like income elasticity, cross-price elasticity can be either positive or negative. A *positive* cross-price elasticity indicates that an increase in the price of X causes the demand for Y to rise. This implies that the goods are substitutes. For McDonald's, Big Macs and Chicken McNuggets are substitutes with a positive cross-price elasticity. In our earlier example, as McDonald's lowered the price of Big Macs, it saw a decline in the quantity of McNuggets sold as consumers substituted between the two meals. If cross-price elasticity turns out to be *negative*, an increase in the price of X causes a decrease in the demand for Y. This implies that the goods are complements. Hot dogs and football games are complements with a negative cross-price elasticity.

As we have already seen, knowing the cross-price elasticity can be a very important part of a company's business strategy. Sony and Toshiba recently competed in the market for high-definition DVD players: Sony's Blu-ray versus Toshiba's HD DVD. Both firms recognized that an important driver of a customer's choice of a DVD player is movie price and availability. No one wants a new high-definition player if there is nothing to watch on it or if the price of movies is expensive. Inexpensive and available movies are a key complement to new DVD players. The cross-price elasticity of movies and high-definition DVD players is strong and negative. Sony won, and some observers think that Sony's ownership of a movie studio gave it an important advantage.

Elasticity of Supply

So far, we have focused on the consumer part of the market. But elasticity also matters on the producer's side.

Elasticity of supply, which measures the response of quantity of a good supplied to a change in price of that good, is defined as

$$\text{elasticity of supply} = \frac{\%\ \text{change in quantity supplied}}{\%\ \text{change in price}}$$

elasticity of supply A measure of the response of quantity of a good supplied to a change in price of that good. Likely to be positive in output markets.

In output markets, the elasticity of supply is likely to be a positive number—that is, a higher price leads to an increase in the quantity supplied, *ceteris paribus*. (Recall our discussion of upward-sloping supply curves in the preceding two chapters.)

The elasticity of supply is a measure of how easily producers can adapt to a price increase and bring increased quantities to market. In some industries, it is relatively easy for firms to increase their output. Ballpoint pens fall into this category, as does most software that has already been developed. For these products, the elasticity of supply is very high. In the oil industry, supply is inelastic, much like demand.

In input markets, however, some interesting problems arise in looking at elasticity. Perhaps the most studied elasticity of all is the **elasticity of labor supply**, which measures the response of labor supplied to a change in the price of labor. Economists have examined household labor supply responses to government programs such as welfare, Social Security, the income tax system, need-based student aid, and unemployment insurance.

In simple terms, the elasticity of labor supply is defined as

elasticity of labor supply A measure of the response of labor supplied to a change in the price of labor.

$$\text{elasticity of labor supply} = \frac{\%\ \text{change in quantity of labor supplied}}{\%\ \text{change in the wage rate}}$$

It seems reasonable at first glance to assume that an increase in wages increases the quantity of labor supplied. That would imply an upward-sloping supply curve and a positive labor supply elasticity, but this is not necessarily so. An increase in wages makes workers better off: They can work the same number of hours and have higher incomes. One of the things workers might like to "buy" with that higher income is more leisure time. "Buying" leisure simply means working fewer hours, and the "price" of leisure is the lost wages. Thus, it is quite possible that to some groups, an increase in wages above some level will lead to a reduction in the quantity of labor supplied.

Looking Ahead

The purpose of this chapter was to convince you that measurement is important. If all we can say is that a change in one economic factor causes another to change, we cannot say whether the change is important or whether a particular policy is likely to work. The most commonly used tool of measurement is elasticity, and the term will recur as we explore economics in more depth.

We now return to the study of basic economics by looking in detail at household behavior. Recall that households *demand* goods and services in product markets but *supply* labor and savings in input or factor markets.

SUMMARY

1. *Elasticity* is a general measure of responsiveness that can be used to quantify many different relationships. If one variable *A* changes in response to changes in another variable *B*, the elasticity of *A* with respect to *B* is equal to the percentage change in *A* divided by the percentage change in *B*.

2. The slope of a demand curve is an inadequate measure of responsiveness because its value depends on the units of measurement used. For this reason, elasticities are calculated using percentages.

PRICE ELASTICITY OF DEMAND *p. 98*

3. *Price elasticity of demand* is the ratio of the percentage change in quantity demanded of a good to the percentage change in price of that good.

4. *Perfectly inelastic* demand is demand whose quantity demanded does not respond at all to changes in price; its numerical value is zero.

5. *Inelastic* demand is demand whose quantity demanded responds somewhat, but not a great deal, to changes in price; its numerical value is between zero and −1.

6. *Elastic* demand is demand in which the percentage change in quantity demanded is larger in absolute value than the percentage change in price. Its numerical value is less than −1.

7. *Unitary elasticity* of demand describes a relationship in which the percentage change in the quantity of a product demanded is the same as the percentage change in price; unitary elasticity has a numerical value of −1.

8. *Perfectly elastic* demand describes a relationship in which a small increase in the price of a product causes the quantity demanded for that product to drop to zero.

CALCULATING ELASTICITIES *p. 100*

9. If demand is elastic, a price increase will reduce the quantity demanded by a larger percentage than the percentage increase in price and total revenue ($P \times Q$) will fall. If demand is inelastic, a price increase will increase total revenue.

10. If demand is elastic, a price cut will cause quantity demanded to increase by a greater percentage than the percentage decrease in price and total revenue will rise. If demand is inelastic, a price cut will cause quantity demanded to increase by a smaller percentage than the percentage decrease in price and total revenue will fall.

THE DETERMINANTS OF DEMAND ELASTICITY *p. 107*

11. The elasticity of demand depends on (1) the availability of substitutes, (2) the importance of the item in individual budgets, and (3) the time frame in question.

OTHER IMPORTANT ELASTICITIES *p. 109*

12. There are several important elasticities. *Income elasticity of demand* measures the responsiveness of the quantity demanded with respect to changes in income. *Cross-price elasticity of demand* measures the response of the quantity of one good demanded to a change in the price of another good. *Elasticity of supply* measures the response of the quantity of a good supplied to a change in the price of that good. The *elasticity of labor supply* measures the response of the quantity of labor supplied to a change in the price of labor.

REVIEW TERMS AND CONCEPTS

cross-price elasticity of demand, *p. 110*

elastic demand, *p. 100*

elasticity, *p. 97*

elasticity of labor supply, *p. 111*

elasticity of supply, *p. 111*

income elasticity of demand, *p. 110*

inelastic demand, *p. 100*

midpoint formula, *p. 102*

perfectly elastic demand, *p. 99*

perfectly inelastic demand, *p. 99*

price elasticity of demand, *p. 99*

unitary elasticity, *p. 100*

PROBLEMS

All problems are available on www.myeconlab.com

1. Fill in the missing amounts in the following table:

	% CHANGE IN PRICE	% CHANGE IN QUANTITY	ELASTICITY
Demand for Ben & Jerry's Ice Cream	+10%	−12%	**a.**
Demand for beer at San Francisco 49ers football games	−20%	**b.**	−.5
Demand for Broadway theater tickets in New York	**c.**	−15%	−1.0
Supply of chickens	+10%	**d.**	+1.2
Supply of beef cattle	−15%	−10%	**e.**

2. Use the table in the preceding problem to defend your answers to the following questions:
   a. Would you recommend that Ben & Jerry's move forward with a plan to raise prices if the company's only goal is to increase revenues?
   b. Would you recommend that beer stands cut prices to increase revenues at 49ers football games next year?

3. Using the midpoint formula, calculate elasticity for each of the following changes in demand by a household.

	P₁	P₂	Q₁	Q₂
Demand for:				
a. Long-distance telephone service	$0.25 per min.	$0.15 per min.	300 min. per month	400 min. per month
b. Orange juice	1.49 per qt	1.89 per qt	14 qt per month	12 qt per month
c. Big Macs	2.89	1.00	3 per week	6 per week
d. Cooked shrimp	$9 per lb	$12 per lb	2 lb per month	1.5 lb per month

4. A sporting goods store has estimated the demand curve for a popular brand of running shoes as a function of price. Use the diagram to answer the questions that follow.

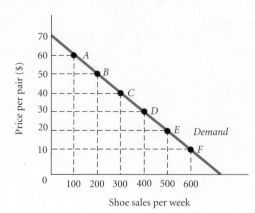

Shoe sales per week

   a. Calculate demand elasticity using the midpoint formula between points *A* and *B*, between points *C* and *D*, and between points *E* and *F*.

   b. If the store currently charges a price of $50, then increases that price to $60, what happens to total revenue from shoe sales (calculate P × Q before and after the price change)? Repeat the exercise for initial prices being decreased to $40 and $20, respectively.
   c. Explain why the answers to a. can be used to predict the answers to b.

5. For each of the following scenarios, decide whether you agree or disagree and explain your answer.
   a. If the elasticity of demand for cocaine is −.2 and the Drug Enforcement Administration succeeds in reducing supply substantially, causing the street price of the drug to rise by 50%, buyers will spend less on cocaine.
   b. Every year Christmas tree vendors bring tens of thousands of trees from the forests of New England to New York City and Boston. During the last two years, the market has been very competitive; as a result, price has fallen by 10 percent. If the price elasticity of demand was −1.3, vendors would lose revenues altogether as a result of the price decline.
   c. If the demand for a good has unitary elasticity, or elasticity is −1, it is always true that an increase in its price will lead to more revenues for sellers taken as a whole.

6. For the following statements, decide whether you agree or disagree and explain your answer.
   a. The demand curve pictured here is elastic.

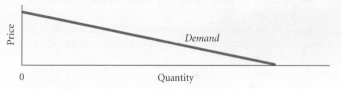

   b. If supply were to increase slightly in the following diagram, prices would fall and firms would earn less revenue.

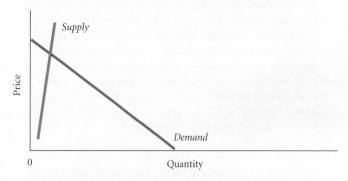

7. Taxicab fares in most cities are regulated. Several years ago taxicab drivers in Boston obtained permission to raise their fares 10 percent, and they anticipated that revenues would increase by about 10 percent as a result. They were disappointed, however. When the commissioner granted the 10 percent increase, revenues increased by only about 5 percent. What can you infer

about the elasticity of demand for taxicab rides? What were taxicab drivers assuming about the elasticity of demand?

*8. Studies have fixed the short-run price elasticity of demand for gasoline at the pump at −0.20. Suppose that international hostilities lead to a sudden cutoff of crude oil supplies. As a result, U.S. supplies of refined gasoline drop 10 percent.
   a. If gasoline were selling for $2.60 per gallon before the cutoff, how much of a price increase would you expect to see in the coming months?
   b. Suppose that the government imposes a price ceiling on gas at $2.60 per gallon. How would the relationship between consumers and gas station owners change?

9. Prior to 2005, it seemed like house prices always rose and never fell. When the demand for housing increases, prices in the housing market rise but not always by very much. For prices to rise substantially, the supply of housing must be relatively inelastic. That is, if the quantity supplied increases rapidly whenever house prices rise, price increases will remain small. Many have suggested government policies to increase the elasticity of supply. What specific policies might hold prices down when demand increases? Explain.

10. For each of the following statements, state the relevant elasticity and state what its value should be (negative, positive, greater than one, zero, and so on).
   a. The supply of labor is inelastic but slightly backward-bending.
   b. The demand for BMWs in an area increases during times of rising incomes just slightly faster than income rises.
   c. The demand for lobsters falls when lobster prices rise (*ceteris paribus*), but the revenue received by restaurants from the sale of lobsters stays the same.
   d. Demand for many goods rise when the price of substitutes rise.
   e. Land for housing development near Youngstown, Ohio, is in plentiful supply. At the current price, there is essentially an infinite supply.

11. [Related to the *Economics in Practice* on p. 108] A number of towns in the United States have begun charging their residents for garbage pickup based on the number of garbage cans filled per week. The town of Chase decided to increase its per-can price from 10 cents to 20 cents per week. In the first week, Chase found that the number of cans that were brought to the curb fell from 550 to 525 (although the city workers complained that the cans were heavier). The town economist ran the numbers, informed the mayor that the demand for disposal was inelastic, and recommended that the city raise the price more to maximize town revenue from the program. Six months later, at a price of 30 cents per can, the number of cans has fallen to 125 and town revenues are down. What might have happened?

12. [Related to the *Economics in Practice* on p. 109] At Frank's Delicatessen, Frank noticed that the elasticity of customers differed in the short and longer term. Frank also noticed that his increase in the price of sandwiches had other effects on his store. In particular, the number of sodas sold declined while the number of yogurts sold went up. How might you explain this pattern?

*Note: Problems marked with an asterisk are more challenging.

13. Describe what will happen to total revenue in the following situations.
   a. Price decreases and demand is elastic.
   b. Price decreases and demand is inelastic.
   c. Price increases and demand is elastic.
   d. Price increases and demand is inelastic.
   e. Price increases and demand is unitary elastic.
   f. Price decreases and demand is perfectly inelastic.
   g. Price increases and demand is perfectly elastic.

14. The cross-price elasticity values for three sets of products are listed in the table below. What can you conclude about the relationships between each of these sets of products?

	PRODUCTS A AND B	PRODUCTS C AND D	PRODUCTS E AND F
Cross-price elasticity	−8.7	+5.5	0.0

15. Income elasticity of demand measures the responsiveness of demand to changes in income. Explain what is happening to demand and what kind of good is being represented in the following situations.
   a. Income is rising, and income elasticity of demand is positive.
   b. Income is rising, and income elasticity of demand is negative.

16. Using the midpoint formula and the following graph, calculate the price elasticity of demand and the price elasticity of supply when the price changes from $4 to $9 and when the price changes from $9 to $15.

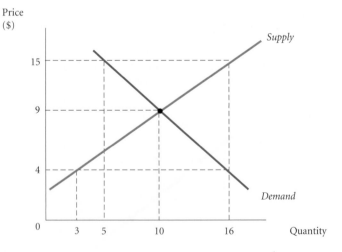

17. Use the following total revenue graph to identify which sections of the total revenue curve reflect elastic demand, inelastic demand, and unitary elastic demand. Explain your answers.

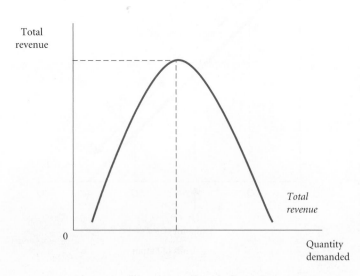

18. For each of the following products, explain whether demand is likely to be elastic or inelastic.
   a. Cigarettes
   b. Tacos
   c. Gasoline
   d. Milk
   e. Honda Accord automobiles
   f. Newspapers

CHAPTER 5 APPENDIX

Point Elasticity (Optional)

Two different elasticities were calculated along the demand curve in Figure 5.3 on p. 104. Between points A and B, we discovered that Herb's demand for lunches in the fancy dining room was very elastic: A price decline of only 10.5 percent resulted in his eating 66.7 percent more lunches in the dining room (elasticity = −6.4). Between points C and D, however, on the same demand curve, we discovered that his demand for meals was very inelastic: A price decline of 40 percent resulted in only a modest increase in lunches consumed of 11.76 percent (elasticity = −0.294).

Now consider the straight-line demand curve in Figure 5A.1. We can write an expression for elasticity at point C as follows:

$$\text{elasticity} = \frac{\%\Delta Q}{\%\Delta P} = \frac{\frac{\Delta Q}{Q} \cdot 100}{\frac{\Delta P}{P} \cdot 100} = \frac{\frac{\Delta Q}{Q_1}}{\frac{\Delta P}{P_1}} = \boxed{\frac{\Delta Q}{\Delta P} \cdot \frac{P_1}{Q_1}}$$

$\Delta Q/\Delta P$ is the *reciprocal* of the slope of the curve. Slope in the diagram is constant along the curve, and it is negative. To calculate the reciprocal of the slope to plug into the previous elasticity equation, we take $Q_1 B$, or M_1, and divide by *minus* the length of line segment CQ_1. Thus,

$$\frac{\Delta Q}{\Delta P} = \frac{M_1}{CQ_1}$$

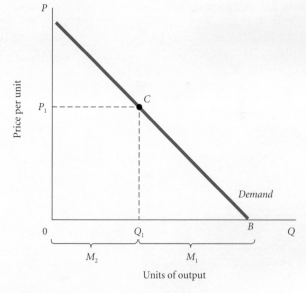

▲ FIGURE 5A.1 Elasticity at a Point Along a Demand Curve

Because the length of CQ_1 is equal to P_1, we can write

$$\frac{\Delta Q}{\Delta P} = \frac{M_1}{P_1}$$

By substituting, we get

$$\text{elasticity} = \frac{M_1}{P_1} \cdot \frac{P_1}{Q_1} = \frac{M_1}{P_1} \cdot \frac{P_1}{M_2} = \boxed{\frac{M_1}{M_2}}$$

(The second equal sign uses the fact that Q_1 equals M_2 in Figure 5A.1.)

Elasticity at point C is simply the ratio of line segment M_1 to line segment M_2. It is easy to see that if we had chosen a point to the left of Q_1, M_1 would have been larger and M_2 would have been smaller, indicating a higher elasticity. If we had chosen a point to the right of Q_1, M_1 would have been smaller and M_2 would have been larger, indicating a lower elasticity.

In Figure 5A.2, you can see that elasticity is unitary (equal to -1) at the midpoint of the demand curve, Q_3. At points to the right, such as Q_2, segment Q_2C (M_1 from Figure 5A.1) is smaller than segment $0Q_1$ (M_2 from Figure 5A.1). This means that the absolute size of the ratio is *less than 1* and that demand is *inelastic* at point A. At points to the left, such as Q_1, segment Q_1C (M_1) is larger than segment $0Q_1$ (M_2). This means that the absolute size of the ratio is *greater than 1* and that demand is elastic at point B.

Compare the results here with the results using the midpoint formula for elasticity for Herb.

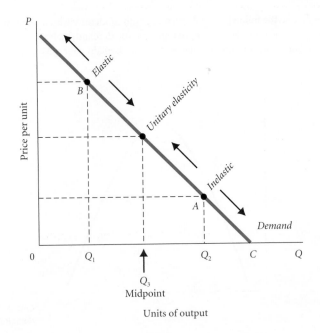

▲ **FIGURE 5A.2** **Point Elasticity Changes Along a Demand Curve**

The Market System
Choices Made by Households and Firms

Now that we have discussed the basic forces of supply and demand, we can explore the underlying behavior of the two fundamental decision-making units in the economy: households and firms.

Figure II.1 presents a diagram of a simple competitive economy. The figure is an expanded version of the circular flow diagram first presented in Figure 3.1 on p. 49. It is designed to guide you through Part II (Chapters 6 through 12) of this book. You will see the

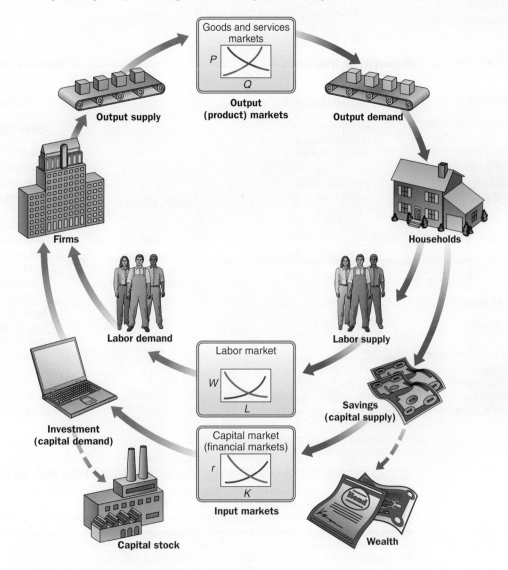

▲ **FIGURE II.1 Firm and Household Decisions**

Households demand in output markets and supply labor and capital in input markets. To simplify our analysis, we have not included the government and international sectors in this circular flow diagram. These topics will be discussed in detail later.

big picture more clearly if you follow this diagram closely as you work your way through this part of the book.

Recall that households and firms interact in two kinds of markets: output (product) markets, shown at the top of Figure II.1, and input (factor) markets, shown at the bottom. Households *demand* outputs and *supply* inputs. In contrast, firms *supply* outputs and *demand* inputs. Chapter 6 explores the behavior of households, focusing first on household demand for outputs and then on household supply in labor and capital markets.

The remaining chapters in Part II focus on firms and the interaction between firms and households. Chapters 7 through 9 analyze the behavior of firms in output markets in both the short run and the long run. Chapter 10 focuses on the behavior of firms in input markets in general, especially the labor and land markets. Chapter 11 discusses the capital market in more detail. Chapter 12 puts all the pieces together and analyzes the functioning of a complete market system. Following Chapter 12, Part III of the book relaxes many assumptions and analyzes market imperfections as well as the potential for and pitfalls of government involvement in the economy. The plan for Chapters 6 through 19 is outlined in Figure II.2.

Recall that throughout this book, all diagrams that describe the behavior of households are drawn or highlighted in *blue*. All diagrams that describe the behavior of firms are drawn or highlighted in *red*. Look carefully at the supply and demand diagrams in Figure II.1; notice that in both the labor and capital markets, the supply curves are blue. The reason is that labor and capital are supplied by households. The demand curves for labor and capital are red because firms demand these inputs for production.

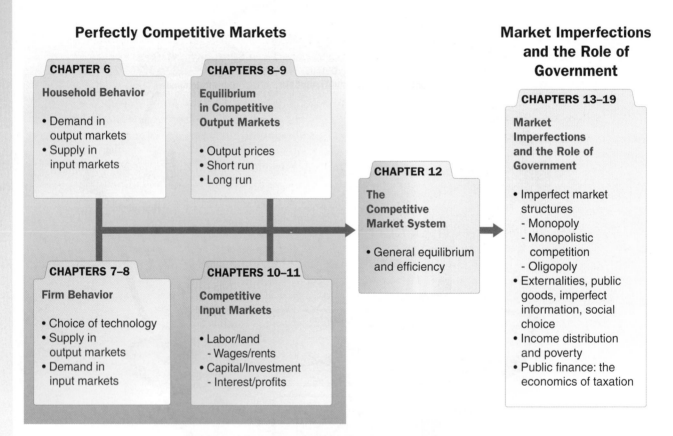

Perfectly Competitive Markets

CHAPTER 6

Household Behavior

- Demand in output markets
- Supply in input markets

CHAPTERS 8–9

Equilibrium in Competitive Output Markets

- Output prices
- Short run
- Long run

CHAPTERS 7–8

Firm Behavior

- Choice of technology
- Supply in output markets
- Demand in input markets

CHAPTERS 10–11

Competitive Input Markets

- Labor/land
  - Wages/rents
- Capital/Investment
  - Interest/profits

CHAPTER 12

The Competitive Market System

- General equilibrium and efficiency

Market Imperfections and the Role of Government

CHAPTERS 13–19

Market Imperfections and the Role of Government

- Imperfect market structures
  - Monopoly
  - Monopolistic competition
  - Oligopoly
- Externalities, public goods, imperfect information, social choice
- Income distribution and poverty
- Public finance: the economics of taxation

▲ **FIGURE II.2 Understanding the Microeconomy and the Role of Government**
To understand how the economy works, it helps to build from the ground up. We start in Chapters 6–8 with an overview of **household** and **firm** decision making in simple perfectly competitive markets. In Chapters 9–11, we see how firms and households interact in **output markets** (product markets) and **input markets** (labor/land and capital) to determine prices, wages, and profits. Once we have a picture of how a simple perfectly competitive economy works, we begin to relax assumptions. Chapter 12 is a pivotal chapter that links perfectly competitive markets with a discussion of market imperfections and the role of government. In Chapters 13–19, we cover the three noncompetitive market structures (monopoly, monopolistic competition, and oligopoly), externalities, public goods, uncertainty and asymmetric information, and income distribution as well as taxation and government finance.

In Figure II.1, much of the detail of the real world is stripped away just as it is on a highway map. A map is a highly simplified version of reality, but it is a very useful tool when you need to know where you are. Figure II.1 is intended to serve as a map to help you understand basic market forces before we add more complicated market structures and government.

Before we proceed with our discussion of household choice, we need to make a few basic assumptions. These assumptions pertain to Chapters 6 through 12.

We first assume that households and firms possess all the information they need to make market choices. Specifically, we assume that households possess knowledge of the qualities and prices of everything available in the market. Firms know all that there is to know about wage rates, capital costs, and output prices. This assumption is often called the assumption of **perfect knowledge**.

The next assumption is **perfect competition**. Perfect competition is a precisely defined form of industry structure. (The word *perfect* here does not refer to virtue. It simply means "total" or "complete.") In a perfectly competitive industry, no single firm has control over prices. That is, no single firm is large enough to affect the market price of its product or the prices of the inputs that it buys. This follows from two characteristics of competitive industries. First, a competitive industry is composed of many firms, each one small relative to the size of the industry. Second, every firm in a perfectly competitive industry produces exactly the same product; the output of one firm cannot be distinguished from the output of the others. Products in a perfectly competitive industry are said to be **homogeneous**.

These characteristics limit the decisions open to competitive firms and simplify the analysis of competitive behavior. Because all firms in a perfectly competitive industry produce virtually identical products and because each firm is small relative to the market, perfectly competitive firms have no control over the prices at which they sell their output. By taking prices as a given, each firm can decide only how much output to produce and how to produce it.

Consider agriculture, the classic example of a perfectly competitive industry. A wheat farmer in South Dakota has absolutely no control over the price of wheat. Prices are determined not by the individual farmers, but by the interaction of many suppliers and many demanders. The only decisions left to the wheat farmer are how much wheat to plant and when and how to produce the crop.

We finally assume that each household is small relative to the size of the market. Households face a set of product prices that they individually cannot control. Prices again are set by the interaction of many suppliers and many demanders.

By the end of Chapter 10, we will have a complete picture of an economy, but it will be based on this set of fairly restrictive assumptions. At first, this may seem unrealistic to you, but keep the following in mind. Much of the economic analysis in the chapters that follow applies to all forms of market structure. Indeed, much of the power of economic reasoning is that it is quite general. As we continue in microeconomics, in Chapters 13 and 14, we will define and explore several different kinds of market organization and structure, including monopoly, oligopoly, and monopolistic competition. Because monopolists, oligopolists, monopolistic competitors, and perfect competitors share the objective of maximizing profits, it should not be surprising that their behavior is in many ways similar. We focus here on perfect competition because many of these basic principles are easier to learn using the simplest of cases.

perfect knowledge The assumption that households possess a knowledge of the qualities and prices of everything available in the market and that firms have all available information concerning wage rates, capital costs, and output prices.

perfect competition An industry structure in which there are many firms, each being small relative to the industry and producing virtually identical products, and in which no firm is large enough to have any control over prices.

homogeneous products Undifferentiated outputs; products that are identical to or indistinguishable from one another.

Household Behavior and Consumer Choice

Every day people in a market economy make decisions. Some of those decisions involve the products they plan to buy: Should you buy a Coke for lunch, a bottle of tea, or just drink water? Should you purchase a laptop computer or stick with your old desktop? Some decisions are about the labor market: Should you continue your schooling or go to work instead? If you do start working, how much should you work? Should you work more when you get a raise or just take it easy? Many

decisions involve a time element. If you decide to buy a laptop, you may have to use your savings or borrow money. That will leave you with fewer choices about what you can buy in the future. On the other hand, the laptop itself is an investment.

To many people, the decisions listed in the previous paragraph seem very different from one another. As you will see in this chapter, however, from an economics perspective, these decisions have a great deal in common. In this chapter, we will develop a set of principles that can be used to understand decisions in the product market and the labor market—decisions for today and for the future.

As you read this chapter, you might want to think about some of the following questions, questions that you will be able to answer by chapter's end. Baseball, even when it was more popular than it is today, was never played year-round. Indeed, no professional sport has a year-round season. Is this break necessary to give the athletes a rest, or is there something about household choice that helps explain this pattern? When the price of gasoline rises, people drive less, but one study suggests that they also switch from brand name products to generics or store brands.[1] Why might this be? Studying household choice will help you understand many decisions that underpin our market economy.

A constant theme that will run through the analysis is the idea of *constrained choice*. That is, the decisions that we make we make under constraints that exist in the marketplace. Household consumption choices are constrained by income, wealth, and existing prices. Household decisions about labor supply and job choice are clearly constrained by the availability of jobs. This was on everyone's minds when the number of unemployed reached 15 million and the unemployment rate hovered at about 10 percent during the 2009–2010 period. In addition, the choices we make in the workforce are constrained by the existing structure of market wages.

Household Choice in Output Markets

Every household must make three basic decisions:

1. How much of each product, or output, to demand
2. How much labor to supply
3. How much to spend today and how much to save for the future

[1] Dora Gicheva, Justine Hastings, and Sofia Villas-Boas, "Revisiting the Income Effect: Gasoline Prices and Grocery Purchases," NBER Working Paper No. 13614, October 2007.

As we begin our look at demand in output markets, you must keep in mind that the choices underlying the demand curve are only part of the larger household choice problem. Closely related decisions about how much to work and how much to save are equally important and must be made simultaneously with output–demand decisions.

The Determinants of Household Demand

As we saw in Chapter 3, several factors influence the quantity of a given good or service demanded by a single household:

- The price of the product
- The income available to the household
- The household's amount of accumulated wealth
- The prices of other products available to the household
- The household's tastes and preferences
- The household's expectations about future income, wealth, and prices

Recall that demand schedules and demand curves express the relationship between quantity demanded and price, *ceteris paribus*. A change in price leads to a movement along a demand curve. Changes in income, in other prices, or in preferences shift demand curves to the left or right. We refer to these shifts as "changes in demand." However, the interrelationship among these variables is more complex than the simple exposition in Chapter 3 might lead you to believe.

The Budget Constraint

Before we examine the household choice process, we need to discuss what choices are open and not open to households. If you look carefully at the list of items that influence household demand, you will see that the first four actually define the set of options available. Information on household income and wealth, together with information on product prices, makes it possible to distinguish those combinations of goods and services that are affordable from those that are not.[2]

budget constraint The limits imposed on household choices by income, wealth, and product prices.

Income, wealth, and prices thus define what we call household **budget constraint**. The budget constraint facing any household results primarily from limits imposed externally by one or more markets. In competitive markets, for example, households cannot control prices; they must buy goods and services at market-determined prices. A household has some control over its income: Its members can choose whether to work, and they can sometimes decide how many hours to work and how many jobs to hold. However, constraints exist in the labor market too. The amount that household members are paid is limited by current market wage rates. Whether they can get a job is determined by the availability of jobs.

Although income does depend, at least in part, on the choices that households make, we will treat it as a given for now. Later in this chapter, we will relax this assumption and explore labor supply choices in more detail.

The income, wealth, and price constraints that surround choice are best illustrated with an example. Consider Barbara, a recent graduate of a midwestern university who takes a job as an account manager at a public relations firm. Let us assume that she receives a salary of $1,000 per month (after taxes) and that she has no wealth and no credit. Barbara's monthly expenditures are limited to her flow of income. Table 6.1 summarizes some of the choices open to her.

TABLE 6.1	Possible Budget Choices of a Person Earning $1,000 per Month after Taxes				
Option	Monthly Rent	Food	Other Expenses	Total	Available?
A	$ 400	$250	$350	$1,000	Yes
B	600	200	200	1,000	Yes
C	700	150	150	1,000	Yes
D	1,000	100	100	1,200	No

---

[2] Remember that we drew the distinction between income and wealth in Chapter 3. *Income* is the sum of household earnings within a given period; it is a flow variable. In contrast, *wealth* is a stock variable; it is what a household owns minus what it owes at a given point in time.

A careful search of the housing market reveals four vacant apartments. The least expensive is a one-room studio with a small kitchenette that rents for $400 per month, including utilities (option A). If she lived there, Barbara could afford to spend $250 per month on food and still have $350 left over for other things.

About four blocks away is a one-bedroom apartment with wall-to-wall carpeting and a larger kitchen. It has more space, but the rent is $600, including utilities. If Barbara took this apartment, she might cut her food expenditures by $50 per month and have only $200 per month left for everything else.

In the same building as the one-bedroom apartment is an identical unit on the top floor of the building with a balcony facing west toward the sunset. The balcony and view add $100 to the monthly rent. To live there, Barbara would be left with only $300 to split between food and other expenses.

Just because she was curious, Barbara looked at a town house in the suburbs that was renting for $1,000 per month. Obviously, unless she could get along without eating or doing anything else that cost money, she could not afford it. The combination of the town house and any amount of food is outside her budget constraint.

Notice that we have used the information that we have on income and prices to identify different combinations of housing, food, and other items that are available to a single-person household with an income of $1,000 per month. We have said nothing about the process of choosing. Instead, we have carved out what is called a **choice set** or **opportunity set**, the set of options that is defined and limited by Barbara's budget constraint.

choice set *or* opportunity set The set of options that is defined and limited by a budget constraint.

Preferences, Tastes, Trade-Offs, and Opportunity Cost So far, we have identified only the combinations of goods and services that are and are not available to Barbara. Within the constraints imposed by limited incomes and fixed prices, however, households are free to choose what they will and will not buy. Their ultimate choices are governed by their individual preferences and tastes.

It will help you to think of the household choice process as a process of allocating income over a large number of available goods and services. Final demand of a household for any single product is just one of many outcomes that result from the decision-making process. Think, for example, of a demand curve that shows a household's reaction to a drop in the price of air travel. During certain periods when people travel less frequently, special fares flood the market and many people decide to take trips that they otherwise would not have taken. However, if you live in Florida and decide to spend $400 to visit your mother in Nashville, you cannot spend that $400 on new clothes, dinners at restaurants, or a new set of tires.

A change in the price of a single good changes the constraints within which households choose, and this may change the entire allocation of income. Demand for some goods and services may rise while demand for others falls. A complicated set of trade-offs lies behind the shape and position of a household demand curve for a single good. Whenever a household makes a choice, it is weighing the good or service that it chooses against all the other things that the same money could buy.

Consider again our young account manager and her options listed in Table 6.1. If she hates to cook, likes to eat at restaurants, and goes out three nights a week, she will probably trade off some housing for dinners out and money to spend on clothes and other things. She will probably rent the studio for $400. She may, however, love to spend long evenings at home reading, listening to classical music, and sipping tea while watching the sunset. In that case, she will probably trade off some restaurant meals, evenings out, and travel expenses for the added comfort of the larger apartment with the balcony and the view. As long as a household faces a limited budget—and all households ultimately do—the real cost of any good or service is the value of the other goods and services that could have been purchased with the same amount of money. The real cost of a good or service is its opportunity cost, and opportunity cost is determined by relative prices.

The Budget Constraint More Formally Ann and Tom are struggling graduate students in economics at the University of Virginia. Their tuition is paid by graduate fellowships. They live as resident advisers in a first-year dormitory, in return for which they receive an apartment and meals. Their fellowships also give them $200 each month to cover all their other expenses. To simplify things, let us assume that Ann and Tom spend their money on only two things: meals at a local Thai restaurant and nights at a local jazz club, The Hungry Ear. Thai meals go for a fixed price of $20 per couple. Two tickets to the jazz club, including espresso, are $10.

As Figure 6.1 shows, we can graphically depict the choices that are available to our dynamic duo. The axes measure the *quantities* of the two goods that Ann and Tom buy. The horizontal axis

▶ **FIGURE 6.1 Budget Constraint and Opportunity Set for Ann and Tom**

A budget constraint separates those combinations of goods and services that are available, given limited income, from those that are not. The available combinations make up the opportunity set.

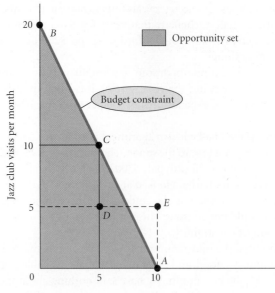

measures the number of Thai meals consumed per month, and the vertical axis measures the number of trips to The Hungry Ear. (Note that price is not on the vertical axis here.) Every point in the space between the axes represents some combination of Thai meals and nights at the jazz club. The question is this: Which of these points can Ann and Tom purchase with a fixed budget of $200 per month? That is, which points are in the opportunity set and which are not?

One possibility is that the students in the dorm are driving Ann and Tom crazy. The two grad students want to avoid the dining hall at all costs. Thus, they might decide to spend all their money on Thai food and none of it on jazz. This decision would be represented by a point *on* the horizontal axis because all the points on that axis are points at which Ann and Tom make no jazz club visits. How many meals can Ann and Tom afford? The answer is simple: When income is $200 and the price of Thai meals is $20, they can afford $200 ÷ $20 = 10 meals. This point is labeled *A* on the budget constraint in Figure 6.1.

Another possibility is that general exams are coming up and Ann and Tom decide to relax at The Hungry Ear to relieve stress. Suppose they choose to spend all their money on jazz and none of it on Thai food. This decision would be represented by a point *on* the vertical axis because all the points on this axis are points at which Ann and Tom eat no Thai meals. How many jazz club visits can they afford? Again, the answer is simple: With an income of $200 and with the price of jazz/espresso at $10, they can go to The Hungry Ear $200 ÷ $10 = 20 times. This is the point labeled *B* in Figure 6.1. The line connecting points *A* and *B* is Ann and Tom's budget constraint.

What about all the points between *A* and *B* on the budget constraint? Starting from point *B*, suppose Ann and Tom give up trips to the jazz club to buy more Thai meals. Each additional Thai meal "costs" two trips to The Hungry Ear. The opportunity cost of a Thai meal is two jazz club trips.

Point *C* on the budget constraint represents a compromise. Here Ann and Tom go to the club 10 times and eat at the Thai restaurant 5 times. To verify that point *C* is on the budget constraint, price it out: 10 jazz club trips cost a total of $10 × 10 = $100, and 5 Thai meals cost a total of $20 × 5 = $100. The total is $100 + $100 = $200.

The budget constraint divides all the points between the axes into two groups: those that can be purchased for $200 or less (the opportunity set) and those that are unavailable. Point *D* on the diagram costs less than $200; point *E* costs more than $200. (Verify that this is true.) The opportunity set is the shaded area in Figure 6.1.

Clearly, both prices and incomes affect the size of a household's opportunity set. If a price or a set of prices falls but income stays the same, the opportunity set gets bigger and the household is better off. If we define **real income** as the set of opportunities to purchase real goods and services, "real income" will have gone up in this case even if the household's money income has not. A consumer's opportunity set expands as the result of a price decrease. On the other hand, when money income increases and prices go up even more, we say that the household's "real income" has fallen.

The concept of real income is very important in macroeconomics, which is concerned with measuring real output and the price level.

real income The set of opportunities to purchase real goods and services available to a household as determined by prices and money income.

The Equation of the Budget Constraint

Yet another way to look at the budget constraint is to write the consumer's problem as an equation. In the previous example, the constraint is that total expenditure on Thai meals plus total expenditure on jazz club visits must be less than or equal to Ann and Tom's income. Total expenditure on Thai meals is equal to the *price* of Thai meals times the number, or *quantity*, of meals consumed. Total expenditure on jazz club visits is equal to the *price* of a visit times the number, or *quantity*, of visits. That is,

$$\$20 \times \text{Thai meals} + \$10 \times \text{jazz visits} \leq \$200$$

If we let X represent the number of Thai meals and we let Y represent the number of jazz club visits and we assume that Ann and Tom spend their entire income on either X or Y, this can be written as follows:

$$20X + 10Y = \$200$$

This is the equation of the budget constraint—the line connecting points A and B in Figure 6.1. Notice that when Ann and Tom spend nothing at the jazz club, $Y = 0$. When you plug $Y = 0$ into the equation of the budget constraint, $20X = 200$ and $X = 10$. Since X is the number of Thai meals, Ann and Tom eat Thai food 10 times. Similarly, when $X = 0$, you can solve for Y, which equals 20. When Ann and Tom eat no Thai food, they can go to the jazz club 20 times.

In general, the budget constraint can be written

$$P_X X + P_Y Y = I,$$

where P_X = the price of X, X = the quantity of X consumed, P_Y = the price of Y, Y = the quantity of Y consumed, and I = household income.[3]

Budget Constraints Change When Prices Rise or Fall Now suppose the Thai restaurant is offering two-for-one certificates good during the month of November. In effect, this means that the price of Thai meals drops to $10 for Ann and Tom. How would the budget constraint in Figure 6.1 change?

First, point B would not change. If Ann and Tom spend all their money on jazz, the price of Thai meals is irrelevant. Ann and Tom can still afford only 20 trips to the jazz club. What has changed is point A, which moves to point A' in Figure 6.2. At the new lower price of $10, if Ann and Tom spent all their money on Thai meals, they could buy twice as many, $200 \div \$10 = 20$. The budget constraint *swivels*, as shown in Figure 6.2.

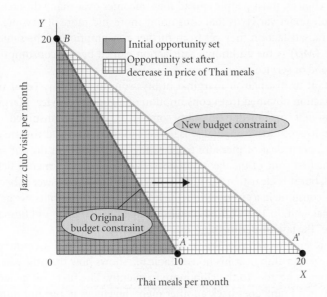

◀ **FIGURE 6.2 The Effect of a Decrease in Price on Ann and Tom's Budget Constraint**

When the price of a good decreases, the budget constraint swivels to the right, increasing the opportunities available and expanding choice.

[3] You can calculate the slope of the budget constraint as $-P_X/P_Y$, the ratio of the price of X to the price of Y. This gives the trade-off that consumers face. In the example, $-P_X/P_Y = -2$, meaning to get another Thai meal, Ann and Tom must give up two trips to the jazz club.

The new, flatter budget constraint reflects the new trade-off between Thai meals and Hungry Ear visits. Now after the price of Thai meals drops to $10, the opportunity cost of a Thai meal is only one jazz club visit. The opportunity set has expanded because at the lower price, more combinations of Thai meals and jazz are available.

Figure 6.2 thus illustrates a very important point. When the price of a single good changes, more than just the quantity demanded of that good may be affected. The household now faces an entirely different problem with regard to choice—the opportunity set has expanded. At the same income of $200, the new lower price means that Ann and Tom might choose more Thai meals, more jazz club visits, or more of both. They are clearly better off. The budget constraint is defined by income, wealth, and prices. Within those limits, households are free to choose, and the household's ultimate choice depends on its own likes and dislikes.

Notice that when the price of meals falls to $10, the equation of the budget constraint changes to $10X + 10Y = 200$, which is the equation of the line connecting points A' and B in Figure 6.2.

The range of goods and services available in a modern society is as vast as consumer tastes are variable, and this makes any generalization about the household choice process risky. Nonetheless, the theory of household behavior that follows is an attempt to derive some logical propositions about the way households make choices.

The Basis of Choice: Utility

Somehow, from the millions of things that are available, each of us manages to sort out a set of goods and services to buy. When we make our choices, we make specific judgments about the relative worth of things that are very different.

During the nineteenth century, the weighing of values was formalized into a concept called utility. Whether one item is preferable to another depends on how much **utility**, or satisfaction, it yields relative to its alternatives. How do we decide on the relative worth of a new puppy or a stereo? a trip to the mountains or a weekend in New York City? working or not working? As we make our choices, we are effectively weighing the utilities we would receive from all the possible available goods.

Certain problems are implicit in the concept of utility. First, it is impossible to measure utility. Second, it is impossible to compare the utilities of different people—that is, we cannot say whether person A or person B has a higher level of utility. Despite these problems, however, the idea of utility helps us better understand the process of choice.

Diminishing Marginal Utility

In making their choices, most people spread their incomes over many different kinds of goods. One reason people prefer variety is that consuming more and more of any one good reduces the marginal, or extra, satisfaction they get from further consumption of the same good. Formally, **marginal utility (MU)** is the additional satisfaction gained by the consumption or use of *one more* unit of a good or service.

It is important to distinguish marginal utility from total utility. **Total utility** is the total amount of satisfaction obtained from consumption of a good or service. Marginal utility comes only from the *last unit* consumed; total utility comes from *all* units consumed.

Suppose you live next to a store that sells homemade ice cream that you are crazy about. Even though you get a great deal of pleasure from eating ice cream, you do not spend your entire income on it. The first cone of the day tastes heavenly. The second is merely delicious. The third is still very good, but it is clear that the glow is fading. Why? The answer is because the more of any one good we consume in a given period, the less satisfaction, or utility, we get from each additional, or marginal, unit. In 1890, Alfred Marshall called this "familiar and fundamental tendency of human nature" the **law of diminishing marginal utility**.

Consider this simple example. Frank loves country music, and a country band is playing seven nights a week at a club near his house. Table 6.2 shows how the utility he derives from the band might change as he goes to the club more frequently. The first visit generates 12 "utils," or units of utility. When Frank goes back another night, he enjoys it, but not quite as much as the first night. The second night by itself yields 10 additional utils. *Marginal utility* is 10, while the *total utility* derived from two nights at the club is 22. Three nights per week at the club provide 28 total utils; the marginal utility of the third night is 6 because total utility rose from 22 to 28. Figure 6.3 graphs total and marginal utility using the data in Table 6.2. Total utility increases up

utility The satisfaction a product yields.

marginal utility (MU) The additional satisfaction gained by the consumption or use of *one more* unit of a good or service.

total utility The total amount of satisfaction obtained from consumption of a good or service.

law of diminishing marginal utility The more of any one good consumed in a given period, the less satisfaction (utility) generated by consuming each additional (marginal) unit of the same good.

TABLE 6.2	Total Utility and Marginal Utility of Trips to the Club Per Week	
Trips to Club	Total Utility	Marginal Utility
1	12	12
2	22	10
3	28	6
4	32	4
5	34	2
6	34	0

through Frank's fifth trip to the club but levels off on the sixth night. Marginal utility, which has declined from the beginning, is now at zero.

Diminishing marginal utility helps explain the reason most sports have limited seasons. Even rabid fans have had enough baseball by late October. Given this fact, it would be hard to sell out ball games for a year-round season. While diminishing marginal utility is a simple and intuitive idea, it has great power in helping us understand the economic world.

Allocating Income to Maximize Utility

How many times in one week would Frank go to the club to hear his favorite band? The answer depends on three things: Frank's income, the price of admission to the club, and the alternatives available. If the price of admission was zero and no alternatives existed, he would probably go to

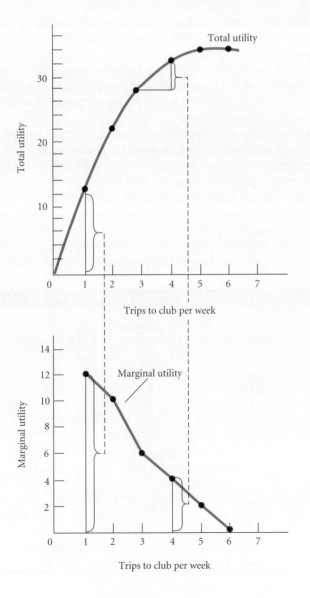

◀ FIGURE 6.3 **Graphs of Frank's Total and Marginal Utility**

Marginal utility is the additional utility gained by consuming one additional unit of a commodity—in this case, trips to the club. When marginal utility is zero, total utility stops rising.

the club five nights a week. (Remember, the sixth night does not increase his utility, so why should he bother to go?) However, Frank is also a basketball fan. His city has many good high school and college teams, and he can go to games six nights a week if he so chooses.

Let us say for now that admission to both the country music club and the basketball games is free—that is, there is no price/income constraint. There is a time constraint, however, because there are only seven nights in a week. Table 6.3 lists Frank's total and marginal utilities from attending basketball games and going to country music clubs. From column 3 of the table, we can conclude that on the first night, Frank will go to a basketball game. The game is worth far more to him (21 utils) than a trip to the club (12 utils).

On the second night, Frank's decision is not so easy. Because he has been to one basketball game this week, the second game is worth less (12 utils as compared to 21 for the first basketball game). In fact, because it is worth the same as a first trip to the club, he is indifferent as to whether he goes to the game or the club. So he splits the next two nights: One night he sees ball game number two (12 utils); the other night he spends at the club (12 utils). At this point, Frank has been to two ball games and has spent one night at the club. Where will Frank go on evening four? He will go to the club again because the marginal utility from a second trip to the club (10 utils) is greater than the marginal utility from attending a third basketball game (9 utils).

Frank is splitting his time between the two activities to maximize total utility. At each successive step, he chooses the activity that yields the most marginal utility. Continuing with this logic, you can see that spending three nights at the club and four nights watching basketball produces total utility of 76 utils each week (28 plus 48). No other combination of games and club trips can produce as much utility.

So far, the only cost of a night of listening to country music is a forgone basketball game and the only cost of a basketball game is a forgone night of country music. Now let us suppose that it costs $3 to get into the club and $6 to go to a basketball game. Suppose further that after paying rent and taking care of other expenses, Frank has only $21 left to spend on entertainment. Typically, consumers allocate limited incomes, or budgets, over a large set of goods and services. Here we have a limited income ($21) being allocated between only two goods, but the principle is the same. Income ($21) and prices ($3 and $6) define Frank's budget constraint. Within that constraint, Frank chooses to maximize utility.

Because the two activities now cost different amounts, we need to find the *marginal utility per dollar* spent on each activity. If Frank is to spend his money on the combination of activities lying within his budget constraint that gives him the most total utility, each night he must choose the activity that gives him the *most utility per dollar spent*. As you can see from column 5 in Table 6.3, Frank gets 4 utils per dollar on the first night he goes to the club (12 utils ÷ $3 = 4 utils per dollar). On night two, he goes to a game and gets 3.5 utils per dollar (21 utils ÷ $6 = 3.5 utils per dollar). On night three, it is back to the club. Then what happens? When all is said and done—work this out for yourself—Frank ends up going to two games and spending three nights at the club. No other combination of activities that $21 will buy yields more utility.

TABLE 6.3   Allocation of Fixed Expenditure per Week Between Two Alternatives

(1) Trips to Club per Week	(2) Total Utility	(3) Marginal Utility (*MU*)	(4) Price (*P*)	(5) Marginal Utility per Dollar (*MU/P*)
1	12	12	$3.00	4.0
2	22	10	3.00	3.3
3	28	6	3.00	2.0
4	32	4	3.00	1.3
5	34	2	3.00	0.7
6	34	0	3.00	0

(1) Basketball Games per Week	(2) Total Utility	(3) Marginal Utility (*MU*)	(4) Price (*P*)	(5) Marginal Utility per Dollar (*MU/P*)
1	21	21	$6.00	3.5
2	33	12	6.00	2.0
3	42	9	6.00	1.5
4	48	6	6.00	1.0
5	51	3	6.00	0.5
6	51	0	6.00	0

The Utility-Maximizing Rule

In general, utility-maximizing consumers spread out their expenditures until the following condition holds:

$$\text{utility-maximizing rule:} \quad \frac{MU_X}{P_X} = \frac{MU_Y}{P_Y} \text{ for all goods,}$$

where MU_X is the marginal utility derived from the last unit of X consumed, MU_Y is the marginal utility derived from the last unit of Y consumed, P_X is the price per unit of X, and P_Y is the price per unit of Y.

To see why this **utility-maximizing rule** is true, think for a moment about what would happen if it were *not* true. For example, suppose MU_X/P_X was greater than MU_Y/P_Y; that is, suppose a consumer purchased a bundle of goods so that the marginal utility from the last dollar spent on X was greater than the marginal utility from the last dollar spent on Y. This would mean that the consumer could increase his or her utility by spending a dollar less on Y and a dollar more on X. As the consumer shifts to buying more X and less Y, he or she runs into diminishing marginal utility. Buying more units of X *decreases* the marginal utility derived from consuming additional units of X. As a result, the marginal utility of another dollar spent on X falls. Now *less* is being spent on Y, and that means its marginal utility *increases*. This process continues until $MU_X/P_X = MU_Y/P_Y$. When this condition holds, there is no way for the consumer to increase his or her utility by changing the bundle of goods purchased.

You can see how the utility-maximizing rule works in Frank's choice between country music and basketball. At each stage, Frank chooses the activity that gives him the most utility per dollar. If he goes to a game, the utility he will derive from the next game—marginal utility—falls. If he goes to the club, the utility he will derive from his next visit falls, and so on.

The principles we have been describing help us understand an old puzzle dating from the time of Plato and familiar to economists beginning with Adam Smith. Adam Smith wrote about it in 1776:

> The things which have the greatest value in use have frequently little or no value in exchange; and on the contrary, those which have the greatest value in exchange have frequently little or no value in use. Nothing is more useful than water: but it will purchase scarce anything; scarce anything can be had in exchange for it. A diamond, on the contrary, has scarce any value in use; but a very great quantity of other goods may frequently be had in exchange for it.[4]

Although diamonds have arguably more than "scarce any value in use" today (for example, they are used to cut glass), Smith's **diamond/water paradox** is still instructive, at least where water is concerned.

The low price of water owes much to the fact that it is in plentiful supply. Even at a price of zero, we do not consume an infinite amount of water. We consume up to the point where *marginal* utility drops to zero. The *marginal* value of water is zero. Each of us enjoys an enormous consumer surplus when we consume nearly free water. At a price of zero, consumer surplus is the entire area under the demand curve. We tend to take water for granted, but imagine what would happen to its price if there were not enough for everyone. It would command a high price indeed.

Diminishing Marginal Utility and Downward-Sloping Demand

The concept of diminishing marginal utility offers one reason people spread their incomes over a variety of goods and services instead of spending all income on one or two items. It also leads us to conclude that demand curves slope downward.

To see why this is so, let us return to our friends Ann and Tom, the struggling graduate students. Recall that they chose between meals at a Thai restaurant and trips to a jazz club. Now think about their demand curve for Thai meals, shown in Figure 6.4. When the price of a meal is $40, they decide not to buy any Thai meals. What they are really deciding is that the utility gained

utility-maximizing rule
Equating the ratio of the marginal utility of a good to its price for all goods.

diamond/water paradox A paradox stating that (1) the things with the greatest value in use frequently have little or no value in exchange and (2) the things with the greatest value in exchange frequently have little or no value in use.

---

[4] Adam Smith, *The Wealth of Nations*, Modern Library Edition (New York: Random House, 1937), p. 28 (1st ed. 1776). The cheapness of water is referred to by Plato in *Euthydemus*, 304 B.C.

▶ **FIGURE 6.4**
Diminishing Marginal Utility and Downward-Sloping Demand

At a price of $40, the utility gained from even the first Thai meal is not worth the price. However, a lower price of $25 lures Ann and Tom into the Thai restaurant 5 times a month. (The utility from the sixth meal is not worth $25.) If the price is $15, Ann and Tom will eat Thai meals 10 times a month—until the marginal utility of a Thai meal drops below the utility they could gain from spending $15 on other goods. At 25 meals a month, they cannot tolerate the thought of another Thai meal even if it is free.

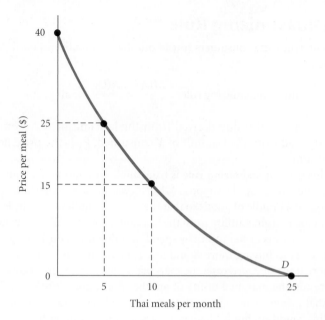

from even that first scrumptious meal each month is not worth the utility that would come from the other things that $40 can buy.

Now consider a price of $25. At this price, Ann and Tom buy five Thai meals. The first, second, third, fourth, and fifth meals each generate enough utility to justify the price. Tom and Ann "reveal" this by buying five meals. After the fifth meal, the utility gained from the next meal is not worth $25.

Ultimately, every demand curve hits the quantity (horizontal) axis as a result of diminishing marginal utility—in other words, demand curves slope downward. How many times will Ann and Tom go to the Thai restaurant if meals are free? Twenty-five times is the answer; and after 25 times a month, they are so sick of Thai food that they will not eat any more even if it is free. That is, marginal utility—the utility gained from the last meal—has dropped to zero. If you think this is unrealistic, ask yourself how much water you drank today.

Income and Substitution Effects

Although the idea of utility is a helpful way of thinking about the choice process, there is an explanation for downward-sloping demand curves that does not rely on the concept of utility or the assumption of diminishing marginal utility. This explanation centers on income and substitution effects.

Keeping in mind that consumers face constrained choices, consider the probable response of a household to a decline in the price of some heavily used product, *ceteris paribus*. How might a household currently consuming many goods be likely to respond to a fall in the price of one of those goods if the household's income, its preferences, and all other prices remained unchanged? The household would face a new budget constraint, and its final choice of all goods and services might change. A decline in the price of gasoline, for example, may affect not only how much gasoline you purchase but also what kind of car you buy, when and how much you travel, where you go, and (not so directly) how many movies you see this month and how many projects around the house you get done.

The Income Effect

Price changes affect households in two ways. First, if we assume that households confine their choices to products that improve their well-being, then a decline in the price of any product, *ceteris paribus*, will make the household unequivocally better off. In other words, if a household continues to buy the same amount of every good and service after the price decrease, it will have income left over. That extra income may be spent on the product whose price has declined, hereafter called good *X*, or on other products. The change in consumption of *X* due to this improvement in well-being is called the *income effect of a price change.*

Suppose you live in Florida and four times a year you fly to Nashville to visit your mother. Suppose further that last year a round-trip ticket to Nashville cost $400. Thus, you spend a total of $1,600 per year on trips to visit Mom. This year, however, increased competition among the airlines has led one airline to offer round-trip tickets to Nashville for $200. Assuming the price remains $200 all year, you can now fly home the same number of times and you will have spent $800 less for airline tickets than you did last year. Now that you are better off, you have additional opportunities. You can fly home a fifth time this year, leaving $600 ($800 − $200) to spend on other things, or you can fly home the same number of times (four) and spend the extra $800 on other things. When the price of something we buy falls, we are *better off.* When the price of something we buy rises, we are *worse off.*

Look back at Figure 6.2 on p. 125. When the price of Thai meals fell, the opportunity set facing Tom and Ann expanded—they were able to afford more Thai meals, more jazz club trips, or more of both. They were unequivocally better off because of the price decline. In a sense, their "real" income was higher.

Now recall from Chapter 3 the definition of a *normal good.* When income rises, demand for normal goods increases. Most goods are normal goods. Because of the price decline, Tom and Ann can afford to buy more. If Thai food is a normal good, a decline in the price of Thai food should lead to an increase in the quantity demanded of Thai food.

The Substitution Effect

The fact that a price decline leaves households better off is only part of the story. When the price of a product falls, that product also becomes *relatively* cheaper. That is, it becomes more attractive relative to potential substitutes. A fall in the price of product *X* might cause a household to shift its purchasing pattern away from substitutes toward *X*. This shift is called the *substitution effect of a price change.*

Earlier we made the point that the "real" cost or price of a good is what one must sacrifice to consume it. This opportunity cost is determined by relative prices. To see why this is so, consider again the choice that you face when a round-trip ticket to Nashville costs $400. Each trip that you take requires a sacrifice of $400 worth of other goods and services. When the price drops to $200, the opportunity cost of a ticket has dropped by $200. In other words, after the price decline, you have to sacrifice only $200 (instead of $400) worth of other goods and services to visit Mom.

To clarify the distinction between the income and substitution, imagine how you would be affected if two things happened to you at the same time. First, the price of round-trip air travel between Florida and Nashville drops from $400 to $200. Second, your income is reduced by $800. You are now faced with new relative prices, but—assuming you flew home four times last year—you are no better off now than you were before the price of a ticket declined. The decrease in the price of air travel has offset your decrease in income.

You are still likely to take more trips home. Why? The opportunity cost of a trip home is now lower, *ceteris paribus*, assuming no change in the prices of other goods and services. A trip to Nashville now requires a sacrifice of only $200 worth of other goods and services, not the $400 worth that it did before. Thus, you will substitute away from other goods toward trips to see your mother.

Everything works in the opposite direction when a price rises, *ceteris paribus*. A price increase makes households worse off. If income and other prices do not change, spending the same amount of money buys less and households will be forced to buy less. This is the income effect. In addition, when the price of a product rises, that item becomes more expensive relative to potential substitutes and the household is likely to substitute other goods for it. This is the substitution effect.

What do the income and substitution effects tell us about the demand curve? Both the income and the substitution effects imply a negative relationship between price and quantity demanded—in other words, downward-sloping demand. When the price of something falls, *ceteris paribus*, we are better off and we are likely to buy more of that good and other goods (income effect). Because lower price also means "less expensive relative to substitutes," we are likely to buy more of the good (substitution effect). When the price of something rises, we are worse off and we will buy less of it (income effect). Higher price also means "more expensive relative to substitutes," and we are likely to buy less of it and more of other goods (substitution effect).[5]

Figure 6.5 summarizes the income and substitution effects of a price change of gasoline prices.

If you recall the example of gasoline prices from early in the chapter, income and substitution effects help us answer the question posed. When gas prices rise, the income effects can cause a fall in the demand for other goods. Since gas is a big part of many budgets, these income effects can be very large. It is the income effect from gasoline price increases that some argue causes consumers to switch away from high-priced brand name products.

▶ **FIGURE 6.5 Income and Substitution Effects of a Price Change**

For normal goods, the income and substitution effects work in the same direction. Higher prices lead to a lower quantity demanded, and lower prices lead to a higher quantity demanded.

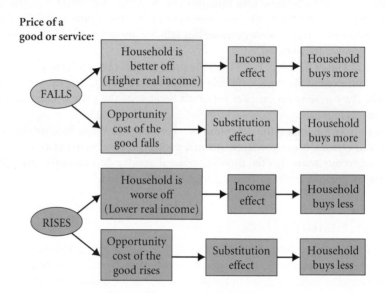

Household Choice in Input Markets

So far, we have focused on the decision-making process that lies behind output demand curves. Households with limited incomes allocate those incomes across various combinations of goods and services that are available and affordable. In looking at the factors affecting choices in the output market, we assumed that income was fixed, or given. We noted at the outset, however, that income is in fact partially determined by choices that households make in input markets. (Look back at Figure II.1 on p. 117.) We now turn to a brief discussion of the two decisions that households make in input markets: the labor supply decision and the saving decision.

The Labor Supply Decision

Most income in the United States is wage and salary income paid as compensation for labor. Household members supply labor in exchange for wages or salaries. As in output markets, households face constrained choices in input markets. They must decide

1. Whether to work
2. How much to work
3. What kind of a job to work at

---

[5] For some goods, the income and substitution effects work in opposite directions. When our income rises, we may buy less of some goods. In Chapter 3, we called such goods *inferior goods*. When the price of an inferior good rises, it is, like any other good, more expensive relative to substitutes and we are likely to replace it with lower-priced substitutes. However, when we are worse off, we increase our demand for inferior goods. Thus, the income effect could lead us to buy more of the good, partially offsetting the substitution effect.

Even if a good is "very inferior," demand curves will slope downward as long as the substitution effect is larger than the income effect. It is possible, at least in theory, for the income effect to be larger. In such a case, a price increase would actually lead to an increase in quantity demanded. This possibility was pointed out by Alfred Marshall in *Principles of Economics*. Marshall attributes the notion of an upward-sloping demand curve to Sir Robert Giffen; for this reason, the notion is often referred to as *Giffen's paradox*. Fortunately or unfortunately, no one has ever demonstrated that a Giffen good has existed.

ECONOMICS IN PRACTICE

Substitution and Market Baskets

In driving to work one day, one of the authors of this text heard the following advertisement for a local grocery store, which we will call Harry's Food.

"Harry's has the best prices in town, and we can prove it! Yesterday we chose Mr. Smith out of our checkout line for a comparison test. Mr. Smith is an average consumer, much like you and me. In doing his weekly grocery shopping yesterday at Harry's, he spent $125. We then sent Mr. Smith to the neighboring competitor with instructions to buy the same market basket of food. When he returned with his food, he saw that his grocery total was $134. You too will see that Harry's can save you money!"

Advertisements like this one are commonplace. As you evaluate the claims in the ad, several things may come to mind. Perhaps Mr. Smith is not representative of consumers or is not much like you. That might make Harry's a good deal for him but not for you. (So your demand curve looks different from Mr. Smith's demand curve.) Or perhaps yesterday was a sale day, meaning yesterday was not typical of Harrys' prices. But there is something more fundamentally wrong with the claims in this ad even if you are just like Mr. Smith and Harry's offers the same prices every day. The fundamental error in this ad is revealed by the work you have done in this chapter.

When Mr. Smith shopped, he presumably looked at the prices of the various food choices offered at the market and tried to do the best he could for his family given those prices and his family's tastes. If we go back to the utility-maximizing rule that you learned in this chapter, we see that Mr. Smith was comparing the marginal utility of each product he consumes relative to its price

in deciding what bundle to buy. In pragmatic terms, if Mr. Smith likes apples and pears about the same, while he was shopping in Harry's, he would have bought the cheaper of the two. When he was sent to the neighboring store, however, he was constrained to buy the same goods that he bought at Harry's. (So he was forced to buy pears even if they were more expensive just to duplicate the bundle.) When we artificially restrict Mr. Smith's ability to substitute goods, we almost inevitably give him a more expensive bundle. The real question is this: Would Mr. Smith have been more happy or less happy with his market basket after spending $125 at Harry's or at its rival? Without knowing more about the shape of Mr. Smith's utility curve and the prices he faces, we cannot answer that question. The dollar comparison in the ad doesn't tell the whole story!

In essence, household members must decide how much labor to supply. The choices they make are affected by:

1. Availability of jobs
2. Market wage rates
3. Skills they possess

As with decisions in output markets, the labor supply decision involves a set of trade-offs. There are basically two alternatives to working for a wage: (1) not working and (2) doing unpaid work. If you do not work, you sacrifice income for the benefits of staying home and reading, watching TV, swimming, or sleeping. Another option is to work, but not for a money wage. In this case, you sacrifice money income for the benefits of growing your own food, raising your children, or taking care of your house.

As with the trade-offs in output markets, your final choice depends on how you value the alternatives available. If you work, you earn a wage that you can use to buy things. Thus, the trade-off is between the value of the goods and services you can buy with the wages you earn versus the value of things you can produce at home—home-grown food, manageable children, clean clothes, and so on—or the value you place on leisure. This choice is illustrated in Figure 6.6. In general, the wage rate can be thought of as the price—or the opportunity cost—of the benefits of either unpaid work or leisure. Just as you choose among different goods by comparing the marginal utility of each relative to its price, you also choose between leisure and other goods by comparing the marginal utility of leisure relative to its price (the wage rate) with the marginal utility of other goods relative to their prices.

▶ **FIGURE 6.6 The Trade-Off Facing Households**

The decision to enter the workforce involves a trade-off between wages (and the goods and services that wages will buy) on the one hand and leisure and the value of nonmarket production on the other hand.

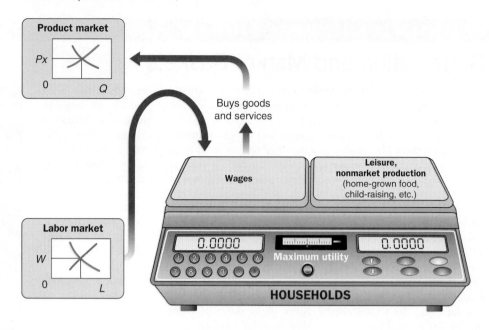

The Price of Leisure

In our analysis in the early part of this chapter, households had to allocate a limited budget across a set of goods and services. Now they must choose among goods, services, and *leisure*.

When we add leisure to the picture, we do so with one important distinction. Trading one good for another involves buying less of one and more of another, so households simply reallocate *money* from one good to the other. "Buying" more leisure, however, means reallocating time between work and nonwork activities. For each hour of leisure that you decide to consume, you give up one hour's wages. Thus, the wage rate is the *price of leisure*.

Conditions in the labor market determine the budget constraints and final opportunity sets that households face. The availability of jobs and these job wage rates determine the final combinations of goods and services that a household can afford. The final choice within these constraints depends on the unique tastes and preferences of each household. Different people place more or less value on leisure—but everyone needs to put food on the table.

Income and Substitution Effects of a Wage Change

labor supply curve A curve that shows the quantity of labor supplied at different wage rates. Its shape depends on how households react to changes in the wage rate.

A **labor supply curve** shows the quantity of labor supplied at different wage rates. The shape of the labor supply curve depends on how households react to changes in the wage rate.

Consider an increase in wages. First, an increase in wages makes households better off. If they work the same number of hours—that is, if they supply the same amount of labor—they will earn higher incomes and be able to buy more goods and services. They can also buy more leisure. If leisure is a normal good—that is, a good for which demand increases as income increases—an increase in income will lead to a higher demand for leisure and a lower labor supply. This is the *income effect of a wage increase*.

However, there is also a potential *substitution effect of a wage increase*. A higher wage rate means that leisure is more expensive. If you think of the wage rate as the price of leisure, each individual hour of leisure consumed at a higher wage costs more in forgone wages. As a result, we would expect households to substitute other goods for leisure. This means working more, or a lower quantity demanded of leisure and a higher quantity supplied of labor.

Note that in the labor market, the income and substitution effects work in *opposite* directions when leisure is a normal good. The income effect of a wage increase implies buying more leisure and working less; the substitution effect implies buying less leisure and working more. Whether households will supply more labor overall or less labor overall when wages rise depends on the relative strength of both the income and the substitution effects.

If the substitution effect is greater than the income effect, the wage increase will increase labor supply. This suggests that the labor supply curve slopes upward, or has a positive slope, like the one in Figure 6.7(a). If the income effect outweighs the substitution effect, however, a higher wage will lead to added consumption of leisure and labor supply will decrease. This implies that the labor supply curve "bends back," as the one in Figure 6.7(b) does.

During the early years of the Industrial Revolution in late eighteenth-century Great Britain, the textile industry operated under what was called the "putting-out" system. Spinning and weaving were done in small cottages to supplement the family farm income—hence the term *cottage industry*. During that period, wages and household incomes rose considerably. Some economic historians claim that this higher income actually led many households to take more leisure and work fewer hours; the empirical evidence suggests a backward-bending labor supply curve.

Just as income and substitution effects helped us understand household choices in output markets, they now help us understand household choices in input markets. The point here is simple: When leisure is added to the choice set, the line between input and output market decisions becomes blurred. In fact, households decide simultaneously how much of each good to consume and how much leisure to consume.

Saving and Borrowing: Present versus Future Consumption

We began this chapter by examining the way households allocate a fixed income over a large number of goods and services. We then pointed out that, at least in part, choices made by households determine income levels. Within the constraints imposed by the market, households decide whether to work and how much to work.

So far, however, we have talked about only the current period—the allocation of current income among alternative uses and the work/leisure choice *today*. Households can also (1) use present income to finance future spending—they can *save*—or (2) use future income to finance present spending—they can *borrow*.

When a household decides to save, it is using current income to finance future consumption. That future consumption may come in 3 years, when you use your savings to buy a car; in 10 years, when you sell stock to put a deposit on a house; or in 45 years, when you retire and begin to receive money from your pension plan. Most people cannot finance large purchases—a house or condominium, for example—out of current income and savings. They almost always borrow money and sign a mortgage. When a household borrows, it is in essence financing a current purchase with future income. It pays back the loan out of future income.

Even in simple economies such as the two-person desert-island economy of Colleen and Bill (see Chapter 2), people must make decisions about *present versus future consumption*. Colleen and Bill could (1) produce goods for today's consumption by hunting and gathering, (2) consume leisure by sleeping on the beach, or (3) work on projects to enhance future consumption opportunities. Building a house or a boat over a 5-year period is trading present

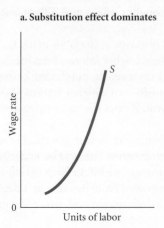

a. Substitution effect dominates

b. Income effect dominates

◀ **FIGURE 6.7 Two Labor Supply Curves**

When the substitution effect outweighs the income effect, the labor supply curve slopes upward (a). When the income effect outweighs the substitution effect, the result is a "backward-bending" labor supply curve: The labor supply curve slopes downward (b).

ECONOMICS IN PRACTICE

What Happens When the Cost of Self-Discovery Falls?

College graduates in 2009 and 2010 entered a difficult job market, with fewer opportunities than their counterparts a few years earlier. As the article below suggests, many ended up taking unpaid internships. Why take an unpaid internship rather than continue to look for paid work?

Many new graduates are quite uncertain about what career to pursue. A first job provides more than a paycheck. It provides an opportunity to learn more about what a career in a particular area looks like and whether it appeals to you. First jobs, in other words, provide a chance to learn about both the world and oneself. When jobs are plentiful, pursuing an unpaid internship in an area you are interested in has a big opportunity cost: the lost wages associated with a full-time job in what might be a less attractive industry. In a world of few paying jobs, the opportunity cost of following your heart in career terms is much lower.

New Experience: Interns Pay to Work For-Profits Finding Flood of Candidates in Poor Job Market

The Boston Globe

Throughout her senior year at Boston College, Brynn Merritt worked part time at Entercom Boston, which owns four radio stations, including WEEI and WRKO. She blogged, called businesses to solicit merchandise for WEEI's Web site, produced ad displays, and sent newsletter e-mail blasts.

For all of this, she was paid nothing.

"I did the same amount of work as a lot of people getting paid did," says Merritt, 22, who graduated this spring. But she's not complaining; in fact, she feels lucky. "I learned a ton," says Merritt, who received a course credit for the internship. "I feel I could go into the business right now."

Unpaid internships have long been offered by nonprofits, but for-profit businesses are increasingly taking advantage of the number of students who, in a tight job market, are willing to forgo a paycheck for practical experience.

Source: The Boston Globe by Bella English. Copyright 2010 by *Globe Newspaper Company - MA*. Reproduced with permission of *Globe Newspaper Company - MA* via Copyright Clearance Center.

consumption for future consumption. As with all of the other choices we have examined in this chapter, the broad principle will be to look at marginal utilities and prices. How much do Colleen and Bill value having something now versus waiting for the future? How much do they gain by waiting?

When a household saves, it usually puts the money into something that will generate income. There is no sense in putting money under your mattress when you can make it work in so many ways: savings accounts, money market funds, stocks, corporate bonds, and so on—many of which are virtually risk-free. When you put your money in any of these places, you are actually lending it out and the borrower pays you a fee for its use. This fee usually takes the form of *interest*. The interest paid is the possible benefit Colleen and Bill get from forgoing current consumption.

Just as changes in wage rates affect household behavior in the labor market, changes in interest rates affect household behavior in capital markets. Higher interest rates mean that borrowing is more expensive—required monthly payments on a newly purchased house or car will be higher. Higher interest rates also mean that saving will earn a higher return: $1,000 invested in a 5 percent savings account or bond yields $50 per year. If rates rise to 10 percent, the annual interest will rise to $100.

What impact do interest rates have on saving behavior? As with the effect of wage changes on labor supply, the effect of changes in interest rates on saving can best be understood in terms of income and substitution effects. Suppose, for example, that I have been saving for a number of years for retirement. Will an increase in interest rates lead to an increase or a decrease in my saving? The answer is not obvious. First, because each dollar saved will earn a higher rate of return, the "price" of spending today in terms of forgone future spending is higher. That is, each dollar that I spend today (instead of saving) costs me more in terms of future consumption because my saving will now earn a higher return. On this score, I will be led to save *more*, which is the substitution effect at work.

However, higher interest rates mean more than that. Higher interest rates mean that it will take less saving today to reach a specific target amount of savings tomorrow. I will not need to save as much for retirement or future consumption as I did before. One hundred dollars put into a savings account with 5 percent compound interest will double in 14 years. If interest was paid at a rate of 10 percent, I would have my $200 in just 7 years. Consequently, I may be led to save less, which is the income effect at work. Higher interest rates mean savers are better off; so higher interest rates may lead to less saving. The final impact of a change in interest rates on saving depends on the relative size of the income and substitution effects. Most empirical evidence indicates that saving tends to increase as the interest rate rises. In other words, the substitution effect is larger than the income effect.

Saving and investment decisions involve a huge and complex set of institutions, the **financial capital market**, in which the suppliers of capital (households that save) and the demand for capital (firms that want to invest) interact. The amount of capital investment in an economy is constrained in the long run by that economy's saving rate. You can think of household *saving* as the economy's supply of capital. When a firm borrows to finance a capital acquisition, it is almost as if households have supplied the capital in exchange for the fee we call interest. We treat capital markets in detail in Chapter 11.[6]

financial capital market
The complex set of institutions in which suppliers of capital (households that save) and the demand for capital (firms wanting to invest) interact.

A Review: Households in Output and Input Markets

In probing the behavior of households in both input and output markets and examining the nature of constrained choice, we went behind the household demand curve using the simplifying assumption that income was fixed and given. Income, wealth, and prices set the limits, or *constraints*, within which households make their choices in output markets. Within those limits, households make their choices on the basis of personal tastes and preferences.

The notion of *utility* helps explain the process of choice. The law of *diminishing marginal utility* partly explains why people seem to spread their incomes over many different goods and services and why demand curves have a negative slope. Another important explanation behind the negative relationship between price and quantity demanded lies in *income effects* and *substitution effects*.

As we turned to input markets, we relaxed the assumption that income was fixed and given. In the labor market, households are forced to weigh the value of leisure against the value of goods and services that can be bought with wage income. Once again, we found household preferences for goods and leisure operating within a set of constraints imposed by the market. Households also face the problem of allocating income and consumption over more than one period of time. They can finance spending in the future with today's income by saving and earning interest, or they can spend tomorrow's income today by borrowing.

We now have a rough sketch of the factors that determine output demand and input supply. (You can review these in Figure II.1 on p. 117.) In the next three chapters, we turn to firm behavior and explore in detail the factors that affect output supply and input demand.

---

[6] Here in Chapter 6, we are looking at a country as if it were isolated from the rest of the world. Very often, however, capital investment is financed by funds loaned or provided by foreign citizens or governments. For example, in recent years, a substantial amount of foreign savings has found its way into the United States for the purchase of stocks, bonds, and other financial instruments. In part, these flows finance capital investment. Also, the United States and other countries that contribute funds to the World Bank and the International Monetary Fund have provided billions in outright grants and loans to help developing countries produce capital. For more information on these institutions, see Chapter 21.

SUMMARY

HOUSEHOLD CHOICE IN OUTPUT MARKETS *p. 121*

1. Every household must make three basic decisions: (1) how much of each product, or output, to demand; (2) how much labor to supply; and (3) how much to spend today and how much to save for the future.

2. Income, wealth, and prices define household *budget constraint.* The budget constraint separates those combinations of goods and services that are available from those that are not. All the points below and to the left of a graph of a household budget constraint make up the *choice set,* or *opportunity set.*

3. It is best to think of the household choice problem as one of allocating income over a large number of goods and services. A change in the price of one good may change the entire allocation. Demand for some goods may rise, while demand for others may fall.

4. As long as a household faces a limited income, the real cost of any single good or service is the value of the next preferred *other* goods and services that could have been purchased with the same amount of money.

5. Within the constraints of prices, income, and wealth, household decisions ultimately depend on preferences—likes, dislikes, and tastes.

THE BASIS OF CHOICE: UTILITY *p. 126*

6. Whether one item is preferable to another depends on how much *utility,* or satisfaction, it yields relative to its alternatives.

7. The *law of diminishing marginal utility* says that the more of any good we consume in a given period of time, the less satisfaction, or utility, we get out of each additional (or marginal) unit of that good.

8. Households allocate income among goods and services to maximize utility. This implies choosing activities that yield the highest marginal utility per dollar. In a two-good world, households will choose to equate the marginal utility per

dollar spent on X with the marginal utility per dollar spent on Y. This is the *utility-maximizing rule.*

INCOME AND SUBSTITUTION EFFECTS *p. 130*

9. The fact that demand curves have a negative slope can be explained in two ways: (1) Marginal utility for all goods diminishes. (2) For most normal goods, both the *income and the substitution effects* of a price decline lead to more consumption of the good.

HOUSEHOLD CHOICE IN INPUT MARKETS *p. 132*

10. In the labor market, a trade-off exists between the value of the goods and services that can be bought in the market or produced at home and the value that one places on leisure. The opportunity cost of paid work is leisure and unpaid work. The wage rate is the price, or opportunity cost, of the benefits of unpaid work or leisure.

11. The income and substitution effects of a change in the wage rate work in opposite directions. Higher wages mean that (1) leisure is more expensive (likely response: people work *more*—substitution effect) and (2) more income is earned in a given number of hours, so some time may be spent on leisure (likely response: people work *less*—income effect).

12. In addition to deciding how to allocate its present income among goods and services, a household may also decide to save or borrow. When a household decides to save part of its current income, it is using current income to finance future spending. When a household borrows, it finances current purchases with future income.

13. An increase in interest rates has a positive effect on saving if the substitution effect dominates the income effect and a negative effect if the income effect dominates the substitution effect. Most empirical evidence shows that the substitution effect dominates here.

REVIEW TERMS AND CONCEPTS

PROBLEMS

All problems are available on www.myeconlab.com

1. For each of the following events, consider how you might react. What things might you consume more or less of? Would you work more or less? Would you increase or decrease your saving? Are your responses consistent with the discussion of household behavior in this chapter?
   a. You have a very close friend who lives in another city, a 3-hour bus ride away. The price of a round-trip ticket rises from $20 to $45.
   b. Tuition at your college is cut 25 percent.

   c. You receive an award that pays you $300 per month for the next 5 years.
   d. Interest rates rise dramatically, and savings accounts are now paying 10% interest annually.
   e. The price of food doubles. (If you are on a meal plan, assume that your board charges double.)
   f. A new business opens up nearby offering part-time jobs at $20 per hour.

2. The following table gives a hypothetical total utility schedule for the Cookie Monster (CM):

# OF COOKIES PER DAY	TOTAL UTILITY PER DAY
0	0
1	100
2	200
3	275
4	325
5	350
6	360
7	360

Calculate the CM's marginal utility schedule. Draw a graph of total and marginal utility. If cookies cost the CM 5 cents each and CM had a good income, what is the maximum number of cookies he would most likely eat in a day?

3. Kamika lives in Chicago but goes to school in Tucson, Arizona. For the last 2 years, she has made four trips home each year. During 2010, the price of a round-trip ticket from Chicago to Tucson increased from $350 to $600. As a result, Kamika decided not to buy a new outfit that year and decided not to drive to Phoenix with friends for an expensive rock concert.
   a. Explain how Kamika's demand for clothing and concert tickets can be affected by an increase in air travel prices.
   b. By using this example, explain why both income and substitution effects might be expected to reduce Kamika's number of trips home.

4. Sketch the following budget constraints:

	P_X	P_Y	INCOME
a.	$20	$50	$1,000
b.	40	50	1,000
c.	20	100	1,000
d.	20	50	2,000
e.	0.25	0.25	7.00
f.	0.25	0.50	7.00
g.	0.50	0.25	7.00

5. On January 1, Professor Smith made a resolution to lose some weight and save some money. He decided that he would strictly budget $100 for lunches each month. For lunch, he has only two choices: the faculty club, where the price of a lunch is $5, and Alice's Restaurant, where the price of a lunch is $10. Every day that he does not eat lunch, he runs 5 miles.
   a. Assuming that Professor Smith spends the $100 each month at either Alice's or the club, sketch his budget constraint. Show actual numbers on the axes.
   b. Last month Professor Smith chose to eat at the club 10 times and at Alice's 5 times. Does this choice fit within his budget constraint? Explain your answer.
   c. Last month Alice ran a half-price lunch special all month. All lunches were reduced to $5. Show the effect on Professor Smith's budget constraint.

6. During 2010, Congress debated the advisability of retaining some or all of the tax cuts signed into law by former President George W. Bush in 2001 and 2003 and set to expire at the end of 2010. By reducing tax rates across the board, take-home pay for all taxpaying workers would increase. The purpose, in part, was to encourage work and increase the supply of labor. Households would respond the way the president hoped, but only if income

effects were stronger than substitution effects. Do you agree or disagree? Explain your answer.

7. Assume that Mei has $100 per month to divide between dinners at a Chinese restaurant and evenings at Zanzibar, a local pub. Assume that going to Zanzibar costs $20 and eating at the Chinese restaurant costs $10. Suppose Mei spends two evenings at Zanzibar and eats six times at the Chinese restaurant.
   a. Draw Mei's budget constraint and show that she can afford six dinners and two evenings at Zanzibar.
   b. Assume that Mei comes into some money and can now spend $200 per month. Draw her new budget constraint.
   c. As a result of the increase in income, Mei decides to spend eight evenings at Zanzibar and eat at the Chinese restaurant four times. What kind of a good is Chinese food? What kind of a good is a night at Zanzibar?
   d. What part of the increase in Zanzibar trips is due to the income effect, and what part is due to the substitution effect? Explain your answer.

8. Decide whether you agree or disagree with each of the following statements and explain your reason:
   a. If the income effect of a wage change dominates the substitution effect for a given household and the household works longer hours following a wage change, wages must have risen.
   b. In product markets, when a price falls, the substitution effect leads to more consumption; but for normal goods, the income effect leads to less consumption.

9. Suppose the price of X is $5 and the price of Y is $10 and a hypothetical household has $500 to spend per month on goods X and Y.
   a. Sketch the household budget constraint.
   b. Assume that the household splits its income equally between X and Y. Show where the household ends up on the budget constraint.
   c. Suppose the household income doubles to $1,000. Sketch the new budget constraint facing the household.
   d. Suppose after the change the household spends $200 on Y and $800 on X. Does this imply that X is a normal or an inferior good? What about Y?

10. For this problem, assume that Joe has $80 to spend on books and movies each month and that both goods must be purchased whole (no fractional units). Movies cost $8 each, and books cost $20 each. Joe's preferences for movies and books are summarized by the following information:

NO. PER MONTH	MOVIES TU	MU	MU/$	NO. PER MONTH	BOOKS TU	MU	MU/$
1	50	—	—	1	22	—	—
2	80	—	—	2	42	—	—
3	100	—	—	3	52	—	—
4	110	—	—	4	57	—	—
5	116	—	—	5	60	—	—
6	121	—	—	6	62	—	—
7	123	—	—	7	63	—	—

   a. Fill in the figures for marginal utility and marginal utility per dollar for both movies and books.
   b. Are these preferences consistent with the law of diminishing marginal utility? Explain briefly.
   c. Given the budget of $80, what quantity of books and what quantity of movies will maximize Joe's level of satisfaction? Explain briefly.

d. Draw the budget constraint (with books on the horizontal axis) and identify the optimal combination of books and movies as point *A*.

e. Now suppose the price of books falls to $10. Which of the columns in the table must be recalculated? Do the required recalculations.

f. After the price change, how many movies and how many books will Joe purchase?

g. Draw the new budget constraint and identify the new optimal combination of books and movies as point *B*.

h. If you calculated correctly, you found that a decrease in the price of books caused Joe to buy more movies as well as more books. How can this be?

11. **[Related to the *Economics in Practice* on *p. 133*]** John's New York–based firm has sent him to work in its Paris office. Recognizing that the cost of living differs between Paris and New York, the company wants to adjust John's salary so that John is as well off (or happy) in Paris as he was in New York. John suggests that he submit a list of the things he bought in New York in a typical month. The firm can use the list to determine John's salary by figuring out how much the same items cost in Paris. Is this a good idea? Explain your answer.

12. **[Related to the *Economics in Practice* on *p. 136*]** Using graphs, show what you would expect to see happen to the labor supply curve facing companies offering unpaid internships as the job market starts to improve.

13. Thomas has allocated $48 per month for entertainment expenses, which he uses either to go bowling or to play billiards. One night of bowling costs Thomas $8, and one night of billiards costs Thomas $4. Use the information in the following graphs to determine how many nights Thomas should spend bowling and how many nights he should play billiards in order to maximize his utility. Explain your answer.

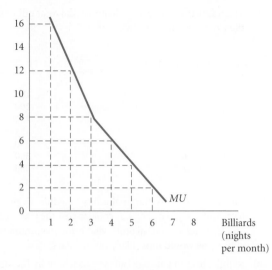

14. For most normal goods, the income effect and the substitution effect work in the same direction; so when the price of a good falls, both the income and substitution effects lead to a higher quantity demanded. How would this change if the good is an inferior good?

15. Explain why in product markets the substitution and income effects work in the same direction for normal goods, but in the labor market, the income and substitution effects work in opposite directions when leisure is considered a normal good.

16. Samantha has $7 to spend on apples and bananas and wants to maximize her utility on her purchase. Based on the data in the table, how many apples and bananas should Samantha purchase, and what is her total utility from the purchase? Does the utility-maximizing rule hold true for her purchase? Explain.

APPLES $1.00			BANANAS $0.50		
QUANTITY	*MU*	*TU*	QUANTITY	*MU*	*TU*
1	28	28	1	12	12
2	24	52	2	10	22
3	20	72	3	8	30
4	16	88	4	6	36
5	12	100	5	4	40
6	8	108	6	2	42
7	4	112	7	0	42
8	0	112	8	–2	40

17. The table shows Regina's marginal utility numbers for hamburgers and pizzas. Regina is trying to decide which item to purchase first, a hamburger or a pizza, knowing that she wants to receive the most utility for each dollar she spends. Assuming she has enough money in her budget to purchase either item, which item should she purchase first?

HAMBURGERS $4		PIZZAS $6	
QUANTITY	*MU*	QUANTITY	*MU*
1	12	1	18
2	8	2	14
3	4	3	8

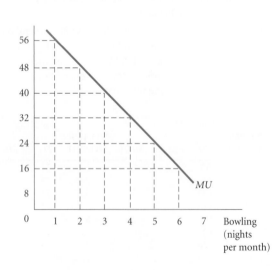

18. Jake and Gonzalo are roommates and have saved a total of $360 to spend on summer entertainment. They have decided to use this money on tickets to baseball games and on tickets to their local amusement park. Their original budget constraint is shown in the graph below. Let X represent amusement park tickets and Y represent baseball tickets.

    a. What is the equation of the original budget constraint?
    b. What is the price of an amusement park ticket? a baseball ticket?
    c. Assume a price change occurs and Jake and Gonzalo now face the new budget constraint. What is the equation of the new budget constraint?
    d. With the new budget constraint, what is the price of an amusement park ticket? a baseball ticket?

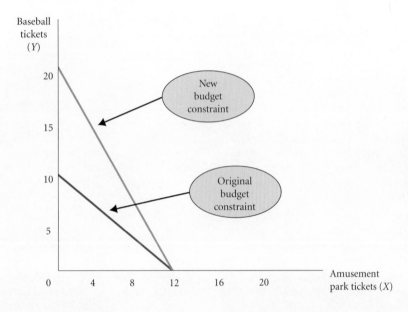

The Production Process: The Behavior of Profit-Maximizing Firms

7

In Chapter 6, we took a brief look at the household decisions that lie behind supply and demand curves. We spent some time discussing household choices: how much to work and how to choose among the wide range of goods and services available within the constraints of prices and income. We also identified some of the influences on household demand in output markets, as well as some of the influences on household supply behavior in input markets.

production The process by which inputs are combined, transformed, and turned into outputs.

We now turn to the other side of the system and examine the behavior of firms. Firms purchase inputs to produce and sell outputs that range from computers to string quartet performances. In other words, they *demand* factors of production in input markets and *supply* goods and services in output markets. In this chapter, we look inside the firm at the production process that transforms inputs into outputs. Although Chapters 7 through 12 describe the behavior of perfectly competitive firms, much of what we say in these chapters also applies to firms that are not perfectly competitive. For example, when we turn to monopoly in Chapter 13, we will be describing firms that are similar to competitive firms in many ways. All firms, whether competitive or not, demand inputs, engage in production, and produce outputs. All firms have an incentive to maximize profits and thus to minimize costs.

Central to our analysis is **production**, the process by which inputs are combined, transformed, and turned into outputs. Firms vary in size and internal organization, but they all take inputs and transform them into goods and services for which there is some demand. For example, an independent accountant combines labor, paper, telephone and e-mail service, time, learning, and a Web site to provide help to confused taxpayers. An automobile plant uses steel, labor, plastic, electricity, machines, and countless other inputs to produce cars. If we want to understand a firm's costs, we first need to understand how it efficiently combines inputs to produce goods and services. Before we begin our discussion of the production process, however, we need to clarify some of the assumptions on which our analysis is based.

Although our discussions in the next several chapters focus on profit-making business firms, it is important to understand that production and productive activity are not confined to private business firms. Households also engage in transforming factors of production (labor, capital, energy, natural resources, and so on) into useful things. When you work in your garden, you are combining land, labor, fertilizer, seeds, and tools (capital) into the vegetables you eat and the flowers you enjoy. The government also combines land, labor, and capital to produce public services for which demand exists: national defense, homeland security, police and fire protection, and education, to name a few.

firm An organization that comes into being when a person or a group of people decides to produce a good or service to meet a perceived demand.

Private business firms are set apart from other producers, such as households and government, by their purpose. A **firm** exists when a person or a group of people decides to produce a good or service to meet a perceived demand. Firms engage in production—that is, they transform inputs into outputs—because they can sell their products for more than it costs to produce them.

The Behavior of Profit-Maximizing Firms

All firms must make several basic decisions to achieve what we assume to be their primary objective—maximum profits.

As Figure 7.1 states, the three decisions that all firms must make include:

1. How much output to supply (quantity of product)
2. How to produce that output (which production technique/technology to use)
3. How much of each input to demand

▶ **FIGURE 7.1 The Three Decisions That All Firms Must Make**

1. How much output to supply	2. Which production technology to use	3. How much of each input to demand

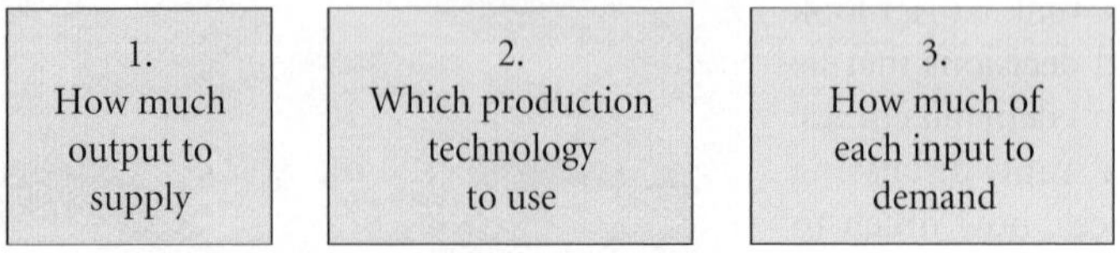

The first and last choices are linked by the second choice. Once a firm has decided how much to produce, the choice of a production method determines the firm's input requirements. If a sweater company decides to produce 5,000 sweaters this month, it knows how many production workers it will need, how much electricity it will use, how much raw yarn to purchase, and how many sewing machines to run.

Similarly, given a technique of production, any set of input quantities determines the amount of output that can be produced. Certainly, the number of machines and workers employed in a sweater mill determines how many sweaters can be produced.

Changing the *technology* of production will change the relationship between input and output quantities. An apple orchard that uses expensive equipment to raise pickers up into the trees will harvest more fruit with fewer workers in a given period of time than an orchard in which pickers use simple ladders. It is also possible that two different technologies can produce the same quantity of output. For example, a fully computerized textile mill with only a few workers running the machines may produce the same number of sweaters as a mill with no sophisticated machines but many workers. A profit-maximizing firm chooses the technology that minimizes its costs for a given level of output.

In this chapter, all firms in a given industry produce the same exact product and we are concerned solely with production. In later chapters, these three basic decisions will be expanded to include the setting of prices and the determination of product quality.

Profits and Economic Costs

profit (economic profit) The difference between total revenue and total cost.

total revenue The amount received from the sale of the product ($q \times P$).

total cost (total economic cost) The total of (1) out-of-pocket costs and (2) opportunity cost of all factors of production.

We assume that firms are in business to make a profit and that a firm's behavior is guided by the goal of maximizing profits. What is profit? **Profit** is the difference between total revenue and total cost:

$$\text{profit} = \text{total revenue} - \text{total cost}$$

Total revenue is the amount received from the sale of the product; it is equal to the number of units sold (q) times the price received per unit (P). **Total cost** is less straightforward to define. We define total cost here to include (1) out-of-pocket costs and (2) opportunity cost of all inputs or factors of production. *Out-of-pocket costs* are sometimes referred to as *explicit costs* or *accounting costs*. These refer to costs as an accountant would calculate them. *Economic costs* include the opportunity cost of every input. These opportunity costs are often referred to as *implicit costs*. The term *profit* will from here on refer to *economic profit*. So whenever we say profit = total revenue − total cost, what we really mean is

$$\text{economic profit} = \text{total revenue} - \text{total economic cost}$$

The reason we take opportunity costs into account is that we are interested in analyzing the behavior of firms from the standpoint of a potential investor or a potential new competitor. If I am thinking about buying a firm or shares in a firm or entering an industry as a new firm, I need to consider the *full* costs of production. For example, if a family business employs three family members but pays them no wage, there is still a cost: the opportunity cost of their labor. In evaluating the business from the outside, these costs must be added if we want to figure out whether the business is successful.

The most important opportunity cost that is included in economic cost is the opportunity cost of capital. The way we treat the opportunity cost of capital is to add a *normal rate of return* to capital as part of economic cost.

Normal Rate of Return   When someone decides to start a firm, that person must commit resources. To operate a manufacturing firm, you need a plant and some equipment. To start a restaurant, you need to buy grills, ovens, tables, chairs, and so on. In other words, you must invest in capital. To start an e-business, you need a host site, some computer equipment, some software, and a Web-site design. Such investment requires resources that stay tied up in the firm as long as it operates. Even firms that have been around a long time must continue to invest. Plant and equipment wear out and must be replaced. Firms that decide to expand must put new capital in place. This is as true of proprietorships, where the resources come directly from the proprietor, as it is of corporations, where the resources needed to make investments come from shareholders.

Whenever resources are used to invest in a business, there is an opportunity cost. Instead of opening a candy store, you could put your funds into an alternative use such as a certificate of deposit or a government bond, both of which earn interest. Instead of using its retained earnings to build a new plant, a firm could earn interest on those funds or pay them out to shareholders.

Rate of return is the annual flow of net income generated by an investment expressed as a percentage of the total investment. For example, if someone makes a $100,000 investment in capital to start a small restaurant and the restaurant produces a flow of profit of $15,000 every year, we say the project has a "rate of return" of 15 percent. Sometimes we refer to the rate of return as the *yield* of the investment.

A **normal rate of return** is the rate that is just sufficient to keep owners and investors satisfied. If the rate of return were to fall below normal, it would be difficult or impossible for managers to raise resources needed to purchase new capital. Owners of the firm would be receiving a rate of return that was lower than what they could receive elsewhere in the economy, and they would have no incentive to invest in the firm.

If the firm has fairly steady revenues and the future looks secure, the normal rate of return should be very close to the interest rate on risk-free government bonds. A firm certainly will not keep investors interested in it if it does not pay them a rate of return at least as high as they can get from a risk-free government or corporate bond. If a firm is rock solid and the economy is steady, it may not have to pay a much higher rate. However, if a firm is in a very speculative industry and the future of the economy is shaky, it may have to pay substantially more to keep its shareholders happy. In exchange for a risk that the business may falter or even fail, the shareholders will expect a higher return.

A normal rate of return is considered a part of the total cost of a business. Adding a normal rate of return to total cost has an important implication: When a firm earns a normal rate of return, it is earning a zero profit as we have defined profit. If the level of profit is positive, the firm is earning an above-normal rate of return on capital.

A simple example will illustrate the concepts of a normal rate of return being part of total cost. Suppose that Sue and Ann decide to start a small business selling turquoise belts in the Denver airport. To get into the business, they need to invest in a fancy pushcart. The price of the pushcart is $20,000 with all the displays and attachments included. Suppose that Sue and Ann estimate that they will sell 3,000 belts each year for $10 each. Further assume that each belt costs $5 from the supplier. Finally, the cart must be staffed by one clerk, who works for an annual wage of $14,000. Is this business going to make a profit?

To answer this question, we must determine total revenue and total cost. First, annual revenue is $30,000 (3,000 belts × $10). Total cost includes the cost of the belts—$15,000 (3,000 belts × $5)—plus the labor cost of $14,000, for a total of $29,000. Thus, on the basis of the annual revenue and cost flows, the firm *seems* to be making a profit of $1,000 ($30,000 − $29,000).

normal rate of return   A rate of return on capital that is just sufficient to keep owners and investors satisfied. For relatively risk-free firms, it should be nearly the same as the interest rate on risk-free government bonds.

What about the $20,000 initial investment in the pushcart? This investment is *not* a direct part of the cost of Sue and Ann's firm. If we assume that the cart maintains its value over time, *the only thing that Sue and Ann are giving up is the interest they might have earned had they not tied up their funds in the pushcart.* That is, the only real cost is the opportunity cost of the investment, which is the forgone interest on the $20,000.

Now suppose that Sue and Ann want a minimum return equal to 10 percent—which is, say, the rate of interest that they could have gotten by purchasing corporate bonds. This implies a normal return of 10 percent, or $2,000 annually (= $20,000 × 0.10) on the $20,000 investment. As we determined earlier, Sue and Ann will earn only $1,000 annually. This is only a 5 percent return on their investment. Thus, they are really earning a below-normal return. Recall that the opportunity cost of capital must be added to total cost in calculating profit. Thus, the total cost in this case is $31,000 ($29,000 + $2,000 in forgone interest on the investment). The level of profit is negative: $30,000 minus $31,000 equals –$1,000. These calculations are summarized in Table 7.1. Because the level of profit is negative, Sue and Ann are actually suffering a loss on their belt business.

TABLE 7.1   Calculating Total Revenue, Total Cost, and Profit

Initial Investment:	$20,000
Market Interest Rate Available:	0.10, or 10%
Total revenue (3,000 belts × $10 each)	**$30,000**
Costs	
Belts from supplier	$15,000
Labor cost	14,000
Normal return/opportunity cost of capital ($20,000 × 0.10)	2,000
Total Cost	**$31,000**
Profit = total revenue − total cost	**−$1,000**[a]

[a]There is a loss of $1,000.

When a firm earns a *positive* level of profit, it is earning more than is sufficient to retain the interest of investors. In fact, positive profits are likely to attract new firms into an industry and cause existing firms to expand.

When a firm suffers a *negative* level of profit—that is, when it incurs a loss—it is earning at a rate below that required to keep investors happy. Such a loss may or may not be a loss as an accountant would measure it. Even if a firm is earning a rate of return of 10 percent, it is earning a below-normal rate of return, or a loss, if a normal return for its industry is 15 percent. Losses may cause some firms to exit the industry; others will contract in size. Certainly, new investment will not flow into such an industry.

Short-Run versus Long-Run Decisions

The decisions made by a firm—how much to produce, how to produce it, and what inputs to demand—all take time into account. If a firm decides that it wants to double or triple its output, it may need time to arrange financing, hire architects and contractors, and build a new plant. Planning for a major expansion can take years. In the meantime, the firm must decide how much to produce within the constraint of its existing plant. If a firm decides to get out of a particular business, it may take time to arrange an orderly exit. There may be contract obligations to fulfill, equipment to sell, and so on. Once again, the firm must decide what to do in the meantime.

A firm's immediate response to a change in the economic environment may differ from its response over time. Consider, for example, a small restaurant with 20 tables that becomes very popular. The immediate problem for the owners is getting the most profit within the constraint of the existing restaurant. The owner might consider adding a few tables or speeding up service to squeeze in a few more customers. Some popular restaurants do not take reservations, forcing people to wait at the bar. This practice increases drink revenues and keeps tables full at all times. At the same time, the owner may be thinking of expanding the current facility, moving to a larger facility, or opening a second restaurant. In the future, the owner might buy the store next door and double the capacity. Such decisions might require negotiating a lease, buying new equipment, and hiring more staff. It takes time to make and implement these decisions.

Because the character of immediate response differs from long-run adjustment, it is useful to define two time periods: the short run and the long run. Two assumptions define the **short run**: (1) a fixed scale (or a fixed factor of production) and (2) no entry into or exit from the industry. First, the short run is defined as that period during which existing firms have some *fixed factor of production*—that is, during which time some factor locks them into their current scale of operations. Second, new firms cannot enter and existing firms cannot exit an industry in the short run. Firms may curtail operations, but they are still locked into some costs even though they may be in the process of going out of business.

Which factor or factors of production are fixed in the short run differs from industry to industry. For a manufacturing firm, the size of the physical plant is often the greatest limitation. A factory is built with a given production rate in mind. Although that rate can be increased, output cannot increase beyond a certain limit in the short run. For a private physician, the limit may be the capacity to see patients; the day has only so many hours. In the long run, the doctor may invite others to join the practice and expand; but for now, in the short run, this sole physician *is* the firm, with a capacity that is the firm's only capacity. For a farmer, the fixed factor may be land. The capacity of a small farm is limited by the number of acres being cultivated.

In the **long run**, there are no fixed factors of production. Firms can plan for any output level they find desirable. They can double or triple output, for example. In addition, new firms can start up operations (enter the industry) and existing firms can go out of business (exit the industry).

No hard-and-fast rule specifies how long the short run is. The point is that firms make two basic kinds of decisions: those that govern the day-to-day operations of the firm and those that involve longer-term strategic planning. Sometimes major decisions can be implemented in weeks. Often, however, the process takes years. In many large firms, different people often make the short- and long-run decisions. A production manager might well be charged with trying to do the best she can with the plant and equipment that she has, while her boss, the division head, figures out whether expansion of the plant is a good idea. In a single proprietorship, one person may wear both hats, thinking simultaneously about how to make the most out of the present while taking steps to improve the future of the business.

> **short run** The period of time for which two conditions hold: The firm is operating under a fixed scale (fixed factor) of production, and firms can neither enter nor exit an industry.

> **long run** That period of time for which there are no fixed factors of production: Firms can increase or decrease the scale of operation, and new firms can enter and existing firms can exit the industry.

The Bases of Decisions: Market Price of Outputs, Available Technology, and Input Prices

As we said earlier, a firm's three fundamental decisions are made with the objective of maximizing profits. Because profits equal total revenues minus total costs, each firm needs to know how much it costs to produce its product and how much its product can be sold for.

To know how much it costs to produce a good or service, a firm needs to know something about the production techniques that are available and about the prices of the inputs required. To estimate how much it will cost to operate a gas station, for instance, a firm needs to know equipment needs, number of workers, kind of building, and so on. The firm also needs to know the going wage rates for mechanics and unskilled laborers, the cost of gas pumps, interest rates, the rents per square foot of land on high-traffic corners, and the wholesale price of gasoline. Of course, the firm also needs to know how much it can sell gasoline and repair services for.

In the language of economics, a firm needs to know three things:

1. The market price of output
2. The techniques of production that are available
3. The prices of inputs

Output price determines potential revenues. The techniques available tell me how much of each input I need, and input prices tell me how much they will cost. Together the available production techniques and the prices of inputs determine costs.

The rest of this chapter and the next chapter focus on costs of production. We begin at the heart of the firm, with the production process. Faced with a set of input prices, firms must decide on the best, or optimal, method of production (Figure 7.2). The **optimal method of production** is the one that minimizes cost. With cost determined and the market price of output known, a firm will make a final judgment about the quantity of product to produce and the quantity of each input to demand.

> **optimal method of production** The production method that minimizes cost.

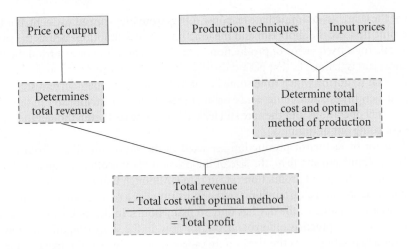

The Production Process

Production is the process through which inputs are combined and transformed into outputs. **Production technology** relates inputs to outputs. Specific quantities of inputs are needed to produce any given service or good. A loaf of bread requires certain amounts of water, flour, and yeast; some kneading and patting; and an oven and gas or electricity. A trip from downtown New York to Newark, New Jersey, can be produced with a taxicab, 45 minutes of a driver's labor, some gasoline, and so on.

Most outputs can be produced by a number of different techniques. You can tear down an old building and clear a lot to create a park in several ways, for example. Five hundred men and women could descend on the park with sledgehammers and carry the pieces away by hand; this would be a **labor-intensive technology**. The same park could be produced by two people with a wrecking crane, a steam shovel, a backhoe, and a dump truck; this would be a **capital-intensive technology**. Similarly, different inputs can be combined to transport people from Oakland to San Francisco. The Bay Area Rapid Transit carries thousands of people simultaneously under San Francisco Bay and uses a massive amount of capital relative to labor. Cab rides to San Francisco require more labor relative to capital; a driver is needed for every few passengers.

In choosing the most appropriate technology, firms choose the one that minimizes the cost of production. For a firm in an economy with a plentiful supply of inexpensive labor but not much capital, the optimal method of production will involve labor-intensive techniques. For example, assembly of items such as running shoes is done most efficiently by hand. That is why Nike produces virtually all its shoes in developing countries where labor costs are very low. In contrast, firms in an economy with high wages and high labor costs have an incentive to substitute away from labor and to use more capital-intensive, or labor-saving, techniques. Suburban office parks use more land and have more open space in part because land in the suburbs is more plentiful and less expensive than land in the middle of a big city.

Production Functions: Total Product, Marginal Product, and Average Product

The relationship between inputs and outputs—that is, the production technology—expressed numerically or mathematically is called a **production function** (or **total product function**). A production function shows units of total product as a function of units of inputs.

Imagine, for example, a small sandwich shop. All the sandwiches made in the shop are grilled, and the shop owns only one grill, which can accommodate only two workers comfortably. As columns 1 and 2 of the production function in Table 7.2 show, one person working alone can produce only 10 sandwiches per hour in addition to answering the phone, waiting on customers, keeping the tables clean, and so on. The second worker can stay at the grill full-time and not worry about anything except making sandwiches. Because the two workers together can produce 25 sandwiches, the second worker can produce $25 - 10 = 15$ sandwiches per hour. A third person trying to use the grill produces crowding, but with careful use of space, more sandwiches can be

production technology
The quantitative relationship between inputs and outputs.

labor-intensive technology Technology that relies heavily on human labor instead of capital.

capital-intensive technology Technology that relies heavily on capital instead of human labor.

production function *or* **total product function** A numerical or mathematical expression of a relationship between inputs and outputs. It shows units of total product as a function of units of inputs.

TABLE 7.2   Production Function

(1) Labor Units (Employees)	(2) Total Product (Sandwiches per Hour)	(3) Marginal Product of Labor	(4) Average Product of Labor (Total Product ÷ Labor Units)
0	0	—	—
1	10	10	10.0
2	25	15	12.5
3	35	10	11.7
4	40	5	10.0
5	42	2	8.4
6	42	0	7.0

produced. The third worker adds 10 sandwiches per hour. Note that the added output from hiring a third worker is less because of the capital constraint, *not* because the third worker is somehow less efficient or hardworking. We assume that all workers are equally capable.

The fourth and fifth workers can work at the grill only while the first three are putting the pickles, onions, and wrapping on the sandwiches they have made. Then the first three must wait to get back to the grill. Worker four adds five sandwiches per hour to the total, and worker five adds just two. Adding a sixth worker adds no output at all: The current maximum capacity of the shop is 42 sandwiches per hour.

Figure 7.3(a) graphs the total product data from Table 7.2. As you look at Table 7.2 and think about marginal product, you should begin to see how important the nature of the production function is to a firm. We see that the sandwich firm that hires a fourth worker will be expanding its sandwich production by five. Is it worth it? That will in turn depend on how much the worker costs and for how much the shop can sell the sandwich. As we proceed to analyze the firm's decision in the next few chapters, we will explore this further.

Marginal Product and the Law of Diminishing Returns
Marginal product is the additional output that can be produced by hiring one more unit of a specific input, holding all other inputs constant. As column 3 of Table 7.2 shows, the marginal product of the first unit of labor in the sandwich shop is 10 sandwiches; the marginal product of the second is 15; the third, 10; and so on. The marginal product of the sixth worker is zero. Figure 7.3(b) graphs the marginal product of labor curve from the data in Table 7.2.

marginal product The additional output that can be produced by adding one more unit of a specific input, *ceteris paribus*.

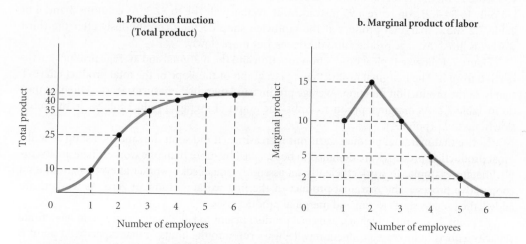

a. Production function
(Total product)

b. Marginal product of labor

▲ **FIGURE 7.3 Production Function for Sandwiches**

A *production function* is a numerical representation of the relationship between inputs and outputs. In Figure 7.3(a), total product (sandwiches) is graphed as a function of labor inputs. The *marginal product* of labor is the additional output that one additional unit of labor produces. Figure 7.3(b) shows that the marginal product of the second unit of labor at the sandwich shop is 15 units of output; the marginal product of the fourth unit of labor is 5 units of output.

The **law of diminishing returns** states that *after a certain point, when additional units of a variable input are added to fixed inputs* (in this case, the building and grill), *the marginal product of the variable input* (in this case, labor) *declines.* The British economist David Ricardo first formulated the law of diminishing returns on the basis of his observations of agriculture in nineteenth-century England. Within a given area of land, he noted, successive "doses" of labor and capital yielded smaller and smaller increases in crop output. The law of diminishing returns is true in agriculture because only so much more can be produced by farming the same land more intensely. In manufacturing, diminishing returns set in when a firm begins to strain the capacity of its existing plant.

At our sandwich shop, diminishing returns set in when the third worker is added. The marginal product of the second worker is actually higher than the first [Figure 7.3(b)]. The first worker takes care of the phone and the tables, thus freeing the second worker to concentrate exclusively on sandwich making. From that point on, the grill gets crowded. It is important to note here that diminishing returns are setting in, not because the third worker is worse than workers one or two (we assume they are identical), but because as we add staff, each has a smaller amount of capital (here a grill) to work with.

Diminishing returns, or *diminishing marginal product,* begin to show up when more and more units of a variable input are added to a fixed input, such as the scale of the plant. Recall that we defined the short run as that period in which some fixed factor of production constrains the firm. It then follows that diminishing returns always apply in the short run and that in the short run, every firm will face diminishing returns. This means that every firm finds it progressively more difficult to increase its output as it approaches capacity production.

Marginal Product versus Average Product **Average product** is the average amount produced by each unit of a variable factor of production. At our sandwich shop with one grill, that variable factor is labor. In Table 7.2, you saw that the first two workers together produce 25 sandwiches per hour. Their average product is therefore 12.5 (25 ÷ 2). The third worker adds only 10 sandwiches per hour to the total. These 10 sandwiches are the *marginal* product of labor. The *average product* of the first three units of labor, however, is 11.7 (the average of 10, 15, and 10). Stated in equation form, the average product of labor is the *total* product divided by total units of labor:

$$\text{average product of labor} = \frac{\text{total product}}{\text{total units of labor}}$$

Average product "follows" marginal product, but it does not change as quickly. If marginal product is above average product, the average rises; if marginal product is below average product, the average falls. Suppose, for example, that you have had six exams and that your average is 86. If you score 75 on the next exam, your average score will fall, but not all the way to 75. In fact, it will fall only to 84.4. If you score a 95 instead, your average will rise to 87.3. As columns 3 and 4 of Table 7.2 show, marginal product at the sandwich shop declines continuously after the third worker is hired. Average product also decreases, but more slowly.

Figure 7.4 shows a typical production function and the marginal and average product curves derived from it. The marginal product curve is a graph of the slope of the total product curve—that is, of the production function. Average product and marginal product start out equal, as they do in Table 7.2. As marginal product climbs, the graph of average product follows it, but more slowly, up to L_1 (point A).

Notice that marginal product starts out increasing. (It did so in the sandwich shop as well.) Most production processes are designed to be run well by more than one worker. Take an assembly line, for example. To work efficiently, an assembly line needs a worker at every station; it's a cooperative process. The marginal product of the first workers is low or zero. As workers are added, the process starts to run and marginal product rises.

At point A (L_1 units of labor), marginal product begins to fall. Because every plant has a finite capacity, efforts to increase production will always run into the limits of that capacity. At point B (L_2 units of labor), marginal product has fallen to equal the average product, which has been increasing. Between point B and point C (between L_2 and L_3 units of labor), marginal product falls below average product and average product begins to follow it *down.* Average product is at its maximum at point B, where it is equal to marginal product. At L_3, more labor yields no more output and marginal product is zero—the assembly line has no more positions, the grill is jammed.

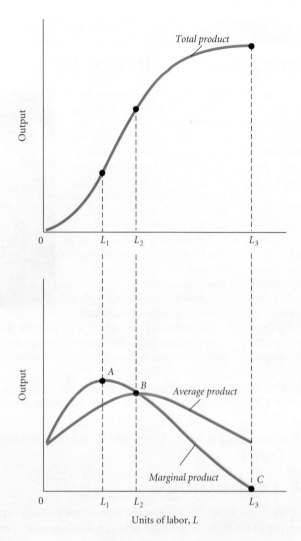

◀ FIGURE 7.4 **Total Average and Marginal Product**

Marginal and average product curves can be derived from total product curves. Average product is at its maximum at the point of intersection with marginal product.

Production Functions with Two Variable Factors of Production

So far, we have considered production functions with only one variable factor of production. However, inputs work together in production. In general, additional capital increases the productivity of labor. Because capital—buildings, machines, and so on—is of no use without people to operate it, we say that capital and labor are *complementary inputs.*

A simple example will clarify this point. Consider again the sandwich shop. If the demand for sandwiches began to exceed the capacity of the shop to produce them, the shop's owner might decide to expand capacity. This would mean purchasing more capital in the form of a new grill.

A second grill would essentially double the shop's productive capacity. The new higher capacity would mean that the sandwich shop would not run into diminishing returns as quickly. With only one grill, the third and fourth workers are less productive because the single grill gets crowded. With two grills, however, the third and fourth workers could produce 15 sandwiches per hour using the second grill. In essence, the added capital raises the *productivity* of labor—that is, the amount of output produced per worker per hour.

Just as the new grill enhances the productivity of workers in the sandwich shop, new businesses and the capital they put in place raise the productivity of workers in countries such as Malaysia, India, and Kenya.

This simple relationship lies at the heart of worries about productivity at the national and international levels. Building new, modern plants and equipment enhances a nation's productivity. In the last decade, China has accumulated capital (that is, built plants and equipment) at a very high rate. The result is growth in the average quantity of output per worker in China.

Learning about Growing Pineapples in Ghana

In this chapter we have focused on the way in which labor, capital, and other inputs are used to produce outputs of various sorts. We have described a somewhat abstract production function, linking specific combinations of inputs and output levels. In reading this chapter, you might have wondered where real people interested in producing something learn about production functions. How does an entrepreneur know what the ideal combination of inputs is to produce a given output?

In a recent interesting article, Timothy Conley from Chicago and Christopher Udry from Yale asked precisely this question in thinking about the production of pineapples in Ghana. What they learned helps us think about the production process more generally.

In farming, as in manufacturing, we need a given combination of labor and capital to produce output, here a crop. The capital doesn't come in the form of a grill, as in the sandwich shop, but tractors, or plows, or shovels. Raw materials include seeds and fertilizer. There are clearly substitution possibilities among these inputs; farmers can weed more and fertilize or water less, for example. How does a farmer know what the right mix of inputs is, given input prices?

Ghana proved to be an interesting place to ask this question. In the 1990s, an area of Ghana changed from an exclusive reliance on maize as the agricultural crop to the development of pineapple farms. This transformation happened slowly over time to various neighborhoods. Conley and Udry found that social learning was key in the process of technology adoption. For farmers in Ghana, the choice of how much fertilizer to use was highly dependent on how much fertilizer their more successful neighbor farmers used. Social learning was especially important for novice pineapple farmers located near more veteran producers.[1]

Social learning obviously plays a role in the diffusion of manufacturing technology as well. It is no accident that many high-tech entrepreneurs began their careers in other high-tech firms where they learned much about the right production techniques.

[1] Timothy Conley and Christopher Udry, "Learning About a New Technology: Pineapples in Ghana," *American Economic Review*, March 2010, 35–69.

Choice of Technology

As our sandwich shop example shows, inputs (factors of production) are complementary. Capital enhances the productivity of labor. Workers in the sandwich shop are more productive when they are not crowded at a single grill. Similarly, labor enhances the productivity of capital. When more workers are hired at a plant that is operating at 50 percent of capacity, previously idle machines suddenly become productive.

However, inputs can also be substituted for one another. If labor becomes expensive, firms can adopt labor-saving technologies; that is, they can substitute capital for labor. Assembly lines can be automated by replacing human beings with machines, and capital can be substituted for land when land is scarce. If capital becomes relatively expensive, firms can substitute labor for capital. In short, most goods and services can be produced in a number of ways through the use of alternative technologies. One of the key decisions that all firms must make is which technology to use.

Consider the choices available to the diaper manufacturer in Table 7.3. Five different techniques of producing 100 diapers are available. Technology *A* is the most labor-intensive, requiring 10 hours of labor and 2 units of capital to produce 100 diapers. (You can think of units of capital as machine hours.) Technology *E* is the most capital-intensive, requiring only 2 hours of labor but 10 hours of machine time.

TABLE 7.3	Inputs Required to Produce 100 Diapers Using Alternative Technologies	
Technology	Units of Capital (*K*)	Units of Labor (*L*)
A	2	10
B	3	6
C	4	4
D	6	3
E	10	2

ECONOMICS IN PRACTICE

How Fast Should a Truck Driver Go?

The trucking business gives us an opportunity to think about choice among technologies in a concrete way.

Suppose you own a truck and use it to haul merchandise for retailers such as Target and Sears. Your typical run is 200 miles, and you hire one person to drive the truck at a cost of $20 per hour. How fast should you instruct him to drive the truck? Consider the cost per trip.

Notice that even with fixed inputs of one truck and one driver, you still have some choices to make. In the language of this chapter, you can think of the choice as one of slow-drive technology (let's say 50 mph) versus fast-drive technology (say, 60 mph).

If the driver's time were the only input, the problem would be simple: Labor costs are minimized if you tell him to drive fast. At 60 mph, a trip takes the driver only 3.33 hours (200 miles divided by 60 mph) and costs you $66.67 given his $20 wage rate. However, at a speed of 50 mph, it takes four hours and costs you $80. With one variable input, the best technology is the one that uses that input most efficiently. In fact, with only one variable input, you would tell the driver to speed regardless of his wage rate.

But, of course, trucks require not only drivers but also fuel, which is where the question gets more interesting. As it turns out, the fuel mileage that a truck gets diminishes with speed beyond about 50 mph. Let's say in this case that the truck gets 15 miles per gallon at 50 mph but only 12 miles per gallon at 60 mph. Now we have a trade-off. When you tell the driver to go fast, your labor costs are lower but your fuel costs are higher.

So what instructions do you give? It should be clear that your instructions depend on the price of fuel. First suppose that fuel costs $3.50 per gallon. If the trucker drives fast, he will get 12 miles per gallon. Since the trucker has to drive 200 miles per trip, he burns 16.66 gallons (200 divided by 12) and total fuel cost is $58.31. Driving fast, the trucker goes 60 miles per hour. You have to pay him for 3.33 hours (200 divided by 60), which at $20 per hour, is a total of $66.67. The total for the trip is $124.98.

On the other hand, if your trucker drives slowly, he will get 15 miles per gallon, which means you need only 13.33 gallons, which costs $46.67. But now it takes more time. He takes four hours, and you must pay him 4 × $20, or $80 per trip. Total cost is now $126.67. Thus, the cost-minimizing solution is to have him drive fast.

Now try a price of $4.50 per gallon. Doing the same calculations, you should be able to show that when driving slowly, the total cost is

$139.99; when driving fast, the cost is $141.63. Thus, the higher fuel price means that you tell the driver to slow down.

Going one step further, you should be able to show that at a fuel price of $4, the trip costs the same whether your trucker drives fast or slowly.

In fact, you should be able to see that at fuel prices in excess of $4 per gallon, you tell your driver to slow down, while at cheaper prices, you tell him to speed up. With more than one input, the choice of technologies often depends on the unit cost of those inputs.

The observation that the optimal "technology" to use in trucking depends on fuel prices is one reason we might expect accident rates to fall with rises in fuel prices (in addition to the fact that everyone drives less when fuel is expensive). Modern technology, in the form of on-board computers, allows a modern trucking firm to monitor driving speed and instruct drivers.

Here is a summary of the cost per trip.

Fuel Price	$3.50	$4.00	$4.50
Drive Fast	$124.97	$133.33	$141.63
Drive Slowly	$126.66	$133.33	$139.99

To choose a production technique, the firm must look to input markets to learn the current market prices of labor and capital. What is the wage rate (P_L), and what is the cost per hour of capital (P_K)? The right choice among inputs depends on how productive an input is and what its price is.

Suppose that labor and capital are both available at a price of $1 per unit. Column 4 of Table 7.4 presents the calculations required to determine which technology is best. The winner is technology C. Assuming that the firm's objective is to maximize profits, it will choose the least-cost technology. Using technology C, the firm can produce 100 diapers for $8. All four of the other technologies produce 100 diapers at a higher cost.

Now suppose that the wage rate (P_L) were to rise sharply, from $1 to $5. You might guess that this increase would lead the firm to substitute labor-saving capital for workers, and you would be right. As column 5 of Table 7.4 shows, the increase in the wage rate means that technology E is now the cost-minimizing choice for the firm. Using 10 units of capital and only 2 units of labor,

TABLE 7.4 Cost-Minimizing Choice Among Alternative Technologies (100 Diapers)

(1) Technology	(2) Units of Capital (K)	(3) Units of Labor (L)	Cost = $(L \times P_L) + (K \times P_K)$ (4) $P_L = \$1$ $P_K = \$1$	(5) $P_L = \$5$ $P_K = \$1$
A	2	10	$12	52
B	3	6	9	33
C	4	4	8	24
D	6	3	9	21
E	10	2	12	20

the firm can produce 100 diapers for $20. All other technologies are now more costly. Notice too from the table that the firm's ability to shift its technique of production softened the impact of the wage increase on its costs. The flexibility of a firm's techniques of production is an important determinant of its costs. Two things determine the cost of production: (1) technologies that are available and (2) input prices. Profit-maximizing firms will choose the technology that minimizes the cost of production given current market input prices.

Looking Ahead: Cost and Supply

So far, we have looked only at a *single* level of output. That is, we have determined how much it will cost to produce 100 diapers using the best available technology when $P_K = \$1$ and $P_L = \$1$ or $5. The best technique for producing 1,000 diapers or 10,000 diapers may be entirely different. The next chapter explores the relationship between cost and the level of output in some detail. One of our main objectives in that chapter is to determine the amount that a competitive firm will choose to *supply* during a given time period.

--- SUMMARY ---

1. Firms vary in size and internal organization, but they all take inputs and transform them into outputs through a process called *production*.

2. In perfect competition, no single firm has any control over prices. This follows from two assumptions: (1) Perfectly competitive industries are composed of many firms, each small relative to the size of the industry, and (2) each firm in a perfectly competitive industry produces *homogeneous products*.

3. The demand curve facing a competitive firm is perfectly elastic. If a single firm raises its price above the market price, it will sell nothing. Because it can sell all it produces at the market price, a firm has no incentive to reduce price.

THE BEHAVIOR OF PROFIT-MAXIMIZING FIRMS *p. 148*

4. Profit-maximizing firms in all industries must make three choices: (1) how much output to supply, (2) how to produce that output, and (3) how much of each input to demand.

5. *Profit* equals total revenue minus total cost. Total cost (economic cost) includes (1) out-of-pocket costs and (2) the opportunity cost of each factor of production, including a normal rate of return on capital.

6. A *normal rate of return* on capital is included in total cost because tying up resources in a firm's capital stock has an opportunity cost. If you start a business or buy a share of

stock in a corporation, you do so because you expect to make a normal rate of return. Investors will not invest their money in a business unless they expect to make a normal rate of return.

7. A positive profit level occurs when a firm is earning an above-normal rate of return on capital.

8. Two assumptions define the *short run*: (1) a fixed scale or fixed factor of production and (2) no entry to or exit from the industry. In the *long run*, firms can choose any scale of operations they want and firms can enter and leave the industry.

9. To make decisions, firms need to know three things: (1) the market price of their output, (2) the production techniques that are available, and (3) the prices of inputs.

THE PRODUCTION PROCESS *p. 152*

10. The relationship between inputs and outputs (the *production technology*) expressed numerically or mathematically is called a *production function* or *total product function*.

11. The *marginal product* of a variable input is the additional output that an added unit of that input will produce if all other inputs are held constant. According to the *law of diminishing returns*, when additional units of a variable input are added to fixed inputs, after a certain point, the marginal product of the variable input will decline.

12. *Average product* is the average amount of product produced by each unit of a variable factor of production. If marginal product is above average product, the average product rises; if marginal product is below average product, the average product falls.

13. Capital and labor are at the same time complementary and substitutable inputs. Capital enhances the productivity of labor, but it can also be substituted for labor.

CHOICE OF TECHNOLOGY *p. 156*

14. One of the key decisions that all firms must make is which technology to use. Profit-maximizing firms will choose the combination of inputs that minimizes costs and therefore maximizes profits.

REVIEW TERMS AND CONCEPTS

average product, *p. 154*

capital-intensive technology, *p. 152*

firm, *p. 148*

labor-intensive technology, *p. 152*

law of diminishing returns, *p. 154*

long run, *p. 151*

marginal product, *p. 153*

normal rate of return, *p. 149*

optimal method of production, *p. 151*

production, *p. 147*

production function *or* total product function, *p. 152*

production technology, *p. 152*

profit (economic profit), *p. 148*

short run, *p. 151*

total cost (total economic cost), *p. 148*

total revenue, *p. 148*

$Profit = total\ revenue - total\ cost$

$Average\ product\ of\ labor = \dfrac{total\ product}{total\ units\ of\ labor}$

PROBLEMS

All problems are available on www.myeconlab.com

1. Consider a firm that uses capital and labor as inputs and sells 5,000 units of output per year at the going market price of $10. Also assume that total labor costs to the firm are $45,000 annually. Assume further that the total capital stock of the firm is currently worth $100,000, that the return available to investors with comparable risks is 10 percent annually, and that there is no depreciation. Is this a profitable firm? Explain your answer.

2. Two former Northwestern University students worked in an investment bank at a salary of $60,000 each for 2 years after they graduated. Together they saved $50,000. After 2 years, they decided to quit their jobs and start a business designing Web sites. They used the $50,000 to buy computer equipment, desks, and chairs. For the next 2 years, they took in $40,000 in revenue each year, paid themselves $10,000 annually each, and rented an office for $18,000 per year. Prior to the investment, their $50,000 was in bonds earning interest at a rate of 10 percent. Are they now earning economic profits? Explain your answer.

3. Suppose that in 2010, you became president of a small non-profit theater company. Your playhouse has 120 seats and a small stage. The actors have national reputations, and demand for tickets is enormous relative to the number of seats available; every performance is sold out months in advance. You are elected because you have demonstrated an ability to raise funds successfully. Describe some of the decisions that you must make in the short run. What might you consider to be your "fixed factor"? What alternative decisions might you be able to make in the long run? Explain.

4. The following table gives total output or total product as a function of labor units used.

LABOR	TOTAL OUTPUT
0	0
1	5
2	9
3	12
4	14
5	15

a. Define diminishing returns.

b. Does the table indicate a situation of diminishing returns? Explain your answer.

5. Suppose that widgets can be produced using two different production techniques, A and B. The following table provides the total input requirements for each of five different total output levels.

	Q = 1		Q = 2		Q = 3		Q = 4		Q = 5	
Tech.	K	L	K	L	K	L	K	L	K	L
A	2	5	1	10	5	14	6	18	8	20
B	5	2	8	3	11	4	14	5	16	6

a. Assuming that the price of labor (P_L) is $1 and the price of capital (P_K) is $2, calculate the total cost of production for each of the five levels of output using the optimal (least-cost) technology at each level.

b. How many labor hours (units of labor) would be employed at each level of output? How many machine hours (units of capital)?

c. Graph total cost of production as a function of output. (Put cost on the *Y*-axis and output, *q*, on the *X*-axis.) Again assume that the optimal technology is used.

d. Repeat a. through c. under the assumption that the price of labor (P_L) rises from \$1 to \$3 while the price of capital (P_K) remains at \$2.

6. A female student who lives on the fourth floor of Bates Hall is assigned to a new room on the seventh floor during her junior year. She has 11 heavy boxes of books and "stuff" to move. Discuss the alternative combinations of capital and labor that might be used to make the move. How would your answer differ if the move were to a new dorm 3 miles across campus and to a new college 400 miles away?

7. The following is a production function.

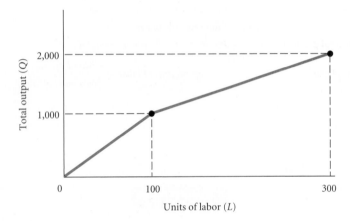

a. Draw a graph of marginal product as a function of output. (*Hint:* Marginal product is the additional number of units of output per unit of labor at each level of output.)

b. Does this graph exhibit diminishing returns? Explain your answer.

8. [Related to the *Economics in Practice* on p. 156] Identical sweaters can be made in one of two ways. With a machine that can be rented for \$50 per hour and a person to run the machine who can be hired at \$25 per hour, five sweaters can be produced in an hour using \$10 worth of wool. Alternatively, I can run the machine with a less skilled worker, producing only four sweaters in an hour with the same \$10 worth of wool. (The less skilled worker is slower and wastes material.) At what wage rate would I choose the less skilled worker?

9. [Related to the *Economics in Practice* on p. 157] When the price of fuel rises, we typically observe fewer accidents. Offer two reasons this might be true.

10. A firm earning zero economic profits is probably suffering losses from the standpoint of general accounting principles. Do you agree or disagree with this argument? Explain why.

11. During the early phases of industrialization, the number of people engaged in agriculture usually drops sharply, even as agricultural output is growing. Given what you know about production technology and production functions, explain this seeming inconsistency.

12. The number of repairs produced by a computer repair shop depends on the number of workers as follows:

NUMBER OF WORKERS	NUMBER OF REPAIRS (PER WEEK)
0	0
1	8
2	20
3	35
4	45
5	52
6	57
7	60

Assume that all inputs (office space, telephone, and utilities) other than labor are fixed in the short run.

a. Add two additional columns to the table and enter the marginal product and average product for each number of workers.

b. Over what range of labor input are there increasing returns to labor? diminishing returns to labor? negative returns to labor?

c. Over what range of labor input is marginal product greater than average product? What is happening to average product as employment increases over this range?

d. Over what range of labor input is marginal product smaller than average product? What is happening to average product as employment increases over this range?

13. Since the end of World War II, manufacturing firms in the United States and in Europe have been moving farther and farther outside of central cities. At the same time, firms in finance, insurance, and other parts of the service sector have been locating near downtown areas in tall buildings. One major reason seems to be that manufacturing firms find it difficult to substitute capital for land, while service-sector firms that use office space do not.

a. What kinds of buildings represent substitution of capital for land?

b. Why do you think that manufacturing firms might find it difficult to substitute capital for land?

c. Why is it relatively easier for a law firm or an insurance company to substitute capital for land?

d. Why is the demand for land likely to be very high near the center of a city?

*e. One of the reasons for substituting capital for land near the center of a city is that land is more expensive near the center. What is true about the relative supply of land near the center of a city? (*Hint:* What is the formula for the area of a circle?)

14. Ted Baxter runs a small, very stable newspaper company in southern Oregon. The paper has been in business for 25 years. The total value of the firm's capital stock is \$1 million, which Ted owns outright. This year the firm earned a total of \$250,000 after out-of-pocket expenses. Without taking the opportunity cost of capital into account, this means that Ted is earning a 25 percent return on his capital. Suppose that risk-free bonds are currently paying a rate of 10 percent to those who buy them.

a. What is meant by the "opportunity cost of capital"?

b. Explain why opportunity costs are "real" costs even though they do not necessarily involve out-of-pocket expenses.

*Note: Problems marked with an asterisk are more challenging.

c. What is the opportunity cost of Ted's capital?

d. How much excess profit is Ted earning?

15. A firm can use three different production technologies, with capital and labor requirements at each level of output as follows:

Daily Output	TECHNOLOGY 1		TECHNOLOGY 2		TECHNOLOGY 3	
	K	L	K	L	K	L
100	3	7	4	5	5	4
150	3	10	4	7	5	5
200	4	11	5	8	6	6
250	5	13	6	10	7	8

a. Suppose the firm is operating in a high-wage country, where capital cost is $100 per unit per day and labor cost is $80 per worker per day. For each level of output, which technology is cheapest?

b. Now suppose the firm is operating in a low-wage country, where capital cost is $100 per unit per day but labor cost is only $40 per unit per day. For each level of output, which technology is cheapest?

c. Suppose the firm moves from a high-wage to a low-wage country but its level of output remains constant at 200 units per day. How will its total employment change?

16. An article on Techspot.com reported on the findings of the marketing research firm iSuppli in its investigation of the cost of the components used to produce the Amazon Kindle 2: "After performing a "teardown," the firm concluded that each Kindle 2 runs approximately $185.49 to produce in-total, or 52% less than its [retail price] of $359." Does this mean that Amazon is making a profit of approximately $173 per Kindle 2?

Source: Matthew DeCarlo, "Teardown reveals production cost of Amazon's Kindle 2," *Techspot.com*, April 22, 2009.

17. The following table represents data for Samantha's Smoothies. Draw a graph showing the total product, marginal product of labor, and average product of labor. Identify where increasing returns, diminishing returns and negative returns set in on the total product curve.

LABOR UNITS (EMPLOYEES)	TOTAL PRODUCT (SMOOTHIES PER HOUR)	MARGINAL PRODUCT OF LABOR	AVERAGE PRODUCT OF LABOR
0	0	—	—
1	50	50	50.0
2	120	70	60.0
3	200	80	66.7
4	250	50	62.5
5	270	20	54.0
6	280	10	46.7
7	260	-20	37.1

18. Which of the following are short-run decisions and which are long-run decisions?

a. General Motors decides to add a second shift to its Arlington, Texas production plant.

b. Gotham Foods International chooses to exit the restaurant industry to concentrate on its wholesale grocery supply business.

c. The Sahara Hotel and Casino in Las Vegas closes two of its three hotel towers in response to low demand.

d. Tony Andretti, owner of Tony the Taxman, hires five new CPAs to work at his tax preparation business.

e. German tool and appliance manufacturer Bosch enters the electric bicycle industry in 2010.

f. General Electric builds a new offshore wind manufacturing plant in the United Kingdom.

19. The data in the table represents annual costs and revenue for Aurora's Orchid Emporium. Aurora works 60 hours a week at the Orchid Emporium. Aurora owns the building that houses the Orchid Emporium, and if she closed the shop, she could rent out the building for $40,000 per year and go to work for Acme Flowers and earn a salary of $30,000 per year. Calculate the economic profit and economic cost for Aurora's Orchid Emporium. Are these figures the same as the accounting cost and accounting profit? Explain.

Wages Paid	$ 22,000
Interest Paid on Loans	8,000
Other Expenditures for Factors of Production	26,000
Total Revenue	115,000

20. Assume that we have a production process that exhibits increasing and then decreasing marginal productivity. That is, as we increase output, the marginal product of labor starts at some level above zero, rises to a maximum, and then eventually falls to zero. Which of the following statements is true? Briefly explain.

a. Total product reaches its highest level where marginal product is equal to average product.

b. Marginal product and average product are equal when marginal product is at its maximum.

c. When marginal product is equal to zero, average product is rising.

d. When marginal product is above average product, average product is rising.

e. When marginal product is equal to average product, output is maximized.

21. Following is information on the production levels of three different firms.

Firm A is currently producing at a quantity where it is experiencing increasing returns.

Firm B is currently producing at a quantity where it is experiencing diminishing returns.

Firm C is currently producing at a quantity where it is experiencing negative returns.

a. If each of the firms cut back on its labor force, what will happen to its marginal product of labor? Why?

b. If each of the firms adds to its labor force, what will happen to its marginal product of labor? Why?

Short-Run Costs and Output Decisions

8

This chapter continues our examination of the decisions that firms make in their quest for profits. You have seen that firms make three specific decisions (Figure 8.1) involving their production. These decisions are:

1. How much output to supply
2. How to produce that output —that is, which production technique/technology to use
3. What quantity of each input to demand

We have assumed so far that firms are in business to earn profits and that they make choices to maximize those profits. (Remember that *profit* refers to economic profit, the difference between revenues and costs—full economic costs.)

In the last chapter, we focused on the production process. This chapter focuses on the *costs* of production. To calculate costs, a firm must know two things: what quantity and combination of inputs it needs to produce its product and how much those inputs cost. (Do not forget that economic costs include a normal return to capital—the opportunity cost of capital.)

Take a moment and look back at the circular flow diagram, Figure II.1 on p. 117. There you can see where we are in our study of the competitive market system. The goal of this chapter is to look behind the supply curve in output markets. It is important to understand, however, that producing output implies demanding inputs at the same time. You can also see in Figure II.1 two of the information sources that firms use in their output supply and input demand decisions: Firms look to *output markets* for the price of output and to *input markets* for the prices of capital and labor.

◀ FIGURE 8.1 **Decisions Facing Firms**

	DECISIONS	are based on	INFORMATION
	1. The quantity of output to *supply*		1. The price of output
	2. How to produce that output (which technique to use)		2. Techniques of production available*
	3. The quantity of each input to *demand*		3. The price of inputs*
			*Determines production costs

Costs in the Short Run

Our emphasis in this chapter is on costs *in the short run only*. Recall that the short run is that period during which two conditions hold: (1) existing firms face limits imposed by some fixed factor of production, and (2) new firms cannot enter and existing firms cannot exit an industry.

In the short run, all firms (competitive and noncompetitive) have costs that they must bear regardless of their output. In fact, some costs must be paid even if the firm stops producing—that is, even if output is zero. These costs are called **fixed costs**, and firms can do nothing in the short run to avoid them or to change them. In the long run, a firm has no fixed costs because it can expand, contract, or exit the industry.

Firms also have certain costs in the short run that depend on the level of output they have chosen. These kinds of costs are called **variable costs**. Total fixed costs and total variable costs together make up **total costs**:

$$TC = TFC + TVC$$

where *TC* denotes total costs, *TFC* denotes total fixed costs, and *TVC* denotes total variable costs. We will return to this equation after discussing fixed costs and variable costs in detail.

Fixed Costs

In discussing fixed costs, we must distinguish between total fixed costs and average fixed costs.

Total Fixed Cost (*TFC*) Total fixed cost is sometimes called *overhead*. If you operate a factory, you must heat the building to keep the pipes from freezing in the winter. Even if no production is taking place, you may have to keep the roof from leaking, pay a guard to protect the building from vandals, and make payments on a long-term lease. There may also be insurance premiums, taxes, and city fees to pay, as well as contract obligations to workers.

Fixed costs represent a larger portion of total costs for some firms than for others. Electric companies, for instance, maintain generating plants, thousands of miles of distribution wires, poles, transformers, and so on. Usually, such plants are financed by issuing bonds to the public—that is, by borrowing. The interest that must be paid on these bonds represents a substantial part of the utilities' operating cost and is a fixed cost in the short run, no matter how much (if any) electricity they are producing.

For the purposes of our discussion in this chapter, we will assume that firms use only two inputs: labor and capital. Although this may seem unrealistic, virtually everything that we will say about firms using these two factors can easily be generalized to firms that use many factors of production. Recall that capital yields services over time in the production of other goods and services. It is the plant and equipment of a manufacturing firm and the computers, desks, chairs, doors, and walls of a law office; it is the software of a Web-based firm and the boat that Bill and Colleen built on their desert island. It is sometimes assumed that capital is a fixed input in the short run and that labor is the only variable input. To be more realistic, however, we will assume that capital has both a fixed *and* a variable component. After all, some capital can be purchased in the short run.

Consider a small consulting firm that employs several economists, research assistants, and secretaries. It rents space in an office building and has a 5-year lease. The rent on the office space can be thought of as a fixed cost in the short run. The monthly electric and heating bills are also essentially fixed (although the amounts may vary slightly from month to month). So are the salaries of the basic administrative staff. Payments on some capital equipment—a large copying machine and the main word-processing system, for instance—can also be thought of as fixed.

The same firm also has costs that vary with output. When there is a great deal of work, the firm hires more employees at both the professional and research assistant levels. The capital used by the consulting firm may also vary, even in the short run. Payments on the computer system do not change, but the firm may rent additional computer time when necessary. The firm can buy additional personal computers, network terminals, or databases quickly if needed. It must pay for the copy machine, but the machine costs more when it is running than when it is not.

Total fixed costs (*TFC*) *or* overhead are those costs that do not change with output even if output is zero. Column 2 of Table 8.1 presents data on the fixed costs of a hypothetical firm. Fixed costs are $1,000 at all levels of output (*q*). Figure 8.2(a) shows total fixed costs as a function of

fixed cost Any cost that does not depend on the firms' level of output. These costs are incurred even if the firm is producing nothing. There are no fixed costs in the long run.

variable cost A cost that depends on the level of production chosen.

total cost (*TC*) Total fixed costs plus total variable costs.

total fixed costs (*TFC*) *or* **overhead** The total of all costs that do not change with output even if output is zero.

output. Because *TFC* does not change with output, the graph is simply a straight horizontal line at $1,000. The important thing to remember here is that firms have no control over fixed costs in the short run.

	TABLE 8.1	Short-Run Fixed Cost (Total and Average) of a Hypothetical Firm	
(1) *q*	(2) *TFC*	(3) *AFC (TFC/q)*
0	$1,000	$ –
1	1,000	1,000
2	1,000	500
3	1,000	333
4	1,000	250
5	1,000	200

Average Fixed Cost (*AFC*)

Average fixed cost (*AFC*) is total fixed cost (*TFC*) divided by the number of units of output (*q*):

$$AFC = \frac{TFC}{q}$$

average fixed cost (*AFC*) Total fixed cost divided by the number of units of output; a per-unit measure of fixed costs.

For example, if the firm in Figure 8.2 produced 3 units of output, average fixed costs would be $333 ($1,000 ÷ 3). If the same firm produced 5 units of output, average fixed cost would be $200 ($1,000 ÷ 5). *Average fixed cost falls as output rises* because the same total is being spread over, or divided by, a larger number of units (see column 3 of Table 8.1). This phenomenon is sometimes called **spreading overhead**.

Graphs of average fixed cost, like that in Figure 8.2(b) (which presents the average fixed cost data from Table 8.1), are downward-sloping curves. Notice that *AFC* approaches zero as the quantity of output increases. If output were 100,000 units, average fixed cost would equal only 1 cent per unit in our example ($1,000 ÷ 100,000 = $0.01). *AFC* never actually reaches zero.

spreading overhead The process of dividing total fixed costs by more units of output. Average fixed cost declines as quantity rises.

Variable Costs

Total Variable Cost (*TVC*)

Total variable cost (*TVC*) is the sum of those costs that vary with the level of output in the short run. To produce more output, a firm uses more inputs. The cost of additional output depends directly on what additional inputs are required and how much they cost.

total variable cost (*TVC*) The total of all costs that vary with output in the short run.

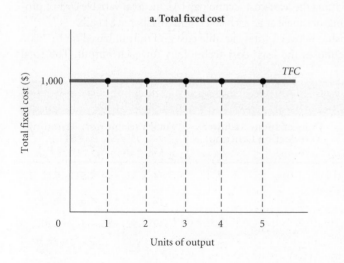
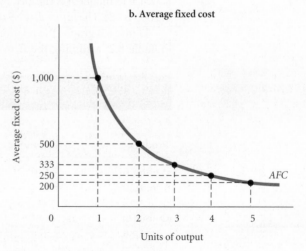

▲ **FIGURE 8.2 Short-Run Fixed Cost (Total and Average) of a Hypothetical Firm**
Average fixed cost is simply total fixed cost divided by the quantity of output. As output increases, average fixed cost declines because we are dividing a fixed number ($1,000) by a larger and larger quantity.

As you saw in Chapter 7, input requirements are determined by technology. Firms generally have a number of production techniques available to them, and the option they choose is assumed to be the one that produces the desired level of output at the least cost. To find out which technology involves the least cost, a firm must compare the total variable costs of producing that level of output using different production techniques.

This is as true of small businesses as it is of large manufacturing firms. Suppose, for example, that you own a small farm. A certain amount of work has to be done to plant and harvest your 120 acres. You might hire four farmhands and divide up the tasks, or you might buy several pieces of complex farm machinery (capital) and do the work single-handedly. Your final choice depends on a number of things. What machinery is available? What does it do? Will it work on small fields such as yours? How much will it cost to buy each piece of equipment? What wage will you have to pay farmhands? How many will you need to hire to get the job done? If machinery is expensive and labor is cheap, you will probably choose the labor-intensive technology. If farm labor is expensive and the local farm equipment dealer is going out of business, you might get a good deal on some machinery and choose the capital-intensive method.

Having compared the costs of alternative production techniques, the firm may be influenced in its choice by the current scale of its operation. Remember, in the short run, a firm is locked into a *fixed* scale of operations. A firm currently producing on a small scale may find that a labor-intensive technique is least costly whether or not labor is comparatively expensive. The same firm producing on a larger scale might find a capital-intensive technique to be less costly.

total variable cost curve A graph that shows the relationship between total variable cost and the level of a firm's output.

The **total variable cost curve** is a graph that shows the relationship between total variable cost and the level of a firm's output (q). At any given level of output, total variable cost depends on (1) the techniques of production that are available and (2) the prices of the inputs required by each technology. To examine this relationship in more detail, let us look at some hypothetical production figures.

Table 8.2 presents an analysis that might lie behind three points on a typical firm's total variable cost curve. In this case, there are two production techniques available, A and B, one somewhat more capital-intensive than the other. We will assume that the price of labor is $1 per unit and the price of capital is $2 per unit. For the purposes of this example, we focus on *variable capital*—that is, on capital that can be changed in the short run. In practice, some capital (such as buildings and large, specialized machines) is fixed in the short run. In our example, we will use K to denote variable capital. Remember, however, that the firm has other capital, capital that is fixed in the short run.

Analysis reveals that to produce 1 unit of output, the labor-intensive technique is least costly. Technique A requires 4 units of both capital and labor, which would cost a total of $12. Technique B requires 6 units of labor but only 2 units of capital for a total cost of only $10. To maximize profits, the firm would use technique B to produce 1 unit. The total variable cost of producing 1 unit of output would thus be $10.

The relatively labor-intensive technique B is also the best method of production for 2 units of output. By using B, the firm can produce 2 units for $18. If the firm decides to produce 3 units of output, however, technique A is cheaper. By using the least-cost technology (A), the total variable cost of production is $24. The firm will use 9 units of capital at $2 each and 6 units of labor at $1 each.

Figure 8.3 graphs the relationship between total variable cost and output based on the data in Table 8.2, assuming the firm chooses the least-cost technology for each output. The total

TABLE 8.2 Derivation of Total Variable Cost Schedule from Technology and Factor Prices

Produce	Using Technique	Units of Input Required (Production Function) K	L	Total Variable Cost Assuming $P_K = \$2, P_L = \$1$ $TVC = (K \times P_K) + (L \times P_L)$
1 unit of output	A	4	4	$(4 \times \$2) + (4 \times \$1) = \$12$
	B	2	6	$(2 \times \$2) + (6 \times \$1) = \boxed{\$10}$
2 units of output	A	7	6	$(7 \times \$2) + (6 \times \$1) = \$20$
	B	4	10	$(4 \times \$2) + (10 \times \$1) = \boxed{\$18}$
3 units of output	A	9	6	$(9 \times \$2) + (6 \times \$1) = \boxed{\$24}$
	B	6	14	$(6 \times \$2) + (14 \times \$1) = \$26$

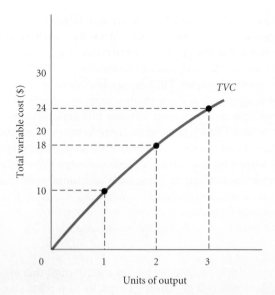

◀ **FIGURE 8.3 Total Variable Cost Curve**

In Table 8.2, total variable cost is derived from production requirements and input prices. A total variable cost curve expresses the relationship between *TVC* and total output.

variable cost curve embodies information about both factor, or input, prices and technology. It shows the cost of production using the best available technique at each output level given current factor prices.

Marginal Cost (*MC*)

The most important of all cost concepts is that of **marginal cost (*MC*)**, the increase in total cost that results from the production of 1 more unit of output. Let us say, for example, that a firm is producing 1,000 units of output per period and decides to raise its rate of output to 1,001. Producing the extra unit raises costs, and the increase—that is, the cost of producing the 1,001st unit—is the marginal cost. Focusing on the "margin" is one way of looking at variable costs: marginal costs reflect changes in variable costs because they vary when output changes. Fixed costs do not change when output changes.

Table 8.3 shows how marginal cost is derived from total variable cost by simple subtraction. The total variable cost of producing the first unit of output is $10. Raising production from 1 unit to 2 units increases total variable cost from $10 to $18; the difference is the marginal cost of the second unit, or $8. Raising output from 2 to 3 units increases total variable cost from $18 to $24. The marginal cost of the third unit, therefore, is $6.

marginal cost (*MC*) The increase in total cost that results from producing 1 more unit of output. Marginal costs reflect changes in variable costs.

TABLE 8.3 Derivation of Marginal Cost from Total Variable Cost

Units of Output	Total Variable Costs ($)	Marginal Costs ($)
0	0	
1	10	10
2	18	8
3	24	6

It is important to think for a moment about the nature of marginal cost. Specifically, marginal cost is the cost of the added inputs, or resources, needed to produce 1 additional unit of output. Look back at Table 8.2 and think about the additional capital and labor needed to go from 1 unit to 2 units. Producing 1 unit of output with technique *B* requires 2 units of capital and 6 units of labor; producing 2 units of output using the same technique requires 4 units of capital and 10 units of labor. Thus, the second unit requires 2 *additional* units of capital and 4 *additional* units of labor. What, then, is the added, or marginal, cost of the second unit? Two units of capital cost $2 each ($4 total) and 4 units of labor cost $1 each (another $4), for a total marginal cost of $8, which is the number we derived in Table 8.3. Although the easiest way to derive marginal cost is to look at total variable cost and subtract, do not lose sight of the fact that when a firm increases its output level, it hires or demands more inputs. *Marginal cost* measures the *additional* cost of inputs required to produce each successive unit of output.

The Shape of the Marginal Cost Curve in the Short Run The assumption of a fixed factor of production in the short run means that a firm is stuck at its current scale of operation (in our example, the size of the plant). As a firm tries to increase its output, it will eventually find itself trapped by that scale. Thus, our definition of the short run also implies that *marginal cost eventually rises with output*. The firm can hire more labor and use more materials—that is, it can add variable inputs—but diminishing returns eventually set in.

Recall from Chapter 7 the sandwich shop with one grill and too many workers trying to prepare sandwiches on it. With a fixed grill capacity, more laborers could make more sandwiches, but the marginal product of each successive cook declined as more people tried to use the grill. If each additional unit of labor adds less and less to total output, *it follows that more labor is needed to produce each additional unit of output*. Thus, each additional unit of output costs more to produce. In other words, *diminishing returns, or decreasing marginal product, imply increasing marginal cost* as illustrated in Figure 8.4.

To reiterate:

> In the short run, every firm is constrained by some fixed input that (1) leads to diminishing returns to variable inputs and (2) limits its capacity to produce. As a firm approaches that capacity, it becomes increasingly costly to produce successively higher levels of output. Marginal costs ultimately increase with output in the short run.

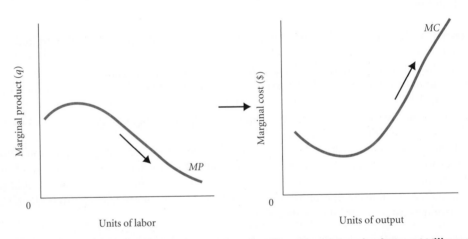

▲ **FIGURE 8.4 Declining Marginal Product Implies That Marginal Cost Will Eventually Rise with Output**

In the short run, every firm is constrained by some fixed factor of production. A fixed factor implies diminishing returns (declining marginal product) and a limited capacity to produce. As that limit is approached, marginal costs rise.

Graphing Total Variable Costs and Marginal Costs Figure 8.5 shows the total variable cost curve and the marginal cost curve of a typical firm. Notice first that the shape of the marginal cost curve is consistent with short-run diminishing returns. At first, *MC* declines, but eventually the fixed factor of production begins to constrain the firm and marginal cost rises. Up to 100 units of output, producing each successive unit of output costs slightly less than producing the one before. Beyond 100 units, however, the cost of each successive unit is greater than the one before. (Remember the sandwich shop.)

More output costs more than less output. Total variable costs (*TVC*), therefore, *always increase* when output increases. Even though the cost of each additional unit changes, *total* variable cost rises when output rises. Thus, the *total* variable cost curve always has a positive slope.

You might think of the total variable cost curve as a staircase. Each step takes you out along the quantity axis by a single unit, and the height of each step is the increase in total variable cost.

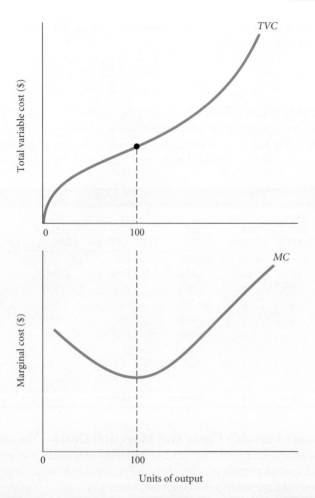

▲ **FIGURE 8.5 Total Variable Cost and Marginal Cost for a Typical Firm**
Total variable costs always increase with output. Marginal cost is the cost of producing each additional unit.
Thus, the marginal cost curve shows how total variable cost changes with single-unit increases in total output.

As you climb the stairs, you are always going up, but the steps have different heights. At first, the stairway is steep, but as you climb, the steps get smaller (marginal cost declines). The 100th stair is the smallest. As you continue to walk out beyond 100 units, the steps begin to get larger; the staircase gets steeper (marginal cost increases).

Remember that the slope of a line is equal to the change in the units measured on the Y-axis divided by the change in the units measured on the X-axis. The slope of a total variable cost curve is thus the change in total variable cost divided by the change in output ($\Delta TVC/\Delta q$). Because marginal cost is by definition the change in total variable cost resulting from an increase in output of one unit ($\Delta q = 1$), *marginal cost actually is the slope of the total variable cost curve*:

$$\text{slope of } TVC = \frac{\Delta TVC}{\Delta q} = \frac{\Delta TVC}{1} = \Delta TVC = MC$$

Notice that up to 100 units, marginal cost decreases and the variable cost curve becomes flatter. The slope of the total variable cost curve is declining—that is, total variable cost increases, but at a *decreasing rate*. Beyond 100 units of output, marginal cost increases and the total variable cost curve gets steeper—total variable costs continue to increase, but at an *increasing rate*.

A more complete picture of the costs of a hypothetical firm appears in Table 8.4. Column 2 shows total variable costs derived from information on input prices and technology. Column 3 derives marginal cost by simple subtraction. For example, raising output from 3 units to 4 units increases variable costs from $24 to $32, making the marginal cost of the fourth unit $8 ($32 − $24). The marginal cost of the fifth unit is $10, the difference between $32 (*TVC*) for 4 units and $42 (*TVC*) for 5 units.

average variable cost (AVC)
Total variable cost divided by the number of units of output.

Average Variable Cost (AVC)   **Average variable cost (AVC)** is total variable cost divided by the number of units of output (q):

$$AVC = \frac{TVC}{q}$$

In Table 8.4, we calculate *AVC* in column 4 by dividing the numbers in column 2 (*TVC*) by the numbers in column 1 (*q*). For example, if the total variable cost of producing 5 units of output is $42, then the average variable cost is $42 ÷ 5, or $8.40. Marginal cost is the cost of 1 *additional unit*. Average variable cost is the total variable cost divided by the total number of units produced.

TABLE 8.4   Short-Run Costs of a Hypothetical Firm

(1) q	(2) TVC	(3) MC (Δ TVC)	(4) AVC (TVC/q)	(5) TFC	(6) TC (TVC + TFC)	(7) AFC (TFC/q)	(8) ATC (TC/q or AFC + AVC)
0	$ 0	$ –	$ –	$1,000	$1,000	$ –	$ –
1	10	10	10	1,000	1,010	1,000	1,010
2	18	8	9	1,000	1,018	500	509
3	24	6	8	1,000	1,024	333	341
4	32	8	8	1,000	1,032	250	258
5	42	10	8.4	1,000	1,042	200	208.4
—	—	—	—	—	—	—	—
—	—	—	—	—	—	—	—
—	—	—	—	—	—	—	—
500	8,000	20	16	1,000	9,000	2	18

Graphing Average Variable Costs and Marginal Costs   The relationship between average variable cost and marginal cost can be illustrated graphically. When marginal cost is *below* average variable cost, average variable cost declines toward it. When marginal cost is *above* average variable cost, average variable cost increases toward it.

Figure 8.6 duplicates the bottom graph for a typical firm in Figure 8.5 but adds average variable cost. As the graph shows, average variable cost *follows* marginal cost but lags behind. As we move from left to right, we are looking at higher and higher levels of output per period. As we increase production, marginal cost—which at low levels of production is above $3.50 per unit—falls as coordination and cooperation begin to play a role. At 100 units of output, marginal cost has fallen to $2.50. Notice that average variable cost falls as well, but not as rapidly as marginal cost.

After 100 units of output, we begin to see diminishing returns. Marginal cost begins to increase as higher and higher levels of output are produced. However, notice that average cost is still falling until 200 units because marginal cost remains below it. At 100 units of output, marginal cost is $2.50 per unit but the *average* variable cost of production is $3.50. Thus, even though marginal cost is rising after 100 units, it is still pulling the average of $3.50 downward.

▶ **FIGURE 8.6 More Short-Run Costs**

When marginal cost is *below* average cost, average cost is declining. When marginal cost is *above* average cost, average cost is increasing. Rising marginal cost intersects average variable cost at the minimum point of *AVC*.

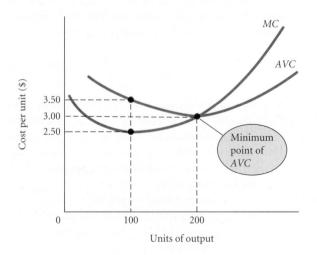

At 200 units, however, marginal cost has risen to $3 and average cost has fallen to $3; marginal and average costs are equal. At this point, marginal cost continues to rise with higher output. From 200 units upward, *MC* is *above AVC* and thus exerts an upward pull on the average variable cost curve. At levels of output below 200 units, marginal cost is below average variable cost and average variable cost decreases as output increases. At levels of output above 200 units, *MC* is above *AVC* and *AVC* increases as output increases. If you follow this logic, you will see that marginal cost intersects average variable cost at the lowest, or minimum, point of *AVC*.

An example using test scores should help you understand the relationship between *MC* and *AVC*. Consider the following sequence of test scores: 95, 85, 92, 88. The average of these four scores is 90. Suppose you get an 80 on your fifth test. This score will drag down your average to 88. Now suppose you get an 85 on your sixth test. This score is higher than 80, but its still *below* your 88 average. As a result, your average continues to fall (from 88 to 87.5) even though your marginal test score rose. If instead of an 85 you get an 89—just one point over your average—you have turned your average around; it is now rising.

Total Costs

We are now ready to complete the cost picture by adding total fixed costs to total variable costs. Recall that

$$TC = TFC + TVC$$

Total cost is graphed in Figure 8.7, where the same vertical distance (equal to *TFC*, which is constant) is simply added to *TVC* at every level of output. In Table 8.4, column 6 adds the total fixed cost of $1,000 to total variable cost to arrive at total cost.

Average Total Cost (*ATC*)   Average total cost (*ATC*) is total cost divided by the number of units of output (*q*):

$$ATC = \frac{TC}{q}$$

Column 8 in Table 8.4 shows the result of dividing the costs in column 6 by the quantities in column 1. For example, at 5 units of output, *total* cost is $1,042; *average* total cost is $1,042 ÷ 5, or $208.40. The average total cost of producing 500 units of output is only $18—that is, $9,000 ÷ 500.

Another, more revealing, way of deriving average total cost is to add average fixed cost and average variable cost together:

$$ATC = AFC + AVC$$

For example, column 8 in Table 8.4 is the sum of column 4 (*AVC*) and column 7 (*AFC*).

average total cost (*ATC*)
Total cost divided by the number of units of output.

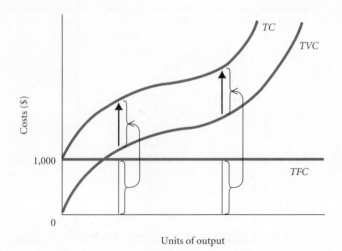

▲ **FIGURE 8.7 Total Cost = Total Fixed Cost + Total Variable Cost**
Adding *TFC* to *TVC* means adding the same amount of total fixed cost to every level of total variable cost. Thus, the total cost curve has the same shape as the total variable cost curve; it is simply higher by an amount equal to *TFC*.

Figure 8.8 derives average total cost graphically for a typical firm. The bottom part of the figure graphs average fixed cost. At 100 units of output, average fixed cost is $TFC/q = \$1,000 \div 100 = \$10$. At 400 units of output, $AFC = \$1,000 \div 400 = \$2.50$. The top part of Figure 8.8 shows the declining AFC added to AVC at each level of output. Because AFC gets smaller and smaller, ATC gets closer and closer to AVC as output increases, but the two lines never meet.

The Relationship Between Average Total Cost and Marginal Cost   The relationship between average *total* cost and marginal cost is exactly the same as the relationship between average *variable* cost and marginal cost. The average total cost curve follows the marginal cost curve but lags behind because it is an average over all units of output. The average total cost curve lags behind the marginal cost curve even more than the average variable cost curve does because the cost of each added unit of production is now averaged not only with the variable cost of all previous units produced but also with fixed costs.

Fixed costs equal $1,000 and are incurred even when the output level is zero. Thus, the first unit of output in the example in Table 8.4 costs $10 in variable cost to produce. The second unit costs only $8 in variable cost to produce. The total cost of 2 units is $1,018; average total cost of the two is ($1,010 + $8)/2, or $509. The marginal cost of the third unit is only $6. The total cost of 3 units is thus $1,024, or $1,018 + $6, and the average total cost of 3 units is ($1,010 + $8 + $6)/3, or $341.

As you saw with the test scores example, marginal cost is what drives changes in average total cost. If marginal cost is *below* average total cost, average total cost will *decline* toward marginal cost. If marginal cost is *above* average total cost, average total cost will *increase*. As a result, marginal cost

▶ FIGURE 8.8 **Average Total Cost = Average Variable Cost + Average Fixed Cost**

To get average total cost, we add average fixed and average variable costs at all levels of output. Because average fixed cost falls with output, an ever-declining amount is added to AVC. Thus, AVC and ATC get closer together as output increases, but the two lines never meet.

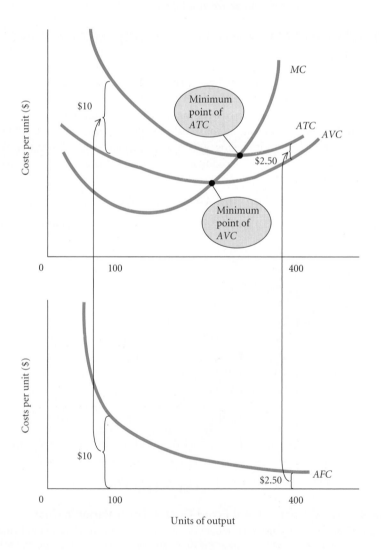

intersects average *total* cost at *ATC*'s minimum point for the same reason that it intersects the average *variable* cost curve at its minimum point.

Short-Run Costs: A Review

Let us now pause to review what we have learned about the behavior of firms. We know that firms make three basic choices: how much product or output to produce or supply, how to produce that output, and how much of each input to demand to produce what they intend to supply. We assume that these choices are made to maximize profits. Profits are equal to the difference between a firm's revenue from the sale of its product and the costs of producing that product: profit = total revenue – total cost.

So far, we have looked only at costs, but costs are just one part of the profit equation. To complete the picture, we must turn to the output market and see how these costs compare with the price that a product commands in the market. Before we do so, however, it is important to consolidate what we have said about costs.

Before a firm does anything else, it needs to know the different methods that it can use to produce its product. The technologies available determine the combinations of inputs that are needed to produce each level of output. Firms choose the technique that produces the desired level of output at the least cost. The cost curves that result from the analysis of all this information show the cost of producing each level of output using the best available technology.

Remember that so far, we have talked only about short-run costs. The curves we have drawn are therefore *short-run cost curves*. The shape of these curves is determined in large measure by the assumptions that we make about the short run, especially the assumption that some fixed factor of production leads to diminishing returns. Given this assumption, marginal costs eventually rise and average cost curves are likely to be U-shaped. Table 8.5 summarizes the cost concepts that we have discussed.

After gaining a complete knowledge of how to produce a product and how much it will cost to produce it at each level of output, the firm turns to the market to find out what it can sell its product for. We now turn our attention to the output market.

TABLE 8.5 A Summary of Cost Concepts		
Term	Definition	Equation
Accounting costs	Out-of-pocket costs or costs as an accountant would define them. Sometimes referred to as *explicit costs*.	—
Economic costs	Costs that include the full opportunity costs of all inputs. These include what are often called *implicit costs*.	—
Total fixed costs (TFC)	Costs that do not depend on the quantity of output produced. These must be paid even if output is zero.	—
Total variable costs (TVC)	Costs that vary with the level of output.	—
Total cost (TC)	The total economic cost of all the inputs used by a firm in production.	$TC = TFC + TVC$
Average fixed costs (AFC)	Fixed costs per unit of output.	$AFC = TFC/q$
Average variable costs (AVC)	Variable costs per unit of output.	$AVC = TVC/q$
Average total costs (ATC)	Total costs per unit of output.	$ATC = TC/q$ $ATC = AFC + AVC$
Marginal costs (MC)	The increase in total cost that results from producing 1 additional unit of output.	$MC = \Delta TC/\Delta q$

ECONOMICS IN PRACTICE

Average and Marginal Costs at a College

Pomona College in California has an annual operating budget of $120 million. With this budget, the college educates and houses 1,500 students. So the average total cost of educating a Pomona student is $80,000 per year, some of which comes from the college endowment and gifts. Suppose college administrators are considering a small increase in the number of students it accepts and believe they could do so without sacrificing quality of teaching and research. Given that the level of tuition and room and board is considerably less than $80,000, can the administrators make a financial case to support such a move?

The key issue here is to recognize that for a college like Pomona—and indeed for most colleges—the average total cost of educating a student is higher than the marginal cost. For a very small increase in the number of students, the course-related expenses probably would not go up at all. These students could

likely be absorbed into existing courses with no added expense for faculty, buildings, or administrators. Housing might be more of a constraint, but even in that regard administrators might find some flexibility. Thus, from a financial perspective, the key question about expansion is not how the average total cost of education compares to the tuition, but how tuition compares to the marginal cost. For this reason, many colleges would, in fact, find it financially advantageous to expand student populations if they could do so without changing the quality and environment of the school.

Suppose that of Pomona's $120 million budget, $60 million was fixed costs: maintenance of the physical campus, basic salaries, and other fixed operating costs. Suppose further that the full marginal cost of providing the education was $40,000 per student and constant. Using these figures, one can easily create the following table and draw the cost curves.

| | | Costs in Dollars | | |
Students	Total Fixed Cost	Total Variable Cost	Total Cost	Average Total Cost
500	$60 million	$ 20 million	$ 80 million	$160,000
1,000	60 million	40 million	100 million	100,000
1,500	60 million	60 million	120 million	80,000
2,000	60 million	80 million	140 million	70,000
2,500	60 million	100 million	160 million	64,000

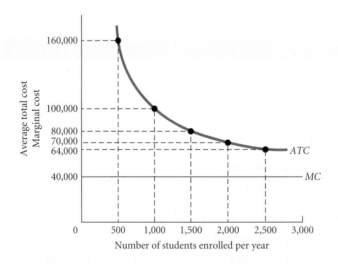

The cost curves also help us understand the downward spiral that can affect colleges as their populations fall. In 2005, Antioch College in Ohio announced that it would be phasing out its undergraduate program. The culprit? Declining attendance caused the average total cost of educating the remaining few students to skyrocket despite attempts to control costs. Given the

inevitability of some fixed costs of education (to educate even a modest student body requires facilities and a college president, for example), as the number of students falls, the average total cost—which is total cost divided by the number of students—rises. For organizations such as colleges and museums, the numbers game is very important to their survival.

Output Decisions: Revenues, Costs, and Profit Maximization

To calculate potential profits, firms must combine their cost analyses with information on potential revenues from sales. After all, if a firm cannot sell its product for more than the cost of production, it will not be in business long. In contrast, if the market gives the firm a price that is significantly greater than the cost it incurs to produce a unit of its product, the firm may have an incentive to expand output. Large profits might also attract new competitors to the market.

Let us now examine in detail how a firm goes about determining how much output to produce. We will begin by examining the decisions of a perfectly competitive firm.

Perfect Competition

Perfect competition exists in an industry that contains many relatively small firms producing identical products. In a perfectly competitive industry, no single firm has any control over prices. In other words, an individual firm cannot affect the market price of its product or the prices of the inputs that it buys. This important characteristic follows from two assumptions. First, a competitive industry is composed of many firms, each small relative to the size of the industry. Second, every firm in a perfectly competitive industry produces **homogeneous products**, which means that one firm's output cannot be distinguished from the output of the others.

These assumptions limit the decisions open to competitive firms and simplify the analysis of competitive behavior. Firms in perfectly competitive industries do not differentiate their products and do not make decisions about price. Instead, each firm takes prices as given—that is, as determined in the market by the laws of supply and demand—and decides only how much to produce and how to produce it.

The idea that competitive firms are "price-takers" is central to our discussion. Of course, we do not mean that firms cannot affix price tags to their merchandise; all firms have this ability. We mean that given the availability of perfect substitutes, any product priced over the market price will not be sold.

These assumptions also imply that the demand for the product of a competitive firm is perfectly elastic (Chapter 5). For example, consider the Ohio corn farmer whose situation is shown in Figure 8.9. The left side of the diagram represents the current conditions in the market. Corn is currently selling for $6.00 per bushel.[1] The right side of the diagram shows the demand for corn as the farmer sees it. If she were to raise her price, she would sell no corn at all; because there are perfect substitutes available, the quantity demanded of her corn would drop to zero. To lower her price would be silly because she can sell all she wants at the current price. (Remember, each farmer's production is very small relative to the entire corn market.)

perfect competition An industry structure in which there are many firms, each small relative to the industry, producing identical products and in which no firm is large enough to have any control over prices. In perfectly competitive industries, new competitors can freely enter and exit the market.

homogenous products Undifferentiated products; products that are identical to, or indistinguishable from, one another.

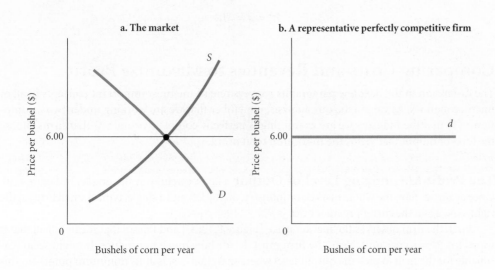

a. The market

b. A representative perfectly competitive firm

◀ **FIGURE 8.9 Demand Facing a Single Firm in a Perfectly Competitive Market**

If a representative firm in a perfectly competitive market raises the price of its output above $6.00, the quantity demanded of *that firm's* output will drop to zero. Each firm faces a perfectly elastic demand curve, *d*.

[1] Capital letters refer to the entire market, and lowercase letters refer to representative firms. For example, in Figure 8.9, the market demand curve is labeled *D* and the demand curve facing the firm is labeled *d*.

In perfect competition, we also assume easy entry—that firms can easily enter and exit the industry. If firms in an industry are earning high profits, new firms are likely to spring up. There are no barriers that prevent a new firm from competing. Fast-food restaurants are quick to spring up when a new shopping center opens, and new gas stations appear when a housing development or a new highway is built. When it became clear a number of years ago that many people would be buying products online, thousands of e-commerce start-ups flooded the Web with new online "shops."

We also assume *easy exit*. When a firm finds itself suffering losses or earning low profits, one option is to go out of business, or exit the industry. Everyone knows a favorite restaurant that went out of business. Changes in cost of production, falling prices from international or regional competition, and changing technology may turn business profits into losses and failure.

The best examples of perfect competition are probably found in agriculture. In that industry, products are absolutely homogeneous—it is impossible to distinguish one farmer's wheat from another's—and prices are set by the forces of supply and demand in a huge national market.

Total Revenue and Marginal Revenue

total revenue (*TR*) The total amount that a firm takes in from the sale of its product: the price per unit times the quantity of output the firm decides to produce ($P \times q$).

Profit is the difference between total revenue and total cost. **Total revenue (*TR*)** is the total amount that a firm takes in from the sale of its product. A perfectly competitive firm sells each unit of product for the same price, regardless of the output level it has chosen. Therefore, total revenue is simply the price per unit times the quantity of output that the firm decides to produce:

$$\text{total revenue} = \text{price} \times \text{quantity}$$
$$TR = P \times q$$

marginal revenue (*MR*) The additional revenue that a firm takes in when it increases output by one additional unit. In perfect competition, $P = MR$.

Marginal revenue (*MR*) is the added revenue that a firm takes in when it increases output by 1 additional unit. If a firm producing 10,521 units of output per month increases that output to 10,522 units per month, it will take in an additional amount of revenue each month. The revenue associated with the 10,522nd unit is the amount for which the firm sells that 1 unit. Thus, for a competitive firm, marginal revenue is equal to the current market price of each additional unit sold. In Figure 8.9, for example, the market price is $6.00. Thus, if the representative firm raises its output from 10,521 units to 10,522 units, its revenue will increase by $6.00.

A firm's *marginal revenue curve* shows how much revenue the firm will gain by raising output by 1 unit at every level of output. The *marginal revenue curve and the demand curve facing a competitive firm are identical*. The horizontal line in Figure 8.9(b) can be thought of as both the demand curve facing the firm and its marginal revenue curve:

$$P^* = d = MR$$

Comparing Costs and Revenues to Maximize Profit

The discussion in the next few paragraphs conveys one of the most important concepts in all of microeconomics. As we pursue our analysis, remember that we are working under two assumptions: (1) that the industry we are examining is perfectly competitive and (2) that firms choose the level of output that yields the maximum total profit.

The Profit-Maximizing Level of Output Look carefully at the graphs in Figure 8.10. Once again, we have the whole market, or industry, on the left and a single, typical small firm on the right. And again the current market price is P^*.

First, the firm observes the market price [Figure 8.10(a)] and knows that it can sell all that it wants for $P^* = \$5$ per unit. Next, the firm must decide how much to produce. It might seem reasonable for the firm to pick the output level where marginal cost is at its minimum point—in this case, at an output of 100 units. Here the difference between marginal revenue, $5.00, and marginal cost, $2.50, is the greatest. As it happens, 100 units is *not* the optimal production level.

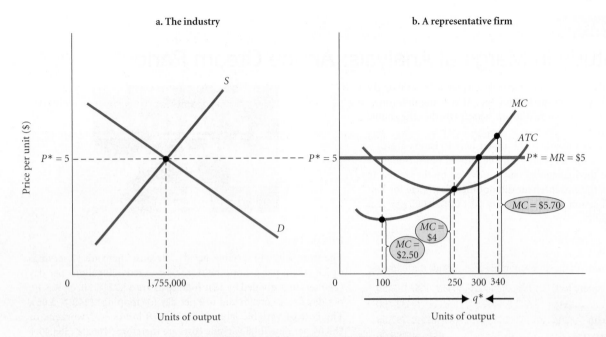

a. The industry   b. A representative firm

▲ FIGURE 8.10 **The Profit-Maximizing Level of Output for a Perfectly Competitive Firm**

If price is above marginal cost, as it is at 100 and 250 units of output, profits can be increased by raising output; each additional unit increases revenues by more than it costs to produce the additional output. Beyond $q^* = 300$, however, added output will reduce profits. At 340 units of output, an additional unit of output costs more to produce than it will bring in revenue when sold on the market. Profit-maximizing output is thus q^*, the point at which $P^* = MC$.

Remember that a firm wants to maximize the difference between *total* revenue and *total* cost, not the difference between *marginal* revenue and *marginal* cost. The fact that marginal revenue is greater than marginal cost at a level of 100 indicates that profit is *not* being maximized. Think about the 101st unit. Adding that single unit to production each period adds $5.00 to revenues but adds only about $2.50 to cost. Profits each period would be higher by about $2.50. Thus, the optimal (profit-maximizing) level of output is clearly higher than 100 units.

Now look at an output level of 250 units. Here, once again, raising output increases profit. The revenue gained from producing the 251st unit (marginal revenue) is still $5, and the cost of the 251st unit (marginal cost) is only about $4. As long as marginal revenue is greater than marginal cost, even though the difference between the two is getting smaller, added output means added profit. Whenever marginal revenue exceeds marginal cost, the revenue gained by increasing output by 1 unit per period exceeds the cost incurred by doing so. This logic leads us to 300 units of output. At 300 units, marginal cost has risen to $5. At 300 units of output, $P^* = MR = MC = \$5$.

Notice that if the firm were to produce *more* than 300 units, marginal cost would rise above marginal revenue. At 340 units of output, for example, the cost of the 341st unit is about $5.70 while that added unit of output still brings in only $5 in revenue, thus reducing profit. It simply does not pay to increase output above the point where marginal cost rises above marginal revenue because such increases will *reduce* profit. The profit-maximizing perfectly competitive firm will produce up to the point where the price of its output is just equal to short-run marginal cost—the level of output at which $P^* = MC$. Thus, in Figure 8.10, the profit-maximizing level of output, q^*, is 300 units.

Keep in mind, though, that all types of firms (not just those in perfectly competitive industries) are profit maximizers. The profit-maximizing output level for *all* firms is the output level where $MR = MC$. In perfect competition, however, $MR = P$, as shown earlier. Hence, for perfectly competitive firms, we can rewrite our profit-maximizing condition as $P = MC$.

Important note: The key idea here is that firms will produce as long as marginal revenue exceeds marginal cost. When marginal cost rises smoothly, as it does in Figure 8.10, the profit-maximizing condition is that MR (or P) *exactly equals MC*. If marginal cost moves up in increments—as it does in the following numerical example—marginal revenue or price may never exactly equal marginal cost. The key idea still holds.

Case Study in Marginal Analysis: An Ice Cream Parlor

The following is a description of the decisions made in 2000 by the owner of a small ice cream parlor in Ohio. After being in business for 1 year, this entrepreneur had to ask herself whether she should stay in business.

The cost figures on which she based her decisions are presented next. These numbers are real, but they do not include one important item: the managerial labor provided by the owner. In her calculations, the entrepreneur did not include a wage for herself, but we will assume an opportunity cost of $30,000 per year ($2,500 per month).

FIXED COSTS

The fixed components of the store's monthly costs include the following:

Rent (1,150 square feet)	$2,012.50
Electricity	325.00
Interest on loan	737.50
Maintenance	295.00
Telephone	65.00
Total	$3,435.00

Not all the items on this list are strictly fixed, however. Electricity costs, for example, would be slightly higher if the store produced more ice cream and stayed open longer, but the added cost would be minimal.

VARIABLE COSTS

The ice cream store's variable costs include two components: (1) behind-the-counter labor costs and (2) cost of making ice cream. The store hires employees at a wage of $5.15 per hour. Including the employer's share of the Social Security tax, the gross cost of labor is $5.54 per hour. Two employees work in the store at all times. The full cost of producing ice cream is $3.27 per gallon. Each gallon contains approximately 12 servings. Customers can add toppings free of charge, and the average cost of the toppings taken by a customer is about $.05:

Gross labor costs	$5.54/hour
Costs of producing one gallon of ice cream (12 servings per gallon)	$3.27
Average cost of added toppings per serving	$.05

REVENUES

The store sells ice cream cones, sundaes, and floats. The average price of a purchase at the store is $1.45. The store is open 8 hours per day, 26 days a month, and serves an average of 240 customers per day:

Average purchase	$1.45
Days open per month	26
Average number of customers per day	240

From the preceding information, it is possible to calculate the store's average monthly profit. Total revenue is equal to 240 customers × $1.45 per customer × 26 days open in an average month: $TR = \$9,048$ per month.

PROFITS

The store sells 240 servings per day. Because there are 12 servings of ice cream per gallon, the store uses exactly 20 gallons per day (240 servings divided by 12). Total costs are $3.27 × 20, or $65.40, per day for ice cream and $12 per day for toppings (240 × $.05). The cost of variable labor is $5.54 × 8 hours × 2 workers, or $88.64 per day. Total variable costs are therefore $166.04 ($65.40 + $12.00 + $88.64) per day. The store is open 26 days a month, so the total variable cost per month is $4,317.04.

Adding fixed costs of $3,435.00 to variable costs of $4,317.04, we get a total cost of operation of $7,752.04 per month. Thus, the firm is averaging a profit of $1,295.96 per month ($9,048.00 − $7,752.04). *This is not an "economic profit" because we have not accounted for the opportunity cost of the owner's time and efforts.* In fact, when we factor in an implicit wage of $2,500 per month for the owner, we see that the store is suffering *losses* of $1,204.04 per month ($1,295.96 − $2,500.00).

Total revenue (*TR*)	$9,048.00
Total fixed cost (*TFC*)	3,435.00
+ Total variable cost (*TVC*)	4,317.04
Total costs (*TC*)	7,752.04
Total profit (*TR* − *TC*)	1,295.96
Adjustment for implicit wage	2,500.00
Economic profit	−1,204.04

Should the entrepreneur stay in business? If she wants to make $2,500 per month and she thinks that nothing about her business will change, she must shut down in the long run. However, two things keep her going: (1) a decision to stay open longer and (2) the hope for more customers in the future.

OPENING LONGER HOURS: MARGINAL COSTS AND MARGINAL REVENUES

The store's normal hours of operation are noon until 8 P.M. On an experimental basis, the owner extends its hours until 11 P.M. for 1 month. The following table shows the average number of additional customers for each of the added hours:

Hours (P.M.)	Customers
8–9	41
9–10	20
10–11	8

Assuming that the late customers spend an average of $1.45, we can calculate the marginal revenue and the marginal cost of staying open longer. The marginal cost of one serving of ice cream is $3.27 divided by 12 = $0.27 + .05 (for topping) = $0.32. (See the table that follows.)

Marginal analysis tells us that the store should stay open for 2 additional hours. Each day that the store stays open from 8 P.M. to 9 P.M. it will make an added profit of $59.45 – $24.20, or $35.25. Staying open from 9 P.M. to 10 P.M. adds $29.00 – $17.48, or $11.52, to profit. Staying open the third hour, however, *decreases* profits because the marginal revenue generated by staying open

from 10 P.M. to 11 P.M. is less than the marginal cost. The entrepreneur decides to stay open for 2 additional hours per day. This adds $46.77 ($35.25 + 11.52) to profits each day, a total of $1,216.02 per month.

By adding the 2 hours, the store turns an economic loss of $1,204.04 per month into a small ($11.98) profit after accounting for the owner's implicit wage of $2,500 per month.

The owner decided to stay in business. She now serves over 350 customers per day, and the price of a dish of ice cream has risen to $2.50 while costs have not changed very much. In 2001, she cleared a profit of nearly $10,000 per month.

Hour (P.M.)	Marginal Revenue (MR)	Marginal Cost (MC)	Added Profit per Hour (MR – MC)
8–9	$1.45 × 41 = $59.45	Ice cream: $0.32 × 41 = $13.12 Labor: 2 × $5.54 = 11.08 Total $24.20	$35.25
9–10	1.45 × 20 = $29.00	Ice cream: $0.32 × 20 = $6.40 Labor: 2 × $5.54 = 11.08 Total $17.48	$11.52
10–11	1.45 × 8 = $11.60	Ice cream: $0.32 × 8 = $2.56 Labor: 2 × $5.54 = 11.08 Total $13.64	–$2.04

A Numerical Example Table 8.6 presents some data for another hypothetical firm. Let us assume that the market has set a $15 unit price for the firm's product. Total revenue in column 6 is the simple product of $P \times q$ (the numbers in column 1 times $15). The table derives total, marginal, and average costs exactly as Table 8.4 did. Here, however, we have included revenues, and we can calculate the profit, which is shown in column 8.

TABLE 8.6 Profit Analysis for a Simple Firm

(1)	(2)	(3)	(4)	(5)	(6) TR	(7) TC	(8) Profit
q	TFC	TVC	MC	P = MR	(P × q)	(TFC + TVC)	(TR – TC)
0	$10	$ 0	$–	$15	$ 0	$10	$–10
1	10	10	10	15	15	20	–5
2	10	15	5	15	30	25	5
3	10	20	5	15	45	30	15
4	10	30	10	15	60	40	20
5	10	50	20	15	75	60	15
6	10	80	30	15	90	90	0

Column 8 shows that a profit-maximizing firm would choose to produce 4 units of output. At this level, profits are $20. At all other output levels, they are lower. Now let us see if "marginal" reasoning leads us to the same conclusion.

First, should the firm produce at all? If it produces nothing, it suffers losses equal to $10. If it increases output to 1 unit, marginal revenue is $15 (remember that it sells each unit for $15) and marginal cost is $10. Thus, it gains $5, reducing its loss from $10 each period to $5.

Should the firm increase output to 2 units? The marginal revenue from the second unit is again $15, but the marginal cost is only $5. Thus, by producing the second unit, the firm gains $10 ($15 – $5) and turns a $5 loss into a $5 profit. The third unit adds $10 to profits. Again, marginal revenue is $15 and marginal cost is $5, an increase in profit of $10, for a total profit of $15.

The fourth unit offers still more profit. Price is still above marginal cost, which means that producing that fourth unit will increase profits. Price, or marginal revenue, is $15, and marginal cost is just $10. Thus, the fourth unit adds $5 to profit. At unit number five, however, diminishing returns push marginal cost above price. The marginal revenue from producing the fifth unit is $15, while marginal cost is now $20. As a result, profit per period drops by $5, to $15 per period. Clearly, the firm will not produce the fifth unit.

The profit-maximizing level of output is thus 4 units. The firm produces as long as price (marginal revenue) is greater than marginal cost. For an in-depth example of profit maximization, see "Case Study in Marginal Analysis: An Ice Cream Parlor" on p. 182.

The Short-Run Supply Curve

Consider how the typical firm shown in Figure 8.10 on p. 181 would behave in response to an increase in price. In Figure 8.11(a), assume that something causes demand to increase (shift to the right), driving price from $5 to $6 and finally to $7. When price is $5, a profit-maximizing firm will choose an output level of 300 in Figure 8.11(b). To produce any less, or to raise output above that level, would lead to a lower level of profit. At $6, the same firm would increase output to 350, but it would stop there. Similarly, at $7, the firm would raise output to 400 units of output.

The *MC* curve in Figure 8.11(b) relates price and quantity supplied. At any market price, the marginal cost curve shows the output level that maximizes profit. A curve that shows how much output a profit-maximizing firm will produce at every price also fits the definition of a supply curve. (Review Chapter 3 if this point is not clear to you.) Thus, the marginal cost curve of a competitive firm is the firm's short-run supply curve.

As you will see, one very important exception exists to this general rule: There is some price level below which the firm will shut down its operations and simply bear losses equal to fixed costs even if price is above marginal cost. This important point is discussed in Chapter 9.

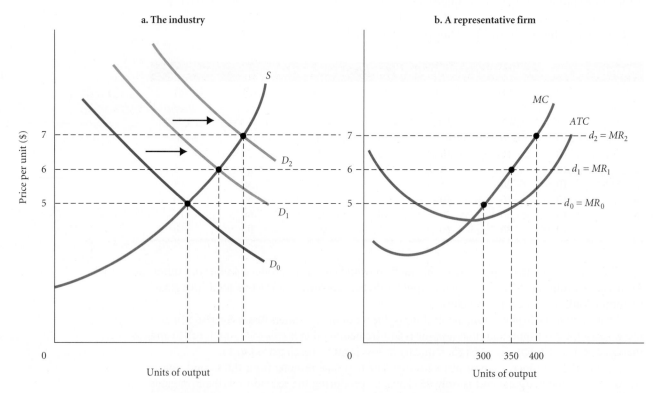

▲ **FIGURE 8.11 Marginal Cost Is the Supply Curve of a Perfectly Competitive Firm**
At any market price,[a] the marginal cost curve shows the output level that maximizes profit. Thus, the marginal cost curve of a perfectly competitive profit-maximizing firm is the firm's short-run supply curve.

[a] This is true except when price is so low that it pays a firm to shut down—a point that will be discussed in Chapter 9.

Looking Ahead

At the beginning of this chapter, we set out to combine information on technology, factor prices, and output prices to understand the supply curve of a competitive firm. We have now accomplished that goal.

Because marginal cost is such an important concept in microeconomics, you should carefully review any sections of this chapter that were unclear to you. Above all, keep in mind that the *marginal cost curve* carries information about both *input prices* and *technology*. The firm looks to output markets for information on potential revenues, and the current market price defines the firm's marginal revenue curve. The point where price (which is equal to marginal revenue in perfect competition) is just equal to marginal cost is the perfectly competitive firm's profit-maximizing level of output. Thus, with one important exception, the marginal cost curve *is* the perfectly competitive firm's supply curve in the short run.

In the next chapter, we turn to the long run. What happens when firms are free to choose their scale of operations without being limited by a fixed factor of production? Without diminishing returns that set in as a result of a fixed scale of production, what determines the shape of cost curves? What happens when new firms can enter industries in which profits are being earned? How do industries adjust when losses are being incurred? How does the structure of an industry evolve over time?

S U M M A R Y

1. Profit-maximizing firms make decisions to maximize profit (total revenue minus total cost).

2. To calculate production costs, firms must know two things: (1) the quantity and combination of inputs they need to produce their product and (2) the cost of those inputs.

COSTS IN THE SHORT RUN p. 168

3. *Fixed costs* are costs that do not change with a firm's output. In the short run, firms cannot avoid fixed costs or change them even if production is zero.

4. *Variable costs* are those costs that depend on the level of output chosen. Fixed costs plus variable costs equal *total costs* ($TC = TFC + TVC$).

5. *Average fixed cost* (AFC) is total fixed cost divided by the quantity of output. As output rises, average fixed cost declines steadily because the same total is being spread over a larger and larger quantity of output. This phenomenon is called *spreading overhead*.

6. Numerous combinations of inputs can be used to produce a given level of output. *Total variable cost* (TVC) is the sum of all costs that vary with output in the short run.

7. *Marginal cost* (MC) is the increase in total cost that results from the production of 1 more unit of output. If a firm is producing 1,000 units, the additional cost of increasing output to 1,001 units is marginal cost. Marginal cost measures the cost of the additional inputs required to produce each successive unit of output. Because fixed costs do not change when output changes, marginal costs reflect changes in variable costs.

8. In the short run, a firm is limited by a fixed factor of production or a fixed scale of a plant. As a firm increases output, it will eventually find itself trapped by that scale. Because of the fixed scale, marginal cost eventually rises with output.

9. Marginal cost is the slope of the total variable cost curve. The total variable cost curve always has a positive slope because total costs always rise with output. However,

increasing marginal cost means that total costs ultimately rise at an increasing rate.

10. *Average variable cost* (AVC) is equal to total variable cost divided by the quantity of output.

11. When marginal cost is above average variable cost, average variable cost is *increasing*. When marginal cost is below average variable cost, average variable cost is *declining*. Marginal cost intersects average variable cost at AVC's minimum point.

12. *Average total cost* (ATC) is equal to total cost divided by the quantity of output. It is also equal to the sum of average fixed cost and average variable cost.

13. When marginal cost is below average total cost, average total cost is declining toward marginal cost. When marginal cost is above average total cost, average total cost is increasing. Marginal cost intersects average total cost at ATC's minimum point.

OUTPUT DECISIONS: REVENUES, COSTS, AND PROFIT MAXIMIZATION p. 179

14. A perfectly competitive firm faces a demand curve that is a horizontal line (in other words, perfectly elastic demand).

15. *Total revenue* (TR) is simply price times the quantity of output that a firm decides to produce and sell. *Marginal revenue* (MR) is the additional revenue that a firm takes in when it increases output by 1 unit.

16. For a perfectly competitive firm, marginal revenue is equal to the current market price of its product.

17. A profit-maximizing firm in a perfectly competitive industry will produce up to the point at which the price of its output is just equal to short-run marginal cost: $P = MC$. The more general profit-maximizing formula is $MR = MC$ ($P = MR$ in perfect competition). The marginal cost curve of a perfectly competitive firm is the firm's short-run supply curve, with one exception (discussed in Chapter 9).

———— REVIEW TERMS AND CONCEPTS ————

average fixed cost (*AFC*), p. 169

average total cost (*ATC*), p. 175

average variable cost (*AVC*), p. 174

fixed cost, p. 168

homogeneous product, p. 179

marginal cost (*MC*), p. 171

marginal revenue (*MR*), p. 180

perfect competition, p. 179

spreading overhead, p. 169

total cost (*TC*), p. 168

total fixed costs (*TFC*) *or* overhead, p. 168

total revenue (*TR*), p. 180

total variable cost (*TVC*), p. 169

total variable cost curve, p. 170

variable cost, p. 168

1. $TC = TFC + TVC$
2. $AFC = TFC/q$

3. Slope of $TVC = MC$
4. $AVC = TVC/q$
5. $ATC = TC/q = AFC + AVC$
6. $TR = P \times q$
7. Profit-maximizing level of output for all firms: $MR = M$
8. Profit-maximizing level of output for perfectly competitive firms: $P = MC$

———————— PROBLEMS ————————

All problems are available on www.myeconlab.com

1. Consider the following costs of owning and operating a car. A $25,000 Ford Taurus financed over 60 months at 7 percent interest means a monthly payment of $495.03. Insurance costs $100 a month regardless of how much you drive. The car gets 20 miles per gallon and uses unleaded regular gasoline that costs $3.50 per gallon. Finally, suppose that wear and tear on the car costs about 15 cents a mile. Which costs are fixed, and which are variable? What is the marginal cost of a mile driven? In deciding whether to drive from New York to Pittsburgh (about 1,000 miles roundtrip) to visit a friend, which costs would you consider? Why?

2. July 23, 2007 LONDON (Reuters)—The final volume of the Harry Potter saga sold more than 11 million copies in the first 24 hours it went on sale in the United States and Britain to become the fastest-selling book in history, publishers said. In book publishing, fixed costs are very high and marginal costs are very low and fairly constant. Suppose that the fixed cost of producing the new Harry Potter volume is $30 million. What is the *average fixed cost* if the publisher produces 5 million copies? 10 million copies? 20 million copies?

   Now suppose that the marginal cost of a Harry Potter book is $1.50 per book and is the same for each book up to 40 million copies. Assume that this includes all variable costs. Explain why in this case marginal cost is a horizontal line, as is average variable cost. What is the *average total cost* of the book if the publisher produces 5 million copies? 10 million copies? 20 million copies?

   Sketch the average fixed cost curve and the average total cost curve facing the publisher.

3. Do you agree or disagree with this statement? Firms minimize costs; thus, a firm earning short-run economic profits will choose to produce at the minimum point on its average total cost function.

4. You are given the following cost data:

   Total fixed costs are 100.

q	TVC
0	0
1	5
2	10
3	20
4	40
5	65
6	95

   If the price of output is $15, how many units of output will this firm produce? What is total revenue? What is total cost? Briefly explain using the concept of marginal cost. What do you think the firm is likely to do in the short run? In the long run?

5. [Related to the *Economics in Practice* on *p. 178*] While charging admission most days of the week, the Museum of Contemporary Art in Los Angeles offers free admission on Thursday evenings. Why do museums often price this way? Why do they choose Thursday rather than Saturday?

6. The following table gives capital and labor requirements for 10 different levels of production.

q	K	L
0	0	0
1	2	5
2	4	9
3	6	12
4	8	15
5	10	19
6	12	24
7	14	30
8	16	37
9	18	45
10	20	54

   a. Assuming that the price of labor (P_L) is $5 per unit and the price of capital (P_K) is $10 per unit, compute and graph total cost, marginal cost, and average variable cost for the firm.

   b. Do the graphs have the shapes that you might expect? Explain.

   c. Using the numbers here, explain the relationship between marginal cost and average variable cost.

   d. Using the numbers here, explain the meaning of "marginal cost" in terms of additional inputs needed to produce a marginal unit of output.

   e. If the output price was $57, how many units of output would the firm produce? Explain.

7. Do you agree or disagree with each of the following statements? Explain your reasons.
   a. For a competitive firm facing a market price above average total cost, the existence of economic profits means that the firm should increase output in the short run even if price is below marginal cost.
   b. If marginal cost is rising with increasing output, average cost must also be rising.
   c. Fixed cost is constant at every level of output except zero. When a firm produces no output, fixed costs are zero in the short run.

8. A firm's cost curves are given in the following table.

q	TC	TFC	TVC	AVC	ATC	MC
0	$100	$100	—	—	—	—
1	130	100	—	—	—	—
2	150	100	—	—	—	—
3	160	100	—	—	—	—
4	172	100	—	—	—	—
5	185	100	—	—	—	—
6	210	100	—	—	—	—
7	240	100	—	—	—	—
8	280	100	—	—	—	—
9	330	100	—	—	—	—
10	390	100	—	—	—	—

   a. Complete the table.
   b. Graph AVC, ATC, and MC on the same graph. What is the relationship between the MC curve and the ATC and between MC and AVC?
   c. Suppose market price is $30. How much will the firm produce in the short run? How much are total profits?
   d. Suppose market price is $50. How much will the firm produce in the short run? What are total profits?

9. A 2010 Georgia Tech graduate inherited her mother's printing company. The capital stock of the firm consists of three machines of various vintages, all in excellent condition. All machines can be running at the same time.

	COST OF PRINTING AND BINDING PER BOOK	MAXIMUM TOTAL CAPACITY (BOOKS) PER MONTH
Machine 1	$1.00	100
Machine 2	2.00	200
Machine 3	3.00	500

   a. Assume that "cost of printing and binding per book" includes *all* labor and materials, including the owner's wages. Assume further that Mom signed a long-term contract (50 years) with a service company to keep the machines in good repair for a fixed fee of $100 per month.
      (1) Derive the firm's marginal cost curve.
      (2) Derive the firm's total cost curve.
   b. At a price of $2.50, how many books would the company produce? What would total revenues, total costs, and total profits be?

10. The following is a total cost curve. Sketch the corresponding marginal cost curve. If the price of output is $3 and there are no fixed costs, what is the profit-maximizing level of output?

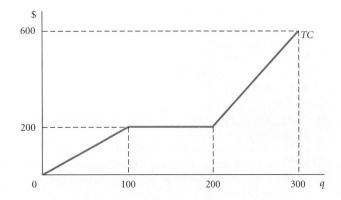

11. The following curve is a production function for a firm that uses just one variable factor of production, labor. It shows total output, or product, for every level of input.
   a. Derive and graph the marginal product curve.
   b. Suppose the wage rate is $4. Derive and graph the firm's marginal cost curve.
   c. If output sells for $6, what is the profit-maximizing level of output? How much labor will the firm hire?

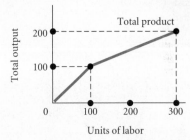

12. [Related to the *Economics in Practice* on p. 182] Elena and Emmanuel live on the Black Sea in Bulgaria and own a small fishing boat. A crew of four is required to take the boat out fishing. The current wage paid to the four crew members is a total of 5,000 levs per day. (A lev is the Bulgarian unit of currency.) Assume that the cost of operating and maintaining the boat is 1,000 levs per day when fishing and zero otherwise. The following schedule gives the appropriate catch for each period during the year.

PERIOD	CATCH PER DAY (KILOGRAMS)
Prime fishing: 180 days	100
Month 7: 30 days	80
Month 8: 30 days	60
Rest of the year	40

The price of fish in Bulgaria is no longer regulated by the government and is now determined in competitive markets. Suppose the price has been stable all year at 80 levs per kilogram.
   a. What is the marginal product of a day's worth of fishing during prime fishing season? during month 7? during month 8?
   b. What is the marginal cost of a kilogram of fish during prime fishing season? during month 7, during month 8, and during the rest of the year?
   c. If you were Elena and Emmanuel, how many months per year would you hire the crew and go out fishing? Explain your answer using marginal logic.

13. For each of the following businesses, what is the likely fixed factor of production that defines the short run?
    a. Potato farm of 160 acres
    b. Chinese restaurant
    c. Dentist in private practice
    d. Car dealership
    e. Bank

14. Explain which of the following is a fixed cost or a variable cost for Southwest Airlines.
    a. The cost of jet fuel used in its airplanes.
    b. The monthly rent on its Dallas, Texas headquarters.
    c. The yearly lease payments on its current inventory of Boeing 737 jets.
    d. The cost of peanuts it serves to passengers.
    e. The salary paid to Laura Wright, Southwest's Senior Vice President of Finance and Chief Financial Officer.
    f. The gate rental fees it pays to McCarran International Airport in Las Vegas, Nevada.

15. Use the information in the graph to find the values for the following costs at an output level of 500.
    a. Total fixed cost
    b. Total variable cost
    c. Total cost
    d. Marginal cost

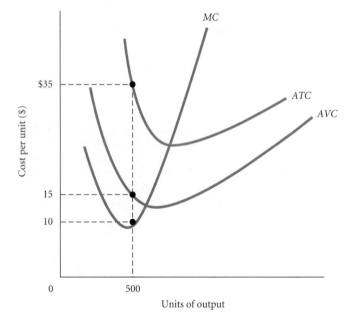

16. Explain how the following events would affect the cost curves in the graph from the previous question.
    a. Hourly wages for employees increase.
    b. The company signs a new 3-year contract with its landlord which lowers its monthly rent by 10 percent.
    c. The company employs a new technology which lowers its utility costs.
    d. The company receives notice of a 5 percent increase in its property insurance rate.
    e. The company's primary supplier of resources implements a 3 percent price increase for all of its supplies.

17. Fill in the columns in the following table. What quantity should a profit-maximizing firm produce? Verify your answer with marginal reasoning.

q	TFC	TVC	MC	P = MR	TR	TC	Profit
0	$20	$0		$22			
1	20	10		22			
2	20	15		22			
3	20	25		22			
4	20	40		22			
5	20	60		22			
6	20	90		22			

18. Use the information from your answer to the previous question to construct a rough plot showing marginal revenue, marginal cost, and average total cost. Also identify the profit-maximizing quantity of output on the graph. You will have to calculate average total cost from the information in the table.

19. Marginal cost represents the increase in total cost that results from producing one more unit of output. Marginal product represents the additional output that can be produced by adding one more unit of a specific input, holding all other inputs constant. What does this imply about the relationship between marginal cost and marginal product?

20. Evaluate the following statement. If the total variable cost of production is the sum of the marginal cost of each additional unit of output, we can calculate the marginal cost by taking the total variable cost of production and dividing it by the quantity of output produced.

Long-Run Costs and Output Decisions

9

The last two chapters discussed the behavior of profit-maximizing competitive firms in the short run. Recall that all firms must make three fundamental decisions: (1) how much output to produce or supply, (2) how to produce that output, and (3) how much of each input to demand.

Firms use information on input prices, output prices, and technology to make the decisions that will lead to the most profit. Because profits equal revenues minus costs, firms must know how much their products will sell for

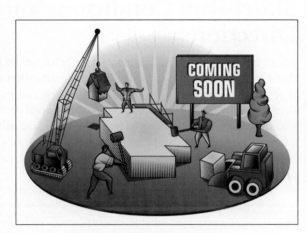

and how much production will cost, using the most efficient technology.

In Chapter 8, we saw how cost curves can be derived from production functions and input prices. Once a firm has a clear picture of its short-run costs, the price at which it sells its output determines the quantity of output that will maximize profit. Specifically, a profit-maximizing perfectly competitive firm will supply output up to the point that price (marginal revenue) equals marginal cost. The marginal cost curve of such a firm is thus the same as its supply curve.

In this chapter, we turn from the short run to the long run. The condition in which firms find themselves in the short run (Are they making profits? Are they incurring losses?) determines what is likely to happen in the long run. Remember that output (supply) decisions in the long run are less constrained than in the short run, for two reasons. First, in the long run, the firm can increase any or all of its inputs and thus has no fixed factor of production that confines its production to a given scale. Second, firms are free to enter industries to seek profits and to leave industries to avoid losses.

In thinking about the relationship between the short run and long run, it is useful to put yourself in the position of a manager of a firm. At times, you will be making what we term *short-run* decisions: You are stuck with a particular factory and set of machines, and your decisions involve asking how best to use those assets to produce output. At the same time, you or another manager at the firm will be doing more strategic *long-run* thinking: Should you be in this business at all, or should you close up shop? In better times, you might consider expanding the operation. In thinking about the long run, you will also have to reckon with other firms entering and exiting the industry. Managers simultaneously make short- and long-run decisions, making the best of the current constraints while planning for the future.

In making decisions or understanding industry structure, the shape of the long-run cost curve is important. As we saw in the short run, a fixed factor of production eventually causes marginal cost to increase along with output. In the long run, all factors can be varied. In the earlier sandwich shop example, in the long run, we can add floor space and grills along with more people to make the sandwiches. Under these circumstances, it is no longer inevitable that increased volume comes with higher costs. In fact, as we will see, long-run cost curves need not slope up at all. You might have wondered why there are only a few automobile and steel companies in the United States but dozens of firms producing books and furniture. Differences in the shapes of the long-run cost curves in those industries do a good job of explaining these differences in the industry structures.

We begin our discussion of the long run by looking at firms in three short-run circumstances: (1) firms that earn economic profits, (2) firms that suffer economic losses but continue to operate to reduce or minimize those losses, and (3) firms that decide to shut down and bear losses just equal to fixed costs. We then examine how these firms make their long-run decisions in response to conditions in their markets.

Although we continue to focus on perfectly competitive firms, *all* firms are subject to the spectrum of short-run profit or loss situations regardless of *market structure*. Assuming perfect competition allows us to simplify our analysis and provides us with a strong background for understanding the discussions of imperfectly competitive behavior in later chapters.

Short-Run Conditions and Long-Run Directions

Before beginning our examination of firm behavior, let us review the concept of profit. Recall that a normal rate of return is included in the definition of total cost (Chapter 7). A *normal rate of return* is a rate that is just sufficient to keep current investors interested in the industry. Because we define *profit* as total revenue minus total cost and because total cost includes a normal rate of return, our concept of profit takes into account the opportunity cost of capital. When a firm is earning an above-normal rate of return, it has a positive profit level; otherwise, it does not. When there are positive profits in an industry, new investors are likely to be attracted to the industry.

When we say that a firm is suffering a *loss*, we mean that it is earning a rate of return that is below normal. Such a firm may be suffering a loss as an accountant would measure it, or it may be earning at a very low—that is, below normal—rate. Investors are not going to be attracted to an industry in which there are losses. A firm that is **breaking even**, or earning a zero level of profit, is one that is earning exactly a normal rate of return. New investors are not attracted, but current ones are not running away either.

breaking even The situation in which a firm is earning exactly a normal rate of return.

With these distinctions in mind, we can say that for any firm, one of three conditions holds at any given moment: (1) The firm is making positive profits, (2) the firm is suffering losses, or (3) the firm is just breaking even. Profitable firms will want to maximize their profits in the short run, while firms suffering losses will want to minimize those losses in the short run.

Maximizing Profits

The best way to understand the behavior of a firm that is currently earning profits is by way of example.

Example: The Blue Velvet Car Wash   When a firm earns revenues in excess of costs (including a normal rate of return), we say it is earning positive or excess profits. Let us consider as an example the Blue Velvet Car Wash. Looking at a few numbers will help you see how the specifics of a business operation translate into economic graphs.

Car washes require a facility. In the case of Blue Velvet, suppose investors have put up $500,000 to construct a building and purchase all the equipment required to wash cars. If the car wash closes, the building and equipment can be sold for its original purchase price, but as long as the firm is in business, that capital is tied up. If the investors could get 10 percent return on their investment in another business, then for them to keep their money in this business, they will also expect 10 percent from Blue Velvet. Thus, the annual cost of the capital needed for the business is $50,000 (10 percent of $500,000).

The car wash is currently servicing 800 cars a week and can be open 50 weeks a year (2 weeks are needed for maintenance). The cost of the basic maintenance contract on the equipment is $50,000 per year, and Blue Velvet has a contract to pay for those services for a year whether it opens the car wash or not. The fixed costs then for the car wash are $100,000 per year: $50,000 for the capital costs and $50,000 for the equipment contract. On a weekly basis, these costs amount to $2,000 per week. If the car wash operates at the level of 800 cars per week, fixed costs are $2.50 per car ($2,000/800).

There are also variable costs associated with the business. To run a car wash, one needs workers and soap and water. Workers can be hired by the hour for $10.00 an hour, and at a customer level of 800 cars per week, each worker can wash 8 cars an hour. At this service level, then, Blue Velvet hires workers for 100 hours and has a wage bill of $1,000. The labor cost of each car wash, when Blue Velvet serves 800 customers, is $1.25 ($10/8).

The number of cars each worker can service depends on the number of cars being worked on. When there is too little business and few workers, no specialization is possible and cars washed per worker fall. With many cars to service, workers start getting in one another's way. We saw that at 800 cars per week, workers could wash 8 each per hour. Later when we graph the operation, we will assume that the number of cars washed per worker rises and then falls, reaching a maximum at a volume less than the current 800 cars.

Every car that is washed costs $0.75 in soap, adding $600 to the weekly bill if 800 car washes are done. Table 9.1 summarizes the costs of Blue Velvet at the 800 washes per week level.

TABLE 9.1 Blue Velvet Car Wash Weekly Costs

TFC Total Fixed Cost		TVC Total Variable Cost (800 Washes)		TC Total Cost (800 Washes)	TR Total Revenue (P = $5)
1. Normal return to investors	$1,000	1. Labor 2. Soap	$1,000 600	TC = TFC + TVC = $2,000 + $1,600 = **$3,600**	TR = $5 × 800 = **$4,000**
2. Other fixed costs (maintenance contract)			**$1,600**		Profit = TR − TC = **$400**
	1,000				
	$2,000				

This car wash business is quite competitive, and the market price for this service at the moment we are considering is $5. (Recall the perfectly elastic demand curve facing a competitive firm we discussed in Chapter 8.) At a service level of 800 cars, as you see from the table, Blue Velvet is making a positive profit of $400 per week. For each car washed, it receives $5 and spends $4.50 ($2.50 in fixed costs + $1.25 in labor costs + $0.75 in soap), for an excess profit of $0.50 per car.

Graphic Presentation For Blue Velvet, we have seen a snapshot of the business as it operates with 800 cars serviced a week. We have also learned a little about the business, which we can use to construct a graphical representation of Blue Velvet to help us see why the firm chose to service 800 cars. Figure 9.1 graphs the performance of Blue Velvet in this first period in which it is making money.

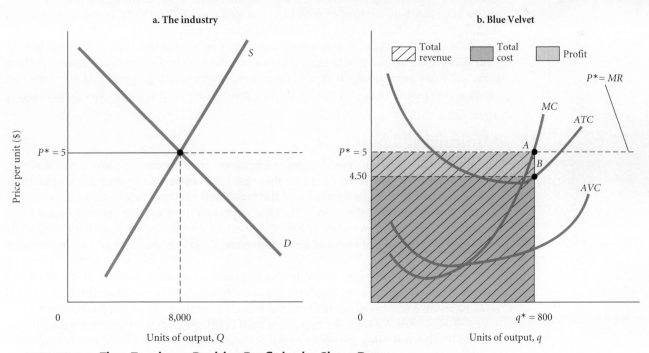

▲ FIGURE 9.1 **Firm Earning a Positive Profit in the Short Run**
A profit-maximizing perfectly competitive firm will produce up to the point where P* = MC. Profit is the difference between total revenue and total cost. At q* = 800, total revenue is $5 × 800 = $4,000, total cost is $4.50 × 800 = $3,600, and profit = $4,000 − $3,600 = $400.

The industry price is $5.00, and we have assumed that the total number of car washes done in the market area in a week is 8,000; so there are 10 firms like Blue Velvet in this competitive marketplace all earning economic profits. There are three key cost curves shown in the graph that represents Blue Velvet. The average variable cost (AVC) curve shows what happens to the per unit costs of workers and the other variable factor, soap, as we change output. Initially as output increases workers can service more cars per hour as they work together, thus causing the AVC to decline, but eventually diminishing returns set in and AVC begins to rise. Now look at the average total cost (ATC) curve. The average total cost curve falls at first in response to the spreading of the fixed costs over more and more units and eventually begins to rise as the inefficiencies in labor take their toll. At the output of 800 washes, the ATC has a value of $4.50. Look back at Table 9.1. The total cost of Blue Velvet at a service level of 800 cars is $3,600. The $4.50 comes from dividing this $3,600 by 800 cars. Finally, we see the marginal cost (MC) curve, which rises after a certain point because of the fixed factor of the building and equipment.

With a price of $5.00, Blue Velvet is producing 800 units and making a profit (the gray box). Blue Velvet is a perfectly competitive firm, and it maximizes profits by producing up to the point where price equals marginal cost, here 800 car washes. Any units produced beyond 800 would add more to cost than they would bring in revenue. Notice Blue Velvet is producing at a level that is larger than the output that minimizes average costs. The high price in the marketplace has induced Blue Velvet to increase its service level even though the result is slightly less labor productivity and thus higher per unit costs.

Both revenues and costs are shown graphically. *Total revenue* (*TR*) is simply the product of price and quantity: $P^* \times q^* = \$5 \times 800 = \$4,000$. On the diagram, total revenue is equal to the area of the rectangle P^*Aq^*0. (The area of a rectangle is equal to its length times its width.) At output q^*, average total cost is $4.50 (point *B*). Numerically, it is equal to the length of line segment q^*B. Because average total cost is derived by dividing total cost by q, we can get back to total cost by *multiplying* average total cost by q. That is,

$$ATC = \frac{TC}{q}$$

and so

$$TC = ATC \times q$$

Total cost (*TC*), then, is $4.50 \times 800 = \$3,600$, the area shaded blue in the diagram. *Profit* is simply the difference between total revenue (*TR*) and total cost (*TC*), or $400. This is the area that is shaded gray in the diagram. This firm is earning positive profits.

A firm, like Blue Velvet, that is earning a positive profit in the short run and expects to continue doing so has an incentive to expand its scale of operation in the long run. Managers in these firms will likely be planning to expand even as they concentrate on producing 800 units. We expect greater output to be produced in the long run as firms react to profits they are earning.

Minimizing Losses

A firm that is not earning a positive profit or breaking even is suffering a loss. Firms suffering losses fall into two categories: (1) those that find it advantageous to shut down operations immediately and bear losses equal to total fixed costs and (2) those that continue to operate in the short run to minimize their losses. The most important thing to remember here is that firms cannot exit the industry in the short run. The firm can shut down, but it cannot get rid of its fixed costs by going out of business. Fixed costs must be paid in the short run no matter what the firm does.

Whether a firm suffering losses decides to produce or not to produce in the short run depends on the advantages and disadvantages of continuing production. If a firm shuts down, it earns no revenue and has no variable costs to bear. If it continues to produce, it both earns revenue and incurs variable costs. Because a firm must bear fixed costs *whether or not* it shuts down, its decision depends *solely on whether total revenue from operating is sufficient to cover total variable cost.*

- If total revenue exceeds total variable cost, the excess revenue can be used to offset fixed costs and reduce losses, and it will pay the firm to keep operating.
- If total revenue is smaller than total variable cost, the firm that operates will suffer losses in excess of fixed costs. In this case, the firm can minimize its losses by shutting down.

Producing at a Loss to Offset Fixed Costs: Blue Velvet Revisited Suppose consumers suddenly decide that car washing is a waste of money and demand falls. The price begins to fall, and Blue Velvet is no longer so profitable. We can see what Blue Velvet's management will decide to do by looking back at Figure 9.1. With an upward-sloping marginal cost curve, as price begins to fall, the Blue Velvet management team first will choose to reduce the number of cars it services. As long as the price is greater than ATC (which is minimized at about $4.35 on the graph), Blue Velvet continues to make a profit. What happens if the price falls below this level, say to $3 per car?

Now Blue Velvet has to decide not only how many cars to wash but whether to be open at all. If the car wash closes, there are no labor and soap costs. But Blue Velvet still has to pay for its unbreakable year-long contract, and it still owns its building, which will take some time to sell. So the fixed costs of $2,000 per week remain. For Blue Velvet, the key question is can it do better than losing $2,000? The answer depends on whether the market price is greater or less than average variable costs—the costs per unit for the variable factors. If the price is greater than the average variable cost, then Blue Velvet can pay for its workers and the soap and have something left for the investors. It will still lose money, but it will be less than $2,000. If price is less than average variable cost, the firm will not only lose its $2,000 but also have added losses on every car it washes. So the simple answer for Blue Velvet is that it should stay open and wash cars as long as it covers its variable costs. Economists call this the **shutdown point**. At all prices above this shutdown point, the marginal cost curve shows the profit-maximizing level of output. At all points below this point, optimal short-run output is zero.

We can now refine our earlier statement, from Chapter 8, that a perfectly competitive firm's marginal cost curve is its short-run supply curve. As we have just seen, a firm will shut down when the market price is less than the minimum point on the AVC curve. Also recall (or notice from the graph) that the marginal cost curve intersects the AVC at AVC's lowest point. It therefore follows that the short-run supply curve of a competitive firm is that portion of its marginal cost curve that lies above its average variable cost curve. For Blue Velvet, the firm will shut down at a price of about $1.50 (reading off the graph).

Figure 9.2 shows the short-run supply curve for the general case of a perfectly competitive firm like Blue Velvet.

shutdown point The lowest point on the average variable cost curve. When price falls below the minimum point on AVC, total revenue is insufficient to cover variable costs and the firm will shut down and bear losses equal to fixed costs.

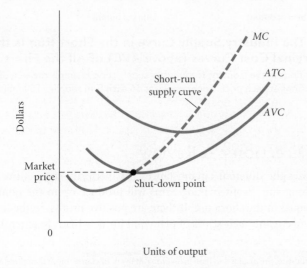

▲ **FIGURE 9.2 Short-Run Supply Curve of a Perfectly Competitive Firm**
At prices below average variable cost, it pays a firm to shutdown rather than continue operating. Thus, the short-run supply curve of a competitive firm is the part of its marginal cost curve that lies *above* its average variable cost curve.

The Short-Run Industry Supply Curve

short-run industry supply curve The sum of the marginal cost curves (above *AVC*) of all the firms in an industry.

Supply in a competitive industry is the sum of the quantity supplied by the individual firms in the industry at each price level. The **short-run industry supply curve** is the sum of the individual firm supply curves—that is, the marginal cost curves (above *AVC*) of all the firms in the industry. Because quantities are being added—that is, because we are finding the total quantity supplied in the industry at each price level—the curves are added horizontally.

Figure 9.3 shows the supply curve for an industry with three identical firms.[1] At a price of $6, each firm produces 150 units, which is the output where $P = MC$. The total amount supplied on the market at a price of $6 is thus 450. At a price of $5, each firm produces 120 units, for an industry supply of 360. Below $4.50, all firms shut down; P is less than *AVC*.

Two things can cause the industry supply curve to shift. In the short run, the industry supply curve shifts if something—a decrease in the price of some input, for instance—shifts the marginal cost curves of all the individual firms simultaneously. For example, when the cost of producing components of home computers decreased, the marginal cost curves of all computer manufacturers shifted downward. Such a shift amounted to the same thing as an outward shift in their supply curves. Each firm was willing to supply more computers at each price level because computers were now cheaper to produce.

In the long run, an increase or decrease in the number of firms—and, therefore, in the number of individual firm supply curves—shifts the total industry supply curve. If new firms enter the industry, the industry supply curve moves to the right; if firms exit the industry, the industry supply curve moves to the left.

We return to shifts in industry supply curves and discuss them further when we take up long-run adjustments later in this chapter.

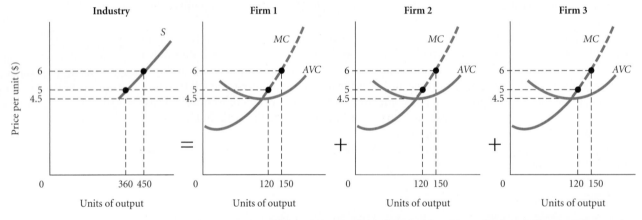

▲ **FIGURE 9.3 The Industry Supply Curve in the Short Run Is the Horizontal Sum of the Marginal Cost Curves (above *AVC*) of All the Firms in an Industry**
If there are only three firms in the industry, the industry supply curve is simply the sum of all the products supplied by the three firms at each price. For example, at $6 each firm supplies 150 units, for a total industry supply of 450.

Long-Run Directions: A Review

Table 9.2 summarizes the different circumstances that perfectly competitive firms may face as they plan for the long run. Profit-making firms will produce up to the point where price and marginal cost are equal in the short run. If there are positive profits, in the long run, there is an incentive for firms to expand their scales of plant and for new firms to enter the industry.

---

[1] Perfectly competitive industries are assumed to have many firms. Many is, of course, more than three. We use three firms here simply for purposes of illustration. The assumption that all firms are identical is often made when discussing a perfectly competitive industry.

TABLE 9.2 Profits, Losses, and Perfectly Competitive Firm Decisions in the Long and Short Run

	Short-Run Condition	Short-Run Decision	Long-Run Decision
Profits	$TR > TC$	$P = MC$: operate	Expand: new firms enter
Losses	1. $TR \geq TVC$	$P = MC$: operate	Contract: firms exit
		(loss < total fixed cost)	
	2. $TR < TVC$	Shut down:	Contract: firms exit
		loss = total fixed cost	

A firm suffering losses will produce if and only if revenue is sufficient to cover total variable cost. Such firms, like profitable firms, will also produce up to the point where $P = MC$. If a firm suffering losses cannot cover total variable cost by operating, it will shut down and bear losses equal to total fixed cost. Whether a firm that is suffering losses decides to shut down in the short run or not, the losses create an incentive to contract in the long run. When firms are suffering losses, they generally exit the industry in the long run.

Thus, the short-run profits of firms cause them to expand or contract when opportunities exist to change their scale of plant. If expansion is desired because economic profits are positive, firms must consider what their costs are likely to be at different scales or operation. (When we use the term "scale of operation," you may find it helpful to picture factories of varying sizes.) Just as firms have to analyze different technologies to arrive at a cost structure in the short run, they must also compare their costs at different scales of plant to arrive at long-run costs. Perhaps a larger scale of operations will reduce average production costs and provide an even greater incentive for a profit-making firm to expand, or perhaps large firms will run into problems that constrain growth. The analysis of long-run possibilities is even more complex than the short-run analysis because more things are variable—scale of plant is not fixed, for example, and there are no fixed costs because firms can exit their industry in the long run. In theory, firms may choose *any* scale of operation; so they must analyze many possible options.

Now let us turn to an analysis of cost curves in the long run.

Long-Run Costs: Economies and Diseconomies of Scale

The shapes of short-run cost curves follow directly from the assumption of a fixed factor of production. As output increases beyond a certain point, the fixed factor (which we usually think of as fixed scale of plant) causes diminishing returns to other factors and thus increasing marginal costs. In the long run, however, there is no fixed factor of production. Firms can choose any scale of production. They can build small or large factories, double or triple output, or go out of business completely.

The shape of a firm's *long-run* average cost curve shows how costs vary with scale of operations. In some firms, production technology is such that increased scale, or size, reduces costs. For others, increased scale leads to higher per-unit costs. When an increase in a firm's scale of production leads to lower average costs, we say that there are **increasing returns to scale**, or **economies of scale**. When average costs do not change with the scale of production, we say that there are **constant returns to scale**. Finally, when an increase in a firm's scale of production leads to higher average costs, we say that there are **decreasing returns to scale, or diseconomies of scale**. Because these economies of scale are a property of production characteristics of the individual firm, they are considered *internal* economies of scale. In the Appendix to this chapter, we talk about *external* economies of scale, which describe economies or diseconomies of scale on an industry-wide basis.

increasing returns to scale, *or* **economies of scale** An increase in a firm's scale of production leads to lower costs per unit produced.

constant returns to scale An increase in a firm's scale of production has no effect on costs per unit produced.

decreasing returns to scale, *or* **diseconomies of scale** An increase in a firm's scale of production leads to higher costs per unit produced.

Increasing Returns to Scale

Technically, the phrase *increasing returns to scale* refers to the relationship between inputs and outputs. When we say that a production function exhibits increasing returns, we mean that a given percentage of increase in inputs leads to a *larger* percentage of increase in the production of output. For example, if a firm doubled or tripled inputs, it would more than double or triple output.

When firms can count on fixed input prices—that is, when the prices of inputs do not change with output levels—increasing returns to scale also means that as output rises, average cost of production falls. The term *economies of scale* refers directly to this reduction in cost per unit of output that follows from larger-scale production.

The Sources of Economies of Scale Most of the economies of scale that immediately come to mind are technological in nature. Automobile production, for example, would be more costly per unit if a firm were to produce 100 cars per year by hand. In the early 1900s, Henry Ford introduced standardized production techniques that increased output volume, reduced costs per car, and made the automobile available to almost everyone. The new technology is not very cost-effective at small volumes of cars, but at larger volumes costs are greatly reduced. Ford's innovation provided a source of scale economics at the plant level of the auto firm.

Some economies of scale result not from technology but from firm-level efficiencies and bargaining power that can come with size. Very large companies, for instance, can buy inputs in volume at discounted prices. Large firms may also produce some of their own inputs at considerable savings, and they can certainly save in transport costs when they ship items in bulk. Wal-Mart has become the largest retailer in the United States in part because of scale economies of this type. Economics of scale have come from advantages of larger *firm* size rather than gains from plant size.

Economies of scale can be seen all around us. A bus that carries 50 people between Vancouver and Seattle uses less labor, capital, and gasoline than 50 people driving 50 different automobiles. The cost per passenger (average cost) is lower on the bus. Roommates who share an apartment are taking advantage of economies of scale. Costs per person for heat, electricity, and space are lower when an apartment is shared than if each person rents a separate apartment.

Example: Economies of Scale in Egg Production Nowhere are economies of scale more visible than in agriculture. Consider the following example. A few years ago a major agribusiness moved to a small Ohio town and set up a huge egg-producing operation. The new firm, Chicken Little Egg Farms Inc., is completely mechanized. Complex machines feed the chickens and collect and box the eggs. Large refrigerated trucks transport the eggs all over the state daily. In the same town, some small farmers still own fewer than 200 chickens. These farmers collect the eggs, feed the chickens, clean the coops by hand, and deliver the eggs to county markets.

Table 9.3 presents some hypothetical cost data for Homer Jones's small operation and for Chicken Little Inc. Jones has his operation working well. He has several hundred chickens and

TABLE 9.3 Weekly Costs Showing Economies of Scale in Egg Production

Jones Farm	Total Weekly Costs
15 hours of labor (implicit value $8 per hour)	$120
Feed, other variable costs	25
Transport costs	15
Land and capital costs attributable to egg production	17
	$177
Total output	2,400 eggs
Average cost	$0.074 per egg

Chicken Little Egg Farms Inc.	Total Weekly Costs
Labor	$ 5,128
Feed, other variable costs	4,115
Transport costs	2,431
Land and capital costs	19,230
	$30,904
Total output	1,600,000 eggs
Average cost	$0.019 per egg

Economies of Scale in the World Marketplace

In this chapter we describe a range of possible long-run cost curves. The form of the long-run production function and possible existence of economies of scale in production have much to say about industrial structure in ways we will explore further in a later chapter.

In a world economy in which trade occurs across geographical boundaries, if economies of scale exist, it is possible to exploit those economies across a very large output base. The 2009 World Development Report from the World Bank has an interesting chapter on scale economies with a few fascinating examples from around the world.

Dongguan is a major manufacturing city in Southeast China, lying between Guangzhou and Shenzhen. A single plant in Dongguan produces more than 30 percent of the world's magnetic recording heads used in hard disk drives. Another plant in the same city produces 60 percent of the electronic learning devices sold in the United States, while a third plant produces 30 million mobile

phones, again all in one plant. Clearly, the scale economies in these three sectors must be very large indeed. Notice in the case of all three examples that products are also light and easy to ship.

spends about 15 hours per week feeding, collecting, delivering, and so on. During the rest of his time, he raises soybeans. We can value Jones's time at $8 per hour because that is the wage he could earn working at a local manufacturing plant. When we add up all Jones's costs, including a rough estimate of the land and capital costs attributable to egg production, we arrive at $177 per week. Total production on the Jones farm runs about 200 dozen, or 2,400, eggs per week, which means that Jones's average cost comes out to $0.074 per egg.

The costs of Chicken Little Inc. are much higher in total; weekly costs run over $30,000. A much higher percentage of costs are capital costs—the firm uses a great many pieces of sophisticated machinery that cost millions to put in place. Total output is 1.6 million eggs per week, and the product is shipped all over the Midwest. The comparatively huge scale of plant has driven average production costs all the way down to $0.019 per egg.

Although these numbers are hypothetical, you can see why small farmers in the United States are finding it difficult to compete with large-scale agribusiness concerns that can realize significant economies of scale.

Many large firms have multiple plants or sites where they produce their goods and services. In our discussion in this chapter, we will distinguish between cost changes that come about because a firm decides to build a large versus a small plant and cost changes that result from firms adding volume to their production by building more plants. Coors originally produced its beer in Colorado in what was, at the time, one of the largest U.S. brewing plants; the firm believed that large size at the plant level brought cost savings. Most electronics companies, on the other hand, produce their output in multiple moderate-sized plants and hope to achieve cost savings through firm size. Both sources of scale economies are important in the economy.

Graphic Presentation   A firm's **long-run average cost curve (*LRAC*)** shows the different scales at which it can choose to operate in the long run. A given point on the *LRAC* tells us the average cost of producing the associated level of output. At that point, the existing scale of plant determines the position and shape of the firm's short-run cost curves. The long-run average cost curve shows the positions of the different sets of short-run curves among which the firm must choose. In making the long-run strategic choice of plant scale, the firm then confronts an associated set of short-run cost curves. The long-run average cost curve is the "envelope" of a series of short-run curves; it "wraps around" the set of all possible short-run curves like an envelope.

When the firm experiences economies of scale, its *LRAC* will decline with output. Figure 9.4 shows short-run and long-run average cost curves for a firm that realizes economies of scale up to about 100,000 units of production and roughly constant returns to scale after that. The 100,000 unit output level in Figure 9.4 is sometimes called the **minimum efficient scale (MES)** of the firm. The

long-run average cost curve (*LRAC*)   The "envelope" of a series of short-run cost curves.

minimum efficient scale (MES)   The smallest size at which the long-run average cost curve is at its minimum.

ECONOMICS IN PRACTICE

Economies of Scale in Solar

Concerns about the environment and interest in sustainable energy have greatly increased the excitement by both consumers and investors in alternative energies such as wind and solar power. For both alternatives, the price of more conventional energy sources, like oil, is very important. As the price of oil rises, solar power, one of the substitutes for oil, becomes more viable. But there are also forces at work on the cost side. As the article below discusses, the process of producing solar panels is subject to scale economies, so that as the use of solar panels increases, the long-run average cost of producing them is likely to fall.

Utility Scale Solar Market Shares, Strategies, and Forecasts, Worldwide, 2010–2016

PR Newswire

Solar energy market driving forces relate to the opportunity to harness a cheap, long lasting, powerful energy source. Solar energy can be used to create electricity in huge quantity. Solar panels are mounted in a weatherproof frame and then mounted in areas with direct exposure to the sun to generate electricity from sunlight.

Solar power systems are composed of solar modules, related power electronics, and other components. Solar panels are used in residential, commercial, and industrial applications. Solar compositions of arrays that make up electric utility grids appear to be the wave of the future. Other solar systems are concentrating systems that leverage thermal transport of heated fluids and utilize traditional steam generators. The demand for solar energy is dependent on lower prices for solar and higher prices for petroleum. A combination of economies of scale being

realized in manufacturing along with increases in the current prices for petroleum will drive solar energy adoption.

Large solar farms are more popular initially, but solar is anticipated to be built out on commercial roof tops in increased quantity. The electricity generated will be fed to local substations and distributed to homes from there.

There is growing global demand for cost-effective and reliable solar power. Molten salt storage and solar electricity generation by use of steam turbines are poised to achieve significant growth. The economies of scale have not yet kicked in and will do so after 100 projects have been built out. The technology promises to be significant because the projects generate so much electricity.

Source: Excerpted from press release "Utility Scale Solar Market Shares, Strategies, and Forecasts, Worldwide, 2010–2016 Now Available at ReportsandReports.com," June 28, 2010.

MES is the smallest size at which the long-run average cost curve is at its minimum. Essentially, it is the answer to the question, how large does a firm have to be to have the best per-unit cost position possible? Consider a firm operating in an industry in which all of the firms in that industry face the long-run average cost curve shown in Figure 9.4. If you want your firm to be cost-competitive in that market, you need to produce at least 100,000 units. At smaller volumes, you will have higher costs than other firms in the industry, which makes it hard for you to stay in the industry. Policy makers are often interested in learning how large MES is relative to the total market for a product, since when MES is large relative to the total market size, we typically expect fewer firms to be in the industry. And, as we will see in the next chapter, competition may be reduced.

Figure 9.4 shows three potential scales of operation, each with its own set of short-run cost curves. Each point on the *LRAC* curve represents the minimum cost at which the associated output level can be produced. Once the firm chooses a scale on which to produce, it becomes locked into one set of cost curves in the short run. If the firm were to settle on scale 1, it would not realize the major cost advantages of producing on a larger scale. By roughly doubling its scale of operations from 50,000 to 100,000 units (scale 2), the firm reduces average costs per unit significantly.

Figure 9.4 shows that at every moment, firms face two different cost constraints. In the long run, firms can change their scale of operation, and costs may be different as a result.

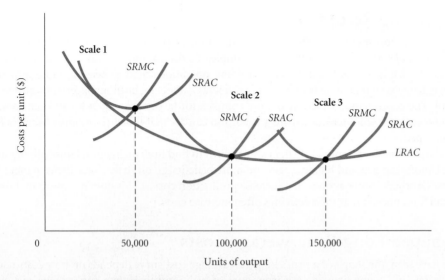

▲ **FIGURE 9.4 A Firm Exhibiting Economies of Scale**
The long-run average cost curve of a firm shows the different scales on which the firm can choose to operate in the long run. Each scale of operation defines a different short run. Here we see a firm exhibiting economies of scale; moving from scale 1 to scale 3 reduces average cost.

However, at any *given* moment, a particular scale of operation exists, constraining the firm's capacity to produce in the short run. That is why we see both short- and long-run curves in the same diagram.

Constant Returns to Scale

Technically, the term *constant returns* means that the quantitative relationship between input and output stays constant, or the same, when output is increased. If a firm doubles inputs, it doubles output; if it triples inputs, it triples output; and so on. Furthermore, if input prices are fixed, constant returns imply that average cost of production does not change with scale. In other words, constant returns to scale mean that the firm's long-run average cost curve remains flat.

The firm in Figure 9.4 exhibits roughly constant returns to scale between scale 2 and scale 3. The average cost of production is about the same in each. If the firm exhibited constant returns at levels above 150,000 units of output, the *LRAC* would continue as a flat, straight line.

Economists have studied cost data extensively over the years to estimate the extent to which economies of scale exist. Evidence suggests that in most industries, firms do not have to be gigantic to realize cost savings from scale economies. In other words, the MES is moderate relative to market size. Perhaps the best example of efficient production on a small scale is the manufacturing sector in Taiwan. Taiwan has enjoyed very rapid growth based on manufacturing firms that employ fewer than 100 workers.

One simple argument supports the empirical result that most industries seem to exhibit constant returns to scale (a flat *LRAC*) after some level of output at least at the level of the plant. Competition always pushes firms to adopt the least-cost technology and scale. If cost advantages result with larger-scale operations, the firms that shift to that scale will drive the smaller, less efficient firms out of business. A firm that wants to grow when it has reached its "optimal" size can do so by building another identical plant. It thus seems logical to conclude that most firms face constant returns to scale at the plant level *as long as* they can replicate their existing plants.

Decreasing Returns to Scale

When average cost increases with scale of production, a firm faces *decreasing returns to scale*, or *diseconomies of scale*. The most often cited example of a diseconomy of scale is bureaucratic inefficiency. As size increases beyond a certain point, operations tend to become more difficult to manage. Large size often entails increased bureaucracy, affecting both managerial incentives and control. The coordination function is more complex for larger firms than for smaller ones, and the chances that it will break down are greater. You can see that this diseconomy of scale is firm-level in type.

A large firm is also more likely than a small firm to find itself facing problems with organized labor. Unions can demand higher wages and more benefits, go on strike, force firms to incur legal expenses, and take other actions that increase production costs. (This does not mean that unions are "bad," but instead that their activities often increase costs.)

U-Shaped Long-Run Average Costs

As we have seen, the shape of a firm's long-run average cost curve depends on how costs react to changes in scale. Some firms do see economies of scale, and their long-run average cost curves slope downward. Most firms seem to have flat long-run average cost curves. Still others encounter diseconomies, and their long-run average cost curves slope upward.

Figure 9.5 describes a firm that exhibits both economies of scale and diseconomies of scale. Average costs decrease with scale of plant up to q^* and increase with scale after that. The *Economics in Practice* on p. 201 discusses the history of the U-shaped curve.

The U-shaped average cost curve looks very much like the short-run average cost curves we have examined in the last two chapters, but do not confuse the two. All short-run average cost curves are U-shaped because we assume a fixed scale of plant that constrains production and drives marginal cost upward as a result of diminishing returns. In the long run, we make no such assumption; instead, we assume that scale of plant can be changed and ask how costs change with scale.

It is important to note that economic efficiency requires taking advantage of economies of scale (if they exist) and avoiding diseconomies of scale. The **optimal scale of plant** is the scale of plant that minimizes average cost. In fact, as we will see next, competition forces firms to use the optimal scale. In Figure 9.5, q^* is the unique optimal scale.

optimal scale of plant The scale of plant that minimizes average cost.

▶ **FIGURE 9.5 A Firm Exhibiting Economies and Diseconomies of Scale**

Economies of scale push this firm's average costs down to q^*. Beyond q^*, the firm experiences diseconomies of scale; q^* is the level of production at lowest average cost, using optimal scale.

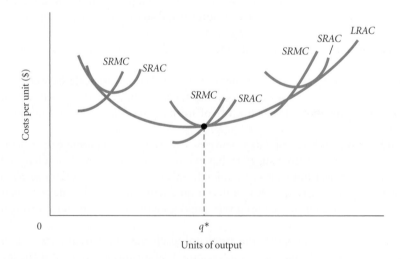

Long-Run Adjustments to Short-Run Conditions

We began this chapter by discussing the different short-run positions in which firms like Blue Velvet may find themselves. Firms can be operating at a profit or suffering economic losses; they can be shut down or producing. The industry is not in long-run equilibrium if firms have an incentive to

ECONOMICS IN PRACTICE

The Long-Run Average Cost Curve: Flat or U-Shaped?

The long-run average cost curve has been a source of controversy in economics for many years. A long-run average cost curve was first drawn as the "envelope" of a series of short-run curves in a classic article written by Jacob Viner in 1931.[1] In preparing that article, Viner gave his draftsman the task of drawing the long-run curve through the minimum points of all the short-run average cost curves.

In a supplementary note written in 1950, Viner commented:

... the error in Chart IV is left uncorrected so that future teachers and students may share the pleasure of many of their predecessors of pointing out that if I had known what an envelope was, I would not have given my excellent draftsman the technically impossible and economically inappropriate task of drawing an *AC* curve which would pass through the lowest cost points of all the *AC* curves yet not rise above any *AC* curve at any point....[2]

While this story is an interesting part of the lore of economics, a more recent debate concentrates on the economic content of this controversy. In 1986, Professor Herbert Simon of Carnegie-Mellon University stated bluntly in an interview for *Challenge* magazine that most textbooks are wrong to use the U-shaped long-run cost curve to predict the size of firms. Simon explained that studies show the firm's cost curves are not U-shaped but instead slope down to the right and then level off.[3]

What difference does it make if the long-run average cost curve has a long flat section with no upturn? In this case, there is no single point on the long-run curve that is the best. Once a firm achieves some scale, it has the same costs no matter how much larger it gets. As Simon tells us, this means we can't predict firm size. But we can still predict industry size: In this situation, we still have forces of profit seeking causing firms to enter and exit until excess profits are zero. The unique industry output is the one that corresponds to a price equal to long-run average cost that also equates supply and demand. Simon is right that this type of cost curve means the economic theory doesn't explain everything, but it still tells us a good deal.

[1] Jacob Viner, "Cost Curves and Supply Curves," *Zeitschrift fur Nationalokonomie*, Vol. 3 (1–1931), 23–46. [2] George J. Stigler and Kenneth E. Boulding, eds., *AEA Readings in Price Theory*, Vol. 6 (Chicago: Richard D. Irwin, 1952), p. 227. [3] Based on interview with Herbert A. Simon, "The Failure of Armchair Economics," *Challenge*, November–December, 1986, 23–24.

enter or exit in the long run. Thus, when firms are earning economic profits (profits above normal, or positive) or are suffering economic losses (profits below normal, or negative), the industry is not at an equilibrium and firms will change their behavior. What firms are likely to do depends in part on costs in the long run. This is why we have spent a good deal of time discussing economies and diseconomies of scale.

We can now put these two ideas together and discuss the actual long-run adjustments that are likely to take place in response to short-run profits and losses.

Short-Run Profits: Moves In and Out of Equilibrium

Consider a competitive market in which demand and costs have been stable for some period and the industry is in equilibrium. The market price is such that firms are earning a normal rate of return and the flow of firms in and out of the industry balances out. Firms are producing as efficiently as possible, and supply equals demand. Figure 9.6 shows this situation at a price of $6 and an output of 200,000 units for an industry with a U-shaped long-run cost curve.

Now suppose demand increases. Perhaps this is the market for green tea, and there has been a news report on the health benefits of the tea. What happens? Managers at the firms notice the demand increase—they too read the paper! But each firm has a fixed capital stock—it owns a set tea plantation, for example. Entry also is impossible in the short run. But existing firms can do something to meet the new demand, even within the constraints of their existing plant. They can hire overtime workers, for example, to increase yield. But this increases average costs. In Figure 9.7, firms will move up their *SRMC* curves as they produce output beyond the level of 2,000. Why do firms do this? Because the increased demand has increased the price. The new higher price makes it worthwhile for the firms to increase their output even though in the short run it is expensive to do so. In fact, the firms increase output as long as the new price is greater than the short-run marginal cost curve. We have noted the new short-run equilibrium in Figure 9.7.

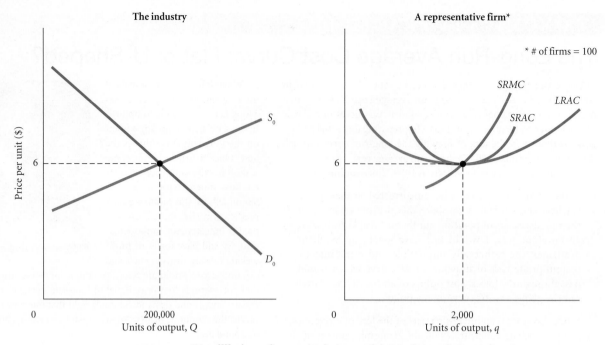

FIGURE 9.6 Equilibrium for an Industry with U-shaped Cost Curves
The individual firm on the right is producing 2,000 units, and so we also know that the industry consists of 100 firms. All firms are identical, and all are producing at the uniquely best output level of 2,000 units.

Again supply equals demand. But there are two important differences. First, and most important, firms are making profits. The profits are noted in the gray-shaded rectangle in Figure 9.8 and are the difference between the new higher price and the new higher average cost. Second, firms are also operating at too large an output level for minimum average cost. Managers in these firms are scrambling to get increased output from a plant designed for a smaller output level.

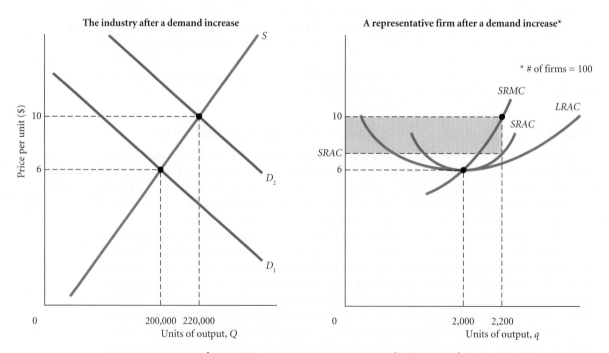

FIGURE 9.7 Industry Response to an Increase in Demand

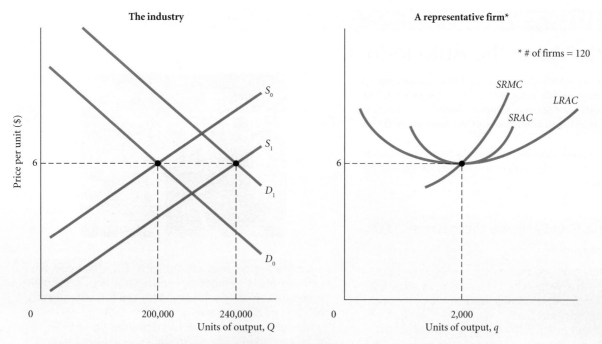

▲ **FIGURE 9.8 New Equilibrium with Higher Demand**

What happens next? Other entrepreneurs observing the industry see the excess profits and enter. Each one enters at a scale of 2,000 because that is the optimal scale in this industry. Perhaps existing firms also build new plants. With each new entry, the industry supply curve (which is just the sum of all the individual firms' supply curves) shifts to the right. More supply is available because there are more firms. Price begins to fall. As long as the price is above $6, each of the firms, both old and new, is making excess profits and more entry will occur. Once price is back to $6, there are no longer excess profits and thus no further entry. Figure 9.8 shows this new equilibrium where supply has shifted sufficiently to return the industry to the original price of $6 at a new quantity level.

Again, notice the characteristics of the final equilibrium: Each individual firm chooses a scale of operations that minimizes its long-run average cost. It operates this plant at an output level that minimizes short-run average cost. In equilibrium, each firm has

$$SRMC = SRAC = LRAC$$

Firms make no excess profits so that

$$P = SRMC = SRAC = LRAC$$

and there are enough firms so that supply equals demand.

Suppose instead of a positive demand shock, the industry experiences an unexpected cut in demand. Precisely the same economic logic holds. When demand falls (shifts to the left), the price falls. In the short run, firms cannot shrink plants, nor can they exit. But with the lower price, firms begin to produce less in their plants than before. In fact, firms cut back production so long as the price they receive is less than their short-run marginal cost. At this point, firms earn losses and are producing at too small a level and thus have higher average cost than before. Some firms drop out, and when they do so, the supply curve shifts to the left. How many firms leave? Enough so that the equilibrium is restored with the price again at $6 and the industry output has fallen reduced to reflect the reduced demand for the product.

The Fortunes of the Auto Industry

In 2010 the majority shareholder in General Motors, once counted among the top Fortune 500 firms, was the U.S. government. The government bought its interest in General Motors as a "reluctant shareholder" to help the firm move out of the bankruptcy that it entered in 2009.

The article below describes the return of the firm to profitability in mid-2010. We can use the tools of this chapter to dig into the lessons of the article.

GM Reports First Quarterly Profit Since 2007
The Wall Street Journal

Ten months after emerging from a government-orchestrated bankruptcy, General Motors Co. on Monday reported its first quarterly profit in three years, driven by dramatic cost reductions and improved global sales.

GM made $863 million in the first three months of 2010, compared with a $6 billion loss a year earlier, a performance that surprised analysts who expected more modest results. Revenue grew 40 percent to $31.5 billion, and the company generated $1 billion in cash.

GM has managed to drive up prices by building fewer vehicles and turning out cars and trucks more desirable to U.S. consumers, such as GM's revamped Chevrolet Equinox crossover, while tighter supply means the company doesn't have to rely on deals to clear out inventory.

Another factor: In North America, GM's factories are operating at 84 percent of capacity, up from less than 40 percent a year ago. Underutilized factories are a major cost drain for auto makers.

The company, meantime, has increased global sales by 24 percent amid rapid growth in emerging markets, including China.

Cost reductions made possible by last year's bankruptcy were a major factor in GM's profit.

Source: The Wall Street Journal, excerpted from "GM Reports First Quarterly Profits Since 2007" by Sharon Terlep. Copyright 2010 by *Dow Jones & Company, Inc.* Reproduced with permission of *Dow Jones & Company, Inc.* via Copyright Clearance Center.

How has GM improved profits? First, demand for autos shifted right as the recession eased and GM built vehicles "more desirable to U.S. consumers," as the article tells us. The demand shift allowed GM to raise prices and allowed it to sell more vehicles. Improved sales also helped on the cost side. The auto industry exhibits large economies of scale due in part to the large capital investment of the assembly lines. In the 2008–2009 recession, the auto industry found itself with excess capacity (the article tells us GM was operating at 40 percent capacity in the trough) and the per unit costs of cars rocketed up. By using more of its capacity, average costs fell, making for better profitability.

The demand shift is only part of the story, however. GM had also taken other actions, both in terms of union wage negotiations and restructuring, to reduce its costs. This had the effect *of shifting down* the long-run average cost curve, further increasing profits. A hard question now being asked is whether these cost reductions will be long lived.

The Long-Run Adjustment Mechanism: Investment Flows Toward Profit Opportunities

The central idea in our discussion of entry, exit, expansion, and contraction is this: In efficient markets, investment capital flows toward profit opportunities. The actual process is complex and varies from industry to industry.

We talked about efficient markets in Chapter 1. In efficient markets, profit opportunities are quickly eliminated as they develop. To illustrate this point, we described driving up to a toll booth and suggested that shorter-than-average lines are quickly eliminated as cars shift into those lines. Profits in competitive industries also are eliminated as new competing firms move into open slots, or perceived opportunities, in the industry.

In practice, the entry and exit of firms in response to profit opportunities usually involve the financial capital market. In capital markets, people are constantly looking for profits. When firms in an industry do well, capital is likely to flow into that industry in a variety of forms. Entrepreneurs start new firms, and firms producing entirely different products may join the competition to break into new markets. It happens all around us. The tremendous success of premium ice cream makers Ben and Jerry's and Häagen-Dazs spawned dozens of competitors. In

ECONOMICS IN PRACTICE

Why Are Hot Dogs So Expensive in Central Park?

Recently, one of the authors of this textbook was walking in Central Park in New York City. Since it was lunchtime and she was hungry, she decided to indulge her secret passion for good old-fashioned hot dogs. Because she did this frequently, she was well aware that the standard price for a hot dog in New York City was $1.50. So she was surprised when she handed the vendor $2 that she received no change back. As it turned out, the price of a hot dog inside the park was $2.00, not the $1.50 vendors charged elsewhere in the city. Since she was trained as an economist, she wanted to know what caused the difference in price.

First, she looked to the demand side of the market. If hot dogs are selling for $2.00 in the park but only $1.50 outside the park, people must be willing and able to pay more for them in the park. Why? Perhaps hot dogs are more enjoyable to people when eaten while walking through Central Park. Hot dogs and "walking through the park" may be complementary goods. Or maybe people who walk in the park at noon are richer.

You might ask, if hot dogs are available outside the park for $1.50, why don't people buy them there and bring them to the park? The fact is that hot dogs are good only when they are hot, and they get cold very quickly. A hot dog purchased 5 minutes away from Central Park will be stone cold by the time someone reaches the park.

But looking at the demand side is not enough to understand a market. We also have to explain the behavior of the hot dog vendors who comprise the supply side of the market. On the supply side, the author knew that the market for hot dogs was virtually perfectly competitive outside the park. First, the product is homogeneous. Essentially all vendors supply the same product: a standard quality-certified hot dog and two varieties of mustard. Second, there is free entry. Since most vendors have wheels on their carts, if the price of hot dogs rises above $1.50 in one part of town, we would expect vendors to move there. The added supply would then push prices back to Price (P) = short-run marginal cost $(SRAC)$ = long-run average cost $(LRAC)$. At P = $1.50, individual vendors around the city must be earning enough to cover average costs including a normal rate of

return (see the discussion in the text on p. 190). If the market price produces excess profits, new vendors will show up to compete those excess profits away.

All of this would suggest that the price of hot dogs should be the same everywhere in New York City. If a vendor is able to charge $2 in the park and has the same costs as a vendor outside the park, he must be earning above-normal profits. After all, the vendor makes $.50 more on each hot dog. Something must be preventing the outside vendors from rolling their carts into the park, which would increase the supply of hot dogs and drive the price back to $1.50.

That something is a more expensive license. In New York, you need a license to operate a hot dog cart, and a license to operate in the park costs more. Since hot dogs are $0.50 more in the park, the added cost of a license each year must be roughly $0.50 per hot dog sold. In fact, in New York City, licenses to sell hot dogs in the park are auctioned off for many thousands of dollars, while licenses to operate in more remote parts of the city cost only about $1,000.

one Massachusetts town of 35,000, a small ice cream store opened to rave reviews, long lines, and high prices and positive profits. Within a year, there were four new ice cream/frozen yogurt stores, no lines, and lower prices. Magic? No, just the natural functioning of competition.

A powerful example of an industry expanding with higher prices and higher economic profits is the housing sector prior to 2007. From the late 1990s until early 2006, the housing market was booming nationally. Demand was shifting to the right for a number of reasons. As it did, housing prices rose substantially and with them the profits being made by builders. As builders responded with higher output, the number of new units started (housing starts) increased to a near record level of over 2.2 million per year in 2005. Construction employment grew to over 7.5 million.

Starting in 2006, housing demand shifted to the left. The inventory of unsold property began to build, and prices started to fall. That turned profits into losses. Home builders cut their production, and many went out of business. These moves had major ramifications for the performance of the whole economy. Go back and look at Figure 9.7 and Figure 9.8. Make sure you understand how these diagrams explain both the expansion and contraction of the housing sector since 2000.

Many believe that part of the explosion of technology-based dot-com companies is due to the ease of entering the sector. All it takes to start a company is an idea, a terminal, and Web access. The number of new firms entering the industry is so large that statistical agencies cannot keep pace.

long-run competitive equilibrium When $P = SRMC = SRAC = LRAC$ and profits are zero.

When there is promise of positive profits, investments are made and output expands. When firms end up suffering losses, firms contract and some go out of business. It can take quite a while, however, for an industry to achieve **long-run competitive equilibrium**, the point at which $P = SRMC = SRAC = LRAC$ and profits are zero. In fact, because costs and tastes are in a constant state of flux, very few industries ever really get there. The economy is always changing. There are always some firms making profits and some firms suffering losses.

This, then, is a story about tendencies:

> Investment—in the form of new firms and expanding old firms—will over time tend to favor those industries in which profits are being made; and over time, industries in which firms are suffering losses will gradually contract from disinvestment.

Output Markets: A Final Word

In the last four chapters, we have been building a model of a simple market system under the assumption of perfect competition. Let us provide just one more example to review the actual response of a competitive system to a change in consumer preferences.

Over the past two decades, Americans have developed a taste for wine in general and for California wines in particular. We know that household demand is constrained by income, wealth, and prices and that income is (at least in part) determined by the choices that households make. Within these constraints, households increasingly choose—or demand—wine. The demand curve for wine has shifted to the right, causing excess demand followed by an increase in price.

With higher prices, wine producers find themselves earning positive profits. *This increase in price and consequent rise in profits is the basic signal that leads to a reallocation of society's resources.* In the short run, wine producers are constrained by their current scales of operation. California has only a limited number of vineyards and only a limited amount of vat capacity, for example.

In the long run, however, we would expect to see resources flow in to compete for these profits, and this is exactly what happens. New firms enter the wine-producing business. New vines are planted, and new vats and production equipment are purchased and put in place. Vineyard owners move into new states—Rhode Island, Texas, and Maryland—and established growers increase production. Overall, more wine is produced to meet the new consumer demand. At the same time, competition is forcing firms to operate using the most efficient technology available.

What starts as a shift in preferences thus ends up as a shift in resources. Land is reallocated, and labor moves into wine production. All this is accomplished without any central planning or direction.

You have now seen what lies behind the demand curves and supply curves in competitive output markets. The next two chapters take up competitive *input* markets and complete the picture.

─────────────── SUMMARY ───────────────

1. For any firm, one of three conditions holds at any given moment: (1) The firm is earning positive profits, (2) the firm is suffering losses, or (3) the firm is just breaking even—that is, earning a normal rate of return and thus zero profits.

SHORT-RUN CONDITIONS AND LONG-RUN DIRECTIONS *p. 190*

2. A firm that is earning positive profits in the short run and expects to continue doing so has an incentive to expand in the long run. Profits also provide an incentive for new firms to enter the industry.

3. In the short run, firms suffering losses are stuck in the industry. They can shut down operations ($q = 0$), but they must still bear fixed costs. In the long run, firms suffering losses can exit the industry.

4. A firm's decision about whether to shut down in the short run depends solely on whether its total revenue from operating is sufficient to cover its total variable cost. If total revenue exceeds total variable cost, the excess can be used to pay some fixed costs and thus reduce losses.

5. Anytime that price is below the minimum point on the average variable cost curve, total revenue will be less than total variable cost, and the firm will shut down. The minimum point on the average variable cost curve (which is also the point where marginal cost and average variable cost intersect) is called the *shutdown point*. At all prices above the shutdown point, the *MC* curve shows the profit-maximizing level of output. At all prices below it, optimal short-run output is zero.

6. The *short-run supply curve* of a firm in a perfectly competitive industry is the portion of its marginal cost curve that lies above its average variable cost curve.

7. Two things can cause the industry supply curve to shift: (1) in the short run, anything that causes marginal costs to change across the industry, such as an increase in the price of a particular input, and (2) in the long run, entry or exit of firms.

LONG-RUN COSTS: ECONOMIES AND DISECONOMIES OF SCALE *p. 195*

8. When an increase in a firm's scale of production leads to lower average costs, the firm exhibits *increasing returns to scale*, or *economies of scale*. When average costs do not change with the scale of production, the firm exhibits *constant returns to scale*. When an increase in a firm's scale of production leads to higher average costs, the firm exhibits *decreasing returns to scale*, or *diseconomies of scale*.

9. A firm's *long-run average cost curve* (*LRAC*) shows the costs associated with different scales on which it can choose to operate in the long run.

LONG-RUN ADJUSTMENTS TO SHORT-RUN CONDITIONS *p. 200*

10. When short-run profits exist in an industry, firms enter and existing firms expand. These events shift the industry supply curve to the right. When this happens, price falls and ultimately profits are eliminated.

11. When short-run losses are suffered in an industry, some firms exit and some firms reduce scale. These events shift the industry supply curve to the left, raising price and eliminating losses.

12. *Long-run competitive equilibrium* is reached when $P = SRMC = SRAC = LRAC$ and profits are zero.

13. In efficient markets, investment capital flows toward profit opportunities.

REVIEW TERMS AND CONCEPTS

breaking even, *p. 190*

constant returns to scale, *p. 195*

decreasing returns to scale *or* diseconomies of scale, *p. 195*

increasing returns to scale *or* economies of scale, *p. 195*

long-run average cost curve (*LRAC*), *p. 197*

long-run competitive equilibrium, *p. 206*

minimum efficient scale (MES), *p. 197*

optimal scale of plant, *p. 200*

short-run industry supply curve, *p. 194*

shutdown point, *p. 193*

long-run competitive equilibrium, $P = SRMC = SRAC = LRAC$

PROBLEMS

All problems are available on www.myeconlab.com

1. For each of the following, decide whether you agree or disagree and explain your answer:
   a. Firms that exhibit constant returns to scale have U-shaped long-run average cost curves.
   b. A firm suffering losses in the short run will continue to operate as long as total revenue at least covers fixed cost.

2. Ajax is a competitive firm operating under the following conditions: Price of output is $5, the profit-maximizing level of output is 20,000 units of output, and the total cost (full economic cost) of producing 20,000 units is $120,000. The firm's *only* fixed factor of production is a $300,000 stock of capital (a building). If the interest rate available on comparable risks is

10 percent, should this firm shut down immediately in the short run? Explain your answer.

3. Explain why it is possible that a firm with a production function that exhibits increasing returns to scale can run into diminishing returns at the same time.

4. Which of the following industries do you think are likely to exhibit large economies of scale? Explain why in each case.
   a. Home building
   b. Electric power generation
   c. Vegetable farming
   d. Software development
   e. Aircraft manufacturing

5. For cases *A* through *F* in the following table, would you (1) operate or shut down in the short run and (2) expand your plant or exit the industry in the long run?

	A	B	C	D	E	F
Total revenue	1,500	2,000	2,000	5,000	5,000	5,000
Total cost	1,500	1,500	2,500	6,000	7,000	4,000
Total fixed cost	500	500	200	1,500	1,500	1,500

6. [Related to the *Economics in Practice* on p. 201] Do you agree or disagree with the following statements? Explain in a sentence or two.
   a. A firm will never sell its product for less than it costs to produce it.
   b. If the short-run marginal cost curve is U-shaped, the long-run average cost curve is likely to be U-shaped as well.

7. The Smythe chicken farm outside Little Rock, Arkansas, produces 25,000 chickens per month. Total cost of production at Smythe Farm is $28,000. Down the road are two other farms. Faubus Farm produces 55,000 chickens a month, and total cost is $50,050. Mega Farm produces 100,000 chickens per month, at a total cost of $91,000. These data suggest that there are significant economies of scale in chicken production. Do you agree or disagree with this statement? Explain your answer.

8. Indicate whether you agree or disagree with the following statements. Briefly explain your answers.
   a. Increasing returns to scale refers to a situation where an increase in a firm's scale of production leads to higher costs per unit produced.
   b. Constant returns to scale refers to a situation where an increase in a firm's scale of production has no effect on costs per unit produced.
   c. Decreasing returns to scale refers to a situation where an increase in a firm's scale of production leads to lower costs per unit produced.

9. You are given the following cost data:

q	TFC	TVC
0	12	0
1	12	5
2	12	9
3	12	14
4	12	20
5	12	28
6	12	38

If the price of output is $7, how many units of output will this firm produce? What is the total revenue? What is the total cost? Will the firm operate or shut down in the short run? in the long run? Briefly explain your answers.

10. The concept of economies of scale refers to lower per-unit production costs at higher levels of output. The easiest way to understand this is to look at whether long-run average cost decreases with output (economies of scale) or whether long-run average cost increases with output (diseconomies of scale). If average cost is constant as output rises, there is constant returns to scale. But the concept of falling unit costs is all around us. Explain how the concept of economies of scale helps shed light on each of the following:
    a. car pooling

    b. doubling up to reduce rent
    c. farming
    d. a single-family car versus public transit
    e. a huge refinery

11. According to its Web site, Netflix is the world's largest online entertainment subscription service. It ships over 2 million DVDs daily to its more than 15 million members. On its Web site, Netflix indicates that its growth strategy is to "focus on subscription growth in order to realize economies of scale." In this business, where do you think scale economies come from?

12. From 2000 to 2005, the home building sector was expanding and new housing construction as measured by housing starts was approaching an all-time high. (At www.census.gov, click "Housing," then click "Construction data.") Big builders such as Lennar Corporation were making exceptional profits. The industry was expanding. Existing home building firms invested in more capacity and raised output. New home building firms entered the industry. From 2006 to 2009, demand for new and existing homes dropped. The inventory of unsold homes grew sharply. Home prices began to fall. Home builders suffered losses, and the industry contracted. Many firms went out of business, and many workers in the construction industry went bankrupt. Use the Internet to verify that all of these events happened. Access www.bls.gov for employment data and www.bea.gov for information on residential construction as part of gross domestic product. What has happened since the beginning of 2010? Has the housing market recovered? Have housing starts stopped falling? If so, at what level? Write a short essay about whether the housing sector is about to expand or contract.

13. [Related to the *Economics in Practice* on p. 205] St. Mark's Square is a beautiful plaza in Venice that is often frequented by both tourists and pigeons. Ringing the piazza are many small, privately owned cafes. In these cafes, a cappuccino costs 7 euros despite the fact that an equally good cappuccino costs only 3 euros a block a way. What is going on here?

14. The following problem traces the relationship between firm decisions, market supply, and market equilibrium in a perfectly competitive market.
    a. Complete the following table for a single firm in the short run.

OUTPUT	TFC	TVC	TC	AVC	ATC	MC
0	$300	$ 0	—	—	—	—
1	—	100	—	—	—	—
2	—	150	—	—	—	—
3	—	210	—	—	—	—
4	—	290	—	—	—	—
5	—	400	—	—	—	—
6	—	540	—	—	—	—
7	—	720	—	—	—	—
8	—	950	—	—	—	—
9	—	1,240	—	—	—	—
10	—	1,600	—	—	—	—

   b. Using the information in the table, fill in the following supply schedule for this individual firm under perfect competition and indicate profit (positive or negative) at each output level. (*Hint:* At each hypothetical price, what is the *MR* of producing 1 more unit of output? Combine this with the *MC* of another unit to figure out the quantity supplied.)

PRICE	QUANTITY SUPPLIED	PROFIT
$ 50	—	——
70	—	——
100	—	——
130	—	——
170	—	——
220	—	——
280	—	——
350	—	——

c. Now suppose there are 100 firms in this industry, all with identical cost schedules. Fill in the market quantity supplied at each price in this market.

PRICE	MARKET QUANTITY SUPPLIED	MARKET QUANTITY DEMANDED
$ 50	—	1,000
70	—	900
100	—	800
130	—	700
170	—	600
220	—	500
280	—	400
350	—	300

d. Fill in the blanks: From the market supply and demand schedules in c., the equilibrium market price for this good is ____ and the equilibrium market quantity is ____. Each firm will produce a quantity of ____ and earn a ____ (profit/loss) equal to ____.

e. In d., your answers characterize the short-run equilibrium in this market. Do they characterize the long-run equilibrium as well? If so, explain why. If not, explain why not (that is, what would happen in the long run to change the equilibrium and why?).

*15. Assume that you are hired as an analyst at a major New York consulting firm. Your first assignment is to do an industry analysis of the tribble industry. After extensive research and two all-nighters, you have obtained the following information:
- *Long-run costs:*
  Capital costs: $5 per unit of output
  Labor costs: $2 per unit of output
- No economies or diseconomies of scale
- Industry currently earning a normal return to capital (profit of zero)
- Industry perfectly competitive, with each of 100 firms producing the same amount of output
- *Total industry output:* 1.2 million tribbles
  Demand for tribbles is expected to grow rapidly over the next few years to a level twice as high as it is now, but (due to short-run diminishing returns) each of the 100 existing firms is likely to be producing only 50 percent more.

a. Sketch the long-run cost curve of a representative firm.
b. Show the current conditions by drawing two diagrams, one showing the industry and one showing a representative firm.
c. Sketch the increase in demand and show how the industry is likely to respond in the short run and in the long run.

16. The following graph shows the supply curve and three different demand curves for a perfectly competitive industry. The table represents cost data for a representative firm in the industry.

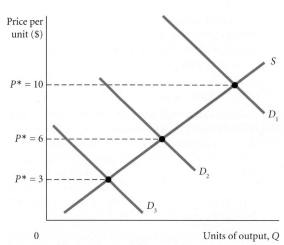

MARKET PRICE	$q^* @ p^* = MC$	$ATC @ p^* = MC$	$AVC @ p^* = MC$
$p^* = 10$	250	$8	$6
$p^* = 6$	175	8	4
$p^* = 3$	100	9	4

a. Use the data in the table and draw a graph for the representative firm in the industry when the industry demand curve is represented by D_1. What is the profit or loss for this firm? Shade in the profit or loss area on the graph.
b. Draw a graph for the representative firm when the industry demand curve falls to D_2. What is the profit or loss for this firm? Shade in the profit or loss area on the graph.
c. Draw a graph for the representative firm when the industry demand curve falls to D_3. What is the profit or loss for this firm? Shade in the profit or loss area on the graph.

17. For each of the three scenarios in the previous question ($p^* = 10$, $p^* = 6$, and $p^* = 3$), explain the long-run incentives for each representative firm in the industry. Also explain what should happen to the size of the industry as a whole.

18. Construct a graph with *AVC*, *ATC*, and *MC* curves. On this graph add a marginal revenue curve for a representative firm in a perfectly competitive industry which is maximizing profits at a price of p^*_1. Add a second marginal revenue curve for a firm which is minimizing losses but continues to produce when the price is p^*_2. Add a third marginal revenue curve for a firm which is shutting down when the price is p^*_3. Explain where you decided to place each of the marginal revenue curves and identify the shutdown point on the graph.

19. The shape of a firm's long-run average cost curve depends on how costs vary with scale of operation. Draw a long-run average cost curve for a firm which exhibits economies of scale, constant returns to scale, and diseconomies of scale. Identify each of these sections of the cost curve and explain why each section exemplifies its specific type of returns to scale.

20. [Related to the *Economics in Practice* on *p. 198*] A new innovation in computer technology is called "cloud computing." With cloud computing, information and software are provided to computers on an "as-needed" basis, much like utilities are provided to homes and businesses. In a statement advocating the advantages of large, public cloud providers like Amazon.com over smaller enterprise data centers, James Hamilton, a vice president at Amazon claimed that "server,

*Note: Problems marked with an asterisk are more challenging.

networking and administration costs the average enterprise five to seven times what it costs a large provider." What does Hamilton's statement imply about the returns to scale in the cloud computing industry?

Source: James Urquhart, "James Hamilton on cloud economies of scale," *cnet.com*, April 28, 2010.

21. The long-run average cost curve for an industry is represented in the following graph. Add short-run average cost curves and short-run marginal cost curves for three firms in this industry, with one firm producing an output of 10,000 units, one firm producing an output of 20,000, and one firm producing an output of 30,000. Label these as Scale 1, Scale 2, and Scale 3, respectively. What is likely to happen to the scale of each of these three firms in the long run?

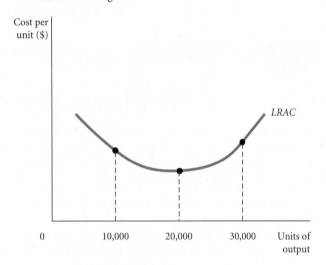

22. On the following graph for a purely competitive industry, Scale 1 represents the short-run production for a representative firm. Explain what is currently happening with firms in this industry in the short run and what will likely happen in the long run.

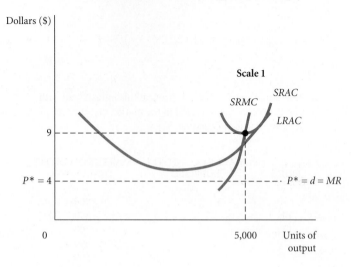

General Equilibrium and the Efficiency of Perfect Competition

12

In the last nine chapters, we have built a model of a simple, perfectly competitive economy. Our discussion has revolved around the two fundamental decision-making units, *households* and *firms*, which interact in two basic market arenas, *input markets* and *output markets*. (Look again at the circular flow diagram, shown in Figure II.1 on p. 117.) By limiting our discussion to perfectly competitive firms, we have been able to examine how the basic decision-making units interact in the two basic market arenas.

Households make constrained choices in both input and output markets. Household income, for example, depends on choices made in input markets: whether to work, how much to work, what skills to acquire, and so on. Input market choices are constrained by such factors as current wage rates, availability of jobs, and interest rates.

Firms are the primary producing units in a market economy. Profit-maximizing firms, to which we have limited our discussion, earn their profits by selling products and services for more than it costs to produce them. With firms, as with households, output markets and input markets cannot be analyzed separately. All firms make three specific decisions simultaneously: (1) how much output to supply, (2) how to produce that output—that is, which technology to use, and (3) how much of each input to demand.

In Chapters 7 through 9, we explored these three decisions from the viewpoint of output markets. We saw that the portion of the marginal cost curve that lies above a firm's average variable cost curve is the supply curve of a perfectly competitive firm in the short run. Implicit in the marginal cost curve is a choice of technology and a set of input demands. In Chapters 10 and 11, we looked at the perfectly competitive firm's three basic decisions from the viewpoint of input markets.

Output and input markets are connected because firms and households make simultaneous choices in both arenas, but there are other connections among markets as well. Firms buy in both capital and labor markets, for example, and they can substitute capital for labor and vice versa. A change in the price of one factor can easily change the demand for other factors. Buying more *capital*, for instance, usually changes the marginal revenue product of *labor* and shifts the labor demand curve. Similarly, a change in the price of a single good or service usually affects household demand for other goods and services, as when a price decrease makes one good more attractive than other close substitutes. The same change also makes households better off when they find that the same amount of income will buy more. Such additional "real income" can be spent on any of the other goods and services that the household buys.

The point here is simple:

> Input and output markets cannot be considered as if they were separate entities or as if they operated independently. Although it is important to understand the decisions of individual firms and households and the functioning of individual markets, we now need to add it all up so we can look at the operation of the system as a whole.

You have seen the concept of equilibrium applied both to markets and to individual decision-making units. In individual markets, supply and demand determine an equilibrium price. Perfectly competitive firms are in short-run equilibrium when price and marginal cost are equal ($P = MC$). In the long run, however, equilibrium in a competitive market is achieved only when economic profits are eliminated. Households are in equilibrium when they have equated the marginal utility per dollar spent on each good to the marginal utility per dollar spent on all other goods. This process of examining the equilibrium conditions in individual markets and for individual households and firms separately is called **partial equilibrium analysis**.

A **general equilibrium** exists when all markets in an economy are in simultaneous equilibrium. An event that disturbs the equilibrium in one market may disturb the equilibrium in many other markets as well. The ultimate impact of the event depends on the way *all* markets adjust to it. Thus, partial equilibrium analysis, which looks at adjustments in one isolated market, may be misleading.

Thinking in terms of a general equilibrium leads to some important questions. Is it possible for all households and firms and all markets to be in equilibrium simultaneously? Are the equilibrium conditions that we have discussed separately compatible with one another? Why is an event that disturbs an equilibrium in one market likely to disturb many other equilibriums simultaneously?

In talking about general equilibrium in the beginning of this chapter, we continue our exercise in *positive economics*—that is, we seek to understand how systems operate without making value judgments about outcomes. Later in the chapter, we turn from positive economics to *normative economics* as we begin to judge the economic system. Are its results good or bad? Can we make them better?

In judging the performance of any economic system, you will recall, it is essential first to establish specific criteria by which to judge. In this chapter, we use two such criteria: *efficiency* and *equity* (fairness). First, we demonstrate the **efficiency** of the allocation of resources—that is, the system produces what people want and does so at the least possible cost—if all the assumptions that we have made thus far hold. When we begin to relax some of our assumptions, however, it will become apparent that free markets may *not* be efficient. Several sources of inefficiency naturally occur within an unregulated market system. In the final part of this chapter, we introduce the potential role of government in correcting market inefficiencies and achieving fairness.

partial equilibrium analysis The process of examining the equilibrium conditions in individual markets and for households and firms separately.

general equilibrium The condition that exists when all markets in an economy are in simultaneous equilibrium.

efficiency The condition in which the economy is producing what people want at least possible cost.

Market Adjustment to Changes in Demand

All economies, particularly market systems, are dynamic: Change occurs all the time. Markets experience shifts of demand, both up and down; costs and technology change; and prices and outputs change. We have spent a lot of time looking at how these changes affect individual markets. But markets are also connected to one another. If capital flows into one market, often that means it is flowing out of another market. If consumers ride trains, often that means they stay off the bus. How do we think about connections across markets?

As we look at the general case, you might find it helpful to keep an example in mind. In 2007, Amazon introduced the Kindle, a small machine that allows a person to read e-books. We could analyze this product introduction in a partial equilibrium setting, considering the responsiveness of potential buyers to price or quality changes in the Kindle. But the introduction of the Kindle and subsequent pricing decisions by Amazon affect other markets as well. E-books substitute in part for printed books. The introduction of the Kindle and subsequent price reductions in the device thus shift the demand for printed books to the left. When the demand for printed books falls, storefront booksellers like Barnes and Noble suffer profit losses. Likely their sales of other products in the stores—complements to their book sales—also decline. Many printed books are ordered over the Web, many in fact through Amazon itself. When demand for these books falls, shipping services like UPS lose business. Printed books are produced using paper. When the demand for books falls, so does the demand for paper, and through that channel the demand for forest products falls.

Nor is the story over there. When Amazon prices the Kindle, it must take into account what is going on in the marketplace for printed books. If Barnes and Noble responds to the shift in its demand by lowering prices of printed books, that move will influence the optimal price for the Kindle. If the fall in demand for paper reduces the cost of paper, the costs of printing books will fall, and that too will lead to a lower price for printed books. Amazon will need to respond to that as well. In a general equilibrium analysis one needs to work through all the feedback loops and connections across industries to get to a final answer.

Figure 12.1 begins our discussion of the more general case of market connections. In the figure we assume that there are two sectors in the economy, X and Y, and that both are currently in long-run equilibrium. Total output in sector X is Q_X^0, the product is selling for a price of P_X^0, and each firm in the industry produces up to where P_X^0 is equal to marginal cost—q_X^0. At that point,

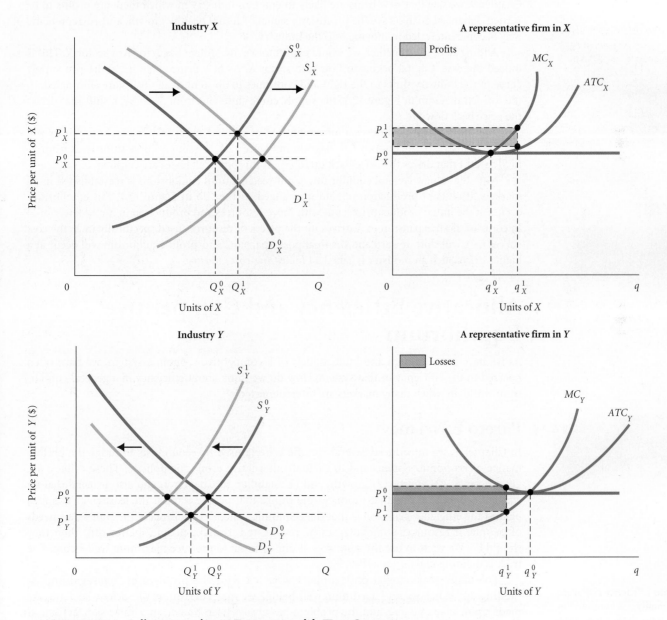

▲ **FIGURE 12.1 Adjustment in an Economy with Two Sectors**
Initially, demand for X shifts from D_X^0 to D_X^1. This shift pushes the price of X up to P_X^1, creating profits.
Demand for Y shifts down from D_Y^0 to D_Y^1, pushing the price of Y down to P_Y^1 and creating losses. Firms have an incentive to leave sector Y and an incentive to enter sector X. Exiting sector Y shifts supply in that industry to S_Y^1, raising price and eliminating losses. Entry shifts supply in X to S_X^1, thus reducing and eliminating profits.

price is just equal to average cost and economic profits are zero. The same condition holds initially in sector Y. The market is in zero profit equilibrium at a price of P_Y^0.

Now assume that a change in consumer preferences (or in the age distribution of the population or in something else) shifts the demand for X out to the right from D_X^0 to D_X^1. That shift drives the price up to P_X^1. If households decide to buy more X, without an increase in income, they must buy *less* of something else. Because everything else is represented by Y in this example, the demand for Y must decline and the demand curve for Y shifts to the left, from D_Y^0 to D_Y^1.

With the shift in demand for X, price rises to P_X^1 and profit-maximizing firms immediately increase output to q_X^1 (the point where $P_X^1 = MC_X$). However, now there are positive profits in X. With the downward shift of demand in Y, price falls to P_Y^1. Firms in sector Y cut back to q_Y^1 (the point where $P_Y^1 = MC_Y$), and the lower price causes firms producing Y to suffer losses.

In the short run, adjustment is simple. Firms in both industries are constrained by their current scales of plant. Firms can neither enter nor exit their respective industries. Each firm in industry X raises output somewhat, from q_X^0 to q_X^1. Firms in industry Y cut back from q_Y^0 to q_Y^1.

In response to the existence of profit in sector X, the capital market begins to take notice. In Chapter 9, we saw that new firms are likely to enter an industry in which there are profits to be earned. Financial analysts see the profits as a signal of future healthy growth, and entrepreneurs may become interested in moving into the industry.

Adding all of this together, we would expect to see investment begin to favor sector X. This is indeed the case: Capital begins to flow into sector X. As new firms enter, the short-run supply curve in the industry shifts to the right and continues to do so until all profits are eliminated. In the top-left diagram in Figure 12.1, the supply curve shifts out from S_X^0 to S_X^1, a shift that drives the price back down to P_X^0.

We would also expect to see a movement out of sector Y because of losses. Some firms will exit the industry. In the bottom-left diagram in Figure 12.1, the supply curve shifts back from S_Y^1 to S_Y^1, a shift that drives the price back up to P_Y^0. At this point, all losses are eliminated.

Note that a new general equilibrium is not reached until equilibrium is reestablished in all markets. If costs of production remain unchanged, as they do in Figure 12.1, this equilibrium occurs at the initial product prices, but with more resources and production in X and fewer in Y. In contrast, if an expansion in X drives up the prices of resources used specifically in X, the cost curves in X will shift upward and the final postexpansion zero-profit equilibrium will occur at a higher price. Such an industry is called an *increasing-cost industry*.

Allocative Efficiency and Competitive Equilibrium

As we have gone through and built models of a competitive economic system, we have often referred to the efficiency of that system. How do we think about efficiency in a general equilibrium world, in which many markets are interconnected?

Pareto Efficiency

In Chapter 1, we introduced several specific criteria used by economists to judge the performance of economic systems and to evaluate alternative economic policies. These criteria are (1) efficiency, (2) equity, (3) growth, and (4) stability. In Chapter 1, you also learned that an *efficient* economy is one that produces the things that people want at the least cost. The idea behind the efficiency criterion is that the economic system exists to serve the wants and needs of people. If resources somehow can be reallocated to make people "better off," then they should be. We want to use the resources at our disposal to produce maximum well-being. The trick is defining *maximum well-being*.

For many years, social philosophers wrestled with the problem of "aggregation," or "adding up." When we say "maximum well-being," we mean maximum *for society*. Societies are made up of many people, and the problem has always been how to maximize satisfaction, or well-being, for all members of society. What has emerged is the now widely accepted concept of *allocative efficiency*, first developed by the Italian economist Vilfredo Pareto in the nineteenth century. Pareto's very precise definition of efficiency is often referred to as **Pareto efficiency** or **Pareto optimality**.

Pareto efficiency *or* Pareto optimality A condition in which no change is possible that will make some members of society better off without making some other members of society worse off.

ECONOMICS IN PRACTICE

Ethanol and Land Prices

The U.S. government provides large subsidies for ethanol, a fuel produced from corn. Proponents of the ethanol subsidies suggest that it is one piece of a policy that can help the United States reduce its dependence on foreign oil. In part, as a result of these subsidies, the midwestern United States has seen a large increase in corn production relative to other grains. The following article traces another of the general equilibrium consequences of the ethanol subsidies: an increase in the price of agricultural land.

Nebraska ethanol boom causing land prices to soar

TheIndependent.com

Ethanol is not only pumping up the price of corn in Nebraska, but also farm real estate market values and cash rent rates values have seen a 14-percent increase, according to the preliminary results of the University of Nebraska-Lincoln's annual Farm Real Estate Market Development Survey.

According to the survey, Nebraska farmland's average value for the year ending Feb. 1 was $1,155 per acre, compared to $1,013 per acre at this time last year, said Bruce Johnson, the UNL agricultural economist who conducts this annual survey.

He said preliminary findings show this was the largest all-land value increase in the past 19 years. It is also the fourth straight year of what Johnson called "solid advances" in land values. He said the state's current all-land average value is more than 50 percent higher than the 2003 level.

Higher prices for corn because of ethanol demand are driving the sharp rise in land prices. By early 2008, Nebraska should have about 25 ethanol plants online, producing 1.2 billion gallons of ethanol and using more than 425 million bushels of corn.

"The demand from rapidly growing ethanol production has triggered the commodity market advances, and, in turn, worked into the agricultural land market dynamic, particularly in the major corn-producing areas of the state," Johnson said.

Source: Robert Pore, robert.pore@theindependent.com. Reprinted with permission.

As we see in the article, a number of markets are affected by the ethanol subsidies. The increase in the demand for ethanol drives up the demand for corn, which in turn increases the demand for land. Since the supply of land is finite, the price of land used to produce corn rises. But what about the rest of the agricultural economy? Increasing land prices increases the cost of other grains, such as wheat. As you learned in Chapter 2, land is a key factor of production. The increase in wheat costs shifts the supply curve to the left, as in the figure below. Wheat prices thus also rise.

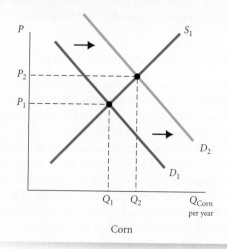

Corn

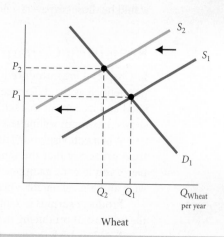

Wheat

Specifically, a change is said to be efficient when it makes some members of society better off without making other members of society worse off. An efficient, or *Pareto optimal*, system is one in which no such changes are possible. An example of a change that makes some people better off and nobody worse off is a simple voluntary exchange. I have apples and you have nuts. I like nuts and you like apples. We trade. We both gain, and no one loses.

For such a definition to have any real meaning, we must answer two questions: (1) What do we mean by "better off"? and (2) How do we account for changes that make some people better off and others worse off?

The answer to the first question is simple. People decide what "better off" and "worse off" mean. I am the only one who knows whether I am better off after a change. If you and I exchange one item for another because I like what you have and you like what I have, we both "reveal" that we are better off after the exchange because we agreed to it voluntarily. If everyone in the neighborhood wants a park and the residents all contribute to a fund to build one, they have consciously changed the allocation of resources and they all are better off for it.

The answer to the second question is more complex. Nearly every change that one can imagine leaves some people better off and some people worse off. If some gain and some lose as the result of a change, and it can be demonstrated that the value of the gains exceeds the value of the losses, then the change is said to be *potentially efficient*. In practice, however, the distinction between a *potentially* and an *actually* efficient change is often ignored and all such changes are simply called *efficient*.

Example: Budget Cuts in Massachusetts   Several years ago, in an effort to reduce state spending, the budget of the Massachusetts Registry of Motor Vehicles was cut substantially. Among other things, the state sharply reduced the number of clerks in each office. Almost immediately Massachusetts residents found themselves waiting in line for hours when they had to register their automobiles or get their driver's licenses.

Drivers and car owners began paying a price: standing in line, which used time and energy that could otherwise have been used more productively. However, before we can make sensible efficiency judgments, we must be able to measure, or at least approximate, the value of both the gains and the losses produced by the budget cut. To approximate the losses to car owners and drivers, we might ask how much people would be willing to pay to avoid standing in those long lines.

One office estimated that 500 people stood in line every day for about 1 hour each. If each person were willing to pay just $2 to avoid standing in line, the damage incurred would be $1,000 (500 × $2) per day. If the registry were open 250 days per year, the reduction in labor force at that office alone would create a cost to car owners, conservatively estimated, of $250,000 (250 × $1,000) per year.

Estimates also showed that taxpayers in Massachusetts saved about $80,000 per year by having fewer clerks at that office. If the clerks were reinstated, there would be some gains and some losses. Car owners and drivers would gain, and taxpayers would lose. However, because we can show that the value of the gains would substantially exceed the value of the losses, it can be argued that reinstating the clerks would be an efficient change. Note that the only *net* losers would be those taxpayers who do not own a car and do not hold driver's licenses.[1]

Revisiting Consumer and Producer Surplus

In Chapter 4 we introduced the concept of consumer and producer surplus. Consumer surplus was defined as the difference between the maximum amount that buyers are willing to pay for a good and its current market price. You can think of a demand curve as defining a boundary that shows maximum willingness to pay per unit at every quantity.

When you visit your favorite sandwich store, it will make you a sandwich and charge you a fixed price. Say that the sandwich is priced at $7. If you really crave sandwiches made at that place, you may be gaining consumer surplus. Indeed, if you were willing to pay $12 for a sandwich and it is selling for a price of $7, you earn a consumer surplus of $5 when you buy it.

Producer surplus is defined as the difference between the current market price of a good and the full cost of producing it. It is, in a way, a measure of profitability.

If you go back to pages 89–91 and review the argument, you will see that demand and supply curves, if left to their own natural adjustments, will lead the markets to an efficient equilibrium. Specifically, they will allocate demand across sectors in a way that maximizes the total surplus (consumer + producer) being generated by the exchange. Any change in quantity imposed on the market will shift the curves (or one of the curves) to the left or the right, and the result will be "deadweight losses."

---

[1] You might wonder whether there are other gainers and losers. What about the clerks? In analysis like this, it is usually assumed that the citizens who pay lower taxes spend their added income on other things. The producers of those other things need to expand to meet the new demand, and they hire more labor. Thus, a contraction of 100 jobs in the public sector will open up 100 jobs in the private sector. If the economy is fully employed, the transfer of labor to the private sector is assumed to create no net gains or losses to the workers.

To really understand the argument that a perfectly competitive economy is economically efficient and will lead to a Pareto efficient set of outcomes requires that we spend more time talking about some of the basic ideas.

The Efficiency of Perfect Competition

All societies answer these basic questions in the design of their economic systems:

1. *What gets produced?* What determines the final mix of output?
2. *How is it produced?* How do capital, labor, and land get divided up among firms? In other words, what is the allocation of resources among producers?
3. *Who gets what is produced?* What determines which households get how much? What is the distribution of output among consuming households?

The following discussion of efficiency uses these three questions and their answers to prove informally that perfect competition is efficient. To demonstrate that the perfectly competitive system leads to an efficient, or Pareto optimal, allocation of resources, we need to show that no changes are possible that will make some people better off without making others worse off. Specifically, we will show that under perfect competition, (1) resources are allocated among firms efficiently, (2) final products are distributed among households efficiently, and (3) the system produces the things that people want.

Efficient Allocation of Resources Among Firms The simple definition of efficiency holds that firms must produce their products using the best available—that is, lowest-cost—technology. If more output could be produced with the same amount of inputs, it would be possible to make some people better off without making others worse off.

The perfectly competitive model we have been using rests on several assumptions that assure us that resources in such a system would indeed be efficiently allocated among firms. Most important of these is the assumption that individual firms maximize profits. To maximize profit, a firm must minimize the cost of producing its chosen level of output. With a full knowledge of existing technologies, firms will choose the technology that produces the output they want at the least cost.

There is more to this story than meets the eye, however. Inputs must be allocated *across* firms in the best possible way. If we find that it is possible, for example, to take capital from firm A and swap it for labor from firm B and produce more product in both firms, then the original allocation was inefficient. Recall our example from Chapter 2. Farmers in Ohio and Kansas both produce wheat and corn. The climate and soil in most of Kansas are best suited to wheat production, and the climate and soil in Ohio are best suited to corn production. Kansas should produce most of the wheat, and Ohio should produce most of the corn. A law that forces Kansas land into corn production and Ohio land into wheat production would result in less of both—an inefficient allocation of resources. However, if markets are free and open, Kansas farmers will naturally find a higher return by planting wheat and Ohio farmers will find a higher return in corn. The free market, then, should lead to an efficient allocation of resources among firms. As you think back on Chapter 2, you should now see that societies operating on the production possibility frontier are efficiently using their inputs.

The same argument can be made more general. Misallocation of resources among firms is unlikely as long as every single firm faces the same set of prices and trade-offs in input markets. Recall from Chapter 10 that perfectly competitive firms will hire additional factors of production as long as their marginal revenue product exceeds their market price. As long as all firms have access to the *same* factor markets and the *same* factor prices, the last unit of a factor hired will produce the same value in each firm. Certainly, firms will use different technologies and factor combinations, but at the margin, no single profit-maximizing firm can get more value out of a factor than that factor's current market price. For example, if workers can be hired in the labor market at a wage of $6.50, *all* firms will hire workers as long as the marginal revenue product (MRP_L) produced by the marginal worker (labor's MRP_L) remains above $6.50. *No* firms will hire labor beyond the point at which MRP_L falls below $6.50. Thus, at equilibrium, additional workers are not worth more than $6.50 to any firm, and switching labor from one firm to another will not produce output of any greater value to society. Each firm has hired the profit-maximizing amount of labor. In short:

> The assumptions that factor markets are competitive and open, that all firms pay the same prices for inputs, and that all firms maximize profits lead to the conclusion that the allocation of resources among firms is efficient.

You should now have a greater appreciation for the power of the price mechanism in a market economy. Each individual firm needs only to make decisions about which inputs to use by looking at its own labor, capital, and land productivity relative to their prices. But because all firms face identical input prices, the market economy achieves efficient input use among firms. Prices are the instrument of Adam Smith's "invisible hand," allowing for efficiency without explicit coordination or planning.

Efficient Distribution of Outputs Among Households
Even if the system is producing the right things and is doing so efficiently, these things still have to get to the right people. Just as open, competitive factor markets ensure that firms do not end up with the wrong inputs, open, competitive output markets ensure that households do not end up with the wrong goods and services.

Within the constraints imposed by income and wealth, households are free to choose among all the goods and services available in output markets. A household will buy a good as long as that good generates utility, or subjective value, greater than its market price. Utility value is revealed in market behavior. You do not go out and buy something unless you are willing to pay *at least* the market price.

Remember that the value you place on any one good depends on what you must give up to have that good. The trade-offs available to you depend on your budget constraint. The trade-offs that are desirable depend on your preferences. If you buy a $300 iPhone, you may be giving up a trip home. If I buy it, I may be giving up four new tires for my car. We have both revealed that the iPhone is worth at least as much to us as all the other things that $300 can buy. As long as we are free to choose among all the things that $300 can buy, we will not end up with the wrong things; it is not possible to find a trade that will make us both better off. Again, the price mechanism plays an important role. Each of us faces the same price for the goods that we choose, and that in turn leads us to make choices that ensure that goods are allocated efficiently among consumers.

> We all know that people have different tastes and preferences and that they will buy very different things in very different combinations. As long as everyone shops freely in the same markets, no redistribution of final outputs among people will make them better off. If you and I buy in the same markets and pay the same prices and I buy what I want and you buy what you want, we cannot possibly end up with the wrong combination of things. Free and open markets are essential to this result.

Producing What People Want: The Efficient Mix of Output
It does no good to produce things efficiently or to distribute them efficiently if the system produces the wrong things. Will competitive markets produce the things that people want?

If the system is producing the wrong mix of output, we should be able to show that producing more of one good and less of another will make people better off. To show that perfectly competitive markets are efficient, we must demonstrate that no such changes in the final mix of output are possible.

The condition that ensures that the right things are produced is $P = MC$. That is, in both the long run and the short run, a perfectly competitive firm will produce at the point where the price of its output is equal to the marginal cost of production. As long as price is above marginal cost, it pays for a firm to increase output. The logic is this: When a firm weighs price and marginal cost, it weighs the value of its product to society *at the margin* against the value of the things that could otherwise be produced with the same resources. Figure 12.2 summarizes this logic.

The argument is quite straightforward. *First, price reflects households' willingness to pay.* By purchasing a good, individual households reveal that it is worth at least as much as the other goods that the same money could buy. Thus, current price reflects the value that households place on a good.

Second, marginal cost reflects the opportunity cost of the resources needed to produce a good. If a firm producing X hires a worker, it must pay the market wage. That wage must be sufficient to

If $P_X > MC_X$, society gains value by producing *more X*.

If $P_X < MC_X$, society gains value by producing *less X*.

| The value placed on good *X* by society through the market, or the social value of a marginal unit of *X*. | $$P_X = MC_X$$ | Market-determined value of resources needed to produce a marginal unit of *X*. MC_X is equal to the opportunity cost of those resources: lost production of other goods or the value of the resources left unemployed (leisure, vacant land, and so on). |

▲ **FIGURE 12.2 The Key Efficiency Condition: Price Equals Marginal Cost**

attract that worker out of leisure or away from firms producing other goods. The same argument holds for capital and land.

Thus, if the price of a good ends up greater than marginal cost, producing more of it will generate benefits to households in excess of opportunity costs, and society gains. Similarly, if the price of a good ends up below marginal cost, resources are being used to produce something that households value less than opportunity costs. Producing less of it creates gains to society.[2]

> Society will produce the efficient mix of output if all firms equate price and marginal cost.

Figure 12.3 shows how a simple competitive market system leads individual households and firms to make efficient choices in input and output markets. For simplicity, the figure assumes only one factor of production, labor. Households weigh the market wage against the value of

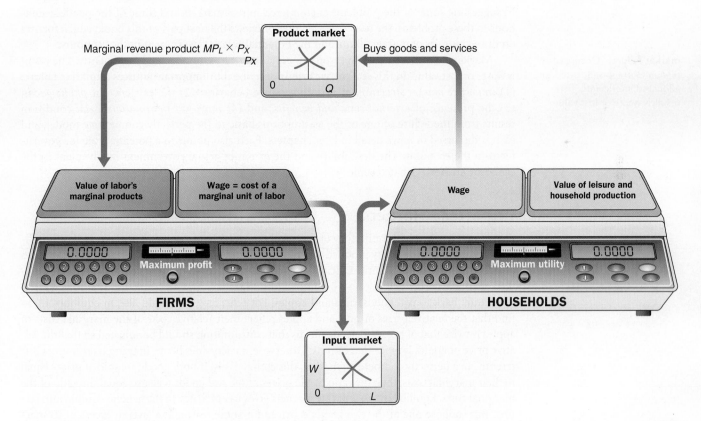

▲ **FIGURE 12.3 Efficiency in Perfect Competition Follows from a Weighing of Values by Both Households and Firms**

---

[2] It is important to understand that firms do not act *consciously* to balance social costs and benefits. In fact, the usual assumption is that firms are self-interested private profit maximizers. It just works out that in perfectly competitive markets, when firms are weighing private benefits against private costs, they are actually (perhaps without knowing it) weighing the benefits and costs to society as well.

leisure and time spent in unpaid household production. However, the wage is a measure of labor's potential product because firms weigh labor cost (wages) against the value of the product produced and hire up to the point at which $W = MRP_L$. Households use wages to buy market-produced goods. Thus, households implicitly weigh the value of market-produced goods against the value of leisure and household production.

When a firm's scale is balanced, it is earning maximum profit; when a household's scale is balanced, it is maximizing utility. Under these conditions, no changes can improve social welfare.

Perfect Competition versus Real Markets

So far, we have built a model of a perfectly competitive market system that produces an efficient allocation of resources, an efficient mix of output, and an efficient distribution of output. The perfectly competitive model is built on a set of assumptions, all of which must hold for our conclusions to be fully valid. We have assumed that all firms and households are price-takers in input and output markets, that firms and households have perfect information, and that all firms maximize profits.

These assumptions do not always hold in real-world markets. When this is the case, the conclusion breaks down that free, unregulated markets will produce an efficient outcome. The remainder of this chapter discusses some inefficiencies that occur naturally in markets and some of the strengths, as well as the weaknesses, of the market mechanism. We also discuss the usefulness of the competitive model for understanding the real economy.

The Sources of Market Failure

In suggesting some of the problems encountered in real markets and some of the possible solutions to these problems, the rest of this chapter previews the next part of this book, which focuses on the economics of market failure and the potential role of government in the economy.

market failure Occurs when resources are misallocated, or allocated inefficiently. The result is waste or lost value.

Market failure occurs when resources are misallocated, or allocated inefficiently. The result is waste or lost value. In this section, we briefly describe four important sources of market failure: (1) *imperfect market structure*, or noncompetitive behavior; (2) the existence of *public goods*; (3) the presence of *external costs and benefits*; and (4) *imperfect information*. Each condition results from the failure of one of the assumptions basic to the perfectly competitive model, and each is discussed in more detail in later chapters. Each also points to a potential role for government in the economy. The desirability and the extent of actual government involvement in the economy are hotly debated subjects.

Imperfect Markets

One of the elements of the efficiency of a perfectly competitive market that we described is the efficient mix of outputs. Society produces the right mix of goods given their costs and the preferences of households in the economy. Efficient mix comes because products are sold at prices equal to their marginal costs.

Think back to two goods, nuts and apples. For efficiency, we would like, in equilibrium, to find that the relative prices of nuts and apples reflect their relative costs. If the marginal costs of apples is twice that of nuts, efficiency means that consumption should be adjusted so that the relative price of apples is twice that of nuts. Otherwise, society does better in using its resources differently. In a perfectly competitive market, this comes easily. If both goods are sold at prices equal to their marginal costs, then the ratio of the prices of the two goods will also equal the ratio of the marginal costs. Equilibrium in separate markets gives us efficiency in the general equilibrium setting. But suppose one of the two goods is priced for some reason at a level in excess of its marginal costs. Now relative prices will no longer reflect relative costs.

So we can see that efficiency of output mix comes from marginal cost pricing. As we will learn in the next few chapters, however, in imperfectly competitive markets, with fewer firms competing and limited entry by new firms, prices will not necessarily equal marginal costs. As a consequence, in a market with firms that have some market power, where firms do not behave as price-takers, we are not guaranteed an efficient mix of output.

Public Goods

A second major source of inefficiency lies in the fact that private producers may not find it in their best interest to produce everything that members of society want because for one reason or another they are unable to charge prices to reflect values people place on those goods. More specifically, there is a whole class of goods and services called **public goods** or **social goods**, that will be underproduced or not produced at all in a completely unregulated market economy.[3]

Public goods are goods and services that bestow collective benefits on society; they are, in a sense, collectively consumed. The classic example is national defense, but there are countless others—police protection, homeland security, preservation of wilderness lands, and public health, to name a few. These things are "produced" using land, labor, and capital just like any other good. Some public goods, such as national defense, benefit the whole nation. Others, such as clean air, may be limited to smaller areas—the air may be clean in a Kansas town but dirty in a Southern California city. Public goods are consumed by everyone, not just by those who pay for them. The inability to exclude nonpayers from consumption of a public good makes it, not surprisingly, hard to charge people a price for the good.

If the provision of public goods were left to private profit-seeking producers with no power to force payment, a serious problem would arise. Suppose, for example, you value some public good, X. If there were a functioning market for X, you would be willing to pay for X. Suppose you are asked to contribute voluntarily to the production of X. Should you contribute? Perhaps you should on moral grounds, but not on the basis of pure self-interest.

At least two problems can get in the way. First, because you cannot be excluded from using X for not paying, you get the good whether you pay or not. Why should you pay if you do not have to? Second, because public goods that provide collective benefits to large numbers of people are expensive to produce, any one person's contribution is not likely to make much difference to the amount of the good ultimately produced. Would the national defense suffer, for example, if you did not pay your share of the bill? Probably not. Thus, nothing happens if you do not pay. The output of the good does not change much, and you get it whether you pay or not. Private provision of public goods fails. A completely laissez-faire market system will not produce everything that all members of a society might want. Citizens must band together to ensure that desired public goods are produced, and this is generally accomplished through government spending financed by taxes. Public goods are the subject of Chapter 16.

public goods, *or* social goods Goods and services that bestow collective benefits on members of society. Generally, no one can be excluded from enjoying their benefits. The classic example is national defense.

Externalities

A third major source of inefficiency is the existence of external costs and benefits. An **externality** is a cost or benefit imposed or bestowed on an individual or a group that is outside, or external to, the transaction—in other words, something that affects a third party. In a city, external costs are pervasive. The classic example is air or water pollution, but there are thousands of others, such as noise, congestion, and your house painted a color that the neighbors think is ugly. Global warming is an externality at the level of the world.

Not all externalities are negative, however. For example, housing investment may yield benefits for neighbors. A farm located near a city provides residents in the area with nice views and a less congested environment.

Externalities are a problem only if decision makers do not take them into account. The logic of efficiency presented earlier in this chapter required that firms weigh social benefits against social costs. If a firm in a competitive environment produces a good, it is because the value of that good to society exceeds the social cost of producing it—this is the logic of $P = MC$. If social costs or benefits are overlooked or left out of the calculations, inefficient decisions result. In essence, if the calculation of either MC or P in the equation is "wrong," equating the two will clearly not lead to an optimal result.

The effects of externalities can be enormous. For years, companies piled chemical wastes indiscriminately into dump sites near water supplies and residential areas. In some locations, those wastes seeped into the ground and contaminated the drinking water. In response to the evidence that smoking damages not only the smoker but also others, governments have increased prohibitions against smoking on airplanes and in public places.

externality A cost or benefit imposed or bestowed on an individual or a group that is outside, or external to, the transaction.

---

[3] Although they are normally referred to as public *goods*, many of the things we are talking about are *services*.

Imperfect Information

imperfect information The absence of full knowledge concerning product characteristics, available prices, and so on.

The fourth major source of inefficiency is **imperfect information** on the part of buyers and sellers. The conclusion that markets work efficiently rests heavily on the assumption that consumers and producers have full knowledge of product characteristics, available prices, and so on. The absence of full information can lead to transactions that are ultimately disadvantageous.

Some products are so complex that consumers find it difficult to judge the potential benefits and costs of purchase. Buyers of life insurance have a very difficult time sorting out the terms of the more complex policies and determining the true "price" of the product. Consumers of almost any service that requires expertise, such as plumbing and medical care, have a hard time evaluating what is needed, much less how well it is done. With imperfect information, prices may no longer reflect individual preferences.

Some forms of misinformation can be corrected with simple rules such as truth-in-advertising regulations. In some cases, the government provides information to citizens; job banks and consumer information services exist for this purpose. In certain industries, such as medical care, there is no clear-cut solution to the problem of noninformation or misinformation. We discuss all these topics in detail in Chapter 16.

Evaluating the Market Mechanism

Is the market system good or bad? Should the government be involved in the economy, or should it leave the allocation of resources to the free market? So far, our information is mixed and incomplete. To the extent that the perfectly competitive model reflects the way markets really operate, there seem to be some clear advantages to the market system. When we relax the assumptions and expand our discussion to include noncompetitive behavior, public goods, externalities, and the possibility of imperfect information, we see at least a potential role for government.

The market system may not provide participants with the incentive to weigh costs and benefits and to operate efficiently. If there are no externalities or if such costs or benefits are properly internalized, firms *will* weigh social benefits and costs in their production decisions. Under these circumstances, the profit motive should provide competitive firms with an incentive to minimize cost and to produce their products using the most efficient technologies. Likewise, competitive input markets should provide households with the incentive to weigh the value of their time against the social value of what they can produce in the labor force.

However, markets are far from perfect. Freely functioning markets in the real world do not always produce an efficient allocation of resources, and this result provides a potential role for government in the economy. Many have called for government involvement in the economy to correct for market failure—that is, to help markets function more efficiently. As you will see, however, many believe that government involvement in the economy creates more inefficiency than it cures.

In addition, we have thus far discussed only the criterion of efficiency, but economic systems and economic policies must be judged by many other criteria, not the least of which is *equity*, or fairness. Indeed, some contend that the outcome of any free market is ultimately unfair because some become rich while others remain poor.

Part III, which follows, explores in greater depth the issue of market imperfections and government involvement in the economy.

SUMMARY

1. Both firms and households make simultaneous choices in input and output markets. For example, input prices determine output costs and affect firms' output supply decisions. Wages in the labor market affect labor supply decisions, income, and ultimately the amount of output households can and do purchase.

2. A *general equilibrium* exists when all markets in an economy are in simultaneous equilibrium. An event that disturbs the equilibrium in one market may disturb the equilibrium in many other markets as well. *Partial equilibrium* analysis can be misleading because it looks only at adjustments in one isolated market.

MARKET ADJUSTMENT TO CHANGES IN DEMAND *p. 254*

3. General equilibrium is reached when equilibrium is established in all markets.

ALLOCATIVE EFFICIENCY AND COMPETITIVE EQUILIBRIUM *p. 256*

4. An *efficient* economy is one that produces the goods and services that people want at the least possible cost. A change is said to be efficient if it makes some members of society better off without making others worse off. An efficient, or *Pareto optimal*, system is one in which no such changes are possible.

5. If a change makes some people better off and some people worse off but it can be shown that the value of the gains exceeds the value of the losses, the change is said to be *potentially efficient* or simply *efficient*.

6. If all the assumptions of perfect competition hold, the result is an efficient, or Pareto optimal, allocation of resources. To prove this statement, it is necessary to show that resources are allocated efficiently among firms, that final products are distributed efficiently among households, and that the system produces what people want.

7. The assumptions that factor markets are competitive and open, that all firms pay the same prices for inputs, and that all firms maximize profits lead to the conclusion that the allocation of resources among firms is efficient.

8. People have different tastes and preferences, and they buy very different things in very different combinations. As long as everyone shops freely in the same markets, no redistribution of outputs among people will make them better off. This leads to the conclusion that final products are distributed efficiently among households.

9. Because perfectly competitive firms will produce as long as the price of their product is greater than the marginal cost of production, they will continue to produce as long as a gain for society is possible. The market thus guarantees that the right things are produced. In other words, the perfectly competitive system produces what people want.

THE SOURCES OF MARKET FAILURE *p. 262*

10. When the assumptions of perfect competition do not hold, the conclusion breaks down that free, unregulated markets will produce an efficient allocation of resources.

11. An imperfectly competitive industry is one in which single firms have some control over price and competition. In all imperfectly competitive industries, output is lower and price is higher than they would be in perfect competition. Imperfect competition is a major source of market inefficiency.

12. *Public*, or *social*, *goods* bestow collective benefits on members of society. Because the benefits of social goods are collective, people cannot, in most cases, be excluded from enjoying them. Thus, private firms usually do not find it profitable to produce public goods. The need for public goods is thus another source of inefficiency.

13. An *externality* is a cost or benefit that is imposed or bestowed on an individual or a group that is outside, or external to, the transaction. If such social costs or benefits are overlooked, the decisions of households or firms are likely to be wrong or inefficient.

14. Market efficiency depends on the assumption that buyers have perfect information on product quality and price and that firms have perfect information on input quality and price. *Imperfect information* can lead to wrong choices and inefficiency.

EVALUATING THE MARKET MECHANISM *p. 264*

15. Sources of market failure—such as imperfect markets, public goods, externalities, and imperfect information—are considered by many to justify the existence of government and governmental policies that seek to redistribute costs and income on the basis of efficiency, equity, or both.

—————— **REVIEW TERMS AND CONCEPTS** ——————

efficiency, *p. 254*
externality, *p. 263*
general equilibrium, *p. 254*
imperfect information, *p. 264*

market failure, *p. 262*
Pareto efficiency *or* Pareto optimality, *p. 256*
partial equilibrium analysis, *p. 254*

public goods *or* social goods, *p. 263*
Key efficiency condition in perfect competition: $P_X = MC_X$

—————— **PROBLEMS** ——————

All problems are available on www.myeconlab.com

1. Numerous times in history, the courts have issued consent decrees requiring large companies to break up into smaller competing companies for violating the antitrust laws. The two best-known examples are American Telephone and Telegraph (AT&T) in the 1980s and Microsoft 20 years later. (AT&T was broken up into the "Baby Bells"; but the Microsoft breakup was successfully appealed, and the breakup never occurred.)

Many argue that breaking up a monopoly is a Pareto-efficient change. This interpretation cannot be so because breaking up a monopoly makes its owners (or shareholders) worse off. Do you agree or disagree? Explain your answer.

2. [Related to the *Economics in Practice* on p. 257] The *Economics in Practice* in this chapter describes the adjustment of the corn and wheat markets to the massive U.S. subsidy given to ethanol production. The subsidy drives up the prices of other agricultural goods such as wheat and substantially raises the value of farmland. How would this story change if oil prices were to rise extensively at the same time? if oil prices were to fall? Trace these changes on the economy using supply and demand curves.

3. For each of the following, tell a story about what is likely to happen in labor and capital markets using the model of the whole economy that we developed over the first 11 chapters.
   a. A sharp drop in demand for automobiles raises the unemployment rate in Flint, Michigan, and cuts into the profits of local gas stations where my nephew lost his job.
   b. As the baby boomers age, many of them are moving back to the city. They are also buying smaller units. This will have a big effect on owners of suburban homes who find their home values falling.
   c. In 2007–2008, the mortgage markets crashed. This led to a serious decline in the availability of credit to buyers who, a couple of years ago, were able to borrow far more than they needed.

4. A medium-sized bakery has just opened in Slovakia. A loaf of bread is currently selling for 14 koruna (the Slovakian currency) over and above the cost of intermediate goods (flour, yeast, and so on). Assuming that labor is the only variable factor of production, the following table gives the production function for the bread.

WORKERS	LOAVES OF BREAD
0	0
1	15
2	30
3	42
4	52
5	60
6	66
7	70

   a. Suppose the current wage rate in Slovakia is 119 koruna per hour. How many workers will the bakery employ?
   b. Suppose the economy of Slovakia begins to grow, incomes rise, and the price of a loaf of bread is pushed up to 20 koruna. Assuming no increase in the price of labor, how many workers will the bakery hire?
   c. An increase in the demand for labor pushes up wages to 125 koruna per hour. What impact will this increase in cost have on employment and output in the bakery at the 20-koruna price of bread?
   d. If all firms behaved like our bakery, would the allocation of resources in Slovakia be efficient? Explain your answer.

5. Country A has soil that is suited to corn production and yields 135 bushels per acre. Country B has soil that is not suited for corn and yields only 45 bushels per acre. Country A has soil that is not suited for soybean production and yields 15 bushels per acre. Country B has soil that is suited for soybeans and yields 35 bushels per acre. In 2004, there was no trade between A and B because of high taxes and both countries together produced huge quantities of corn and soybeans. In 2005, taxes were eliminated because of a new trade agreement. What is likely to happen? Can you justify the trade agreement on the basis of Pareto efficiency? Why or why not?

6. Do you agree or disagree with each of the following statements? Explain your answer.
   a. Housing is a public good and should be produced by the public sector because private markets will fail to produce it efficiently.
   b. Monopoly power is inefficient because large firms will produce too much product, dumping it on the market at artificially low prices.
   c. Medical care is an example of a potentially inefficient market because consumers do not have perfect information about the product.

7. The point of scalping is to find someone who wants a ticket more than the person who presently has it. Whenever two different prices exist in a market, arbitrage opportunities (buy and then sell at a higher price) are there. Professional scalpers buy up tickets when they are first offered to the public, while some buy them on the street the night of the event. They can sell any ticket, even those in short supply, *at some price*. When many people want to go to an event that has a limited supply of tickets, the scalping price can be quite high. Go online and find scalping agencies like Stub-Hub and Ace Tickets. See if you can find an event for which the scalping price is much higher than the original price. What determines whether the event is worth the higher price?

   It is argued that scalping is efficient. Explain that argument. Others ask how could it be efficient "if only rich people can afford to go to most games?" Do you agree? Why or why not?

8. Which of the following are examples of Pareto-efficient changes? Explain your answers.
   a. Cindy trades her laptop computer to Bob for his old car.
   b. Competition is introduced into the electric industry, and electricity rates drop. A study shows that benefits to consumers are larger than the lost monopoly profits.
   c. A high tax on wool sweaters deters buyers. The tax is repealed.
   d. A federal government agency is reformed, and costs are cut 23 percent with no loss of service quality.

9. A major source of chicken feed in the United States is anchovies, small fish that can be scooped out of the ocean at low cost. Every 7 years, when the anchovies disappear to spawn, producers must turn to grain, which is more expensive, to feed their chickens. What is likely to happen to the cost of chicken when the anchovies disappear? What are substitutes for chicken? How are the markets for these substitutes affected? Name some complements to chicken. How are the markets for these complements affected? How might the allocation of farmland be changed as a result of the disappearance of anchovies?

10. Suppose two passengers end up with a reservation for the last seat on a train from San Francisco to Los Angeles. Two alternatives are proposed:
    a. Toss a coin
    b. Sell the ticket to the highest bidder

    Compare the two options from the standpoint of efficiency and equity.

11. Assume that there are two sectors in an economy: goods (*G*) and services (*S*). Both sectors are perfectly competitive, with large numbers of firms and constant returns to scale. As income rises, households spend a larger portion of their income on *S* and a smaller portion on *G*. Using supply and demand curves for both sectors and a diagram showing a representative firm in

each sector, explain what would happen to output and prices in the short run and the long run in response to an increase in income. (Assume that the increase in income causes demand for *G* to shift left and demand for *S* to shift right.) In the long run, what would happen to employment in the goods sector? in the service sector? (*Hint:* See Figure 12.2 on p. 261.)

12. Which of the following are actual Pareto-efficient changes? Explain briefly.
    a. You buy three oranges for $1 from a street vendor.
    b. You are near death from thirst in the desert and must pay a passing vagabond $10,000 for a glass of water.
    c. A mugger steals your wallet.
    d. You take a taxi ride in downtown Manhattan during rush hour.

13. Each instance that follows is an example of one of the four types of market failure discussed in this chapter. In each case, identify the type of market failure and defend your choice briefly.
    a. An auto repair shop convinces you that you need a $2,000 valve job when all you really need is an oil change.
    b. Everyone in a neighborhood would benefit if an empty lot were turned into a park, but no entrepreneur will come forward to finance the transformation.
    c. A bar opens next to your apartment building and plays loud music on its patio every night until 4 A.M.
    d. The only two airlines flying direct between St. Louis and Atlanta make an agreement to raise their prices.

14. Two factories in the same town hire workers with the same skills. Union agreements require factory A to pay its workers $10 per hour, while factory B must pay $6 per hour. Each factory hires the profit-maximizing number of workers. Is the allocation of labor between these two factories efficient? Explain why or why not.

15. Explain why resources are allocated efficiently among firms and why output is distributed efficiently among households in perfectly competitive markets.

16. Under what condition would society benefit from more of a good being produced, and under what condition would society benefit from less of a good being produced?

17. James lives on a cul-de-sac where he and all his neighbors park on the street. After his car was vandalized, James decided to install motion-sensitive lighting on the front of his house. Now any movement activates the lights, which shine across the entire parking area on the street. Explain why the installation of the lights might lead to an inefficient outcome.

18. Briefly explain whether each of the following represents a public good.
    a. A chef salad sold at the cafeteria in the county courthouse
    b. Palm trees planted along the median of the Pacific Coast Highway
    c. A Doppler radar station built at Chicago's O'Hare International Airport
    d. A new roller coaster at Cedar Point, an amusement park in Sandusky, Ohio
    e. A new fleet of police cars for the Oklahoma City Police Department
    f. The Vietnam Memorial in Washington, D.C.

19. Explain the difference between a positive externality and a negative externality. Can both types of externalities result in market failure? Why or why not?

Monopoly and Antitrust Policy

13

In 1911 the U.S. Supreme Court found that Standard Oil of New Jersey, the largest oil company in the United States, was a monopoly and ordered that it be divided up. In 1999 a U.S. court similarly found that Microsoft had exercised monopoly power and ordered it to change a series of its business practices. In 2010 the Federal Trade Commission—one of the government agencies empowered to protect consumers—argued that Google possessed monopoly power and should also be restrained by the government in its business practices. What do we mean by a monopoly, and why might the government and the courts try to control monopolists? Have our ideas on what constitutes a monopoly changed over time with new technology?

In earlier chapters, we described in some detail the workings and benefits of perfect competition. Market competition among firms producing undifferentiated or homogeneous products limits the choices of firms. Firms decide how much to produce and how to produce, but in setting prices, they look to the market. Moreover, because of entry and competition, firms do no better than earn the opportunity cost of capital in the long run. For firms such as Google and Microsoft, economic decision making is richer and so is the potential for profit making.

In the next three chapters, we explore markets in which competition is limited, either by the fewness of firms or by product differentiation. After a brief discussion of market structure in general, this chapter will focus on monopoly markets. Chapter 14 will cover oligopolies, while Chapter 15 will deal with monopolistic competition.

Imperfect Competition and Market Power: Core Concepts

In the competitive markets we have been studying all firms charge the same price. With many firms producing identical or homogeneous products, consumers have many choices, and those choices constrain the pricing of individual firms. This same competition also means that firms in the long run earn only a normal return on their capital. In **imperfectly competitive** markets, on the other hand, the absence of numerous competitors or the existence of product differentiation creates situations in which firms can at times raise their prices and not lose all their customers. These firms can be said to have **market power**. In these markets we may observe firms earning excess profits, and we may see firms producing different variants of a product and charging different prices for those variants. Studying these markets is especially interesting because we now have to think not only about pricing behavior, but also about how firms choose product quality and type.

imperfectly competitive industry An industry in which individual firms have some control over the price of their output.

market power An imperfectly competitive firm's ability to raise price without losing all of the quantity demanded for its product.

Forms of Imperfect Competition and Market Boundaries

Once we move away from perfectly competitive markets, with its assumption of many firms and undifferentiated products, there is a range of other possible market structures. At one extreme lies the monopoly. A *monopoly* is an industry with a single firm in which the entry of new firms is blocked. An *oligopoly* is an industry in which there is a small number of firms, each large enough so that its presence affects prices. Firms that differentiate their products in industries with many producers and free entry are called *monopolistic competitors*. We begin our discussion in this chapter with monopoly.

What do we mean when we say that a monopoly firm is the only firm in the industry? In practice, given the prevalence of branding, many firms, especially in the consumer products markets, are alone in producing a specific product. Procter & Gamble (P&G), for example, is the only producer of Ivory soap. Coca-Cola is the only producer of Coke Classic. And yet we would call neither firm monopolistic because for both, many other firms produce products that are *close substitutes*. Instead of drinking Coke, we could drink Pepsi; instead of washing with Ivory, we could wash with Dove. To be meaningful, therefore, our definition of a monopolistic industry must be more precise. We define a **pure monopoly** as an industry (1) with a single firm that produces a product for which there are *no close substitutes* and (2) in which significant barriers to entry prevent other firms from entering the industry to compete for profits.

As we think about the issue of product substitutes and market power, it is useful to recall the structure of the competitive market. Consider a firm producing an undifferentiated brand of hamburger meat, Brand X hamburger. As we show in Figure 13.1 the demand this firm faces is horizontal, perfectly elastic. The demand for hamburgers as a whole, however, likely slopes down. While there are substitutes for hamburgers, they are not perfect and some people will continue to consume hamburgers even if they cost more than other foods. As we broaden the category we are considering, the substitution possibilities *outside* the category fall, and demand becomes quite inelastic, as for example for food in general. If a firm were the only producer of Brand X hamburger, it would have no market power: If it raised its price, people would just switch to Brand Z hamburger. A firm that produced all the hamburgers in the United States, on the other hand, might have some market power: It could perhaps charge more than other beef-product producers and still sell hamburgers. A firm that controlled all of the food in the United States would likely have substantial market power since we all must eat!

In practice, figuring out which products are close substitutes for one another to determine market power can be difficult. Are hamburgers and hot dogs close substitutes so that a hamburger monopoly would have little power to raise prices? Are debit cards and checks close

pure monopoly An industry with a single firm that produces a product for which there are no close substitutes and in which significant barriers to entry prevent other firms from entering the industry to compete for profits.

▶ **FIGURE 13.1**

The Boundary of a Market and Elasticity

We can define an industry as broadly or as narrowly as we like. The more broadly we define the industry, the fewer substitutes there are; thus, the less elastic the demand for that industry's product is likely to be. A monopoly is an industry with one firm that produces a product for which there are *no close substitutes*. The producer of Brand X hamburger cannot properly be called a monopolist because this producer has no control over market price and there are many substitutes for Brand X hamburger.

Demand for Brand X hamburger

Demand for hamburger

Demand for beef

Demand for meat

Demand for food

substitutes for credit cards so that credit card firms have little market power? The courts in a recent antitrust case said no. Is Microsoft a monopoly, or does it compete with Linux and Apple for software users? These are questions that occupy considerable time for economists, lawyers, and the antitrust courts. The *Economics in Practice* on p. 287 discusses the antitrust rules that pertain to the National Football League.

Price and Output Decisions in Pure Monopoly Markets

Consider a market with a single firm producing a good for which there are few substitutes. How does this profit-maximizing monopolist choose its output levels? At this point we assume the monopolist cannot price-discriminate. It sells its product to all demanders at the same price. (*Price discrimination* means selling to different consumers or groups of consumers at different prices and will be discussed later in this chapter.)

Assume initially that our pure monopolist buys in competitive input markets. Even though the firm is the only one producing for its product market, it is only one among many firms buying factors of production in input markets. The local telephone company must hire labor like any other firm. To attract workers, the company must pay the market wage; to buy fiber-optic cable, it must pay the going price. In these input markets, the monopolistic firm is a price-taker.

On the cost side of the profit equation, a pure monopolist does not differ from a perfect competitor. Both choose the technology that minimizes the cost of production. The cost curve of each represents the minimum cost of producing each level of output. The difference arises on the revenue, or demand, side of the equation, where we begin our analysis.

Demand in Monopoly Markets

A perfectly competitive firm, you will recall, can sell all it wants to sell at the market price. The firm is a small part of the market. The demand curve facing such a firm is thus a horizontal line. Raising the price of its product means losing all demand because perfect substitutes are available. The perfectly competitive firm has no incentive to charge a lower price either since it can sell all it wants at the market price.

A monopolist is different. It does not constitute a small part of the market; it *is* the market. The firm no longer looks at a market price to see what it can charge; it sets the market price. How does it do so? Even a firm that is a monopolist in its own market will nevertheless compete with other firms in other markets for a consumer's dollars. Even a monopolist thus loses some customers when it raises its price. The monopolist sets its price by looking at the trade-off in terms of profit earned between getting more money for each unit sold versus selling fewer units.

Shortly we will look at exactly how a monopolist thinks about this trade-off. But before we become more formal, it is interesting to think about the business decisions of the competitive firm versus a monopolist. For a competitive firm, the market provides a lot of information; in effect, all the firm needs to do is figure out if, given its costs, it can make money at the current market price. A monopolist needs to learn about the demand curve for its product. When the iPod first came out, Apple had to figure out how much individuals would be willing to pay for this new product. What did its demand curve look like? Firms like Apple have quite sophisticated marketing departments that survey potential consumers, collect data from related markets, and even do a bit of trial and error to learn what their demand curves really look like.

Marginal Revenue and Market Demand We learned in Chapter 7 that the competitive firm maximizes its profit by continuing to produce output so long as marginal revenue exceeds marginal cost. Under these conditions, incremental units add more to the plus, or revenue, side than they add to the minus, or cost, side. The same general rule is true for the monopolist: A monopolist too will maximize profits by expanding output so long as marginal revenue exceeds marginal cost. The key difference in the two cases lies in the definition of marginal revenue.

For a competitive firm marginal revenue is simply the price, as we discussed in Chapter 7. Every unit that the firm sells, it sells at the going market price. The competitive firm is a very small part of the overall market, and its behavior has no effect on the overall market price. So the incremental or marginal revenue from each new unit sold is simply the price. In the case of a monopolist, however, the monopolist is the market. If that firm decides to double its output, market output will double, and it is easy to see that the only way the firm will be able to sell twice the output is to lower its price. The fact that a monopolist's output decisions influence market prices means that price and marginal revenue will diverge. The simplest way to see this is via a bit of arithmetic.

Consider the hypothetical demand schedule in Table 13.1. Column 3 lists the total revenue that the monopoly would take in at different levels of output. If it were to produce 1 unit, that unit would sell for $10, and total revenue would be $10. Two units would sell for $9 each, in which case total revenue would be $18. As column 4 shows, marginal revenue from the second unit would be $8 ($18 minus $10). Notice that the marginal revenue from increasing output from 1 unit to 2 units ($8) is *less* than the price of the second unit ($9).

TABLE 13.1 Marginal Revenue Facing a Monopolist			
(1)	(2)	(3)	(4)
Quantity	Price	Total Revenue	Marginal Revenue
0	$11	0	—
1	10	$10	$10
2	9	18	8
3	8	24	6
4	7	28	4
5	6	30	2
6	5	30	0
7	4	28	−2
8	3	24	−4
9	2	18	−6
10	1	10	−8

Now consider what happens when the firm considers setting production at 4 units instead of 3. The fourth unit would sell for $7, but because the firm cannot price discriminate, it must sell *all* 4 units for $7 each. Had the firm chosen to produce only 3 units, it could have sold those 3 units for $8 each. Thus, offsetting the revenue gain of $7 is a revenue loss of $3—that is, $1 for each of the 3 units that would have sold at the higher price. The marginal revenue of the fourth unit is $7 minus $3, or $4, which is considerably below the price of $7. (Remember, unlike a monopoly, a perfectly competitive firm does not have to charge a lower price to sell more. Thus, $P = MR$ in competition.) For a monopolist, an increase in output involves not only producing more and selling it, but also reducing the overall price of its output.

Marginal revenue can also be derived by looking at the change in total revenue as output changes by 1 unit. At 3 units of output, total revenue is $24. At 4 units of output, total revenue is $28. Marginal revenue is the difference, or $4.

Moving from 6 to 7 units of output actually reduces total revenue for the firm. At 7 units, marginal revenue is negative. Although it is true that the seventh unit will sell for a positive price ($4), the firm must sell all 7 units for $4 each (for a total revenue of $28). If output had been restricted to 6 units, each would have sold for $5. Thus, offsetting the revenue gain of $4 is a revenue loss of $6—that is, $1 for each of the 6 units that the firm would have sold at the higher price. Increasing output from 6 to 7 units actually decreases revenue by $2. Figure 13.2

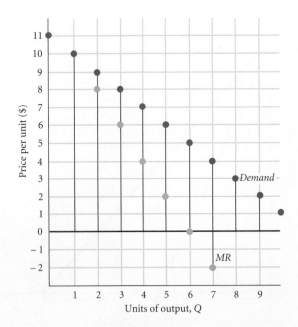

▲ **FIGURE 13.2 Marginal Revenue Curve Facing a Monopolist**

At every level of output except 1 unit, a monopolist's marginal revenue (*MR*) is below price. This is so because (1) we assume that the monopolist must sell all its product at a single price (no price discrimination) and (2) to raise output and sell it, the firm must lower the price it charges. Selling the additional output will raise revenue, but this increase is offset somewhat by the lower price charged for all units sold. Therefore, the increase in revenue from increasing output by 1 (the marginal revenue) is less than the price.

graphs the marginal revenue schedule derived in Table 13.1. Notice that at every level of output except 1 unit, marginal revenue is *below* price. Marginal revenue turns from positive to negative after 6 units of output. When the demand curve is a straight line, the marginal revenue curve bisects the quantity axis between the origin and the point where the demand curve hits the quantity axis, as in Figure 13.3.

Look carefully at Figure 13.3. The marginal revenue curve shows the change in total revenue that results as a firm moves along the segment of the demand curve that lies directly above it. Consider starting at a price in excess of point A per period in the top panel of Figure 13.3. Here total revenue (shown in the bottom panel) is zero because nothing is sold. To begin selling, the firm must lower the product price. Marginal revenue is positive, and total revenue begins to increase. To sell increasing quantities of the good, the firm must lower its price more and more. As output increases between zero and Q^* and the firm moves down its demand curve from point *A* to point *B*, marginal revenue remains positive and total revenue continues to increase. The quantity of output (Q) is rising, which tends to push total revenue ($P \times Q$) *up*. At the same time, the price of output (P) is falling, which tends to push total revenue ($P \times Q$) *down*. Up to point *B*, the effect of increasing Q dominates the effect of falling P and total revenue rises: Marginal revenue is positive (above the quantity axis).[1]

What happens as we look at output levels greater than Q^*—that is, farther down the demand curve from point *B* toward point *C*? We are still lowering P to sell more output, but at levels greater than Q^*, marginal revenue is negative, and total revenue in the bottom panel starts to fall. Beyond Q^*, the effect of cutting price on total revenue is larger than the effect of

---

[1] Recall from Chapter 4 that if the percentage change in Q is greater than the percentage change in P as you move along a demand curve, the absolute value of elasticity of demand is greater than 1. Thus, as we move along the demand curve in Figure 13.3 between point *A* and point *B*, demand is *elastic*.

▶ **FIGURE 13.3**

Marginal Revenue and Total Revenue

A monopoly's marginal revenue curve bisects the quantity axis between the origin and the point where the demand curve hits the quantity axis. A monopoly's *MR* curve shows the change in total revenue that results as a firm moves along the segment of the demand curve that lies exactly above it.

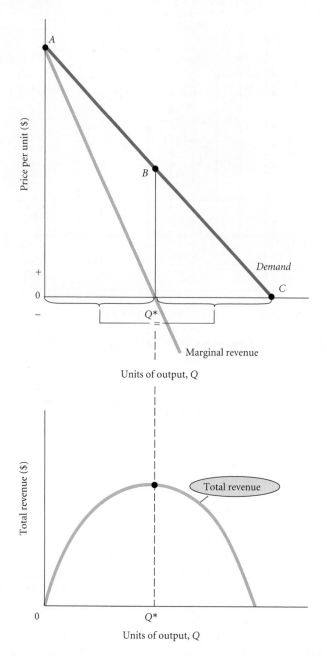

increasing quantity. As a result, total revenue ($P \times Q$) falls. At point *C*, revenue once again is at zero, this time because price has dropped to zero.[2]

The Monopolist's Profit-Maximizing Price and Output   We have spent much time defining and explaining marginal revenue because it is an important factor in the monopolist's choice of profit-maximizing price and output. Figure 13.4 superimposes a demand curve and the marginal revenue curve derived from it over a set of cost curves. In determining price and output, a monopolistic firm must go through the same basic decision process that a competitive firm goes through. Any profit-maximizing firm will raise its production as long as the added revenue from the increase outweighs the added cost. All firms, including monopolies, raise output as long as marginal revenue is greater than marginal cost. Any positive difference between marginal revenue and marginal cost can be thought of as marginal profit.

---

[2] Beyond Q^*, between points *B* and *C* on the demand curve in Figure 13.3, the decline in price must be bigger in percentage terms than the increase in quantity. Thus, the absolute value of elasticity beyond point *B* is less than 1: Demand is inelastic. At point *B*, marginal revenue is zero; the decrease in *P* exactly offsets the increase in *Q*, and elasticity is unitary or equal to −1.

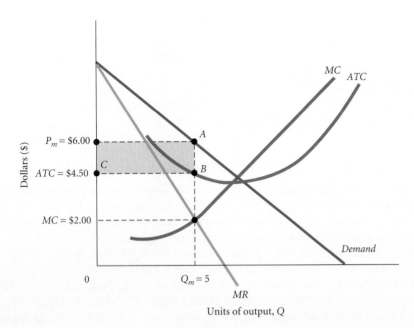

◀ FIGURE 13.4 **Price and Output Choice for a Profit-Maximizing Monopolist**

A profit-maximizing monopolist will raise output as long as marginal revenue exceeds marginal cost. Maximum profit is at an output of 5 units per period and a price of $6. Above 5 units of output, marginal cost is greater than marginal revenue; increasing output beyond 5 units would reduce profit. At 5 units, $TR = P_m AQ_m0$, $TC = CBQ_m0$, and profit = $P_m ABC$.

The optimal price/output combination for the monopolist in Figure 13.4 is $P_m = \$6$ and $Q_m = 5$ units, the quantity at which the marginal revenue curve and the marginal cost curve intersect. At any output below 5, marginal revenue is greater than marginal cost. At any output above 5, increasing output would reduce profits because marginal cost exceeds marginal revenue. This leads us to conclude that the profit-maximizing level of output for a monopolist is the one at which marginal revenue equals marginal cost: $MR = MC$.

Because marginal revenue for a monopoly lies below the demand curve, the final price chosen by the monopolist will be above marginal cost. ($P_m = \$6.00$ is greater than $MC = \$2.00$.) At 5 units of output, price will be fixed at $6 (point A on the demand curve), which is as much as the market will bear, and total revenue will be $P_m \times Q_m = \$6 \times 5 = \$30$ (area $P_m AQ_m0$). Total cost is the product of average total cost and units of output, $\$4.50 \times 5 = \$22.50$ (area CBQ_m0). Total profit is the difference between total revenue and total cost, $\$30 - \$22.50 = \$7.50$. In Figure 13.4, total profit is the area of the gray rectangle $P_m ABC$.

Our discussion about the optimal output level for a monopolist points to a common misconception. Even monopolists face constraints on the prices they can charge. Suppose a single firm controlled the production of bicycles. That firm would be able to charge more than could be charged in a competitive marketplace, but the power to raise prices has limits. As the bike price rises, we will see more people buying inline skates or walking. A particularly interesting case comes from monopolists who sell durable goods, goods that last for some period of time. Microsoft is the only producer for Windows, the operating system that dominates the personal computer (PC) market. But when Microsoft tries to sell a new version of that operating system (for example, Windows 7, which it introduced in 2010), its price is constrained by the fact that many of the potential consumers it seeks already have an old operating system. If the new price is too high, consumers will stay with the older version. Some monopolists may face quite elastic demand curves as a result of the characteristics of the product they sell.

The Absence of a Supply Curve in Monopoly   In perfect competition, the supply curve of a firm in the short run is the same as the portion of the firm's marginal cost curve that lies above the average variable cost curve. As the price of the good produced by the firm changes, the perfectly competitive firm simply moves up or down its marginal cost curve in choosing how much output to produce.

As you can see, however, Figure 13.4 contains nothing that we can point to and call a supply curve. The amount of output that a monopolist produces depends on its marginal cost curve *and* on the shape of the demand curve that it faces. In other words, the amount of output that a monopolist supplies is not independent of the shape of the demand curve. A monopoly firm has no supply curve that is independent of the demand curve for its product.

To see why, consider what a firm's supply curve means. A supply curve shows the quantity of output the firm is willing to supply at each price. If we ask a monopolist how much output she is willing to supply at a given price, the monopolist will say that her supply behavior depends not only on marginal cost but also on the marginal revenue associated with that price. To know what that marginal revenue would be, the monopolist must know what her demand curve looks like.

In sum, in perfect competition, we can draw a firm's supply curve without knowing anything more than the firm's marginal cost curve. The situation for a monopolist is more complicated: A monopolist sets both price and quantity, and the amount of output that it supplies depends on its marginal cost curve and the demand curve that it faces.

Perfect Competition and Monopoly Compared

One way to understand monopoly is to compare equilibrium output and price in a perfectly competitive industry with the output and price that would be chosen if the same industry were organized as a monopoly. To make this comparison meaningful, let us exclude from consideration any technological advantage that a single large firm might enjoy.

We begin our comparison with a perfectly competitive industry made up of a large number of firms operating with a production technology that exhibits constant returns to scale in the long run. (Recall that *constant returns to scale* means that average cost is the same whether the firm operates one large plant or many small plants.) Figure 13.5 shows a perfectly competitive industry at long-run equilibrium, a condition in which price is equal to long-run average costs and in which there are no profits.

Suppose the industry were to fall under the control of a single price monopolist. The monopolist now owns one firm with many plants. However, technology has not changed, only the location of decision-making power has. To analyze the monopolist's decisions, we must derive the consolidated cost curves now facing the monopoly.

The marginal cost curve of the new monopoly will be the horizontal sum of the marginal cost curves of the smaller firms, which are now branches of the larger firm. That is, to get the large firm's *MC* curve, at each level of *MC*, we add together the output quantities from each separate plant. To understand why, consider this simple example. Suppose there is perfect competition and the industry is made up of just two small firms, A and B, each with upward-sloping marginal cost curves. Suppose for firm A, *MC* = $5 at an output of 10,000 units and for firm B, *MC* = $5 at an output of 20,000 units. If these firms were merged, what would be the marginal cost of the 30,000th unit of output per period? The answer is $5 because the new larger firm

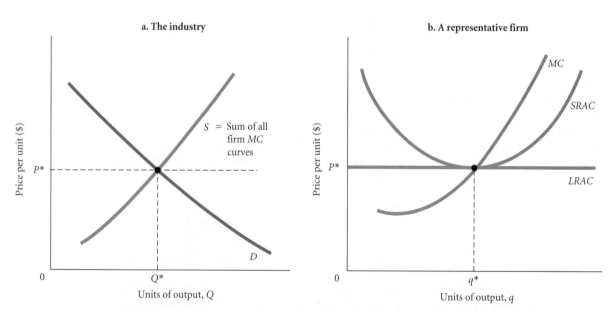

a. The industry   b. A representative firm

▲ **FIGURE 13.5 A Perfectly Competitive Industry in Long-Run Equilibrium**
In a perfectly competitive industry in the long run, price will be equal to long-run average cost. The market supply curve is the sum of all the short-run marginal cost curves of the firms in the industry. Here we assume that firms are using a technology that exhibits constant returns to scale: *LRAC* is flat. Big firms enjoy no cost advantage.

would produce 10,000 units in plant A and 20,000 in plant B. This means that the marginal cost curve of the new firm is *exactly the same curve* as the supply curve in the industry when it was competitively organized. (Recall from Chapter 9 that the industry supply curve in a perfectly competitive industry is the sum of the marginal cost curves [above average variable cost] of all the individual firms in that industry.)[3]

Figure 13.6 illustrates the cost curves, marginal revenue curve, and demand curve of the consolidated monopoly industry. If the industry were competitively organized, total industry output would have been $Q_c = 4,000$ and price would have been $P_c = \$3$. These price and output decisions are determined by the intersection of the competitive supply curve, S_c, and the market demand curve.

No longer faced with a price that it cannot influence, however, the monopolist can choose any price/quantity combination along the demand curve. The output level that maximizes profits to the monopolist is $Q_m = 2,500$—the point at which marginal revenue intersects marginal cost. Output will be priced at $P_m = \$4$. To increase output beyond 2,500 units or to charge a price below $4 (which represents the amount consumers are willing to pay) would reduce profit. Relative to a perfectly competitive industry, a monopolist restricts output, charges higher prices, and earns positive profits. In the long run, the monopolist will close plants.

Also remember that all we did was transfer decision-making power from the individual small firms to a consolidated owner. The new firm gains nothing technologically by being big.

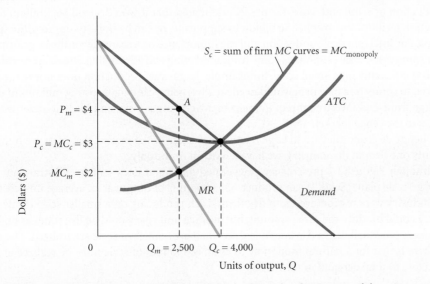

▲ **FIGURE 13.6 Comparison of Monopoly and Perfectly Competitive Outcomes for a Firm with Constant Returns to Scale**

In the newly organized monopoly, the marginal cost curve is the same as the supply curve that represented the behavior of all the independent firms when the industry was organized competitively. Quantity produced by the monopoly will be less than the perfectly competitive level of output, and the monopoly price will be higher than the price under perfect competition. Under monopoly, $P = P_m = \$4$ and $Q = Q_m = 2,500$. Under perfect competition, $P = P_c = \$3$ and $Q = Q_c = 4,000$.

Monopoly in the Long Run: Barriers to Entry

What will happen to a monopoly in the long run? Of course, it is possible for a monopolist to suffer losses. Just because a firm is the only producer in a market does not guarantee that anyone will buy its product. Monopolists can end up going out of business just like competitive firms. If, on the contrary, the monopolist is earning positive profits (a rate of return above the normal return to capital), as in Figure 13.4, we would expect other firms to enter as they do in competitive markets. In fact,

---

[3] The same logic will show that the average cost curve of the consolidated firm is the sum of the average cost curves of the individual plants.

many markets that end up competitive begin with an entrepreneurial idea and a short-lived monopoly position. In the mid-1970s, a California entrepreneur named Gary Dahl "invented" and marketed the Pet Rock. Dahl had the market to himself for about 6 months, during which time he earned millions before scores of competitors entered, driving down the price and profits. (In the end, this product, perhaps not surprisingly, disappeared). *For a monopoly to persist, some factor or factors must prevent entry.* We turn now to a discussion of those factors, commonly termed **barriers to entry**.

barriers to entry Factors that prevent new firms from entering and competing in imperfectly competitive industries.

Return for a moment to Figure 13.4 on p. 275. In that graph, we see that the monopolist is earning a positive economic profit. Such profits can persist only if other firms cannot enter this industry and compete them away. The term *barriers to entry* is used to describe the set of factors that prevent new firms from entering a market with excess profits. Monopoly can persist only in the presence of entry barriers.

Economies of Scale   In Chapter 9, we described production technologies in which average costs fall with output increases. In situations in which those scale economies are very large relative to the overall market, the cost advantages associated with size can give rise to monopoly power.

Scale economies come in a number of different forms. Providing cable service requires laying expensive cable; conventional telephones require the installation of poles and wires. For these cases, there are clear cost advantages in having only one set of physical apparatuses. Once a firm has laid the wire, providing service to one more customer is very inexpensive. The semiconductor industry is another case in which production favors the large firms. In 2007, Intel, the world leader in production of semiconductors for the PC, estimated that it would spend $6.2 billion for new production facilities and another $6 billion to support its research efforts to improve the speed of its chips. For Intel, physical production and the importance of research favor the large firm.

In some cases, scale economies come from marketing and advertising. Breakfast cereal can be produced efficiently on a small scale, for example; large-scale production does not reduce costs. However, to compete, a new firm would need an advertising campaign costing millions of dollars. The large front-end investment requirement in advertising is risky and likely to deter would-be entrants to the cereal market.

natural monopoly An industry that realizes such large economies of scale in producing its product that single-firm production of that good or service is most efficient.

When scale economies are so large relative to the size of the market that costs are minimized with only one firm in the industry, we have a **natural monopoly**.

Although Figure 13.7 presents an exaggerated picture, it does serve to illustrate our point. One large-scale plant (Scale 2) can produce 500,000 units of output at an average unit cost of $1. If the industry were restructured into five firms, each producing on a smaller scale (Scale 1), the industry could produce the same amount, but average unit cost would be five times as high ($5). Consumers potentially see a considerable gain when economies of scale are realized. The critical point here is that for a natural monopoly to exist, economies of scale must be realized at a scale that is close to total demand in the market.

▶ **FIGURE 13.7**
A Natural Monopoly

A natural monopoly is a firm in which the most efficient scale is very large. Here, average total cost declines until a single firm is producing nearly the entire amount demanded in the market. With one firm producing 500,000 units, average total cost is $1 per unit. With five firms each producing 100,000 units, average total cost is $5 per unit.

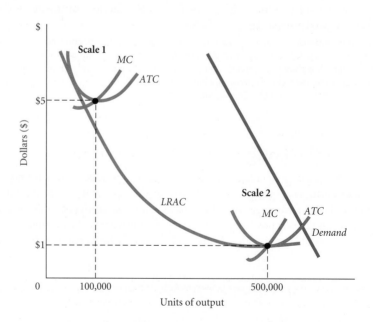

Notice in Figure 13.7 that the long-run average cost curve continues to decline until it almost hits the market demand curve. If at a price of $1 market demand is 5 *million* units of output, there would be no reason to have only one firm in the industry. Ten firms could each produce 500,000 units, and each could reap the full benefits of the available economies of scale.

Historically, natural monopolies in the United States have been regulated by the state. Public utility commissions in each state monitor electric companies and locally operating telephone companies, regulating prices so that the benefits of scale economies are realized without the inefficiencies of monopoly power. The *Economics in Practice* on p. 280 describes the current debate over the regulation of cable television.

Patents **Patents** are legal barriers that prevent entry into an industry by granting exclusive use of the patented product or process to the inventor. Patents are issued in the United States under the authority of Article I, Section 8, of the Constitution, which gives Congress the power to "promote the progress of science and the useful arts, by securing for limited times to authors and inventors the exclusive right to their respective writings and discoveries." Patent protection in the United States is currently granted for a period of 20 years.

patent A barrier to entry that grants exclusive use of the patented product or process to the inventor.

Patents provide an incentive for invention and innovation. New products and new processes are developed through research undertaken by individual inventors and by firms. Research requires resources and time, which have opportunity costs. Without the protection that a patent provides, the results of research would become available to the general public quickly. If research did not lead to expanded profits, less research would be done. On the negative side though, patents do serve as a barrier to competition and they slow down the benefits of research flowing through the market to consumers.

The expiration of patents after a given number of years represents an attempt to balance the benefits of firms and the benefits of households: On the one hand, it is important to stimulate invention and innovation; on the other hand, invention and innovation do society less good when their benefits to the public are constrained.[4]

In recent years, public attention has been focused on the high costs of health care. One factor contributing to these costs is the high price of many prescription drugs. Equipped with newly developed tools of bioengineering, the pharmaceutical industry has been granted thousands of patents for new drugs. When a new drug for treating a disease is developed, the patent holder can charge a high price for the drug. The drug companies argue that these rewards are justified by high research and development costs; others say that these profits are the result of a monopoly protected by the patent system.

Government Rules Patents provide one example of a government-enforced regulation that creates monopoly. For patents, the justification for such intervention is to promote innovation. In some cases, governments impose entry restrictions on firms as a way of controlling activity. In most parts of the United States, governments restrict the sale of alcohol. In fact, in some states (Iowa, Maine, New Hampshire, and Ohio), liquor can be sold only through state-controlled and managed stores. Most states operate lotteries as monopolists. However, when large economies of scale do not exist in an industry or when equity is not a concern, the arguments in favor of government-run monopolies are much weaker. One argument is that the state wants to prevent private parties from encouraging and profiting from "sin," particularly in cases in which society at large can be harmed. Another argument is that government monopolies are a convenient source of revenues.

Ownership of a Scarce Factor of Production You cannot enter the diamond-producing business unless you own a diamond mine. There are not many diamond mines in the world, and most are already owned by a single firm, the DeBeers Company of South Africa. At one time, the Aluminum Company of America (now Alcoa) owned or controlled virtually 100 percent of the known bauxite deposits in the world and until the 1940s monopolized the production and distribution of aluminum. Obviously, if production requires a particular input and one firm owns the entire supply of that input, that firm will control the industry. Ownership alone is a barrier to entry.

---

[4] Another alternative is *licensing*. With licensing, the new technology is used by all producers and the inventor splits the benefits with consumers. Because forcing the non-patent-holding producers to use an inefficient technology results in waste, some analysts have proposed adding mandatory licensing to the current patent system. A key question here involves determining the right licensing fee.

ECONOMICS IN PRACTICE

Managing the Cable Monopoly

Many people subscribe to cable television. Cable systems bundle a collection of network and cable stations and offer them to viewers as packages, ranging from a basic service with only a modest number of offerings to much-expanded premium services. In the last 20 years, the cable system has grown to a multibillion dollar industry covering most of the country.

What you might not realize about the cable system is that it consists of a network of local monopolies. In any given area, typically just one cable company is in operation. Historically, this monopoly was justified as a natural monopoly, reflecting the expensive cable that needed to be laid to serve the population and the fact that once the cable was laid, the costs of providing service to a new consumer was modest.

What you also may not realize is that when you pay your cable bill, part of your payment goes to your home city. In fact, cities negotiate with the various cable companies to give one of them the right to be the monopoly supplier of cable service in return for a fee that is typically on the order of 5 percent of the cable revenues. Once a firm has bought the right to be a local cable company, it must follow a set of rules, particularly with regard to the availability and price of the basic cable.

One of the hot debates in 2008 was in the cable industry. Cable companies offer programs bundled rather than à la carte programs. Keith Martin, the commissioner of the Federal Communications Commission, which oversees cable, pushed to have cable unbundled, largely in response to parents who were concerned about inappropriate television shows coming into their homes as part of a bundle. What economic logic would justify bundling programs in this way?

Here it is helpful to think about costs again. Once a television show is produced, distributing it to another customer has a zero marginal cost up to the capacity level of the cable. Thus, from a cable company's point of view, having a large customer base for the various shows is typically a profitable strategy. Suppose

100 viewers valued doctor shows at $2 a week each and lawyer shows at $1.50 each, while another 100 viewers had the opposite preference. To maximize revenue with à la carte pricing, the cable company would charge $1.50 for each show, giving it 200 viewers per show for a revenue of $600 (200 viewers × 2 shows each × $1.50). If the cable company sells the bundle for $3.50, all viewers buy and it earns $700. If the cable company sells the bundle for $3, its revenue is still the original $600 but now all of its customers are better off and can watch two programs instead of one. When the cost of distributing a good with high fixed costs is zero, bundling is often a way to make both producers and consumers better off.

network externalities
The value of a product to a consumer increases with the number of that product being sold or used in the market.

Network Effects How much value do you get from a telephone or a fax machine? It will depend on how many other people own a machine that can communicate with yours. Products such as these, in which benefits of ownership are a function of how many other people are part of the network, are subject to **network externalities**. For phones and faxes, the network effects are direct. For products such as the Windows operating system and the Xbox, network effects may be indirect. Having a large consumer base increases consumer valuation by encouraging the development of complementary goods. When many people own an Xbox, game developers have an incentive to create games for the system. Good games increase the value of the system. In the case of online interactive games like Zygna's Farmville, some observers have argued that the size of the playing community creates large network effects.

How does the existence of network effects create a barrier to entry? In this situation, a firm that starts early and builds a large product base will have an advantage over a newcomer. Microsoft's dominant position in the operating system market reflects network effects in this business. The high concentration in the game console market (Microsoft, Nintendo, and Sony control this market) also comes from network effects.

The Social Costs of Monopoly

So far, we have seen that a monopoly produces less output and charges a higher price than a competitively organized industry if no large economies of scale exist for the monopoly. We have also seen the way in which barriers to entry can allow monopolists to persist over time. You are probably thinking at this point that producing less and charging more to earn positive profits is not likely to be in the best interests of consumers, and you are right.

Inefficiency and Consumer Loss

In Chapter 12, we argued that price must equal marginal cost ($P = MC$) for markets to produce what people want. This argument rests on two propositions: (1) that price provides a good approximation of the social value of a unit of output and (2) that marginal cost, in the absence of externalities (costs or benefits to external parties not weighed by firms), provides a good approximation of the product's social opportunity cost. In a pure monopoly, price is above the product marginal cost. When this happens, the firm is underproducing from society's point of view. Society would be better off if the firm produced more and charged a lower price. Monopoly leads to an inefficient mix of output.

A slightly simplified version of the monopoly diagram appears in Figure 13.8, which shows how we might make a rough estimate of the size of the loss to social welfare that arises from monopoly. (For clarity, we will ignore the short-run cost curves and assume constant returns to scale in the long run.) Under competitive conditions, firms would produce output up to $Q_c = 4,000$ units and price would ultimately settle at $P_c = \$2$, equal to long-run average cost. Any price above \$2 will mean positive profits, which would be eliminated by the entry of new competing firms in the long run. (You should remember all this from Chapter 9.)

A monopoly firm in the same industry, however, would produce only $Q_m = 2,000$ units per period and charge a price of $P_m = \$4$ because $MR = MC$ at $Q_m = 2,000$ units. The monopoly would make a profit equal to total revenue minus total cost, or $P_m \times Q_m$ minus $ATC \times Q_m$. Profit

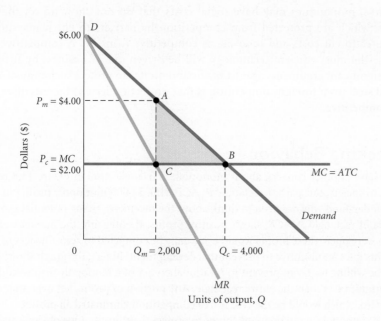

▲ **FIGURE 13.8 Welfare Loss from Monopoly**
A demand curve shows the amounts that people are willing to pay at each potential level of output. Thus, the demand curve can be used to approximate the benefits to the consumer of raising output above 2,000 units. *MC* reflects the marginal cost of the resources needed. The triangle *ABC* roughly measures the net social gain of moving from 2,000 units to 4,000 units (or the loss that results when monopoly decreases output from 4,000 units to 2,000 units).

to the monopoly is thus equal to the area P_mACP_c, or \$4,000. [(\$4 $\times$ 2,000) $-$ (\$2 $\times$ 2,000) $=$ \$8,000 $-$ \$4,000 $=$ \$4,000. Remember that $P_c = ATC$ in this example.]

Now consider the gains and losses associated with increasing price from \$2 to \$4 and cutting output from 4,000 units to 2,000 units. As you might guess, the winner will be the monopolist and the loser will be the consumer, but let us see how it works out.

At P_c = \$2, the price under perfect competition, there are no profits. Consumers are paying a price of \$2, but the demand curve shows that many are willing to pay more than that. For example, a substantial number of people would pay \$4 or more. Those people willing to pay more than \$2 are receiving what we earlier called a *consumer surplus*. Consumer surplus is the difference between what households are willing to pay for a product and the current market price. The demand curve shows approximately how much households are willing to pay at each level of output. Thus, the area of triangle DBP_c gives us a rough measure of the "consumer surplus" being enjoyed by households when the price is \$2. Consumers willing to pay exactly \$4 get a surplus equal to \$2. Those who place the highest value on this good—that is, those who are willing to pay the most (\$6)—get a surplus equal to DP_c, or \$4.

Now the industry is reorganized as a monopoly that cuts output to 2,000 units and raises price to \$4. The big winner is the monopolist, who ends up earning profits equal to \$4,000. The big losers are the consumers. Their "surplus" now shrinks from the area of triangle DBP_c to the area of triangle DAP_m. Part of that loss (which is equal to $DBP_c - DAP_m$, or the area P_mABP_c) is covered by the monopolist's gain of P_mACP_c, but not all of it. The loss to consumers exceeds the gain to the monopoly by the area of triangle ABC ($P_mABP_c - P_mACP_c$), which roughly measures the net loss in social welfare associated with monopoly power in this industry. Because the area of a triangle is half its base times its height, the welfare loss is 1/2 $\times$ 2,000 $\times$ \$2 = \$2,000. If we could push price back down to the competitive level and increase output to 4,000 units, consumers would gain more than the monopolist would lose and the gain in social welfare would approximate the area of ABC, or \$2,000.

In this example, the presence of a monopoly also causes an important change in the distribution of real income. In Figure 13.8, area P_mACP_c is a profit of \$4,000 flowing every period to the monopolist. If price were pushed down to \$2 by competition or regulation, those profits would pass to consumers in the form of lower prices. Society may value this resource transfer on equity grounds in addition to efficiency grounds.

Of course, monopolies may have social costs that do not show up on these graphs. Monopolies, which are protected from competition by barriers to entry, may not face the same pressures to cut costs and innovate as competitive firms do. A competitive firm that does not use the most efficient technology will be driven out of business by firms that do. One of the significant arguments against tariffs and quotas to protect such industries as automobiles and steel from foreign competition is that protection lessens the incentive to be efficient and competitive.

Rent-Seeking Behavior

Economists have another concern about monopolies. Triangle ABC in Figure 13.8 represents a real net loss to society, but part of rectangle P_mACP_c (the \$4,000 monopoly profit) may also end up lost. To understand why, we need to think about the incentives facing potential monopolists.

The area of rectangle P_mACP_c shows positive profits. If entry into the market were easy and competition were open, these profits would eventually be competed to zero. Owners of businesses earning profits have an incentive to prevent this development. In fact, the graph shows how much they would be willing to pay to prevent it. A rational owner of a monopoly firm would be willing to pay any amount less than the entire rectangle. Any portion of profits left over after expenses is better than zero, which would be the case if free competition eliminated all profits.

Potential monopolists can do many things to protect their profits. One obvious approach is to push the government to impose restrictions on competition. A classic example is the behavior of taxicab driver organizations in New York and other large cities. To operate a cab legally in New York City, you need a license. The city tightly controls the number of licenses available. If entry into the taxi business were open, competition would hold down cab fares to the cost of operating cabs. However, cab drivers have become a powerful lobbying force and have muscled the city into restricting the number of licenses issued. This restriction keeps fares high and preserves monopoly profits.

There are countless other examples. The steel industry and the automobile industry spend large sums lobbying Congress for tariff protection.[5] Some experts claim that establishment of the now-defunct Civil Aeronautics Board in 1937 to control competition in the airline industry and extensive regulation of trucking by the I.C.C. prior to deregulation in the 1970s came about partly through industry efforts to restrict competition and preserve profits.

This kind of behavior, in which households or firms take action to preserve positive profits, is called **rent-seeking behavior**. Recall from Chapter 10 that rent is the return to a factor of production in strictly limited supply. Rent-seeking behavior has two important implications.

rent-seeking behavior
Actions taken by households or firms to preserve positive profits.

First, this behavior consumes resources. Lobbying and building barriers to entry are not costless activities. Lobbyists' wages, expenses of the regulatory bureaucracy, and the like must be paid. Periodically faced with the prospect that the city of New York will issue new taxi licenses, cab owners and drivers have become so well organized that they can bring the city to a standstill with a strike or even a limited job action. Indeed, positive profits may be completely consumed through rent-seeking behavior that produces nothing of social value; all it does is help to preserve the current distribution of income.

Second, the frequency of rent-seeking behavior leads us to another view of government. So far, we have considered only the role that government might play in helping to achieve an efficient allocation of resources in the face of market failure—in this case, failures that arise from imperfect market structure. Later in this chapter we survey the measures government might take to ensure that resources are efficiently allocated when monopoly power arises. However, the idea of rent-seeking behavior introduces the notion of **government failure**, in which the government becomes the tool of the rent seeker and the allocation of resources is made even less efficient than before.

government failure Occurs when the government becomes the tool of the rent seeker and the allocation of resources is made even less efficient by the intervention of government.

This idea of government failure is at the center of **public choice theory**, which holds that governments are made up of people, just as business firms are. These people—politicians and bureaucrats—can be expected to act in their own self-interest, just as owners of firms do. We turn to the economics of public choice in Chapter 16.

public choice theory An economic theory that the public officials who set economic policies and regulate the players act in their own self-interest, just as firms do.

Price Discrimination

So far in our discussion of monopoly, we have assumed that the firm faces a known downward-sloping demand curve and must choose a *single price* and a single quantity of output. Indeed, the reason that price and marginal revenue are different for a monopoly and the same for a perfectly competitive firm is that if a monopoly decides to sell more output, it must lower price in order to do so.

In the real world, however, there are many examples of firms that charge different prices to different groups of buyers. Charging different prices to different buyers is called **price discrimination**. The motivation for price discrimination is fairly obvious: If a firm can identify those who are willing to pay a higher price for a good, it can earn more profit from them by charging a higher price. The idea is best illustrated using the extreme case where a firm knows what each buyer is willing to pay. A firm that charges the maximum amount that buyers are willing to pay for each unit is practicing **perfect price discrimination**.

price discrimination Charging different prices to different buyers.

Figure 13.9 is similar to Figure 13.8. For simplicity, assume a firm with a constant marginal cost equal to $2 per unit. A non-price-discriminating monopolist would have to set one and only one price. That firm would face the marginal revenue curve shown in the diagram and would produce as long as MR is above MC: Output would be Q_m, and price would be set at $4 per unit. The firm would earn an economic profit of $2 per unit for every unit up to Q_m. Consumers would enjoy a consumer surplus equal to the shaded area. Consumer A, for example, is willing to pay $5.75 but has to pay only $4.00.

perfect price discrimination Occurs when a firm charges the maximum amount that buyers are willing to pay for each unit.

Now consider what would happen if the firm could charge each consumer the maximum amount that that consumer was willing to pay. In Figure 13.9(a), if the firm could charge consumer A a price of $5.75, the firm would earn $3.75 in profit on that unit and the consumer would get no consumer surplus. Going on to consumer B, if the firm could determine B's

---

[5] A tariff is a tax on imports designed to give a price advantage to domestic producers.

▶ **FIGURE 13.9**

Price Discrimination

In Figure 13.9(a), consumer A is willing to pay $5.75. If the price-discriminating firm can charge $5.75 to A, profit is $3.75. A monopolist who cannot price discriminate would maximize profit by charging $4. At a price of $4.00, the firm makes $2.00 in profit and consumer A enjoys a consumer surplus of $1.75. In Figure 13.9(b), for a perfectly price-discriminating monopolist, the demand curve is the same as marginal revenue. The firm will produce as long as $MR > MC$, up to Q_c. At Q_c, profit is the entire shaded area and consumer surplus is zero.

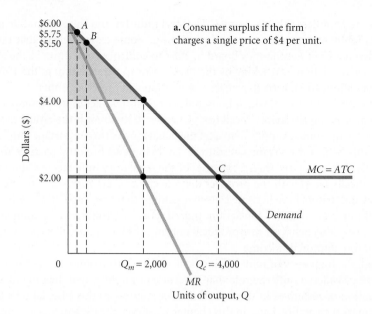

a. Consumer surplus if the firm charges a single price of $4 per unit.

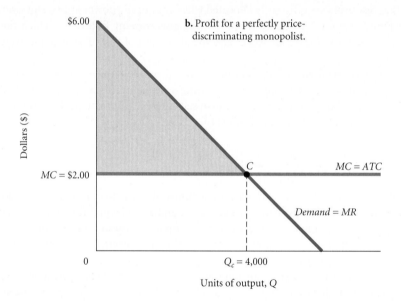

b. Profit for a perfectly price-discriminating monopolist.

maximum willingness to pay and charge $5.50, profit would be $3.50 and consumer surplus for B would again be zero. This would continue all the way to point C on the demand curve, where total profit would be equal to the entire area under the demand curve and above the $MC = ATC$ line, as shown in Figure 13.9(b).

Another way to look at the diagram in Figure 13.9(b) is to notice that the demand curve actually becomes the same as the marginal revenue curve. When a firm can charge the maximum that anyone is willing to pay *for each unit*, that price *is* marginal revenue. There is no need to draw a separate MR curve as there was when the firm could charge only one price to all consumers. Once again, profit is the entire shaded area and consumer surplus is zero.

It is interesting to note that a perfectly price-discriminating monopolist will actually produce the *efficient* quantity of output—Q_c in Figure 13.9(b), which is the same as the amount that would be produced had the industry been perfectly competitive. The firm will continue to produce as long as benefits to consumers exceed marginal cost; it does not stop at Q_m in Figure 13.9(a). But when a monopolist can perfectly price discriminate, it reaps all the net benefits from higher production. There is no deadweight loss, but there is no consumer surplus either.

Examples of Price Discrimination

Examples of price discrimination are all around us. It used to be that airlines routinely charged those who stayed over Saturday nights a much lower fare than those who did not. Business travelers generally travel during the week, often are unwilling to stay over Saturdays, and generally are willing to pay more for tickets.

Airlines, movie theaters, hotels, and many other industries routinely charge a lower price for children and the elderly. The reason is that children and the elderly generally have a lower willingness to pay. Telephone companies have so many ways of targeting different groups that it is difficult to know what they are really charging.

In each case, the objective of the firm is to segment the market into different identifiable groups, with each group having a different elasticity of demand. Doing so requires firms to ensure that different customers are kept separated, so that they cannot trade with one another. It can be shown, although we will not present the analysis here, that the optimal strategy for a firm that can sell in more than one market is to charge higher prices in markets with low demand elasticities.

Remedies for Monopoly: Antitrust Policy

As we have just seen, the exercise of monopoly power can bring with it considerable social costs. On the other hand, as our discussion of entry barriers suggested, at times, monopolies may bring with them benefits associated with scale economies or innovation gains. Sometimes monopolies result from the natural interplay of market and technological forces, while at other times firms actively and aggressively pursue monopoly power, doing their best to eliminate the competition. In the United States, the rules set out in terms of what firms can and cannot do in their markets are contained in two pieces of antitrust legislation: the Sherman Act passed in 1890 and the Clayton Act passed in 1914.

Major Antitrust Legislation

The following are some of the major antitrust legislation that have been passed in the United States.

The Sherman Act of 1890   The substance of the Sherman Act is contained in two short sections:

> *Section 1.* Every contract, combination in the form of trust or otherwise, or conspiracy, in restraint of trade or commerce among the several States, or with foreign nations, is hereby declared to be illegal....
>
> *Section 2.* Every person who shall monopolize, or attempt to monopolize, or combine or conspire with any other person or persons, to monopolize any part of the trade or commerce among the several States, or with foreign nations, shall be deemed guilty of a misdemeanor, and, on conviction thereof, shall be punished by fine not exceeding five thousand dollars, or by imprisonment not exceeding one year, or by both said punishments, in the discretion of the court.

For our treatment of monopoly, the relevant part of the Sherman Act is Section 2, the rule against monopolization or attempted monopolization. The language of the act is quite broad, so it is the responsibility of the courts to judge conduct that is legal and conduct that is illegal. As a firm competes in the hopes of winning business, what kind of behavior is acceptable hard competition and what is not? Two different administrative bodies have the responsibility for initiating actions on behalf of the U.S. government against individuals or companies thought to be in violation of the antitrust laws. These agencies are the Antitrust Division of the Justice Department and the Federal Trade Commission (FTC). In addition, private citizens can initiate antitrust actions.

In 1911, two major antitrust cases were decided by the Supreme Court. The two companies involved, Standard Oil and American Tobacco, seemed to epitomize the textbook definition of monopoly, and both appeared to exhibit the structure and the conduct outlawed by the Sherman Act. Standard Oil controlled about 91 percent of the refining industry, and although the exact figure is still disputed, the American Tobacco Trust probably controlled between 75 percent and 90 percent of the market for all tobacco products except cigars. Both companies had used tough tactics to swallow up competition or to drive it out of business. Not surprisingly, the Supreme Court found both firms guilty of violating Sections 1 and 2 of the Sherman Act and ordered their dissolution.[6]

rule of reason The criterion introduced by the Supreme Court in 1911 to determine whether a particular action was illegal ("unreasonable") or legal ("reasonable") within the terms of the Sherman Act.

The Court made clear, however, that the Sherman Act did not outlaw every action that seemed to restrain trade, only those that were "unreasonable." In enunciating this **rule of reason**, the Court seemed to say that structure alone was not a criterion for unreasonableness. Thus, it was possible for a near-monopoly not to violate the Sherman Act as long as it had won its market using "reasonable" tactics.

Subsequent court cases confirmed that a firm could be convicted of violating the Sherman Act only if it had exhibited *unreasonable conduct*. Between 1911 and 1920, cases were brought against Eastman Kodak, International Harvester, United Shoe Machinery, and United States Steel. The first three companies controlled overwhelming shares of their respective markets, and the fourth controlled 60 percent of the country's capacity to produce steel. Nonetheless, all four cases were dismissed on the grounds that these companies had shown no evidence of "unreasonable conduct."

New technologies have also created challenges for the courts in defining reasonable conduct. Perhaps the largest antitrust case recently has been the case launched by the U.S. Department of Justice against Microsoft. By the 1990s, Microsoft had more that 90 percent of the market in operating systems for PCs. The government argued that Microsoft had achieved this market share through illegal dealing, while Microsoft argued that the government failed to understand the issues associated with competition in a market with network externalities and dynamic competition. In the end, the case was settled with a *consent decree* in July 1994. A consent decree is a formal agreement between a prosecuting government and defendants that must be approved by the courts. Such decrees can be signed before, during, or after a trial and are often used to save litigation costs. In the case of Microsoft, under the consent decree, it agreed to give computer manufacturers more freedom to install software from other software companies. In 1997, Microsoft found itself charged with violating the terms of the consent decree and was back in court. In 2000, the company was found guilty of violating the antitrust laws and a judge ordered it split into two companies. But Microsoft appealed; and the decision to split the company was replaced with a consent decree requiring Microsoft to behave more competitively, including a provision that computer makers would have the ability to sell competitors' software without fear of retaliation. In the fall of 2005, Microsoft finally ended its antitrust troubles in the United States after agreeing to pay RealNetworks $761 million to settle one final lawsuit.

In 2005, Advanced Micro Devices (AMD) brought suit against Intel, which has an 80 percent share of the x-86 processors used in most of the world's PCs. AMD alleged anticompetitive behavior and attempted monopolization. At present in the United States, private antitrust cases, brought by one firm against another, are 20-plus times more common than government-led cases.

The Clayton Act and the Federal Trade Commission, 1914 Designed to strengthen the Sherman Act and to clarify the rule of reason, the **Clayton Act** of 1914 outlawed a number of specific practices. First, it made *tying contracts* illegal. Such contracts force a customer to buy one product to obtain another. Second, it limited mergers that would "substantially lessen competition or tend to create a monopoly." Third, it banned *price discrimination*—charging different customers different prices for reasons other than changes in cost or matching competitors' prices.

Clayton Act Passed by Congress in 1914 to strengthen the Sherman Act and clarify the rule of reason, the act outlawed specific monopolistic behaviors such as tying contracts, price discrimination, and unlimited mergers.

Federal Trade Commission (FTC) A federal regulatory group created by Congress in 1914 to investigate the structure and behavior of firms engaging in interstate commerce, to determine what constitutes unlawful "unfair" behavior, and to issue cease-and-desist orders to those found in violation of antitrust law.

The **Federal Trade Commission (FTC)**, created by Congress in 1914, was established to investigate "the organization, business conduct, practices, and management" of companies that engage in interstate commerce. At the same time, the act establishing the commission added another vaguely worded prohibition to the books: "Unfair methods of competition in commerce are hereby declared unlawful." The determination of what constituted "unfair" behavior was left up to the commission. The FTC was also given the power to issue "cease-and-desist orders" where it found behavior in violation of the law.

---

[6] *United States v. Standard Oil Co. of New Jersey*, 221 U.S. 1 (1911); *United States v. American Tobacco Co.*, 221 U.S. 106 (1911).

ECONOMICS IN PRACTICE

Antitrust Rules Cover the NFL

Most people recognize that a sports league like the National Football League is big business, but not everyone realizes that it is subject to antitrust laws. But, as the article below indicates, one of the biggest cases facing the Supreme Court in 2009–2010 involved the NFL.

The NFL's practice had been to negotiate as a single unit with apparel companies that wished to sell apparel like hats and T-shirts with football logos. Of course this meant that apparel companies could not play the New York Giants against the Indianapolis Colts in signing deals. American Needle, a large apparel company, sued. In its defense, the NFL argued that in its negotiations with companies like Reebok and American Needle, it faced competition from baseball and basketball leagues that kept it from extracting too high a price for its logos. In essence, the NFL argued that in the sports-logo hat market a New York Yankees hat was a pretty good substitute for a New York Giants hat. The court saw it differently.

American Needle: High Court Delivers 9–0 Shutout Against NFL

The Wall Street Journal

Wow. Turns out the big antitrust case of the 2009–2010 Supreme Court term, American Needle v. NFL, didn't provide much of a matchup.

American Needle clobbered the league, in a unanimous 9–0 decision penned by Justice John Paul Stevens. We had no dissents and no concurrences. This was an unadulterated blowout. This was the 1940 NFL Championship game; the 1986 Super Bowl.

The case pitted American Needle, Inc., an apparel manufacturer, against the NFL. The dispute started back in 2000 when the NFL signed an exclusive apparel licensing deal with Reebok International, now a unit of Adidas AG.

American Needle, which had individual licensing deals with NFL teams, sued, arguing the NFL's exclusive deal with Reebok violated antitrust rules. The NFL argued that it is a single entity with 32 teams that compete with each other in football but not in business, where the teams collectively compete with other sports and forms of entertainment. American Needle countered by arguing that the league was actually a collection of 32 independent entities—i.e., all the teams.

The Seventh Circuit in 2008 ruled for the NFL, prompting the appeal.

The Supreme Court on Monday essentially ruled that the NFL is composed of 32 separate business entities.

Source: The Wall Street Journal, from "American Needle: High Court Delivers 9–0 Shutout Against NFL" by Ashby Jones. Copyright 2010 by *Dow Jones & Company, Inc.* Reproduced with permission of *Dow Jones & Company, Inc.* via Copyright Clearance Center.

Nonetheless, the legislation of 1914 retained the focus on *conduct*; thus, the rule of reason remained central to all antitrust action in the courts.

Imperfect Markets: A Review and a Look Ahead

A firm has *market power* when it exercises some control over the price of its output or the prices of the inputs that it uses. The extreme case of a firm with market power is the pure monopolist. In a pure monopoly, a single firm produces a product for which there are no close substitutes in an industry in which all new competitors are barred from entry.

Our focus in this chapter on pure monopoly (which occurs rarely) has served a number of purposes. First, the monopoly model describes a number of industries quite well. Second, the monopoly case illustrates the observation that imperfect competition leads to an inefficient allocation of resources. Finally, the analysis of pure monopoly offers insights into the more commonly encountered market models of monopolistic competition and oligopoly, which we discussed briefly in this chapter and will discuss in detail in the next two chapters.

SUMMARY

1. A number of assumptions underlie the logic of perfect competition. Among them: (1) A large number of firms and households are interacting in each market; (2) firms in a given market produce undifferentiated, or homogeneous, products; and (3) new firms are free to enter industries and compete for profits. The first two imply that firms have no control over input prices or output prices; the third implies that opportunities for positive profit are eliminated in the long run.

IMPERFECT COMPETITION AND MARKET POWER: CORE CONCEPTS *p. 269*

2. A market in which individual firms have some control over price is imperfectly competitive. Such firms exercise *market power*. The three forms of *imperfect competition* are monopoly, oligopoly, and monopolistic competition.

3. A *pure monopoly* is an industry with a single firm that produces a product for which there are no close substitutes and in which there are significant *barriers to entry*.

4. Market power means that firms must make four decisions instead of three: (1) how much to produce, (2) how to produce it, (3) how much to demand in each input market, and (4) *what price to charge for their output*.

5. Market power does not imply that a monopolist can charge any price it wants. Monopolies are constrained by market demand. They can sell only what people will buy and only at a price that people are willing to pay.

PRICE AND OUTPUT DECISIONS IN PURE MONOPOLY MARKETS *p. 271*

6. In perfect competition, many firms supply homogeneous products. With only one firm in a monopoly market, however, there is no distinction between the firm and the industry—the firm *is* the industry. The market demand curve is thus the firm's demand curve, and the total quantity supplied in the market is what the monopoly firm decides to produce.

7. For a monopolist, an increase in output involves not just producing more and selling it but also reducing the price of its output to sell it. Thus, marginal revenue, to a monopolist, is not equal to product price, as it is in competition. Instead, marginal revenue is lower than price because to raise output 1 unit *and to be able to sell* that 1 unit, the firm must lower the price it charges to all buyers.

8. A profit-maximizing monopolist will produce up to the point at which marginal revenue is equal to marginal cost ($MR = MC$).

9. Monopolies have no identifiable supply curves. They simply choose a point on the market demand curve. That is, they choose a price and quantity to produce, which depend on both the marginal cost and the shape of the demand curve.

10. In the short run, monopolists are limited by a fixed factor of production, just as competitive firms are. Monopolies that do not generate enough revenue to cover costs will go out of business in the long run.

11. Compared with a competitively organized industry, a monopolist restricts output, charges higher prices, and earns positive profits. Because *MR* always lies below the demand curve for a monopoly, monopolists always charge a price higher than *MC* (the price that would be set by perfect competition).

12. Barriers to entry prevent new entrants from competing away industry excess profits.

13. Forms of barriers to entry include economies of scale, patents, government rules, ownership of scarce factors, and network effects.

14. When a firm exhibits economies of scale so large that average costs continuously decline with output, it may be efficient to have only one firm in an industry. Such an industry is called a *natural monopoly*.

THE SOCIAL COSTS OF MONOPOLY *p. 281*

15. When firms price above marginal cost, the result is an inefficient mix of output. The decrease in consumer surplus is larger than the monopolist's profit, thus causing a net loss in social welfare.

16. Actions that firms take to preserve positive profits, such as lobbying for restrictions on competition, are called rent seeking. *Rent-seeking behavior* consumes resources and adds to social cost, thus reducing social welfare even further.

PRICE DISCRIMINATION *p. 283*

17. Charging different prices to different buyers is called *price discrimination*. The motivation for price discrimination is fairly obvious: If a firm can identify those who are willing to pay a higher price for a good, it can earn more profit from them by charging a higher price.

18. A firm that charges the maximum amount that buyers are willing to pay for each unit is practicing *perfect price discrimination*.

19. A perfectly price-discriminating monopolist will actually produce the *efficient* quantity of output.

20. Examples of price discrimination are all around us. Airlines routinely charge travelers who stay over Saturday nights a much lower fare than those who do not. Business travelers generally travel during the week, often are unwilling to stay over Saturdays, and generally are willing to pay more for tickets.

REMEDIES FOR MONOPOLY: ANTITRUST POLICY *p. 285*

21. Governments have assumed two roles with respect to imperfectly competitive industries: (1) They *promote* competition and restrict market power, primarily through antitrust laws and other congressional acts; and (2) they *restrict* competition by regulating industries.

22. In 1914, Congress passed the *Clayton Act*, which was designed to strengthen the Sherman Act and to clarify what specific forms of conduct were "unreasonable" restraints of trade. In the same year, the *Federal Trade Commission* was established and given broad power to investigate and regulate unfair methods of competition.

REVIEW TERMS AND CONCEPTS

barrier to entry, *p. 278*

Clayton Act, *p. 286*

Federal Trade Commission (FTC), *p. 286*

government failure, *p. 283*

imperfectly competitive industry, *p. 269*

market power, *p. 269*

natural monopoly, *p. 278*

network externalities, *p. 280*

patent, *p. 279*

perfect price discrimination, *p. 283*

price discrimination, *p. 283*

public choice theory, *p. 283*

pure monopoly, *p. 270*

rent-seeking behavior, *p. 283*

rule of reason, *p. 286*

PROBLEMS

All problems are available on www.myeconlab.com  myeconlab

1. Do you agree or disagree with each of the following statements? Explain your reasoning.
   a. For a monopoly, price is equal to marginal revenue because a monopoly has the power to control price.
   b. Because a monopoly is the only firm in an industry, it can charge virtually any price for its product.
   c. It is always true that when demand elasticity is equal to −1, marginal revenue is equal to 0.

2. Explain why the marginal revenue curve facing a competitive firm differs from the marginal revenue curve facing a monopolist.

3. Assume that the potato chip industry in the Northwest in 2009 was competitively structured and in long-run competitive equilibrium; firms were earning a normal rate of return. In 2010, two smart lawyers quietly bought up all the firms and began operations as a monopoly called "Wonks." To operate efficiently, Wonks hired a management consulting firm, which estimated long-run costs and demand. These results are presented in the following figure.

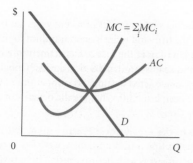

($\sum_i MC_i$ = the horizontal sum of the marginal cost curves of the individual branches/firms.)
   a. Indicate 2009 output and price on the diagram.
   b. By assuming that the monopolist is a profit-maximizer, indicate on the graph total revenue, total cost, and total profit after the consolidation.
   c. Compare the perfectly competitive outcome with the monopoly outcome.
   d. In 2010, an old buddy from law school files a complaint with the Antitrust Division of the Justice Department claiming that Wonks has monopolized the potato chip industry.

Justice concurs and prepares a civil suit. Suppose you work in the White House and the president asks you to prepare a brief memo (two or three paragraphs) outlining the issues. In your response, be sure to include:
   (1) The economic justification for action.
   (2) A proposal to achieve an efficient market outcome.

4. Willy's Widgets, a monopoly, faces the following demand schedule (sales in widgets per month):

PRICE	$20	$30	$40	$50	$60	$70	$80	$90	$100
QUANTITY DEMANDED	40	35	30	25	20	15	10	5	0

   Calculate marginal revenue over each interval in the schedule—for example, between $q = 40$ and $q = 35$. Recall that marginal revenue is the added revenue from an additional *unit* of production/sales and assume that *MR* is constant within each interval.

   If marginal cost is constant at $20 and fixed cost is $100, what is the profit-maximizing level of output? (Choose one of the specific levels of output from the schedule.) What is the level of profit? Explain your answer using marginal cost and marginal revenue.

   Repeat the exercise for *MC* = $40.

5. The following diagram illustrates the demand curve facing a monopoly in an industry with no economies or diseconomies of scale and no fixed costs. In the short and long run *MC* = *ATC*. Copy the diagram and indicate the following:

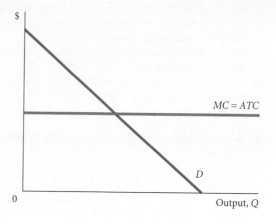

   a. Optimal output
   b. Optimal price
   c. Total revenue
   d. Total cost
   e. Total monopoly profits
   f. Total "excess burden" or "welfare costs" of the monopoly (briefly explain)

6. The following diagram shows the cost structure of a monopoly firm as well as market demand. Identify on the graph and calculate the following:
   a. Profit-maximizing output level
   b. Profit-maximizing price
   c. Total revenue
   d. Total cost
   e. Total profit or loss

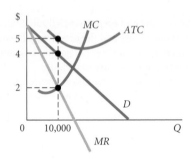

7. Consider the following monopoly that produces paperback books:

$$\text{fixed costs} = \$1,000$$
$$\text{marginal cost} = \$1 \text{ (and is constant)}$$

   a. Draw the average total cost curve and the marginal cost curve on the same graph.
   b. Assume that all households have the same demand schedule given by the following relationship:

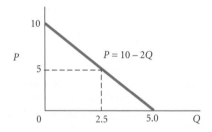

   Assuming 400 households are in the economy, draw the market demand curve and the marginal revenue schedule facing the monopolist.
   c. What is the monopolist's profit-maximizing output? What is the monopolist's price?
   d. What is the "efficient price," assuming no externalities?
   e. Suppose the government "imposed" the efficient price by setting a ceiling on price at the efficient level. What is the long-run output of the monopoly?
   f. Suggest an alternative approach for achieving an efficient outcome.

*8. In Taiwan, there is only one beer producer, a government-owned monopoly called Taiwan Beer. Suppose that the company were run in a way to maximize profit for the government. That is, assume that it behaved like a private profit-maximizing monopolist. Assuming demand and cost conditions are given on the following diagram, at what level would Taiwan Beer target output and what price would it charge?

   Now suppose Taiwan Beer decided to begin competing in the highly competitive American market. Assume further that Taiwan maintains import barriers so that American producers cannot sell in Taiwan but that they are not immediately reciprocated. Assuming Taiwan Beer can sell all that it can produce in the American market at a price $P = P_{US}$ indicate the following:
   a. Total output
   b. Output sold in Taiwan
   c. New price in Taiwan
   d. Total sold in the United States
   e. Total profits
   f. Total profits on U.S. sales
   g. Total profits on Taiwan sales

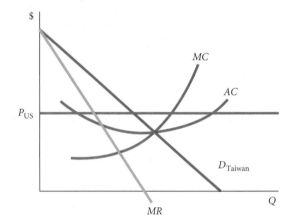

9. One of the big success stories of recent years has been Google. Research the firm and write a memorandum to the head of the Antitrust Division of the Justice Department presenting the case for and against antitrust action against Google. In what ways has Google acted to suppress competition? What private suits have been brought? What are the benefits of a strong, profitable Google?

10. [Related to the *Economics in Practice* on p. 280] When cable television was first introduced, there were few substitutes for it, particularly in areas with poor reception of network TV. In the current environment, a number of companies from outside the industry (for example, AT&T) have begun to develop new ways to compete with cable. What effect should we expect this to have on the cable companies?

11. [Related to the *Economics in Practice* on p. 287] Explain how the Supreme Court ruling in American Needle v. NFL exemplifies the "rule of reason" provision of the Sherman Act of 1890.

*Note: Problems marked with an asterisk are more challenging.

12. Black Eyed Peas was a rock band that stood at the top of the charts for sales in 2010 when its song "I Gotta Feeling" was downloaded over 7 million times. The path to success for a rock band involves reducing the elasticity of demand that it faces and building barriers to entry. That sounds like economic babble, but it has a lot of meaning. Using the language of economics and the concepts presented in this chapter, explain why lowering the elasticity of demand and building barriers to entry are exactly what Black Eyed Peas is trying to do.

13. The diagram below shows a firm (industry) that earns a normal return to capital if organized competitively. Price in the market place is P_c under competition. We assume at first that marginal cost is fixed at $50 per unit of output and that there are no economies or diseconomies of scale. [The equation of the demand curve facing the industry is $P = 100 - 1/180\ Q$].

Calculate the total revenue to the competitive firms, assuming free entry. What is total cost under competition? Calculate consumer surplus under competition.

Now assume that you bought all the firms in this industry, combining them into a single-firm monopoly protected from entry by a patent. Calculate the profit-maximizing price, P_m, total revenue from the monopoly, total cost, profit, and consumer surplus. Also compare the competitive and monopoly outcomes. Calculate the dead weight loss from monopoly. What potential remedies are available?

14. Explain why a monopoly faces no supply curve.

15. Suppose Gloria has the only franchise for a McDonald's restaurant in Laughlin, Nevada, a city with a population of roughly 8,100. Does the fact that Gloria has the only McDonald's in town necessarily mean this represents a monopoly? Explain.

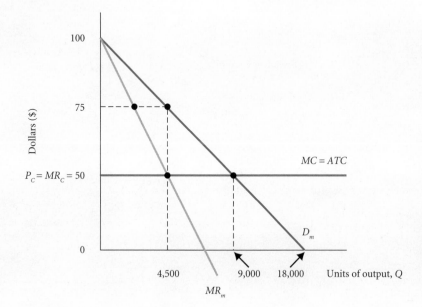

Oligopoly 14

We have now examined two "pure" market structures. At one extreme is *perfect competition*, a market structure in which many firms, each small relative to the size of the market, produce undifferentiated products and have no market power at all. Each competitive firm takes price as given and faces a perfectly elastic demand for its product. At the other extreme is *pure monopoly*, a market structure in which only one firm is the industry. The

monopoly holds the power to set price and is protected against competition by barriers to entry. Its market power would be complete if it did not face the discipline of the market demand curve. Even a monopoly, however, must produce a product that people want and are willing to pay for.

Most industries in the United States fall somewhere between these two extremes. In the next two chapters, we focus on two types of industries in which firms exercise some market power but at the same time face competition: oligopoly and monopolistic competition. In this chapter, we cover oligopolies, and in Chapter 15, we turn to monopolistic competition.

An **oligopoly** is an industry dominated by a few firms that, by virtue of their individual sizes, are large enough to influence the market price. Oligopolies exist in many forms. Consider the following cases:

In the United States, 90 percent of the music produced and sold comes from one of four studios: Universal, Sony, Warner, or EMI. The competition among these four firms is intense, but most of it involves the search for new talent and the marketing of that talent. Although studios compete less on price, Radiohead's 2007 campaign to have consumers set their own price in buying its new CD may result in a shake-up of the industry.

Stents are small metal devices used to prop open coronary arteries once they have been unblocked by angioplasty surgery. In the United States, the $1 billion stent market is dominated by three firms: Boston Scientific, Johnson & Johnson, and Medtronic. Among the three, there is fierce competition in the area of research and development (R&D) as they try to develop new, improved products. In 2007, Johnson & Johnson tried marketing its stents directly to patients, with an advertisement during the Dallas Cowboys–New York Jets Thanksgiving Day football game. On the other hand, we see very little price competition among these firms.

Airlines are another oligopolistic industry, but price competition can be fierce. When Southwest enters a new market, travelers often benefit from large price drops.

In 2010 Amazon found its position in the market for handheld readers threatened as the Kindle was joined by both the Nook and the iPad.

What we see in these examples is the complexity of competition among oligopolists. Oligopolists compete with one another not only in price but also in developing new products, marketing and advertising those products, and developing complements to use with the products.

oligopoly A form of industry (market) structure characterized by a few dominant firms. Products may be homogenous or differentiated.

At times, in some industries, competition in any of these areas can be fierce; in the other industries, there seems to be more of a "live and let live" attitude. The complex interdependence among oligopolists combined with the wide range of strategies that they use to compete makes them difficult to analyze. To find the right strategy, firms need to anticipate the reactions of their customers and their rivals to what the firms do. If I raise my price, will my rivals follow me? If they do not, will my customers leave, or are they attracted enough to what I produce that they will continue to purchase from me? If Universal decides to dramatically cut prices of its music and redo its contracts with artists so that they earn more revenue from concerts, will Sony imitate that strategy? If Sony does, how will that affect Universal? As you can see, these are hard, although interesting, questions. This chapter will introduce you to a range of different models from the fields of game theory and competitive strategy to help you answer these questions.

The four cases just described differ not only in how firms compete but also in some of the fundamental features of their industries. Before we describe the formal models of the way oligopoly firms interact, it is useful to provide a few tools that can be used to analyze the *structure* of the industries to which those firms belong. Knowing more of the structure of an industry can help us figure out which of the models we describe will be most helpful. For this exercise, we will rely on some of the tools developed in the area of competitive strategy used in business schools and in management consulting.

Market Structure in an Oligopoly

Five Forces model A model developed by Michael Porter that helps us understand the five competitive forces that determine the level of competition and profitability in an industry.

One of the standard models used in the competitive strategy area to look at the structure of an oligopoly industry is the **Five Forces model** developed by Michael Porter of Harvard University. Figure 14.1 illustrates the model.

The five forces help us explain the relative profitability of an industry and identify in which area firm rivalry is likely to be most intense.

The center box of the figure focuses on the competition among the existing firms in the industry. In the competitive market, that box is so full of competitors that no individual firm needs to think strategically about any other individual firm. In the case of monopoly, the center box has only one firm. In an oligopoly, there are a small number of firms and each of those firms will spend time thinking about how it can best compete against the other firms.

What characteristics of the existing firms should we look at to see how that competition will unfold? An obvious structural feature of an industry to consider is the number and size distribution of those firms. Do the top two firms have 90 percent of the market or only 20 percent? Is there one very large firm and a few smaller competitors, or are firms similar in size? Table 14.1 shows the distribution of market shares in a range of different U.S. industries, based on census data using value of shipments. Market share can also be constructed using employment data. We can see that even within industries that are highly *concentrated*, there are differences. Ninety percent of U.S. beer is made by the top four firms (Anheuser-Busch itself produces 50 percent of the beer sold in the

▶ **FIGURE 14.1**
Forces Driving Industry Competition

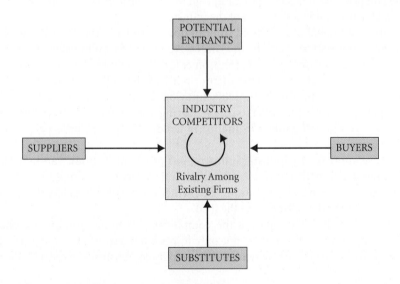

TABLE 14.1	Percentage of Value of Shipments Accounted for by the Largest Firms in High-Concentration Industries, 2002		
Industry Designation	Four Largest Firms	Eight Largest Firms	Number of Firms
Primary copper	99	100	10
Cigarettes	95	99	15
Household laundry equipment	93	100	13
Cellulosic man-made fiber	93	100	8
Breweries	90	94	344
Electric lamp bulbs	89	94	57
Household refrigerators and freezers	85	95	18
Small arms ammunition	83	89	109
Cereal breakfast foods	82	93	45
Motor vehicles	81	91	308

Source: U.S. Department of Commerce, Bureau of the Census, 2002 Economic Census, *Concentration Ratios: 2002* ECO2-315R-1, May 2006.

United States), but there is a relatively large fringe of much smaller firms. In the copper industry, we find only large firms. As we will see shortly in the models, with fewer firms, all else being equal competition is reduced.

We are also interested in the size distribution of firms among the top firms. Again, looking at the beer industry, while Anheuser-Busch produces half of the U.S. beer consumed, MillerCoors (a recently merged pair) is now up to 30 percent of the market, giving us a two-firm **concentration ratio** of 80 percent. In the market for conventional DVD players, Sony controls 20 percent of the market, but the next three or four firms in the industry have similar shares. When we discuss the price leadership model of oligopoly, we will highlight this question of size distribution. In our discussion of government merger policy, we will discuss measures other than the concentration ratio that can be used to measure firm shares.

concentration ratio The share of industry output in sales or employment accounted for by the top firms.

The final feature of existing firms that we want to look at is the amount of product differentiation we see in the industry. Are the firms all making the same product, or are the products very different from one another? This takes us back to the issue of how close products are as substitutes, a topic introduced in Chapter 13 in the description of monopoly. How different are Actavision's Guitar Hero and Electronic Arts' Rock Band? Does Farmville compete, or are there really different markets for casual and dedicated gamers as some claim? The more differentiated products made by oligopolists are, the more their behavior will resemble that of the monopolist.

Now look at the boxes to the north and south of the competitive rivalry box in Figure 14.1. To the north, we see potential entrants. In the last chapter, we described the major sources of entry barriers. When entry barriers are low, new firms can come in to compete away any excess profits that existing firms are earning. In an oligopoly, we find that the threat of entry by new firms can play an important role in how competition in the industry unfolds. In some cases, the threat alone may be enough to make an industry with only a few firms behave like a perfectly competitive firm. Markets in which entry and exit are easy so that the threat of potential entry holds down prices to a competitive level are known as **contestable markets**.

Consider, for example, a small airline that can move its capital stock from one market to another with little cost. Cape Air flies between Boston, Martha's Vineyard, Nantucket, and Cape Cod during the summer months. During the winter, the same planes are used in Florida, where they fly up and down that state's west coast between Naples, Fort Meyers, Tampa, and other cities. A similar situation may occur when a new industrial complex is built at a fairly remote site and a number of trucking companies offer their services. Because the trucking companies' capital stock is mobile, they can move their trucks somewhere else at no great cost if business is not profitable. Existing firms in this market are continuously faced with the threat of competition. In contestable markets, even large oligopolistic firms end up behaving like perfectly competitive firms. Prices are pushed to long-run average cost by competition, and positive profits do not persist.

contestable markets Markets in which entry and exit are easy.

To the south of the competitor box, we see substitutes. For oligopolists—just like the monopolists described in the last chapter—the availability of substitute products outside the industry will limit the ability of firms to earn high profits.

ECONOMICS IN PRACTICE

Why Are Record Labels Losing Key Stars Like Madonna?

How can we use the Five Forces model to help us understand the competition record labels face? Notice first that the defectors from the labels—Madonna, Radiohead, and Nine Inch Nails—are well-known stars. For the record labels, these stars are suppliers. As these stars gain in popularity, they can drive harder bargains with the record labels. (This is one reason record labels sign artists to multiple record contracts, but no contract lasts forever.) While the supply of unknown singers is likely quite elastic, the supply of branded stars like Madonna is much more inelastic. Some people would argue that venues such as YouTube reduce the power of the record labels, even for young artists, by providing low-cost exposure. Here, YouTube serves as a *substitute* for the record labels from the perspective of the unknown artists. Buyers are also gaining power. With easy access to downloaded music, often pirated, listeners are willing to spend less on music and concerts play a bigger role in generating revenue for artists. Most observers think that the sum of these changes brought by new technology will be negative for record label profits.

Madonna (and the Internet) Disrupts Another Business

Wall Street Journal

Madonna has always had a keen eye for the latest trends and her new megadeal is no exception. But this time it's not due to the latest musical styles she's embracing. It's the fact that the Internet is disrupting traditional business models.

Rather than renewing her contract with her longtime record label Warner Bros., the Material Girl is signing a 10-year, $120-million deal with a concert-promotion company, the *Journal* reports. The promoter, Live Nation, probably won't make that back by selling the three albums worth of music Madonna's agreed to record for them. Instead, it intends to make a profit by selling everything from concert tickets to Madonna-brand perfumes to corporate sponsorships.

It's a textbook example of how the Internet is disrupting an industry. The record labels used to be the key players in the music industry. Getting music to fans meant negotiating a complex supply chain that included printing records and delivering them to stores. Looking at it this way, the record labels are more or less distribution companies. Yes, it's a simplified view, but it also makes it easier to see the broader implications, because most successful companies have had to master two skills: making stuff and distributing stuff.

The Internet is the world's most efficient distribution channel, which makes it a threat to any business whose business model relies on getting product to customers. In the case of the music industry, anyone can now distribute their music over the Internet for little or no cost. This, in turn, changes the value of recorded music. Madonna and bands like Radiohead and Nine Inch Nails realize that the best way to make money is to use their music as a way to promote their overall brands.

The music industry is just the most obvious example of the way the Internet is changing the way an industry distributes, values, and indeed defines its product. Newspapers—including the Business Technology Blog's employer—are going through their own version of this disruption right now. And it's just a matter of time before it impacts other industries.

Now take a look at the horizontal boxes in Figure 14.1. One of the themes in this book has been the way in which input and output markets are linked. Firms that sell in the product market also buy in the input market. Conditions faced by firms in their input markets are described in the left-hand box, suppliers. The circular flow diagram in Chapter 3 emphasizes this point. We see this same point in the Five Forces horizontal boxes. Airlines, which have some market power in the airline industry, face strong oligopolists when they try to buy or lease airplanes. In the airplane market, Boeing and Airbus control almost the entire market for commercial airplanes. In the market for leasing planes, GE has a dominant position. When a firm with market power faces another firm with market power in the input markets, interesting bargaining dynamics may result in terms of who ends up with the profits.

Finally, on the right side of the Five Forces diagram, we see the buyer or consumer—in some ways the most important part of the schema. Buyer preferences, which we studied as we looked at individual demand and utility functions—help to determine how successful a firm will be when it tries to differentiate its products. Some buyers can also exert bargaining power, even when faced with a relatively powerful seller. When people think of buyers, they usually think of the retail buyer of consumer goods. These buyers typically have little power. But many products in the U.S. economy are sold to other firms, and in many of these markets firms face highly concentrated buyers. Intel sells its processors to the relatively concentrated personal computer market, in which Dell has a large share. Proctor & Gamble (P&G) sells its consumer products to Wal-Mart, which currently controls 25 percent of the retail grocery market. Wal-Mart's power has enormous effects on how P&G can compete in its markets.

We have now identified a number of the key features of an oligopolistic industry. Understanding these features will help us predict the strategies firms will use to compete with their rivals for business. We turn now to some of the models of oligopolistic behavior.

Oligopoly Models

Because many different types of oligopolies exist, a number of different oligopoly models have been developed. The following provides a sample of the alternative approaches to the behavior (or conduct) of oligopolistic firms. As you will see, all kinds of oligopolies have one thing in common: The behavior of any given oligopolistic firm depends on the behavior of the other firms in the industry composing the oligopoly.

The Collusion Model

In Chapter 13, we examined what happens when a perfectly competitive industry falls under the control of a single profit-maximizing firm. We saw that when many competing firms act independently, they produce more, charge a lower price, and earn less profit than if they had acted as a single unit. If these firms get together and agree to cut production and increase price—that is, if firms can agree *not* to price compete—they will have a bigger total-profit pie to carve up. When a group of profit-maximizing oligopolists colludes on price and output, the result is the same as it would be if a monopolist controlled the entire industry. That is, the colluding oligopoly will face market demand and produce only up to the point at which marginal revenue and marginal cost are equal ($MR = MC$) and price will be set above marginal cost.

A group of firms that gets together and makes price and output decisions jointly is called a **cartel**. Perhaps the most familiar example of a cartel today is the Organization of Petroleum Exporting Countries (OPEC). The OPEC cartel consists of 13 countries, including Saudi Arabia and Kuwait, that agree on oil production levels. As early as 1970, the OPEC cartel began to cut petroleum production. Its decisions in this matter led to a 400 percent increase in the price of crude oil on world markets during 1973 and 1974.

cartel A group of firms that gets together and makes joint price and output decisions to maximize joint profits.

OPEC is a cartel of governments. Cartels consisting of firms, by contrast, are illegal under U.S. antitrust laws described in Chapter 13. Price fixing has been defined by courts as any agreement among individual competitors concerning prices. All agreements aimed at fixing prices or output levels, regardless of whether the resulting prices are high, are illegal. Moreover, price fixing is a criminal offense, and the penalty for being found guilty can involve jail time as well as fines. In the 1950s, a group of 12 executives from five different companies in the electrical equipment industry were found guilty of a price-fixing scheme to rotate winning bids among the firms. All were fined and sentenced to jail. In 2005, a former executive from Bayer AG, a major German pharmaceutical company, was sentenced to four months in jail and given a $50,000 fine for price fixing. In 2007, the U.S. government launched suits charging price fixing against a number of firms in industries ranging from car rentals to board game manufacturers. Despite the clear illegality of price fixing, the lure of profits seems to attract some executives to agree on prices.

For a cartel to work, a number of conditions must be present. First, demand for the cartel's product must be inelastic. If many substitutes are readily available, the cartel's price increases may become self-defeating as buyers switch to substitutes. Here we see the importance of understanding the substitutes box in Figure 14.1. Second, the members of the cartel must play by the rules. If a cartel is holding up prices by restricting output, there is a big incentive for members to cheat by increasing output. Breaking ranks can mean huge profits.

Incentives of the various members of a cartel to "cheat" on the cartel rather than cooperate highlights the role of the size distribution of firms in an industry. Consider an industry with one large firm and a group of small firms that has agreed to charge relatively high prices. For each firm, the price will be above its marginal cost of production. Gaining market share by selling more units is thus very appealing. On the other hand, if every firm drops prices to gain a market share, the cartel will collapse. For small players in an industry, the attraction of the added market share is often hard to resist, while the top firms in the industry have more to lose if the cartel collapses and have less added market share to gain. In most cartels, it is the small firms that begin pricing at below cartel prices.

Collusion occurs when price- and quantity-fixing agreements are explicit, as in a cartel. **Tacit collusion** occurs when firms end up fixing prices without a specific agreement or when such agreements are implicit. A small number of firms with market power may fall into the practice of setting similar prices or following the lead of one firm without ever meeting or setting down formal agreements. The fewer and more similar the firms, the easier it will be for tacit collusion to occur. As we will see later in this chapter, antitrust laws also play a role in trying to discourage tacit collusion.

tacit collusion   Collusion occurs when price- and quantity-fixing agreements among producers are explicit. *Tacit collusion* occurs when such agreements are implicit.

The Price-Leadership Model

In another form of oligopoly, one firm dominates an industry and all the smaller firms follow the leader's pricing policy—hence its name **price leadership**. If the dominant firm knows that the smaller firms will follow its lead, it will derive its own demand curve by subtracting from total market demand the amount of demand that the smaller firms will satisfy at each potential price.

The price-leadership model is best applied when the industry is made up of one large firm and a number of smaller competitive firms. Under these conditions, we can think of the dominant firm as maximizing profit subject to the constraint of market demand *and* subject to the behavior of the smaller competitive firms. Smaller firms then can essentially sell all they want at this market price. The difference between the quantity demanded in the market and the amount supplied by the smaller firms is the amount that the dominant firm will produce.

Under price leadership, the quantity demanded in the market will be produced by a mix of the smaller firms and the dominant firm. Contrast this situation with that of the monopolist. For a monopolist, the only constraint it faces comes from consumers, who at some price will forgo the good the monopolist produces. In an oligopoly, with a dominant firm practicing price leadership, the existence of the smaller firms (and their willingness to produce output) is also a constraint. For this reason, the output expected under price leadership lies between that of the monopolist and the competitive firm, with prices also set between the two price levels.

The fact that the smaller firms constrain the behavior of the dominant firm suggests that that firm might have an incentive to try to push those smaller firms out of the market by buying up or merging with the smaller firms. We have already seen in the monopoly chapter how moving from many firms to one firm can help a firm increase profits, even as it reduces social welfare. Antitrust rules governing mergers, discussed later in this chapter, reflect the potential social costs of such mergers. An alternative way for a dominant firm to reduce the number of smaller firms in its industry is through aggressive price setting. Rather than accommodate the small firms, as is done in the price-leadership situation, the dominant firm can try cutting prices aggressively until the smaller firms leave. The practice by which a large, powerful firm tries to drive smaller firms out of the market by temporarily selling at an artificially low price is called *predatory pricing*. Such behavior can be very expensive for the larger firm and is often ineffective. Changing prices below average variable costs to push other firms out of an industry in the expectation of later recouping through price increases is also illegal under antitrust laws.

price leadership   A form of oligopoly in which one dominant firm sets prices and all the smaller firms in the industry follow its pricing policy.

The Cournot Model

A very simple model that illustrates the idea of interdependence among firms in an oligopoly is the Cournot model, introduced in the 19th century by the mathematician Antoine Augustin Cournot. The model is based on Cournot's observations of competition between two producers of spring water. Despite the age of the model and some if its restrictive assumptions, the intuition that emerges from it has proven to be helpful to economists and policy makers.

The original Cournot model focused on an oligopoly with only two firms producing identical products and not colluding. A two-firm oligopoly is known as a **duopoly**. The key feature of an oligopoly, compared to the competitive firm, is that a firm's optimal decisions depend on the actions of the other individual firms in its industry. In a duopoly, the right output choice for each of the two firms will depend on what the other firm does. Cournot provides us with one way to model how firms take each other's behavior into account.

duopoly   A two-firm oligopoly.

Return to the monopoly example that we used in the previous chapter in Figure 13.8 on p. 281, reproduced here as Figure 14.2(a). Marginal cost is constant at $2, and the demand curve facing the monopolist firm is the downward-sloping market demand curve. Recall that the marginal revenue curve lies below the demand curve because in order to increase sales the monopoly firm must lower its per-unit price. In this example, the marginal revenue curve hits zero at an output of 3,000 units. In this market, the monopolist maximizes profits at a quantity of 2,000 units and a price of $4 as we saw in the last chapter. What happens in this market if, instead of having one monopoly firm, we have a Cournot duopoly? What does the duopoly equilibrium look like?

In choosing the optimal output, the monopolist had only to consider its own costs and the demand curve that it faced. The duopolist has another factor to consider: how much output will its rival produce? The more the rival produces, the less market is left for the other firm in the duopoly. In the Cournot model, each firm looks at the market demand, subtracts what it expects the rival firm to produce, and chooses its output to maximize its profits based on the market that is left.

Let's illustrate the Cournot duopoly solution to this problem with two firms, Firm A and Firm B. Recall the key feature of the duopoly: Firms must take each other's output into account when choosing their own output. Given this feature, it is helpful to look at how each firm's optimal output might vary with its rival's output. In Figure 14.2(b), we have drawn two *reaction functions*, showing each firm's optimal, profit-maximizing output as it depends on its rival's output. The Y-axis shows levels of Firm A's output, denoted q_A, and the X-axis shows Firm B's output, denoted as q_B.

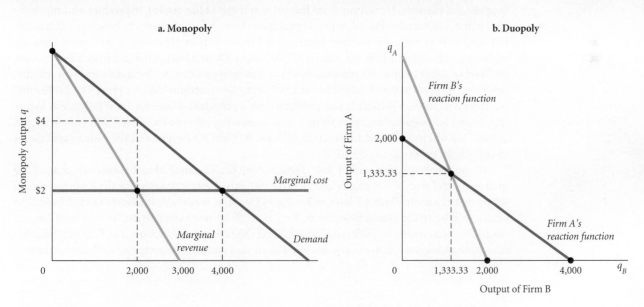

▲ **FIGURE 14.2 Graphical Depiction of the Cournot Model**
The left graph shows a profit-maximizing output of 2,000 units for a monopolist with marginal cost of $2. The right graph shows output of 1,333.33 units *each* for two duopolists with the same marginal cost of $2, facing the same demand curve. Total industry output increases as we go from the monopolist to the Cournot duopolists, but it does not rise as high as the competitive output (here 4,000 units).

Several of the points along Firm A's reaction function should look familiar. Consider the point where Firm A's reaction function crosses the vertical axis. At this point, Firm A's task is to choose the optimal output assuming Firm B produces 0. But we know what this point is from solving the monopoly problem. If Firm B produces nothing, then Firm A is a monopolist and it optimally produces 2,000 units. So *if* Firm A expects Firm B to produce 0, it should produce 2,000 to maximize its profits.

Look at the point at which Firm A's reaction function crosses the horizontal axis. At this point Firm B is producing 4,000 units. Look back at Figure 14.2(a). At an output level of 4,000 units the market price is $2, which is the marginal cost of production. If Firm A expects Firm B to produce 4,000 units, there is no profitable market left for Firm A and it will produce 0. If you start there, where the output of Firm B (measured on the horizontal axis) is 4,000 units each period, and you let Firm B's output fall moving to the left, Firm A will find it in its interest to increase output. If you carefully figure out what Firms A's profit-maximizing output is at every possible level of output for Firm B, you will discover that Firm A's reaction function is just a downward-sloping line between 2,000 on the *Y*-axis and 4,000 on the *X*-axis. The downward slope reflects the way in which firm A chooses its output. It looks at the market demand, subtracts its rival's output, and then chooses its own optimal output. The more the rival produces, the less market is profitably left for the other firm in the duopoly.

Next, we do the same thing for Firm B. How much will Firm B produce if it maximizes profit and accepts Firm A's output as given? Since the two firms are exactly alike in costs and type of product, Firm B's reaction function looks just like Firm A's: When Firm B thinks it is alone in the market (Firm A's output on the vertical axis is 0) it produces the monopoly output of 2,000; when Firm B thinks Firm A is going to produce 4,000 units, it chooses to produce 0.

As you can see, the two reaction functions cross. Each firm's reaction function shows what it wants to do, conditional on the other firm's output. At the point of intersection, each firm is doing the best it can, given the actual output of the other firm. This point is sometimes called the *best response equilibrium*. As you can see from the graph, the Cournot duopoly equilibrium to this problem occurs when each firm is producing 1,333.33 units for an industry total of 2,666.66. This output is more than the original monopolist produced in this market, but less than the 4,000 units that a competitive industry would produce.

It turns out that the crossing point is the only equilibrium point in Figure 14.2(b). To see why, consider what happens if you start off with a monopoly and then let a second firm compete. Suppose, for example, Firm A expected Firm B to stay out of the market, to produce nothing, leaving Firm A as a monopolist. With that expectation, Firm A would choose to produce 2,000 units. But now look at Firm B's reaction function. If Firm A is now producing 2,000 units, Firm B's profit-maximizing output is not zero, it is 1,000 units. Draw a horizontal line from Firm A's output level of 2,000 to Firm B's reaction function and then go down to the *X*-axis and you will discover that Firm B's optimal output lies at 1,000 units. So an output level for Firm A of 2,000 units is not an equilibrium because it was predicated on a production level for Firm B that was incorrect. Going one step further, with Firm B now producing 1,000 units, Firm A will cut back from 2,000. This will in turn lead to a further increase in Firm B's output and the process will go on until both are producing 1,333.33.

As we have seen, the output level predicted by the Cournot model is between that of the monopoly and that of a perfectly competitive industry. Later extensions of the Cournot model tell us that the more firms we have, behaving as Cournot predicted, the closer output (and thus prices) will be to the competitive levels. This type of intuitive result is one reason the Cournot model has been widely used despite its simplified view of firm interaction. The field of game theory, to which we now turn, offers a more sophisticated and complete view of firm interactions.

Game Theory

The firms in Cournot's model do not anticipate the moves of the competition. Instead, they try to guess the output levels of their rivals and then choose optimal outputs of their own. But notice, the firms do not try to anticipate or influence what the rival firms will do in response to their own actions. In many situations, it does not seem realistic for firms to just take their rival's output as independent of their own. We might think that Intel, recognizing how important Advanced Micro Devices (AMD) is in the processor market, would try to influence AMD's business decisions. **Game theory** is a subfield of economics that analyzes the choices made by rival firms, people, and even governments when they are trying to maximize their own well-being while anticipating and reacting to the actions of others in their environment.

Game theory began in 1944 with the work of mathematician John von Neumann and economist Oskar Morgenstern who published path-breaking work in which they analyzed a set of problems, or *games*, in which two or more people or organizations pursue their own interests and in which neither one of them can dictate the outcome. Game theory has become an increasingly popular field of study and research. The notions of game theory have been applied to analyses of firm behavior, politics, international relations, nuclear war, military strategy, and foreign policy. In 1994, the Nobel Prize in Economic Science was awarded jointly to three early game theorists: John F. Nash of Princeton University, John C. Harsanyi of the University of California at Berkeley, and Reinhard Selten of the University of Bonn. You may have seen the movie *A Beautiful Mind* about John Nash and his contribution to game theory.

Game theory begins by recognizing that in all conflict situations, there are decision makers (or players), rules of the game, and payoffs (or prizes). Players choose strategies without knowing with certainty what strategy the opposition will use. At the same time, though, some information that indicates how their opposition may be "leaning" may be available to the players. Most centrally, understanding that the other players are also trying to do their best will be helpful in predicting their actions.

Figure 14.3 illustrates what is called a payoff matrix for a simple game. Each of two firms, A and B, must decide whether to mount an expensive advertising campaign. If each firm decides not to advertise, it will earn a profit of $50,000. If one firm advertises and the other does not, the firm that does will increase its profit by 50 percent (to $75,000) while driving the competition into the loss column. If both firms decide to advertise, they will each earn profits of $10,000. They may generate a bit more demand by advertising, but not enough to offset the expense of the advertising.

If firms A and B could collude (and we assume that they cannot), their optimal strategy would be to agree not to advertise. That solution maximizes the joint profits to both firms. If both firms do not advertise, joint profits are $100,000. If both firms advertise, joint profits are only $20,000. If only one of the firms advertises, joint profits are $75,000 − $25,000 = $50,000.

We see from Figure 14.3 that each firm's *payoff* depends on what the other firm does. In considering what firms should do, however, it is more important to ask whether a firm's *strategy* depends on what the other firm does. Consider A's choice of strategy. Regardless of what B does, it pays A to advertise. If B does not advertise, A makes $25,000 more by advertising than by not advertising. Thus, A will advertise. If B does advertise, A must advertise to avoid a loss. The same logic holds for B. Regardless of the strategy pursued by A, it pays B to advertise. A **dominant strategy** is one that is best no matter what the opposition does. In this game, both players have a dominant strategy, which is to advertise.

game theory   Analyzes the choices made by rival firms, people, and even governments when they are trying to maximize their own well-being while anticipating and reacting to the actions of others in their environment.

dominant strategy   In game theory, a strategy that is best no matter what the opposition does.

◀ **FIGURE 14.3 Payoff Matrix for Advertising Game**

Both players have a dominant strategy. If B does not advertise, A will because $75,000 beats $50,000. If B does advertise, A will also advertise because a profit of $10,000 beats a loss of $25,000. A will advertise regardless of what B does. Similarly, B will advertise regardless of what A does. If A does not advertise, B will because $75,000 beats $50,000. If A does advertise, B will too because a $10,000 profit beats a loss of $25,000.

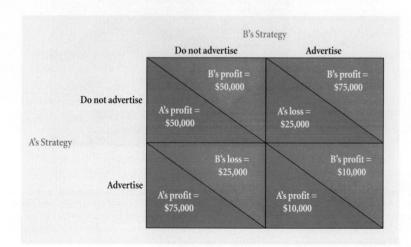

B's Strategy

	Do not advertise	Advertise
Do not advertise	B's profit = $50,000 / A's profit = $50,000	B's profit = $75,000 / A's loss = $25,000
Advertise	B's loss = $25,000 / A's profit = $75,000	B's profit = $10,000 / A's profit = $10,000

A's Strategy

prisoners' dilemma   A game in which the players are prevented from cooperating and in which each has a dominant strategy that leaves them both worse off than if they could cooperate.

The result of the game in Figure 14.4 is an example of what is called a **prisoners' dilemma**. The term comes from a game in which two prisoners (call them Ginger and Rocky) are accused of robbing the local 7-Eleven together, but the evidence is shaky. If both confess, they each get 5 years in prison for armed robbery. If each one refuses to confess, they are convicted of a lesser charge, shoplifting, and get 1 year in prison each. The problem is that the district attorney has offered each of them a deal independently. If Ginger confesses and Rocky does not, Ginger goes free and Rocky gets 7 years. If Rocky confesses and Ginger does not, Rocky goes free and Ginger gets 7 years. The payoff matrix for the prisoners' dilemma is given in Figure 14.4.

By looking carefully at the payoffs, you may notice that both Ginger and Rocky have dominant strategies: to confess. That is, Ginger is better off confessing regardless of what Rocky does and Rocky is better off confessing regardless of what Ginger does. The likely outcome is that both will confess even though they would be better off if they both kept their mouths shut. There are many cases in which we see games like this one. In a class that is graded on a curve, all students might consider agreeing to moderate their performance. But incentives to "cheat" by studying would be hard to resist. In an oligopoly, the fact that prices tend to be higher than marginal costs provides incentives for firms to "cheat" on output—restricting agreements by selling additional units.

Is there any way out of this dilemma? There may be, under circumstances in which the game is played over and over. Look back at Figure 14.3. The best joint outcome is not to advertise. But the power of the dominant strategy makes it hard to get to the top-left corner. Suppose firms interact over and over again for many years. Now opportunities for cooperating are richer. Suppose firm A decided not to advertise for one period to see how firm B would respond. If firm B continued to advertise, A would have to resume advertising to survive. Suppose B decided to match A's strategy. In this case, both firms might—with no explicit collusion—end up not advertising after A figures out what B is doing. We return to this in the discussion of repeated games, which follows.

There are many games in which one player does not have a dominant strategy, but in which the outcome is predictable. Consider the game in Figure 14.5(a) in which C does not have a dominant strategy. If D plays the left strategy, C will play the top strategy. If D plays the right strategy, C will play the bottom strategy. What strategy will D choose to play? If C knows the options, it will see that D has a dominant strategy and is likely to play that same strategy. D does better playing the right-hand strategy regardless of what C does. D can guarantee a $100 win by choosing right and is guaranteed to win nothing by playing left. Because D's behavior is predictable (it will play the right-hand strategy), C will play bottom. When all players are playing their best strategy *given* what their competitors are doing, the result is called a **Nash equilibrium**, named after John Nash. We have already seen one example of a Nash equilibrium in the Cournot model.

Nash equilibrium   In game theory, the result of all players' playing their best strategy given what their competitors are doing.

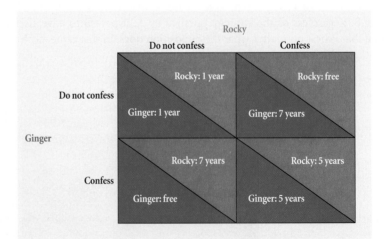

▲ **FIGURE 14.4** **The Prisoners' Dilemma**

Both players have a dominant strategy and will confess. If Rocky does *not* confess, Ginger will because going free beats a year in jail. Similarly, if Rocky *does* confess, Ginger will confess because 5 years in the slammer is better than 7. Rocky has the same set of choices. If Ginger does *not* confess, Rocky will because going free beats a year in jail. Similarly, if Ginger *does* confess, Rocky also will confess because 5 years in the slammer is better than 7. Both will confess *regardless* of what the other does.

a. Original Game

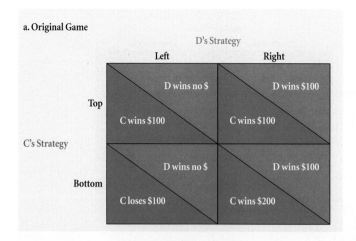

b. New Game

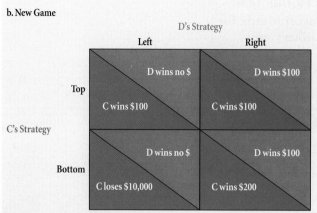

▲ **FIGURE 14.5 Payoff Matrixes for Left/Right–Top/Bottom Strategies**

In the original game (*a*), C does not have a dominant strategy. If D plays left, C plays top; if D plays right, C plays bottom. D, on the other hand, *does* have a dominant strategy: D will play right regardless of what C does. If C believes that D is rational, C will predict that D will play right. If C concludes that D will play right, C will play bottom. The result is a Nash equilibrium because each player is doing the best that it can *given* what the other is doing.

In the new game (*b*), C had better be very sure that D will play right because if D plays left and C plays bottom, C is in big trouble, losing $10,000. C will probably play top to minimize the potential loss if the probability of D's choosing left is at all significant.

Now suppose the game in Figure 14.5(a) were changed. Suppose all the payoffs are the same except that if D chooses left and C chooses bottom, C loses $10,000, as shown in Figure 14.5(b). While D still has a dominant strategy (playing right), C now stands to lose a great deal by choosing bottom on the off chance that D chooses left instead. When uncertainty and risk are introduced, the game changes. C is likely to play top and guarantee itself a $100 profit instead of playing bottom and risk losing $10,000 in the off chance that D plays left. A **maximin strategy** is a strategy chosen by a player to maximize the minimum gain that it can earn. In essence, one who plays a maximin strategy assumes that the opposition will play the strategy that does the most damage.

maximin strategy   In game theory, a strategy chosen to maximize the minimum gain that can be earned.

Repeated Games

Clearly, games are not played once. Firms must decide on advertising budgets, investment strategies, and pricing policies continuously. Pepsi and Coca-Cola have competed against each other for 100 years, in countries across the globe. While explicit collusion violates the antitrust statutes, strategic reaction does not. Yet strategic reaction in a repeated game may have the same effect as tacit collusion.

Consider the game in Figure 14.6. Suppose British Airways and Lufthansa were competing for business on the New York to London route during the off-season. To lure travelers, they were offering low fares. The question is how much to lower fares. Both airlines were considering a deep reduction to a fare of $400 round-trip or a moderate one to $600. Suppose costs are such that each $600 ticket produces profit of $400 and each $400 ticket produces profit of $200.

Clearly, demand is sensitive to price. Assume that studies of demand elasticity have determined that if *both* airlines offer tickets for $600, they will attract 6,000 passengers per week (3,000 for each airline) and each airline will make a profit of $1.2 million per week ($400 dollar profit times 3,000 passengers). However, if both airlines offer deeply reduced fares of $400, they will attract 2,000 additional customers per week for a total of 8,000 (4,000 for each airline). While they will have more passengers, each ticket brings in less profit and total profit falls to $800,000 per week ($200 profit times 4,000 passengers). In this example, we can make some inferences about demand elasticity. With a price cut from $600 to $400, revenues fall from $3.6 million (6,000 passengers times $600) to $3.2 million (8,000 passengers times $400). We know from Chapter 5 that if a price cut reduces revenue, we are operating on an *inelastic* portion of the demand curve.

▶ **FIGURE 14.6**

Payoff Matrix for Airline Game

In a single play, both British Airways (BA) and Lufthansa Airlines (LA) have dominant strategies. If LA prices at $600, BA will price at $400 because $1.6 million beats $1.2 million. If, on the other hand, LA prices at $400, BA will again choose to price at $400 because $800,000 beats zero. Similarly, LA will choose to price at $400 regardless of which strategy BA chooses.

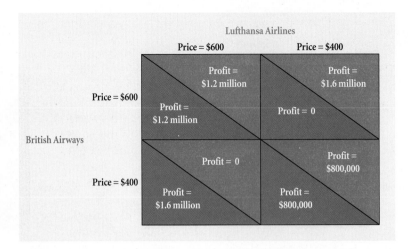

What if the two airlines offer different prices? To keep things simple, we will ignore brand loyalty and assume that whichever airline offers the lowest fare gets all of the 8,000 passengers. If British Airways offers the $400 fare, it will sell 8,000 tickets per week and make $200 profit each, for a total of $1.6 million. Since Lufthansa holds out for $600, it sells no tickets and makes no profit. Similarly, if Lufthansa were to offer tickets for $400, it would make $1.6 million per week while British Airways would make zero.

Looking carefully at the payoff matrix in Figure 14.6, do you conclude that either or both of the airlines have a dominant strategy? In fact, both do. If Lufthansa prices at $600, British Airways will price at the lower fare of $400, because $1.6 million per week is more than $1.2 million. On the other hand, if Lufthansa offers the deep price cut, British Airways must do so as well. If British Airways does not, it will earn nothing, and $800,000 beats nothing! Similarly, Lufthansa has a dominant strategy to offer the $400 fare because it makes more regardless of what British Airways does.

The result is that both airlines will offer the greatly reduced fare and each will make $800,000 per week. This is a classic prisoners' dilemma. If they were permitted to collude on price, they would both charge $600 per ticket and make $1.2 million per week instead—a 50 percent increase.

It was precisely this logic that led American Airlines President Robert Crandall to suggest to Howard Putnam of Braniff Airways in 1983, "I think this is dumb as hell...to sit here and pound the @#%* out of each other and neither one of us making a @#%* dime." ... "I have a suggestion for you, raise your @#%* fares 20 percent. I'll raise mine the next morning."

Since competing firms are prohibited from even talking about prices, Crandall got into trouble with the Justice Department when Putnam turned over a tape of the call in which these comments were made. But could they have colluded without talking to each other? Suppose prices are announced each week at a given time. It is like playing the game in Figure 14.6 a number of times in succession, a repeated game. After a few weeks of making $800,000, British Airways raises its price to $600. Lufthansa knows that if it sits on its $400 fare, it will double its profit from $800,000 to $1.6 million per week. But what is British Airways up to? It must know that its profit will drop to zero unless Lufthansa raises its fare too. The fare increase could just be a signal that both firms would be better off at the higher price and that if one leads and can count on the other to follow, they will both be better off. The strategy to respond in kind to a competitor is called a **tit-for-tat strategy**.

tit-for-tat strategy A repeated game strategy in which a player responds in kind to an opponent's play.

If Lufthansa figures out that British Airways will play the same strategy that Lufthansa is playing, both will end up charging $600 per ticket and earning $1.2 million instead of charging $400 and earning only $800,000 per week even though there has been no explicit price fixing.

A Game with Many Players: Collective Action Can Be Blocked by a Prisoner's Dilemma

Some games have many players and can result in the same kinds of prisoners' dilemmas as we have just discussed. The following game illustrates how coordinated collective action in everybody's interest can be blocked under some circumstances.

Suppose I am your professor in an economics class of 100 students. I ask you to bring $10 to class. In front of the room I place two boxes marked Box A and Box B. I tell you that you must put the sum of $10 split any way you would like in the two boxes. You can put all $10 in Box A and nothing in Box B. You can put all $10 in Box B and nothing in Box A. On the other hand, you can put $2.50 in Box A and $7.50 in Box B. Any combination totaling $10 is all right, and I am the only person who will ever know how you split up your money.

At the end of the class, every dollar put into Box A will be returned to the person who put it in. You get back exactly what you put in. But Box B is special. I will add 20 cents to Box B for every dollar put into it. That is, if there is $100 in the box, I will add $20. But here is the wrinkle: The money that ends up in Box B, *including* my 20 percent contribution, will be divided equally among everyone in the class regardless of the amount that an individual student puts in.

You can think of Box A as representing a private market where we get what we pay for. We pay $10, and we get $10 in value back. Think of Box B as representing something we want to do collectively where the benefits go to all members of the class regardless of whether they have contributed. In Chapter 12, we discussed the concept of a *public good*. People cannot be excluded from enjoying the benefits of a public good once it is produced. Examples include clean air, a lower crime rate from law enforcement, and national defense. You can think of Box B as representing a public good.

Now where do you put your money? If you were smart, you would call a class meeting and get everyone to agree to put his or her entire $10 in Box B. Then everybody would walk out with $12. There would be $1,000 in the box, I would add $200, and the total of $1,200 would be split evenly among the 100 students.

But suppose you were not allowed to get together, in the same way that Ginger and Rocky were kept in separate cells in the jailhouse? Further suppose that everyone acts in his or her best interest. Everyone plays a strategy that maximizes the amount that he or she walks out with. If you think carefully, the dominant strategy for each class member is to put all $10 in Box A. *Regardless of what anyone else does*, you get more if you put all your money into Box A than you would get from any other split of the $10. And if you put all your money into A, no one will walk out of the room with more money than you will!

How can this be? It is simple. Suppose everyone else puts the $10 in B but you put your $10 in A. Box B ends up with $990 plus a 20 percent bonus from me of $198, for a grand total of $1,188, just $12 short of the maximum possible of $1,200. What do you get? Your share of Box B—which is $11.88, *plus* your $10 back, for a total of $21.88. Pretty slimy but clearly optimal for you. If you had put all your money into B, you would get back only $12. You can do the same analysis for cases in which the others split up their income in any way, and the optimal strategy is still to put the whole $10 in Box A.

Here is another way to think about it is: What part of what you ultimately get out is linked to or dependent upon what you put in? For every dollar you put in A, you get a dollar back. For every dollar *you yourself* put in B, you get back only 1 cent, one one-hundredth of a dollar, because your dollar gets split up among all 100 members of the class.

Thus, the game is a classic prisoners' dilemma, where collusion if it could be enforced would result in an optimal outcome but where dominant strategies result in a suboptimal outcome.

How do we break this particular dilemma? We call a town meeting (class meeting) and pass a law that requires us to contribute to the production of public goods by paying taxes. Then, of course, we run the risk that government becomes a player. We will return to this theme in Chapters 16 and 18.

To summarize, oligopoly is a market structure that is consistent with a variety of behaviors. The only necessary condition of oligopoly is that firms are large enough to have some control over price. Oligopolies are concentrated industries. At one extreme is the cartel, in which a few firms get together and jointly maximize profits—in essence, acting as a monopolist. At the other extreme, the firms within the oligopoly vigorously compete for small, contestable markets by moving capital quickly in response to observed profits. In between are a number of alternative models, all of which emphasize the interdependence of oligopolistic firms.

ECONOMICS IN PRACTICE

Price Fixing in Digital Music

In 2010 the Second Circuit Court of Appeals decided to reinstate a case from several years ago alleging that the major music labels had colluded to keep the prices of digital downloads higher than they otherwise would be. Earlier cases had found no direct evidence of any price conspiracy. In contrast to some price fixing cases, there was no trail of secret meetings or phone calls, no "smoking gun" as the lawyers often say. Instead, as the following article makes clear, the court relied on economic evidence: the failure of the major record labels to markedly reduce music prices despite the drastic reductions in costs associated with moving from compact discs to digital music.

RIAA Digital Music Price-Fixing Case Reinstated

ZeroPaid.com

It's been an open secret that record labels have long colluded with one another to ensure maximum profits with limited competition and consumer choice. A group of plaintiffs has taken the RIAA to court over the matter, and after initially having to watch the case dismissed at the District Court level back in 2008, has now convinced a three-judge panel at the Second Circuit Court of Appeals to reinstate the case.

One of the major points of evidence of collusion is that the price of digital music is still too similar to physical CDs despite the obviously drastic reduction in price associated with distributing it, something file-sharers have argued all along.

The judges note:

Moreover, the pricing of CDs accounted for costs such as copying the compact discs; producing the CD case, labels and anti-shoplifting packaging; shipping, both to the distributor and then to record stores; labor, such as shelving CDs and staffing cash registers; and damaged and unsold inventory. All of these costs were eliminated with Internet Music. However, these dramatic cost reductions were not accompanied by dramatic price reductions for Internet Music, as would be expected in a competitive market.

In other words, an album that once fetched $15 on store shelves should now cost much less being that the label has much fewer costs to recoup.

Source: Reprinted with permission from Zeropaid, Inc.

Oligopoly and Economic Performance

How well do oligopolies perform? Should they be regulated or changed? Are they efficient, or do they lead to an inefficient use of resources? On balance, are they good or bad?

With the exception of the contestable-markets model, all the models of oligopoly we have examined lead us to conclude that concentration in a market leads to pricing above marginal cost and output below the efficient level. When price is above marginal cost at equilibrium, consumers are paying more for the good than it costs to produce that good in terms of products forgone in other industries. To increase output would be to create value that exceeds the social cost of the good, but profit-maximizing oligopolists have an incentive not to increase output.

Entry barriers in many oligopolistic industries also prevent new capital and other resources from responding to profit signals. Under competitive conditions or in contestable markets, positive profits would attract new firms and thus increase production. This does not happen in most oligopolistic industries. The problem is most severe when entry barriers exist and firms explicitly or tacitly collude. The results of collusion are identical to the results of a monopoly. Firms jointly maximize profits by fixing prices at a high level and splitting up the profits.

On the other hand, it is useful to ask why oligopolies exist in an industry in the first place and what benefits larger firms might bring to a market. When there are economies of scale, larger and fewer firms bring cost efficiencies even as they reduce price competition.

Vigorous product competition among oligopolistic competitors may produce variety and lead to innovation in response to the wide variety of consumer tastes and preferences. The connection between market structure and the rate of innovation is the subject of some debate in research literature.

Industrial Concentration and Technological Change

One of the major sources of economic growth and progress throughout history has been technological advance. Innovation, both in methods of production and in the creation of new and better products, is one of the engines of economic progress. Much innovation starts with R&D efforts undertaken by firms in search of profit.

Several economists, notably Joseph Schumpeter and John Kenneth Galbraith, argued in works now considered classics that industrial concentration, where a relatively small number of firms control the marketplace, actually increases the rate of technological advance. As Schumpeter put it in 1942:

> As soon as we...inquire into the individual items in which progress was most conspicuous, the trail leads not to the doors of those firms that work under conditions of comparatively free competition but precisely to the doors of the large concerns ...and a shocking suspicion dawns upon us that big business may have had more to do with creating that standard of life than keeping it down.[1]

This interpretation caused the economics profession to pause and take stock of its theories. The conventional wisdom had been that concentration and barriers to entry insulate firms from competition and lead to sluggish performance and slow growth.

The evidence concerning where innovation comes from is mixed. Certainly, most small businesses do not engage in R&D and most large firms do. When R&D expenditures are considered as a percentage of sales, firms in industries with high concentration ratios spend more on R&D than firms in industries with low concentration ratios.

Many oligopolistic companies do considerable research. In the opening segment of this chapter, we noted three firms dominated the medical devices market—Johnson & Johnson, Boston Scientific, and Medtronic. Each of these firms spends more than 10 percent of its revenues on R&D. Johnson & Johnson alone spent $8 billion on R&D in 2007. Microsoft spends a similar amount.

However, the "high-tech revolution" grew out of many tiny start-up operations. Companies such as Sun Microsystems, Cisco Systems, and even Microsoft barely existed only a generation ago. The new biotechnology firms that are just beginning to work miracles with genetic engineering are still tiny operations that started with research done by individual scientists in university laboratories.

Significant ambiguity on this subject remains. Indeed, there may be no right answer. Technological change seems to come in fits and starts, sometimes from small firms and sometimes from large ones.

The Role of Government

As we suggested earlier, one way that oligopolies increase the market concentration is through mergers. Not surprisingly, the government has passed laws to control the growth of market power through mergers.

---

[1] J. A. Schumpeter, *Capitalism, Socialism, and Democracy* (New York: Harper, 1942); and J. K. Galbraith, *American Capitalism* (Boston: Houghton Mifflin, 1952).

Regulation of Mergers

The Clayton Act of 1914 (as mentioned in Chapter 13) had given government the authority to limit mergers that might "substantially lessen competition in an industry." The **Celler-Kefauver Act** (1950) enabled the Justice Department to monitor and enforce these provisions. In the early years of the Clayton Act, firms that wanted to merge knew there was a risk of government opposition. Firms could spend large amounts of money on lawyers and negotiation. Firms could spend resources on negotiations only to have the government take the firms to court.

In 1968, the Justice Department issued its first guidelines designed to reduce uncertainty about the mergers it would find acceptable. The 1968 guidelines were strict. For example, if the largest four firms in an industry controlled 75 percent or more of a market, an acquiring firm with a 15 percent market share would be challenged if it wanted to acquire a firm that controlled as little as an additional 1 percent of the market.

In 1982, the Antitrust Division—in keeping with President Reagan's hands-off policy toward big business—issued a new set of guidelines. Revised in 1984, they remain in place today. The standards are based on a measure of market structure called the **Herfindahl-Hirschman Index (HHI)**. The HHI is calculated by expressing the market share of each firm in the industry as a percentage, squaring these figures, and summing. For example, in an industry in which two firms each control 50 percent of the market, the index is

$$50^2 + 50^2 = 2,500 + 2,500 = 5,000$$

For an industry in which four firms each control 25 percent of the market, the index is

$$25^2 + 25^2 + 25^2 + 25^2 = 625 + 625 + 625 + 625 = 2,500$$

Table 14.2 shows HHI calculations for several hypothetical industries. The Justice Department's courses of action, summarized in Figure 14.7, are as follows: If the Herfindahl-Hirschman Index is less than 1,000, the industry is considered unconcentrated and any proposed merger will go unchallenged by the Justice Department. If the index is between 1,000 and 1,800, the department will challenge any

TABLE 14.2	Calculation of a Simple Herfindahl-Hirschman Index for Four Hypothetical Industries, Each with No More Than Four Firms				
	Percentage Share of:				Herfindahl Hirschman Index
	Firm 1	Firm 2	Firm 3	Firm 4	
Industry A	50	50	–	–	$50^2 + 50^2 = 5,000$
Industry B	80	10	10	–	$80^2 + 10^2 + 10^2 = 6,600$
Industry C	25	25	25	25	$25^2 + 25^2 + 25^2 + 25^2 = 2,500$
Industry D	40	20	20	20	$40^2 + 20^2 + 20^2 + 20^2 = 2,800$

▶ **FIGURE 14.7**
Department of Justice Merger Guidelines (revised 1984)

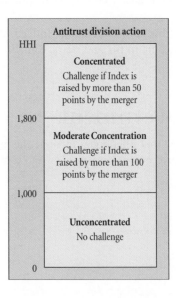

merger that would increase the index by over 100 points. Herfindahl indexes above 1,800 mean that the industry is considered concentrated already, and the Justice Department will challenge any merger that pushes the index up more than 50 points.

You should be able to see that the HHI combines two features of an industry that we identified as important in our Five Forces discussion: the number of firms in an industry and their relative sizes.

In the previous arithmetic example, we looked at the share of the market controlled by each of several firms. Before we can make these calculations, however, we have to answer another question: How do we define the market? What are we taking a share of? Think back to our discussion of market power in Chapter 13. Coca-Cola has a "monopoly" in the production of Coke but is one of several firms making cola products, one of many more firms making soda in general, and one of hundreds of firms making beverages. Coca-Cola's market power depends on how much substitutability there is among cola products, among sodas in general, and among beverages in general. Before the government can calculate an HHI, it must *define the market*, a task that involves figuring out which products are good substitutes for the products in question.

An interesting example of the difficulty in defining markets and the use of the HHI in merger analysis comes from the 1997 opposition by the FTC to the proposed merger between Staples and Office Depot. At that time, Office Depot and Staples were the number one and number two firms, respectively, in terms of market share in dedicated sales of office supplies. The FTC argued that in sales of office supplies, office superstores such as Office Depot and Staples had a strong advantage in the mind of the consumer. As a result of the one-stop shopping that they offered, it was argued that other stores selling stationery were not good substitutes for the sales of these two stores. So the FTC defined the market over which it intended to calculate the HHI to decide on the merger as the sale of office supplies in office superstores. Practically, this meant that stationery sold in the corner shop or in Wal-Mart was not part of the market, not a substantial constraint on the pricing of Office Depot or Staples. Using this definition, depending on where in the United States one looked, the HHI resulting from the proposed merger was between 5,000 and 10,000, clearly above the threshold. Economists working for Staples, on the other hand, argued that the market should include all sellers of office supplies. By that definition, a merger between Office Depot and Staples would result in a HHI well below the threshold since these two firms together controlled only 5 percent of the total market and the HHI in the overall market was well below 1,000. In the end, the merger was not allowed.

In Table 14.3, we present HHIs for a few different markets. Notice in one case—Las Vegas gaming—that the market has both a product and a geographic component. This definition, which was used by the government in one merger case, assumes that casinos in Las Vegas do not effectively compete with casinos in Atlantic City, for example. Other markets (for example, beer) are national markets. In general, the broader the definition of the market, the lower the HHI.

TABLE 14.3

Industry Definition	Some Sample HHIs
Beer	3,525
Ethanol	326
Las Vegas gaming	1,497
Critical care patient monitors	2,661

In 1997, the Department of Justice and the FTC issued joint *Horizontal Merger Guidelines*, updating and expanding the 1984 guidelines. The most interesting part of the new provisions is that the government examines each potential merger to determine whether it enhances the firms' power to engage in "coordinated interaction" with other firms in the industry. The guidelines define "coordinated interaction" as

> actions by a group of firms that are profitable for each of them only as the result of the accommodating reactions of others. This behavior includes tacit or express collusion, and may or may not be lawful in and of itself. [2]

---

[2] U.S. Department of Justice, Federal Trade Commission, *Horizontal Merger Guidelines*, 2005.

A Proper Role?

Certainly, there is much to guard against in the behavior of large, concentrated industries. Barriers to entry, large size, and product differentiation all lead to market power and to potential inefficiency. Barriers to entry and collusive behavior stop the market from working toward an efficient allocation of resources.

For several reasons, however, economists no longer attack industry concentration with the same fervor they once did. First, even firms in highly concentrated industries can be pushed to produce efficiently under certain market circumstances. Second, the benefits of product differentiation and product competition are real. After all, a constant stream of new products and new variations of old products comes to the market almost daily. Third, the effects of concentration on the rate of R&D spending are, at worst, mixed. It is true that large firms do a substantial amount of the total research in the United States. Finally, in some industries, substantial economies of scale simply preclude a completely competitive structure.

In addition to the debate over the desirability of industrial concentration, there is a never-ending debate concerning the role of government in regulating markets. One view is that high levels of concentration lead to inefficiency and that government should act to improve the allocation of resources—to help the market work more efficiently. This logic has been used to justify the laws and other regulations aimed at moderating noncompetitive behavior.

An opposing view holds that the clearest examples of effective barriers to entry are those created by government. This view holds that government regulation in past years has been ultimately anticompetitive and has made the allocation of resources less efficient than it would have been with no government involvement. Recall from Chapter 13 that those who earn positive profits have an incentive to spend resources to protect themselves and their profits from competitors. This *rent-seeking* behavior may include using the power of government.

Complicating the debate further is international competition. Increasingly, firms are faced with competition from foreign firms in domestic markets at the same time they are competing with other multinational firms for a share of foreign markets. We live in a truly global economy today. Thus, firms that dominate a domestic market may be fierce competitors in the international arena. This has implications for the proper role of government. Some contend that instead of breaking up AT&T, the government should have allowed it to be a bigger, stronger international competitor. We will return to this debate in a later chapter.

SUMMARY

MARKET STRUCTURE IN AN OLIGOPOLY *p. 294*

1. An *oligopoly* is an industry dominated by a few firms that, by virtue of their individual sizes, are large enough to influence market price. The behavior of a single oligopolistic firm depends on the reactions it expects of all the other firms in the industry. Industrial strategies usually are very complicated and difficult to generalize about.

2. The Five Forces model is a helpful way to organize economic knowledge about the structure of oligopolistic industries. By gathering data on an industry's structure in terms of the existing rivals, new entrants, substitutes, and buyer and supplier characteristics, we can better understand the sources of excess profits in an industry.

OLIGOPOLY MODELS *p. 297*

3. When firms collude, either explicitly or tacitly, they jointly maximize profits by charging an agreed-to price or by setting output limits and splitting profits. The result is the same as it would be if one firm monopolized the industry: The firm will produce up to the point at which $MR = MC$, and price will be set above marginal cost.

4. The *price-leadership* model of oligopoly leads to a result similar but not identical to the collusion model. In this organization, the dominant firm in the industry sets a price and allows competing firms to supply all they want at that price. An oligopoly with a dominant price leader will produce a level of output between what would prevail under competition and what a monopolist would choose in the same industry. An oligopoly will also set a price between the monopoly price and the competitive price.

5. The *Cournot model* of oligopoly is based on three assumptions: (1) that there are few firms in an industry, (2) that each firm takes the output of the other as a given, and (3) that firms maximize profits. The model holds that a series of output-adjustment decisions leads to a final level of output between that which would prevail under perfect competition and that which would be set by a monopoly.

GAME THEORY *p. 300*

6. *Game theory* analyzes the behavior of firms as if their behavior were a series of strategic moves and counter-moves. It helps us understand the problem of oligopoly

but leaves us with an incomplete and inconclusive set of propositions about the likely behavior of individual oligopolistic firms.

OLIGOPOLY AND ECONOMIC PERFORMANCE *p. 306*

7. Concentration in markets often leads to price above marginal cost and output below the efficient level. Market concentration, however, can also lead to gains from economies of scale and may promote innovation.

THE ROLE OF GOVERNMENT *p. 307*

8. The *Clayton Act* of 1914 (see Chapter 13) gave the government the authority to limit mergers that might "substantially lessen competition in an industry." The *Celler-Kefauver Act* (1950) enabled the Justice Department to move against a proposed merger. Currently, the Justice Department uses the *Herfindahl-Hirschman Index* to determine whether it will challenge a proposed merger.

9. Some argue that the regulation of mergers is no longer a proper role for government.

--- **REVIEW TERMS AND CONCEPTS** ---

--- **PROBLEMS** ---

All problems are available on www.myeconlab.com

1. Which of the following industries would you classify as an oligopoly? Which would you classify as monopolistically competitive? Explain your answer. If you are not sure, what information do you need to know to decide?
   a. Athletic shoes
   b. Restaurants
   c. Watches
   d. Aircraft
   e. Ice cream

2. [Related to the *Economics in Practice* on p. 296] In the last decade, many movie theaters have closed and others have seen a fall in yearly revenues. Use the Five Forces apparatus to analyze why this might have occurred.

3. Which of the following markets are likely to be perfectly contestable? Explain your answers.
   a. Shipbuilding
   b. Trucking
   c. Housecleaning services
   d. Wine production

4. Assume that you are in the business of building houses. You have analyzed the market carefully, and you know that at a price of $120,000, you will sell 800 houses per year. In addition, you know that at any price above $120,000, no one will buy your houses because the government provides equal-quality houses to anyone who wants one at $120,000. You also know that for every $20,000 you lower your price, you will be able to sell an additional 200 units. For example, at a price of $100,000, you can sell 1,000 houses; at a price of $80,000, you can sell 1,200 houses; and so on.
   a. Sketch the demand curve that your firm faces.

   b. Sketch the effective marginal revenue curve that your firm faces.
   c. If the marginal cost of building a house is $100,000, how many will you build and what price will you charge? What if *MC* = $85,000?

5. The matrix in Figure 1 on the following page shows payoffs based on the strategies chosen by two firms. If they collude and hold prices at $10, each firm will earn profits of $5 million. If A cheats on the agreement, lowering its price, but B does not, A will get 75 percent of the business and earn profits of $8 million and B will lose $2 million. Similarly, if B cheats and A does not, B will earn $8 million and A will lose $2 million. If both firms cut prices, they will end up with $2 million each in profits.

   Which strategy minimizes the maximum potential loss for A and for B? If you were A, which strategy would you choose? Why? If A cheats, what will B do? If B cheats, will A do? What is the most likely outcome of such a game? Explain.

6. The payoff matrixes in Figure 2 on the following page show the payoffs for two games. The payoffs are given in parentheses. The figure on the left refers to the payoff to A; the figure on the right refers to the payoff to B. Hence, (2, 25) means a $2 payoff to A and a $25 payoff to B.
   a. Is there a dominant strategy in each game for each player?
   b. If game 1 were repeated a large number of times and you were A and you could change your strategy, what might you do?
   c. Which strategy would you play in game 2? Why?

7. Between 2008 and 2010, dozens of lawsuits were brought or reinstated against U.S. firms for conspiracy to fix prices of things as diverse as pharmaceuticals, baby products, digital music, and eggs. Choose one of these lawsuits or cases and

describe the economic and legal issues. What are the details of the case? What law was allegedly violated? How was the case settled? Was justice done? Explain your answer.

8. Suppose we have an industry with two firms producing the same product. Firm A produces 90 units, while firm B produces 10 units. The price in the market is $100, and both firms have marginal costs of production of $50. What incentives do the two firms have to lower prices as a way of trying to get consumers to switch the firm they buy from? Which firm is more likely to lower its price?

9. For each of the following, state whether you agree or disagree. Explain your reasoning.
   a. Oligopolies are always bad for society.
   b. The beer industry has a few large firms and many small firms. Therefore, we would not call it an oligopoly.

10. The following table represents the market share percentage for each firm in a hypothetical industry.

Firm	A	B	C	D	E	F	G
Market Share	12	8	20	25	4	25	6

   a. Calculate the four-firm concentration ratio for this industry.
   b. Calculate the Herfindahl-Hirschman Index (HHI) for this industry.
   c. Would the Justice Department consider this industry as unconcentrated, moderately concentrated, or concentrated? Why?

   d. Suppose firms *E* and *G* wanted to merge. What would be the value of the HHI following this merger? Would the Justice Department most likely challenge this merger? Why or why not?

11. Bernie and Leona were arrested for money laundering and were interrogated separately by the police. Bernie and Leona were each presented with the following independent offers. If one confesses and the other doesn't, the one who confesses will go free and the other will receive a 20-year prison sentence; if both confess, each will receive a 10-year prison sentence. Bernie and Leona both know that without any confessions, the police only have enough evidence to convict them of the lesser crime of tax evasion, and each would then receive a 2-year prison sentence.
   a. Use the above information to construct a payoff matrix for Bernie and Leona.
   b. What is the dominant strategy for Bernie and for Leona? Why?
   c. Based on your response to the previous question, what prison sentence will each receive?

12. Explain whether you agree or disagree with the following statement. If all firms in an industry successfully engage in collusion, the resulting profit-maximizing price and output would be the same as if the industry was a monopoly.

13. What is the *Cournot* model? How does the output decision in the *Cournot* model differ from the output decision in a monopoly?

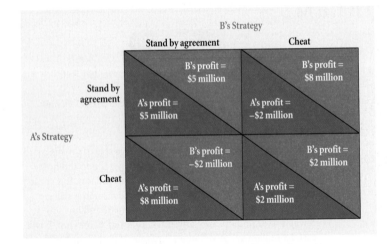

▲ **FIGURE 1**

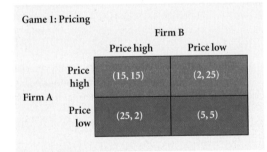

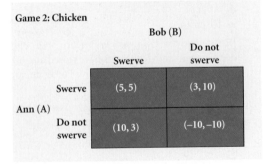

▲ **FIGURE 2**

International Trade, Comparative Advantage, and Protectionism

20

Over the last 40 years, international transactions have become increasingly important to the U.S. economy. In 1970, imports represented only about 7 percent of U.S. gross domestic product (GDP). The share is now around 15 percent. In 2010, the United States imported about $180 billion worth of goods and services each month. The increased trade we observe in the United States is mirrored throughout the world. From 1980 to 2009, world trade in real terms grew more than sixfold. This trend has been especially rapid in the newly industrialized Asian economies, but many developing countries such as Malaysia and Vietnam have been increasing their openness to trade.

The "internationalization" or "globalization" of the U.S. economy has occurred in the private and public sectors, in input and output markets, and in firms and households. Once uncommon, foreign products are now everywhere, from the utensils we eat with to the cars we drive. Chinese textiles and Indian software are commonplace. It might surprise you to learn that many of the cut flowers sold in the United States are grown in Africa and South America. In fact, most products today are made in a number of countries. Back in Chapter 1, we presented an *Economics in Practice* that described the production of Apple's iPod. An iPod contains 451 parts made in countries scattered around the world including Korea, Japan, China, and the United States. The bottom of the iPod has the following information: "Assembled in China; Designed in California." Suzuki makes cars in Hungary and employs workers from Romania and Slovakia. Honda started producing Japanese motorcycles in Ohio in 1977 with 64 employees in Marysville. The company now employs over 12,000 workers who assemble Honda automobiles. Bose is based in the United States but has its electronic components assembled in Mexico.

At the same time, the United States exports billions of dollars' worth of agricultural goods, aircraft, and industrial machinery. Korea imports substantial amounts of U.S. beef. In addition, the United States exports and imports large quantities of services. When a Pakistani student enrolls in an American college or university, or a sick woman from Chile seeks medical attention in a U.S. hospital, or a Kenyan hires a lawyer in Miami to help him with a real estate deal, or a

TABLE 20.1
U.S. Balance of Trade (Exports Minus Imports), 1929–2009 (Billions of Dollars)

	Exports Minus Imports
1929	+0.4
1933	+0.1
1945	−0.8
1955	+0.5
1960	+4.2
1965	+5.6
1970	+4.0
1975	+16.0
1976	−1.6
1977	−23.1
1978	−25.4
1979	−22.5
1980	−13.1
1981	−12.5
1982	−20.0
1983	−51.7
1984	−102.7
1985	−115.2
1986	−132.5
1987	−145.0
1988	−110.1
1989	−87.9
1990	−77.6
1991	−27.0
1992	−32.8
1993	−64.4
1994	−92.7
1995	−90.7
1996	−96.3
1997	−101.4
1998	−161.8
1999	−262.1
2000	−382.1
2001	−371.0
2002	−427.2
2003	−504.1
2004	−618.7
2005	−722.7
2006	−769.3
2007	−713.8
2008	−707.8
2009	−392.4

Source: U.S. Department of Commerce, Bureau of Economic Analysis.

trade surplus The situation when a country exports more than it imports.

trade deficit The situation when a country imports more than it exports.

tourist from Indonesia eats at a restaurant in New York City, the United States is exporting a service. Similarly, when a student from the United States takes her junior year abroad in Scotland, or a tourist stays in a hotel in Singapore or gets a massage at a spa in Jamaica, the United States is importing a service.

Nor are the patterns of trade that we observe in one period set in stone. Consider the case of textiles and apparel. As recently as 2000, Mexico was the major supplier to the United States of textiles and apparel with almost 15 percent of total U.S. imports in this category. By 2006, China had overtaken Mexico's lead with 29 percent of the share of U.S. textile and apparel imports. The Dominican Republic and Honduras, which had been the fourth and fifth largest sources of U.S. imports, respectively, had been replaced by Bangladesh and Indonesia. In 2004, for the first time, India became one of the top five exporters to the United States in this category.

In addition to the fact that goods and services (outputs) flow easily across borders, so too do inputs: capital and labor. Certainly, it is very easy to buy financial assets abroad. Millions of Americans own shares in foreign stocks or have invested in bonds issued by foreign countries. At the same time, millions of foreigners have put money into the U.S. stock and bond markets.

A new phenomenon, outsourcing, is also changing the nature of the global labor market. It is now simple and very common for a customer service call to a software company from a user of its product in Bend, Oregon, to be routed to Bangalore, India, where a young, ambitious Indian man or woman provides assistance to a customer over the Internet. The Internet has in essence made it possible for labor to flow smoothly across international borders.

The inextricable connection of the U.S. economy to the economies of the rest of the world has had a profound impact on the discipline of economics and is the basis of one of its most important insights: All economies, regardless of their size, depend to some extent on other economies and are affected by events outside their borders.

To get you more acquainted with the international economy, this chapter discusses the economics of international trade. First, we describe the recent tendency of the United States to import more than it exports. Next, we explore the basic logic of trade. Why should the United States or any other country engage in international trade? Finally, we address the controversial issue of protectionism. Should a country provide certain industries with protection in the form of import quotas or tariffs, which are taxes imposed on imports? Should a country help a domestic industry compete in international markets by providing subsidies?

Trade Surpluses and Deficits

Until the 1970s, the United States generally exported more than it imported. When a country exports more than it imports, it runs a **trade surplus**. When a country imports more than it exports, it runs a **trade deficit**. Table 20.1 shows that before 1976 the United States generally ran a trade surplus. This changed in 1976, and since 1976 the United States has run a trade deficit. The deficit reached a local peak of $145.0 billion in 1987, fell to $27.0 billion in 1991, and then rose dramatically to over $700 billion by 2005. By 2009, the trade deficit had fallen to just under $400 billion, as U.S. imports declined more than U.S. exports during the recession.

The large trade deficits in the middle and late 1980s sparked political controversy that continues today. Foreign competition hit U.S. markets hard. Less expensive foreign goods—among them steel, textiles, and automobiles—began driving U.S. manufacturers out of business, and thousands of jobs were lost in important industries. Cities such as Pittsburgh, Youngstown, and Detroit had major unemployment problems. In more recent times, the outsourcing of software development to India has caused complaints from white-collar workers.

The natural reaction to trade-related job dislocation is to call for protection of U.S. industries. Many people want the president and Congress to impose taxes and import restrictions that would make foreign goods less available and more expensive, protecting U.S. jobs. This argument is not new. For hundreds of years, industries have petitioned governments for protection and societies have debated the pros and cons of free and open trade. For the last century and a half, the principal argument against protection has been the theory of comparative advantage, first discussed in Chapter 2.

The Economic Basis for Trade: Comparative Advantage

Perhaps the best-known debate on the issue of free trade took place in the British Parliament during the early years of the nineteenth century. At that time, the landed gentry—the landowners—controlled Parliament. For a number of years, imports and exports of grain had been subject to a set of tariffs, subsidies, and restrictions collectively called the **Corn Laws**. Designed to discourage imports of grain and to encourage exports, the Corn Laws' purpose was to keep the price of food high. The landlords' incomes, of course, depended on the prices they got for what their land produced. The Corn Laws clearly worked to the advantage of those in power.

With the Industrial Revolution, a class of wealthy industrial capitalists emerged. The industrial sector had to pay workers at least enough to live on, and a living wage depended greatly on the price of food. Tariffs on grain imports and export subsidies that kept grain and food prices high increased the wages that capitalists had to pay, cutting into their profits. The political battle raged for years. However, as time went by, the power of the landowners in the House of Lords was significantly reduced. When the conflict ended in 1848, the Corn Laws were repealed.

On the side of repeal was David Ricardo, a businessman, economist, member of Parliament, and one of the fathers of modern economics. Ricardo's principal work, *Principles of Political Economy and Taxation*, was published in 1817, two years before he entered Parliament. Ricardo's **theory of comparative advantage**, which he used to argue against the Corn Laws, claimed that trade enables countries to specialize in producing the products they produce best. According to the theory specialization and free trade will benefit all trading partners (real wages will rise), even those that may be absolutely less efficient producers. This basic argument remains at the heart of free-trade debates even today, as policy makers argue about the effects of tariffs on agricultural development in sub-Saharan Africa and the gains and losses from outsourcing software development to India.

The easiest way to understand the theory of comparative advantage is to examine a simple two-person society. Suppose Bill and Colleen, stranded on a deserted island in Chapter 2, have only two tasks to accomplish each week: gathering food to eat and cutting logs to construct a house. If Colleen could cut more logs than Bill in a day and Bill could gather more berries and fruits, specialization would clearly benefit both of them.

But suppose Bill is slow and clumsy and Colleen is better at cutting logs *and* gathering food. Ricardo's point is that it still pays for them to specialize. They can produce more in total by specializing than they can by sharing the work equally. We now turn to look at the application of the powerful idea of comparative advantage to international trade.

Absolute Advantage versus Comparative Advantage

A country enjoys an **absolute advantage** over another country in the production of a good if it uses fewer resources to produce that good than the other country does. Suppose country A and country B produce wheat, but A's climate is more suited to wheat and its labor is more productive. Country A will produce more wheat per acre than country B and use less labor in growing it and bringing it to market. Country A enjoys an absolute advantage over country B in the production of wheat.

A country enjoys a **comparative advantage** in the production of a good if that good can be produced at lower cost *in terms of other goods*. Suppose countries C and D both produce wheat and corn and C enjoys an absolute advantage in the production of both—that is, C's climate is better than D's and fewer of C's resources are needed to produce a given quantity of both wheat and corn. Now C and D must each choose between planting land with either wheat or corn. To produce more wheat, either country must transfer land from corn production; to produce more corn, either country must transfer land from wheat production. The cost of wheat in each country can be measured in bushels of corn, and the cost of corn can be measured in bushels of wheat.

Suppose that in country C, a bushel of wheat has an opportunity cost of 2 bushels of corn. That is, to produce an additional bushel of wheat, C must give up 2 bushels of corn. At the same time, producing a bushel of wheat in country D requires the sacrifice of only 1 bushel of corn. Even though C has an *absolute* advantage in the production of both products, D enjoys a *comparative* advantage in the production of wheat because the *opportunity cost* of producing wheat is lower in D. Under these circumstances, Ricardo claims, D can benefit from trade if it specializes in the production of wheat.

Corn Laws The tariffs, subsidies, and restrictions enacted by the British Parliament in the early nineteenth century to discourage imports and encourage exports of grain.

theory of comparative advantage Ricardo's theory that specialization and free trade will benefit all trading partners (real wages will rise), even those that may be absolutely less efficient producers.

absolute advantage The advantage in the production of a good enjoyed by one country over another when it uses fewer resources to produce that good than the other country does.

comparative advantage The advantage in the production of a good enjoyed by one country over another when that good can be produced at lower cost in terms of other goods than it could be in the other country.

Gains from Mutual Absolute Advantage To illustrate Ricardo's logic in more detail, suppose Australia and New Zealand each have a fixed amount of land and do not trade with the rest of the world. There are only two goods—wheat to produce bread and cotton to produce clothing. This kind of two-country/two-good world does not exist, but its operations can be generalized to many countries and many goods.

To proceed, we have to make some assumptions about the preferences of the people living in New Zealand and the people living in Australia. If the citizens of both countries walk around naked, there is no need to produce cotton, so all the land can be used to produce wheat. However, assume that people in both countries have similar preferences with respect to food and clothing: The populations of both countries use both cotton and wheat, and preferences for food and clothing are such that both countries consume equal amounts of wheat and cotton.

Finally, we assume that each country has only 100 acres of land for planting and that land yields are as given in Table 20.2. New Zealand can produce 3 times the wheat that Australia can on 1 acre of land, and Australia can produce 3 times the cotton that New Zealand can in the same space. New Zealand has an absolute advantage in the production of wheat, and Australia has an absolute advantage in the production of cotton. In cases like this, we say the two countries have *mutual absolute advantage*.

TABLE 20.2 Yield per Acre of Wheat and Cotton

	New Zealand	Australia
Wheat	6 bushels	2 bushels
Cotton	2 bales	6 bales

If there is no trade and each country divides its land to obtain equal units of cotton and wheat production, each country produces 150 bushels of wheat and 150 bales of cotton. New Zealand puts 75 acres into cotton but only 25 acres into wheat, while Australia does the reverse (Table 20.3).

TABLE 20.3 Total Production of Wheat and Cotton Assuming No Trade, Mutual Absolute Advantage, and 100 Available Acres

	New Zealand	Australia
Wheat	25 acres × 6 bushels/acre = 150 bushels	75 acres × 2 bushels/acre = 150 bushels
Cotton	75 acres × 2 bales/acre = 150 bales	25 acres × 6 bales/acre = 150 bales

We can organize the same information in graphic form as production possibility frontiers for each country. In Figure 20.1, which presents the positions of the two countries before trade, each country is constrained by its own resources and productivity. If Australia put all its land into cotton, it would produce 600 bales of cotton (100 acres × 6 bales/acre) and no wheat; if it put all its land into wheat, it would produce 200 bushels of wheat (100 acres × 2 bushels/acre) and no cotton. The opposite is true for New Zealand. Recall from Chapter 2 that a country's production possibility frontier represents all combinations of goods that can be produced, given the country's resources and state of technology. Each country must pick a point along its own production possibility curve.

When both countries have an absolute advantage in the production of one product, it is easy to see that specialization and trade will benefit both. Australia should produce cotton, and New Zealand should produce wheat. Transferring all land to wheat production in New Zealand yields 600 bushels, while transferring all land to cotton production in Australia yields 600 bales. An agreement to trade 300 bushels of wheat for 300 bales of cotton would double both wheat and cotton consumption in both countries. (Remember, before trade, both countries produced 150 bushels of wheat and 150 bales of cotton. After trade, each country will have 300 bushels of wheat and 300 bales of cotton to consume. Final production and trade figures are provided in Table 20.4 and Figure 20.2.) Trade enables both countries to move beyond their previous resource and productivity constraints.

The advantages of specialization and trade seem obvious when one country is technologically superior at producing one product and another country is technologically superior at producing another product. However, let us turn to the case in which one country has an absolute advantage in the production of *both* goods.

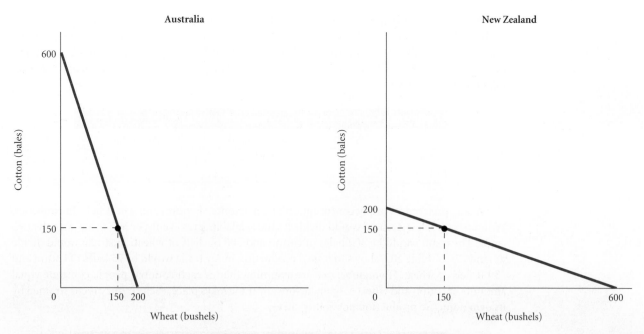

▲ FIGURE 20.1 **Production Possibility Frontiers for Australia and New Zealand Before Trade**

Without trade, countries are constrained by their own resources and productivity.

TABLE 20.4 Production and Consumption of Wheat and Cotton After Specialization					
	Production			Consumption	
	New Zealand	Australia		New Zealand	Australia
Wheat	100 acres × 6 bushels/acre 600 bushels	0 acres 0	Wheat	300 bushels	300 bushels
Cotton	0 acres 0	100 acres × 6 bales/acre 600 bales	Cotton	300 bales	300 bales

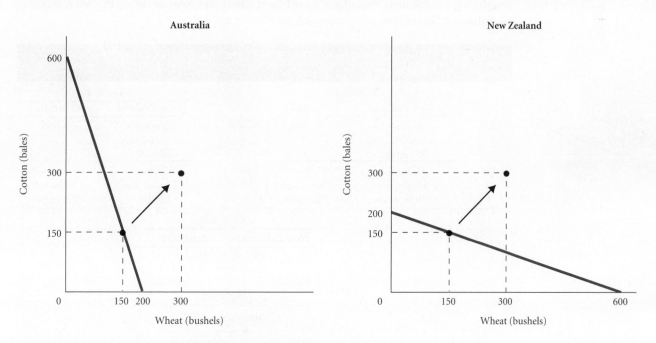

▲ FIGURE 20.2 **Expanded Possibilities After Trade**

Trade enables both countries to move beyond their own resource constraints—beyond their individual production possibility frontiers.

Gains from Comparative Advantage   Table 20.5 contains different land yield figures for New Zealand and Australia. Now New Zealand has a considerable absolute advantage in the production of both cotton and wheat, with 1 acre of land yielding 6 times as much wheat and twice as much cotton as 1 acre in Australia. Ricardo would argue that *specialization and trade are still mutually beneficial.*

TABLE 20.5 Yield per Acre of Wheat and Cotton		
	New Zealand	Australia
Wheat	6 bushels	1 bushel
Cotton	6 bales	3 bales

Again, preferences imply consumption of equal units of cotton and wheat in both countries. With no trade, New Zealand would divide its 100 available acres evenly, or 50/50, between the two crops. The result would be 300 bales of cotton and 300 bushels of wheat. Australia would divide its land 75/25. Table 20.6 shows that final production in Australia would be 75 bales of cotton and 75 bushels of wheat. (Remember, we are assuming that in each country, people consume equal amounts of cotton and wheat.) Again, before any trade takes place, each country is constrained by its own domestic production possibility curve.

TABLE 20.6 Total Production of Wheat and Cotton Assuming No Trade and 100 Available Acres		
	New Zealand	Australia
Wheat	50 acres × 6 bushels/acre	75 acres × 1 bushel/acre
	300 bushels	75 bushels
Cotton	50 acres × 6 bales/acre	25 acres × 3 bales/acre
	300 bales	75 bales

Imagine we are at a meeting of trade representatives of both countries. As a special adviser, David Ricardo is asked to demonstrate that trade can benefit both countries. He divides his demonstration into three stages, which you can follow in Table 20.7. For Ricardo to be correct about the gains from specialization, it must be true that moving resources around in the two countries generates more than the 375 bushels of wheat and bales of cotton that we had before specialization. To see how this is managed, we move in stages.

TABLE 20.7 Realizing a Gain from Trade When One Country Has a Double Absolute Advantage						
	STAGE 1				STAGE 2	
	New Zealand	Australia			New Zealand	Australia
Wheat	50 acres × 6 bushels/acre 300 bushels	0 acres 0	Wheat		75 acres × 6 bushels/acre 450 bushels	0 acres 0
Cotton	50 acres × 6 bales/acre 300 bales	100 acres × 3 bales/acre 300 bales	Cotton		25 acres × 6 bales/acre 150 bales	100 acres × 3 bales/acre 300 bales

	STAGE 3	
	New Zealand	Australia
Wheat	100 bushels (trade) →	
	350 bushels	100 bushels
	(after trade)	
Cotton	200 bales (trade) ←	
	350 bales	100 bales
	(after trade)	

In Stage 1, let Australia move all its land into cotton production, where it is least disadvantaged. Australia would then produce 300 bales of cotton, as we see Stage 1 of Table 20.7. Now the question is whether Ricardo can help us use New Zealand's land to add at least 75 bales of cotton to the total while producing more than the original 375 bushels of wheat. In Stage 2, Ricardo tells New Zealand to use 25 acres to produce cotton and 75 acres for wheat production. With that allocation of land, New Zealand produces 450 bushels of wheat (far more than the total produced in the nonspecialization case by both countries) and 150 bales of cotton, leaving us with 450 bales of cotton as well. Specialization has increased the world production of both wheat and cotton by 75 units! With trade, which we show in Stage 3 for the case in which both countries prefer equal consumption of the two goods, both countries can be better off than they were earlier.

Why Does Ricardo's Plan Work?   To understand why Ricardo's scheme works, let us return to the definition of comparative advantage.

The real cost of producing cotton is the wheat that must be sacrificed to produce it. *When we think of cost this way, it is less costly to produce cotton in Australia than to produce it in New Zealand, even though an acre of land produces more cotton in New Zealand.* Consider the "cost" of 3 bales of cotton in the two countries. In terms of opportunity cost, 3 bales of cotton in New Zealand cost 3 bushels of wheat; in Australia, 3 bales of cotton cost only 1 bushel of wheat. Because 3 bales are produced by 1 acre of Australian land, to get 3 bales, an Australian must transfer 1 acre of land from wheat to cotton production. Because an acre of land produces a bushel of wheat, losing 1 acre to cotton implies the loss of 1 bushel of wheat. *Australia has a comparative advantage in cotton production* because its opportunity cost, in terms of wheat, is lower than New Zealand's. This is illustrated in Figure 20.3.

Conversely, New Zealand has a comparative advantage in wheat production. A unit of wheat in New Zealand costs 1 unit of cotton, while a unit of wheat in Australia costs 3 units of cotton. When countries specialize in producing goods in which they have a comparative advantage, they maximize their combined output and allocate their resources more efficiently.

Terms of Trade

Ricardo might suggest a number of options for exchanging wheat and cotton to the trading partners. The one we just examined benefited both partners; in percentage terms, Australia made out slightly better. Other deals might have been more advantageous to New Zealand.

The ratio at which a country can trade domestic products for imported products is the **terms of trade**. The terms of trade determine how the gains from trade are distributed among trading partners. In the case just considered, the agreed-to terms of trade were 1 bushel of wheat for 2 bales of cotton. Such terms of trade benefit New Zealand, which can get 2 bales of cotton for each bushel of wheat. If it were to transfer its own land from wheat to cotton, it would get only 1 bale of cotton. The same terms of trade benefit Australia, which can get 1 bushel of wheat for 2 bales of cotton. A direct transfer of its own land would force it to give up 3 bales of cotton for 1 bushel of wheat.

terms of trade   The ratio at which a country can trade domestic products for imported products.

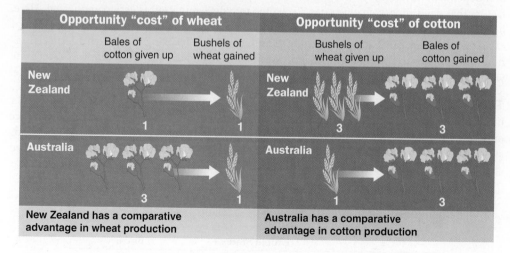

◀ FIGURE 20.3
Comparative Advantage Means Lower Opportunity Cost
The real cost of cotton is the wheat sacrificed to obtain it. The cost of 3 bales of cotton in New Zealand is 3 bushels of wheat (a half acre of land must be transferred from wheat to cotton—refer to Table 20.5). However, the cost of 3 bales of cotton in Australia is only 1 bushel of wheat. Australia has a comparative advantage over New Zealand in cotton production, and New Zealand has a comparative advantage over Australia in wheat production.

If the terms of trade changed to 3 bales of cotton for every bushel of wheat, only New Zealand would benefit. At those terms of trade, *all* the gains from trade would flow to New Zealand. Such terms do not benefit Australia at all because the opportunity cost of producing wheat domestically is *exactly the same* as the trade cost: A bushel of wheat costs 3 bales of cotton. If the terms of trade went the other way—1 bale of cotton for each bushel of wheat—only Australia would benefit. New Zealand gains nothing because it can already substitute cotton for wheat at that ratio. To get a bushel of wheat domestically, however, Australia must give up 3 bales of cotton, and one-for-one terms of trade would make wheat much less costly for Australia.

Both parties must have something to gain for trade to take place. In this case, you can see that both Australia and New Zealand will gain when the terms of trade are set between 1:1 and 3:1, cotton to wheat.

Exchange Rates

The examples used thus far have shown that trade can result in gains to both parties. When trade is free—unimpeded by government-instituted barriers—patterns of trade and trade flows result from the independent decisions of thousands of importers and exporters and millions of private households and firms.

Private households decide whether to buy Toyotas or Chevrolets, and private firms decide whether to buy machine tools made in the United States or machine tools made in Taiwan, raw steel produced in Germany or raw steel produced in Pittsburgh.

But how does this trade actually come about? Before a citizen of one country can buy a product made in another country or sold by someone in another country, a currency swap must take place. Consider Shane, who buys a Toyota from a dealer in Boston. He pays in dollars, but the Japanese workers who made the car receive their salaries in yen. Somewhere between the buyer of the car and the producer, a currency exchange must be made. The regional distributor probably takes payment in dollars and converts them into yen before remitting the proceeds to Japan.

To buy a foreign-produced good, a consumer, or an intermediary, has to buy foreign currency. The price of Shane's Toyota in dollars depends on the price of the car stated in yen and the dollar price of yen. You probably know the ins and outs of currency exchange very well if you have ever traveled in another country.

In June 2010, the British pound was worth $1.48. Now suppose you are in London having dinner. On the menu is a nice bottle of wine for 15 pounds. How can you figure out whether you want to buy it? You know what dollars will buy in the United States, so you have to convert the price into dollars. Each pound will cost you $1.48, so 15 pounds will cost you $1.48 × 15 = $22.20.

exchange rate The ratio at which two currencies are traded. The price of one currency in terms of another.

The attractiveness of foreign goods to U.S. buyers and of U.S. goods to foreign buyers depends in part on the **exchange rate**, the ratio at which two currencies are traded. In May 2008, the British pound was worth $1.97, and that same bottle of wine would have cost $29.55.

To understand the patterns of trade that result from the actions of hundreds of thousands of independent buyers and sellers—households and firms—we must know something about the factors that determine exchange rates. Exchange rate determination is very complicated. Here, however, we can demonstrate two things. First, for any pair of countries, there is a range of exchange rates that can lead automatically to both countries' realizing the gains from specialization and comparative advantage. Second, within that range, the exchange rate will determine which country gains the most from trade. In short, exchange rates determine the terms of trade.

Trade and Exchange Rates in a Two-Country/Two-Good World   Consider first a simple two-country/two-good model. Suppose both the United States and Brazil produce only two goods—raw timber and rolled steel. Table 20.8 gives the current prices of both goods as domestic buyers see them. In Brazil, timber is priced at 3 reals (R) per foot and steel is priced at 4 R per meter. In the United States, timber costs $1 per foot and steel costs $2 per meter.

TABLE 20.8 Domestic Prices of Timber (per Foot) and Rolled Steel (per Meter) in the United States and Brazil		
	United States	Brazil
Timber	$1	3 Reals
Rolled steel	$2	4 Reals

Suppose U.S. and Brazilian buyers have the option of buying at home or importing to meet their needs. The options they choose will depend on the exchange rate. For the time being, we will ignore transportation costs between countries and assume that Brazilian and U.S. products are of equal quality.

Let us start with the assumption that the exchange rate is \$1 = 1 R. From the standpoint of U.S. buyers, neither Brazilian steel nor Brazilian timber is competitive at this exchange rate. A dollar buys a foot of timber in the United States, but if converted into a real, it will buy only one-third of a foot. The price of Brazilian timber to an American is \$3 because it will take \$3 to buy the necessary 3 R. Similarly, \$2 buys a meter of rolled steel in the United States, but the same \$2 buys only half a meter of Brazilian steel. The price of Brazilian steel to an American is \$4, twice the price of domestically produced steel.

At this exchange rate, however, Brazilians find that U.S.-produced steel and timber are less expensive than steel and timber produced in Brazil. Timber at home—Brazil—costs 3 R, but 3 R buys \$3, which buys 3 times as much timber in the United States. Similarly, steel costs 4 R at home, but 4 R buys \$4, which buys twice as much U.S.-made steel. At an exchange rate of \$1 = 1 R, Brazil will import steel and timber and the United States will import nothing.

However, now suppose the exchange rate is 1 R = \$0.25. This means that 1 dollar buys 4 R. At this exchange rate, the Brazilians buy timber and steel at home and the Americans import both goods. At this exchange rate, Americans must pay a dollar for a foot of U.S. timber, but the same amount of timber can be had in Brazil for the equivalent of \$0.75. (Because 1 R costs \$0.25, 3 R can be purchased for \$0.75.) Similarly, steel that costs \$2 per meter in the United States costs an American half as much in Brazil because \$2 buys 8 R, which buys 2 meters of Brazilian steel. At the same time, Brazilians are not interested in importing because both goods are cheaper when purchased from a Brazilian producer. In this case, the United States imports both goods and Brazil imports nothing.

So far we can see that at exchange rates of \$1 = 1 R and \$1 = 4 R, we get trade flowing in only one direction. Let us now try an exchange rate of \$1 = 2 R, or 1 R = \$0.50. First, Brazilians will buy timber in the United States. Brazilian timber costs 3 R per foot, but 3 R buys \$1.50, which is enough to buy 1.5 feet of U.S. timber. Buyers in the United States will find Brazilian timber too expensive, but Brazil will import timber from the United States. At this same exchange rate, however, both Brazilian and U.S. buyers will be indifferent between Brazilian and U.S. steel. To U.S. buyers, domestically produced steel costs \$2. Because \$2 buys 4 R, a meter of imported Brazilian steel also costs \$2. Brazilian buyers also find that steel costs 4 R, whether domestically produced or imported. Thus, there is likely to be no trade in steel.

What happens if the exchange rate changes so that \$1 buys 2.1 R? While U.S. timber is still cheaper to both Brazilians and Americans, Brazilian steel begins to look good to U.S. buyers. Steel produced in the United States costs \$2 per meter, but \$2 buys 4.2 R, which buys more than a meter of steel in Brazil. When \$1 buys more than 2 R, trade begins to flow in both directions: Brazil will import timber, and the United States will import steel.

If you examine Table 20.9 carefully, you will see that trade flows in both directions as long as the exchange rate settles between \$1 = 2 R and \$1 = 3 R. Stated the other way around, trade will flow in both directions if the price of a real is between \$0.33 and \$0.50.

TABLE 20.9 Trade Flows Determined by Exchange Rates

Exchange Rate	Price of Real	Result
\$1 = 1 R	\$ 1.00	Brazil imports timber and steel.
\$1 = 2 R	.50	Brazil imports timber.
\$1 = 2.1 R	.48	Brazil imports timber; United States imports steel.
\$1 = 2.9 R	.34	Brazil imports timber; United States imports steel.
\$1 = 3 R	.33	United States imports steel.
\$1 = 4 R	.25	United States imports timber and steel.

Exchange Rates and Comparative Advantage If the foreign exchange market drives the exchange rate to anywhere between 2 and 3 R per dollar, the countries will automatically adjust and comparative advantage will be realized. At these exchange rates, U.S. buyers begin buying all their steel in Brazil. The U.S. steel industry finds itself in trouble. Plants close, and U.S. workers begin to lobby for tariff protection against Brazilian steel. At the same time, the U.S. timber industry does well, fueled by strong export demand from Brazil. The timber-producing sector expands. Resources, including capital and labor, are attracted into timber production.

The opposite occurs in Brazil. The Brazilian timber industry suffers losses as export demand dries up and Brazilians turn to cheaper U.S. imports. In Brazil, lumber companies turn to the government and ask for protection from cheap U.S. timber. However, steel producers in Brazil are happy. They are not only supplying 100 percent of the domestically demanded steel but also selling to U.S. buyers. The steel industry expands, and the timber industry contracts. Resources, including labor, flow into steel.

With this expansion-and-contraction scenario in mind, let us look again at our original definition of comparative advantage. If we assume that prices reflect resource use and resources can be transferred from sector to sector, we can calculate the opportunity cost of steel/timber in both countries. In the United States, the production of a meter of rolled steel consumes twice the resources that the production of a foot of timber consumes. Assuming that resources can be transferred, the opportunity cost of a meter of steel is 2 feet of timber (Table 20.8). In Brazil, a meter of steel uses resources costing 4 R, while a unit of timber costs 3 R. To produce a meter of steel means the sacrifice of only four-thirds (or one and one-third) feet of timber. Because the opportunity cost of a meter of steel (in terms of timber) is lower in Brazil, we say that Brazil has a comparative advantage in steel production.

Conversely, consider the opportunity cost of timber in the two countries. Increasing timber production in the United States requires the sacrifice of half a meter of steel for every foot of timber—producing a meter of steel uses $2 worth of resources, while producing a foot of timber requires only $1 worth of resources. Nevertheless, each foot of timber production in Brazil requires the sacrifice of three-fourths of a meter of steel. Because the opportunity cost of timber is lower in the United States, the United States has a comparative advantage in the production of timber. If exchange rates end up in the right ranges, the free market will drive each country to shift resources into those sectors in which it enjoys a comparative advantage. Only in a country with a comparative advantage will those products be competitive in world markets.

The Sources of Comparative Advantage

Specialization and trade can benefit all trading partners, even those that may be inefficient producers in an absolute sense. If markets are competitive and if foreign exchange markets are linked to goods-and-services exchange, countries will specialize in producing products in which they have a comparative advantage.

So far, we have said nothing about the sources of comparative advantage. What determines whether a country has a comparative advantage in heavy manufacturing or in agriculture? What explains the actual trade flows observed around the world? Various theories and empirical work on international trade have provided some answers. Most economists look to **factor endowments**—the quantity and quality of labor, land, and natural resources of a country—as the principal sources of comparative advantage. Factor endowments seem to explain a significant portion of actual world trade patterns.

The Heckscher-Ohlin Theorem

Eli Heckscher and Bertil Ohlin, two Swedish economists who wrote in the first half of the twentieth century, expanded and elaborated on Ricardo's theory of comparative advantage. The **Heckscher-Ohlin theorem** ties the theory of comparative advantage to factor endowments. It assumes that products can be produced using differing proportions of inputs and that inputs are mobile between sectors in each economy but that factors are not mobile *between* economies. According to this theorem, a country has a comparative advantage in the production of a product if that country is relatively well endowed with inputs used intensively in the production of that product.

factor endowments The quantity and quality of labor, land, and natural resources of a country.

Heckscher-Ohlin theorem A theory that explains the existence of a country's comparative advantage by its factor endowments: A country has a comparative advantage in the production of a product if that country is relatively well endowed with inputs used intensively in the production of that product.

This idea is simple. A country with a great deal of good fertile land is likely to have a comparative advantage in agriculture. A country with a large amount of accumulated capital is likely to have a comparative advantage in heavy manufacturing. A country well-endowed with human capital is likely to have a comparative advantage in highly technical goods.

Other Explanations for Observed Trade Flows

Comparative advantage is not the only reason countries trade. It does not explain why many countries import and export the same kinds of goods. The United States, for example, exports and imports automobiles.

Just as industries within a country differentiate their products to capture a domestic market, they also differentiate their products to please the wide variety of tastes that exists worldwide. The Japanese automobile industry, for example, began producing small, fuel-efficient cars long before U.S. automobile makers did. In doing so, the Japanese auto industry developed expertise in creating products that attracted a devoted following and considerable brand loyalty. BMWs, made mostly in Germany, and Volvos, made mostly in Sweden, also have their champions in many countries. Just as product differentiation is a natural response to diverse preferences within an economy, it is also a natural response to diverse preferences across economies. Paul Krugman did some of the earliest work in this area, sometimes called New Trade Theory.

New trade theory also relies on the idea of comparative advantage. If the Japanese developed skills and knowledge that gave them an edge in the production of fuel-efficient cars, that knowledge can be thought of as a very specific kind of capital that is not currently available to other producers. The Volvo company invested in a form of intangible capital called *goodwill*. That goodwill, which may come from establishing a reputation for safety and quality over the years, is one source of the comparative advantage that keeps Volvos selling on the international market. Some economists distinguish between gains from *acquired comparative advantages* and gains from *natural comparative advantages*.

Trade Barriers: Tariffs, Export Subsidies, and Quotas

Trade barriers—also called *obstacles to trade*—take many forms. The three most common are tariffs, export subsidies, and quotas. All are forms of **protection** shielding some sector of the economy from foreign competition.

A **tariff** is a tax on imports. The average tariff on imports into the United States is less than 5 percent. Certain protected items have much higher tariffs. For example, in 2009 President Obama imposed a tariff of 35 percent on tire imports from China.

Export subsidies—government payments made to domestic firms to encourage exports—can also act as a barrier to trade. One of the provisions of the Corn Laws that stimulated Ricardo's musings was an export subsidy automatically paid to farmers by the British government when the price of grain fell below a specified level. The subsidy served to keep domestic prices high, but it flooded the world market with cheap subsidized grain. Foreign farmers who were not subsidized were driven out of the international marketplace by the artificially low prices.

Farm subsidies remain a part of the international trade landscape today. Many countries continue to appease their farmers by heavily subsidizing exports of agricultural products. The political power of the farm lobby in many countries has had an important effect on recent international trade negotiations aimed at reducing trade barriers. The prevalence of farm subsidies in the developed world has become a major rallying point for less developed countries as they strive to compete in the global marketplace. Many African nations, in particular, have a comparative advantage in agricultural land. In producing agricultural goods for export to the world marketplace, however, they must compete with food produced on heavily subsidized farms in Europe and the United States. Countries such as France have particularly high farm subsidies,

protection The practice of shielding a sector of the economy from foreign competition.

tariff A tax on imports.

export subsidies Government payments made to domestic firms to encourage exports.

which, it argues, helps preserve the rural heritage of France. One side effect of these subsidies, however, is to make it more difficult for some of the poorer nations in the world to compete. Some have argued that if developed nations eliminated their farm subsidies, this would have a much larger effect on the economies of some African nations than is currently achieved by charitable aid programs.

dumping A firm's or an industry's sale of products on the world market at prices below its own cost of production.

Closely related to subsidies is **dumping**. Dumping occurs when a firm or industry sells its products on the world market at prices lower than its cost of production. Charges of dumping are often brought by a domestic producer that believes itself to be subject to unfair competition. In the United States, claims of dumping are brought before the International Trade Commission. In 2007, for example, a small manufacturer of thermal paper charged China and Germany with dumping. In 2006, the European Union charged China with dumping shoes. In 2009, China brought a dumping charge against U.S. chicken producers. Determining whether dumping has actually occurred can be difficult. Domestic producers argue that foreign firms will dump their product in the United States, drive out American competitors, and then raise prices, thus harming consumers. Foreign exporters, on the other hand, claim that their prices are low simply because their costs are low and that no dumping has occurred. Figuring out the costs for German thermal paper or Chinese shoes is not easy. In the case of the Chinese shoe claim, for example, the Chinese government pointed out that shoes are a very labor-intensive product and that given China's low wages, it should not be a surprise that it is able to produce shoes very cheaply. In other words, the Chinese claim that shoes are an example of the theory of comparative advantage at work rather than predatory dumping.

quota A limit on the quantity of imports.

A **quota** is a limit on the quantity of imports. Quotas can be mandatory or voluntary, and they may be legislated or negotiated with foreign governments. The best-known voluntary quota, or "voluntary restraint," was negotiated with the Japanese government in 1981. Japan agreed to reduce its automobile exports to the United States by 7.7 percent, from the 1980 level of 1.82 million units to 1.68 million units. Many quotas limit trade around the world today. Perhaps the best-known recent case is the textile quota imposed in August 2005 by the European Union on imports of textiles from China. Because China had exceeded quotas that had been agreed to earlier in the year, the EU blocked the entry of Chinese-produced textiles into Europe; as a result, more than 100 million garments piled up in European ports.

U.S. Trade Policies, GATT, and the WTO

Smoot-Hawley tariff The U.S. tariff law of the 1930s, which set the highest tariffs in U.S. history (60 percent). It set off an international trade war and caused the decline in trade that is often considered one of the causes of the worldwide depression of the 1930s.

The United States has been a high-tariff nation, with average tariffs of over 50 percent, for much of its history. The highest were in effect during the Great Depression following the **Smoot-Hawley tariff**, which pushed the average tariff rate to 60 percent in 1930. The Smoot-Hawley tariff set off an international trade war when U.S. trading partners retaliated with tariffs of their own. Many economists say the decline in trade that followed was one of the causes of the worldwide depression of the 1930s.[1]

General Agreement on Tariffs and Trade (GATT) An international agreement signed by the United States and 22 other countries in 1947 to promote the liberalization of foreign trade.

In 1947, the United States, with 22 other nations, agreed to reduce barriers to trade. It also established an organization to promote liberalization of foreign trade. The **General Agreement on Tariffs and Trade (GATT)** proved to be very successful in helping reduce tariff levels and encourage trade. In 1986, GATT sponsored a round of world trade talks known as the Uruguay Round that were focused on reducing trade barriers further. After much debate, the Uruguay Round was signed by the U.S. Congress in 1993 and became a model for multilateral trade agreements.

World Trade Organization (WTO) A negotiating forum dealing with rules of trade across nations.

In 1995, the **World Trade Organization (WTO)** was established as a negotiating forum to deal with the rules of trade established under GATT and other agreements. It remains the key institution focused on facilitating freer trade across nations and negotiating trade disputes. The WTO consists of 153 member nations and serves as a negotiating forum for countries as they work through complexities of trade under the Uruguay Round and other agreements. At this time, the WTO is the central institution for promoting and facilitating free trade.

Doha Development Agenda An initiative of the World Trade Organization focused on issues of trade and development.

While the WTO was founded to promote free trade, its member countries clearly have different incentives as they confront trade cases. In recent years, differences between developed and developing countries have come to the fore. In 2001, at a WTO meeting in Doha, Qatar, the WTO launched a new initiative, the **Doha Development Agenda**, to deal with some of the issues that intersect the areas of trade and development. In 2007, the Doha Development Agenda continued to struggle over

---

[1] See especially Charles Kindleberger, *The World in Depression 1929–1939* (London: Allen Lane, 1973).

the issue of agriculture and farm subsidies that were described earlier in this chapter. The less developed countries, with sub-Saharan Africa taking the lead, seek to eliminate all farm subsidies currently paid by the United States and the European Union. The EU has, for its part, tried to push the less developed countries toward better environmental policies as part of a broader free trade package. As of 2010, the Doha declaration remained stalled.

The movement in the United States has been away from tariffs and quotas and toward freer trade. The Reciprocal Trade Agreements Act of 1934 authorized the president to negotiate trade agreements on behalf of the United States. As part of trade negotiations, the president can confer *most-favored-nation status* on individual trading partners. Imports from countries with most-favored-nation status are taxed at the lowest negotiated tariff rates. In addition, in recent years, several successful rounds of tariff-reduction negotiations have reduced trade barriers to their lowest levels ever.

Despite this general trend toward freer trade, most American presidents in the last 50 years have made exceptions to protect one economic sector or another. Eisenhower and Kennedy restricted imports of Japanese textiles; Johnson restricted meat imports to protect Texas beef producers; Nixon restricted steel imports; Reagan restricted automobiles from Japan. In early 2002, President George W. Bush imposed a 30 percent tariff on steel imported from the EU. In 2003, the WTO ruled that these tariffs were unfair and allowed the EU to slap retaliatory tariffs on U.S. products. Shortly thereafter, the steel tariffs were rolled back, at least on EU steel. At present, the United States has high tariffs on sugar-based ethanol, an energy source competitive with corn-based ethanol, and on tires imported from China.

Economic Integration

Economic integration occurs when two or more nations join to form a free-trade zone. In 1991, the European Community (EC, or the Common Market) began forming the largest free-trade zone in the world. The economic integration process began that December, when the 12 original members (the United Kingdom, Belgium, France, Germany, Italy, the Netherlands, Luxembourg, Denmark, Greece, Ireland, Spain, and Portugal) signed the Maastricht Treaty. The treaty called for the end of border controls, a common currency, an end to all tariffs, and the coordination of monetary and political affairs. The **European Union (EU)**, as the EC is now called, has 27 members (for a list, see the Summary, p. 429). On January 1, 1993, all tariffs and trade barriers were dropped among the member countries. Border checkpoints were closed in early 1995. Citizens can now travel among member countries without passports.

The United States is not a part of the EU. However, in 1988, the United States (under President Reagan) and Canada (under Prime Minister Mulroney) signed the **U.S.-Canadian Free Trade Agreement**, which removed all barriers to trade, including tariffs and quotas, between the two countries in 1998.

During the last days of the George H. W. Bush administration in 1992, the United States, Mexico, and Canada signed the **North American Free Trade Agreement (NAFTA)**, with the three countries agreeing to establish all of North America as a free-trade zone. The agreement eliminated all tariffs over a 10- to 15-year period and removed restrictions on most investments. During the presidential campaign of 1992, NAFTA was hotly debated. Both Bill Clinton and George Bush supported the agreement. Industrial labor unions that might be affected by increased imports from Mexico (such as those in the automobile industry) opposed the agreement, while industries whose exports to Mexico might increase as a result of the agreement—for example, the machine tool industry—supported it. Another concern was that Mexican companies were not subject to the same environmental regulations as U.S. firms, so U.S. firms might move to Mexico for this reason.

NAFTA was ratified by the U.S. Congress in late 1993 and went into effect on the first day of 1994. The U.S. Department of Commerce estimated that as a result of NAFTA, trade between the United States and Mexico increased by nearly $16 billion in 1994. In addition, exports from the United States to Mexico outpaced imports from Mexico during 1994. In 1995, however, the agreement fell under the shadow of a dramatic collapse of the value of the peso. U.S. exports to Mexico dropped sharply, and the United States shifted from a trade surplus to a large trade deficit with Mexico. Aside from a handful of tariffs, however, all of NAFTA's commitments were fully implemented by 2003, and an 8-year report signed by all three countries declared the pact a success. The report concludes, "Eight years of expanded trade, increased employment and investment, and enhanced opportunity for the citizens of all three countries have demonstrated that NAFTA works and will continue to work." In 2007, trade among the NAFTA nations reached $930 billion.

economic integration Occurs when two or more nations join to form a free-trade zone.

European Union (EU) The European trading bloc composed of 27 countries (of the 27 countries in the EU, 16 have the same currency—the euro).

U.S.-Canadian Free Trade Agreement An agreement in which the United States and Canada agreed to eliminate all barriers to trade between the two countries by 1998.

North American Free Trade Agreement (NAFTA) An agreement signed by the United States, Mexico, and Canada in which the three countries agreed to establish all North America as a free-trade zone.

ECONOMICS IN PRACTICE

Tariff Wars

In the recent recession we have again seen political pressure aimed at imposing tariffs. These pressures have been especially strong in the case of China, whose export growth to the United States and the EU has been very strong. In the case of the EU's tariff on Chinese shoes, pressure from Italian shoemakers played a substantial role.

China Complains to WTO About EU Tariffs

The Wall Street Journal

China filed a complaint against European Union shoe tariffs at the World Trade Organization on Thursday, as Beijing continued its legal assault on what it says is unfair Western protectionism.

China's exports have been growing since the 1990s, particularly after the country joined the WTO in 2001. Eight years later, China passed Germany to become the world's top exporter. That status comes with a price: China is now the leading target for protectionist measures, according to Global Trade Alert, an independent monitor.

As the fitful economic recovery has put some domestic jobs and profits at risk, the EU and the U.S. have sought to stem the flow of Chinese imports with special duties. Added to existing tariffs, the duties are meant to make Chinese goods too expensive for consumers to afford.

China isn't taking the restrictions lying down. From a new office near WTO headquarters in Geneva, Beijing is playing hardball. It is paying top dollar to engage premium counsel, some trade lawyers say.

In September, China reacted to President Barack Obama's tariffs on tire imports with a complaint against the U.S. China has also put restrictions on imports of U.S. poultry and auto parts.

Early Friday, China's Commerce Ministry said it had made a preliminary decision to impose antidumping duties on some U.S. chicken products from Feb. 13, the eve of the Lunar New Year, China's biggest holiday. Companies named in the statement include Pilgrim's Pride and Tyson Foods Inc.

In the EU case, China is taking on one of the most important tariff increases ever levied, which has taken a bite out of its expansive shoe industry. The 16.5% tariffs are antidumping duties, meant to punish goods that are sold below cost and hurt the sales of domestic producers.

The EU duties were inaugurated in 2006 and extended for 15 months in December 2009. At the same time, shoe imports from Vietnam were hit with a 10% tariff.

The EU tariffs were passed after fierce lobbying by Italy on behalf of its domestic shoemakers. Italy traded votes in other debates with EU members in exchange for support for the tariffs, EU officials say.

Source: The Wall Street Journal, excerpted from "China Complains to WTO About EU Tariffs" by John W. Miller. Copyright 2010 by *Dow Jones & Company, Inc.* Reproduced with permission of *Dow Jones & Company, Inc.* via Copyright Clearance Center.

Free Trade or Protection?

One of the great economic debates of all time revolves around the free-trade-versus-protection controversy. We briefly summarize the arguments in favor of each.

The Case for Free Trade

In one sense, the theory of comparative advantage *is* the case for free trade. Trade has potential benefits for all nations. A good is not imported unless its net price to buyers is below the net price of the domestically produced alternative. When the Brazilians in our earlier example found U.S. timber less expensive than their own, they bought it, yet they continued to pay the same price for homemade steel. Americans bought less expensive Brazilian steel, but they continued to buy domestic timber at the same lower price. Under these conditions, *both Americans and Brazilians ended up paying less and consuming more.*

At the same time, resources (including labor) move out of steel production and into timber production in the United States. In Brazil, resources (including labor) move out of timber production and into steel production. The resources in both countries are used more efficiently.

Tariffs, export subsidies, and quotas, which interfere with the free movement of goods and services around the world, reduce or eliminate the gains of comparative advantage.

We can use supply and demand curves to illustrate this. Suppose Figure 20.4 shows domestic supply and demand for textiles. In the absence of trade, the market clears at a price of $4.20. At equilibrium, 450 million yards of textiles are produced and consumed.

Assume now that textiles are available at a world price of $2. This is the price in dollars that Americans must pay for textiles from foreign sources. If we assume that an unlimited quantity of textiles is available at $2 and there is no difference in quality between domestic and foreign textiles, no domestic producer will be able to charge more than $2. In the absence of trade barriers, the world price sets the price in the United States. As the price in the United States falls from $4.20 to $2.00, the quantity demanded by consumers increases from 450 million yards to 700 million yards, but the quantity supplied by domestic producers drops from 450 million yards to 200 million yards. The difference, 500 million yards, is the quantity of textiles imported.

The argument for free trade is that each country should specialize in producing the goods and services in which it enjoys a comparative advantage. If foreign producers can produce textiles at a much lower price than domestic producers, they have a comparative advantage. As the world price of textiles falls to $2, domestic (U.S.) quantity supplied drops and resources are transferred to other sectors. These other sectors, which may be export industries or domestic industries, are not shown in Figure 20.4a. It is clear that the allocation of resources is more efficient at a price of $2. Why should the United States use domestic resources to produce what foreign producers can produce at a lower cost? U.S. resources should move into the production of the things it produces best.

Now consider what happens to the domestic price of textiles when a trade barrier is imposed. Figure 20.4b shows the effect of a set tariff of $1 per yard imposed on imported textiles. The tariff raises the domestic price of textiles to $2 + $1 = $3. The result is that some of the gains from trade are lost. First, consumers are forced to pay a higher price for the same good. The quantity of

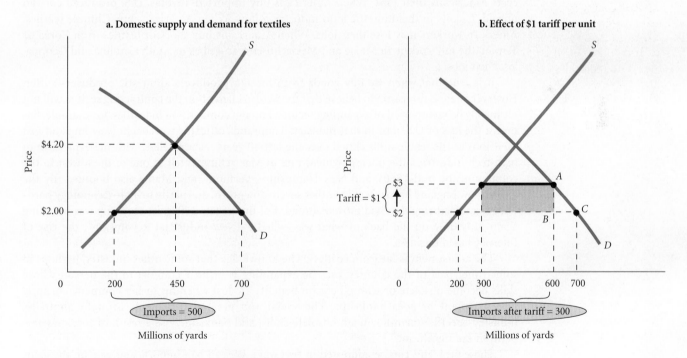

▲ FIGURE 20.4 **The Gains from Trade and Losses from the Imposition of a Tariff**
A tariff of $1 increases the market price facing consumers from $2 per yard to $3 per yard. The government collects revenues equal to the gray shaded area in **b**. The loss of efficiency has two components. First, consumers must pay a higher price for goods that could be produced at lower cost. Second, marginal producers are drawn into textiles and away from other goods, resulting in inefficient domestic production. The triangle labeled ABC in **b** is the dead weight loss or excess burden resulting from the tariff.

textiles demanded drops from 700 million yards under free trade to 600 million yards because some consumers are not willing to pay the higher price. Notice in Figure 20.4b the triangle labeled ABC. This is the deadweight loss or excess burden resulting from the tariff. Absent the tariff, these 100 added units of textiles would have generated benefits in excess of the $2 that each one cost.

At the same time, the higher price of textiles draws some marginal domestic producers who could not make a profit at $2 into textile production. (Recall that domestic producers do not pay a tariff.) As the price rises to $3, the quantity supplied by domestic producers rises from 200 million yards to 300 million yards. The result is a decrease in imports from 500 million yards to 300 million yards.

Finally, the imposition of the tariff means that the government collects revenue equal to the shaded area in Figure 20.4b. This shaded area is equal to the tariff rate per unit ($1) times the number of units imported after the tariff is in place (300 million yards). Thus, receipts from the tariff are $300 million.

What is the final result of the tariff? Domestic producers receiving revenues of only $2 per unit before the tariff was imposed now receive a higher price and earn higher profits. However, these higher profits are achieved at a loss of efficiency. Trade barriers prevent a nation from reaping the benefits of specialization, push it to adopt relatively inefficient production techniques, and force consumers to pay higher prices for protected products than they would otherwise pay.

The Case for Protection

A case can also be made in favor of tariffs and quotas. Over the course of U.S. history, protectionist arguments have been made so many times by so many industries before so many congressional committees that it seems all pleas for protection share the same themes. We describe the most frequently heard pleas next.

Protection Saves Jobs   The main argument for protection is that foreign competition costs Americans their jobs. When Americans buy imported Toyotas, U.S. produced cars go unsold. Layoffs in the domestic auto industry follow. When Americans buy Chinese textiles, American workers may lose their jobs. When Americans buy shoes or textiles from Korea or Taiwan, the millworkers in Maine and Massachusetts, as well as in South Carolina and Georgia, lose their jobs.

It is true that when we buy goods from foreign producers, domestic producers suffer. However, there is no reason to believe that the workers laid off in the contracting sectors will not ultimately be reemployed in expanding sectors. Foreign competition in textiles, for example, has meant the loss of U.S. jobs in that industry. Thousands of textile workers in New England lost their jobs as the textile mills closed over the last 40 years. Nevertheless, with the expansion of high-tech industries, the unemployment rate in Massachusetts fell to one of the lowest in the country in the mid-1980s, and New Hampshire, Vermont, and Maine also boomed. By the 1990s, New England had suffered another severe downturn, due partly to high-technology hardware manufacturing that had moved abroad. But by the late 1990s, its economy was booming again, this time on the back of what was called a "New Industrial Revolution": the rise of Internet-based business.

The adjustment is far from costless. The knowledge that some other industry, perhaps in some other part of the country, may be expanding is of little comfort to the person whose skills become obsolete or whose pension benefits are lost when his or her company abruptly closes a plant or goes bankrupt. The social and personal problems brought about by industry-specific unemployment, obsolete skills, and bankruptcy as a result of foreign competition are significant.

These problems can be addressed in two ways. We can ban imports and give up the gains from free trade, acknowledging that we are willing to pay premium prices to save domestic jobs in industries that can produce more efficiently abroad, or we can aid the victims of free trade in a constructive way, helping to retrain them for jobs with a future. In some instances, programs to relocate people in expanding regions may be in order. Some programs deal directly with the transition without forgoing the gains from trade.

ECONOMICS IN PRACTICE

A Petition

While most economists argue in favor of free trade, it is important to recognize that some groups are likely to lose from freer trade. Arguments by the losing groups against trade have been around for hundreds of years. In the following article, you will find an essay by a French satirist of the nineteenth century, Frederic Bastiat, complaining about the unfair competition that the sun provides to candle makers. You see that the author proposes a quota, as opposed to a tariff, on the sun.

From the Manufacturers of Candles, Tapers, Lanterns, Sticks, Street Lamps, Snuffers, and Extinguishers, and from Producers of Tallow, Oil, Resin, Alcohol, and Generally of Everything Connected with Lighting.

To the Honourable Members of the Chamber of Deputies.

Gentlemen:

You are on the right track. You reject abstract theories and [have] little regard for abundance and low prices. You concern yourselves mainly with the fate of the producer. You wish to free him from foreign competition, that is, to reserve the *domestic market* for *domestic industry*.

We come to offer you a wonderful opportunity for your—what shall we call it? Your theory? No, nothing is more deceptive than theory. Your doctrine? Your system? Your principle? But you dislike doctrines, you have a horror of systems, as for principles, you deny that there are any in political economy; therefore we shall call it your practice—your practice without theory and without principle.

We are suffering from the ruinous competition of a rival who apparently works under conditions so far superior to our own for the production of light that he is *flooding* the *domestic market* with it at an incredibly low price; for the moment he appears, our sales cease, all the consumers turn to him, and a branch of French industry whose ramifications are innumerable is all at once reduced to complete stagnation. This rival, which is none other than the sun, is waging war on us so mercilessly we suspect he is being stirred up against us by perfidious Albion (excellent diplomacy nowadays!), particularly because he has for that haughty island a respect that he does not show for us. [A reference to Britain's reputation as a foggy island.]

We ask you to be so good as to pass a law requiring the closing of all windows, dormers, skylights, inside and outside

Screening out the sun would increase the demand for candles. Should candlemakers be protected from unfair competition?

shutters, curtains, casements, bull's-eyes, deadlights, and blinds—in short, all openings, holes, chinks, and fissures through which the light of the sun is wont to enter houses, to the detriment of the fair industries with which, we are proud to say, we have endowed the country, a country that cannot, without betraying ingratitude, abandon us today to so unequal a combat.

Source: An Open Letter to the French Parliament by Frederic Bastiat (1801–1850), originally published in 1845.

Some Countries Engage in Unfair Trade Practices Attempts by U.S. firms to monopolize an industry are illegal under the Sherman and Clayton acts. If a strong company decides to drive the competition out of the market by setting prices below cost, it would be aggressively prosecuted by the Antitrust Division of the Justice Department. However, the argument goes, if we will not allow a U.S. firm to engage in predatory pricing or monopolize an industry or a market, can we stand by and let a German firm or a Japanese firm do so in the name of free trade? This is a legitimate argument and one that has gained significant favor in recent years. How should we respond when a large international company or a country behaves strategically against a domestic firm or industry? Free trade may be the best solution when everybody plays by the rules, but sometimes we have to fight back. The WTO is the vehicle currently used to negotiate disputes of this sort.

Cheap Foreign Labor Makes Competition Unfair   Let us say that a particular country gained its "comparative advantage" in textiles by paying its workers low wages. How can U.S. textile companies compete with companies that pay wages that are less than a quarter of what U.S. companies pay? Questions like this are often asked by those concerned with competition from China and India.

First, remember that wages in a competitive economy reflect productivity: a high ratio of output to units of labor. Workers in the United States earn higher wages because they are more productive. The United States has more capital per worker; that is, the average worker works with better machinery and equipment and its workers are better trained. Second, trade flows not according to *absolute* advantage, but according to *comparative* advantage: All countries benefit, even if one country is more efficient at producing everything.

Protection Safeguards National Security   Beyond saving jobs, certain sectors of the economy may appeal for protection for other reasons. The steel industry has argued for years with some success that it is vital to national defense. In the event of a war, the United States would not want to depend on foreign countries for a product as vital as steel. Even if we acknowledge another country's comparative advantage, we may want to protect our own resources.

Virtually no industry has ever asked for protection without invoking the national defense argument. Testimony that was once given on behalf of the scissors and shears industry argued that "in the event of a national emergency and imports cutoff, the United States would be without a source of scissors and shears, basic tools for many industries and trades essential to our national defense." The question lies not in the merit of the argument, but in just how seriously it can be taken if *every* industry uses it.

Protection Discourages Dependency   Closely related to the national defense argument is the claim that countries, particularly small or developing countries, may come to rely too heavily on one or more trading partners for many items. If a small country comes to rely on a major power for food or energy or some important raw material in which the large nation has a comparative advantage, it may be difficult for the smaller nation to remain politically neutral. Some critics of free trade argue that larger countries, such as the United States, Russia, and China have consciously engaged in trade with smaller countries to create these kinds of dependencies.

Therefore, should small, independent countries consciously avoid trading relationships that might lead to political dependence? This objective may involve developing domestic industries in areas where a country has a comparative disadvantage. To do so would mean protecting that industry from international competition.

Environmental Concerns   In recent years, concern about the environment has led some people to question advantages of free trade. Some environmental groups, for example, argue that the WTO's free trade policies may harm the environment. The central argument is that poor countries will become havens for polluting industries that will operate their steel and auto factories with few environmental controls.

These issues are quite complex, and there is much dispute among economists about the interaction between free trade and the environment. One relatively recent study of sulphur dioxide, for example, found that in the long run, free trade reduces pollution, largely by increasing the income of countries; richer countries typically choose policies to improve the environment.[2] Thus, while free trade and increased development initially may cause pollution levels to rise, in the long run, prosperity is a benefit to the environment. Many also argue that there are complex trade-offs to be made between pollution control and problems such as malnutrition and health for poor countries. The United States and Europe both traded off faster economic growth and income against cleaner air and water at earlier times in their development. Some argue that it is unfair for the developed countries to impose their preferences on other countries facing more difficult trade-offs.

Nevertheless, the concern with global climate change has stimulated new thinking in this area. A recent study by the Tyndall Centre for Climate Change Research in Britain found that in 2004, 23 percent of the greenhouse gas emissions produced by China were created in the production of

---

[2] Werner Antweiler, Brian Copeland, and M. Scott Taylor, "Is Free Trade Good for the Environment?" *AER*, September, 2001.

exports. In other words, these emissions come not as a result of goods that China's population is enjoying as its income rises, but as a consequence of the consumption of the United States and Europe, where most of these goods are going. In a world in which the effects of carbon emissions are global and all countries are not willing to sign binding global agreements to control emissions, trade with China may be a way for developed nations to avoid their commitments to pollution reduction. Some have argued that penalties could be imposed on high-polluting products produced in countries that have not signed international climate control treaties as a way to ensure that the prices of goods imported this way reflect the harm that those products cause the environment.[3] Implementing these policies is, however, likely to be very complex, and some have argued that it is a mistake to bundle trade and environmental issues. As with other areas covered in this book, there is still disagreement among economists as to the right answer.

Protection Safeguards Infant Industries   Young industries in a given country may have a difficult time competing with established industries in other countries. In a dynamic world, a protected **infant industry** might mature into a strong industry worldwide because of an acquired, but real, comparative advantage. If such an industry is undercut and driven out of world markets at the beginning of its life, that comparative advantage might never develop.

infant industry A young industry that may need temporary protection from competition from the established industries of other countries to develop an acquired comparative advantage.

Yet efforts to protect infant industries can backfire. In July 1991, the U.S. government imposed a 62.67 percent tariff on imports of active-matrix liquid crystal display screens (also referred to as "flat-panel displays" used primarily for laptop computers) from Japan. The Commerce Department and the International Trade Commission agreed that Japanese producers were selling their screens in the U.S. market at a price below cost and that this dumping threatened the survival of domestic laptop screen producers. The tariff was meant to protect the infant U.S. industry until it could compete head-on with the Japanese.

Unfortunately for U.S. producers of laptop computers and for consumers who purchase them, the tariff had an unintended (although predictable) effect on the industry. Because U.S. laptop screens were generally recognized to be of lower quality than their Japanese counterparts, imposition of the tariff left U.S. computer manufacturers with three options: (1) They could use the screens available from U.S. producers and watch sales of their final product decline in the face of *higher-quality* competition from abroad, (2) they could pay the tariff for the higher-quality screens and watch sales of their final product decline in the face of *lower-priced* competition from abroad, or (3) they could do what was most profitable for them to do—move their production facilities abroad to avoid the tariff completely. The last option is what Apple and IBM did. In the end, not only were the laptop industry and its consumers hurt by the imposition of the tariff (due to higher costs of production and to higher laptop computer prices), but the U.S. screen industry was hurt as well (due to its loss of buyers for its product) by a policy specifically designed to help it.

The case for free trade has been made across the world as increasing numbers of countries have joined the world marketplace. Figure 20.5 traces the path of tariffs across the world from

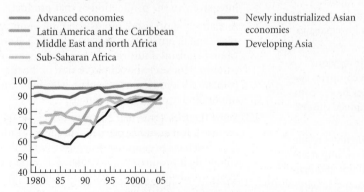

Changes in Openness to Trade Over Time across the World

—— Advanced economies
—— Latin America and the Caribbean
—— Middle East and north Africa
—— Sub-Saharan Africa
—— Newly industrialized Asian economies
—— Developing Asia

◀ FIGURE 20.5 **Trade Openness Across the World (Index is 100 minus the average effective tariff rate in the region.)**

Source: International Monetary Fund, *2007 World Economic Outlook.*
Trade openness is measured as 100 minus the average effective tariff rate in the region.

---

[3] Judith Chevalier, "A Carbon Cap That Starts in Washington," *New York Times*, December 16, 2007.

1980–2005. The lines show an index of trade openness, calculated as 100 minus the tariff rate. (So higher numbers mean lower tariffs.) We see rapid reductions in the last 25 years across the world, most notably in countries in the emerging and developing markets.

An Economic Consensus

You now know something about how international trade fits into the structure of the economy.

Critical to our study of international economics is the debate between free traders and protectionists. On one side is the theory of comparative advantage, formalized by David Ricardo in the early part of the nineteenth century. According to this view, all countries benefit from specialization and trade. The gains from trade are real, and they can be large; free international trade raises real incomes and improves the standard of living.

On the other side are the protectionists, who point to the loss of jobs and argue for the protection of workers from foreign competition. Although foreign competition can cause job loss in specific sectors, it is unlikely to cause net job loss in an economy and workers will, over time, be absorbed into expanding sectors. Foreign trade and full employment can be pursued simultaneously. Although economists disagree about many things, the vast majority of them favor free trade.

SUMMARY

1. All economies, regardless of their size, depend to some extent on other economies and are affected by events outside their borders.

TRADE SURPLUSES AND DEFICITS *p. 410*

2. Until the 1970s, the United States generally exported more than it imported—it ran a *trade surplus*. In the mid-1970s, the United States began to import more merchandise than it exported—a *trade deficit*.

THE ECONOMIC BASIS FOR TRADE: COMPARATIVE ADVANTAGE *p. 411*

3. The *theory of comparative advantage*, dating to David Ricardo in the nineteenth century, holds that specialization and free trade will benefit all trading partners, even those that may be absolutely less efficient producers.

4. A country enjoys an *absolute advantage* over another country in the production of a product if it uses fewer resources to produce that product than the other country does. A country has a *comparative advantage* in the production of a product if that product can be produced at a lower cost in terms of other goods.

5. Trade enables countries to move beyond their previous resource and productivity constraints. When countries specialize in producing those goods in which they have a comparative advantage, they maximize their combined output and allocate their resources more efficiently.

6. When trade is free, patterns of trade and trade flows result from the independent decisions of thousands of importers and exporters and millions of private households and firms.

7. The relative attractiveness of foreign goods to U.S. buyers and of U.S. goods to foreign buyers depends in part on *exchange rates*, the ratios at which two currencies are traded for each other.

8. For any pair of countries, there is a range of exchange rates that will lead automatically to both countries realizing the gains from specialization and comparative advantage. Within that range, the exchange rate will determine which country gains the most from trade. This leads us to conclude that exchange rates determine the terms of trade.

9. If exchange rates end up in the right range (that is, in a range that facilitates the flow of goods between nations), the free market will drive each country to shift resources into those sectors in which it enjoys a comparative advantage. Only those products in which a country has a comparative advantage will be competitive in world markets.

THE SOURCES OF COMPARATIVE ADVANTAGE *p. 418*

10. The *Heckscher-Ohlin theorem* looks to relative *factor endowments* to explain comparative advantage and trade flows. According to the theorem, a country has a comparative advantage in the production of a product if that country is relatively well endowed with the inputs that are used intensively in the production of that product.

11. A relatively short list of inputs—natural resources, knowledge capital, physical capital, land, and skilled and unskilled labor—explains a surprisingly large portion of world trade patterns. However, the simple version of the theory of comparative advantage cannot explain why many countries import and export the same goods.

12. Some theories argue that comparative advantage can be acquired. Just as industries within a country differentiate their products to capture a domestic market, they also differentiate their products to please the wide variety of tastes that exists worldwide. This theory is consistent with the theory of comparative advantage.

TRADE BARRIERS: TARIFFS, EXPORT SUBSIDIES, AND QUOTAS *p. 419*

13. Trade barriers take many forms. The three most common are *tariffs, export subsidies*, and *quotas*. All are forms of *protection* through which some sector of the economy is shielded from foreign competition.

14. Although the United States has historically been a high-tariff nation, the general movement is now away from tariffs and quotas. The *General Agreement on Tariffs and Trade (GATT)*, signed by the United States and 22 other countries in 1947, continues in effect today; its purpose is to reduce barriers to world trade and keep them down. Also important are the *U.S.-Canadian Free Trade Agreement*, signed in 1988, and the *North American Free Trade Agreement*, signed by the United States, Mexico, and Canada in the last days of the George H. W. Bush administration in 1992, taking effect in 1994.

15. The *World Trade Organization (WTO)* was set up by GATT to act as a negotiating forum for trade disputes across countries.

16. The *European Union (EU)* is a free-trade bloc composed of 27 nations: Austria, Belgium, Bulgaria, Cyprus, the Czech Republic, Denmark, Estonia, Finland, France, Germany, Greece, Hungary, Ireland, Italy, Latvia, Lithuania, Luxembourg, Malta, the Netherlands, Poland, Portugal, Romania, Slovakia, Slovenia, Spain, Sweden, and the United Kingdom. Many economists believe that the advantages of free trade within the bloc, a reunited Germany, and the ability to work well as a bloc will make the EU the most powerful player in the international marketplace in the coming decades.

FREE TRADE OR PROTECTION? *p. 422*

17. In one sense, the theory of comparative advantage is the case for free trade. Trade barriers prevent a nation from reaping the benefits of specialization, push it to adopt relatively inefficient production techniques, and force consumers to pay higher prices for protected products than they would otherwise pay.

18. The case for protection rests on a number of propositions, one of which is that foreign competition results in a loss of domestic jobs, but there is no reason to believe that the workers laid off in the contracting sectors will not be ultimately reemployed in other expanding sectors. This adjustment process is far from costless, however.

19. Other arguments for protection hold that cheap foreign labor makes competition unfair; that some countries engage in unfair trade practices; that free trade might harm the environment; and that protection safeguards the national security, discourages dependency, and shields *infant industries*. Despite these arguments, most economists favor free trade.

REVIEW TERMS AND CONCEPTS

absolute advantage, *p. 411*

comparative advantage, *p. 411*

Corn Laws, *p. 411*

Doha Development Agenda, *p. 420*

dumping, *p. 420*

economic integration, *p. 421*

European Union (EU), *p. 421*

exchange rate, *p. 416*

export subsidies, *p. 419*

factor endowments, *p. 418*

General Agreement on Tariffs and Trade (GATT), *p. 420*

Heckscher-Ohlin theorem, *p. 418*

infant industry, *p. 427*

North American Free Trade Agreement (NAFTA), *p. 421*

protection, *p. 419*

quota, *p. 420*

Smoot-Hawley tariff, *p. 420*

tariff, *p. 419*

terms of trade, *p. 415*

theory of comparative advantage, *p. 411*

trade deficit, *p. 410*

trade surplus, *p. 410*

U.S.-Canadian Free Trade Agreement, *p. 421*

World Trade Organization (WTO), *p. 420*

PROBLEMS

All problems are available on www.myeconlab.com

1. Suppose Germany and France each produce only two goods, guns and butter. Both are produced using labor alone. Assuming both countries are at full employment, you are given the following information:

Germany: 10 units of labor required to produce 1 gun
5 units of labor required to produce 1 pound of butter
Total labor force: 1,000,000 units

France: 15 units of labor required to produce 1 gun
10 units of labor required to produce 1 pound of butter
Total labor force: 750,000 units

 a. Draw the production possibility frontiers for each country in the absence of trade.

 b. If transportation costs are ignored and trade is allowed, will France and Germany engage in trade? Explain.

 c. If a trade agreement was negotiated, at what rate (number of guns per unit of butter) would they agree to exchange?

2. The United States and Russia each produce only bearskin caps and wheat. Domestic prices are given in the following table:

	RUSSIA	UNITED STATES	
Bearskin caps	10 Ru	$ 7	Per hat
Wheat	15 Ru	$10	Per bushel

On April 1, the Zurich exchange listed an exchange rate of $1 = 1 Ru.
  a. Which country has an absolute advantage in the production of bearskin caps? wheat?
  b. Which country has a comparative advantage in the production of bearskin caps? wheat?
  c. If the United States and Russia were the only two countries engaging in trade, what adjustments would you predict assuming exchange rates are freely determined by the laws of supply and demand?

3. The following table shows imports and exports of goods during 2009 for the United States:

	EXPORTS	IMPORTS
Total	1,068.0	1,575.0
Civilian aircraft	35.0	10.0
Apparel, household goods—textile	5.0	74.0
Crude oil	1.0	189.0
Vehicles, parts, and engines	82.0	158.0
Foods, feeds, and beverages	94.0	81.0

All figures are rounded to the nearest billion dollars.
Source: www.census.gov.

What, if anything, can you conclude about the comparative advantage that the United States has relative to its trading partners in the production of goods? What stories can you tell about the wide disparities in apparel and aircraft?

4. The following table gives recent figures for yield per acre in Illinois and Kansas:

	WHEAT	SOYBEANS
Illinois	48	39
Kansas	40	24

Source: U.S. Department of Agriculture, *Crop Production.*

  a. If we assume that farmers in Illinois and Kansas use the same amount of labor, capital, and fertilizer, which state has an absolute advantage in wheat production? soybean production?
  b. If we transfer land out of wheat into soybeans, how many bushels of wheat do we give up in Illinois per additional bushel of soybeans produced? in Kansas?
  c. Which state has a comparative advantage in wheat production? in soybean production?
  d. The following table gives the distribution of land planted for each state in millions of acres in the same year.

	TOTAL ACRES UNDER TILL	WHEAT	SOYBEANS
Illinois	22.9	1.9 (8.3%)	9.1 (39.7%)
Kansas	20.7	11.8 (57.0%)	1.9 (9.2%)

Are these data consistent with your answer to part c? Explain.

5. You can think of the United States as a set of 50 separate economies with no trade barriers. In such an open environment, each state specializes in the products that it produces best.
  a. What product or products does your state specialize in?
  b. Can you identify the source of the comparative advantage that lies behind the production of one or more of these products (for example, a natural resource, plentiful cheap labor, or a skilled labor force)?
  c. Do you think that the theory of comparative advantage and the Heckscher-Ohlin theorem help to explain why your state specializes the way that it does? Explain your answer.

6. Australia and the United States produce white and red wines. Current domestic prices for each wine are given in the following table:

	AUSTRALIA	UNITED STATES
White wine	5 AU$	10 US$
Red wine	10 AU$	15 US$

Suppose the exchange rate is 1 AU$ = 1 US$.
  a. If the price ratios within each country reflect resource use, which country has a comparative advantage in the production of red wine? white wine?
  b. Assume that there are no other trading partners and that the only motive for holding foreign currency is to buy foreign goods. Will the current exchange rate lead to trade flows in both directions between the two countries? Explain.
  c. What adjustments might you expect in the exchange rate? Be specific.
  d. What would you predict about trade flows between Australia and the United States after the exchange rate has adjusted?

7. Some empirical trade economists have noted that for many products, countries are both importers and exporters. For example, the United States both imports and exports shirts. How do you explain this?

8. [Related to the *Economics in Practice* on p. 422] Review the *Economics in Practice* on p. 422. Despite the reduction in tariffs brought about by the passage of trade agreements such as GATT, the recent recession has generated political pressure in many countries to again impose import tariffs, with this pressure especially strong in the case of imports from China. Why would a recession create pressure to impose tariffs? Who is likely to be in favor of imposing these tariffs, and who might be in favor of reducing or eliminating them? Do some research on the imposition of tariffs during the recent recession. Did many countries actually impose new tariffs on imports? What has been the response of the WTO and countries like China to the imposition of these tariffs?

9. [Related to the *Economics in Practice* on p. 425] When a president presents a trade agreement for ratification to Congress, many domestic industries fight the ratification. In 2005, the United States was negotiating the Central America-Dominican Republic Free Trade Agreement (CAFTA-DR). Write a brief essay on the U.S. political opposition to CAFTA-DR in 2004 and 2005. What industries in the United States opposed the trade agreement? Is it fair to compare the arguments of these industries to the arguments posed by the candle makers?

10. The following graph represents the domestic supply and demand for coffee a number of years ago.
  a. In the absence of trade, what is the equilibrium price and equilibrium quantity?

b. The government opens the market to free trade, and Columbia enters the market, pricing coffee at $1 per pound. What will happen to the domestic price of coffee? What will be the new domestic quantity supplied and domestic quantity demanded? How much coffee will be imported from Columbia?

c. After numerous complaints from domestic coffee producers, the government imposes a $0.50 per pound tariff on all imported coffee. What will happen to the domestic price of coffee? What will be the new domestic quantity supplied and domestic quantity demanded? How much coffee will now be imported from Columbia?

d. How much revenue will the government receive from the $0.50 per pound tariff?

e. Who ultimately ends up paying the $0.50 per pound tariff? Why?

11. Refer to the previous problem. Assume the market is opened to trade and Columbia still enters the market by pricing coffee at $1.00 per pound. But as a response to complaints from domestic coffee producers, instead of imposing a $0.50 per pound tariff, the government imposes an import quota of 50 million pounds on Columbian coffee. How will the results of the quota differ from the results of the tariff?

12. The nation of Pixley has an absolute advantage in everything it produces compared to the nation of Hooterville. Could these two nations still benefit by trading with each other? Explain.

13. Evaluate the following statement: If lower exchange rates increase a nation's exports, the government should do everything in its power to ensure that the exchange rate for its currency is as low as possible.

14. Since the 1960s, the United States has had an embargo in place on Cuba, virtually eliminating all trade between the two countries. Suppose the United States decided to lift the embargo on exports to Cuba while maintaining the embargo on Cuban imports. Explain whether this one-sided change would benefit neither country, just one country, or both countries?

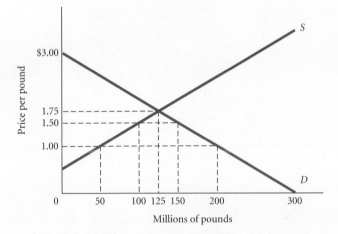

Glossary

ability-to-pay principle A theory of taxation holding that citizens should bear tax burdens in line with their ability to pay taxes. *p. 393*

absolute advantage A producer has an absolute advantage over another in the production of a good or service if he or she can produce that product using fewer resources. *p. 28 p. 411*

adverse selection A situation in which asymmetric information results in high-quality goods or high-quality consumers being squeezed out of transactions because they cannot demonstrate their quality. *p. 358*

asymmetric information One of the parties to a transaction has information relevant to the transaction that the other party does not have. *p. 357*

average fixed cost (*AFC*) Total fixed cost divided by the number of units of output; a per-unit measure of fixed costs. *p. 169*

average product The average amount produced by each unit of a variable factor of production. *p. 154*

average tax rate Total amount of tax paid divided by total income. *p. 391*

average total cost (*ATC*) Total cost divided by the number of units of output. *p. 175*

average variable cost (*AVC*) Total variable cost divided by the number of units of output. *p. 174*

barriers to entry Factors that prevent new firms from entering and competing in imperfectly competitive industries. *p. 278*

behavioral economics A branch of economics that uses the insights of psychology and economics to investigate decision making. *p. 317*

benefits-received principle A theory of fairness holding that taxpayers should contribute to government (in the form of taxes) in proportion to the benefits they receive from public expenditures. *p. 393*

black market A market in which illegal trading takes place at market-determined prices. *p. 84*

bond A contract between a borrower and a lender, in which the borrower agrees to pay the loan at some time in the future, along with interest payments along the way. *p. 236*

brain drain The tendency for talented people from developing countries to become educated in a developed country and remain there after graduation. *p. 437*

breaking even The situation in which a firm is earning exactly a normal rate of return. *p. 190*

budget constraint The limits imposed on household choices by income, wealth, and product prices. *p. 122*

capital Things that are produced and then used in the production of other goods and services. *p. 25 p. 233*

capital flight The tendency for both human capital and financial capital to leave developing countries in search of higher expected rates of return elsewhere with less risk. *p. 436*

capital income Income earned on savings that have been put to use through financial capital markets. *p. 237*

capital market The input/factor market in which households supply their savings, for interest or for claims to future profits, to firms that demand funds to buy capital goods. *p. 49 p. 236*

capital stock For a single firm, the current market value of the firm's plant, equipment, inventories, and intangible assets. *p. 234*

capital-intensive technology Technology that relies heavily on capital instead of human labor. *p. 152*

cartel A group of firms that gets together and makes joint price and output decisions to maximize joint profits. *p. 297*

Cartesian coordinate system A common method of graphing two variables that makes use of two perpendicular lines against which the variables are plotted. *p. 18 p. 22*

Celler-Kefauver Act Extended the government's authority to control mergers. *p. 308*

***ceteris paribus,* or all else equal** A device used to analyze the relationship between two variables while the values of other variables are held unchanged. *p. 11*

choice set *or* opportunity set The set of options that is defined and limited by a budget constraint. *p. 123*

Clayton Act Passed by Congress in 1914 to strengthen the Sherman Act and clarify the rule of reason, the act outlawed specific monopolistic behaviors such as tying contracts, price discrimination, and unlimited mergers. *p. 286*

Coase theorem Under certain conditions, when externalities are present, private parties can arrive at the efficient solution without government involvement. *p. 334*

command economy An economy in which a central government either directly or indirectly sets output targets, incomes, and prices. *p. 40*

commitment device Actions that individuals take in one period to try to control their behavior in a future period. *p. 317*

comparative advantage A producer has a comparative advantage over another in the production of a good or service if he or she can produce that product at a lower *opportunity cost*. *p. 29 p. 411*

compensating differentials Differences in wages that result from differences in working conditions. Risky jobs usually pay higher wages; highly desirable jobs usually pay lower wages. *p. 368*

complements, complementary goods Goods that "go together"; a decrease in the price of one results in an increase in demand for the other and vice versa. *p. 55*

concentration ratio The share of industry output in sales or employment accounted for by the top firms. *p. 295*

constant returns to scale An increase in a firm's scale of production has no effect on costs per unit produced. *p. 195*

constant-cost industry An industry that shows no economies or diseconomies of scale as the industry grows. Such industries have flat, or horizontal, long-run supply curves. *p. 212 p. 213*

consumer goods Goods produced for present consumption. *p. 32*

consumer sovereignty The idea that consumers ultimately dictate what will be produced (or not produced) by choosing what to purchase (and what not to purchase). *p. 41*

consumer surplus The difference between the maximum amount a person is willing to pay for a good and its current market price. *p. 89*

contestable markets Markets in which entry and exit are easy. *p. 295*

Corn Laws The tariffs, subsidies, and restrictions enacted by the British Parliament in the early nineteenth century to discourage imports and encourage exports of grain. *p. 411*

cross-price elasticity of demand A measure of the response of the quantity of one good demanded to a change in the price of another good. *p. 110*

deadweight loss The total loss of producer and consumer surplus from underproduction or overproduction. *p. 92*

decreasing returns to scale, *or* diseconomies of scale An increase in a firm's scale of production leads to higher costs per unit produced. *p. 195*

decreasing-cost industry An industry that realizes external economies—that is, average costs decrease as the industry grows. The long-run supply curve for such an industry has a negative slope. *p. 212 p. 213*

demand curve A graph illustrating how much of a given product a household would be willing to buy at different prices. *p. 51*

demand schedule A table showing how much of a given product a household would be willing to buy at different prices. *p. 51*

demand-determined price The price of a good that is in fixed supply; it is determined exclusively by what households and firms are willing to pay for the good. *p. 224*

depreciation The amount by which an asset's value falls in a given period. *p. 236*

depreciation of a currency The fall in value of one currency relative to another. *p. 224*

derived demand The demand for resources (inputs) that is dependent on the demand for the outputs those resources can be used to produce. *p. 215*

descriptive economics The compilation of data that describe phenomena and facts. *p. 10*

diamond/water paradox A paradox stating that (1) the things with the greatest value in use frequently have little or no value in exchange and (2) the things with the greatest value in exchange frequently have little or no value in use. *p. 129*

diminishing marginal utility The more of any one good consumed in a given period, the less incremental satisfaction is generated by consuming a marginal or incremental unit of the same good. *p. 354*

Doha Development Agenda An initiative of the World Trade Organization focused on issues of trade and development. *p. 420*

dominant strategy In game theory, a strategy that is best no matter what the opposition does. *p. 301*

drop-in-the-bucket problem   A problem intrinsic to public goods: The good or service is usually so costly that its provision generally does not depend on whether any single person pays. *p. 342*

dumping   A firm's or an industry's sale of products on the world market at prices below its own cost of production. *p. 420*

duopoly   A two-firm oligopoly. *p. 299*

economic growth   An increase in the total output of an economy. It occurs when a society acquires new resources or when it learns to produce more using existing resources. *p. 14   p. 36*

economic income   The amount of money a household can spend during a given period without increasing or decreasing its net assets. Wages, salaries, dividends, interest income, transfer payments, rents, and so on are sources of economic income. *p. 370*

economic integration   Occurs when two or more nations join to form a free-trade zone. *p. 421*

economic theory   A statement or set of related statements about cause and effect, action and reaction. *p. 10*

economics   The study of how individuals and societies choose to use the scarce resources that nature and previous generations have provided. *p. 2*

efficiency   In economics, allocative efficiency. An efficient economy is one that produces what people want at the least possible cost. *p. 13   p. 254*

efficient market   A market in which profit opportunities are eliminated almost instantaneously. *p. 3*

elastic demand   A demand relationship in which the percentage change in quantity demanded is larger than the percentage change in price in absolute value (a demand elasticity with an absolute value greater than 1). *p. 100*

elasticity   A general concept used to quantify the response in one variable when another variable changes. *p. 97*

elasticity of labor supply   A measure of the response of labor supplied to a change in the price of labor. *p. 111*

elasticity of supply   A measure of the response of quantity of a good supplied to a change in price of that good. Likely to be positive in output markets. *p. 111*

empirical economics   The collection and use of data to test economic theories. *p. 13*

entrepreneur   A person who organizes, manages, and assumes the risks of a firm, taking a new idea or a new product and turning it into a successful business. *p. 48*

equilibrium   The condition that exists when quantity supplied and quantity demanded are equal. At equilibrium, there is no tendency for price to change. In the macroeconomic goods market, equilibrium occurs when planned aggregate expenditure is equal to aggregate output. *p. 66*

equity   Fairness. *p. 14   p. 367*

estate   The property that a person owns at the time of his or her death. *p. 396*

estate tax   A tax on the total value of a person's estate. *p. 396*

European Union (EU)   The European trading bloc composed of 27 countries. *p. 421*

excess burden   The amount by which the burden of a tax exceeds the total revenue collected. Also called deadweight loss. *p. 402*

excess demand *or* shortage   The condition that exists when quantity demanded exceeds quantity supplied at the current price. *p. 66*

excess supply *or* surplus   The condition that exists when quantity supplied exceeds quantity demanded at the current price. *p. 68*

expected rate of return   The annual rate of return that a firm expects to obtain through a capital investment. *p. 243*

expected utility   The sum of the utilities coming from all possible outcomes of a deal, weighted by the probability of each occurring. *p. 355*

expected value   The sum of the payoffs associated with each possible outcome of a situation weighted by its probability of occurring. *p. 354*

export promotion   A trade policy designed to encourage exports. *p. 441*

export subsidies   Government payments made to domestic firms to encourage exports. *p. 419*

external economies and diseconomies   When industry growth results in a decrease of long-run average costs, there are *external economies*; when industry growth results in an increase of long-run average costs, there are *external diseconomies*. *p. 210   p. 213*

externality   A cost or benefit imposed or bestowed on an individual or a group that is outside, or external to, the transaction. *p. 263   p. 329*

factor endowments   The quantity and quality of labor, land, and natural resources of a country. *p. 418*

factor substitution effect   The tendency of firms to substitute away from a factor whose price has risen and toward a factor whose price has fallen. *p. 222*

factors of production (*or* factors)   The inputs into the process of production. Another term for resources. Land, labor, and capital are the three key factors of production. *p. 25   p. 49*

fair game *or* fair bet   A game whose expected value is zero. *p. 354*

fallacy of composition   The erroneous belief that what is true for a part is necessarily true for the whole. *p. 13*

favored customers   Those who receive special treatment from dealers during situations of excess demand. *p. 84*

Federal Trade Commission (FTC)   A federal regulatory group created by Congress in 1914 to investigate the structure and behavior of firms engaging in interstate commerce, to determine what constitutes unlawful "unfair" behavior, and to issue cease-and-desist orders to those found in violation of antitrust law. *p. 286*

financial capital market   The complex set of institutions in which suppliers of capital (households that save) and the demand for capital (firms wanting to invest) interact. *p. 137   p. 237*

firm   An organization that comes into being when a person or a group of people decides to produce a good or service to meet a perceived demand. A firm transforms resources (inputs) into products (outputs). Firms are the primary producing units in a market economy. *p. 48   p. 148*

Five Forces model   A model developed by Michael Porter that helps us understand the five competitive forces that determine the level of competition and profitability in an industry. *p. 294*

fixed cost   Any cost that does not depend on the firms' level of output. These costs are incurred even if the firm is producing nothing. There are no fixed costs in the long run. *p. 168*

food stamps   Vouchers that have a face value greater than their cost and that can be used to purchase food at grocery stores. *p. 383*

free enterprise   The freedom of individuals to start and operate private businesses in search of profits. *p. 41*

free-rider problem   A problem intrinsic to public goods: Because people can enjoy the benefits of public goods whether or not they pay for them, they are usually unwilling to pay for them. *p. 342*

game theory   Analyzes the choices made by rival firms, people, and even governments when they are trying to maximize their own well-being while anticipating and reacting to the actions of others in their environment. *p. 301*

General Agreement on Tariffs and Trade (GATT)   An international agreement signed by the United States and 22 other countries in 1947 to promote the liberalization of foreign trade. *p. 420*

general equilibrium   The condition that exists when all markets in an economy are in simultaneous equilibrium. *p. 254*

Gini coefficient   A commonly used measure of the degree of inequality of income derived from a Lorenz curve. It can range from 0 to a maximum of 1. *p. 372*

government failure   Occurs when the government becomes the tool of the rent seeker and the allocation of resources is made even less efficient by the intervention of government. *p. 283*

graph   A two-dimensional representation of a set of numbers, or data. *p. 17   p. 22*

Heckscher-Ohlin theorem   A theory that explains the existence of a country's comparative advantage by its factor endowments: A country has a comparative advantage in the production of a product if that country is relatively well endowed with inputs used intensively in the production of that product. *p. 418*

Herfindahl-Hirschman Index (HHI)   An index of market concentration found by summing the square of percentage shares of firms in the market. *p. 308*

homogenous products   Undifferentiated products; products that are identical to, or indistinguishable from, one another. *p. 119   p. 179*

horizontal differentiation   Products differ in ways that make them better for some people and worse for others. *p. 316*

households   The consuming units in an economy. *p. 48*

human capital   A form of intangible capital that includes the skills and other knowledge that workers have or acquire through education and training and that yields valuable services to a firm over time. *p. 234   p. 368*

imperfect information   The absence of full knowledge concerning product characteristics, available prices, and so on. *p. 264*

imperfectly competitive industry   An industry in which individual firms have some control over the price of their output. *p. 269*

import substitution   An industrial trade strategy that favors developing local industries that can manufacture goods to replace imports. *p. 440*

impossibility theorem A proposition demonstrated by Kenneth Arrow showing that no system of aggregating individual preferences into social decisions will always yield consistent, nonarbitrary results. *p. 346*

income The sum of all a household's wages, salaries, profits, interest payments, rents, and other forms of earnings in a given period of time. It is a flow measure. *p. 54*

income elasticity of demand A measure of the responsiveness of demand to changes in income. *p. 110*

increasing returns to scale, *or* **economies of scale** An increase in a firm's scale of production leads to lower costs per unit produced. *p. 195*

increasing-cost industry An industry that encounters external diseconomies—that is, average costs increase as the industry grows. The long-run supply curve for such an industry has a positive slope. *p. 212 p. 213*

Indifference curve A set of points, each point representing a combination of goods X and Y, all of which yield the same total utility. *p. 141 p. 145*

industrial policy A policy in which governments actively pick industries to support as a base for economic development. *p. 439*

Industrial Revolution The period in England during the late eighteenth and early nineteenth centuries in which new manufacturing technologies and improved transportation gave rise to the modern factory system and a massive movement of the population from the countryside to the cities. *p. 4*

inelastic demand Demand that responds somewhat, but not a great deal, to changes in price. Inelastic demand always has a numerical value between zero and –1. *p. 100*

infant industry A young industry that may need temporary protection from competition from the established industries of other countries to develop an acquired comparative advantage. *p. 427*

inferior goods Goods for which demand tends to fall when income rises. *p. 54*

injunction A court order forbidding the continuation of behavior that leads to damages. *p. 336*

input *or* **factor markets** The markets in which the resources used to produce goods and services are exchanged. *p. 48*

inputs *or* **resources** Anything provided by nature or previous generations that can be used directly or indirectly to satisfy human wants. *p. 26*

intangible capital Nonmaterial things that contribute to the output of future goods and services. *p. 234*

interest The payments made for the use of money; The fee that borrowers pay to lenders for the use of their funds. *p. 237*

interest rate Interest payments expressed as a percentage of the loan. *p. 238*

International Monetary Fund (IMF) An international agency whose primary goals are to stabilize international exchange rates and to lend money to countries that have problems financing their international transactions. *p. 439*

investment The process of using resources to produce new capital; New capital additions to a firm's capital stock. Although capital is measured at a given point in time (a stock), investment is measured over a period of time (a flow). The flow of investment increases the capital stock. *p. 32 p. 235*

isocost line A graph that shows all the combinations of capital and labor available for a given total cost. *p. 163 p. 165*

isoquant A graph that shows all the combinations of capital and labor that can be used to produce a given amount of output. *p. 162 p. 165*

labor market The input/factor market in which households supply work for wages to firms that demand labor. *p. 49*

labor supply curve A curve that shows the quantity of labor supplied at different wage rates. Its shape depends on how households react to changes in the wage rate. *p. 134*

labor theory of value Stated most simply, the theory that the value of a commodity depends only on the amount of labor required to produce it. *p. 379*

labor-intensive technology Technology that relies heavily on human labor instead of capital. *p. 152*

laissez-faire economy Literally from the French: "allow [them] to do." An economy in which individual people and firms pursue their own self-interest without any central direction or regulation. *p. 40*

land market The input/factor market in which households supply land or other real property in exchange for rent. *p. 49*

law of demand The negative relationship between price and quantity demanded: As price rises, quantity demanded decreases; as price falls, quantity demanded increases. *p. 52*

law of diminishing marginal utility The more of any one good consumed in a given period, the less satisfaction (utility) generated by consuming each additional (marginal) unit of the same good. *p. 126*

law of diminishing returns When additional units of a variable input are added to fixed inputs after a certain point, the marginal product of the variable input declines. *p. 154*

law of supply The positive relationship between price and quantity of a good supplied: An increase in market price will lead to an increase in quantity supplied, and a decrease in market price will lead to a decrease in quantity supplied. *p. 61*

liability rules Laws that require A to compensate B for damages imposed. *p. 336*

logrolling Occurs when congressional representatives trade votes, agreeing to help each other get certain pieces of legislation passed. *p. 347*

long run That period of time for which there are no fixed factors of production: Firms can increase or decrease the scale of operation, and new firms can enter and existing firms can exit the industry. *p. 151*

long-run average cost curve (LRAC) The "envelope" of a series of short-run cost curves. *p. 197*

long-run competitive equilibrium When $P = SRMC = SRAC = LRAC$ and profits are zero. *p. 206*

long-run industry supply curve (LRIS) A graph that traces out price and total output over time as an industry expands. *p. 212 p. 213*

Lorenz curve A widely used graph of the distribution of income, with cumulative percentage of households plotted along the horizontal axis and cumulative percentage of income plotted along the vertical axis. *p. 371*

macroeconomics The branch of economics that examines the economic behavior of aggregates—income, employment, output, and so on—on a national scale. *p. 7*

marginal cost (MC) The increase in total cost that results from producing 1 more unit of output. Marginal costs reflect changes in variable costs. *p. 171*

marginal damage cost (MDC) The additional harm done by increasing the level of an externality-producing activity by 1 unit. If producing product X pollutes the water in a river, *MDC* is the additional cost imposed by the added pollution that results from increasing output by 1 unit of X per period. *p. 333*

marginal private cost (MPC) The amount that a consumer pays to consume an additional unit of a particular good. *p. 333*

marginal product The additional output that can be produced by adding one more unit of a specific input, *ceteris paribus*. *p. 153*

marginal product of labor (MP$_L$) The additional output produced by 1 additional unit of labor. *p. 216*

Marginal rate of substitution MU_X/MU_Y; the ratio at which a household is willing to substitute good Y for good X. *p. 141 p. 145*

marginal rate of technical substitution The rate at which a firm can substitute capital for labor and hold output constant. *p. 162 p. 165*

marginal rate of transformation (MRT) The slope of the production possibility frontier (ppf). *p. 35*

marginal revenue (MR) The additional revenue that a firm takes in when it increases output by one additional unit. In perfect competition, $P = MR$. *p. 180*

marginal revenue product (MRP) The additional revenue a firm earns by employing 1 additional unit of input, *ceteris paribus*. *p. 217*

marginal social cost (MSC) The total cost to society of producing an additional unit of a good or service. *MSC* is equal to the sum of the marginal costs of producing the product and the correctly measured damage costs involved in the process of production. *p. 330*

marginal tax rate The tax rate paid on any additional income earned. *p. 391*

marginal utility (MU) The additional satisfaction gained by the consumption or use of one more unit of a good or service. *p. 126*

marginalism The process of analyzing the additional or incremental costs or benefits arising from a choice or decision. *p. 3*

market The institution through which buyers and sellers interact and engage in exchange. *p. 40*

market demand The sum of all the quantities of a good or service demanded per period by all the households buying in the market for that good or service. *p. 58*

market failure Occurs when resources are misallocated, or allocated inefficiently. The result is waste or lost value. *p. 262 p. 329*

market power An imperfectly competitive firm's ability to raise price without losing all of the quantity demanded for its product. *p. 269*

market signaling Actions taken by buyers and sellers to communicate quality in a world of uncertainty. *p. 360*

market supply The sum of all that is supplied each period by all producers of a single product. *p. 65*

maximin strategy In game theory, a strategy chosen to maximize the minimum gain that can be earned. *p. 303*

mechanism design A contract or an institution that aligns the interests of two parties in a transaction. A piece rate, for example, creates incentives for a worker to work hard, just as his or her superior wants. A co-pay in the health care industry encourages more careful use of health care, just as the insurance company wants. *p. 363*

Medicaid *and* Medicare In-kind government transfer programs that provide health and hospitalization benefits: Medicare to the aged and their survivors and to certain of the disabled, regardless of income, and Medicaid to people with low incomes. *p. 383*

microeconomics The branch of economics that examines the functioning of individual industries and the behavior of individual decision-making units—that is, firms and households. *p. 6*

midpoint formula A more precise way of calculating percentages using the value halfway between P_1 and P_2 for the base in calculating the percentage change in price and the value halfway between Q_1 and Q_2 as the base for calculating the percentage change in quantity demanded. *p. 102*

minimum efficient scale (MES) The smallest size at which the long-run average cost curve is at its minimum. *p. 197*

minimum wage A price floor set for the price of labor; the lowest wage that firms are permitted to pay workers. *p. 86 p. 368*

model A formal statement of a theory, usually a mathematical statement of a presumed relationship between two or more variables. *p. 10*

money income The measure of income used by the Census Bureau. Because money income excludes noncash transfer payments and capital gains income, it is less inclusive than economic income. *p. 371*

monopolistic competition A common form of industry (market) structure in the United States, characterized by a large number of firms, no barriers to entry, and product differentiation. *p. 314*

moral hazard Arises when one party to a contract changes behavior in response to that contract and thus passes on the costs of that behavior change to the other party. *p. 362*

movement along a demand curve The change in quantity demanded brought about by a change in price. *p. 58*

movement along a supply curve The change in quantity supplied brought about by a change in price. *p. 63*

Nash equilibrium In game theory, the result of all players' playing their best strategy given what their competitors are doing. *p. 302*

natural experiment Selection of a control versus experimental group in testing the outcome of an intervention is made as a result of an exogenous event outside the experiment itself and unrelated to it. *p. 444*

natural monopoly An industry that realizes such large economies of scale in producing its product that single-firm production of that good or service is most efficient. *p. 278*

negative relationship A relationship between two variables, X and Y, in which a decrease in X is associated with an increase in Y and an increase in X is associated with a decrease in Y. *p. 19 p. 22*

network externalities The value of a product to a consumer increases with the number of that product being sold or used in the market. *p. 280*

nonexcludable A characteristic of most public goods: Once a good is produced, no one can be excluded from enjoying its benefits. *p. 342*

nonrival in consumption A characteristic of public goods: One person's enjoyment of the benefits of a public good does not interfere with another's consumption of it. *p. 341*

normal goods Goods for which demand goes up when income is higher and for which demand goes down when income is lower. *p. 54*

normal rate of return A rate of return on capital that is just sufficient to keep owners and investors satisfied. For relatively risk-free firms, it should be nearly the same as the interest rate on risk-free government bonds. *p. 149*

normative economics An approach to economics that analyzes outcomes of economic behavior, evaluates them as good or bad, and may prescribe courses of action. Also called *policy economics*. *p. 9*

North American Free Trade Agreement (NAFTA) An agreement signed by the United States, Mexico, and Canada in which the three countries agreed to establish all North America as a free-trade zone. *p. 421*

Ockham's razor The principle that irrelevant detail should be cut away. *p. 11*

oligopoly A form of industry (market) structure characterized by a few dominant firms. Products may be homogenous or differentiated. *p. 293*

opportunity cost The best alternative that we forgo, or give up, when we make a choice or a decision. *p. 2 p. 27*

optimal level of provision for public goods The level at which society's total willingness to pay per unit is equal to the marginal cost of producing the good. *p. 345*

optimal method of production The production method that minimizes cost. *p. 151*

optimal scale of plant The scale of plant that minimizes average cost. *p. 200*

origin On a Cartesian coordinate system, the point at which the horizontal and vertical axes intersect. *p. 18 p. 22*

output effect of a factor price increase (decrease) When a firm decreases (increases) its output in response to a factor price increase (decrease), this decreases (increases) its demand for all factors. *p. 224*

outputs Goods and services of value to households. *p. 26*

Pareto efficiency *or* Pareto optimality A condition in which no change is possible that will make some members of society better off without making some other members of society worse off. *p. 256*

partial equilibrium analysis The process of examining the equilibrium conditions in individual markets and for households and firms separately. *p. 254*

patent A barrier to entry that grants exclusive use of the patented product or process to the inventor. *p. 279*

payoff The amount that comes from a possible outcome or result. *p. 354*

perfect competition An industry structure in which there are many firms, each being small relative to the industry and producing virtually identical products, and in which no firm is large enough to have any control over prices. In perfectly competitive industries, new competitors can freely enter and exit the market. *p. 119 p. 179*

perfect knowledge The assumption that households possess a knowledge of the qualities and prices of everything available in the market and that firms have all available information concerning wage rates, capital costs, and output prices. *p. 119*

perfect price discrimination Occurs when a firm charges the maximum amount that buyers are willing to pay for each unit. *p. 283*

perfect substitutes Identical products. *p. 55*

perfectly elastic demand Demand in which quantity drops to zero at the slightest increase in price. *p. 99*

perfectly inelastic demand Demand in which quantity demanded does not respond at all to a change in price. *p. 99*

physical, *or* tangible, capital Material things used as inputs in the production of future goods and services. The major categories of physical capital are nonresidential structures, durable equipment, residential structures, and inventories. *p. 233*

positive economics An approach to economics that seeks to understand behavior and the operation of systems without making judgments. It describes what exists and how it works. *p. 9*

positive relationship A relationship between two variables, X and Y, in which a decrease in X is associated with a decrease in Y, and an increase in X is associated with an increase in Y. *p. 19 p. 22*

post hoc, ergo propter hoc Literally, "after this (in time), therefore because of this." A common error made in thinking about causation: If Event A happens before Event B, it is not necessarily true that A caused B. *p. 12*

poverty line The officially established income level that distinguishes the poor from the nonpoor. It is set at three times the cost of the Department of Agriculture's minimum food budget. *p. 375*

Preference map A consumer's set of indifference curves. *p. 142 p. 145*

present discounted value (PDV) *or* present value (PV) The present discounted value of R dollars to be paid *t* years in the future is the amount you need to pay today, at current interest rates, to ensure that you end up with *R* dollars *t* years from now. It is the current market value of receiving *R* dollars in *t* years. *p. 249 p. 251*

price ceiling A maximum price that sellers may charge for a good, usually set by government. *p. 82*

price discrimination Charging different prices to different buyers. *p. 283*

price elasticity of demand The ratio of the percentage of change in quantity demanded to the percentage of change in price; measures the responsiveness of quantity demanded to changes in price. *p. 99*

price floor A minimum price below which exchange is not permitted. *p. 86*

price leadership A form of oligopoly in which one dominant firm sets prices and all the smaller firms in the industry follow its pricing policy. *p. 298*

price rationing The process by which the market system allocates goods and services to consumers when quantity demanded exceeds quantity supplied. *p. 79*

principle of neutrality All else equal, taxes that are neutral with respect to economic decisions (that is, taxes that do not distort economic decisions) are generally preferable to taxes that distort economic decisions. Taxes that are not neutral impose excess burdens. *p. 402*

principle of second best The fact that a tax distorts an economic decision does not always imply that such a tax imposes an excess burden. If there are previously existing distortions, such a tax may actually improve efficiency. *p. 405*

prisoners' dilemma A game in which the players are prevented from cooperating and in which each has a dominant strategy that leaves them both worse off than if they could cooperate. *p. 302*

producer surplus The difference between the current market price and the full cost of production for the firm. *p. 90*

product differentiation A strategy that firms use to achieve market power. Accomplished by producing products that have distinct positive identities in consumers' minds. *p. 315*

product *or* output markets The markets in which goods and services are exchanged. *p. 48*

production The process that transforms scarce resources into useful goods and services. *p. 25 p. 147*

production function *or* total product function A numerical or mathematical expression of a relationship between inputs and outputs. It shows units of total product as a function of units of inputs. *p. 152*

production possibility frontier (ppf) A graph that shows all the combinations of goods and services that can be produced if all of society's resources are used efficiently. *p. 33*

production technology The quantitative relationship between inputs and outputs. *p. 152*

productivity of an input The amount of output produced per unit of that input. *p. 216*

profit The difference between revenues and costs. *p. 61 p. 148*

progressive tax A tax whose burden, expressed as a percentage of income, increases as income increases. *p. 390*

property income Income from the ownership of real property and financial holdings. It takes the form of profits, interest, dividends, and rents. *p. 369*

proportional tax A tax whose burden is the same proportion of income for all households. *p. 390*

protection The practice of shielding a sector of the economy from foreign competition. *p. 419*

public assistance, *or* welfare Government transfer programs that provide cash benefits to: (1) families with dependent children whose incomes and assets fall below a very low level, and (2) the very poor regardless of whether they have children. *p. 382*

public choice theory An economic theory that the public officials who set economic policies and regulate the players act in their own self-interest, just as firms do. *p. 283*

public goods, (*or* social *or* collective goods) Goods and services that bestow collective benefits on members of society. Generally, no one can be excluded from enjoying their benefits. The classic example is national defense. *p. 263 p. 341*

pure monopoly An industry with a single firm that produces a product for which there are no close substitutes and in which significant barriers to entry prevent other firms from entering the industry to compete for profits. *p. 270*

pure rent The return to any factor of production that is in fixed supply. *p. 224*

quantity demanded The amount (number of units) of a product that a household would buy in a given period if it could buy all it wanted at the current market price. *p. 50*

quantity supplied The amount of a particular product that a firm would be willing and able to offer for sale at a particular price during a given time period. *p. 61*

queuing Waiting in line as a means of distributing goods and services: a nonprice rationing mechanism. *p. 83*

quota A limit on the quantity of imports. *p. 420*

random experiment (Sometimes referred to as a randomized experiment.) A technique in which outcomes of specific interventions are determined by using the intervention in a randomly selected subset of a sample and then comparing outcomes from the exposed and control group. *p. 444*

ration coupons Tickets or coupons that entitle individuals to purchase a certain amount of a given product per month. *p. 84*

Rawlsian justice A theory of distributional justice that concludes that the social contract emerging from the "original position" would call for an income distribution that would maximize the well-being of the worst-off member of society. *p. 379*

real income The set of opportunities to purchase real goods and services available to a household as determined by prices and money income. *p. 124*

regressive tax A tax whose burden, expressed as a percentage of income, falls as income increases. *p. 390*

rent-seeking behavior Actions taken by households or firms to preserve positive profits. *p. 283*

risk premium The maximum price a risk-averse person will pay to avoid taking a risk. *p. 348*

risk-averse Refers to a person's preference of a certain payoff over an uncertain one with the same expected value. *p. 356*

risk-loving Refers to a person's preference for an uncertain deal over a certain deal with an equal expected value. *p. 356*

risk-neutral Refers to a person's willingness to take a bet with an expected value of zero. *p. 356*

rule of reason The criterion introduced by the Supreme Court in 1911 to determine whether a particular action was illegal ("unreasonable") or legal ("reasonable") within the terms of the Sherman Act. *p. 286*

scarce Limited. *p. 2*

shift of a demand curve The change that takes place in a demand curve corresponding to a new relationship between quantity demanded of a good and price of that good. The shift is brought about by a change in the original conditions. *p. 58*

shift of a supply curve The change that takes place in a supply curve corresponding to a new relationship between quantity supplied of a good and the price of that good. The shift is brought about by a change in the original conditions. *p. 64*

shock therapy The approach to transition from socialism to market capitalism that advocates rapid deregulation of prices, liberalization of trade, and privatization. *p. 451*

short run The period of time for which two conditions hold: The firm is operating under a fixed scale (fixed factor) of production, and firms can neither enter nor exit an industry. *p. 151*

short-run industry supply curve The sum of the marginal cost curves (above *AVC*) of all the firms in an industry. *p. 194*

shut-down point The lowest point on the average variable cost curve. When price falls below the minimum point on *AVC*, total revenue is insufficient to cover variable costs and the firm will shut down and bear losses equal to fixed costs. *p. 193*

slope A measurement that indicates whether the relationship between variables is positive or negative and how much of a response there is in *Y* (the variable on the vertical axis) when *X* (the variable on the horizontal axis) changes. *p. 19 p. 22*

Smoot-Hawley tariff The U.S. tariff law of the 1930s, which set the highest tariffs in U.S. history (60 percent). It set off an international trade war and caused the decline in trade that is often considered one of the causes of the worldwide depression of the 1930s. *p. 420*

social capital, *or* infrastructure Capital that provides services to the public. Most social capital takes the form of public works (roads and bridges) and public services (police and fire protection). *p. 234*

social choice The problem of deciding what society wants. The process of adding up individual preferences to make a choice for society as a whole. *p. 346*

social overhead capital Basic infrastructure projects such as roads, power generation, and irrigation systems. *p. 439*

Social Security system The federal system of social insurance programs. It includes three separate programs that are financed through separate trust funds: the Old Age and Survivors Insurance (OASI) program, the Disability Insurance (DI) program, and the Health Insurance (HI), or Medicare program. *p. 381*

sources side/uses side The impact of a tax may be felt on one or the other or on both sides of the income equation. A tax may cause net income to fall (damage on the sources side), or it may cause prices of goods and services to rise so that income buys less (damage on the uses side). *p. 397*

spreading overhead The process of dividing total fixed costs by more units of output. Average fixed cost declines as quantity rises. *p. 169*

stability A condition in which national output is growing steadily, with low inflation and full employment of resources. *p. 14*

stock A share of stock is an ownership claim on a firm, entitling its owner to a profit share. *p. 238*

substitutes Goods that can serve as replacements for one another; when the price of one increases, demand for the other increases. *p. 55*

sunk costs Costs that cannot be avoided because they have already been incurred. *p. 3*

supply curve A graph illustrating how much of a product a firm will sell at different prices. *p. 62*

supply schedule A table showing how much of a product firms will sell at alternative prices. *p. 61*

tacit collusion Collusion occurs when price- and quantity-fixing agreements among producers are explicit. *Tacit collusion* occurs when such agreements are implicit. *p. 298*

tariff A tax on imports. *p. 419*

tax base The measure or value upon which a tax is levied. *p. 389*

tax incidence The ultimate distribution of a tax burden. *p. 396*

tax rate structure The percentage of a tax base that must be paid in taxes—25 percent of income, for example. *p. 389*

tax shifting Occurs when households can alter their behavior and do something to avoid paying a tax. *p. 397*

technological change The introduction of new methods of production or new products intended to increase the productivity of existing inputs or to raise marginal products. *p. 228*

terms of trade The ratio at which a country can trade domestic products for imported products. *p. 415*

theory of comparative advantage Ricardo's theory that specialization and free trade will benefit all trading parties, even those that may be "absolutely" more efficient producers. *p. 28 p. 411*

Tiebout hypothesis An efficient mix of public goods is produced when local land/ housing prices and taxes come to reflect consumer preferences just as they do in the market for private goods. *p. 346*

time series graph A graph illustrating how a variable changes over time. *p. 17 p. 22*

tit-for-tat strategy A repeated game strategy in which a player responds in kind to an opponent's play. *p. 304*

total cost (*TC*) Total fixed costs plus total variable costs. *p. 168*

total cost (total economic cost) The total of (1) out-of-pocket costs and (2) opportunity cost of all factors of production. *p. 148*

total fixed costs (*TFC*) *or* overhead The total of all costs that do not change with output even if output is zero. *p. 168*

total revenue (*TR*) The amount received from the sale of the product; The price per unit times the quantity of output the firm decides to produce ($P \times q$). *p. 148 p. 180*

total utility The total amount of satisfaction obtained from consumption of a good or service. *p. 126*

total variable cost (*TVC*) The total of all costs that vary with output in the short run. *p. 169*

total variable cost curve A graph that shows the relationship between total variable cost and the level of a firm's output. *p. 170*

trade deficit Occurs when a country's exports of goods and services are less than its imports of goods and services in a given period. *p. 410*

trade surplus The situation when a country exports more than it imports. *p. 410*

tragedy of commons The idea that collective ownership may not provide the proper private incentives for efficiency because individuals do not bear the full costs of their own decisions but do enjoy the full benefits. *p. 449*

transfer payments Cash payments made by the government to people who do not supply goods, services, or labor in exchange for these payments. They include Social Security benefits, veterans' benefits, and welfare payments. *p. 370*

U.S.-Canadian Free Trade Agreement An agreement in which the United States and Canada agreed to eliminate all barriers to trade between the two countries by 1998. *p. 421*

unemployment compensation A state government transfer program that pays cash benefits for a certain period of time to laid-off workers who have worked for a specified period of time for a covered employer. *p. 383*

unitary elasticity A demand relationship in which the percentage change in quantity of a product demanded is the same as the percentage change in price in absolute value (a demand elasticity of –1). *p. 100*

utilitarian justice The idea that "a dollar in the hand of a rich person is worth less than a dollar in the hand of a poor person." If the marginal utility of income declines with income, transferring income from the rich to the poor will increase total utility. *p. 379*

utility The satisfaction a product yields. *p. 126*

utility possibilities frontier A graphic representation of a two-person world that shows all points at which I's utility can be increased only if J's utility is decreased. *p. 376*

utility-maximizing rule Equating the ratio of the marginal utility of a good to its price for all goods. *p. 129*

variable A measure that can change from time to time or from observation to observation. *p. 10*

variable cost A cost that depends on the level of production chosen. *p. 168*

vertical differentiation A product difference that, from everyone's perspective, makes a product better than rival products. *p. 318*

vicious-circle-of-poverty hypothesis Suggests that poverty is self-perpetuating because poor nations are unable to save and invest enough to accumulate the capital stock that would help them grow. *p. 436*

voting paradox A simple demonstration of how majority-rule voting can lead to seemingly contradictory and inconsistent results. A commonly cited illustration of the kind of inconsistency described in the impossibility theorem. *p. 347*

wealth *or* net worth The total value of what a household owns minus what it owes. It is a stock measure. *p. 54*

World Bank An international agency that lends money to individual countries for projects that promote economic development. *p. 439*

World Trade Organization (WTO) A negotiating forum dealing with rules of trade across nations. *p. 420*

X-axis On a Cartesian coordinate system, the horizontal line against which a variable is plotted. *p. 18 p. 22*

X-intercept The point at which a graph intersects the X-axis. *p. 18 p. 22*

Y-axis On a Cartesian coordinate system, the vertical line against which a variable is plotted. *p. 18 p. 22*

Y-intercept The point at which a graph intersects the Y-axis. *p. 18 p. 22*

Index

Photo Credits